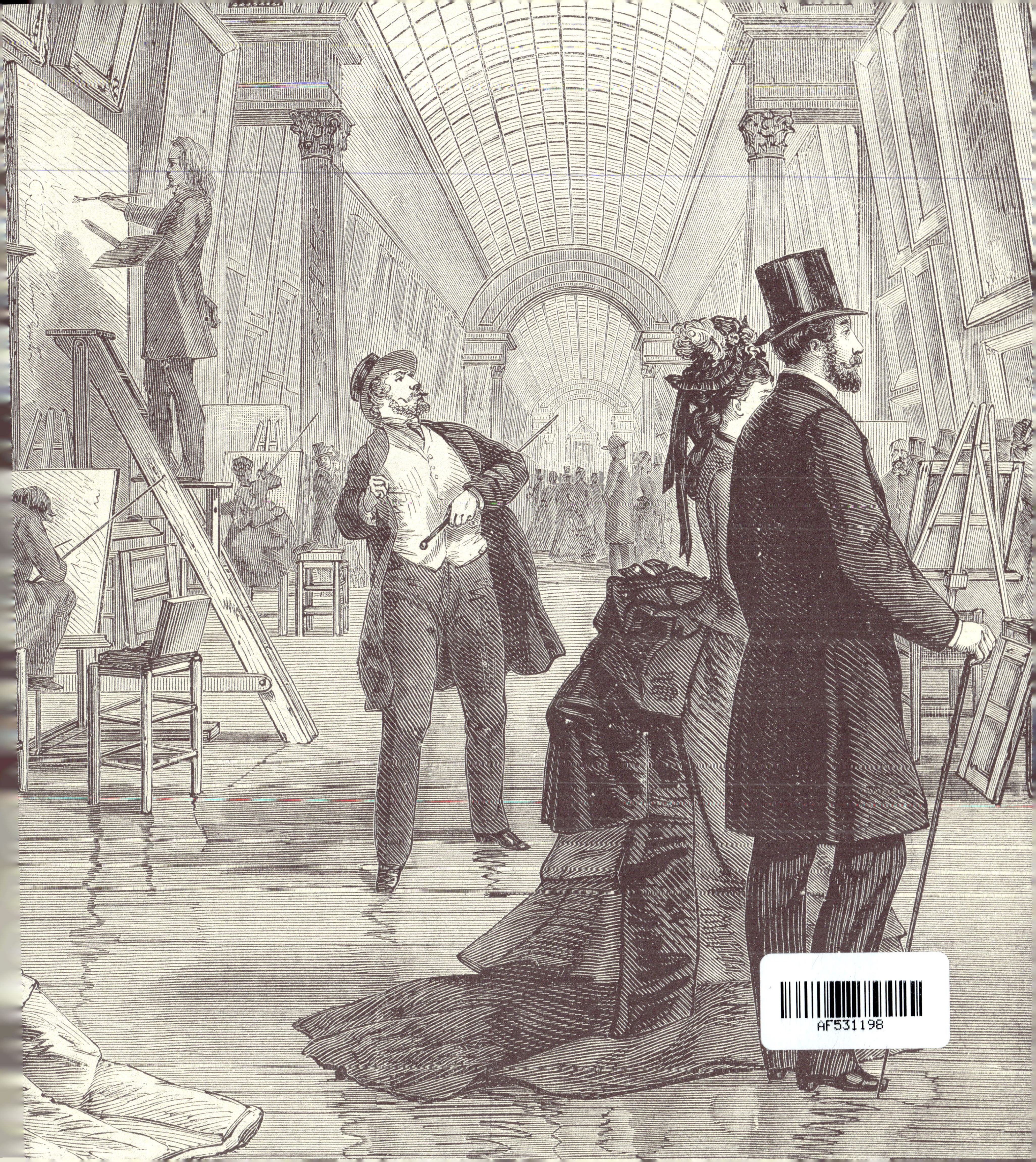

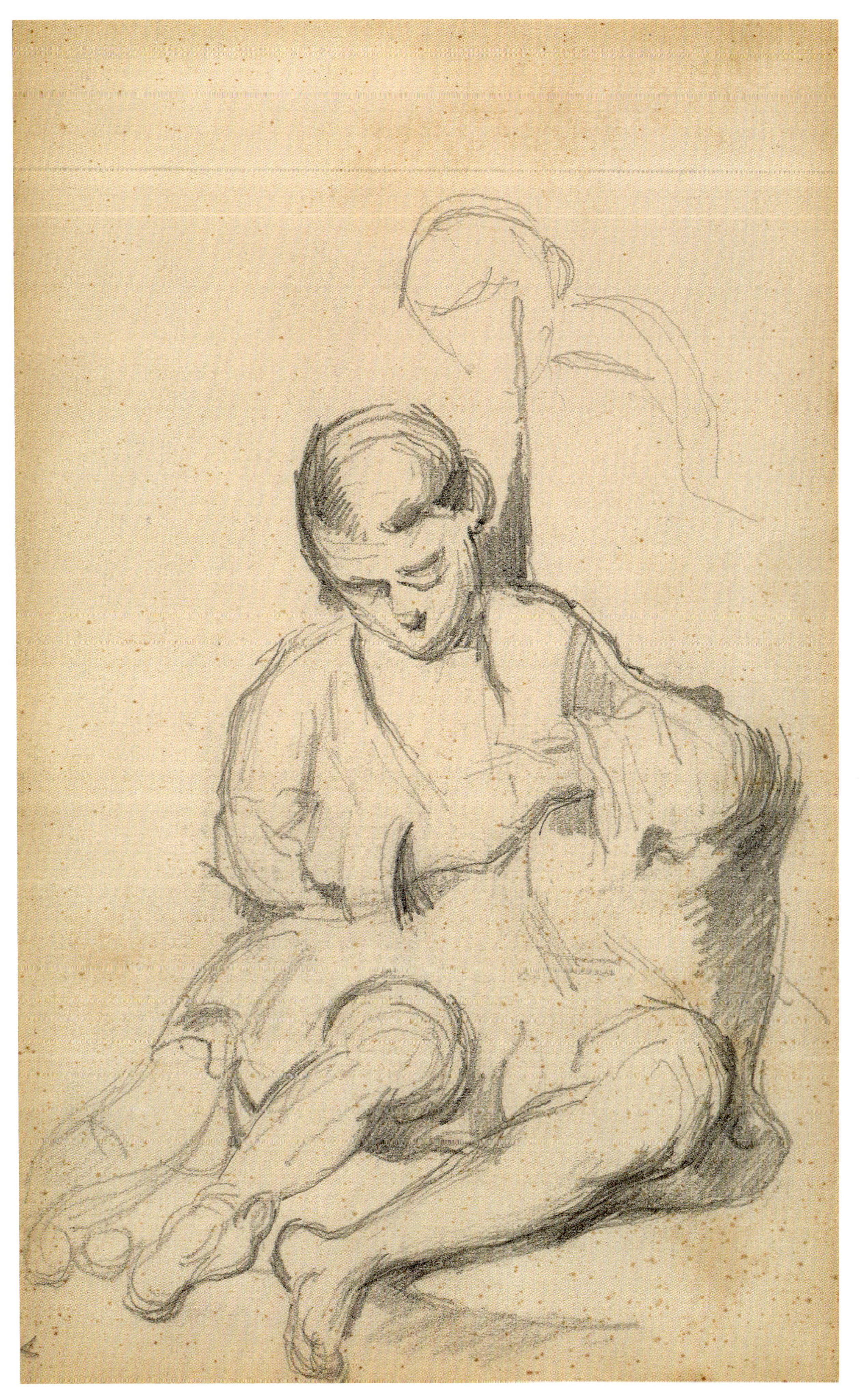

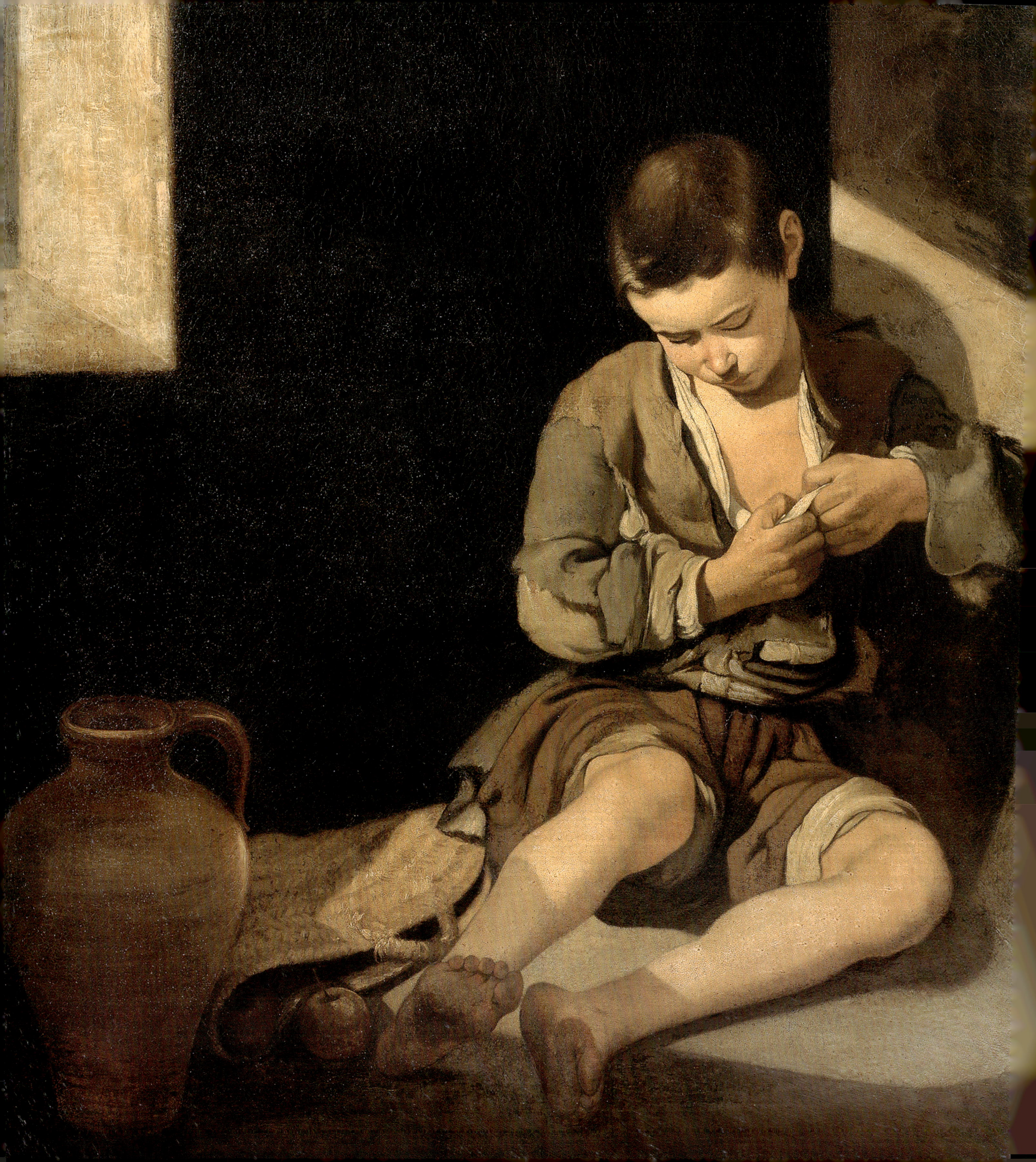

Inspiring Impressionism
The Impressionists and the Art of the Past

Edited by
Ann Dumas

with
Xavier Bray
Michael Clarke
John Collins
Angelica Daneo
John House
Frances Suzman Jowell
Richard Rand
Lesley Stevenson

Denver Art Museum

Yale University Press
New Haven and London

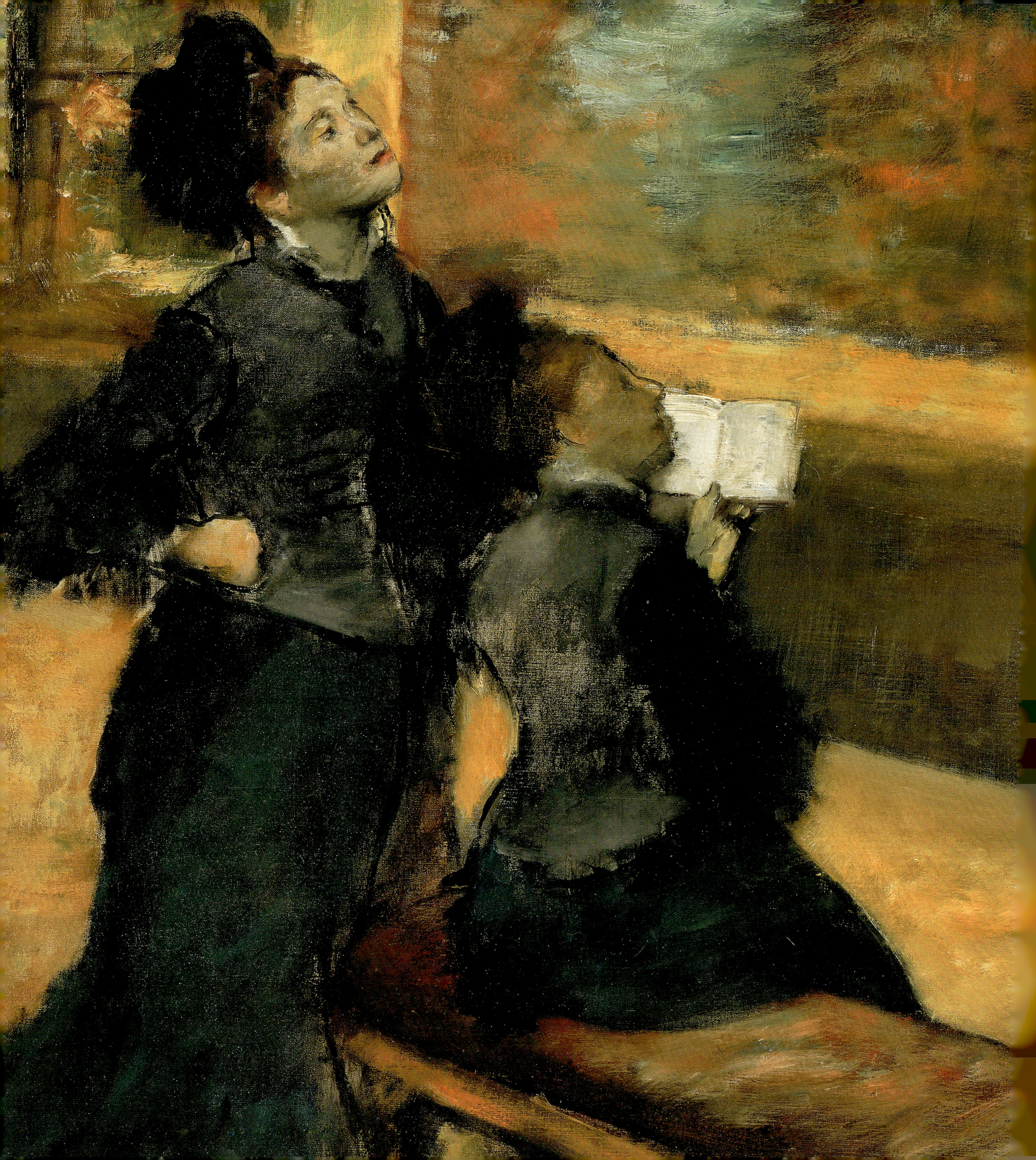

Contents

6 Lenders to the Exhibition
7 Sponsor's Statement
8 Directors' Foreword
11 Acknowledgments

15 **Old Art into New: The Impressionists and the Reinvention of Tradition**
Ann Dumas

79 **Impressionism and the Golden Age of Dutch Art**
Frances Suzman Jowell

111 **Sketches of Spain: The Spanish Old Masters and the French Impressionists**
Xavier Bray

135 **Painted in an Hour: Impressionism and Eighteenth-Century French Art**
Richard Rand

157 **Impressions of Old Masters: The Landscape Tradition**
Michael Clarke

183 **In Search of the Past: The Case of Still Life**
Lesley Stevenson

205 **Genre: Painting without a Subject?**
John House

217 **An Elegant Alliance: Impressionist Portraiture and the Art of the Past**
John Collins

242 **Chronology: 1849–1910**
Angelica Daneo

257 Checklist of the Exhibition
262 Bibliography
272 Index
279 Photographic Credits

Lenders to the Exhibition

Albright-Knox Art Gallery, Buffalo, New York
The Art Institute of Chicago
Ashmolean Museum, University of Oxford, England
The Baltimore Museum of Art
The Barker Welfare Foundation, Glen Head, New York
The Berger Collection at the Denver Art Museum
Bibliothèque nationale de France, Paris
Brooklyn Museum
Ny Carlsberg Glyptotek, Copenhagen
Collection of Rhoda and David T. Chase
Chrysler Museum of Art, Norfolk, Virginia
Columbus Museum of Art
The Corcoran Gallery of Art, Washington, D.C.
Dallas Museum of Art
The Dixon Gallery and Gardens, Memphis
Dulwich Picture Gallery, London
Ferens Art Gallery, Hull City Museums and Art Galleries
Fine Arts Museums of San Francisco
Fitzwilliam Museum, Cambridge
Galleria Borghese, Rome
Gemäldegalerie, Staatliche Museen zu Berlin
J. Paul Getty Museum, Los Angeles
Glasgow City Council (Museums), The Stirling Maxwell Collection, Pollok House
Richard Green Gallery, London
High Museum of Art, Atlanta
The Israel Museum, Jerusalem
Joslyn Art Museum, Omaha, Nebraska
William I. Koch, Palm Beach, Florida
Koninklijk Museum voor Schone Kunsten, Antwerp
Jocelyn Kress and Jedediah H. Kress Turner
Kunsthistorisches Museum, Vienna
The Metropolitan Museum of Art, New York
The Morgan Library & Museum, New York
Musée Calvet, Avignon
Musée de Grenoble
Musée des Beaux-Arts, Tours
Musée d'Orsay, Paris
Musée du Louvre, Paris
Musée Fabre, Montpellier
Musée Marmottan Monet, Paris, France
Museum of Fine Arts, Boston
The Museum of Fine Arts, Houston
Nasjonalmuseet for Kunst, Arkitektur og Design, Oslo
Nationalgalerie, Staatliche Museen zu Berlin
The National Gallery, London
National Gallery of Art, Washington, D.C.
National Gallery of Canada, Ottawa
National Gallery of Scotland, Edinburgh
Nationalmuseum, Stockholm
The Nelson-Atkins Museum of Art, Kansas City, Missouri
Petit Palais, Musée des Beaux-Arts de la Ville de Paris
Philadelphia Museum of Art
The Phillips Collection, Washington, D.C.
Portland Art Museum, Oregon
Portand Museum of Art, Maine
Princeton University Art Museum
Private collection
Private collection, San Francisco
Dr. Hans Riegel Stiftung, Austria
Seattle Art Museum
Shelburne Museum, Shelburne, Vermont
Smith College Museum of Art, Northampton, Massachusetts
Statens Museum for Kunst, Copenhagen
Sterling and Francine Clark Art Institute, Williamstown, Massachusetts
Tate, London
Toledo Museum of Art
Virginia Museum of Fine Arts, Richmond
Wadsworth Atheneum Museum of Art, Hartford, Connecticut
The Walters Art Museum, Baltimore

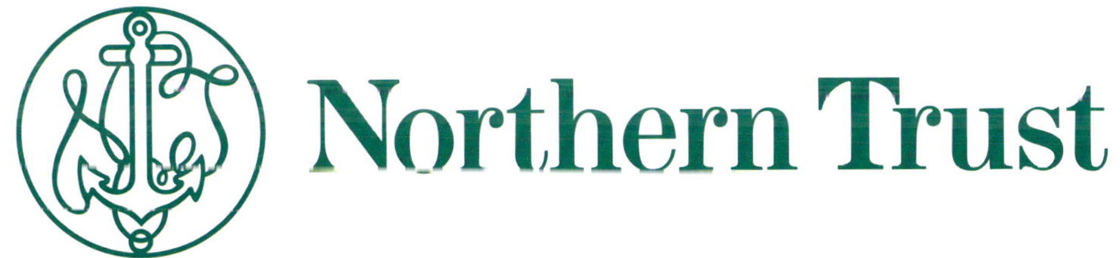

Since 1889, Northern Trust has advanced a culture of caring and a commitment to invest in the communities we serve. We believe that the arts play a vital role in our communities—enhancing the quality of life, providing a learning opportunity, and enriching our cultural experiences.

We are proud to make these timeless works of art accessible to community members in Denver, Atlanta, and Seattle who might not otherwise have such an opportunity to see how Impressionism is deeply rooted in the styles and motifs of the early masters.

Northern Trust is proud to be the National Tour Sponsor of *Inspiring Impressionism,* a multi-year traveling art exhibition that explores the influence that old master painters such as Raphael and Titian had on Impressionists including Monet and Degas.

We applaud the Denver Art Museum, the High Museum of Art, Atlanta, and the Seattle Art Museum for their collaboration in bringing this one-of-a-kind exhibition to thousands of attendees. On behalf of Northern Trust, I invite you to enjoy this important exhibition—and to learn how the works of the old master painters inspired a generation of Impressionists.

William A. Osborn
Chairman and Chief Executive Officer
Northern Trust Corporation

Directors' Foreword

We are proud and pleased to present exclusively in Atlanta, Denver, and Seattle *Inspiring Impressionism: The Impressionists and the Art of the Past,* the first exhibition fully to explore the important relationship between the Impressionists and earlier masters.

The art of the Impressionists is familiar to most museum visitors. Less familiar is the debt these painters owed to earlier art. This exhibition will show how often beneath the Impressionists' commitment to innovation and to capturing contemporary life there lay a deep exploration and understanding of the art from the past. Artists such as Manet, Degas, Monet, Renoir, Cézanne, Pissarro, Cassatt, and Morisot were captivated and influenced by artists and artistic styles from the past, especially seventeenth-century Dutch and Spanish and eighteenth-century French art, as these movements were reassessed in the nineteenth century. These experiences of earlier art had an impact on their style and choice of subjects and reinforced their pictorial aims as they sought to create a new, modern art.

Although scholars have written extensively on the response of individual Impressionist artists to the art of the past, museum visitors have rarely had the opportunity to explore these connections within the context of an exhibition that presents the work of most of the Impressionist artists collectively.

Inspiring Impressionism: The Impressionists and the Art of the Past features approximately one hundred works of art, including sixty-five by Impressionist painters and thirty-five by earlier artists. Organized over the past six years, the show includes works from nearly seventy museums and private collections in Europe and the United States. We owe an enormous debt to all of the institutional and private lenders who agreed to participate in this project.

We would also like to express our sincerest appreciation to co-curators Ann Dumas, Consultant Curator at the Royal Academy of Arts, London, and Timothy J. Standring, Deputy Director for Collections and Programs at the Denver Art Museum, for their dedication and enthusiasm which brought this exhibition about. David Brenneman, Director of Collections and Exhibitions at the High Museum of Art, and Chiyo Ishikawa, Deputy Director and Curator of European Painting and Sculpture at the Seattle Art Museum, both contributed much to this project, as did educators Pat Rodewald and Julia Forbes in Atlanta, Patty Williams in Denver, and Sandra Jackson-Dumont and Jill Rullkoetter in Seattle.

Exhibitions of this scale require considerable financial assistance, and we would very much like to thank the following for their support: our national sponsor, Northern Trust; the National Endowment for the Humanities for awarding this project both Planning and Implementation Grants; the Samuel H. Kress Foundation; and the Friends of Painting and Sculpture at the Denver Art Museum. The exhibition is supported by an indemnity from the Federal Council on the Arts and the Humanities. We thank Christopher Fykyn, Nicholas Maclean, and Michael Simpson for providing third-party insurance values.

Michael Shapiro
Nancy and Holcombe T. Green, Jr. Director
High Museum of Art

Lewis I. Sharp
Frederick and Jan Mayer Director
Denver Art Museum

Mimi Gardner Gates
Illsley Ball Nordstrom Director
Seattle Art Museum

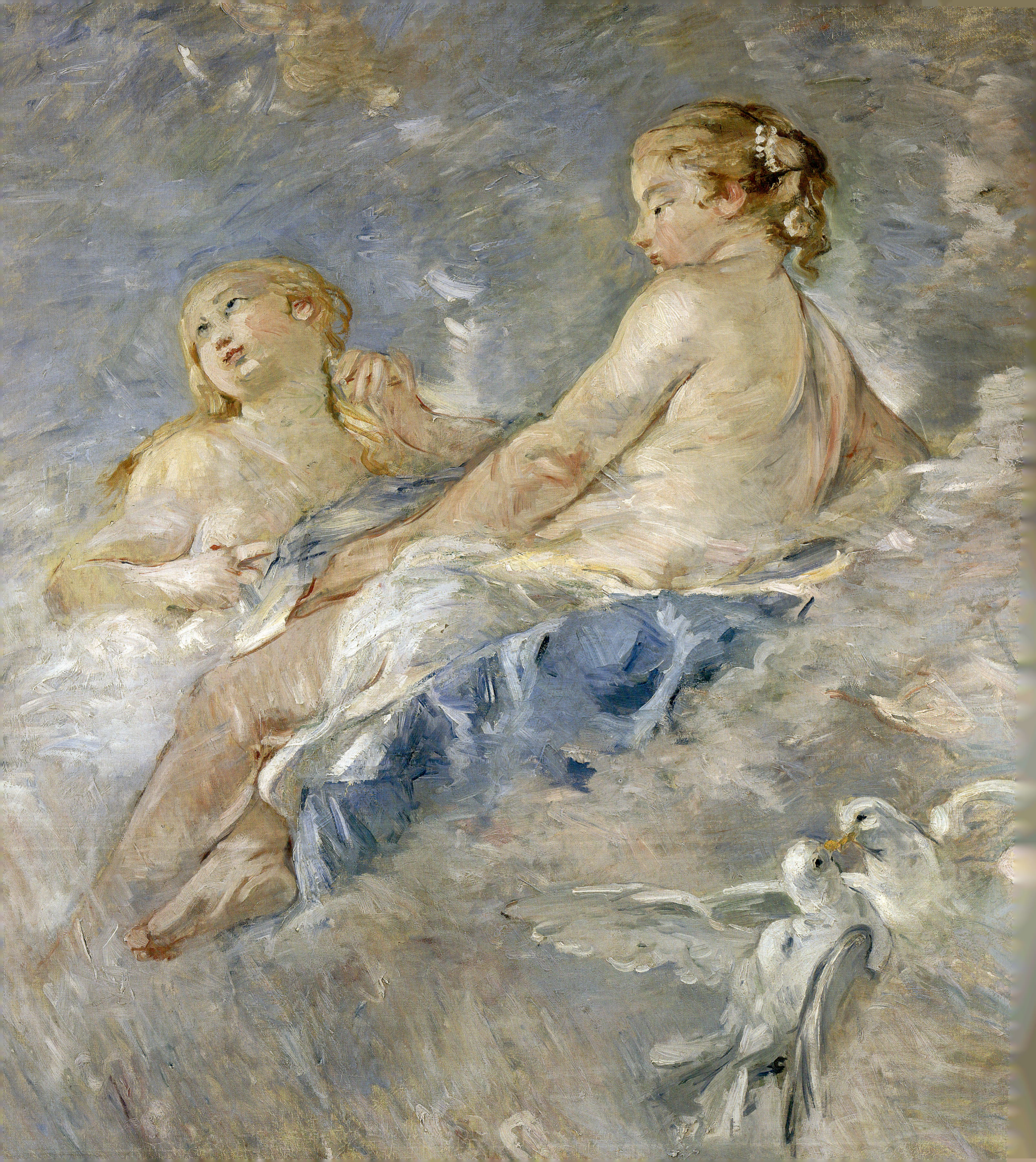

Acknowledgments

Inspiring Impressionism: The Impressionists and the Art of the Past, the exhibition and the book, have been made possible by the efforts of many people. The multiple and fascinating ways in which the Impressionist artists explored earlier art is a rich and complex subject. Over the past six years, as we have traveled many miles to seek out the works of art that would bring this story to life in the most telling way, we have been most fortunate to have had the support of many remarkable people. We thank the following organizations and individuals, without whom *Inspiring Impressionism* would not have been realized.

The owners of the marvelous works of art presented in the exhibition merit our special thanks because they were willing to part with some of their most treasured works of art. These institutions and their generous staff members include: Paul Huvenne and Dries Beheydt at the Koninklijk Museum voor Schone Kunsten in Antwerp; Hans Riegel in Austria; Sylvain Boyer, Odile Cavalier, and Alban Rudelin at the Musée Calvet in Avignon; Doreen Bolger, Jay M. Fisher, Allison C. Perkins, Katherine Rothkopf, Sona Johnston, Brianna Bedigian, and Angelique Weger at The Baltimore Museum of Art; Gary Vikan, Regine Schulz, Eik Kahng, and Michael Gunn at The Walters Art Museum in Baltimore; Peter-Klaus Schuster and Elke Schwichtenberg at the Alte Nationalgalerie in Berlin; Bernd Lindemann, Roberto Contini, Julie Rowlins, and Norbert Ludwig at the Gemäldegalerie in Berlin; Malcolm Rogers, George Shackelford, Erica Hirshler, Kim Pashko, and Erin M. A. Schleigh at the Museum of Fine Arts, Boston; Arnold L. Lehman, Marc Mayer, Marilyn Kushner, Elisa Flynn, Jennifer Lesslie, and Ruth Janson at the Brooklyn Museum; Louis Grachos, Kenneth Wayne, and David J. Chan at the Albright-Knox Art Gallery in Buffalo; Duncan Robinson, David Scrase, Jane Monroe, and Emily Higgins at The Fitzwilliam Museum in Cambridge, England; James Cuno, Douglas W. Druick, Larry J. Feinberg, and Aimee L. Marshall at The Art Institute of Chicago; Nannette V. Maciejunes, Dominique Vasseur, and Jenny Wilkinson at the Columbus Museum of Art; Flemming Friborg and Claus Grønne at the Ny Carlsberg Glyptotek in Copenhagen; Allis Helleland, Hanne Møller, and Eva Maria Gertung at the Statens Museum for Kunst in Copenhagen; John R. Lane, Dorothy Kosinski, and Jeff Zilm at the Dallas Museum of Art; Michael Clarke, Rachel Travers, and Shona Corner at the National Gallery of Scotland in Edinburgh; Mark O'Neill, Robert Wenley, Celine Blair, Jeff Dunn, Robert Ferguson, and Winnie Tyrrell at the Glasgow City Council (Museums); Sarane H.

Ross and Susan M. De Maio at The Barker Welfare Foundation in Glen Head, New York; Guy Tosatto, Isabelle Varloteaux, and Lionel Dutruc at the Musée de Grenoble; Willard Holmes, Eric Zafran, and Adria Patterson at the Wadsworth Atheneum Museum of Art in Hartford, Connecticut; Peter C. Marzio, Edgar Peters Bowron, Erika Franek, Marty Stein, and Margaret C. McKee at The Museum of Fine Arts, Houston; Brian Hayton, Kirsten Simister, Laura Turner, and Edward Whitley at the Ferens Art Gallery, Hull City Museums and Art Galleries; James S. Snyder, Adina Kamien-Kazhdan, Stephanie Rachum, and Gioia Sztulman at The Israel Museum, Jerusalem; Marc F. Wilson, Ian Kennedy, Julie Mattsson, and Stacey Sherman at The Nelson-Atkins Museum of Art in Kansas City, Missouri; Jonathan Green at Richard Green Gallery in London; Ian Dejardin, Margaret Reid, Mella Shaw, and Fulvio Rubesa at the Dulwich Picture Gallery in London; Charles Saumarez Smith, David Jaffé, Christopher Riopelle, Xavier Bray, Marjorie E. Wieseman, Simona Pizzi, and Margaret Daly at The National Gallery in London; Nicholas Serota, Alex Beard, and Matthew Gale at the Tate in London; Michael Brand, Deborah Gribbon (former Director), Scott Schaefer, Scott Allan, Jon L. Seydl, Sally Hibbard, Emily Horton, and Jacklyn Burns at the J. Paul Getty Museum in Los Angeles; Jay Kamm and Neil O'Brien at The Dixon Gallery and Gardens in Memphis; Michel Hilaire, Florence Hudowicz, and Assie Guillaume at the Musée Fabre in Montpellier; Philippe de Montebello, Gary Tinterow, Walter Liedtke, Jim Voorhies, Lisa Cain, Frances Redding Wallace, Sandra Wiskari, Deanna Cross, and Julie Zeftel at The Metropolitan Museum of Art in New York; Charles E. Pierce Jr., Cara Dufour Denison, Patricia Courtney, and Eva Soos at The Morgan Library & Museum in New York; Jocelyn Kress in New York; William J. Hennessey, Jeff Harrison, Catherine Jordan Wass, and Irene Roughton at the Chrysler Museum of Art in Norfolk; Jessica Nicoll, Linda Muehlig, and Louise A. Laplante at the Smith College Museum of Art in Northampton, Massachusetts; J. Brooks Joyner, John Wilson III, and Penelope Smith at the Joslyn Art Museum in Omaha, Nebraska; Sune Nordgren, Sidsel Helliesen, Nils Messel, Torill Bjordal, and Christa E. Köressaar at the Nasjonalmuseet for Kunst, Arkitektur og Design in Oslo; Pierre Théberge, David Franklin, John Collins, Delphine Bishop, Mike Steinhauer, Marie-Claude Rousseau, and France Beauregard at the National Gallery of Canada in Ottawa; Christopher Brown, Jon Whiteley, Geraldine Glynn, Aisha Gibbons, and Amanda Turner at the Ashmolean Museum in Oxford; William I. Koch in Palm Beach; Jean-Noël Jeanneney, Brigitte Robin-Loiseau, Cyril Chazal, and Franck Bougamont at the Bibliothèque nationale de France in Paris; Serge Lemoine, Caroline Mathieu, and Sylvie Patry at the Musée d'Orsay in Paris; Henri Loyrette, Vincent Pomarède, and Olivier Meslay at the Musée du Louvre in Paris; Gilles Chazal, Hubert Cavaniol, and Delphine Desveaux at the Musée du Petit Palais in Paris; Waring Hopkins at the Galerie Hopkins-Custot in Paris; Yves and Daphne Rouart in Paris; Anne d'Harnoncourt, Joseph Rishel, Innis Howe Shoemaker, Shannon N. Schuler, Jennifer Vanim, and Holly Frisbee at the Philadelphia Museum of Art; Daniel O'Leary, Ellie Vuilleumier, Stephanie Doben, and Allyson Humphrey at the Portland Museum of Art in Portland, Maine; Brian Ferriso, Bruce Guenther, Penelope Hunter-Stiebel, and Ann Eichelberg at the Portland Art Museum in Portland, Oregon; Susan M. Taylor, Betsy J. Rosasco, Maureen McCormick, Alexia Hughes, Karen Richter, and Nicole Gordon at the Princeton University Art Museum; Alexander Lee Nyerges, Michael Brand (former Director), Mitchell Merling, Mary Sullivan, and Howell Perkins at the Virginia Museum of Fine Arts in Richmond; Anna Coliva at the Galleria Borghese in Rome; Claudio Strinati at the Soprintendenza per il Polo Museale Romano in Rome; John E. Buchanan Jr., Harry S. Parker III (former Director), Robert Futernick, Lynn Federle Orr, Robert Flynn Johnson, Maria Reilly, and Sue Grinols at the Fine Arts Museums of San Francisco; Stephan Jost, Deborah Dunlap Shenk (former Interim President), Jean Burks, Barbara Rathburn, and Julie B. Sopher at the Shelburne Museum in Shelburne, Vermont; Solfrid Söderlind, Torsten Gunnarsson, Wolfgang Nittnaus, Karin Sidén, Per Hedström, Karin Blomberg, Lillie Johansson, Gunilla Vogt, Suzanne Mohr Rydqvist, and Anne Behrens at the Nationalmuseum in Stockholm; Don Bacigalupi, Lawrence W. Nichols, Karen Serota, and Nicole M. Rivette at the Toledo Museum of Art; Philippe Le Leyzour at the Musée des Beaux-Arts in Tours; Wilfried Seipel, Karl Schütz, Wolfgang Prohaska, Ruperta Pichler, and Ilse Jung at the Kunsthistorisches Museum in Vienna; Paul Greenhalgh, Kathryn M. Keane, Jacquelyn Serwer, and Andrea Romeo at The Corcoran Gallery of Art in Washington; Earl A. Powell III, Philip Conisbee, Arthur Wheelock, Stephanie Belt, and Barbara Goldstein Wood at the National Gallery of Art in Washington; Jay Gates, Eliza Rathbone, Joseph Holbach, and Sarah Anderson at The Phillips Collection in Washington; Rhoda Chase in West Hartford; Michael Conforti, Richard Rand, Monique Le Blanc, and Merry L. Armata at the Sterling and Francine Clark Art Institute in Williamstown, Massachusetts.

An outstanding group of scholars contributed to this catalogue, and we thank them for their thoughtful suggestions, stimulating essays, and collegial support: Xavier Bray, Michael Clarke, John Collins,

Angelica Daneo, John House, Frances Suzman Jowell, Richard Rand, and Lesley Stevenson.

Early on in the planning of the exhibition, we benefited greatly from many participants in two workshops on the topic of Impressionism and the art of the past held in Colorado and in London. Participants in Denver were David Brenneman, Chiyo Ishikawa, Patricia Mainardi, Mitchell Merling, Richard Rand, and the late Robert Rosenblum; and in London, Michael Clarke, John House, Frances Jowell, Christopher Lloyd, Christopher Riopelle, Richard Thomson, Gary Tinterow, and Jon Whitely.

We are also grateful to our many colleagues who contributed in significant ways to the advancement of this project: Colin Bailey, Joseph Baillio, Alberto Bellucci, Sergio Benedetti, Till-Holger Borchert, Maria del Mar Borobia Guerrero, Paloma Botin, Tatjana Bosnjak, Richard Brettell, Hilton Brown, Hugo Chapman, Laura Coyle, Mark Curley, Tatjana Cvjetićanin, Alan Darr, Marianne Delafond, Noelle DeLage, Douglas Druick, Claudia Einecke, Catherine Evans, Oliver Fairclough, Walter Feilchenfeldt, Robert Fergusson, Gabriele Finaldi, Matthieu Gilles, Marco Goldin, Brad Goldstein, Antony V. Griffiths, Gloria Groom, Vivien Hamilton, Christoph Heinrich, John B. Henry III, Michael Ann Holly, R. Bruce Hutton, Guido Jansen, Sophie Jugie, Simon Kelly, Richard Kendall, George Keyes, David Koetser, Michael Komanecky, Dragana Kovacic, Mark Ledbury, Catherine Lepdor, Clay Lewis, Tomàs Llorens, Katherine Maier, J. Patrice Marandel, Werner and Gabrielle Merzbacher, James Mitchell, Charles S. Moffett, Lawrence W. Nichols, Alessandro Nicosia, Patrick Noon, Jan Patten, Matthieu Pinette, Sylvie Ramond, Jonathan Ree, Theodore Reff, Elaine Rice Bachmann, Pierre Rosenberg, Howard Shaw, Martina Sitt, Guillermo Solana, Nicola Spinosa, Irina Subotic, Ann Sumner, Desmond Shawe-Taylor, Richard Thomson, Richard Shiff, Charles L. Venable, Roger Ward, Malcolm Warner, Betty Weiss, Liz Westerfield, Ully Wille, and Miguel Zugaza. We apologize if we have missed anyone.

Exhibitions happen because of the dedication and commitment of our colleagues. Administration of the exhibition was carried out at the Denver Art Museum, whose director, Lewis Sharp, encouraged us every step of the way. Our sincere thanks go to Angelica Daneo, Assistant Curator, whose clear understanding of the issues, attention to detail (especially with loan requests), and consummate organizational skills added immeasurably to the project; she is to be commended as well for the Chronology. Thanks, too, to Marnie Gloor, who by creative, cheerful, and diligent efforts also aided considerably in the realization of this catalogue; Patty Williams, whose lifetime of experience made sure that the visitor's experience would not be forgotten; Michael Assaf and Kara Kudzma, who kept the project within budget; registrars Lori Iliff and Laura Paulick Moody, who withstood a checklist that seemingly never closed; Rebeka Ceravolo and Kate Merkel, who were invaluable research assistants for the Chronology; and Ama Mills-Robertson and Nicole Parks, who managed the rights and reproductions requests for the catalogue with the help of Maria Laura Novas and Benjamin H. Rose, interns. We would also like to thank the colleagues who helped in different ways: Cindy Abramson, Kristin Altman, Megan Cooke, Jennifer Darling, Christina Hixson, Georgia Johnston, Andrea Kalivas-Fulton, Dan Kohl, Liz Larter, Janet Meredith, Lehlan Murray, Suzanna Moran, Sarah Nuese, Chiara Robinson, Jeff Wells, and Bruce Wyman. Jessie Turner, a researcher based in London, coordinated with the curators and the Denver team tirelessly and imaginatively; she found potential works for the show and helped prepare educational materials and aspects of the catalogue.

We would like to thank Ed Marquand and all the staff at Marquand Books, who produced the catalogue. In particular, we are indebted to John Hubbard for the handsome design, Sara Billups, Marissa Meyer, and Marie Weiler. The catalogue was superbly edited by Fronia W. Simpson.

We would also like to thank our colleagues at the High Museum of Art in Atlanta and the Seattle Art Museum who added much to the project: in Atlanta, Michael Shapiro, David Brenneman, Jody Cohen, and Patricia Rodewald; and in Seattle, Mimi Gardner Gates, Chiyo Ishikawa, Zora Hutlova Foy, and Sandra Jackson-Dumont.

Ann Dumas and Timothy J. Standring

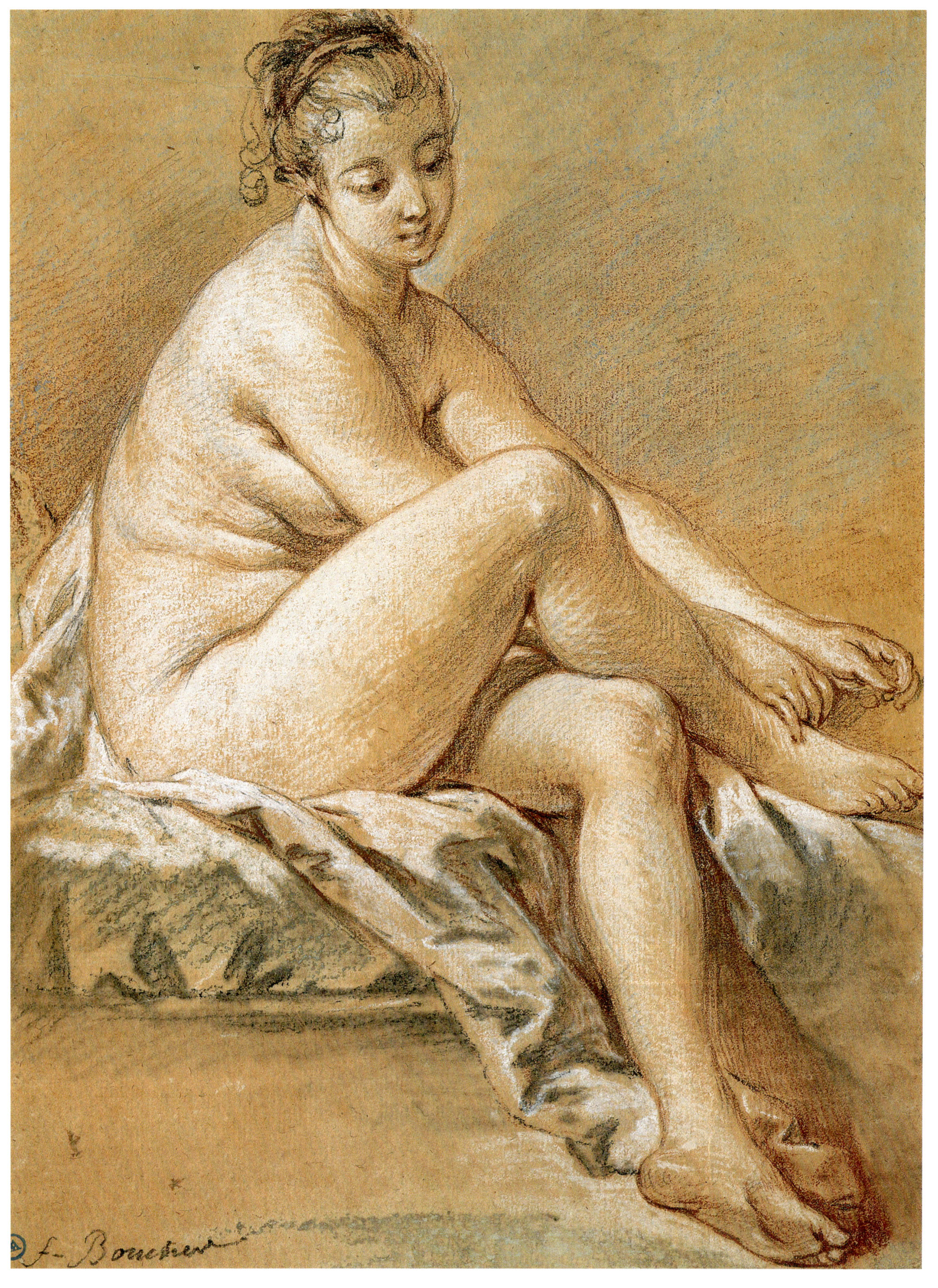
f. Boucher

Ann Dumas

The Impressionists
and the Reinvention
of Tradition

Old Art into New

The public and several of the more conservative critics were startled when the Impressionists' first group exhibition opened in April 1874 in the former studios of the photographer Nadar on the boulevard des Capucines in Paris. The paintings seemed to be a provocative rejection of all the qualities most revered in the art of the old masters and still preserved in the work of contemporary academic artists: draftsmanship, flawless surface, harmonious composition, and subjects drawn from religion, history, or mythology. It is difficult from our remove today to recapture the novelty and excitement of Impressionism when it was new. But the bright colors, unedifying, contemporary subjects—a mundane stretch of countryside or a busy Paris boulevard, for instance—and the sheer lack of finish of the works on display suggested that here was a group of rebels daring to present mere sketches as if they were finished paintings suitable for public exhibition. These were, in Charles Baudelaire's phrase, "les peintres de la vie moderne" (the painters of modern life).[1] The artists' agenda seemed to be a complete break with the art of the past. Pissarro once declared that he wanted to burn down the Louvre, and Monet would remark dismissively that he had never had time to visit that great museum.[2]

Looking closely at the careers of the Impressionist artists represented in this exhibition—Frédéric Bazille (1841–1870), Mary Cassatt (1844–1926), Paul Cézanne (1839–1906), Edgar Degas (1834–1917), Édouard Manet (1832–1883), Claude Monet (1840–1926), Berthe Morisot (1841–1895), Camille Pissarro (1830–1903), Pierre-Auguste Renoir (1841–1919), and Alfred Sisley (1839–1899)—we discover that, rather than turning their backs on earlier art, they engaged with it in a variety of ways, from direct copying to the most discreet assimilation, and from overt homage to irreverent parody, as they sought to articulate a revolutionary, contemporary realism in their own work. Even their boldest attempts to create a wholly new form of art were grounded in a profound awareness of the traditions and conventions that they were rejecting. This is not surprising, perhaps, since artists have always had to work with and against the traditions they inherit. Manet's deep understanding of older art, for example, possessed both a respectful and a rebellious component. This makes him an indispensable part of the present survey, even though he never exhibited with the Impressionists (who nevertheless regarded him as a pioneer and mentor). Or again, Degas's seemingly casual, off-center fragments of contemporary life that captivate us with their almost cinematic realism were rooted in a thorough study of older art, especially the masters of the Italian Renaissance. Cézanne found a model for his vigorous draftsmanship in Baroque sculpture and painting, while Morisot's translucent technique and feminine subjects are directly descended from the airy world of the French Rococo.

This exhibition and the essays in the accompanying catalogue set out to explore the rich and varied connections between the work of the Impressionists and the art of the European traditions that they studied and transformed in their still lifes, landscapes, domestic scenes, portraits, and nudes. First, though, we need to consider how to define "older art." After some deliberation, the exhibition curators decided not to include artists of the earlier nineteenth century, in particular Jean-Auguste-Dominique Ingres (1780–1867), Eugène Delacroix (1798–1863), and Camille Corot (1796–1875), although all three were unquestionably of the greatest importance to the Impressionists of the next generation. We felt that our account would be more sharply focused if the Impressionists were separated unambiguously from earlier art, for which the cutoff point here is 1789, the year of the French Revolution, which brought to an end the ancien régime. (It should be remembered, however, that such a break between the art of the early nineteenth century and earlier schools is an invention of modern auction house catalogues and would not have been perceived as a caesura in the nineteenth century.) In any case, the earlier nineteenth-century artists named above can be viewed as conduits of old master traditions: Ingres as the heir to the purity of line characteristic of Raphael (1483–1520); Corot as the perpetuator of classical landscape à la Claude Lorrain (1604/5–1682); and Delacroix as the successor to the expressive color and technique of Peter Paul Rubens (1577–1640).

Three essays in the catalogue are devoted to the major historical revivals that run through the exhibition like leitmotifs: seventeenth-century Spanish art, seventeenth-century Dutch art, and eighteenth-century French art. All three were reassessed in the mid-nineteenth century, thus providing new routes into the art of the past and profoundly shaping the ways in which both the Impressionists and their more conservative contemporaries viewed and approached these traditions.

This is by no means the first exhibition to look at the way in which the Impressionists used older art. The historical reception of works of art has for some time played an important role in revisionist art history.[3] *Inspiring Impressionism: The Impressionists and the Art of the Past* takes its place in this development by exploring a broad range of the Impressionists' responses to older art. One section of the exhibition is devoted to direct copies of motifs—sometimes only a figure or a detail—from old master works. The exhibition then broadens its scope to investigate more generic responses to composition, style, and technique. To some extent, every exhibition is a construct. By presenting Impressionist and old master works together, *Inspiring Impressionism* undertakes something that occurred only infrequently in the nineteenth century, and then usually in the context of an auction of a private collection or a sale. Moreover, there is often no hard evidence that an individual Impressionist painter knew directly the specific old master work or works with which the present exhibition suggests his or her work is related. Yet our aim is not to pinpoint sources by establishing connections between specific works but to show older paintings that could have possessed prototypical significance for the Impressionists, whether the debt was direct or indirect, acknowledged or unacknowledged.

In the nineteenth century knowledge of past art was considered an essential part of an academic artist's education. Young artists hoping to make a career in Paris would aim to enter the prestigious École des Beaux-Arts, where they would follow a rigorous training based

Fig. 1
Visit to the Museum, 1808
Bibliothèque nationale de France

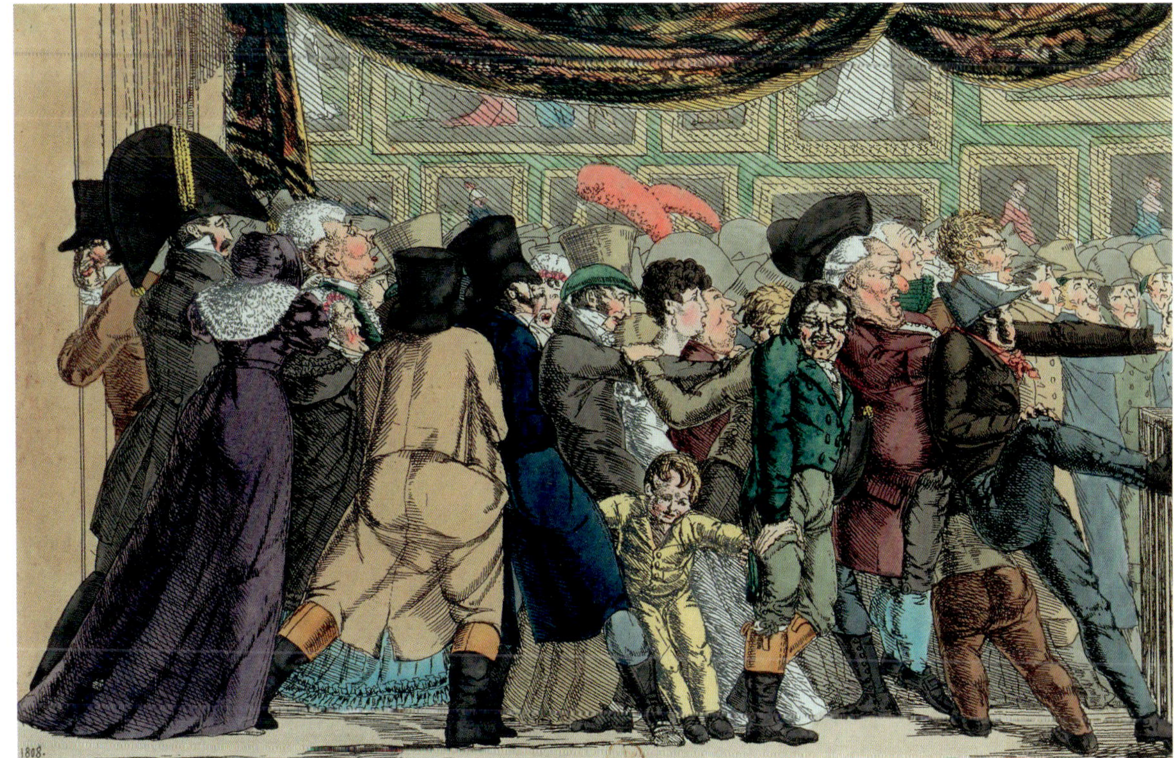

on copying older art, first drawing from plaster casts and paintings before being allowed to progress to the living model. The most talented students would compete for the coveted Prix de Rome, which entitled them to live and study in Rome, honing their technique and enlarging their repertoire of subjects and compositions through assiduous study of the great works of art to be found in the Eternal City's churches and palaces. The terms of the prize required them to send to Paris an *envoi*, an accurate copy of a great Renaissance painting, preferably by Raphael, the quintessential embodiment of the academic tradition.

The advent of the public museum dramatically expanded artists' opportunities to learn from the art of the past. The Louvre opened its doors as the Musée Central des Arts in August 1793, during the Reign of Terror. It was followed by the Pinacoteca di Brera in Milan in 1809, in 1815 by what is now the Rijksmuseum in Amsterdam, in 1819 by the Museo del Prado in Madrid, in 1824 by the National Gallery in London, and in 1830 by the Alte Museum in Berlin. But of all these new palaces of culture, the Louvre was the most splendid. Its collections, displayed in palatial galleries around the Salon Carré, were profuse, rich, and eclectic and included masterpieces of Italian art and of the Northern and French Schools, among them works by Rubens, Claude, Caravaggio (1573–1610), Jan van Eyck (d. 1441), and Nicolas Poussin (1594–1665). As soon as the new museum opened its doors, enthusiastic crowds rushed to see what had previously been locked away in the palaces of kings and wealthy collectors (fig. 1). A measure of the value attached to copying is the fact that five days in the new ten-day week of the Revolutionary calendar were initially set aside for copyists, with the public admitted on only three days.[4] So many artists flocked to set up their easels in the galleries and make copies of the magnificent collections now on view (fig. 2) that their numbers had to be restricted.

Such was the popularity of copies in the first half of the nineteenth century that many artists were able to make a career solely as copyists, executing commissions from the State and from private clients who wanted their own Raphael, for example. A special taste for fine copies—"l'esprit musée"—developed among cultivated collectors.[5] The politician Louis-Adolphe Thiers, for example, who was responsible for suppressing the Paris Commune in 1871, filled his apartment with small-scale replicas of great works.[6] Thiers's friend Charles Blanc, minister of fine arts and founder of the journal the *Gazette des Beaux-Arts,* institutionalized the academic copy when he opened the Musée des Copies in the Palais de l'Industrie

Fig. 2
Winslow Homer (1836–1910)
Art Students and Copyists in the Louvre Gallery, Paris, 1868
Wood engraving on paper, 9 x 13¾ in. (22.9 x 34.9 cm)
Bowdoin College Museum of Art, Brunswick, Maine. Museum and College Purchase, Hamlin, Quinby, and Special Funds

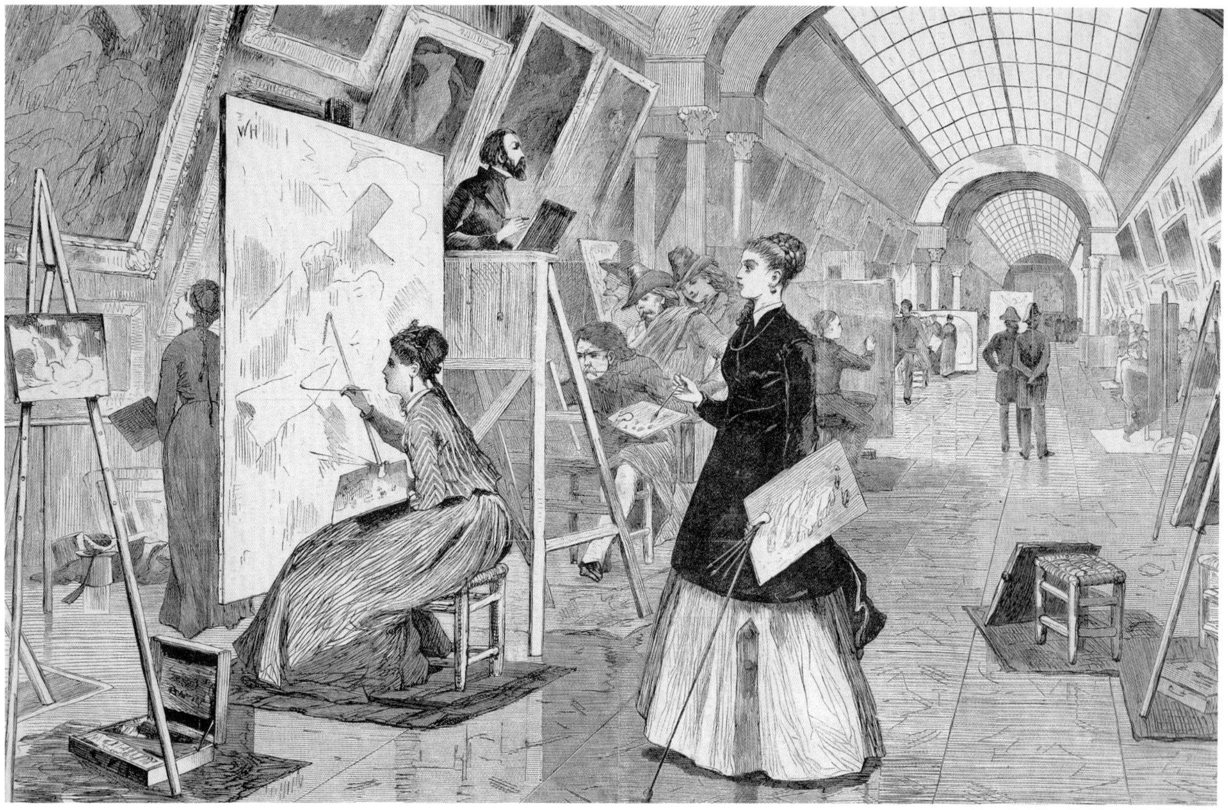

on the Champs-Élysées in 1873.[7] The motives behind the creation of the Musée des Copies, which was devoted entirely to copies after the old masters produced by living artists on commission from the State, were conservative and defensive in that the museum aimed to demonstrate the superiority of painted copies over photographs, which were on the rise, and to protect the academic tradition, which was under threat.[8] The Musée des Copies survived a mere eight months, closing in December 1873 after Blanc had been removed from his post by the new conservative government. Only five months later the Impressionists held their first group exhibition, which challenged all the values to which the Musée des Copies owed its existence.

The museum as a repository of great art and a custodian of visual memory was central to nineteenth-century culture, with countless artists traveling to see the Louvre and the new museums in other European cities. Where else did they have access to the art of the past? Temporary exhibitions (although fewer than today), auction sales, and displays of dealers' gallery stocks provided additional opportunities. Accustomed as we are to the ready availability of color reproductions of works of art—in books and on computer screens, posters, and postcards—it is easy to forget that things were quite different in the nineteenth century. Black-and-white reproductive prints added to the expanding image bank of great paintings. Often, though, such prints were of rather poor quality, like the wood engravings reproduced in Blanc's *Histoire des peintres de toutes les écoles,* an encyclopedic series of biographies of the old masters published from 1861 to 1876 in the *Gazette des Beaux-Arts*.[9] Yet they formed an extremely important source of subjects and compositions for painters, despite the inherent lack of color and brushwork. Black-and-white photographs of old master paintings were also becoming available, including those produced in Florence by Alinari and in Paris by Jean Laurent, who in 1863 published a series of photographs of works in the Prado.[10]

The future Impressionists who embarked on artistic training in Paris in the 1860s did not generally take the established academic route. "Institutions, stipends, and honours are made only for idiots, pranksters, and rogues. . . . Let them go the École, let them have a raft of professors. I don't give a damn"[11]—such was Cézanne's contempt for the academic system that prevailed when he arrived in Paris from his native Aix-en-Provence at the age of twenty-two in

1861. Although Pissarro, Degas, and Renoir briefly attended classes at the École des Beaux-Arts, most of the others received their early training, such as it was, in informal open studios, where, in return for a few francs, they were provided with a studio, a model, and occasional guidance from the master. Rejected by the École des Beaux-Arts in 1861 and again in 1862, Cézanne pursued traditional training in draftsmanship at a studio of this kind, the Académie Suisse, where he made friends with Pissarro. Renoir enrolled in the studio run by the Swiss history painter Charles Gleyre (1806–1874), where he met Monet, Sisley, and the talented Frédéric Bazille (who was to be killed at the age of twenty-nine in 1870 during the Franco-Prussian War). Gleyre, although known for academic, historical subjects, differed from his more unbending peers by fostering his pupils' individuality and urging them to paint out of doors and mix their colors on the spot. In thus promoting an awareness of natural effects and spontaneous working methods, he addressed two concerns fundamental to the Impressionist enterprise.

Even when trying to make their mark at the Salon—the huge, official State-sponsored annual exhibitions that represented an artist's primary opportunity to be recognized and sell work—a number of the future Impressionists flouted convention by slapping paint onto the canvas thickly with a palette knife. The most striking example of this deliberate affront to academic expectations is Cézanne's dark, tormented pictures of the 1860s. Despite such iconoclasm, a number of the Impressionists-to-be supplemented their classes in informal studios with extensive copying in the Louvre. Degas and Renoir had known the museum since childhood. Renoir had grown up in the old quarter sandwiched between the Louvre and the Tuileries Palace, and the museum's masterpieces remained a touchstone for him throughout his life. When the young Morisot announced her desire to become a painter, her mother's first thought was to enroll her as a copyist in the Louvre. Cassatt is shown studying works in the Louvre in two paintings (cat. 35, p. 152) and two etchings by her friend Degas, *Mary Cassatt at the Louvre: The Etruscan Gallery* and *Mary Cassatt at the Louvre: The Paintings Gallery,* both of 1879–80.[12] Shortly after arriving in Paris, Cézanne began spending his afternoons at the Louvre, copying works by Rubens, Giorgione (c. 1476/78–1510), Titian (c. 1487/90–1576), and Paolo Veronese (1528–1588). He would continue to make drawings in the Louvre, as well as the museum of plaster casts, the Musée du Trocadéro, producing nearly four hundred copies in all. "The Louvre is the book where we learn to read,"[13] he would later recall.

Italian art of the High Renaissance remained the basis of academic practice, but Spanish, Dutch, and French Rococo painting proved more relevant to most of the artists of Impressionism, with the exceptions of Manet and Degas. Both had received a more academically orientated training, and Italian art was of fundamental importance to them. Manet had studied for six years at the École des Beaux-Arts as a pupil of the unconventional academic history painter Thomas Couture (1815–1879), who encouraged an eclectic approach to the art of the past. Manet made two brief trips to Florence and Rome in 1853, when he also visited the Netherlands. In 1857 he returned to Italy, immersing himself in the art of Titian, Domenico Ghirlandaio (1449–1494), Michelangelo (1475–1564), and others.[14] The synoptic brio of the drawings of details from old master paintings he made on these journeys reveals a strikingly precocious individuality.

During the 1860s Manet produced a dazzling series of paintings that, while addressing his friend Baudelaire's demand for a new "painter of modern life," demonstrate the wealth of ideas that the artist was absorbing from the past. Two of his most important early paintings are clearly indebted to Italian models. His startlingly real portrayal of a model in the role of a contemporary Parisian prostitute, *Olympia* (1861; Musée d'Orsay, Paris), harshly updates Titian's sensual reclining Venuses. No less shocking at the time was his *Luncheon on the Grass* of 1863 (fig. 3), a picnic scene with two male students accompanied by two female companions, one wearing only a slip, and the other, in the foreground, naked and staring boldly out at the viewer. This, of course, is Manet's best-known and most brilliant transformation of old master sources. As he explained to his friend the writer Antonin Proust, his intention had been to create a modern version of Titian's *Le Concert champêtre,* of about 1509, in the Louvre (fig. 4). The public, scandalized when the painting was shown at the Salon des Refusés in 1863 (an exhibition put on to display the unusually large number of works rejected at the official Salon in that year), generally failed to detect the other impeccable old master pedigree behind the group of figures: two river gods from an engraving by Marcantonio Raimondi (c. 1480–c. 1534) after a lost cartoon by Raphael, *The Judgment of Paris* (fig. 5). Manet's staged contemporary tableau thus looks both to the past and to the present, and his witty parody both acknowledges and subverts his venerable sources.

Degas's early copies of Italian art are more respectful toward their sources. "The masters must be copied over and over again, and it is only after proving yourself a good copyist that you should

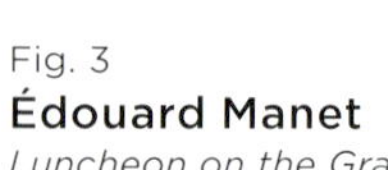

Fig. 3
Édouard Manet
Luncheon on the Grass, 1863
Oil on canvas, 81⅞ x 104⅛ in.
(208 x 264.5 cm), Musée d'Orsay,
Paris, France

Fig. 4
Titian (Tiziano Vecellio)
(c. 1488–1576)
Le Concert champêtre
Oil on canvas, 53½ x 41⅜ in.
(136 x 105 cm), Musée du Louvre,
Paris, France

Fig. 5
Marcantonio Raimondi
(c. 1480–c. 1534), after Raphael
The Judgment of Paris
Engraving, $11\frac{7}{16}$ x 17 in. (29.1 x 43.2 cm)
National Gallery of Art, Washington,
Gift of W. G. Russell Allen, 1941.1.63

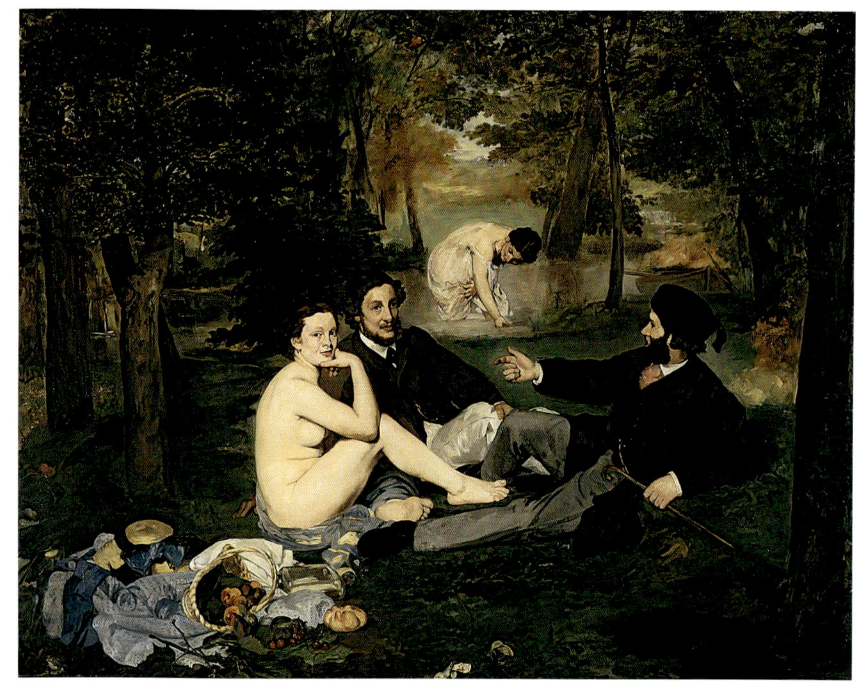

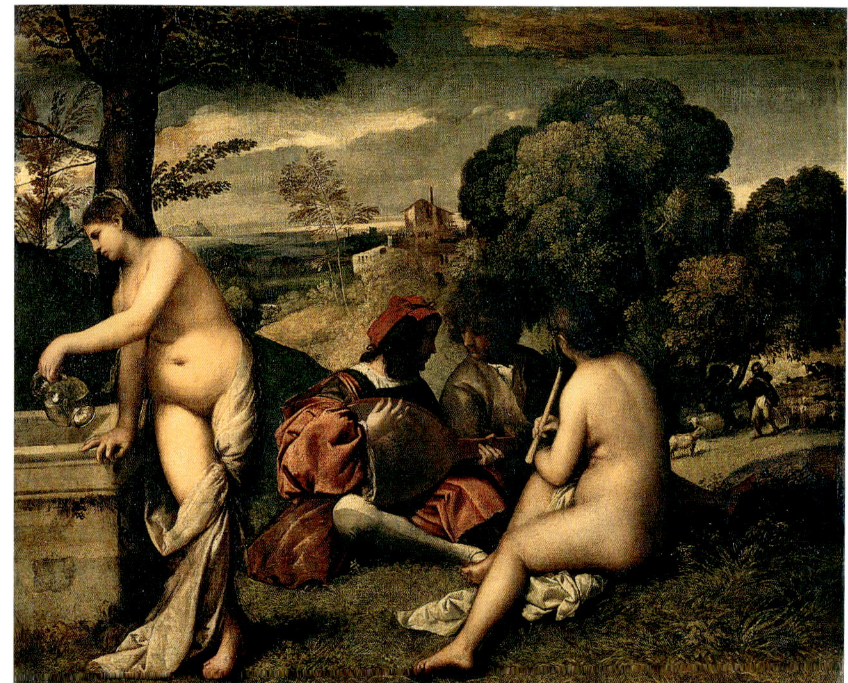

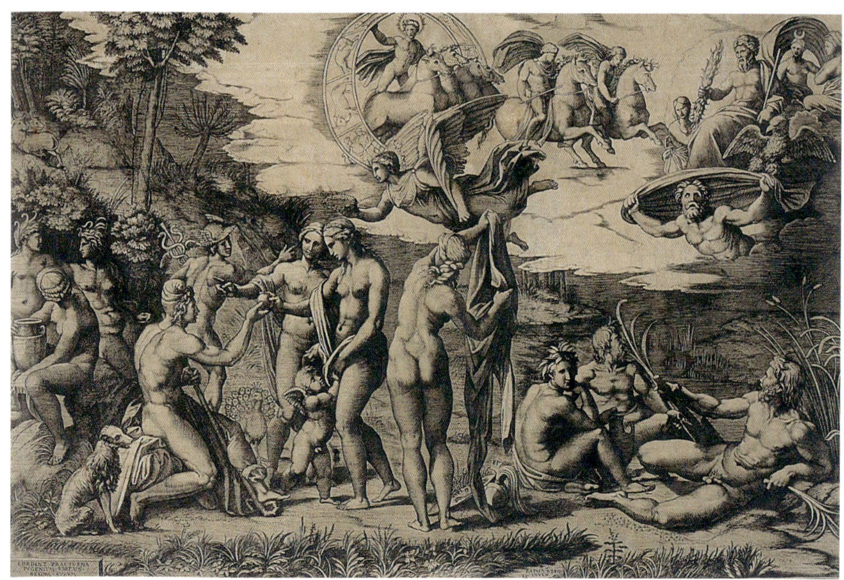

reasonably be permitted to draw a radish from nature"[15] is typical of the opinions that Degas voiced on a number of occasions. He studied with Louis Lamothe, a pupil of Hippolyte Flandrin and also of Ingres, Raphael's principal nineteenth-century disciple. Between 1857 and 1861 Degas spent extensive periods with his relatives in Naples and Florence or traveling throughout Italy filling his notebooks with studies of items that ranged from Roman antiquities to paintings by Giotto through Raphael—an activity that schooled him in the incisive draftsmanship that would underpin his art for the rest of his life. At least eighty drawings in the studio sales held in 1918, after his death, were after Italian Renaissance subjects.[16] At the Uffizi in Florence, a red chalk drawing of an unknown woman, at the time attributed to Leonardo da Vinci (1452–1519) but now usually given to Bachiacca (Francesco Umbertini; 1494–1557), inspired Degas to make a drawing that formed the basis of a large, confident painting in which he allowed himself the license of color, although the pose, expression, and details of the costume remain faithful to the original sixteenth-century drawing (cat. 30, p. 23).

Back in Paris, Degas pursued his intensive study of the old masters, especially of the Italian School, making numerous copies at the Cabinet des Estampes in the Bibliothèque impériale, the École des Beaux-Arts, and the Louvre. In 1861 he created a full-scale copy of Mantegna's *Calvary* of about 1457–59 (cat. 33, p. 24). With its fresh, modern aura, this freely painted oil sketch is anything but a painstaking, academic replica, and one recalls that Degas once remarked: "The air in the paintings of the old masters is not air that one can breathe."[17] What attracted him to Mantegna's painting was not the details but the overall design, the choreographed groupings of the figures, their relation to the space around them, and the broad contrasts between areas of warm and cool color. The Italian artist remained an inspiration to Degas throughout his career. More than thirty years after copying the *Calvary*, he again turned to a Mantegna in the Louvre, producing a free version of *Minerva Chasing Vice from the Garden of Virtue* of 1502[18] at a time when he was fascinated by the techniques of Renaissance oil painting, particularly the use of glazes, which he adapted to his work in pastel.

Degas himself named Mantegna as a source of inspiration for *The Daughter of Jephthah* (cat. 31, p. 25), the largest of four ambitious history paintings that occupied him during the 1860s as he attempted to gain recognition at the Salon. He likewise acknowledged that the work of another Italian artist, Veronese, inspired this brilliant composition, in which, as Degas explained, he combined "the spirit and love of Mantegna with the verve and color of Veronese."[19] Degas also made a small, loosely painted copy of the right-hand side of Veronese's *The Finding of Moses* (cat. 32, p. 27), anticipating, perhaps, the eloquent use of the fragment that characterizes his mature work.[20]

Degas was not alone in his admiration for Veronese's "verve and color." Undaunted by the complex arrangements of figures and stormy sky in Veronese's *Calvary,* the nineteen-year-old Morisot made a thoroughly competent copy of it in 1860 (cat. 66, p. 26), two years after she had first registered to copy in the Louvre.[21] Cézanne, too, was seduced by Veronese's glowing color and bravura technique. His flamboyant early masterpiece, *The Feast (The Orgy)* of 1867–70 (private collection) clearly pays homage to the great sixteenth-century Venetian magician of sumptuous pageantry while hovering on the edge of parody. Again, Renoir loved Veronese all his life, and on his last visit to the Louvre, in 1919, was particularly moved by *The Marriage at Cana* (1562–63).

While Degas was adhering in his copies and historical compositions of the 1860s to traditional concepts of high art based on the Italian Renaissance, art historians and some of the finest writers of the day were busy rehabilitating seventeenth-century Spanish and Dutch art and that of the French Rococo. In his *Histoire des peintres de toutes les écoles,* Blanc covered all the major schools. Théophile Thoré (also known as Thoré-Bürger; 1807–1869), a republican who interpreted older art from a polemical, left-wing position, acquired special authority as a prophetic critic. A powerful advocate for seventeenth-century Dutch art, he had a decisive influence on the way it was received from the 1860s on. Dutch art encapsulated his notion of "an art for mankind," an art that, in contrast to what he saw as the empty idealization of the Italian School, valued and found beauty in the commonplace life of its own time. Guidebooks, too, played an important role in influencing what the public saw. In 1858 Thoré published *Musées de la Hollande,* the first of two guides to Dutch museums that encouraged the readers to go and visit for themselves. In 1866 he published an essay on Johannes Vermeer (1632–1675), a painter who had fallen into almost total oblivion in the eighteenth century and the early nineteenth. This was followed in 1868 by an important study of Frans Hals (1581/85–1666), in which Thoré approached the artist's work from a new and influential perspective, praising his sincerity and the spontaneity of his technique. More surprisingly, Thoré defended the Rococo art of François Boucher (1703–1770), Jean-Honoré Fragonard (1732–1806), and Jean-Antoine Watteau (1684–1721), masters of the ancien régime whom

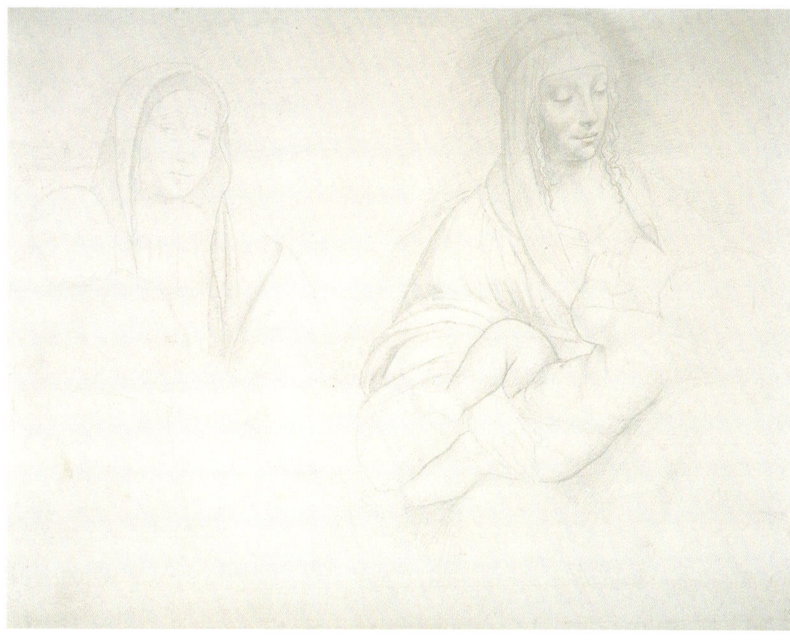

Cat. 29
Edgar Degas
Studies after Two Italian Madonnas, c. 1859–60

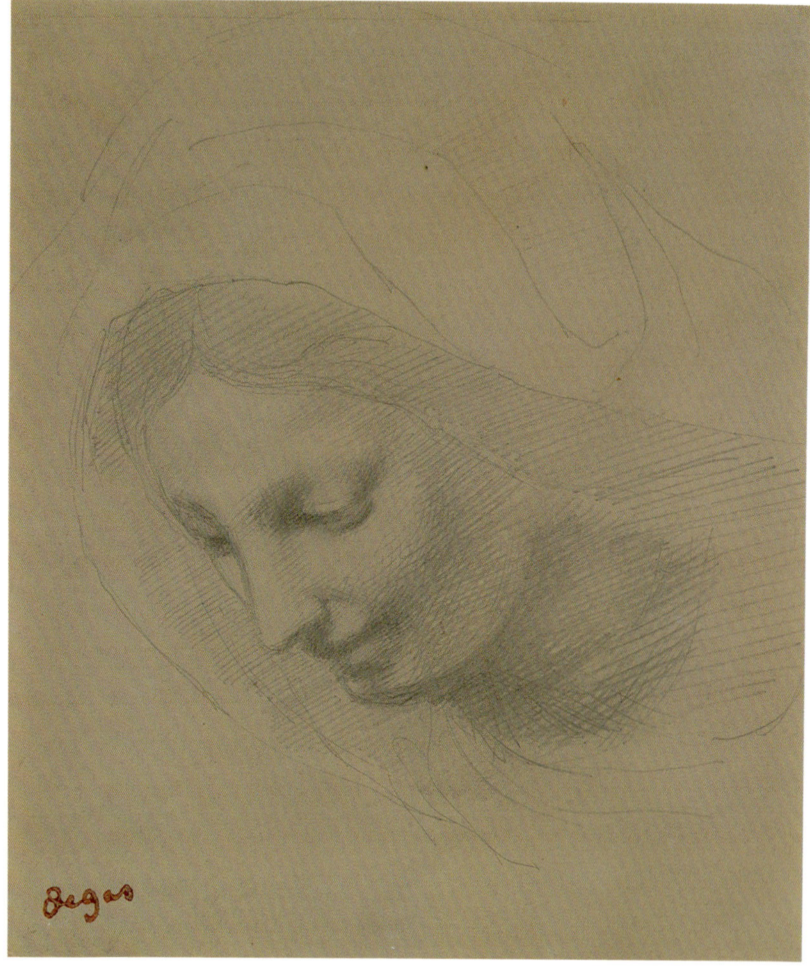

Cat. 27
Edgar Degas
Head of the Virgin after Solario's "Virgin of the Green Cushion" (Louvre), c. 1857

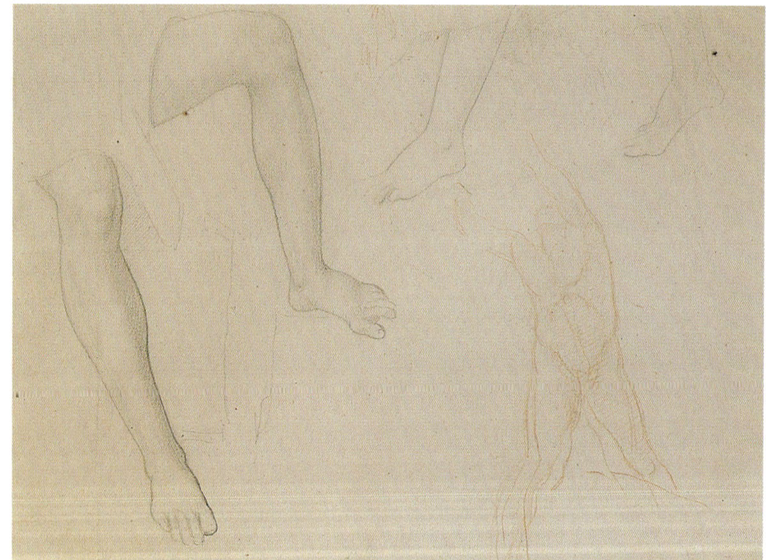

Cat. 25 (recto)
Edgar Degas
Studies of Legs and Feet and of a Figure, c. 1854

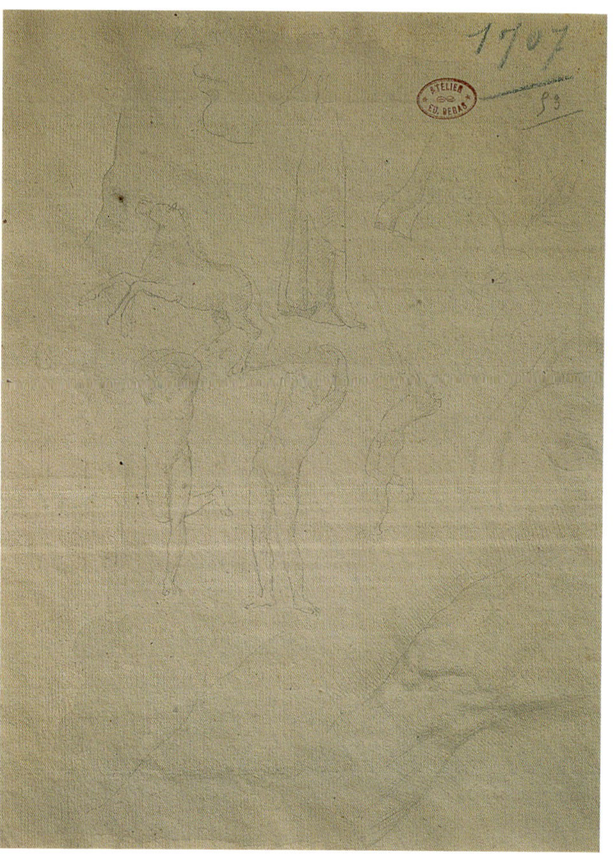

Cat. 25 (verso)
Edgar Degas
Studies of Nude Man, a Horse, and a Knee, c. 1854

Cat. 30
Edgar Degas
Portrait of a Young Woman, after a 16th-century Florentine drawing, c. 1858–59

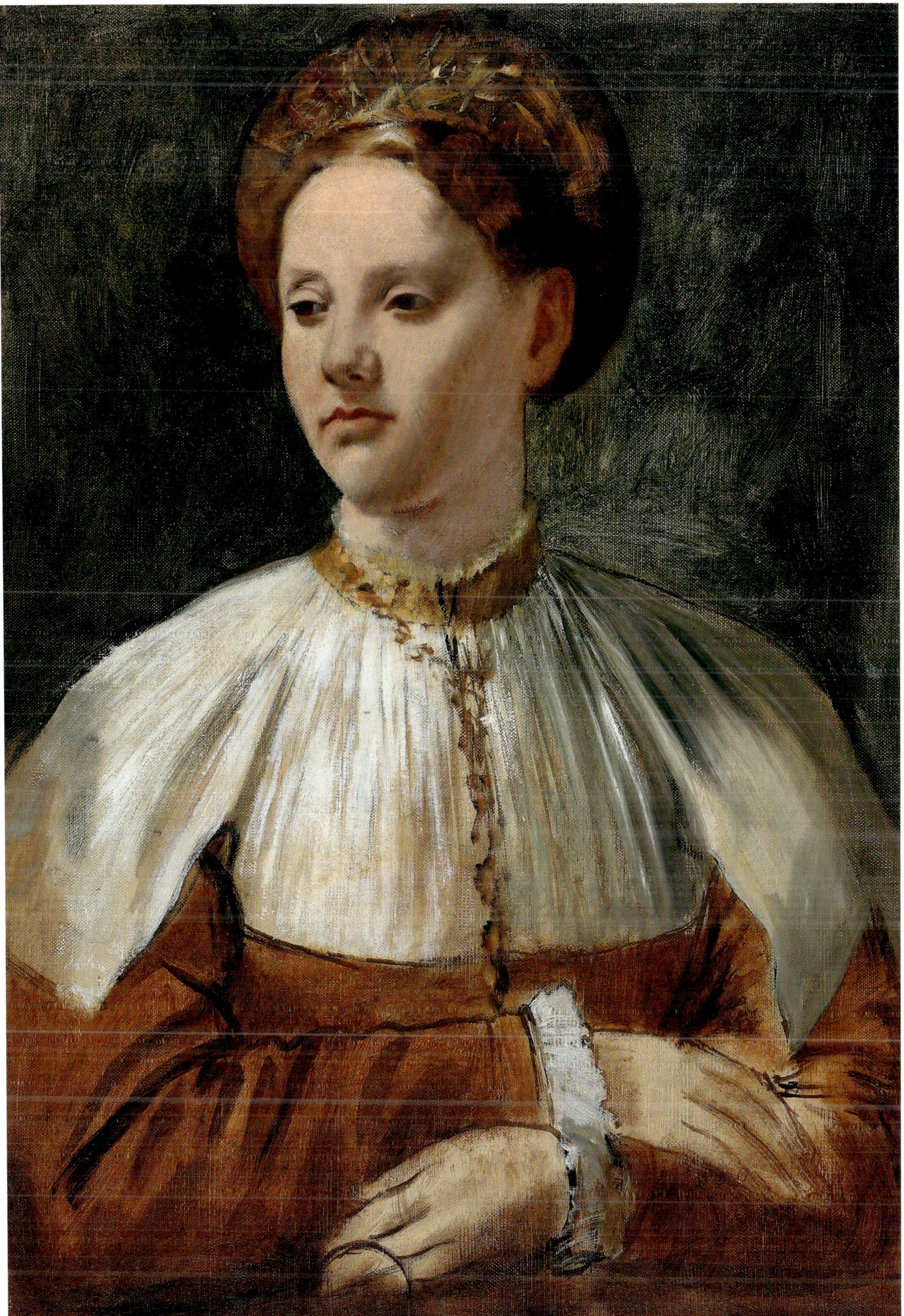

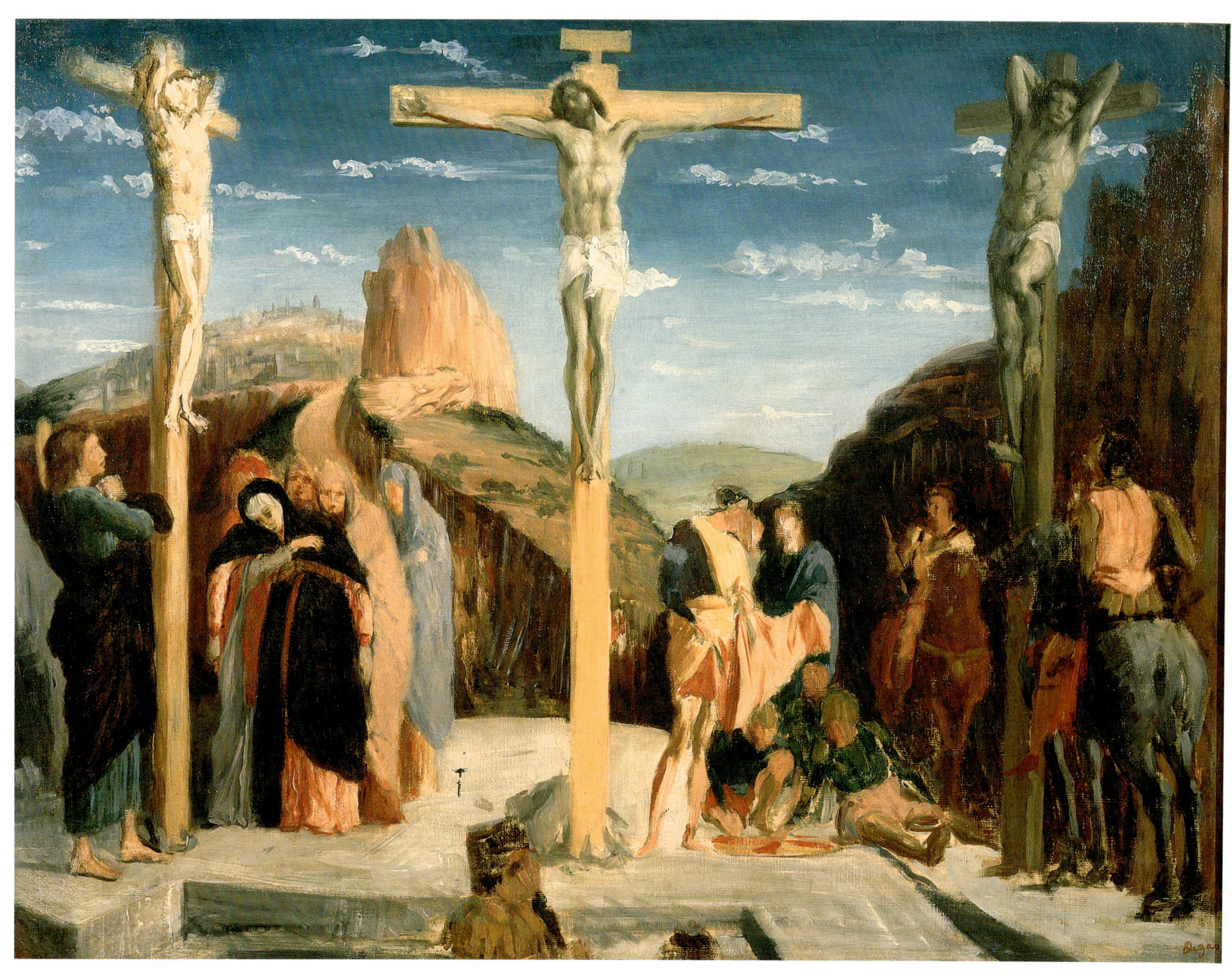

Cat. 33
Edgar Degas
The Calvary, copy after Mantegna, 1861

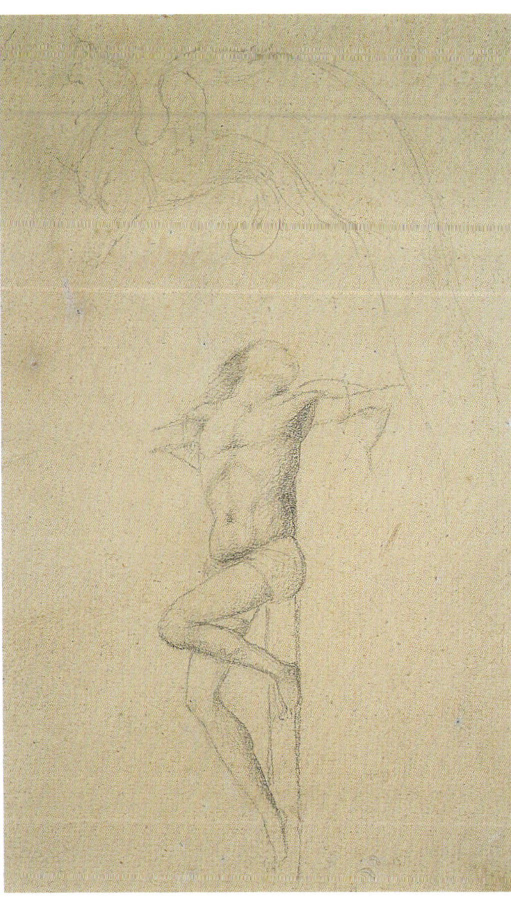

Cat. 26
Edgar Degas
Study of One of the Thieves in Mantegna's "Crucifixion," c. 1855

Cat. 31
Edgar Degas
The Daughter of Jephthah, 1859–60

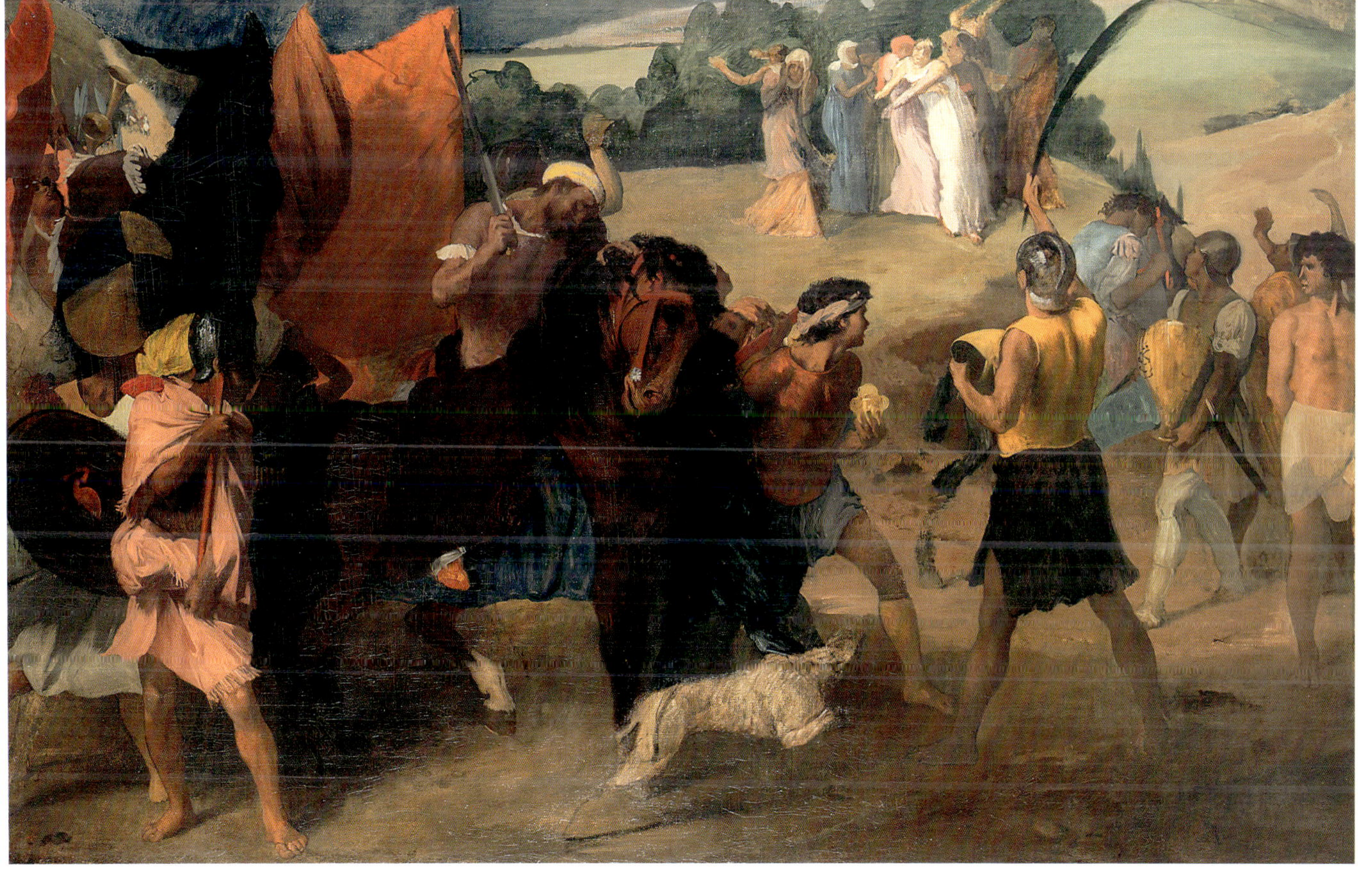

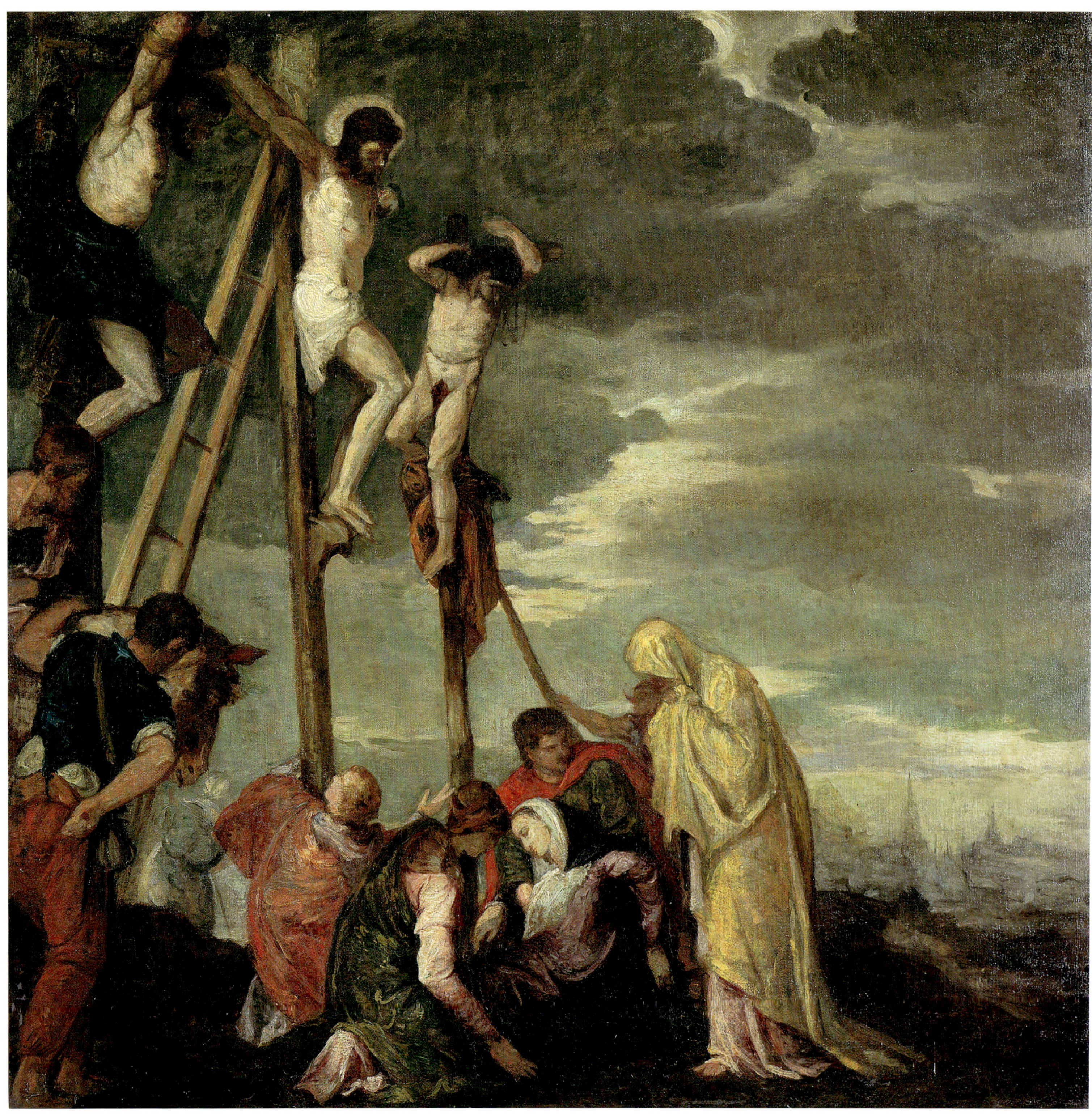

Cat. 66
Berthe Morisot
The Calvary, 1860

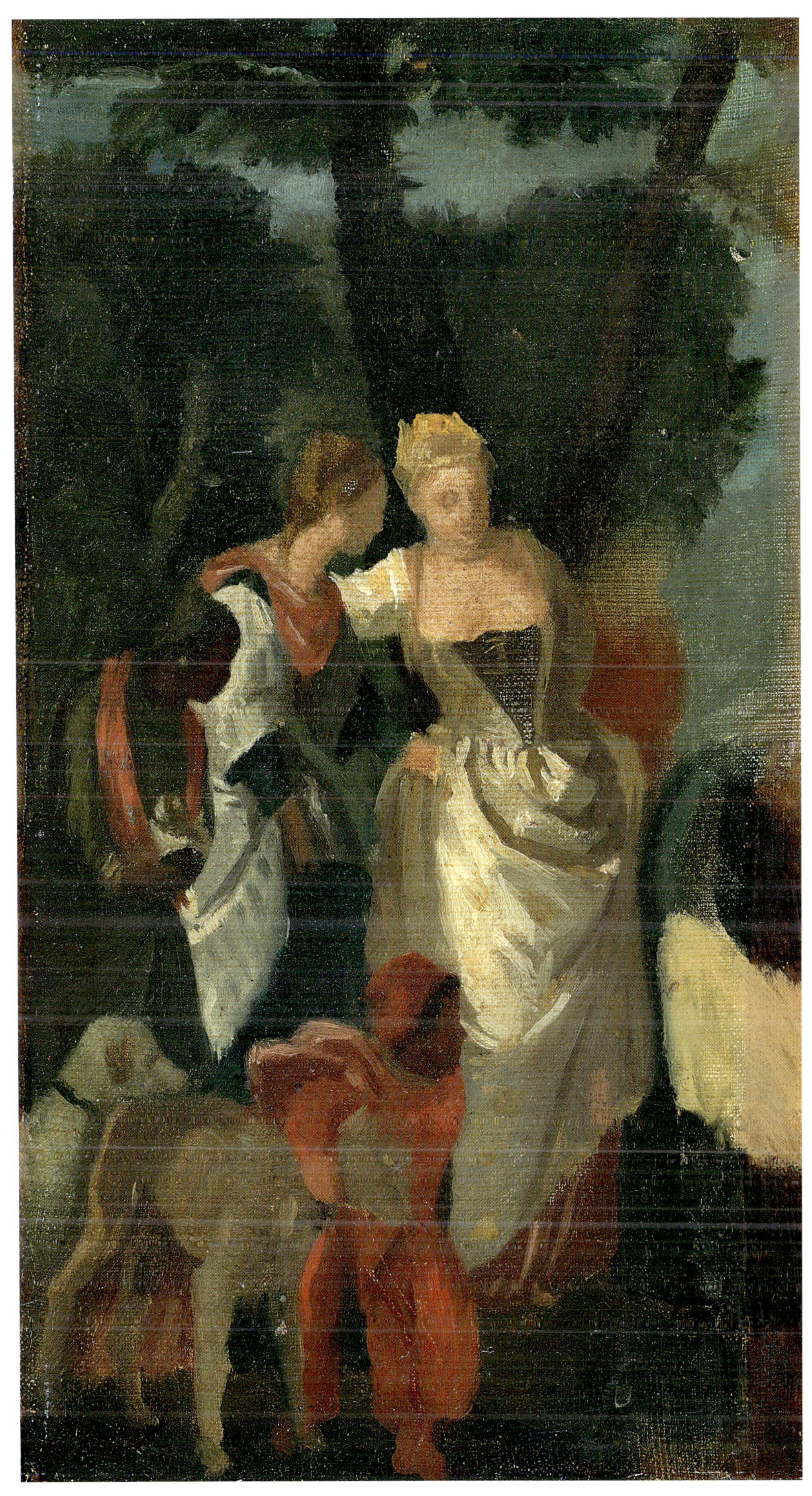

Cat. 32
Edgar Degas
Copy after "The Finding of Moses" by Veronese, late 1860s

Cat. 100
School of Diego Rodríguez de Silva y Velázquez
Meeting of Thirteen People

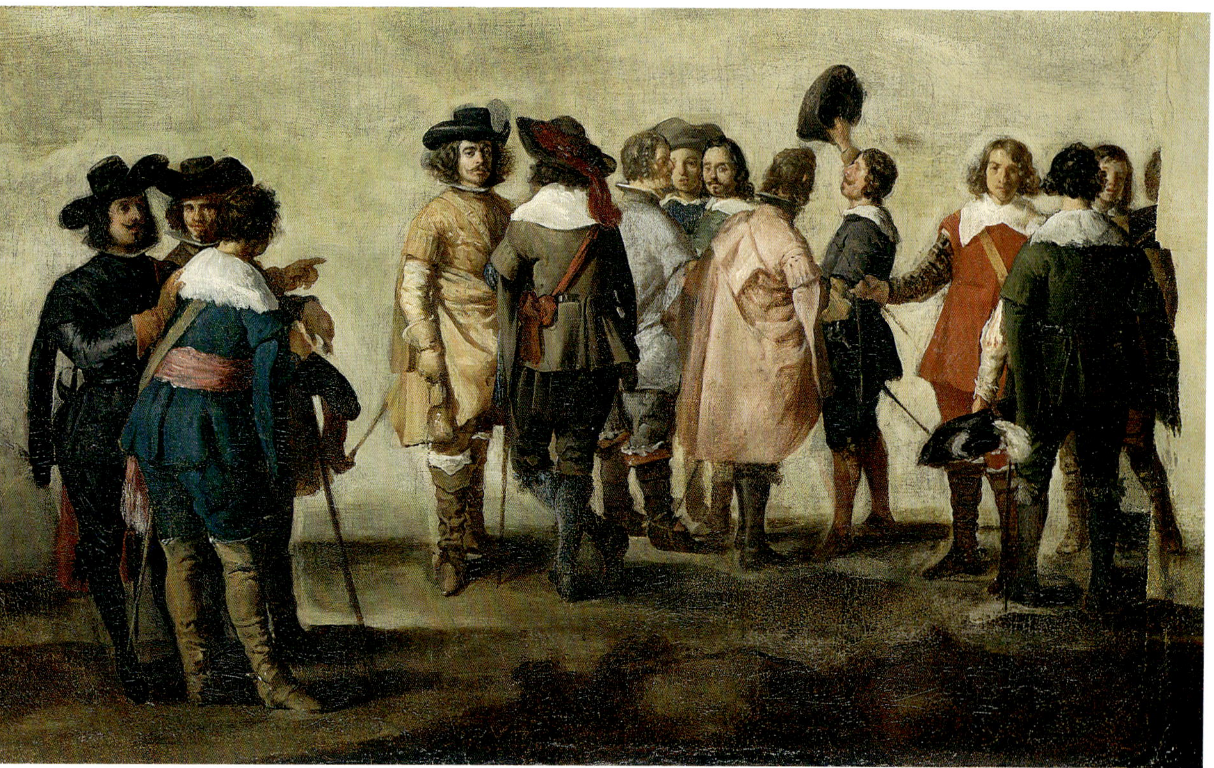

the Revolution had caused to fall from favor because their work seemed frivolous, artificial, and aristocratic. Thoré managed to make Watteau fit into his left-wing scheme of things—"before him people painted princesses and he painted shepherdesses"[22]—and he admired the Rococo artists in general for their essentially French qualities. These views were echoed by the brothers Jules and Edmond de Goncourt, famous diarists and novelists of the Naturalist School, in their brilliant *L'Art du XVIIIe siècle,* which included separate monographs on Watteau, Boucher, Jean-Siméon Chardin (1699–1779), George de La Tour (1593–1652), Jean-Baptiste Greuze (1725–1805), and Fragonard. Like Thoré, the Goncourts pioneered a new style of heightened, emotive, and highly persuasive writing about art.[23] The Goncourts wrote vividly of the charm of a vanished, more graceful age, a nostalgia expressed in a vogue for the eighteenth century not only in fine art but also in the decorative arts, in fashion, and in the fancy dress balls presided over by Empress Eugénie and later by Renoir's patron Madame Charpentier, who would attend Rococo soirées dressed as Marie-Antoinette.

The revival in the critical fortunes of seventeenth-century Dutch and Spanish and French Rococo art struck a chord with the emerging generation of Impressionists and seemed to sanction their rejection of academic notions of finish and elevated subject matter in favor of free, expressive painting and accessible, everyday scenes of contemporary life. The authority of Raphael was now usurped by Fragonard, Hals, and, above all, Diego Rodríguez de Silva y Velázquez (1599–1660). Chances to study great works of art from these schools at firsthand were greatly enhanced in 1869, when a spectacular collection of eighteenth-century French and seventeenth-century Dutch art amassed by the physician Louis La Caze went on view at the Louvre. The collection contained many small-scale, freely brushed works that attracted the Impressionists, along with such famous paintings as Hals's *The Gypsy* (fig. 23), Watteau's *Gilles* (1721), and four of Fragonard's *portraits de fantaisie* (e.g., fig. 60), which were celebrated for their bravura technique.

Spanish culture had fascinated French writers, musicians, and artists since Napoleon's invasion of the Iberian Peninsula in 1808. Growing enthusiasm for *espagnolisme* was fueled by the display of an outstanding collection of Spanish paintings, known as the Musée Espagnole, at the Louvre from 1838 to 1848.[24] At midcentury authors fostering the vogue for Spanish art included Thoré, who wrote extensively on Velázquez, and Blanc, who published the Spanish volume of his *Histoire des peintres de toutes les écoles* in 1869. Cassatt,

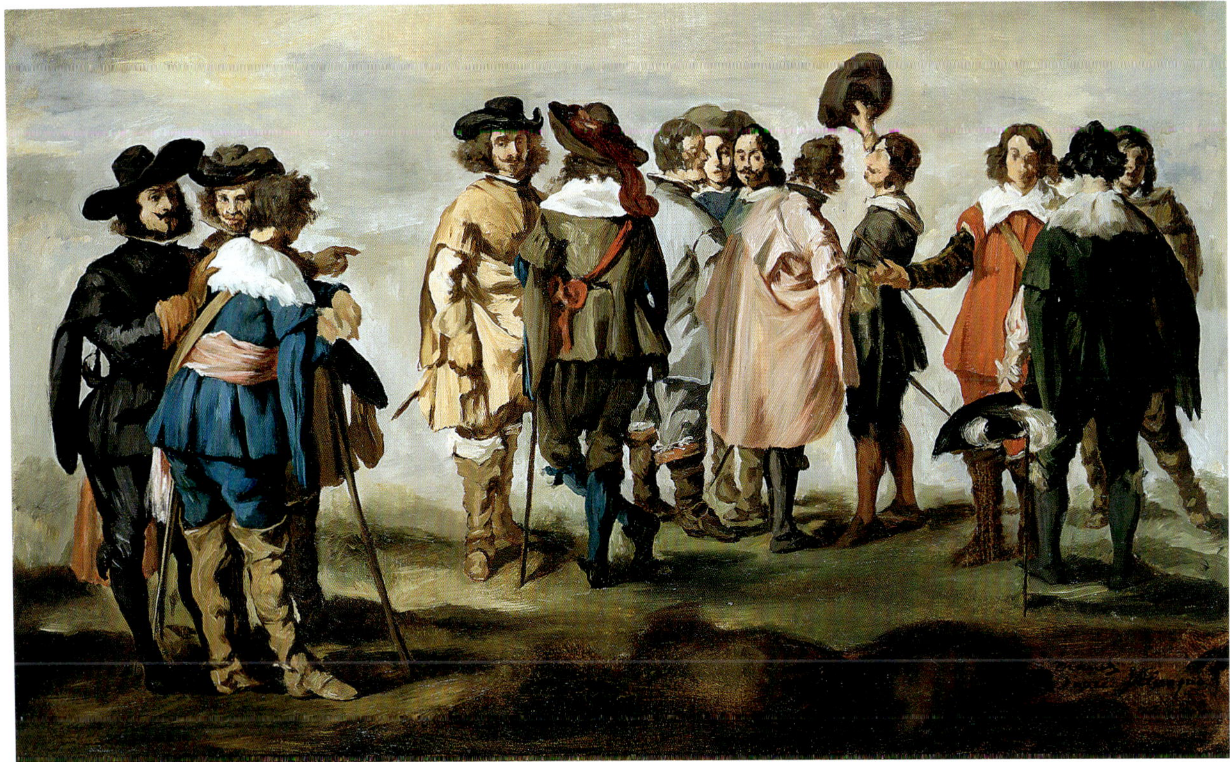

Cat. 48
Édouard Manet
The Little Cavaliers, c. 1859–60

Cézanne, Degas, Morisot, and Renoir all responded to the lure of Spain, but the painter most captivated by Spanish art in the 1860s was Manet.

On a brief visit to Spain in September 1865, Manet, although impressed by El Greco (1541–1614) and Francisco de Goya (1746–1828), was bowled over by Velázquez.[25] Long before traveling to Spain, Manet had studied Spanish paintings in the Louvre, attracted by their truthfulness and lack of idealization. About 1859 he had copied *Meeting of Thirteen People* (then attributed to Velázquez), an immensely popular work because it was seen as a realistic portrayal of seventeenth-century figures—a gathering of artists that includes Bartolomé Esteban Murillo (1617/18–1682) and Velázquez himself at the left (cat. 100, p. 28; cat. 48, p. 29).[26] Although close to the original, Manet's copy, which he titled *The Little Cavaliers,* has a more modern feel owing to its looser handling and heightened color. Moreover, the way in which the figures are strung out informally across an empty landscape with no apparent narrative link anticipates the enigmatic disconnectedness of Manet's mature work. *Meeting of Thirteen People* is one of a number of paintings by Velázquez of which Manet made etchings in the 1860s (cat. 49, p. 30), perhaps in emulation of Goya, some of whose etchings after Velázquez he owned. A few years later, Renoir would pay homage both to the notion of *espagnolisme* and to Manet by incorporating Manet's etching after Velázquez's *Meeting of Thirteen People* in his *Still Life with Bouquet* (cat. 79, p. 31).

Another painting in the Louvre that was extremely popular in the nineteenth century, both with artists and the public at large, was a portrait dating from about 1653 of the Infanta Margarita, daughter of Philip IV of Spain. Now considered a product of Velázquez's workshop, the painting is of very high quality, and nineteenth-century observers valued it as an example of the master's virtuoso brushwork. Renoir claimed that "All of the art of painting is in it [the Infanta's pink sash],"[27] and some art historians have seen a homage to the portrait in Renoir's famous *La Loge* (fig. 47). *Infanta Margarita* was certainly in his thoughts when he portrayed a contemporary French girl, Romaine Lacaux, in 1864 (fig. 6). One of Renoir's most enchanting child portraits, this canvas emulates the naturalism and fluid handling that he admired in Velázquez's portraits of the Spanish Infantas (cat. 99, p. 33). Manet and Degas rose to the challenge of capturing the dazzling technique of *Infanta Margarita* in the relatively intractable medium of etching. Degas's etching stays closer to the letter of the original, whereas Manet's interpretation is freer, more abstracted, and perhaps closer to its spirit (cat. 52, p. 117).[28]

Cat. 49
Édouard Manet
The Little Cavaliers, 1860, pl. 2 from the portfolio *Eight Etchings by Manet,* 1862

Cat. 79
Pierre-Auguste Renoir
Still Life with Bouquet, 1871

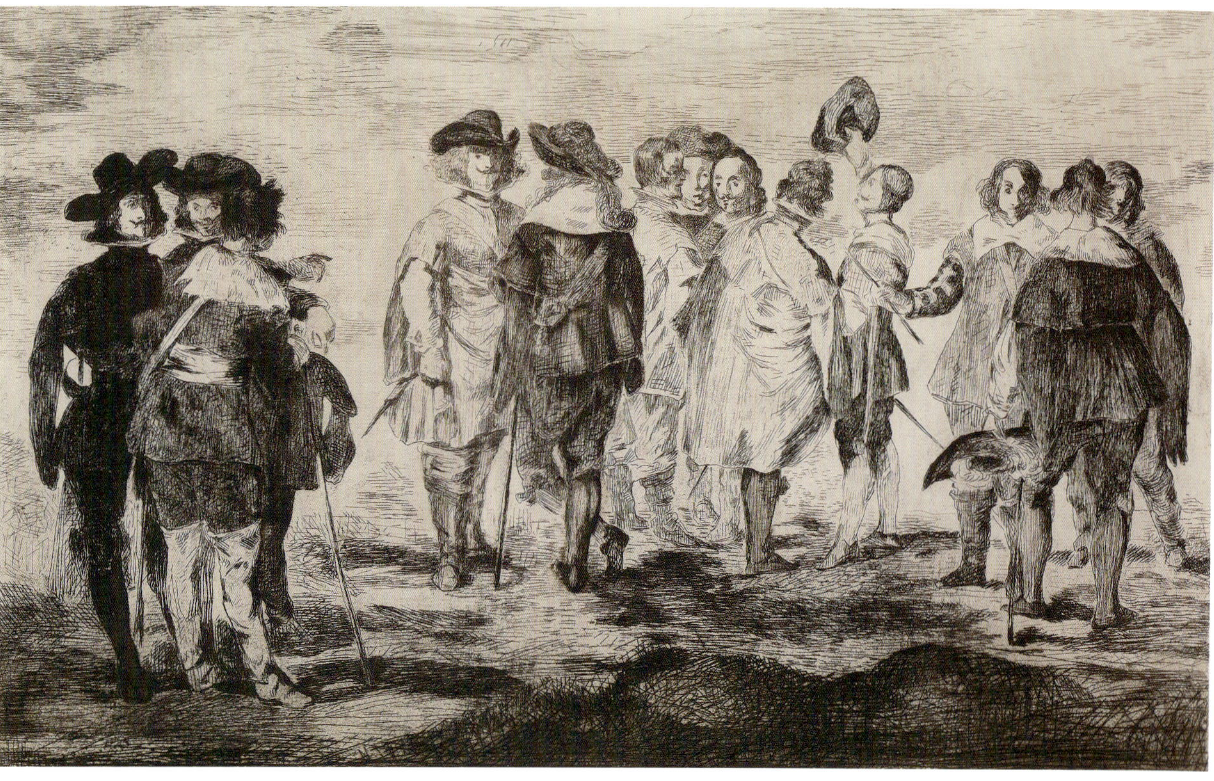

Murillo also had a considerable impact on French artists of the nineteenth century, when, possibly, he was valued more highly than at any time since. *The Beggar Boy* of about 1650 (cat. 69, p. 35), for example, was another work notably popular with copyists (fig. 7), but it also inspired a drawing by Cézanne in which the artist focused on the complex pose of the child (cat. 12, p. 35).

Manet again occupies center stage in the taste for seventeenth-century Dutch art that developed in the 1860s. In his disarmingly direct portrait of Victorine Meurent (cat. 54, p. 220), his favorite model of the 1860s, who had posed for the unashamedly naked *parisienne* in *Luncheon on the Grass* (fig. 3), the thick, creamy paint and frankness of the sitter's gaze immediately recall portraits by Hals, who was a key reference for Manet (cat. 43, p. 220). A year or two before, he had painted his large *Fishing* (cat. 51, p. 36), in which he pays homage to Flemish painters, especially Rubens, in a characteristic blend of witty historicizing and modernity. Alluding to the images of Rubens and his wife Hélène Fourment as they appear in the Flemish artist's *Park of the Château de Steen,* Manet identifies with Rubens by depicting himself and his fiancée, the Dutch Suzanne Leenhoff, in seventeenth-century costume in a setting that, while recognizably the Seine and its banks, also evokes two landscapes by Annibale Carracci (1560–1609) in the Louvre and the landscapes by Rubens that Manet knew from reproductions in the Flemish volume of Blanc's *Histoire des peintres de toutes les écoles* (figs. 8–10).[29] This was not the only time that Manet's wide-ranging visual imagination juggled easily with a number of different sources in a single work.[30] Rubens's freely brushed, small-scale sketches in oil, several of which entered the Louvre in the 1860s, must have been in his mind when he dashed off his *Study for the "Surprised Nymph"* (cat. 50, p. 38), the study for the large, finished painting in Buenos Aires (1859–61; Museo Nacional de Bellas Artes, Buenos Aires), in which the pose recasts that of Susannah in versions of *Susannah and the Elders* by Rubens (cat. 92, p. 39), as well as that of other prototypes such as Boucher's *Bath of Diana* (fig. 16), which Manet had copied in 1852.

A radical shift in the Impressionists' attitude to the art of the past became noticeable when they found their true voice in the early 1870s and emerged unequivocally as the painters of modern life. Feeling a compulsive need to rid themselves of the conventional languages of painting, of the weight of "past looking,"[31] they now eschewed overt references to older art in an attempt to heighten the immediacy and impact of their principal subjects: landscape and contemporary urban life. The American painter Lilla Cabot Perry

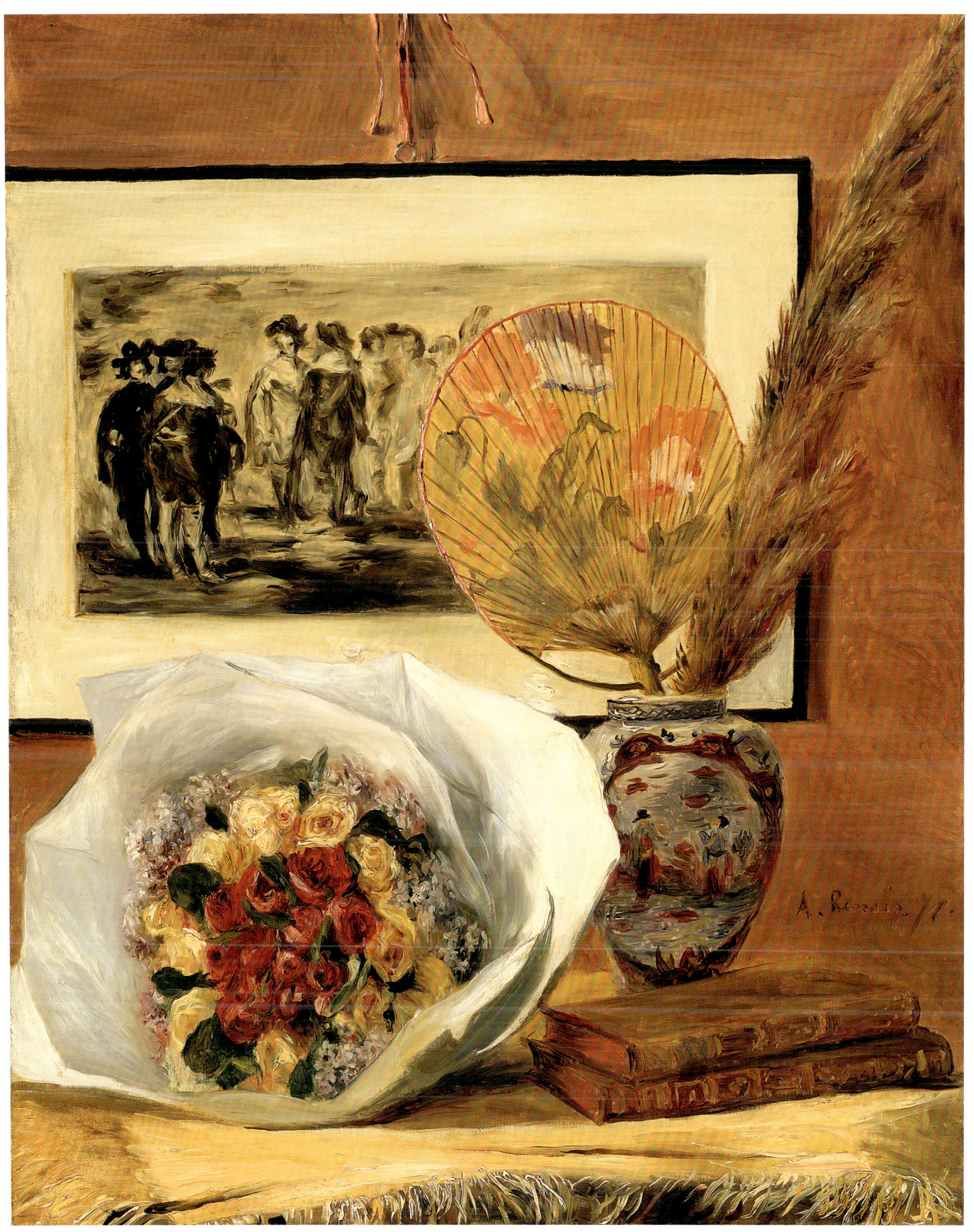
A. Renoir. 71.

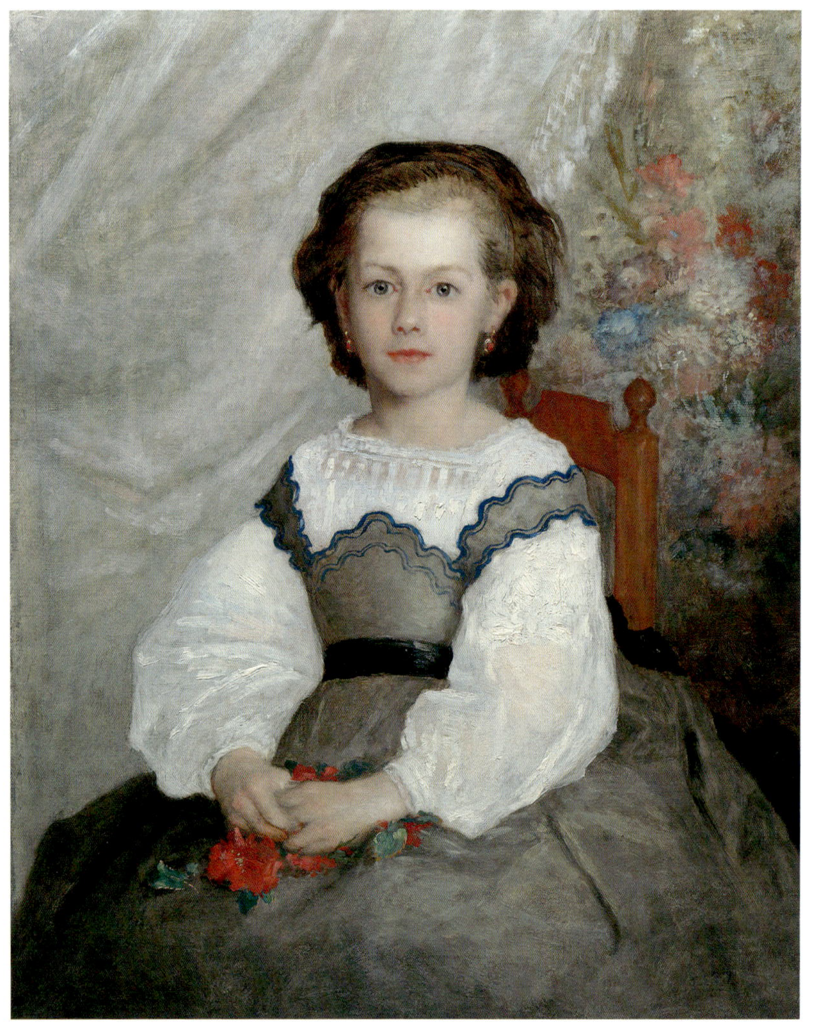

Fig. 6
Pierre-Auguste Renoir
Romaine Lacaux, 1864
Oil on fabric, 32 x 25⅝ in. (81.3 x 65 cm)
The Cleveland Museum of Art, Gift of
Hanna Fund, 1942.1065

Cat. 99
Diego Rodríguez de Silva y Velázquez and Workshop
Infanta Margarita Teresa, c. 1664

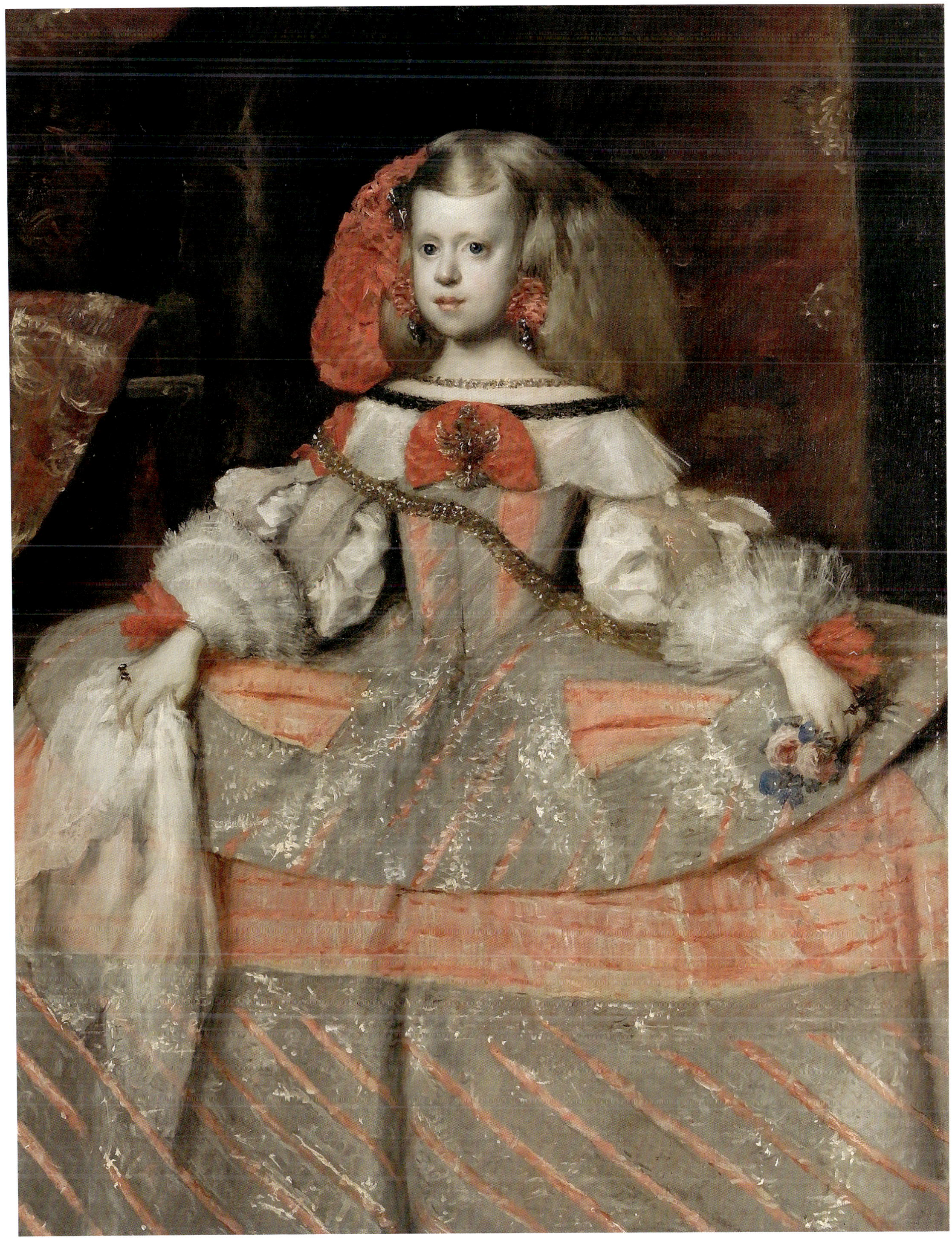

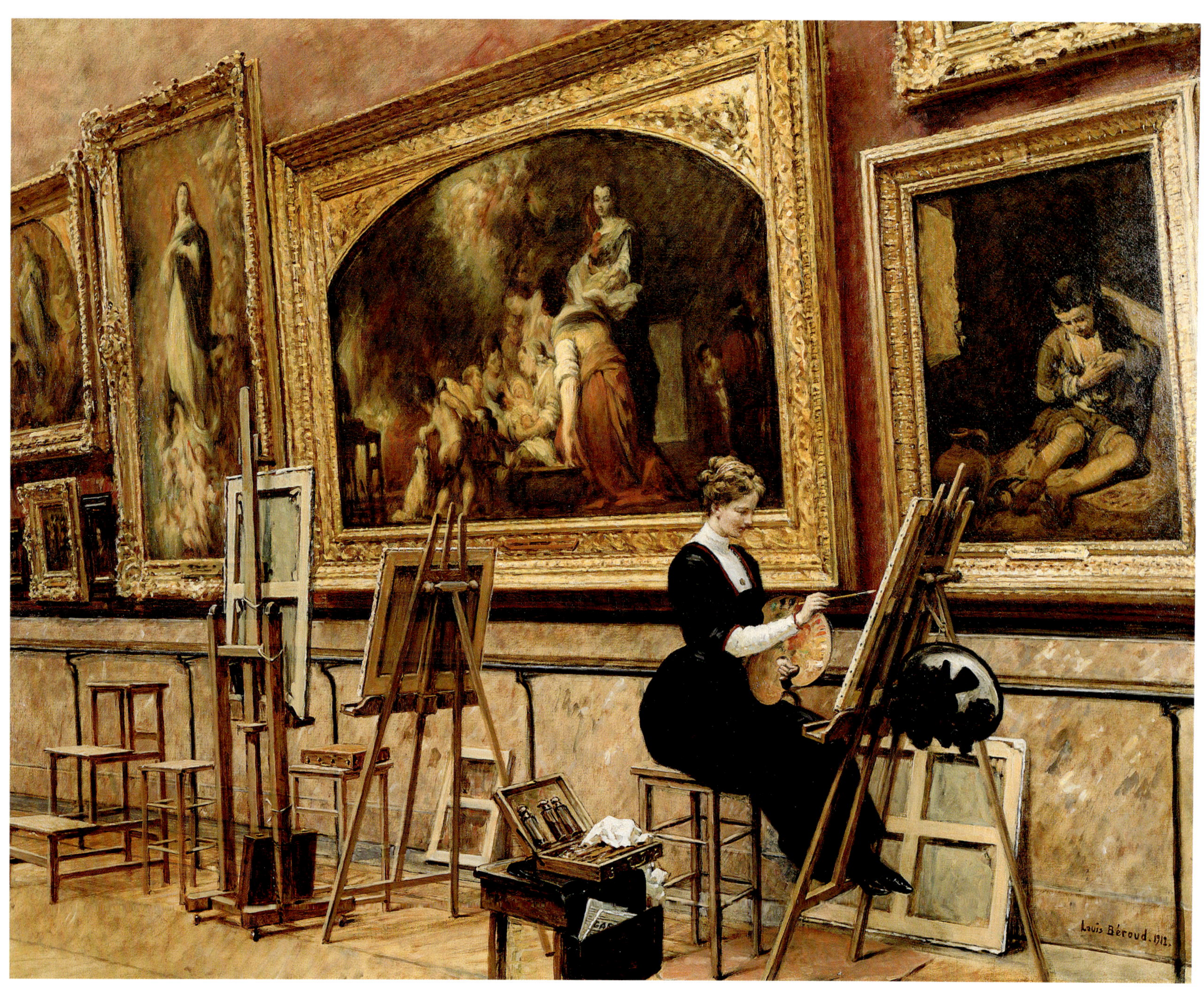

Fig. 7
Louis Beroud (1852–1930)
At the Louvre—Copying Murillo, 1912
Oil on canvas, 51½ x 63½ in. (130.8 x 161.3 cm)
Private collection

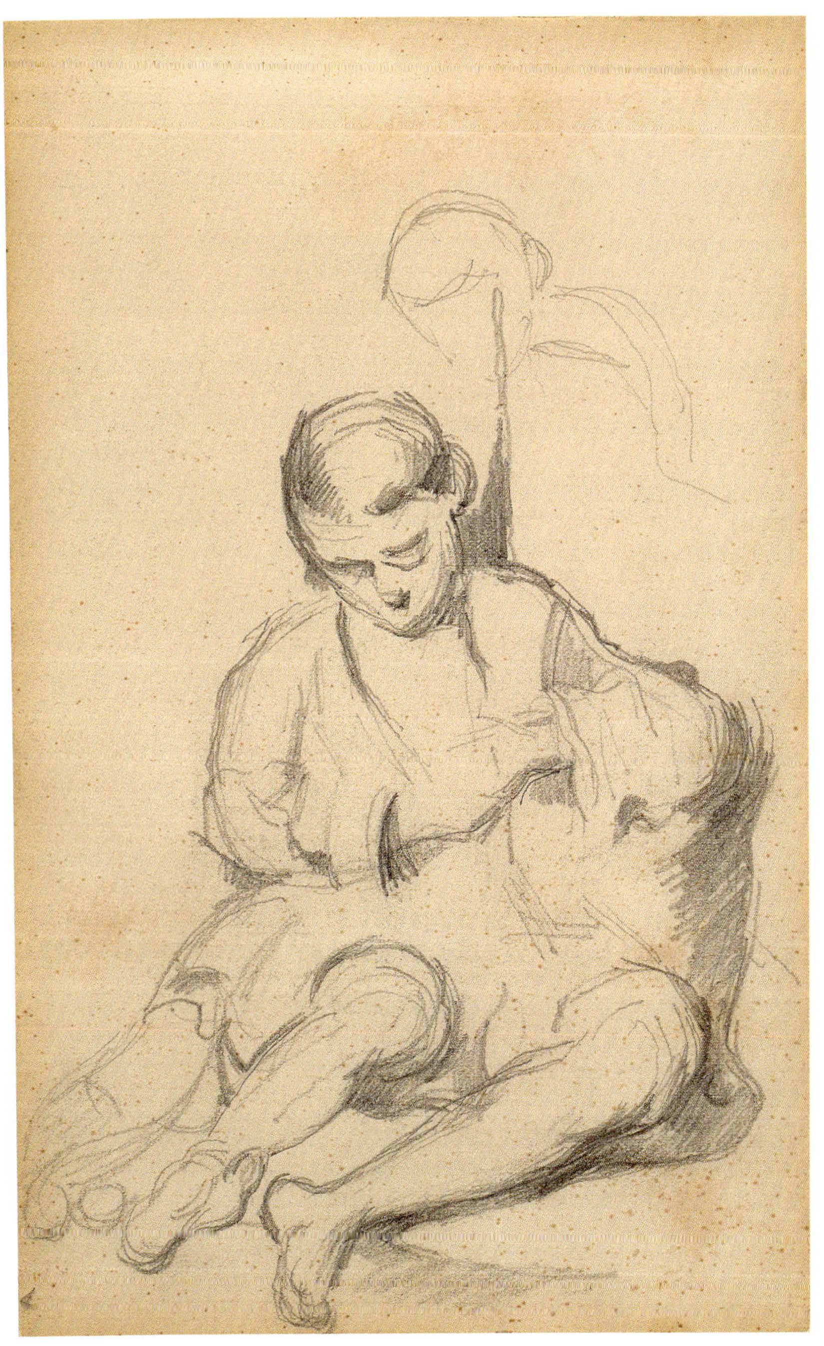

Cat. 12
Paul Cézanne
Boy Searching for Lice, after Murillo,
c. 1882–85

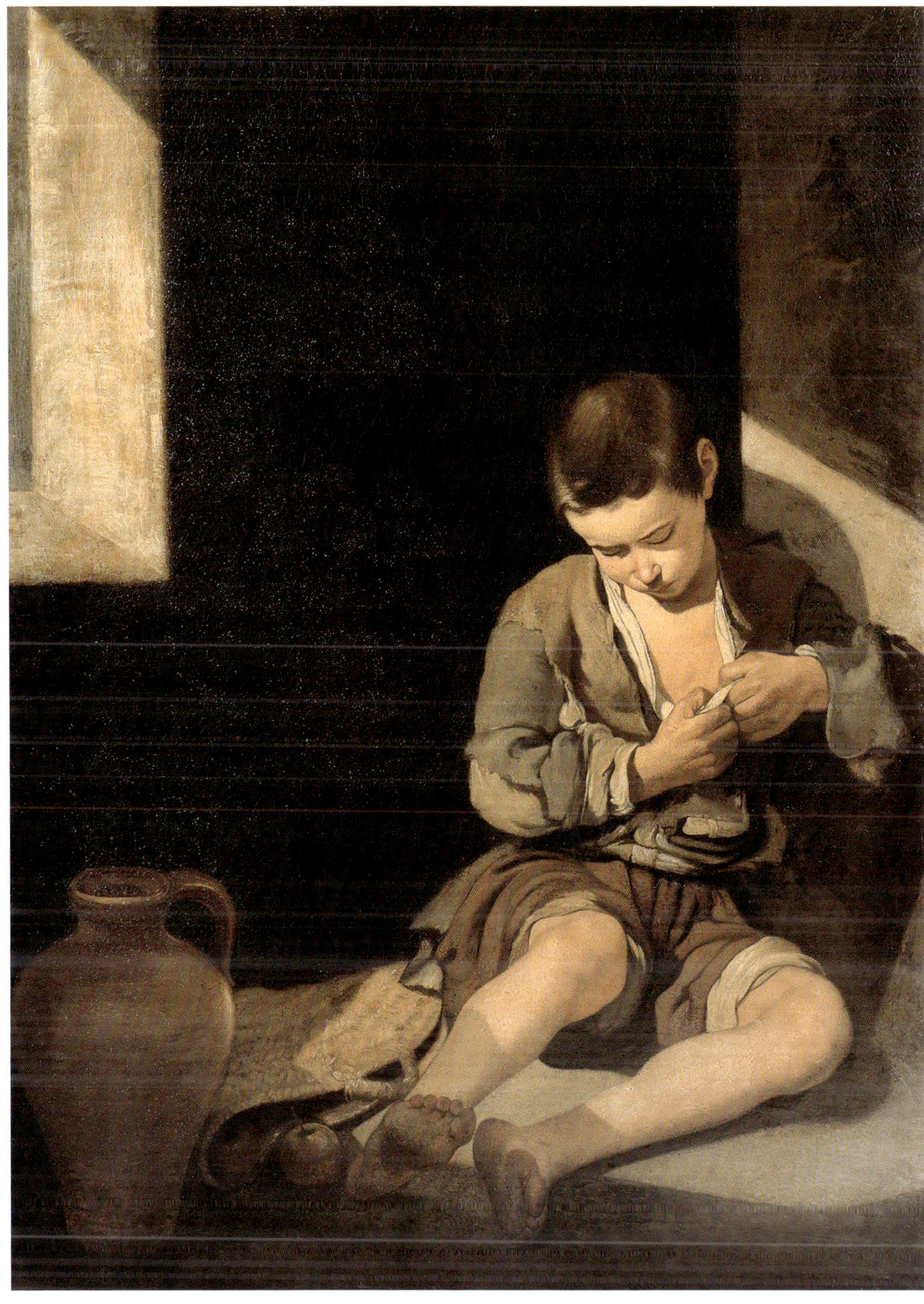

Cat. 69
After Bartolomé Esteban Murillo
The Beggar Boy

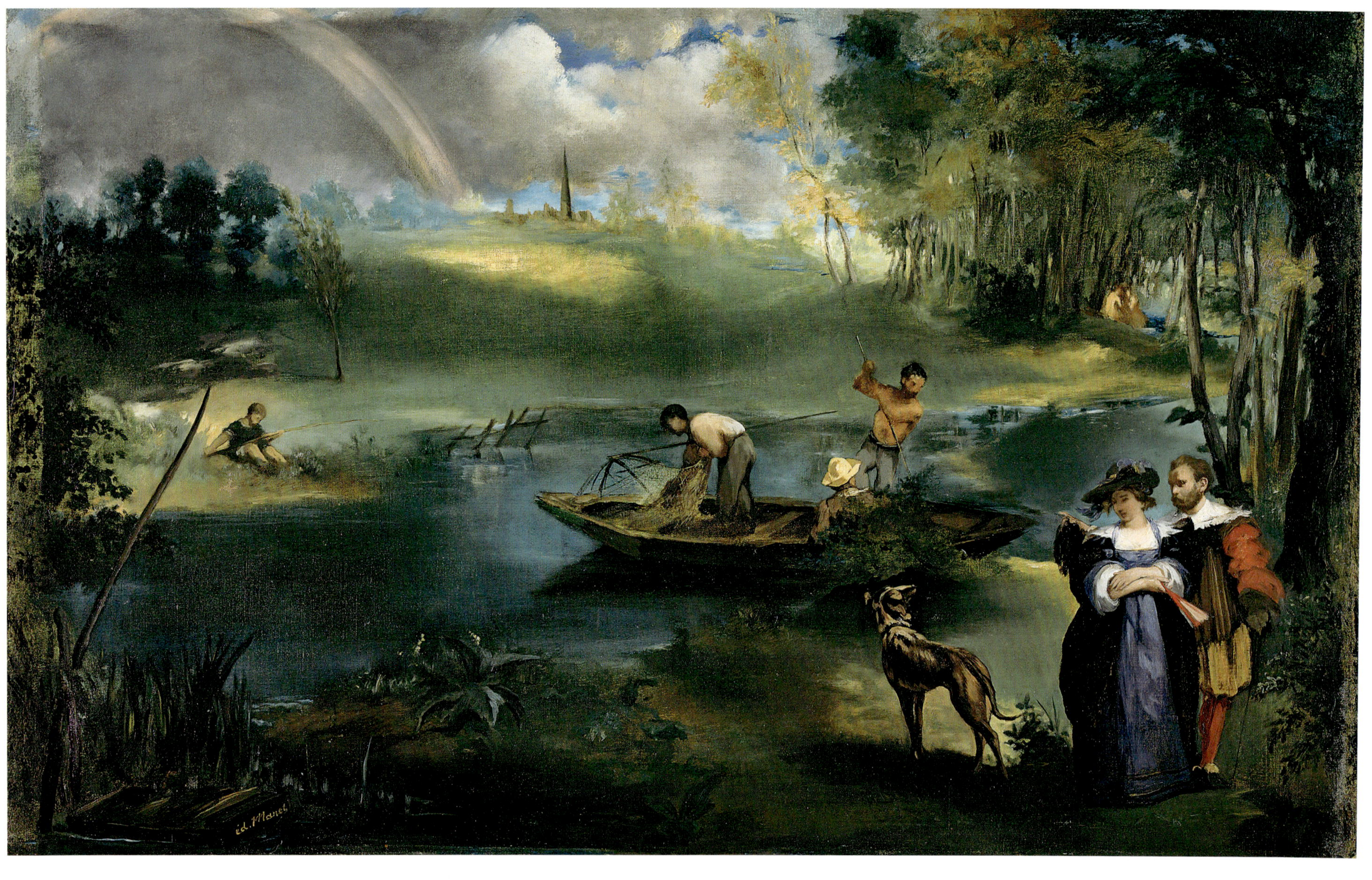

Cat. 51
Édouard Manet
Fishing, 1861–63

Figs. 8–10
Engraving after Annibale Carracci, *Landscape.* From Blanc, *Histoire des peintres de toutes les écoles (depuis la Renaissance jusqu'à nos jours), École bolognaise* (Paris: Librairie Renouard, 1874). Bibliothèque nationale de France, Paris

Engraving after Peter Paul Rubens, *The Château Steen.* From Blanc, *Histoire des peintres de toutes les écoles (depuis la Renaissance jusqu'à nos jours), École flamande* (Paris: Jules Renouard, 1864). Bibliothèque nationale de France, Paris

Engraving after Peter Paul Rubens, *The Rainbow.* From Blanc, *Histoire des peintres de toutes les écoles (depuis la Renaissance jusqu'à nos jours), École flamande* (Paris: Jules Renouard, 1864). Bibliothèque nationale de France, Paris

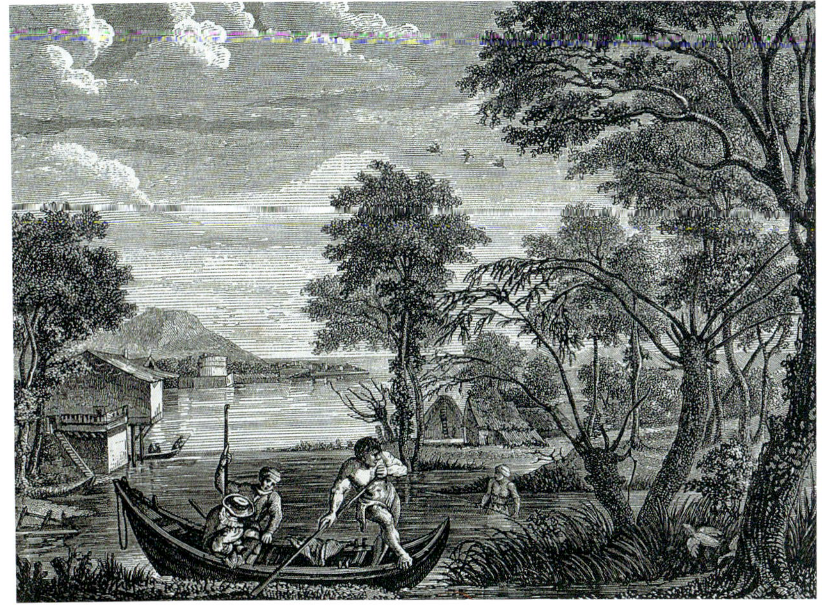

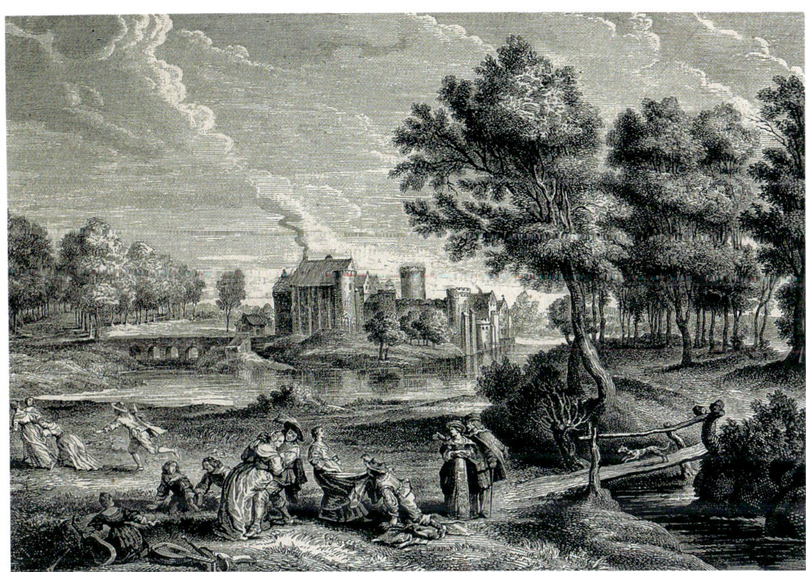

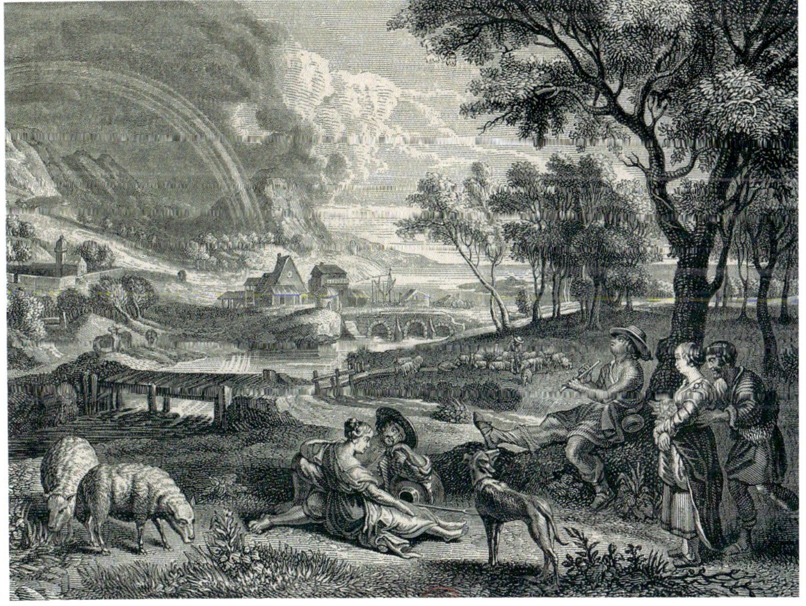

remembered Monet saying in 1889 that he wished he had been born blind and then suddenly regained his sight so as to be able to see the world without knowing the meaning of objects.[32] Cézanne expressed similar views when he spoke of painting only "what we see, forgetting everything that existed before us." Although Cézanne was himself a lifelong habitué of the Louvre, he considered that too much knowledge could hamper a fresh response to the thing observed: "We must not . . . be satisfied with retaining the beautiful formulas of our illustrious predecessors. Let us go forth to study beautiful nature, let us try to free our minds from them, let us strive to express ourselves according to our personal temperament."[33] Closely linked to these notions of seeing the world afresh was the concept that the work of art should express the artist's individuality. Art, in Émile Zola's well-known dictum, was "nature seen through a temperament."[34]

Forgetting was at the heart of Impressionist ideology in the 1870s and early 1880s.[35] In 1876, the year of the second Impressionist exhibition, two important publications made the case for innocent looking. The pamphlet *La Nouvelle Peinture* (*The New Painting*) by Edmond Duranty, a Naturalist writer and close friend of Degas, urged artists to ignore the examples of others and to be true to themselves, to turn away from traditional subjects and to focus on modern life. Duranty described the Impressionists as "trying to create from scratch a wholly modern art, an art imbued with our surroundings, our sentiments, and the things of our age."[36] In "The Impressionists and Édouard Manet," Manet's friend the poet Stéphane Mallarmé advocated the same conscious naïveté. "Each work should be a new creation of the mind, the eye should forget all it has seen, and learn anew from the lesson before it. It should abstract itself from memory, seeing only that which it looks upon, and that as for the first time."[37]

The new art of the Impressionists developed at a time of dynamic social change. In Paris the structures of the old order had literally been torn down when Baron Haussmann demolished buildings to make way for the broad boulevards that are still a feature of the city. Many other radical changes were undermining the traditional structures of French society: a huge migration from the countryside to the cities, growing industrialization, and the rise of a new and prosperous bourgeoisie all had an enormous impact on Paris, both transforming it into a glittering modern metropolis and fostering an appreciation of the contrasting values of the countryside. To capture a fresh response to nature and the exciting urban kaleidoscope, the Impressionists devised a vivid new pictorial language of bright color and small, broken brushstrokes that created the impression of

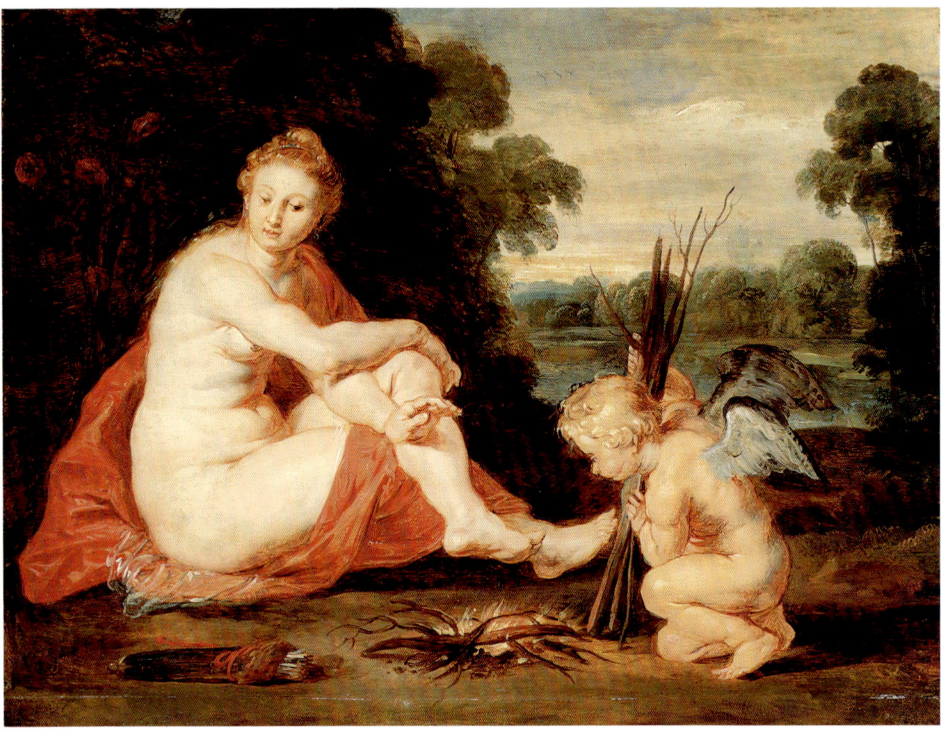

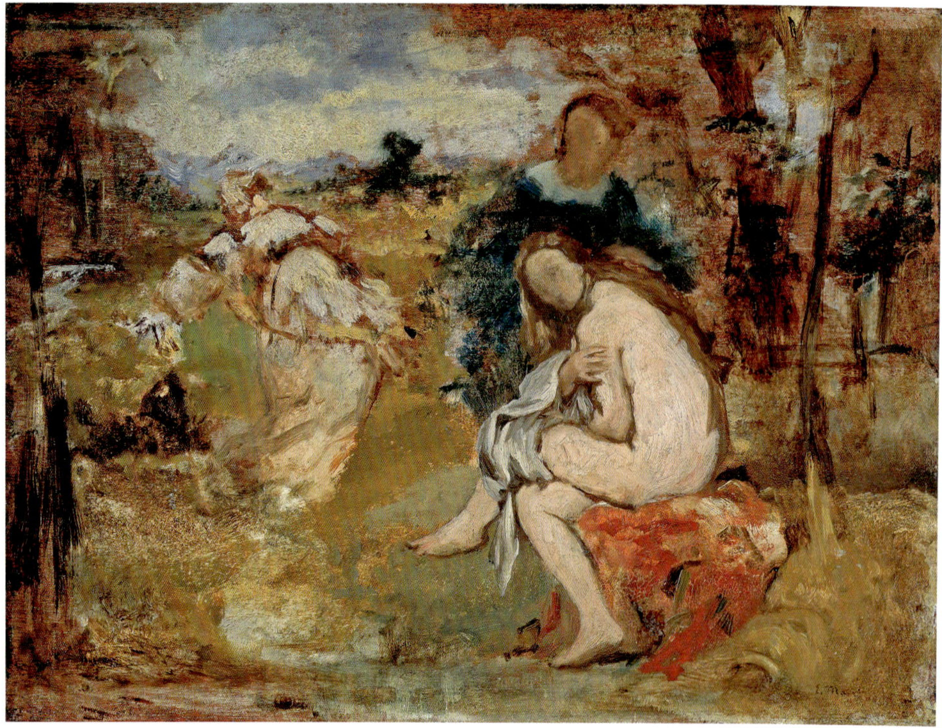

Cat. 93
Follower of Sir Peter Paul Rubens
Venus and Cupid Warming Themselves (Venus frigida), c. 1610–20

Cat. 50
Édouard Manet
Study for the "Surprised Nymph," 1860–61

spontaneity. They avoided the meticulous detail, clear outlines, and tonal modeling typical of the academic tradition and applied paint in nondescriptive visible touches all over the surface of a picture. They broke with the academic convention of dark grounds, often priming their canvases in various shades of tinted white to achieve maximum luminosity. In the quest for vibrant color, they were helped by the high chroma colorants that became available as a result of advances in chemistry and by ready-mixed pigments in portable tubes that facilitated plein air painting. New hog-bristle brushes in a variety of shapes—as compared with the soft, round, sable brushes used by the old masters—helped to give Impressionist paintings their characteristically lively, variegated surface textures.[38] The mark of the brush—the *touche*—now ceased to be a descriptive tool and became the defining element in artists' expression of their immediate response to what they saw.

In their compositions the Impressionists used antiacademic strategies to suggest direct engagement with the real world. Typically, they rejected the one-point perspective that creates the illusion of a window onto the world common in old master painting, instead

Cat. 92
Sir Peter Paul Rubens
Susannah and the Elders, 1607

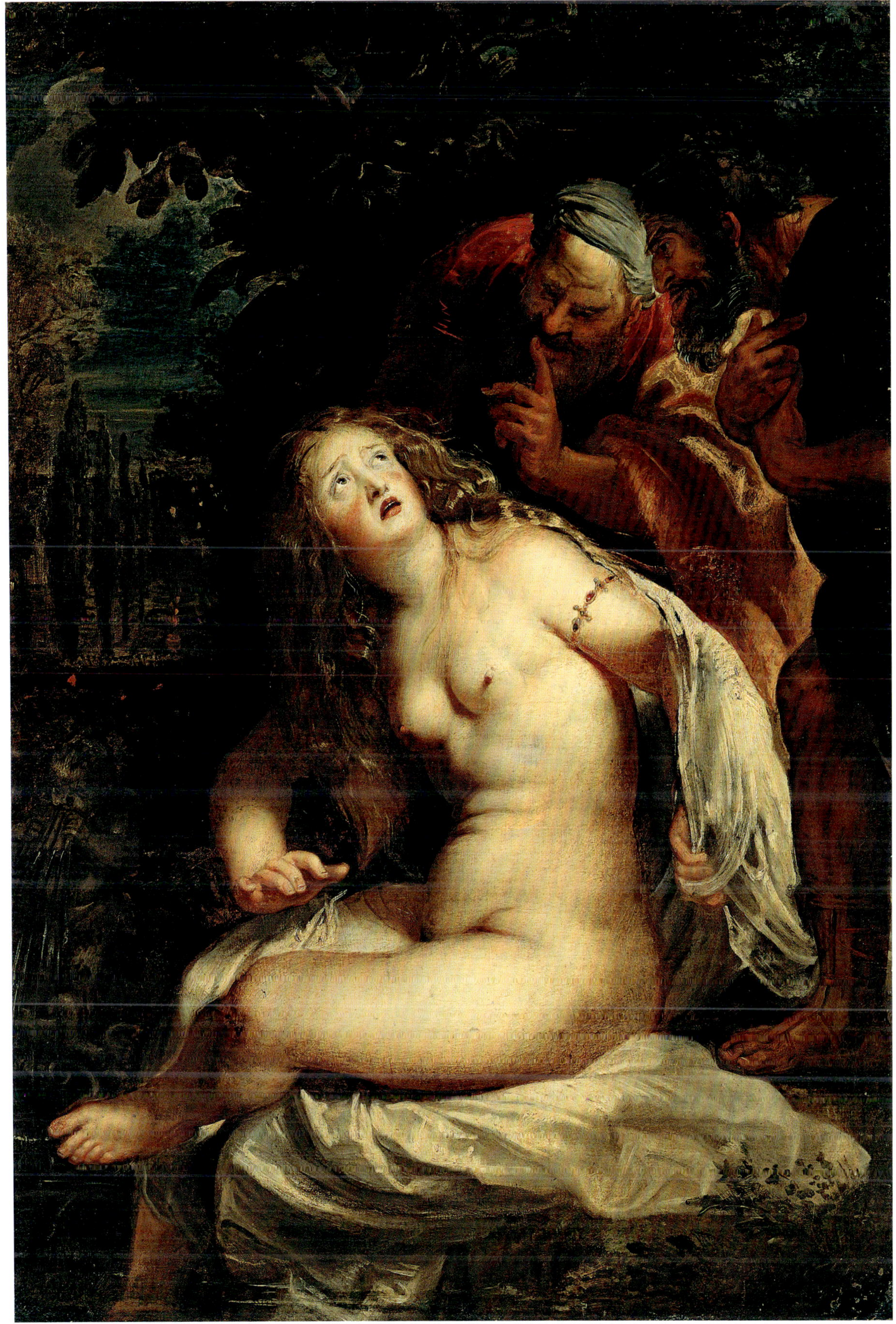

collapsing the space between near and far to grant more or less equal emphasis to all the elements in a composition. They developed a shifting perspective that could encompass different viewpoints and unusual angles of vision, evoking a visual equivalent of the experience of the Baudelairian flâneur immersing himself in the varied texture of everyday life.

This new way of painting was, on the face of it, avowedly antihistorical. Yet no artist can break completely with the past, and the work of the Impressionists time and again evinces lingering echoes of the old masters in subject, composition, and technique. Degas, an artist both forward looking and anachronistic, offers a fascinating case study of Impressionist attitudes to tradition. He pursued the most daringly innovative compositional strategies of all the Impressionists. Borrowing from the conventions of Japanese ukiyo-e prints, which were immensely popular in nineteenth-century Paris, he adopted plunging perspectives and cropped edges to create seemingly random, fragmentary views of Parisian cafés and cabarets, of dancers rehearsing backstage, and of horses and riders at the races—all glimpsed as if from the corner of the eye. Despite such radical modernity, the old masters were never far from Degas's thoughts. "No art was ever less spontaneous than mine," he asserted. "What I do is the result of reflection and the study of the great masters; of inspiration, spontaneity, temperament . . . I know nothing."[39] So when, with this in mind, we look again at these fleeting vignettes of Parisian life, we discover that the figures are drawn with the razor-sharp clarity that we associate with Mantegna or Raphael (or Degas's more immediate mentor Ingres) and that his compositions have been as carefully planned as a mythological scene by Poussin.

Just how consistently the example of older art was on Degas's mind is demonstrated by the words recorded by Edmond de Goncourt in connection with one of the artist's modern dance subjects, *The Rehearsal* of about 1874. "While standing on tiptoe to demonstrate the dancers' steps," Goncourt remembered, Degas spoke of "the tender softness of Velázquez and the silhouetted flatness of Mantegna,"[40] referring to the influence of Velázquez in melding forms with the surrounding atmosphere and acknowledging a debt to Mantegna in linear design.[41] Sometimes a drawing made in Degas's youth lingered in his memory to resurface many years later. The intertwining figures of two men conversing, for instance, sketched from Raphael's *The School of Athens* in Rome in the 1850s (cat. 77, p. 41; cat. 24, p. 41), is boldly refreshed four decades later in a charcoal drawing of two dancers (*Harlequin and Colombine,* private collection).[42]

Less surprisingly perhaps, the ghosts of the past hovered over Impressionist painting in the more traditional domains of still life and portraiture. The studied abandon of an opulent bouquet by the seventeenth-century master of decorative still-life Jean-Baptiste Monnoyer (c. 1634–1699), a favorite of Louis XIV, is recaptured in the formality of Bazille's large-scale flower piece (cat. 65, p. 43; cat. 4, p. 42), while Monet's splendid *Still Life with Flowers and Fruit* (cat. 59, p. 44) brings a new naturalism to the subject. Nineteenth-century still-life painters greatly admired Chardin for his harmonious arrangements of humble objects and for his mastery of color and light. The inspiration of exquisite works like the little basket of plums (cat. 22, p. 45) can be clearly sensed in Renoir's *Still Life with Peaches and Grapes* (cat. 82, p. 45), in which the soft play of light defines the colors and forms of the peaches in the blue-and-white porcelain dish, offset by bunches of grapes strewn casually over the table. Chardin's legacy is also felt in Manet's *Le Sauman (The Salmon)* (cat. 55, p. 46), although the crisp folds of the white tablecloth, the gleaming textures of silvery fish, transparent glass, and white porcelain, and especially the detail of the half-peeled lemon are closer to a Dutch master of the genre like Pieter Claesz (1596/97–1661)—an example of Manet's sophisticatedly eclectic response to older art, as mentioned above. In *The Salmon* the rumpled tablecloth and tipped-up bowl combine with old master references to introduce a disquieting note characteristic of Manet's unique, modern sensibility. More opulent Dutch table pieces, such as *A Table of Desserts* (1640; Musée du Louvre, Paris) by Jan Davidsz de Heem (1606/7–1684) and *Banquet Still Life* (cat. 6, p. 189) by Abraham Hendricksz van Beyeren (1620/21–1690), seem to lie behind some of Cézanne's great orchestrations of color and form in his late still lifes (cat. 17, p. 192). The intense observation that Spanish artists brought to still life can also be felt in Sisley's *The Pike* (cat. 39, p. 47; cat. 96, p. 47).

The Impressionists rejuvenated genre painting through fresh observation of the world around them. Seventeenth-century Dutch and Flemish genre scenes, often filtered through the example of Chardin, offered a potent model. In the eighteenth century Chardin had appealed to aristocratic collectors, but the writers principally responsible for reviving interest in his work in the nineteenth century—Thoré and the Goncourts—regarded him as a precursor of the naturalism of their own day. This perspective struck a special chord with Pissarro, who painted working country people throughout his life. His servant girls recall Chardin's kitchen maids (cat. 75, p. 48; cat. 20, p. 49), but they also engage with the tradition of women

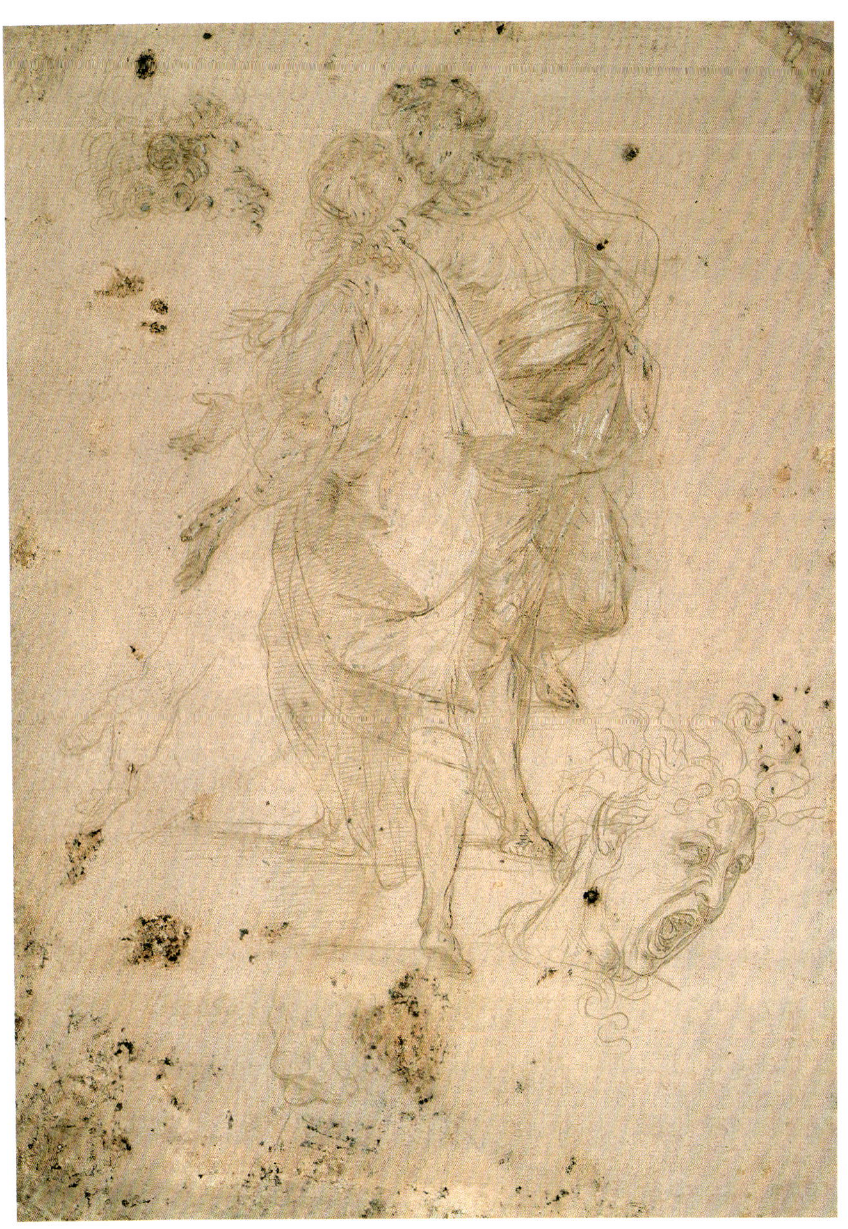

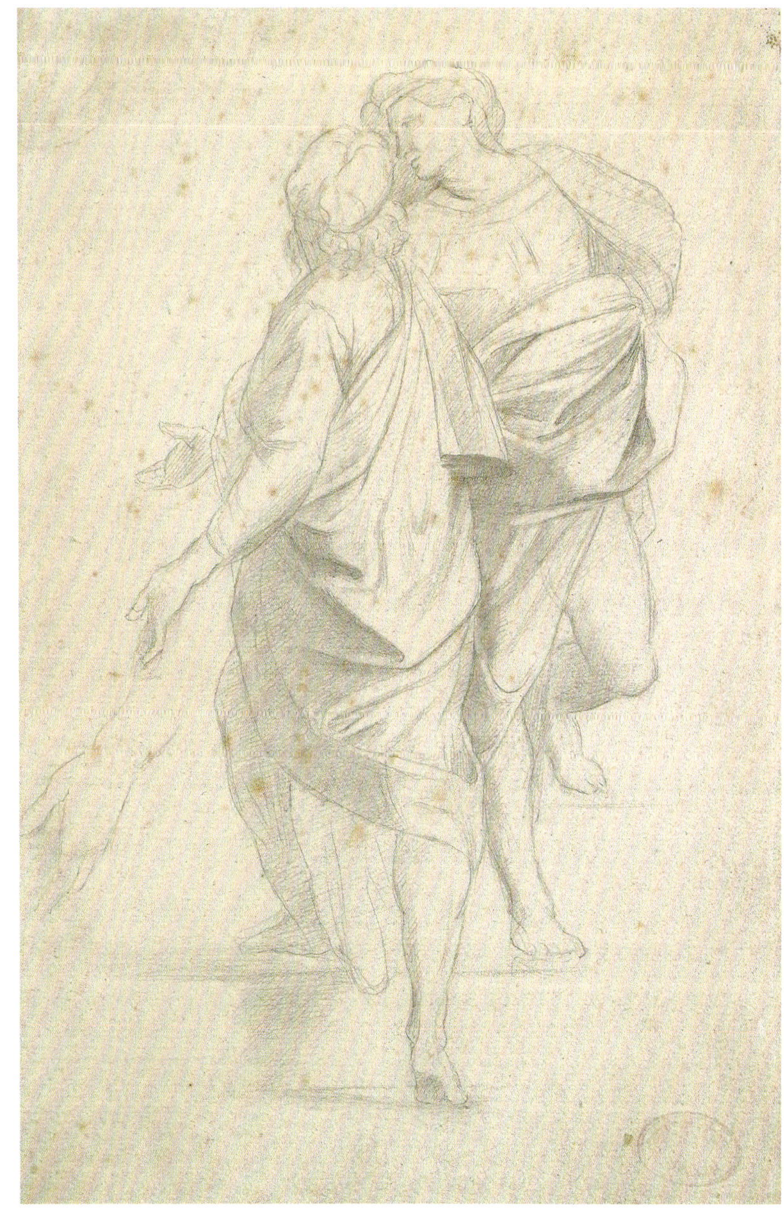

Cat. 77
Raphael Santi
Two Men Conversing on a Flight of Steps and *A Head Shouting*, c. 1509

Cat. 24
Edgar Degas
Two Figures Standing on a Flight of Steps, after Raphael, c. 1853–54

Cat. 4
Frédéric Bazille
Flowers, 1868

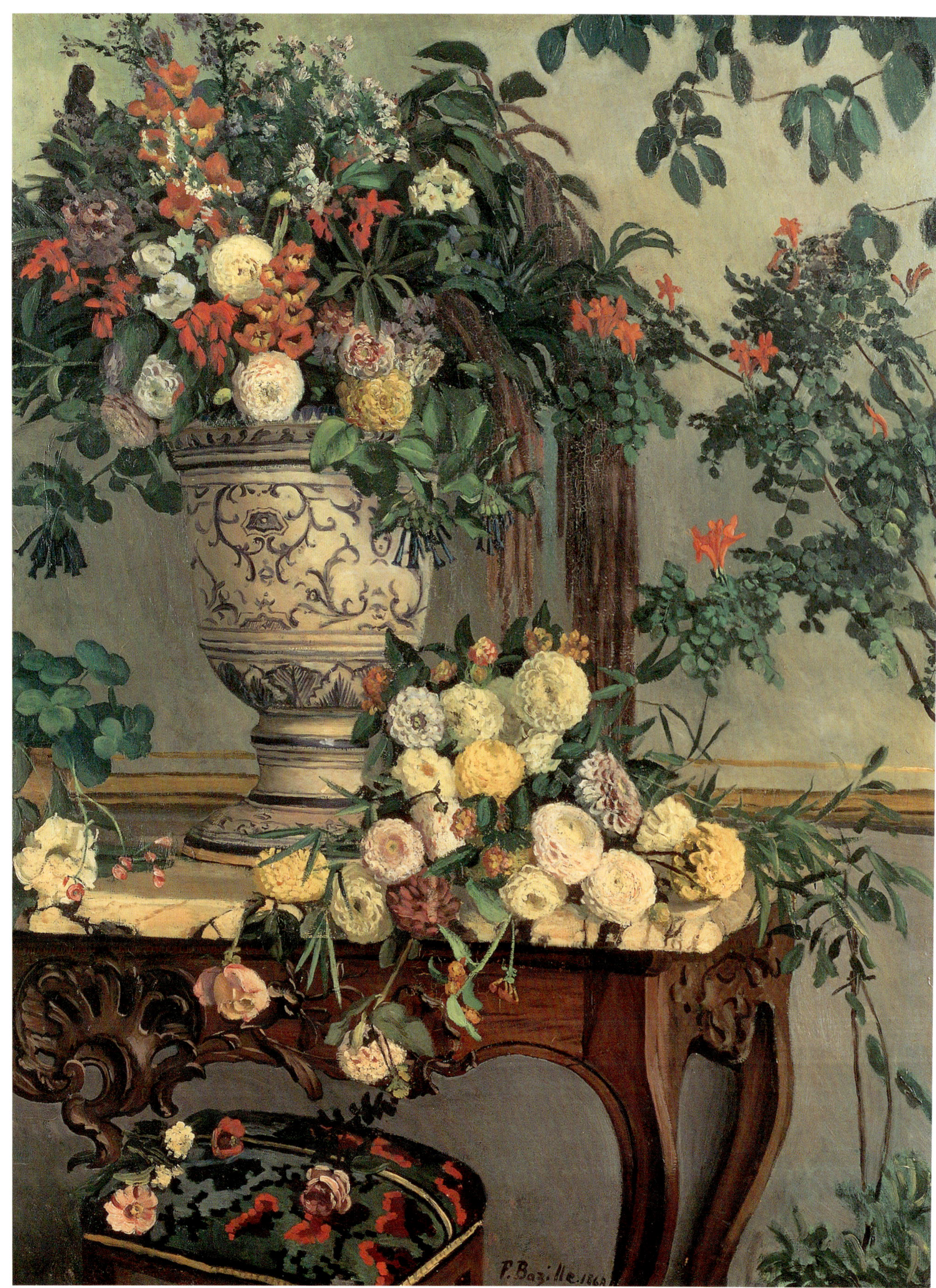

Cat. 65
Jean-Baptiste Monnoyer
Vase of Flowers on a Marble Table

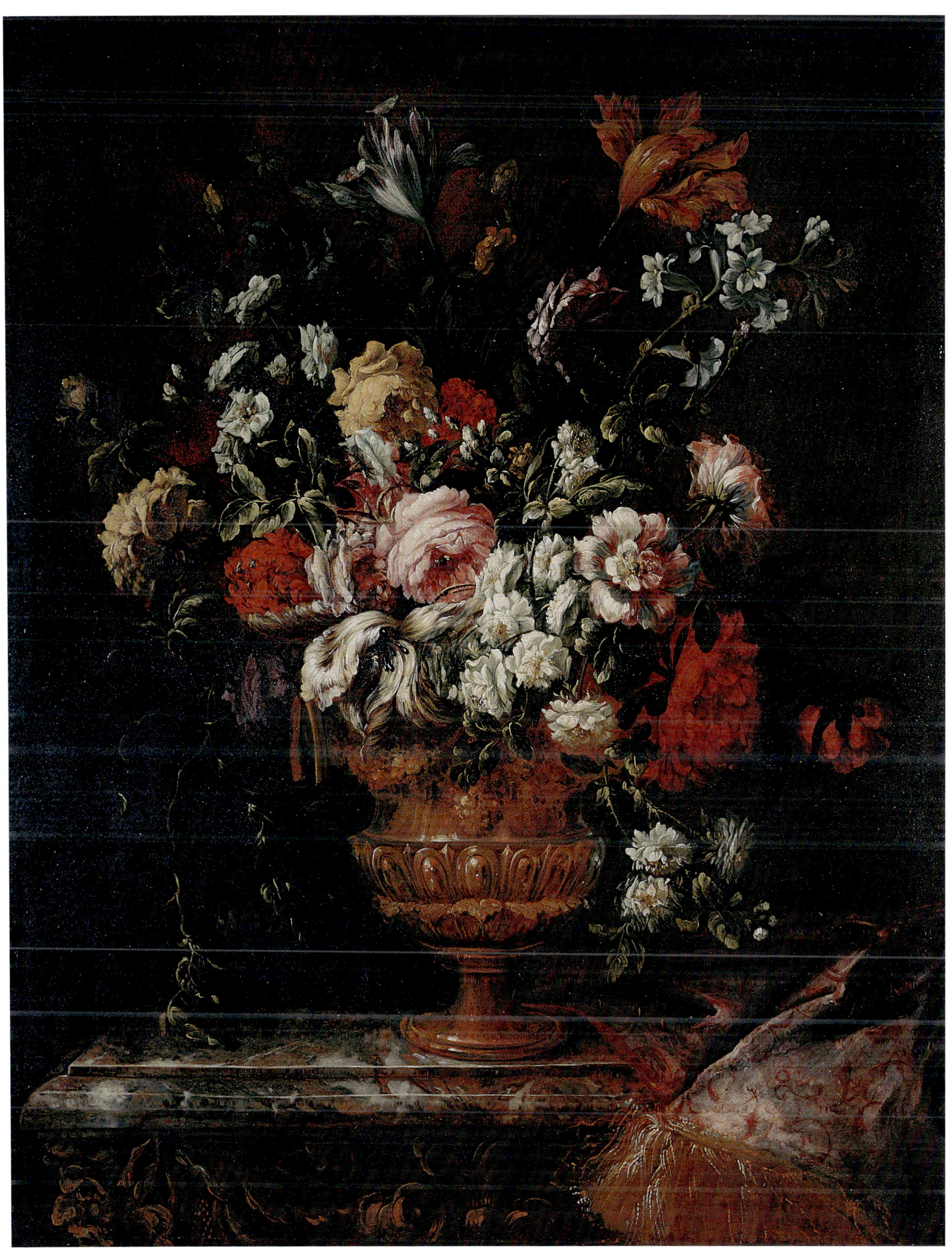

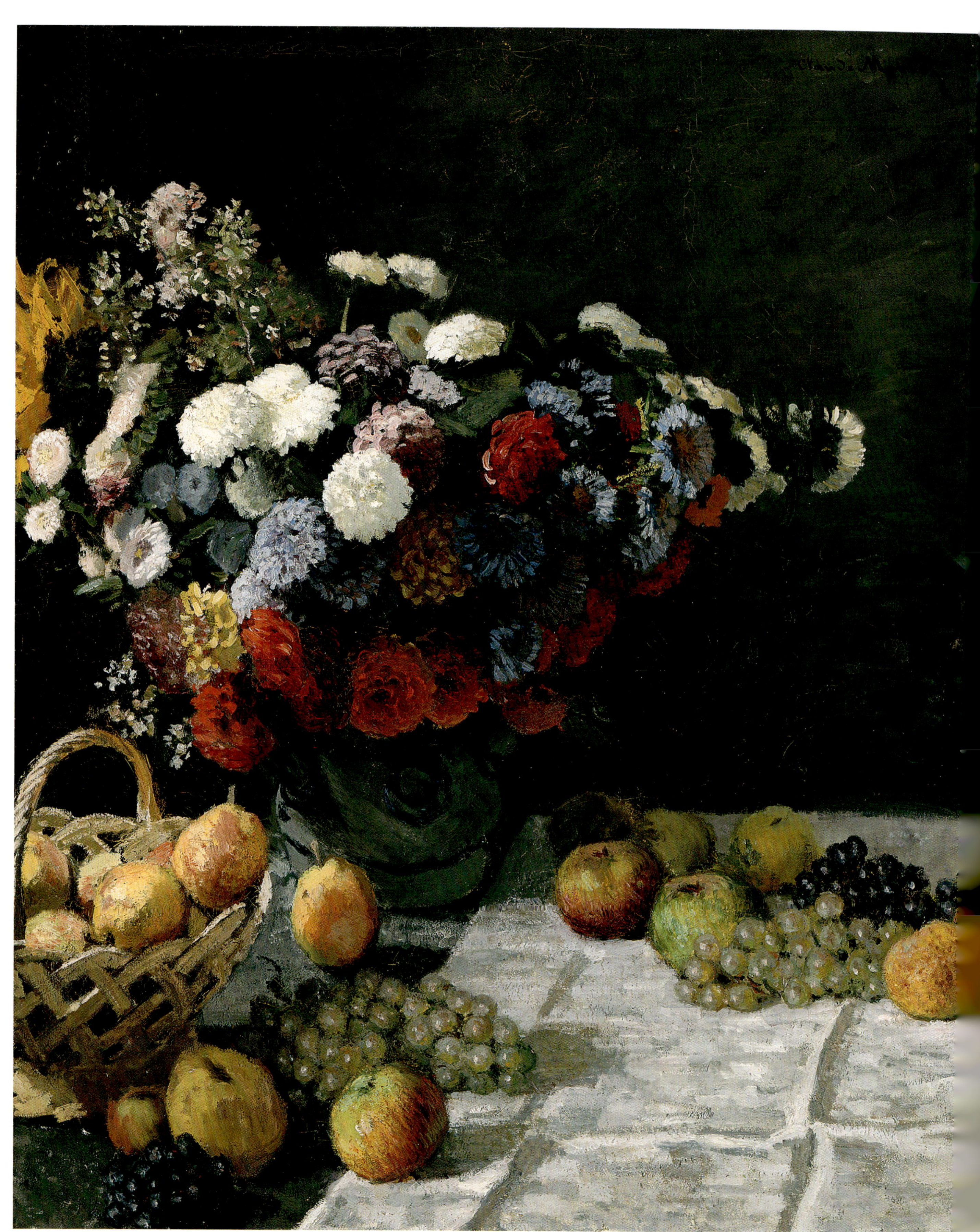

Cat. 59
Claude Monet
Still Life with Flowers and Fruit, 1869

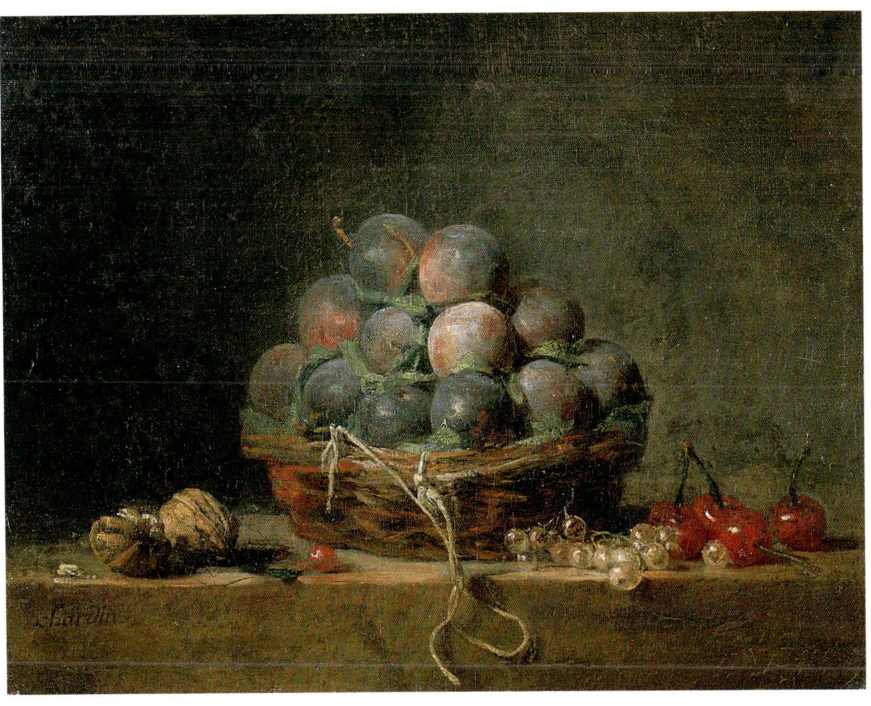

Cat. 22
Jean-Siméon Chardin
Basket of Plums, c. 1765

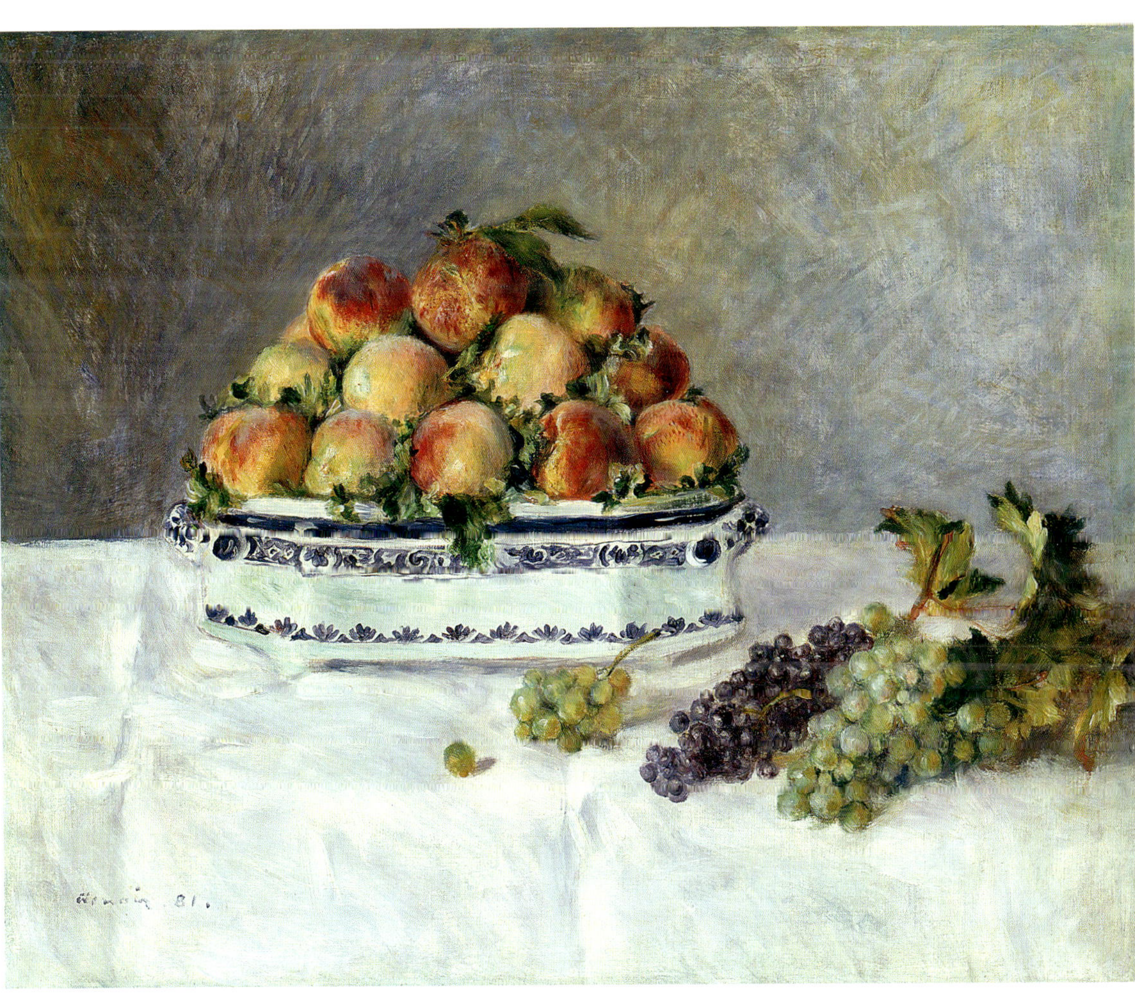

Cat. 82
Pierre-Auguste Renoir
Still Life with Peaches and Grapes, 1881

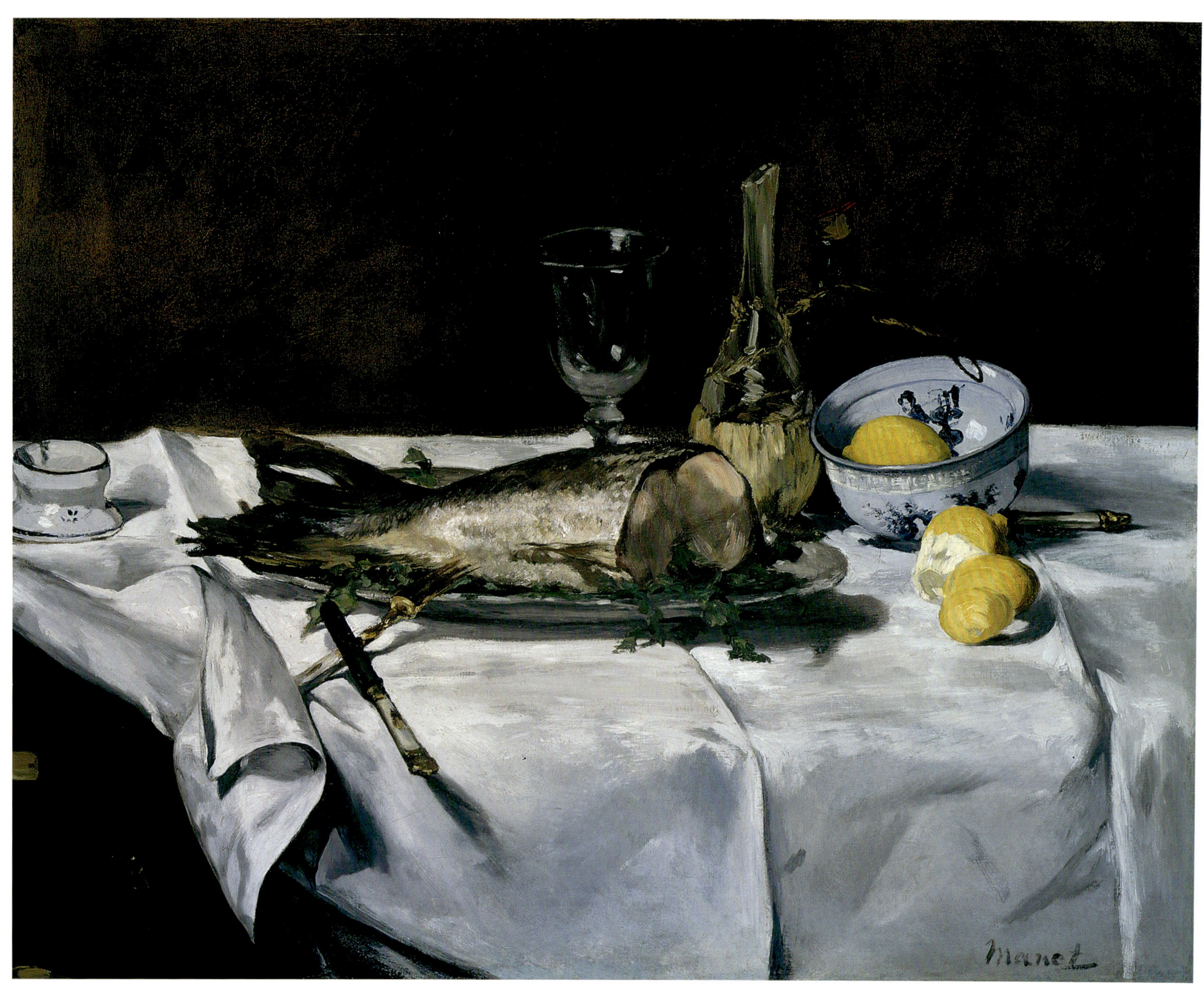

Cat. 55
Édouard Manet
Le Saumon (The Salmon), c. 1864–65

Cat. 96
Alfred Sisley
The Pike, 1888

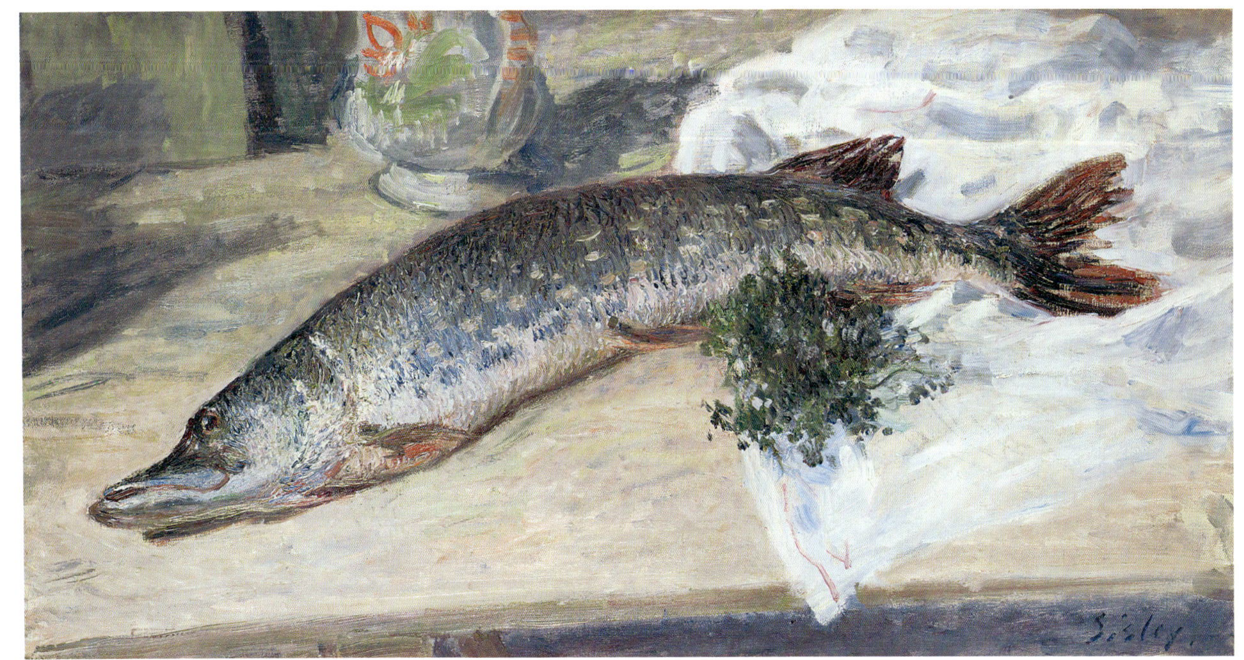

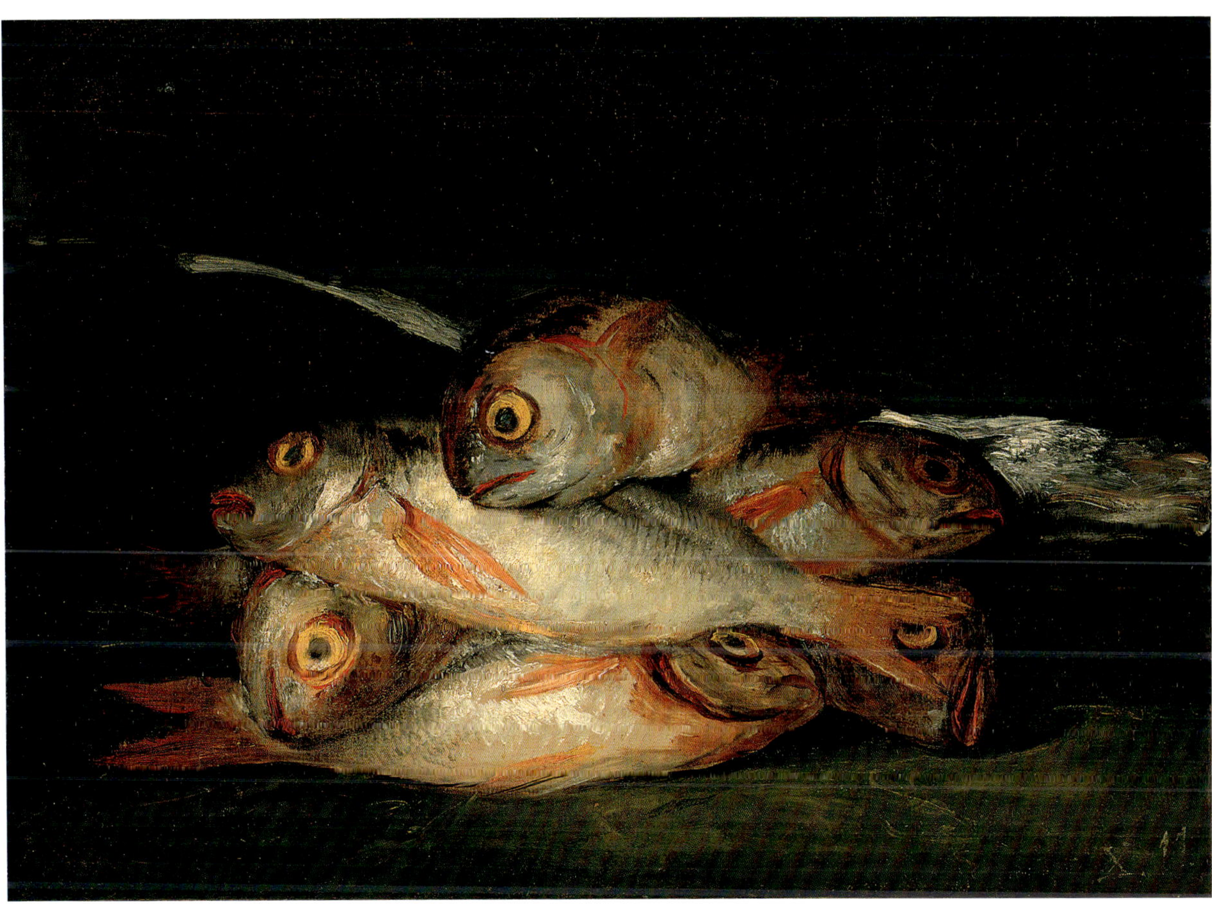

Cat. 39
Francisco de Goya
Still Life with Golden Bream, 1808–12

Cat. 75
Camille Pissarro
The Little Country Maid, 1882

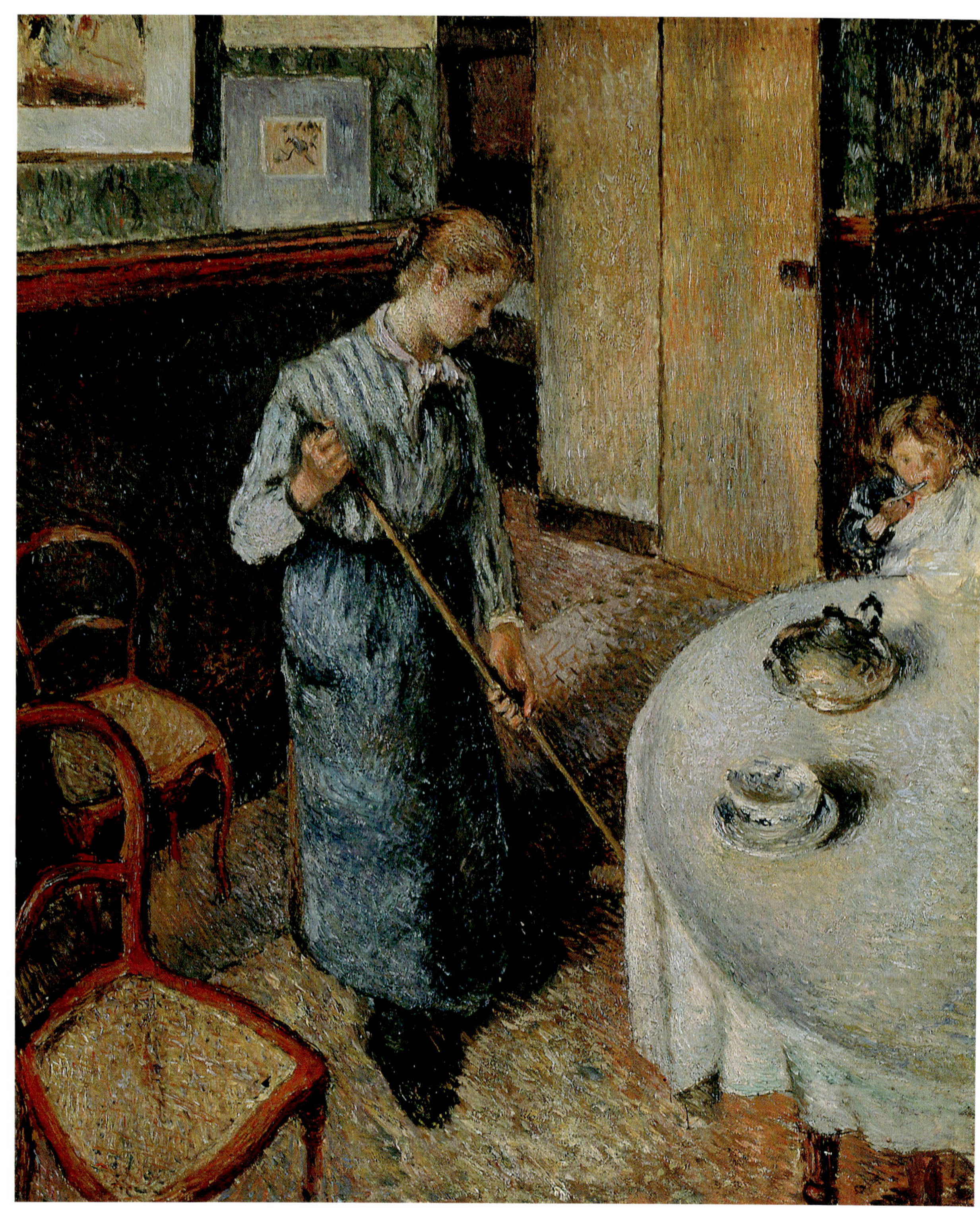

Cat. 20
Jean-Siméon Chardin
The Scullery Maid, 1738

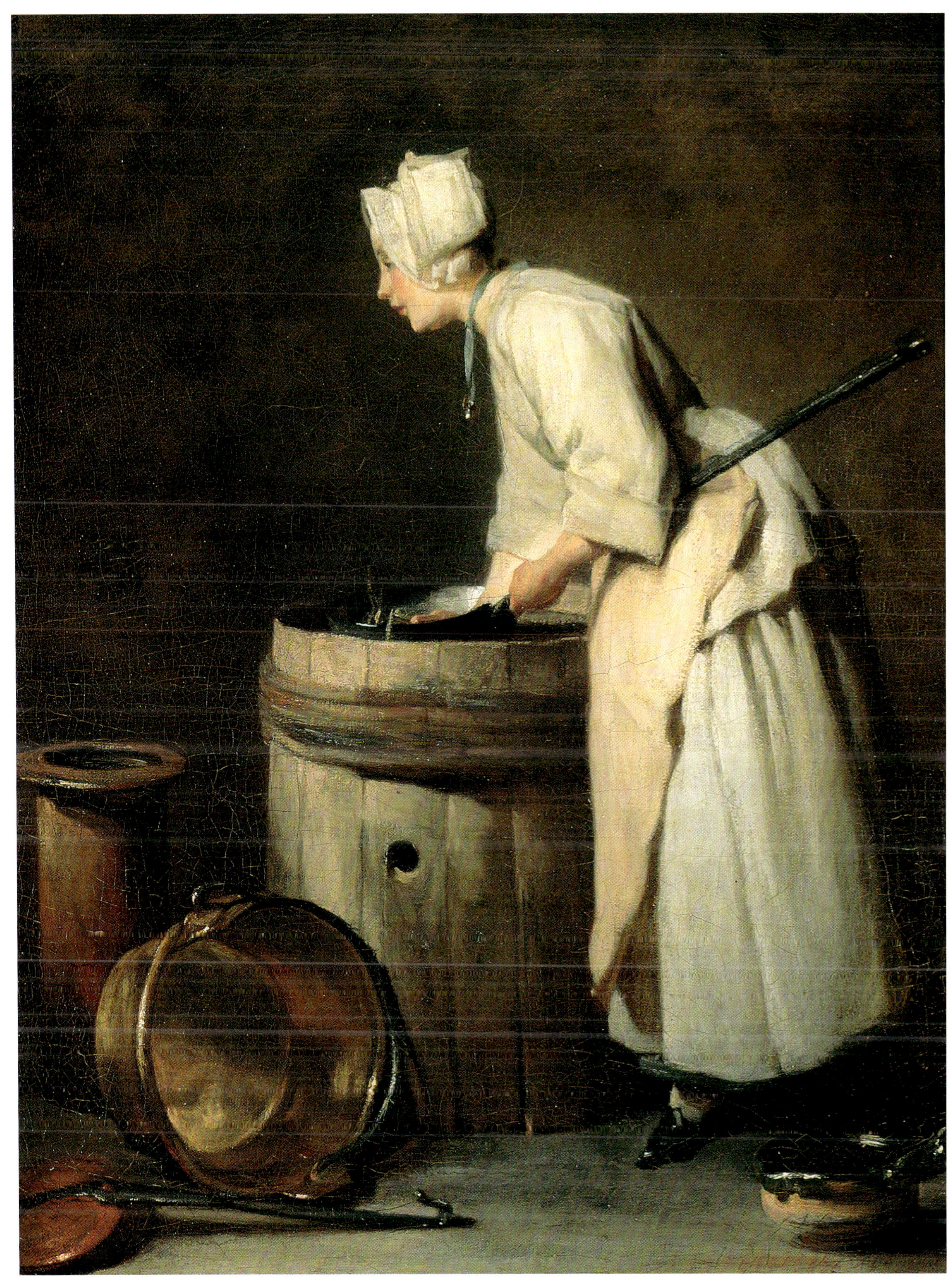

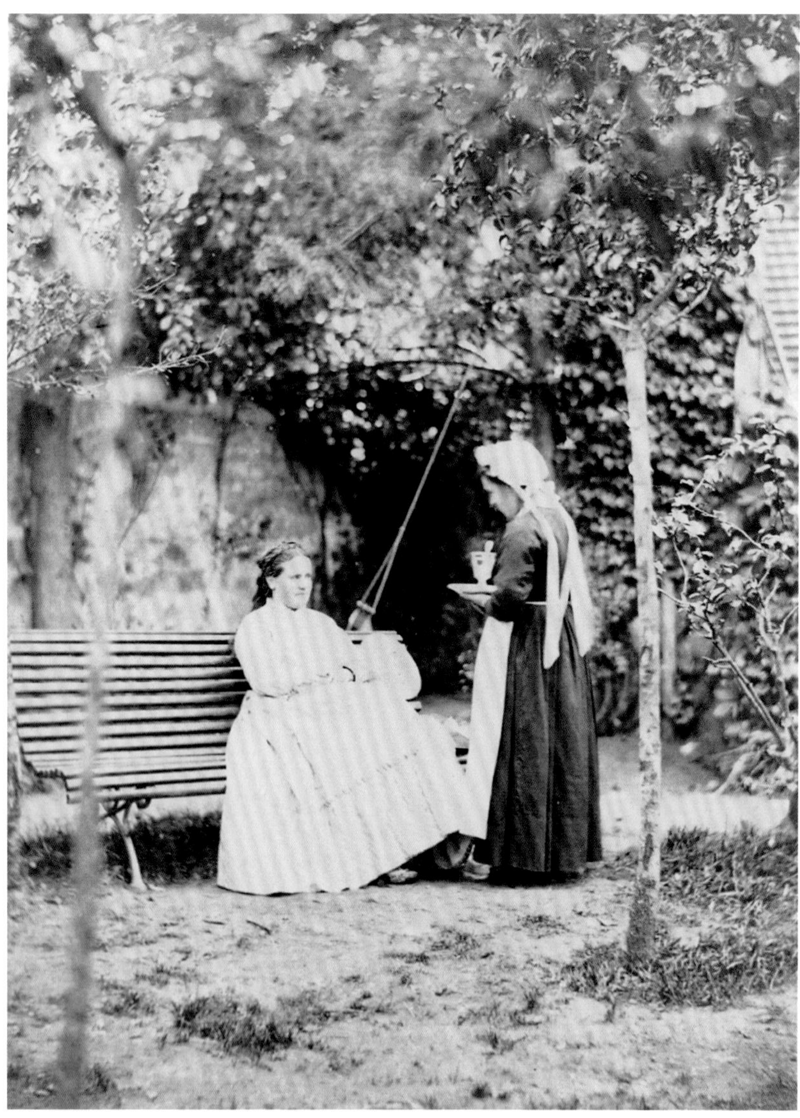

Fig. 11
Julie Pissarro and the Maid at Pontoise, c. 1872–75
Photograph, 8¼ x 6¼ in. (20.9 x 15.8 cm)
Lionel and Sandrine Pissarro Archives, Paris

Cat. 72
Camille Pissarro
The Maidservant, 1867

shown performing domestic tasks in courtyards or kitchens familiar from the paintings of Pieter de Hooch (1629–1684) and other Dutch genre painters (cat. 72, p. 51; fig. 11).

Impressionist painters turned to eighteenth-century French models when addressing the established genre subjects of sewing, reading, and music making. Cassatt's *Mrs. Duffee Seated on a Striped Sofa, Reading* (cat. 10, p. 230) adapts Rococo ideals of *sensibilité* to a modern sitter and alludes to such distinguished precedents as Fragonard's *A Young Girl Reading* (cat. 38, p. 231), not only in its subject matter but also in its mood of quiet self-absorption, in details of its dress, and in its fluent handling—an aspect of Fragonard's work much admired by the Impressionists. Renoir, who was steeped in eighteenth-century art, seems to have had Greuze in mind when painting an intimate portrait of his young son Jean drawing (cat. 88, p. 52; cat. 41, p. 52), while in *Christine Lerolle Embroidering* (cat. 87, p. 53), an affectionate portrayal of the daughter of his friend the artist and collector Henri Lerolle, he merges genre and portraiture in a strategy also adopted by other Impressionists.[43] The well-established pedigree of images of women sewing in a domestic environment stretched back to such examples of seventeenth-century Dutch genre painting as *The Seamstress* by Cornelis Bisschop (cat. 7, p. 53), though a more celebrated source for the pose and the meditative stillness in Renoir's painting was Vermeer's *The Lace Maker* (fig. 20), which had entered the Louvre in 1870 and reputedly was one of Renoir's favorite paintings.

Renoir and Morisot were the artists for whom eighteenth-century French art had the strongest appeal. As a teenager, Renoir had been an apprentice painter of porcelain and was often called on to copy details of compositions by Boucher, Fragonard, and Watteau, an activity that awakened an enthusiasm for the elegance and lightness of the French Rococo that never left him. Even in the 1870s, when, like his fellow Impressionists, Renoir was engaged primarily with themes taken from contemporary Paris, he often viewed these subjects through an eighteenth-century lens. In his famous modern-life tableau, *Ball at the Moulin de la Galette* of 1876 (fig. 12), the feathery touch and luminous palette bring the magic of Watteau's enchanted domains to a contemporary Montmartre dance hall.

Morisot had a special affinity with the high-keyed color and brio of eighteenth-century French painting. In 1884 she made a rather faithful copy of a detail of Boucher's *Venus Asking Vulcan for Arms* of 1757 in the Louvre (cat. 67, p. 142) and hung it above the fireplace in her living room.[44] If anything, Morisot heightens the Rococo feel

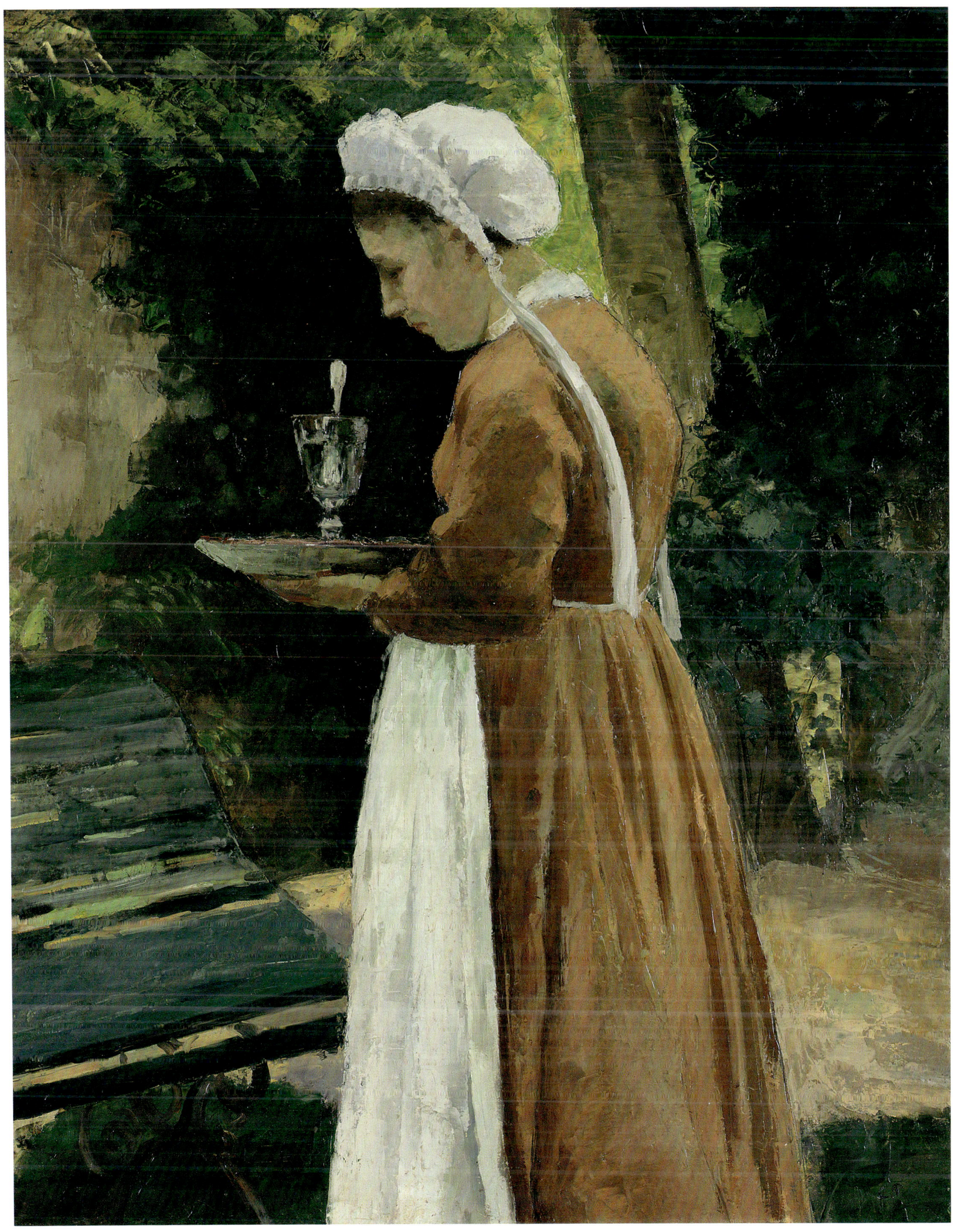

Cat. 88
Pierre-Auguste Renoir
The Artist's Son, Jean, Drawing, 1901

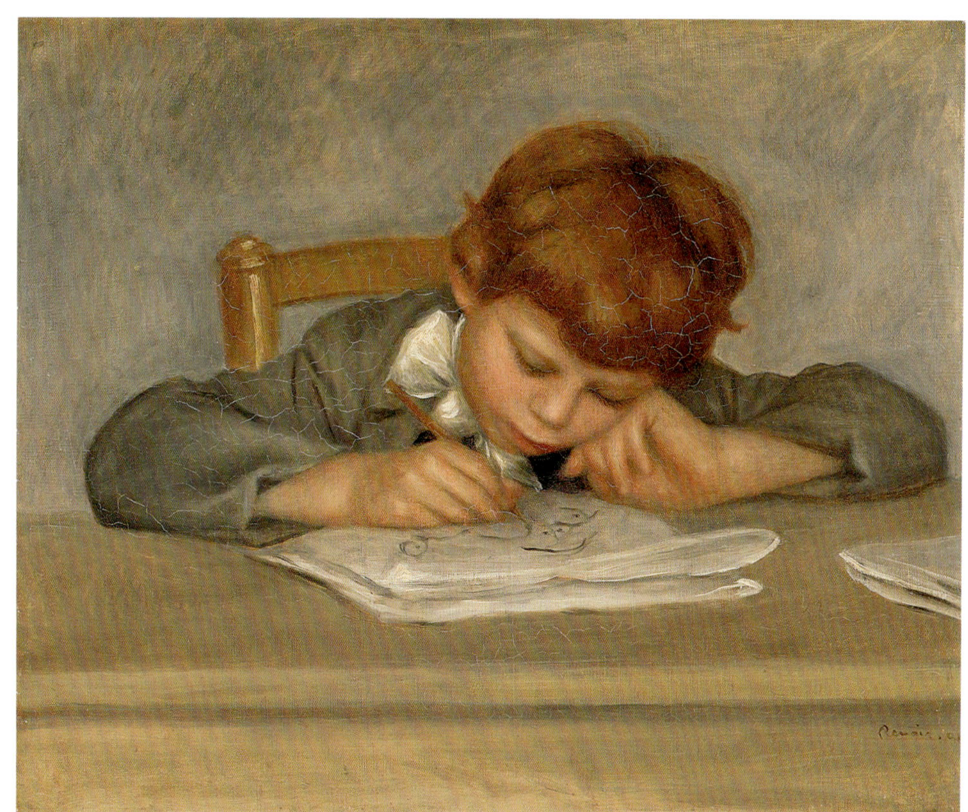

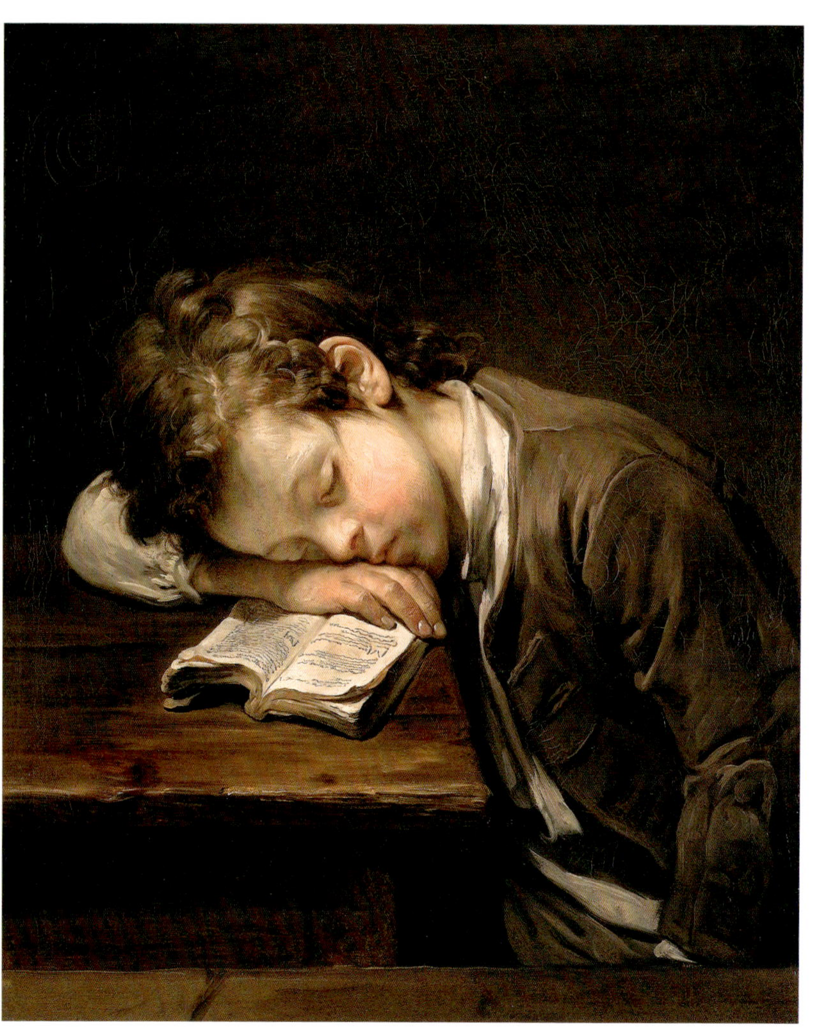

Cat. 41
Jean-Baptiste Greuze
A Schoolboy Sleeping on His Book, 1755

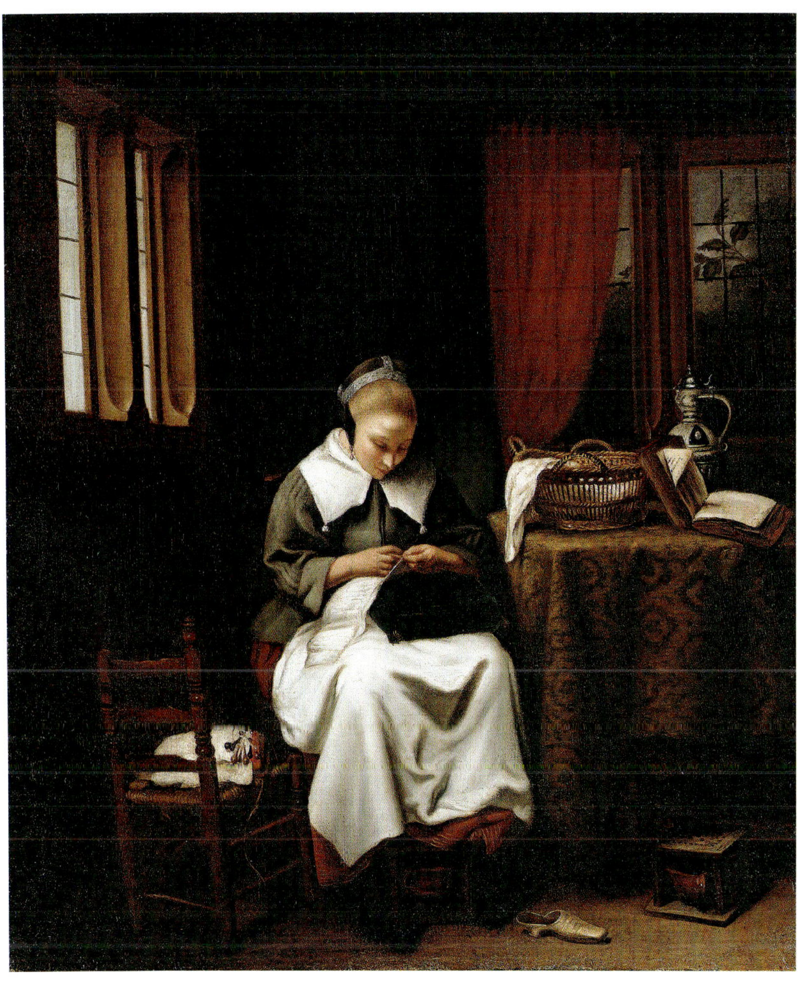

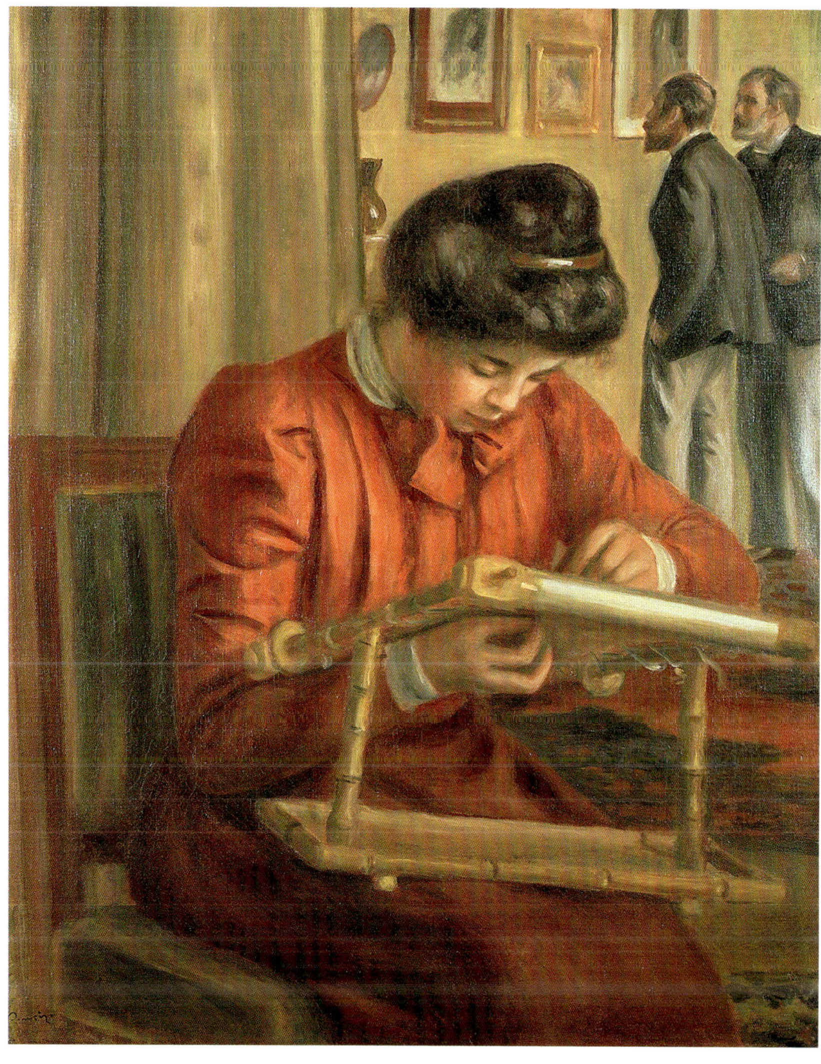

Cat. 7
Cornelis Bisschop
The Seamstress, 17th century

Cat. 87
Pierre-Auguste Renoir
Christine Lerolle Embroidering, c. 1895–98

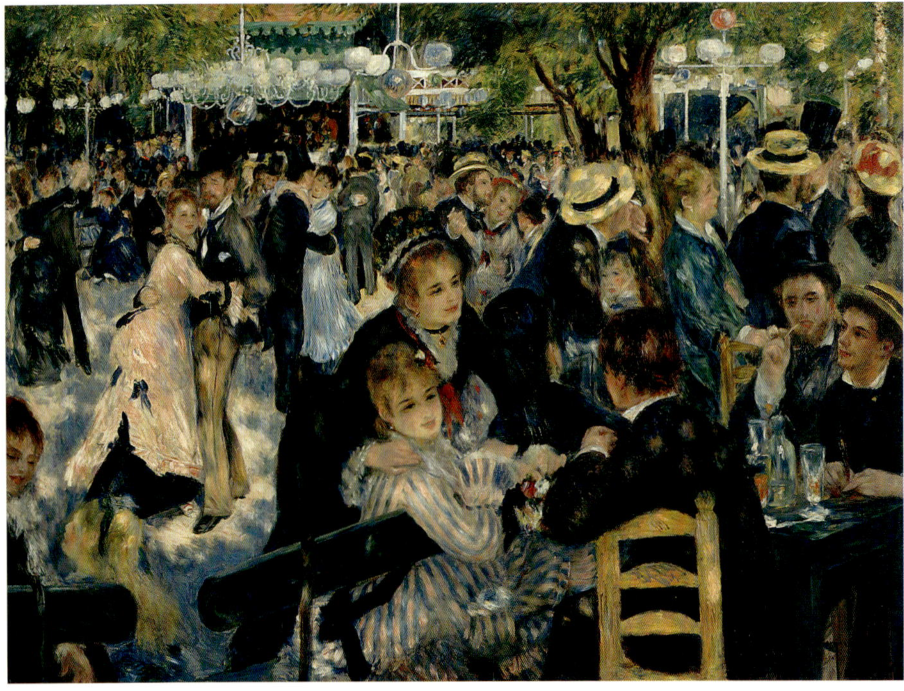

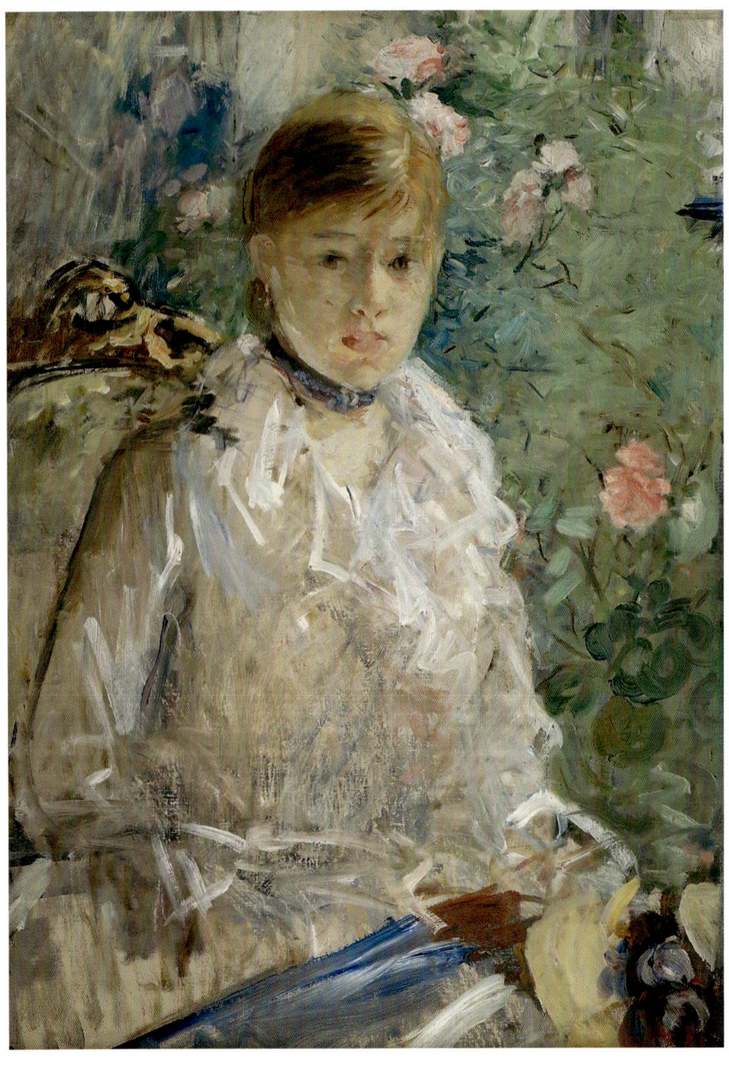

Fig. 12
Pierre-Auguste Renoir
Ball at the Moulin de la Galette, 1876
Oil on canvas, 51⅝ x 68⅞ in.
(131 x 175 cm)
Musée d'Orsay, Paris, France

Fig. 13
Berthe Morisot
Young Woman by a Window (Summer), 1879
Oil on canvas, 29⅞ x 24 in. (76 x 61 cm)
Musée Fabre, Montpellier Agglomération

of the original by emphasizing the sweetness of Boucher's blues and pinks and, above all, painting with the frothy, bravura brushwork typical of her mature style. Morisot was often linked with Fragonard by contemporary commentators, especially in response to the portraits and figures she exhibited in 1880 at the fifth Impressionist exhibition. Describing *Young Woman by a Window,* also called *Summer* (fig. 13), Philippe Burty, for instance, enthused: "Berthe Morisot handles the palette and brush with a truly astonishing delicacy. Since the eighteenth century, since Fragonard, no one at all has used clearer tones with such intelligent assurance."[45]

One feature of eighteenth-century French painting, the fête champêtre, immortalized by Watteau, Jean-Baptiste-Joseph Pater (1695–1736), Nicolas Lancret (1690–1743), Jean-Baptiste Huet (1745–1811), and others, was adapted to modern bourgeois life by Renoir in images showing young women in white dresses disporting themselves with their suitors in pastoral settings (cat. 80, p. 55; cat. 45, p. 56). Morisot and Monet evoked this theme less consciously, perhaps, in their pictures of gardens and country meadows (cat. 68, p. 57; cat. 63, p. 57).

The notion of the "innocent eye" described above was fundamental to the Impressionists' concept of landscape painting. Cézanne spoke of painting only "what we see, forgetting everything that existed before us." But despite this determination on the painters' part to cast aside the art of the museums and look only at the luminous outdoors, we find that Impressionist landscapes are often rooted in earlier art, notably that of seventeenth-century Dutch artists, who favored more humble scenery observed without the artificial conventions of the classical landscapes of Poussin and Claude. The Impressionists were not the first to adapt seventeenth-century Dutch landscape modes to contemporary French scenery—the so-called Barbizon School, including Charles-François Daubigny (1817–1878), Jean-François Millet (1814–1875), and Théodore Rousseau (1812–1867),

The painting illustrated below was mistakenly omitted from the catalogue *Inspiring Impressionism: The Impressionists and the Art of the Past*. It will be on display at the Denver Art Museum and the Seattle Art Museum only.

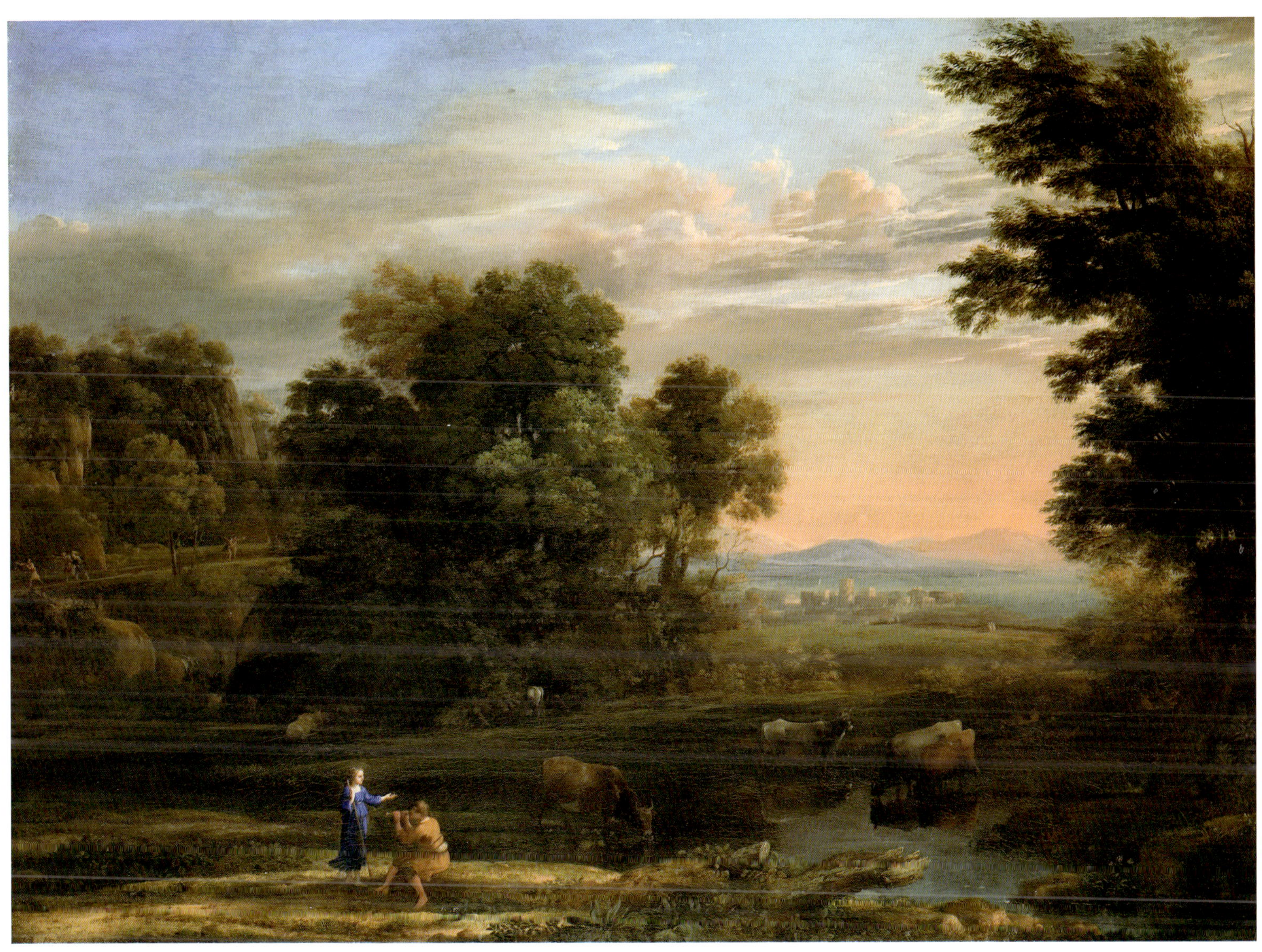

Claude Lorrain
French, 1604/5–1682
Landscape with Cowherd Piping, 1649–50
Oil on canvas, 39 × 53½ in. (99 × 135.9 cm)
On loan to the Denver Art Museum: in honor of Mr. and Mrs. Rush Kress by their children, 5.2006

Cat. 80
Pierre-Auguste Renoir
Confidences, c. 1873

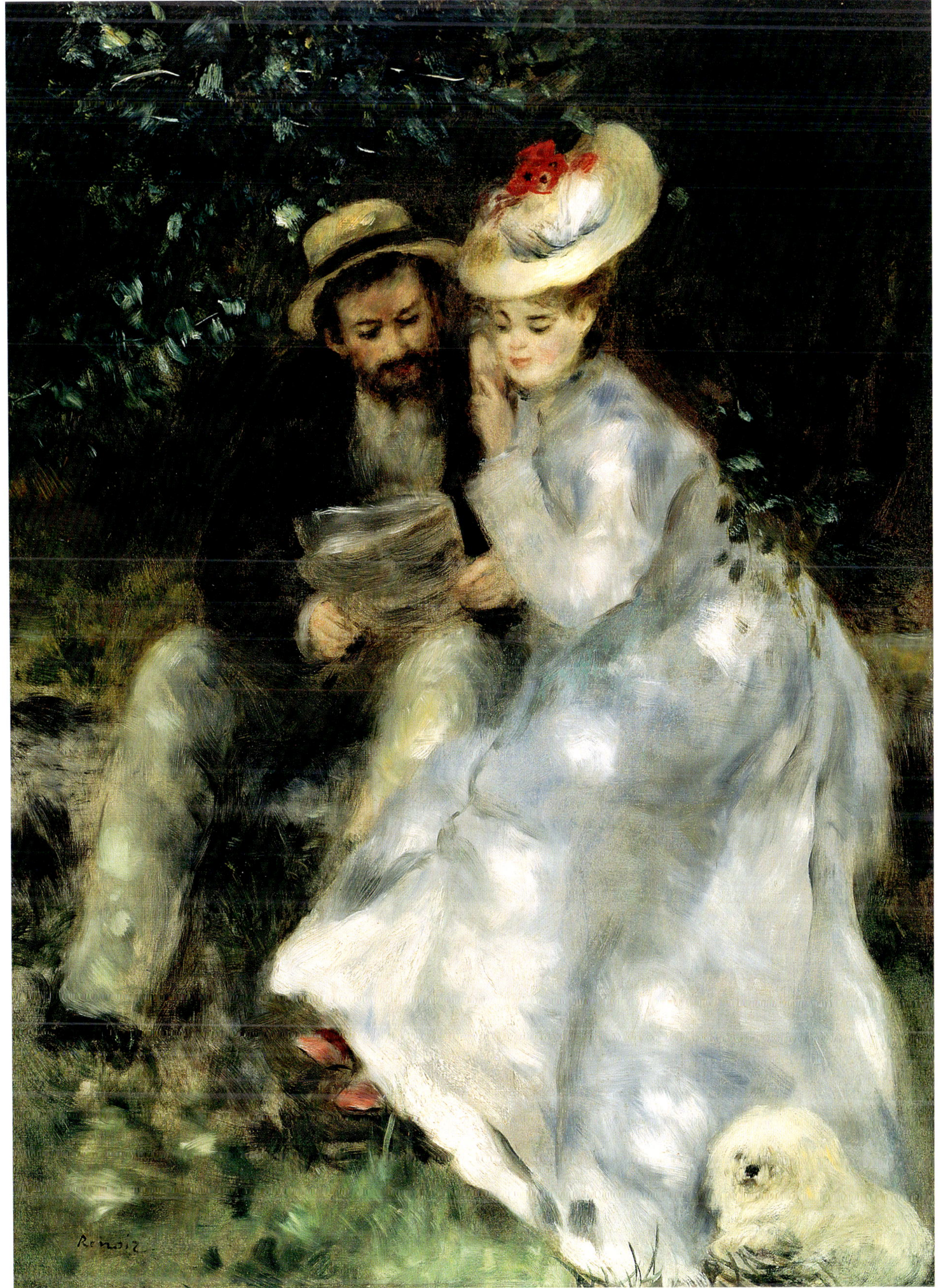

Cat. 45
Jean-Baptiste Huet
Young Couple in a Landscape

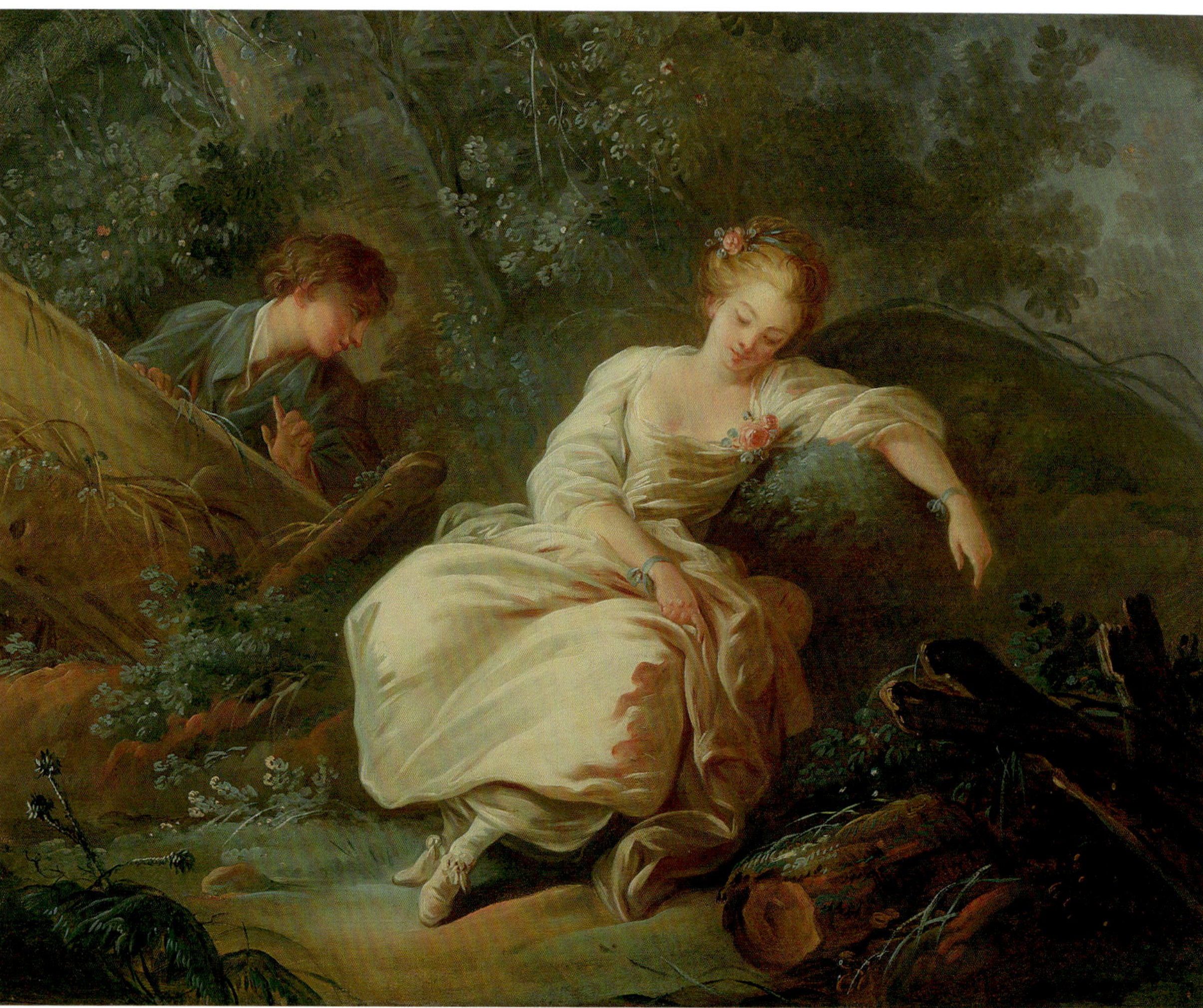

had done so in the 1840s, a connection that was highlighted by the painter and art critic Eugène Fromentin (1820–1876) in his *Les Maîtres d'autrefois*—but, unlike their predecessors, the Impressionists employed high-key color and a lively touch instead of a dark-toned "old master" palette.

Of all the Impressionists Monet seemed to be the most estranged from the art of the museums. In 1867, on a rare occasion when he applied to copy in the Louvre, he turned his back on the pictures on view and painted what he could see from the window (*Garden of the Princess,* 1867; Allen Memorial Art Museum, Oberlin, Ohio). And a letter written to his friend Bazille when he was a young artist making his first plein air landscapes in Normandy stresses the importance of "not resembling anyone" and expressing only what one feels oneself.[46] Yet Monet was not ignorant of older art; he simply sought to suppress his knowledge of it in the interests of a direct response to the motif.[47] He traveled to the Netherlands in 1871 (when he went to the Trippenhuis in Amsterdam, which housed the present Rijksmuseum's collections until 1885)[48] and returned in 1874 and 1886. The Dutch landscape, with its wide horizons, high skies, and canals and windmills, inspired a group of landscapes in 1874 (cat. 64, p. 60), and earlier Dutch painting seems to have left traces in Monet's work, even if the debt remained unacknowledged. The receding road, for instance, a motif common to both Dutch and Barbizon landscape painting, was taken up by Monet, Pissarro, and Sisley in the early 1870s (cat. 73, p. 59).

The most celebrated example of the receding road in seventeenth-century Dutch art is *The Avenue at Middelharnis* of 1689 by Meindert Hobbema (1638–1709; fig. 35), which was acquired by the National Gallery, London, in 1871, the year that Monet and Pissarro went there to escape the Paris Commune, and it is tempting to assume that they

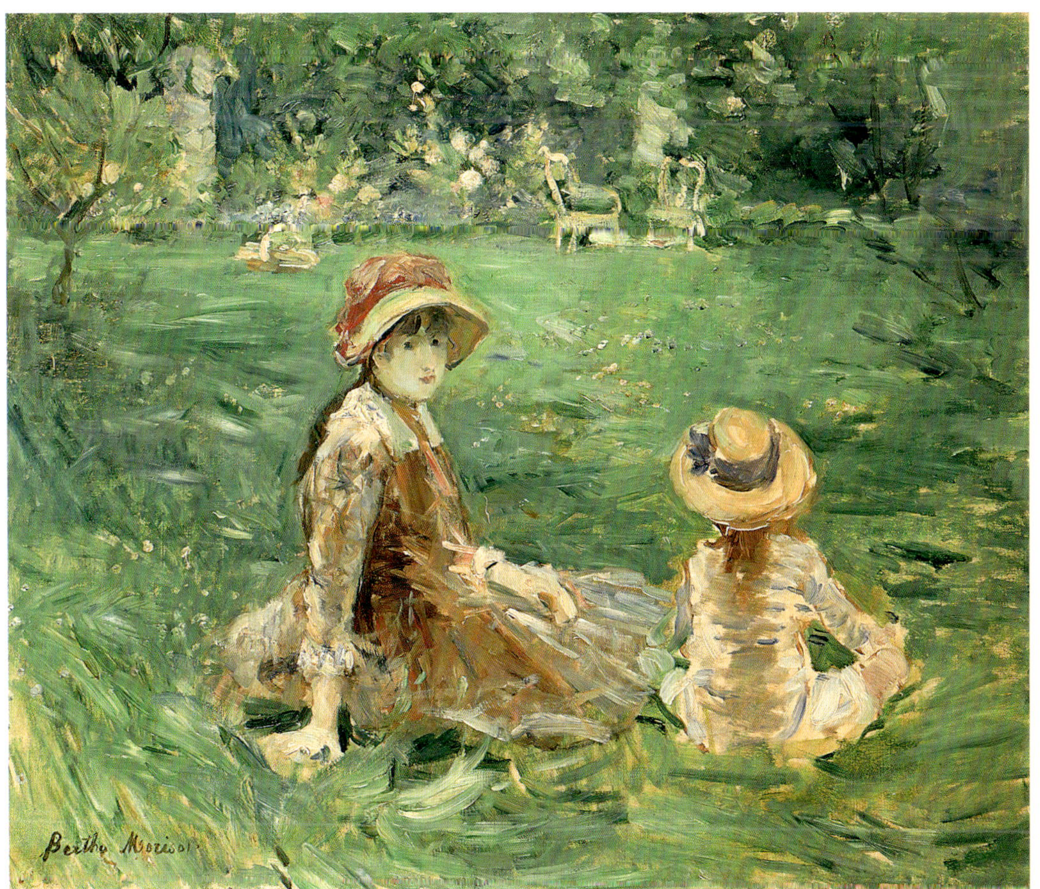

Cat. 68
Berthe Morisot
In the Garden at Maurecourt, c. 1884

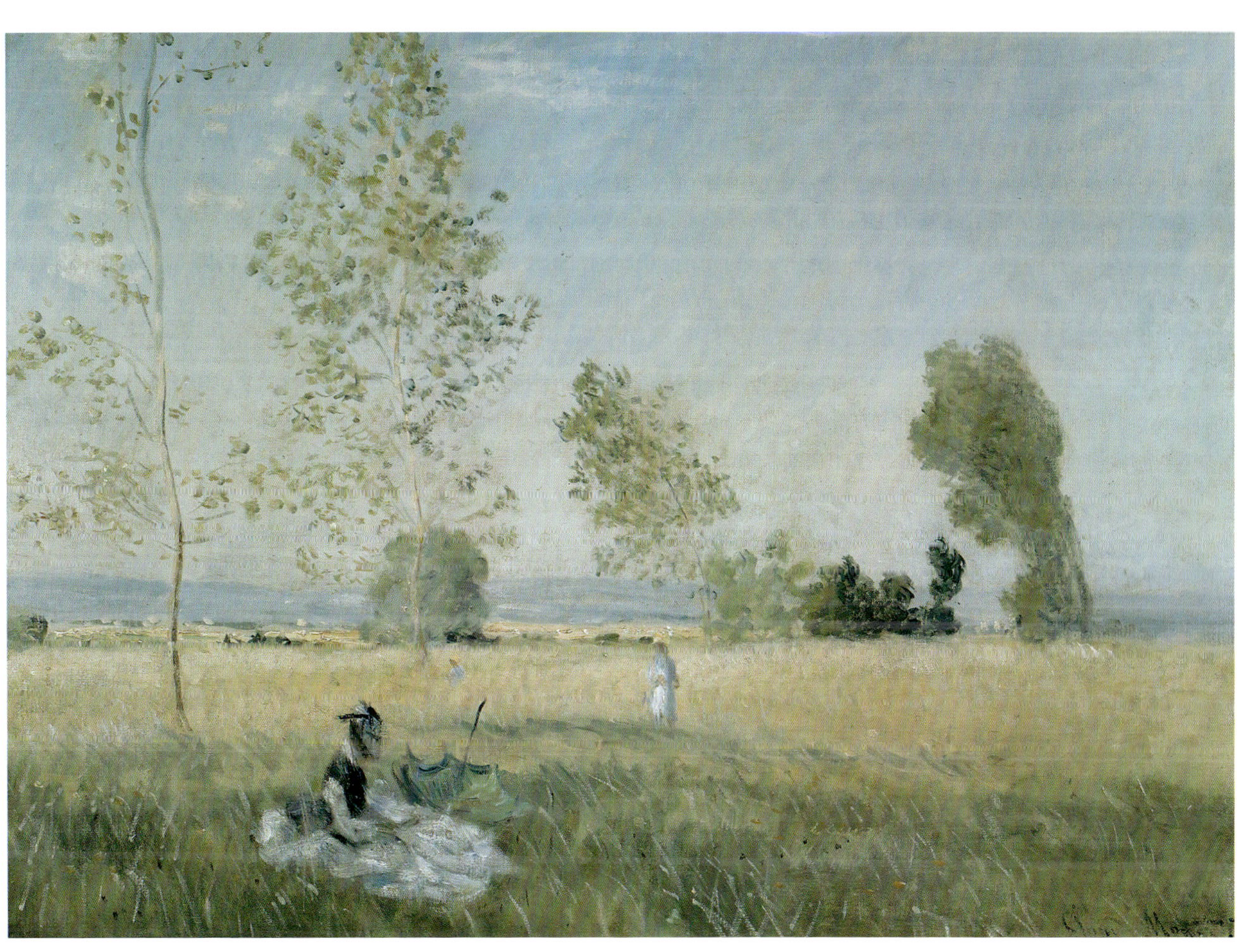

Cat. 63
Claude Monet
Summer, 1874

saw and were impressed by it. (Sisley could certainly have seen it when he was in London in 1874.) In Monet's and Sisley's river views one senses the heritage of Salomon van Ruysdael (1600/1603–1670) and Jan van Goyen (1596–1656), exponents of tranquil river scenery and damp skies rendered in soft tones of green and gray (cat. 62, p. 177; cat. 94, p. 176). Moreover, Monet's *The Zuiderkerk, Amsterdam (Looking up the Groenburgwal)* (cat. 64, p. 60) would seem to revive the genre of Dutch townscape as practiced by Hobbema and other seventeenth-century Dutch masters (cat. 44, p. 61).

Viewed in their entirety, statements by the Impressionists reveal the contradiction at the heart of their enterprise: a quest for visual innocence versus an awareness of the art of the past. Cézanne, despite avowedly attempting to forget that he had ever seen a picture, constantly had recourse to museums and reproductions for inspiration to continue his adventurous quest. When he claimed that he wished "to redo Poussin after nature,"[49] he was referring to a countertrend in landscape painting that looked to the classical tradition established in France by Poussin and Claude rather than to seventeenth-century Dutch art. Cézanne's statement, reported at secondhand by younger artists who interviewed him in his final years, has given rise to much speculation and commentary.[50] Without question, he admired Poussin and copied his works.[51] In 1864 he registered at the Louvre to copy *Et in Arcadia Ego,* and he kept a reproduction of this painting in his studio in Aix until the end of his life.[52] Occasional features in some of Cézanne's landscapes suggest classical conventions—for example, a pine branch extending across the foreground that frames a distant view of the artist's most persistently depicted motif, the Mont Sainte-Victoire, or the warmth of the Mediterranean light—but, on the whole, his handling, his palette, and the general atmosphere of his landscapes are quite different from a work by Poussin. One senses that Cézanne's late landscapes evolved in a highly personal process that blended direct observation of nature, work in the studio, and knowledge of the old masters.[53] But his Poussin statement remains puzzling. Perhaps it can be best interpreted as expressing his aspiration to achieve pictorial coherence and inner harmony and, in doing so, to align himself in a general way with the French classical tradition, which was the subject of considerable cultural debate around 1900.[54]

Another great artist of the French Baroque who fascinated Cézanne was a fellow Provençal, the sculptor Pierre Puget (1620–1694). He admired Puget's work for its dynamic vigor—"I understand that he had the *mistral* in him," and "He knew how to bring marble to life," Cézanne is reputed to have remarked.[55] Cézanne made numerous drawings after Puget's sculptures, including the *Gallic Hercules* (Musée du Louvre, Paris). A group of pencil, oil, and watercolor studies that Cézanne made after a little plaster putto in his possession (cat. 36, p. 62; this is not the actual one Cézanne owned but identical to it), which was then thought to be by Puget but now more commonly attributed to François Du Quesnoy (1594–1643), reveals that his concerns were far removed from those of an academic copy. Exploring the figure from a variety of viewpoints (cat. 14, p. 64; cat. 15, p. 64; cat. 18, p. 65), he was preoccupied with its contrapposto twist and the flow of energy pulsing through the sculpture, capturing them vividly in two dimensions, not by careful outlining but by repeated, broken, cursive lines. Two great still lifes featuring the putto (for one, see cat. 16, p. 63) focus on a probing analysis of the forms and their relation to the surrounding space, a scrutiny so intense, particularly in the version at the Courtauld, that it generates visual tensions, distortions, and disjunctions adumbrating the more radical undermining of spatial convention in the work of the Cubists in the early twentieth century.

In the early 1880s a number of Impressionists began to feel a need to locate themselves within a continuum of European painting, to "reinvent" themselves as the "old masters" of their time. They had become dissatisfied with what they saw as the overly ephemeral character of Impressionism. Its lack of solid draftsmanship and composition and its failure to encompass deeper meanings led them to seek new approaches, which often entailed a reassessment of older art. "I wanted to make of Impressionism something solid and lasting like the art of the museums,"[56] Cézanne recalled. Renoir echoed these sentiments when he admitted to his dealer Ambroise Vollard that he had reached the end of Impressionism.[57] Among other things, this change of attitude signaled a move away from contemporary subjects drawn from everyday life toward more timeless, universal, and classicizing themes, such as the nude and maternity.

Perhaps the conservative cultural climate of late-nineteenth-century France combined with its Catholic revival to encourage a resurgence of mother and child imagery. Cassatt, an American who spent her entire artistic career in France, is the chief Impressionist exponent of this venerable subject. She had acquired a profound knowledge of Italian Renaissance art from private collections in Paris and from travels in Italy.[58] The traditional iconography of the Virgin and Child worshiped by a donor clearly inspired her modern domestic scene *The Family* (cat. 47, p. 66; cat. 11, p. 67).

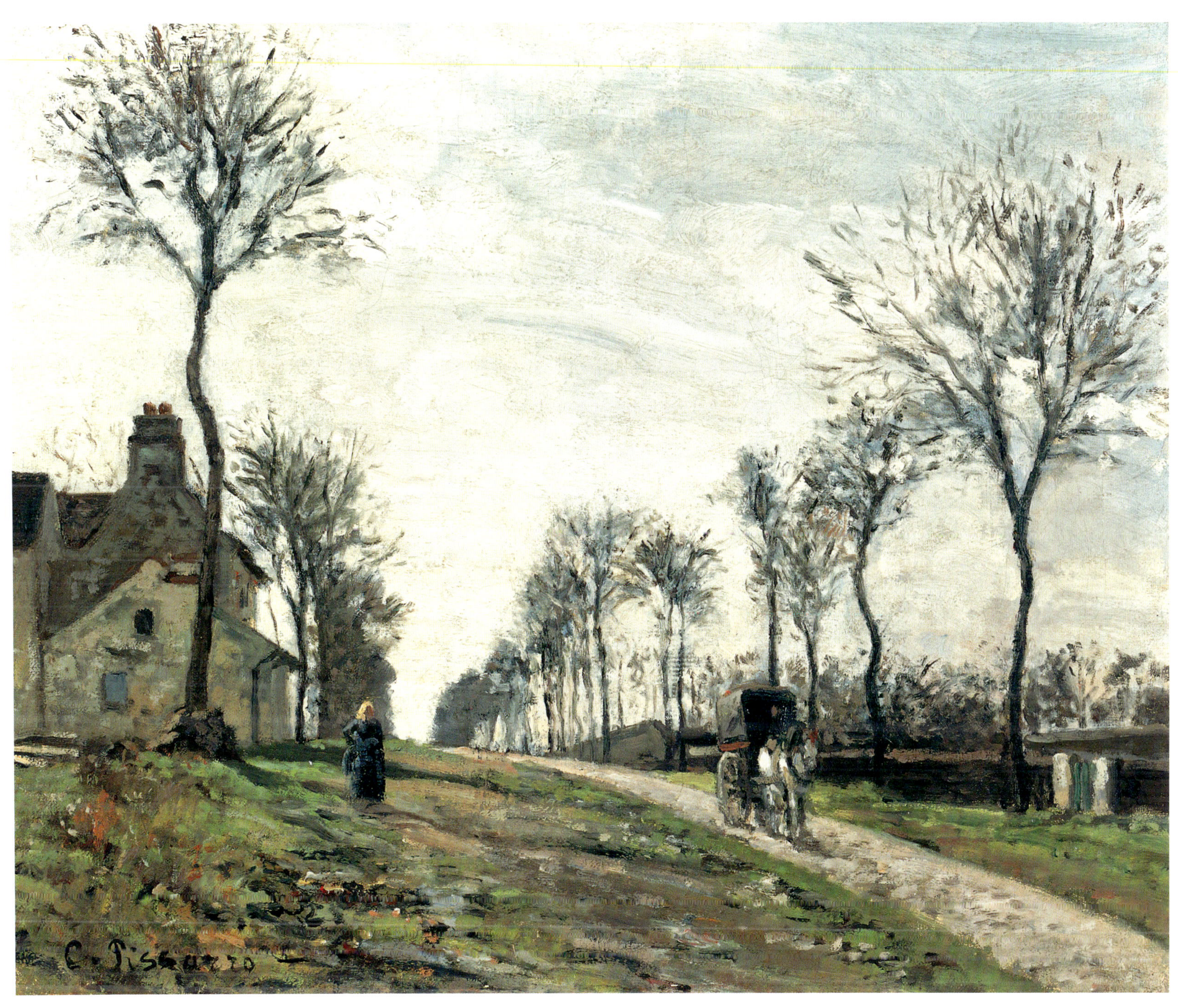

Cat. 73
Camille Pissarro
The Marly Road, c. 1870

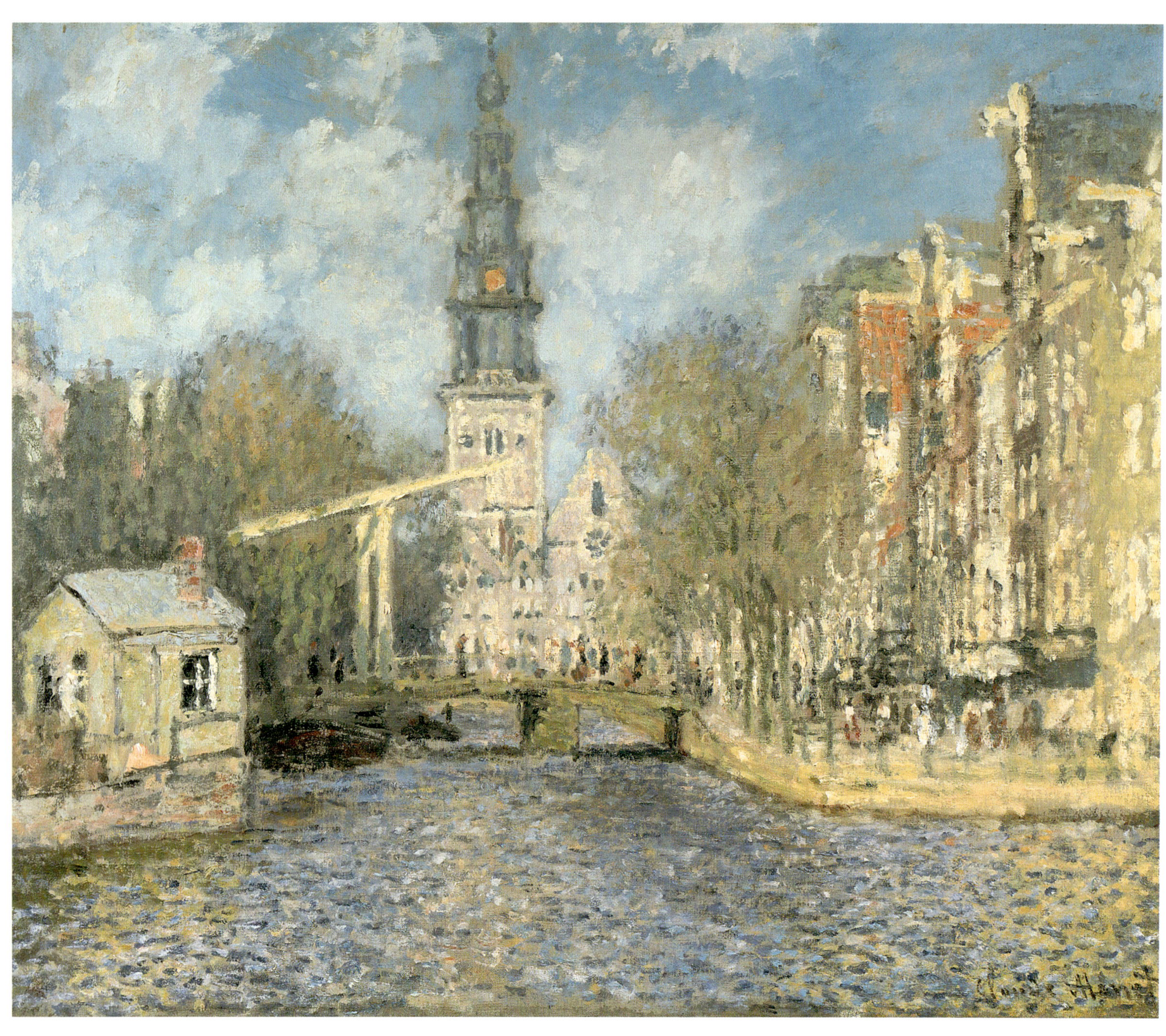

Cat. 64
Claude Monet
The Zuiderkerk, Amsterdam (Looking up the Groenburgwal), c. 1874

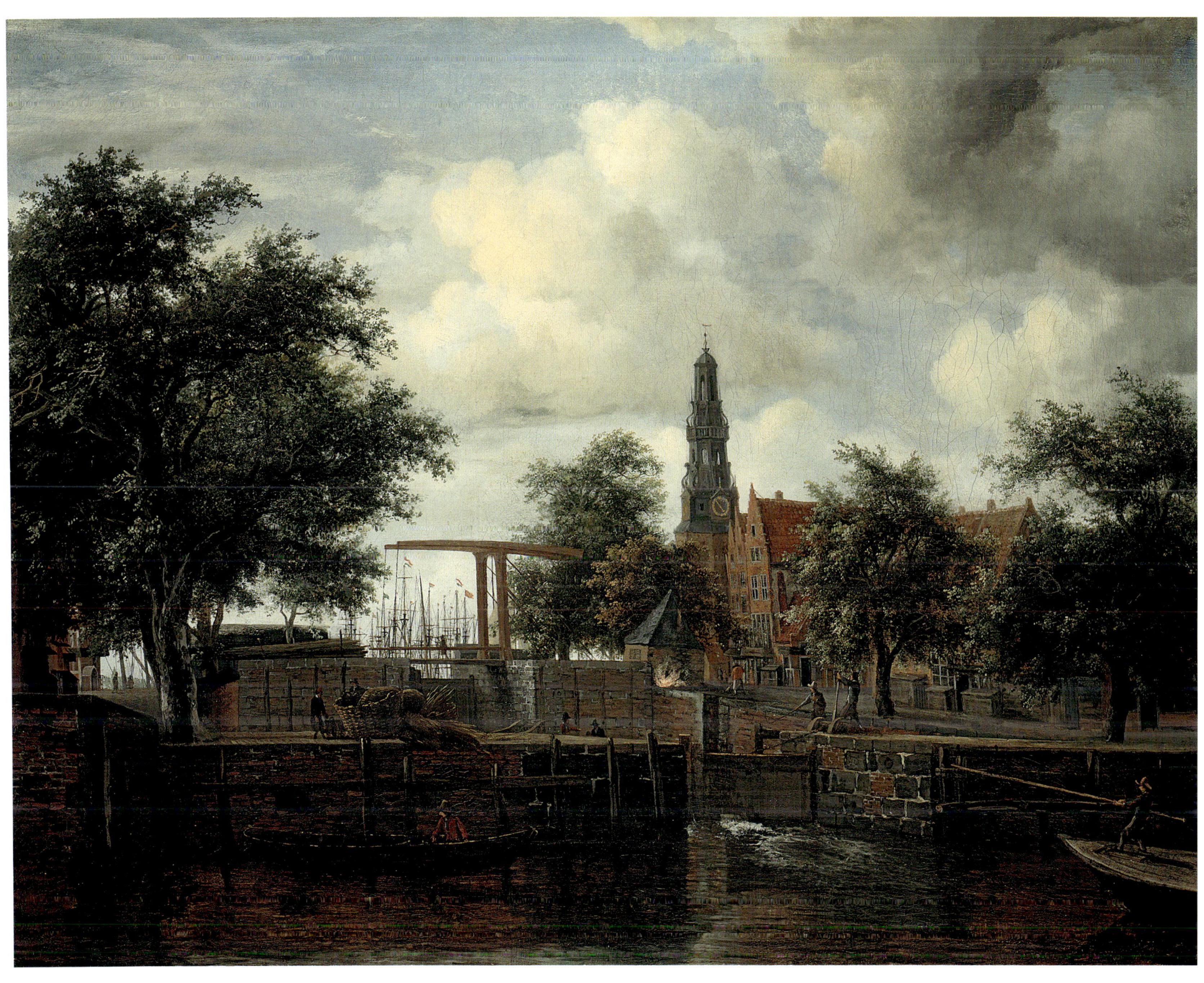

Cat. 44
Meindert Hobbema
The Haarlem Lock, Amsterdam,
c. 1663–65

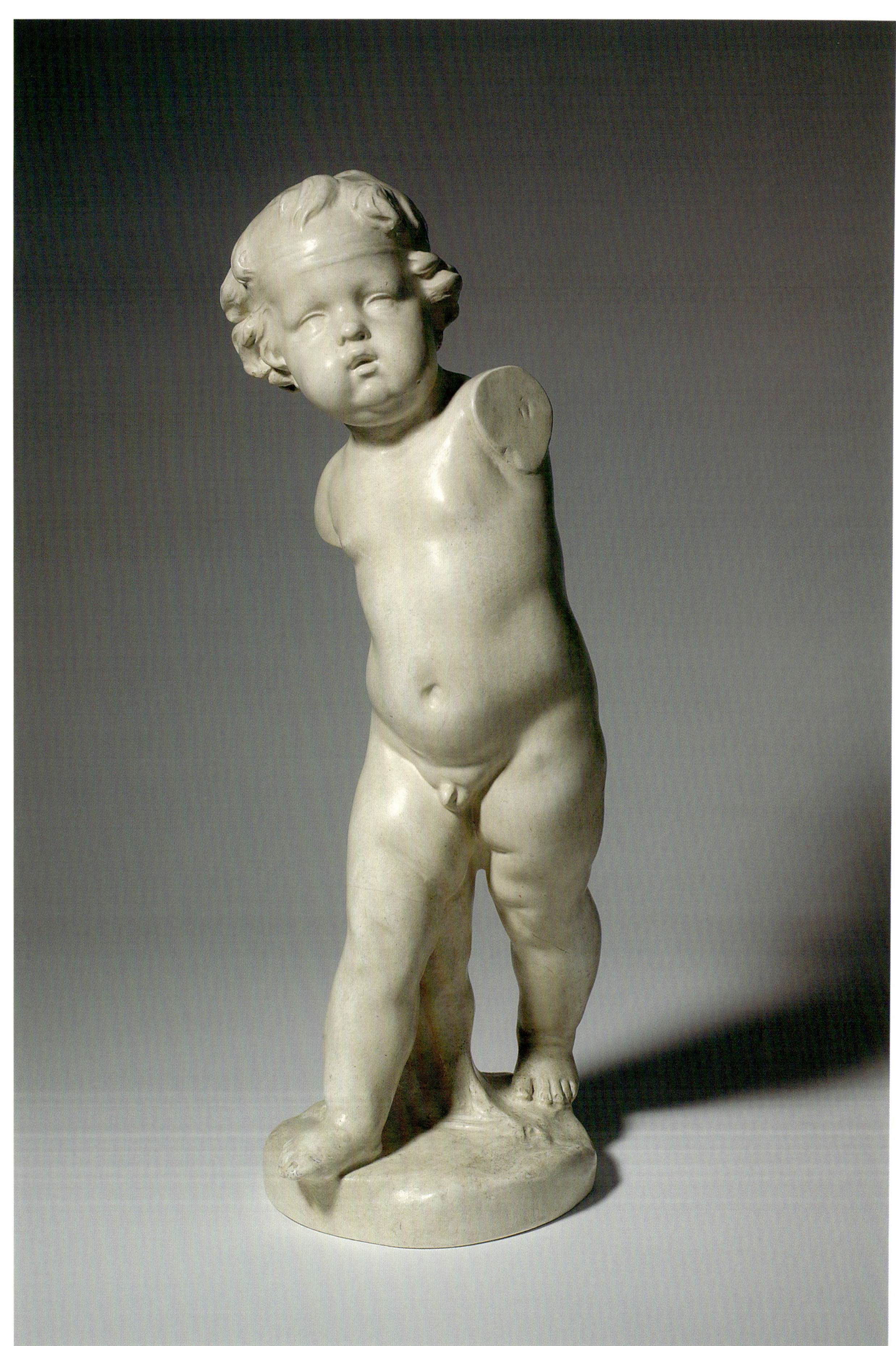

Cat. 36
After François Du Quesnoy
Putto

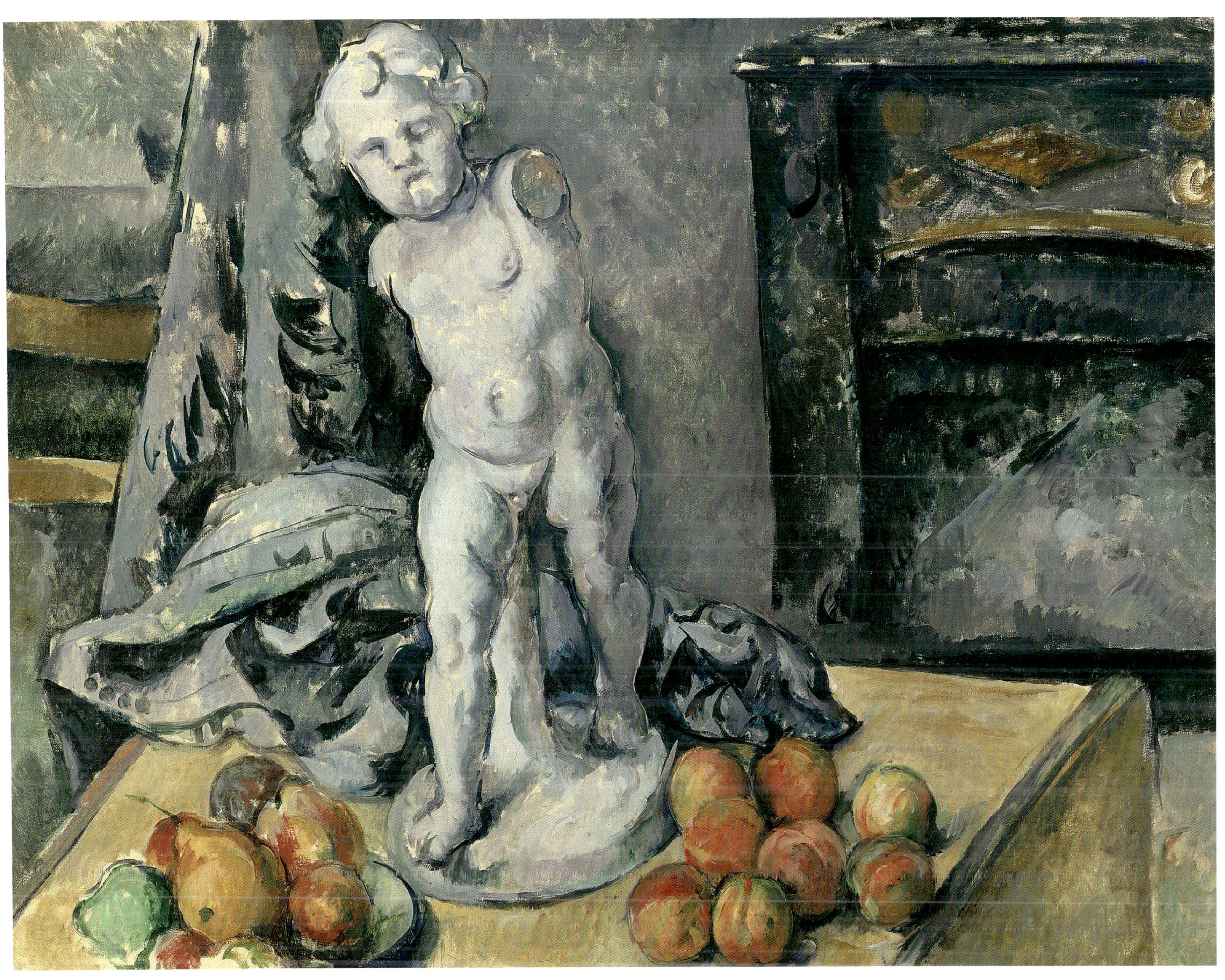

Cat. 16
Paul Cézanne
Still Life with Statuette, 1894–95

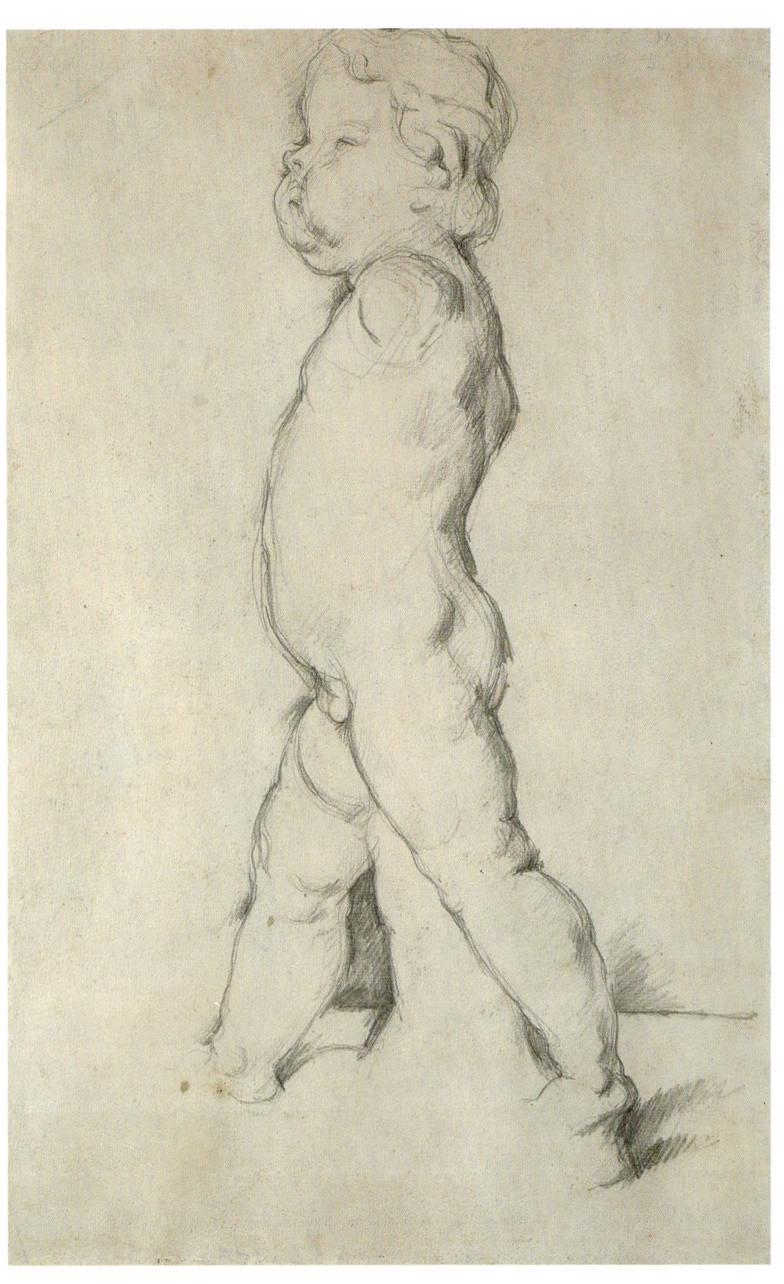

Cat. 14
Paul Cézanne
Plaster Cast of a Putto, c. 1890

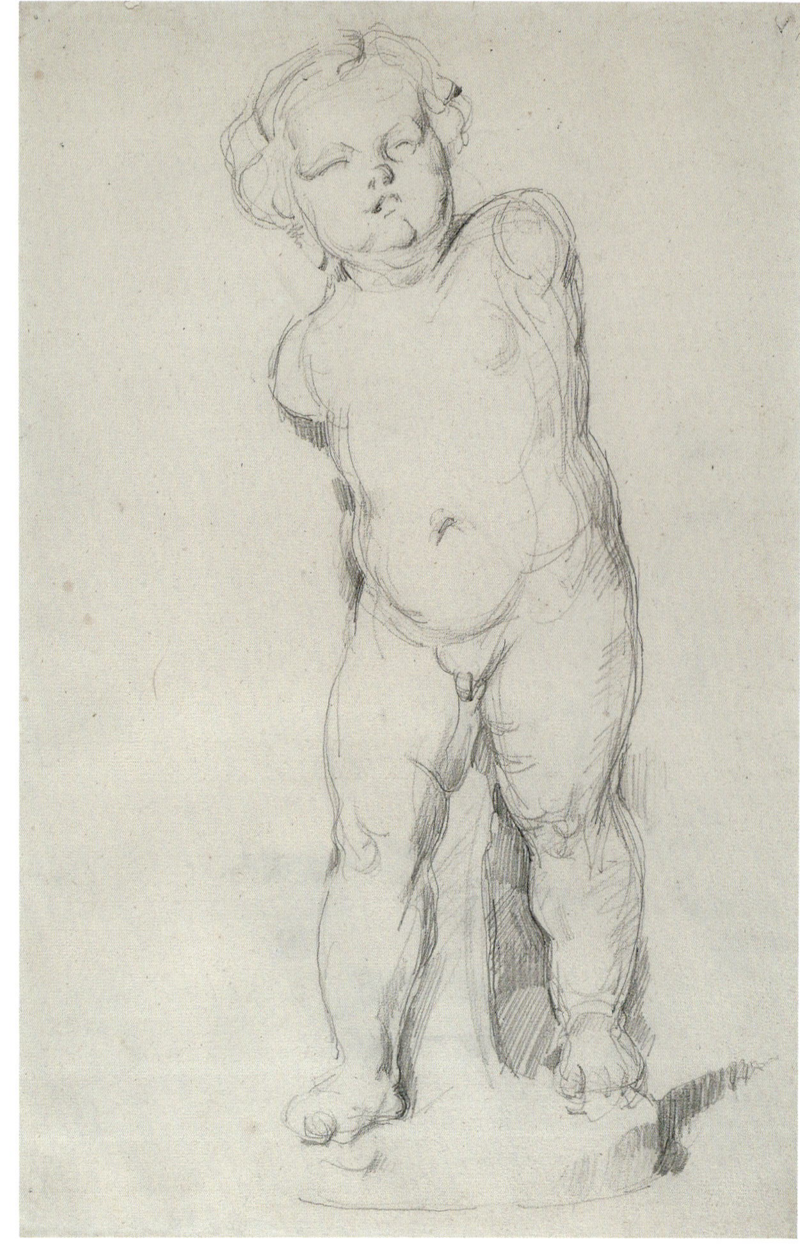

Cat. 15
Paul Cézanne
The Plaster Cupid (recto) and *Study of Drapery* (verso), 1890–95

Cat. 18
Paul Cézanne
The Plaster Cupid, 1900–1904

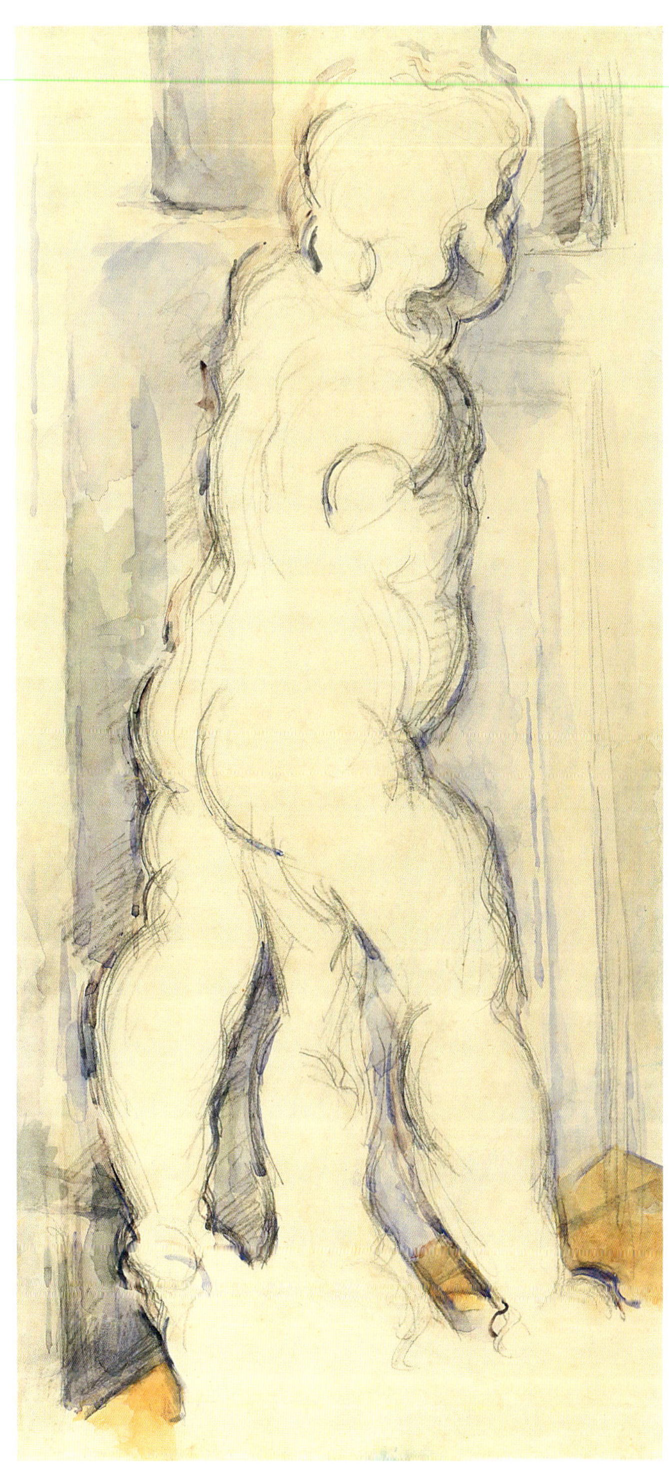

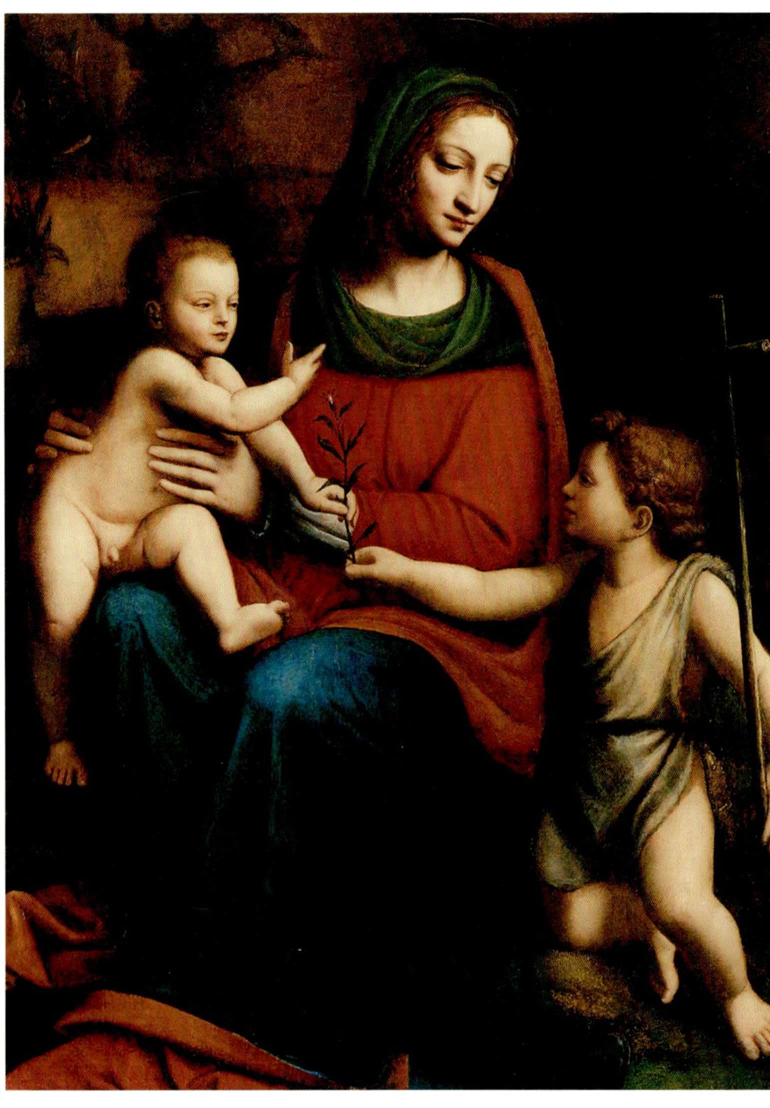

Cat. 47
Bernardino Luini
Madonna and Child with the Infant Saint John, c. 1515–20

Cat. 11
Mary Cassatt
The Family, 1893

Renoir, with his conservative views about women's role in society, was also particularly responsive to the maternity theme. His tender portrayal of his son Jean cradled by Gabrielle, a woman who worked for many years in the Renoir household, amounts to an intimate, secular variation on the sacred prototype (cat. 86, p. 69). In his resplendent late portrait of Madame Thurnyssen, the wife of a German art collector, and her daughter Josefina, painted in Munich in the summer of 1910, the Madonna and Child theme is again a strong undercurrent, despite the worldliness of the sitters (cat. 89, p. 68). The astute German art historian and critic Julius Meier-Graefe hit the nail on the head when he observed rather tartly: "One could think of it as a new type of Madonna and Child with the mother having no intimation of the child's godliness."[59] Stylistically, this is Renoir at his most opulent and expansive. In his youth Renoir had copied *Hélène Fourment and Two of Her Children* (1635–36; Musée du Louvre, Paris). In Munich he had the chance to study the great works by Rubens in the Alte Pinakothek and was especially captivated by *Hélène Fourment and Her Eldest Son, Frans* (fig. 14), on which his *Madame Thurnyssen* is so clearly based. "See the pictures by Rubens in Munich; there is the most glorious fullness and the most beautiful colour, and the layer of paint is very thin," Renoir told the American critic Walter Pach.[60] And to Vollard he remarked: "One day, at the Louvre, I noticed that Rubens had obtained more by a simple rubbing than I did with all my heavy layers."[61] Along with the vibrating surfaces of Titian's late work, Rubens's ample forms and thin washes of warm color provided an inspiration to the aging artist as he developed his final style.

The beginnings of Renoir's late fascination with the great masters can be traced back a decade and a half to 1881, when his quest for a more rigorous alternative to Impressionism had led him to Italy to study the work of Raphael at firsthand. He attempted to revive the art of the museums in a large painting of bathers in a landscape on which he worked for a number of years (fig. 15). Raphael's firm contours, flawless brushwork, and the mythical world of such works as *The Triumph of Galatea* (Villa Farnesina, Rome) preside over Renoir's *The Large Bathers.* This monumental composition, in which surprisingly contemporary-looking Parisian nymphs frolic in an Impressionist landscape, marked a turning point in the artist's career and launched a series of bather compositions that would preoccupy him until his death, in 1917.

The Italian Renaissance was not, however, the only inspiration behind Renoir's bathers. A relief by the French sculptor François Girardon (1628–1715) provided the model for the figures, and one of

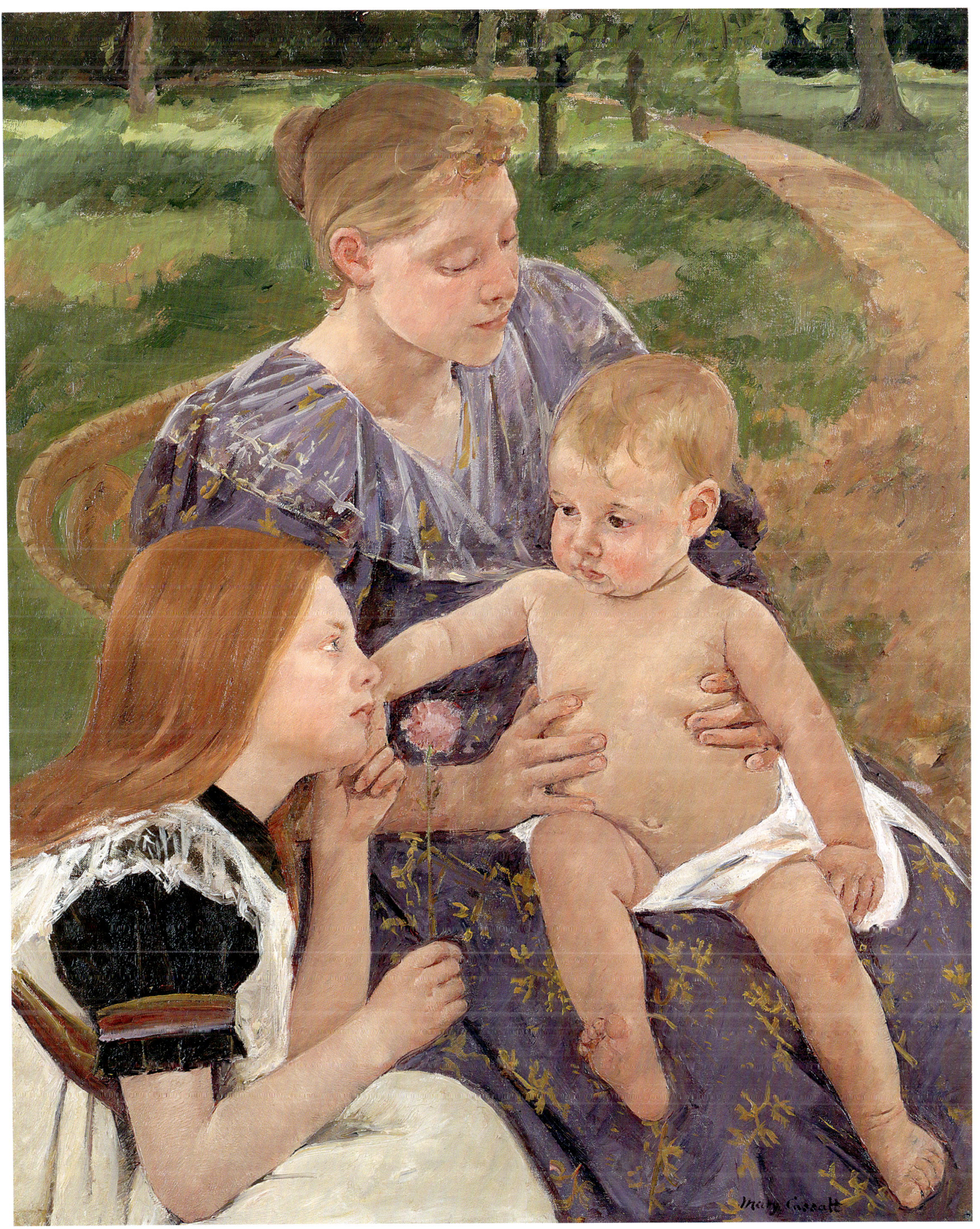
Mary Cassatt

Cat. 89
Pierre-Auguste Renoir
Mother and Child (Madame Thurneyssen and Her Daughter), 1910

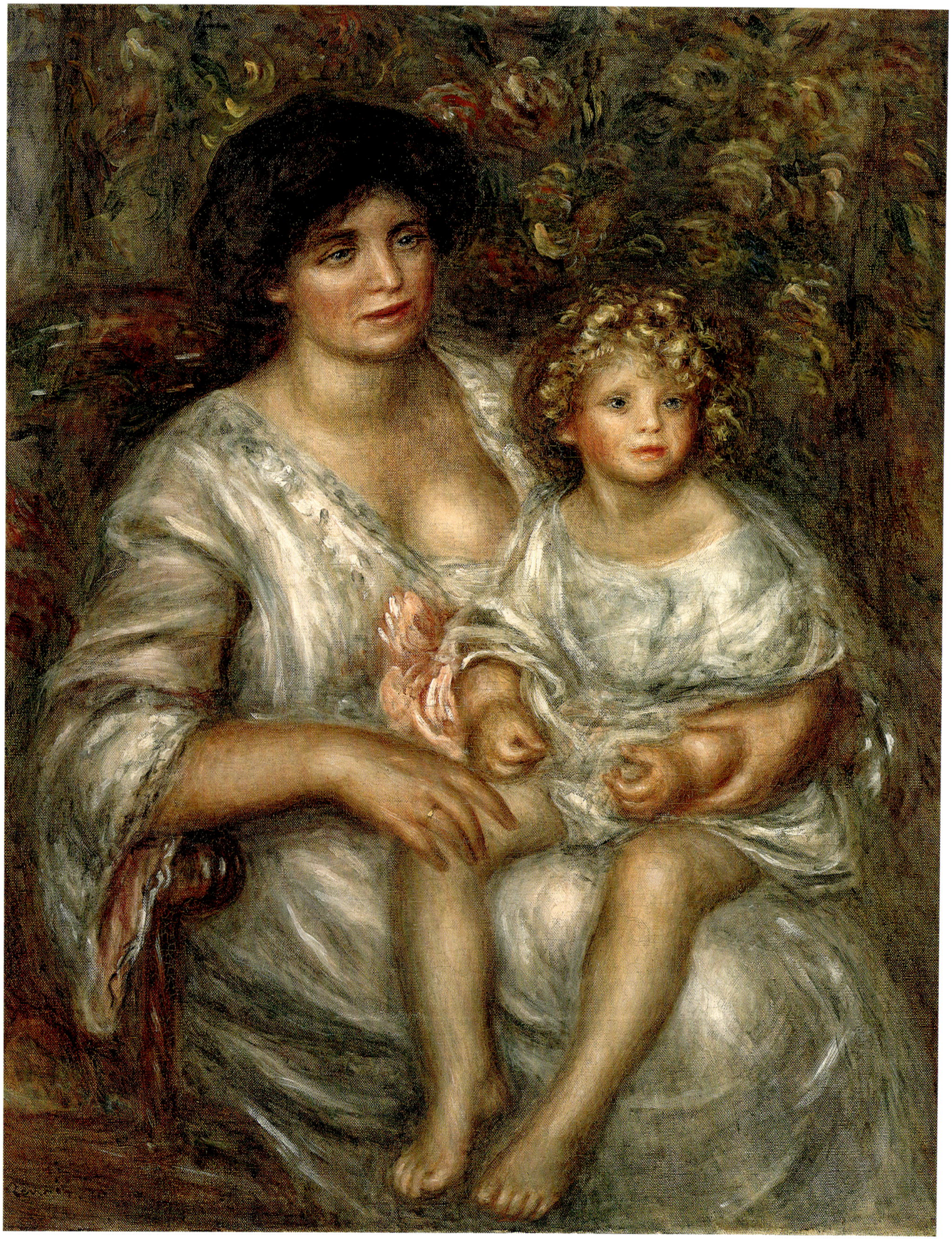

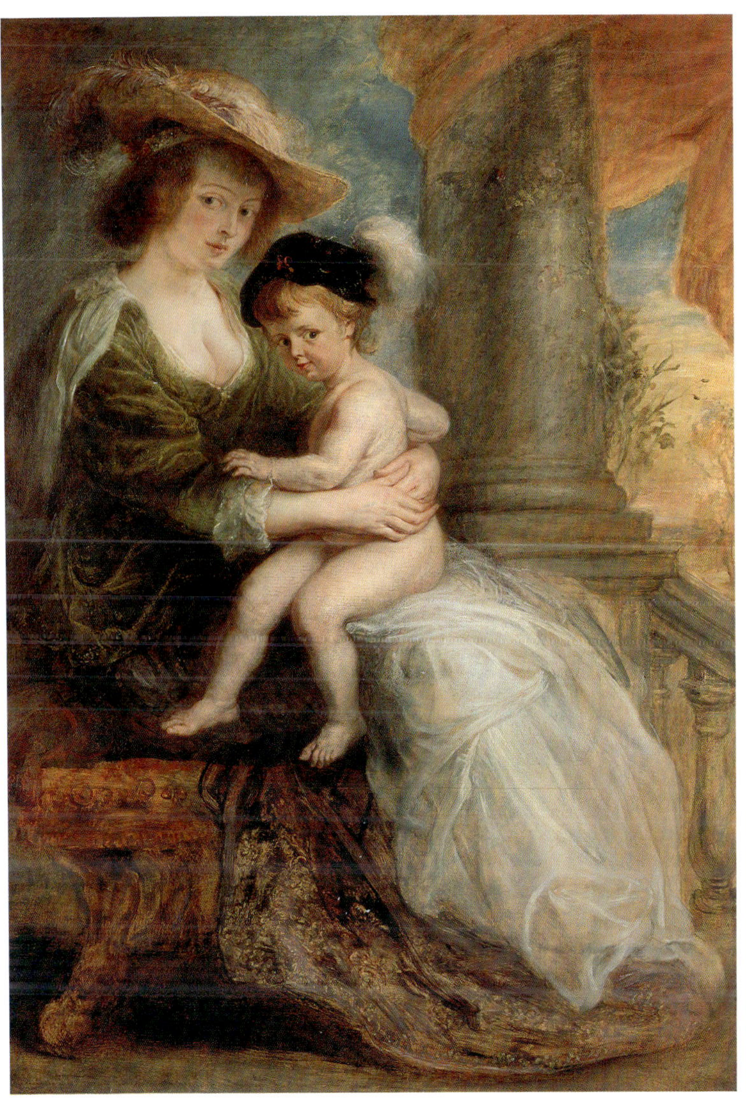

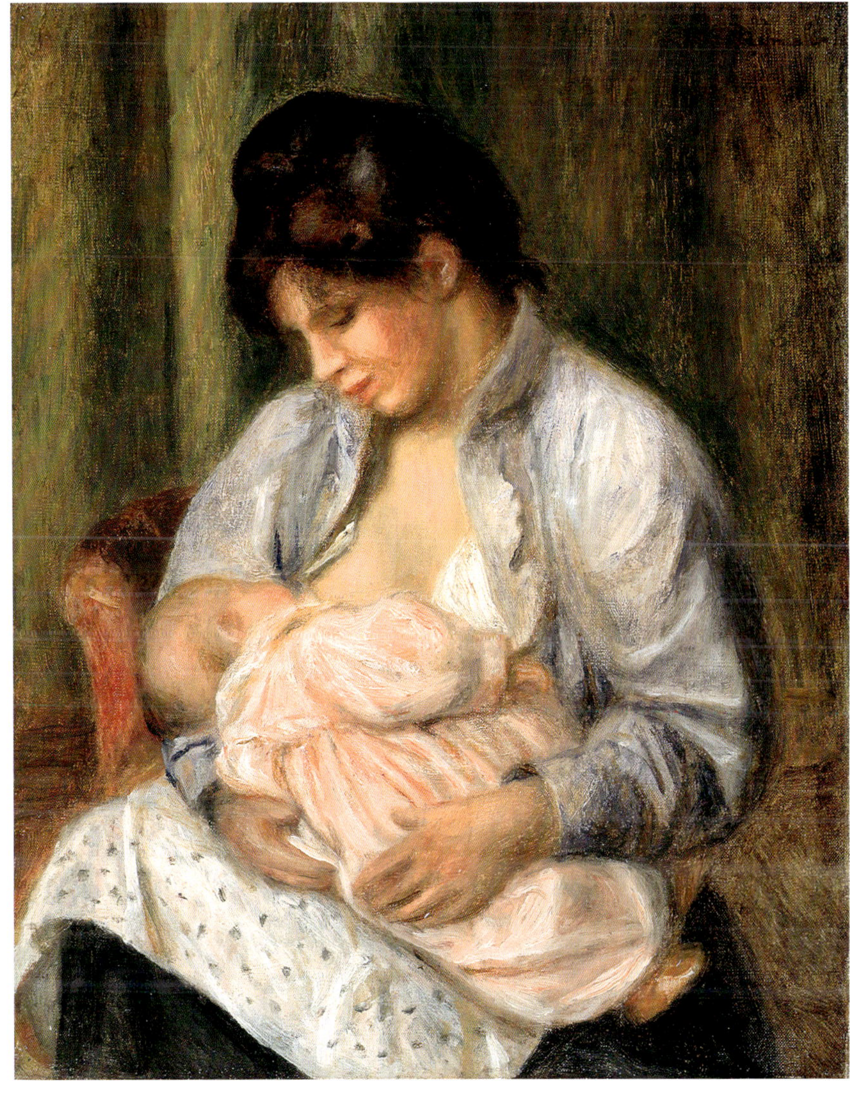

Fig. 14
Sir Peter Paul Rubens
Hélène Fourment and Her Eldest Son, Frans, c. 1635
Oil on wood, 57½ x 40⅛ in. (146 x 102 cm)
Alte Pinakothek, Munich

Cat. 86
Pierre-Auguste Renoir
A Woman Nursing a Child, c. 1893

Fig. 15
Pierre-Auguste Renoir
The Large Bathers, 1884–87
Oil on canvas, 46⅜ x 67¼ in.
(117.8 x 170.8 cm)
Philadelphia Museum of Art, The Mr. and Mrs. Carroll S. Tyson, Jr., Collection, 1963

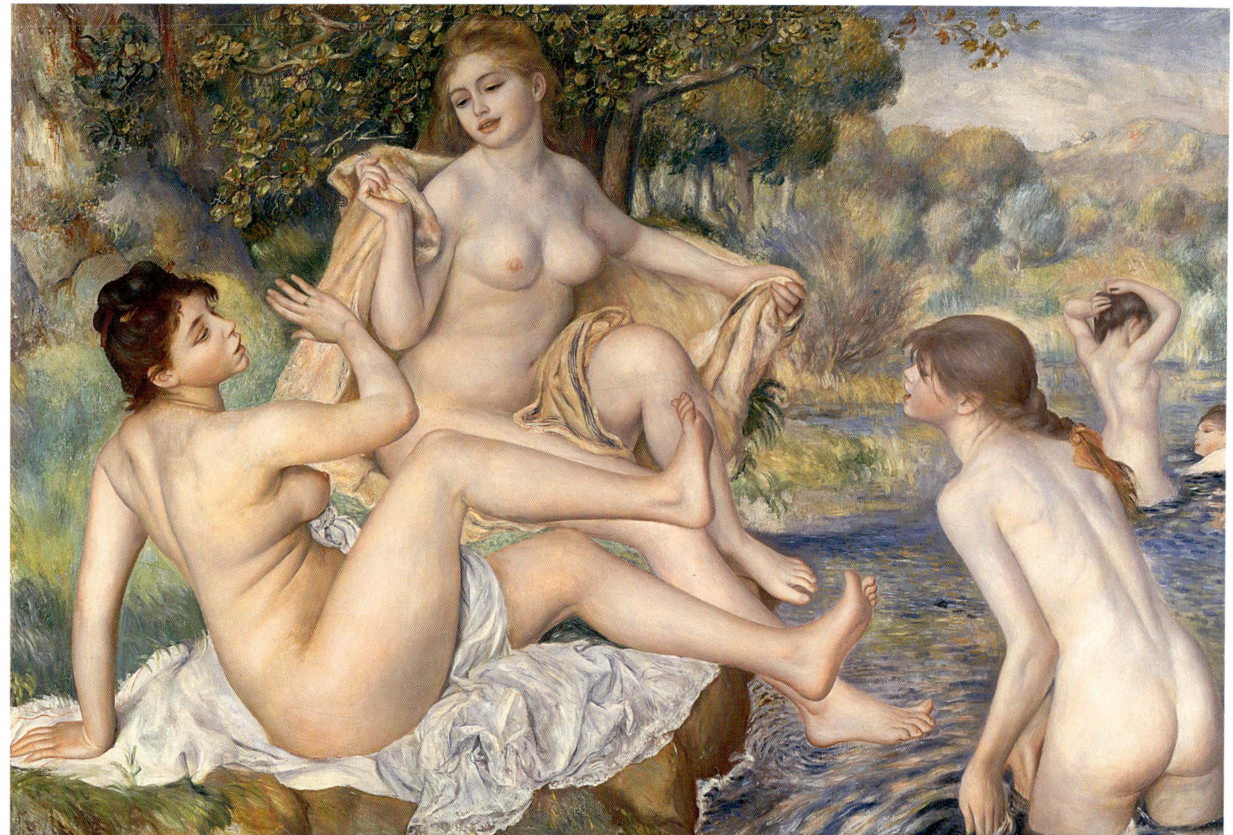

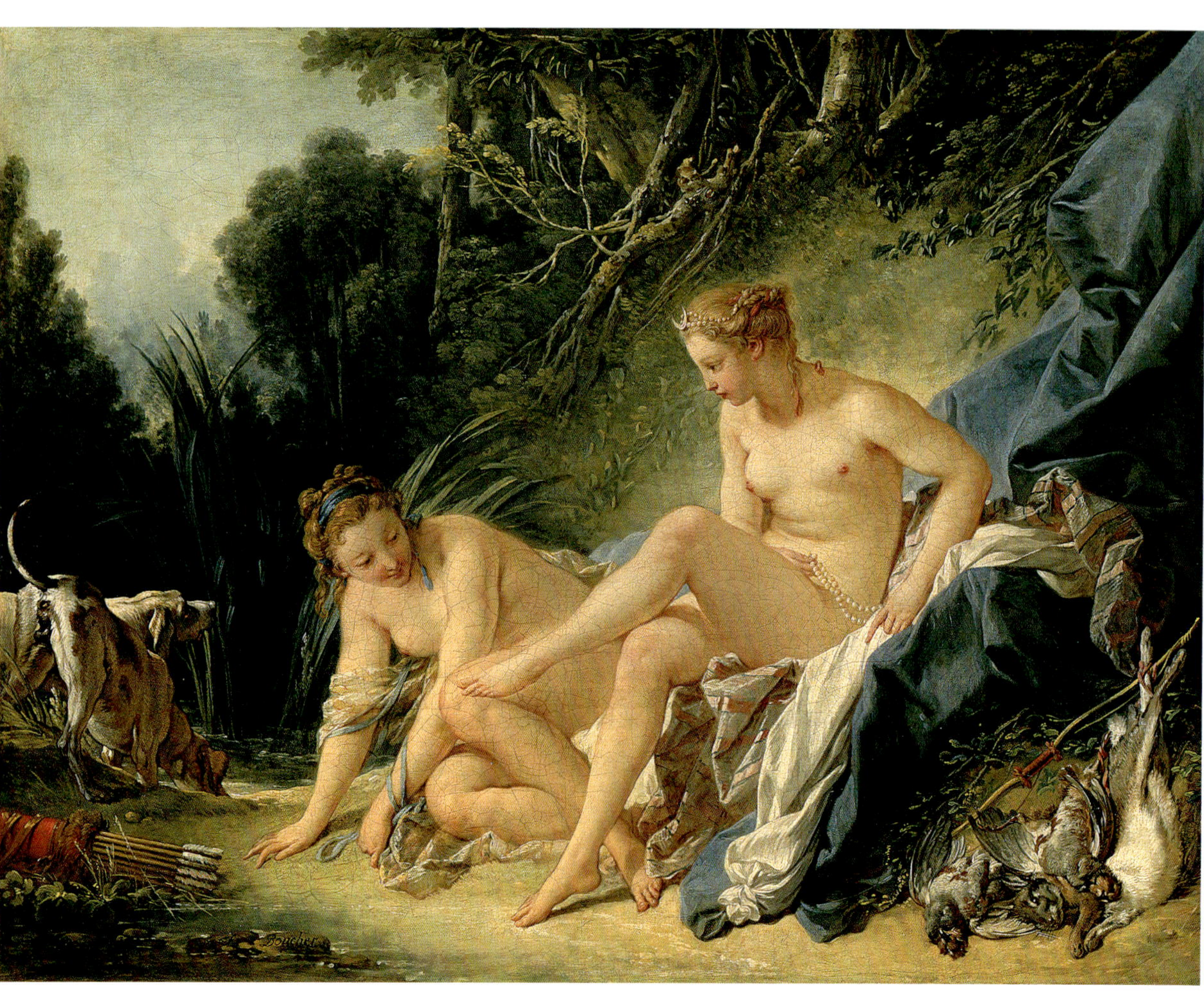

Fig. 16
François Boucher
Bath of Diana, 1742
Oil on canvas, 22 x 28¾ in. (56 x 73 cm)
Musée du Louvre, Paris, France

his favorite works in the Louvre, Boucher's *Bath of Diana* (fig. 16) also played an important role in his reappraisal of the bather theme in the early 1880s. (Boucher's painting appears to have exerted a particular fascination on artists of the day: it was one of the first works to be copied by Manet, and Cézanne had a reproduction of it in his studio.) True to his old master aspirations, Renoir made a number of preparatory drawings for his major *Bathers* canvas, some of them executed in red chalk, a technique favored by Boucher and other eighteenth-century artists (cat. 8).

By the 1890s, Renoir's "hard-edged" style yielded to a fluid melding of figure and ground. Now Titian became a primary inspiration, especially *Venus and the Organist* (fig. 17), which the French artist admired greatly when he visited the Prado in 1892: "The limpidity of the flesh, one wants to caress it. In front of this one feels all the joy that Titian felt when painting."[62] In contrast to Manet's *Olympia,* a brazen contemporary Venus who, thirty years earlier, had punctured the ideals embodied by Titian, Renoir's *Nude on a Couch* (cat. 91, p. 72) is a resplendent and respectful emulation of his mentor's fluid technique and rich color. With the monumental grandeur of *Seated Bather* (cat. 90, p. 75), Renoir invokes the other god of his late years—Rubens.

Renoir's interest in the female nude was paralleled by both Cézanne and Degas. As mature artists, all three looked to the example of the old masters, especially Titian, Rubens, and Veronese, in seeking to locate themselves in the tradition of post-Renaissance painting. Cézanne worked both with and against tradition when engaging with the time-honored subject of the bather. His copying in the Louvre had furnished him with a vast resource of nudes, ranging from the sculptures of Michelangelo and Puget to the paintings of Rubens and Poussin, on which he could draw as he constructed his reinterpretation of the great mythological scenes he admired. Removed from a narrative context, his bathers become primitive presences in a remote and strangely troubling arcadia.

Degas's late nudes, especially the pastels, display a chromatic brilliance that pays homage to Titian and the Venetian masters. Yet their strained, unconventional poses, in which one senses a lingering memory of violent old master narratives, seem to shatter the canons of classical beauty. In wrestling with this timeless subject of the nude, both Degas and Cézanne may have been torn between an ingrained reverence for the older art and a compulsion to explore the theme on their own, modern terms. It could be argued that the art of the past became a burden, even a torment, to the two artists as they strove to

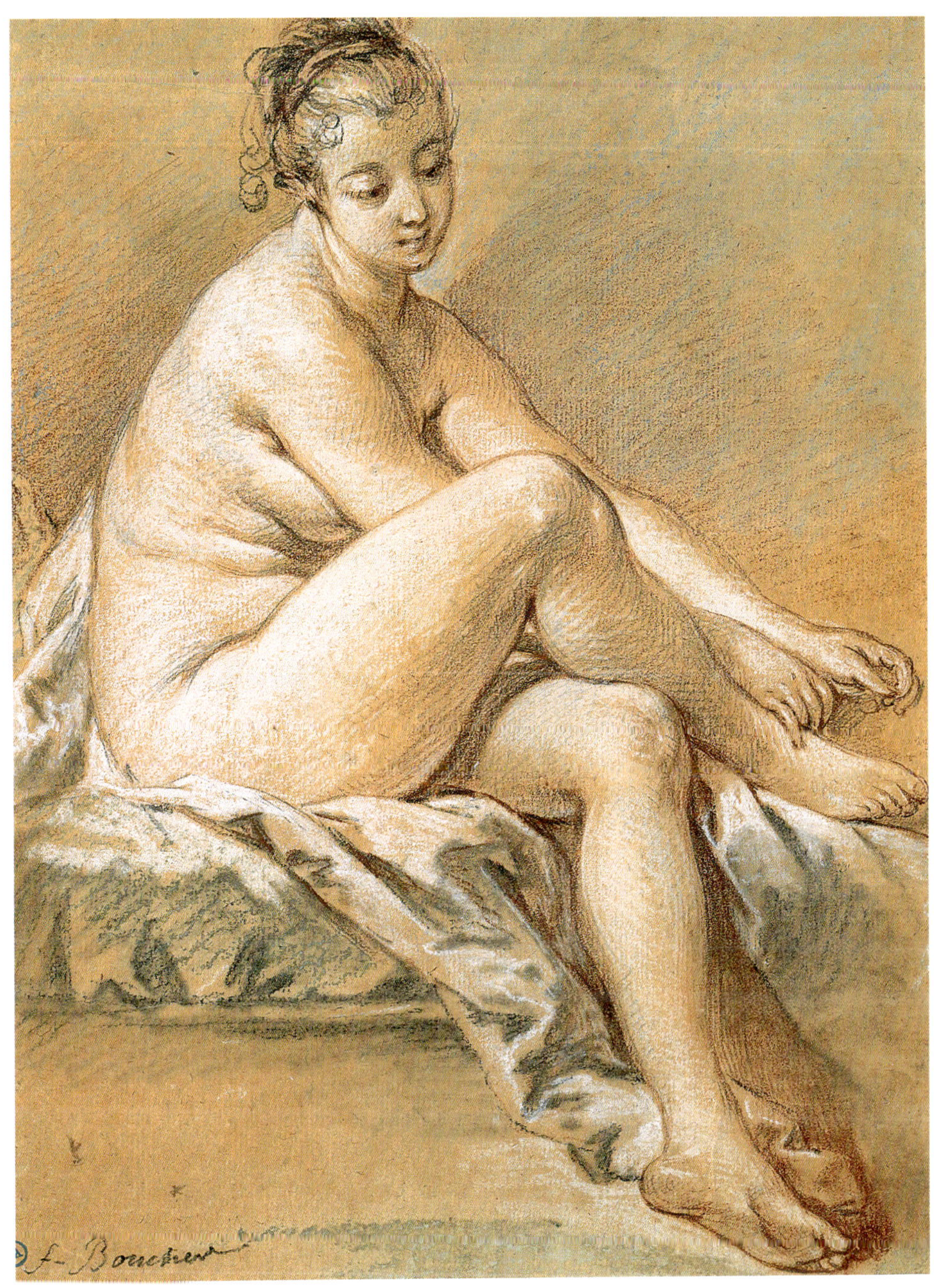

Cat. 8
François Boucher
Seated Nude, 1749

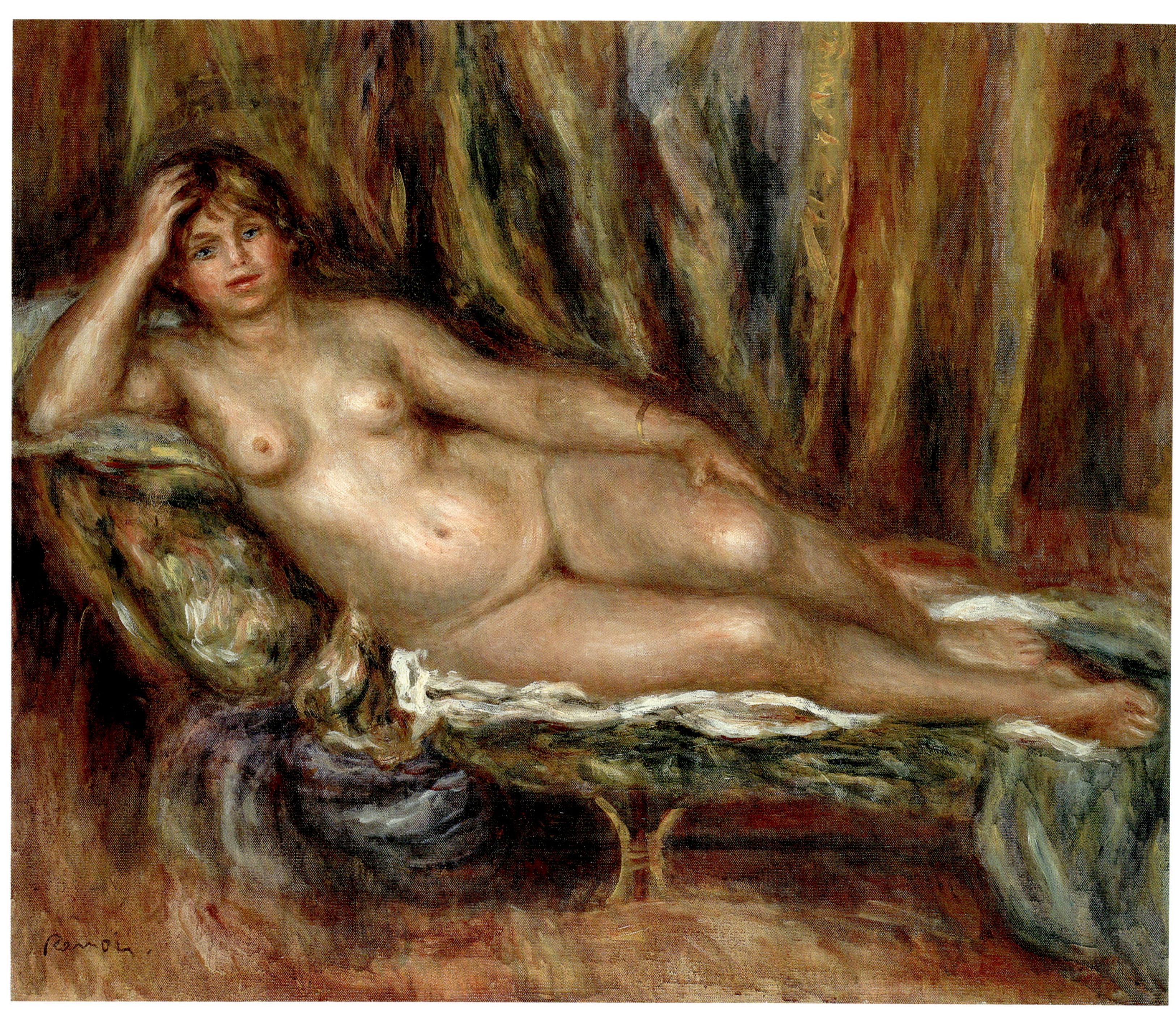

Cat. 91
Pierre-Auguste Renoir
Nude on a Couch, 1915

Fig. 17
Titian (c. 1488–1576)
Venus and the Organist, c. 1548
Oil on canvas, 54⅜ × 87½ in.
(138 × 222.4 cm)
Museo del Prado, Madrid

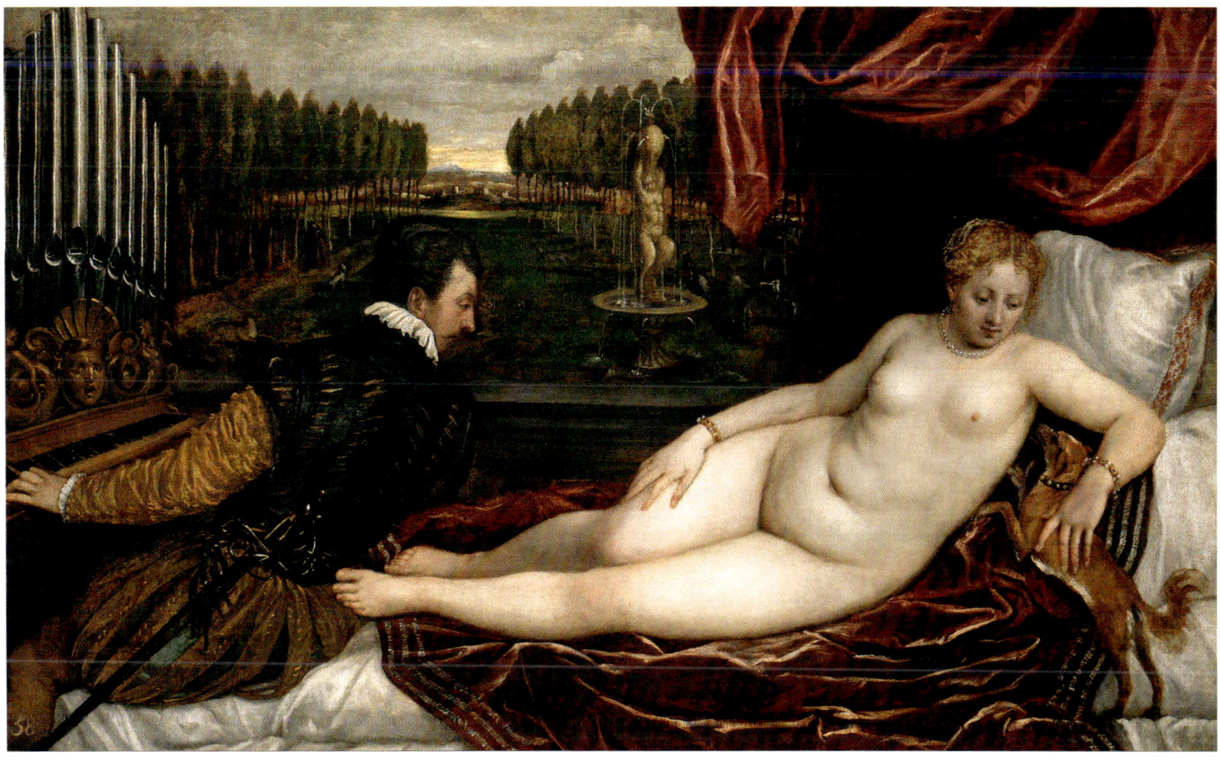

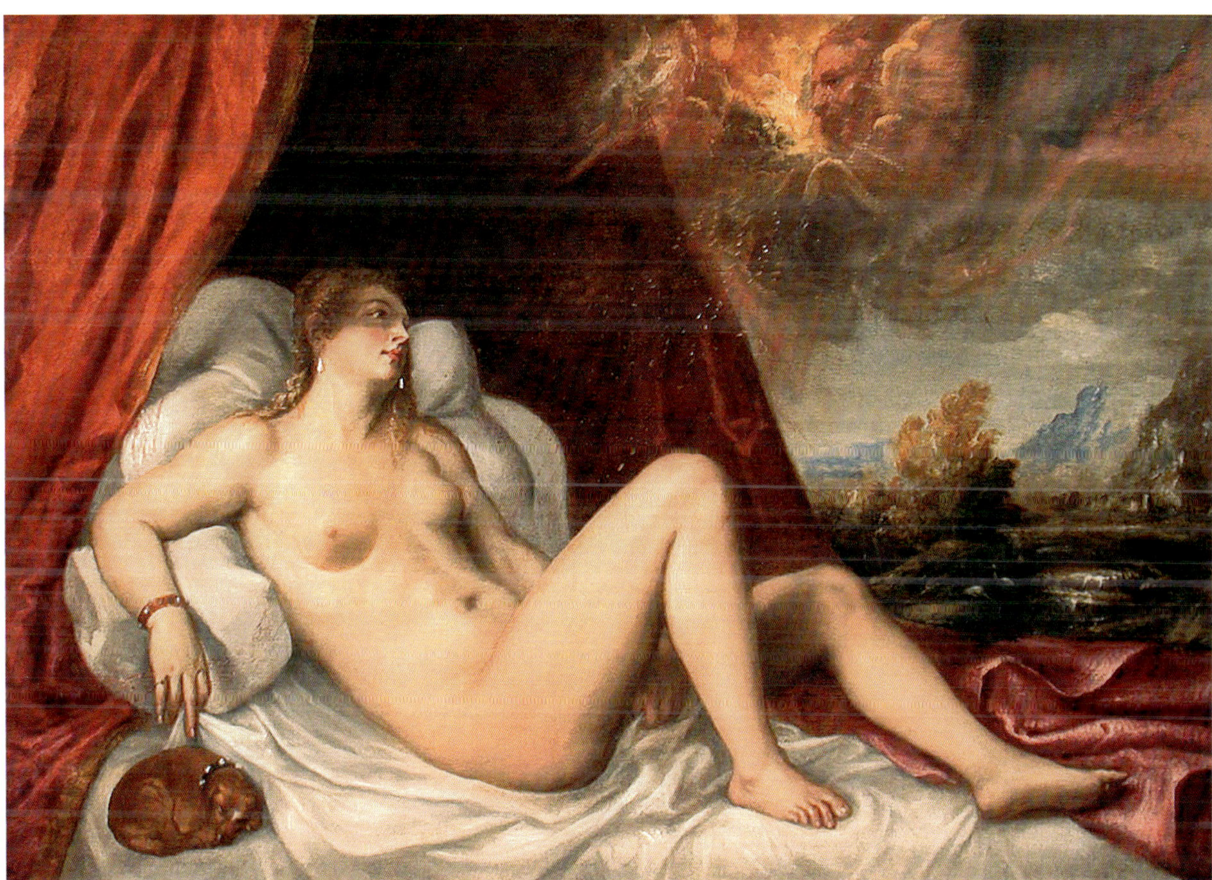

Cat. 97
Titian and Workshop
Danaë, after 1554

Cat. 85
Pierre-Auguste Renoir
A Bather, c. 1885–90

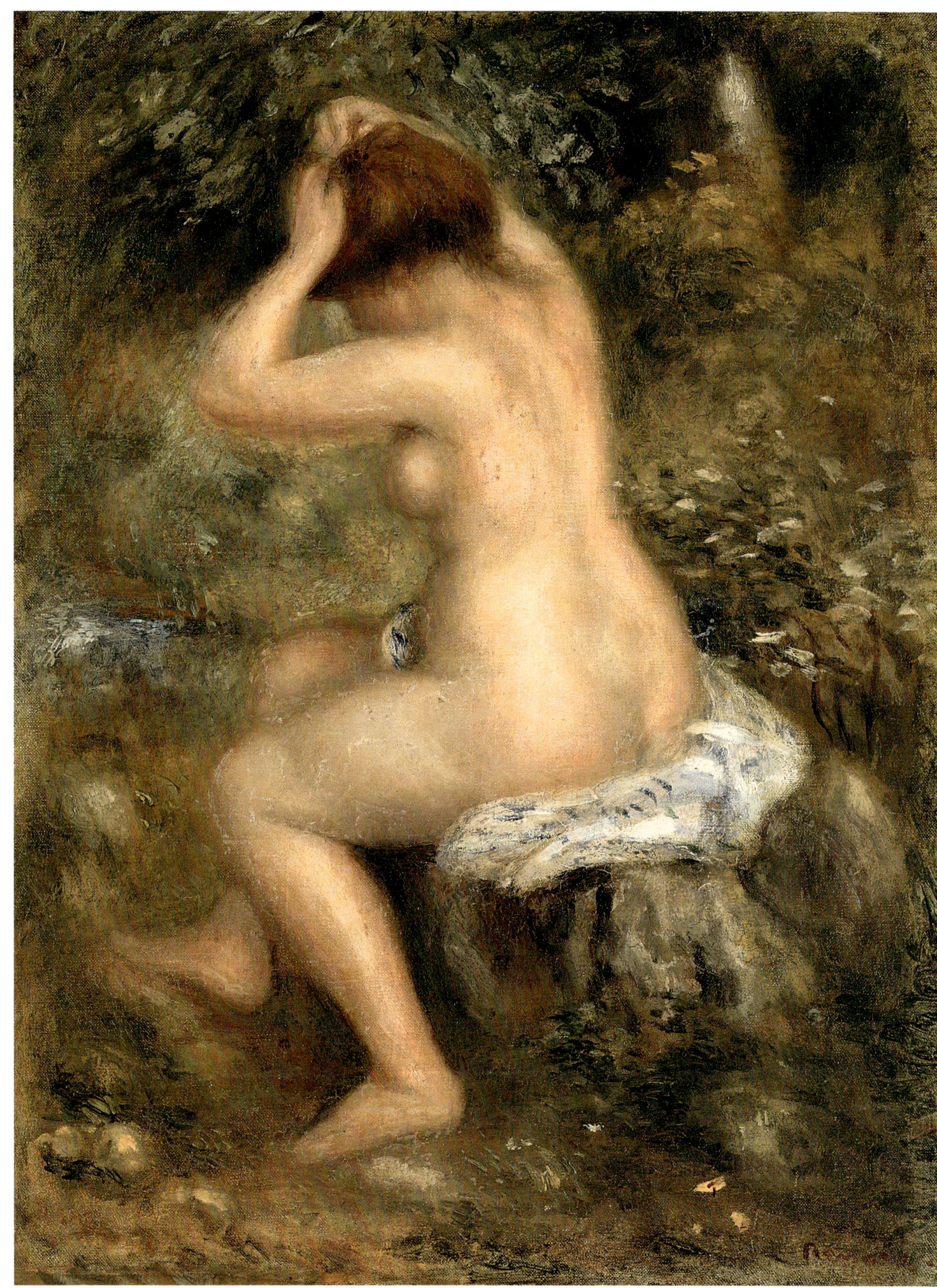

Cat. 90
Pierre-Auguste Renoir
Seated Bather, 1914

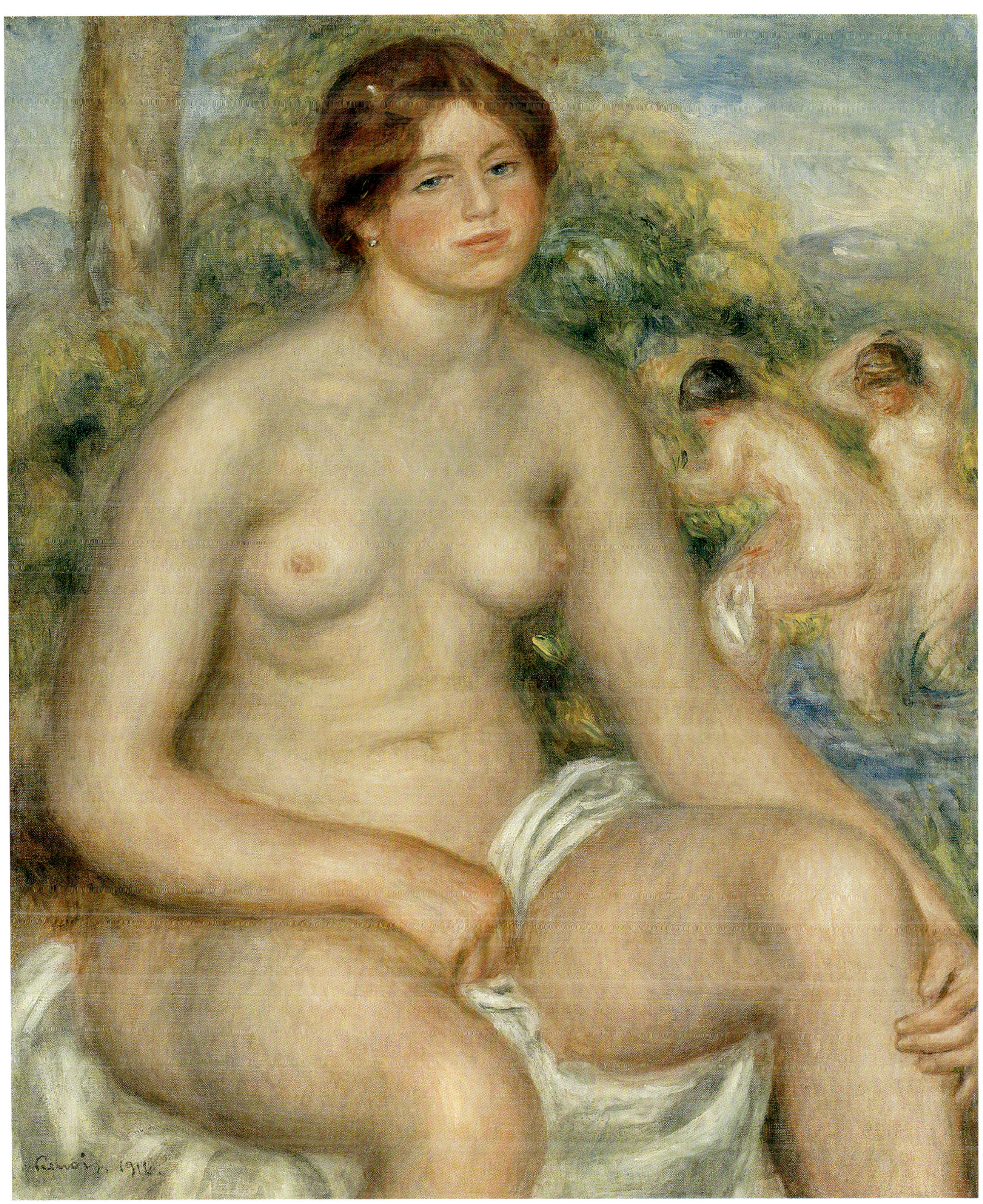

Fig. 18
Edgar Degas
After the Bath (Woman Drying Herself), c. 1896
Oil on canvas, 35¼ x 46 in. (89.5 x 116.8 cm)
Philadelphia Museum of Art, Purchased with funds from the estate of George D. Widener, 1980

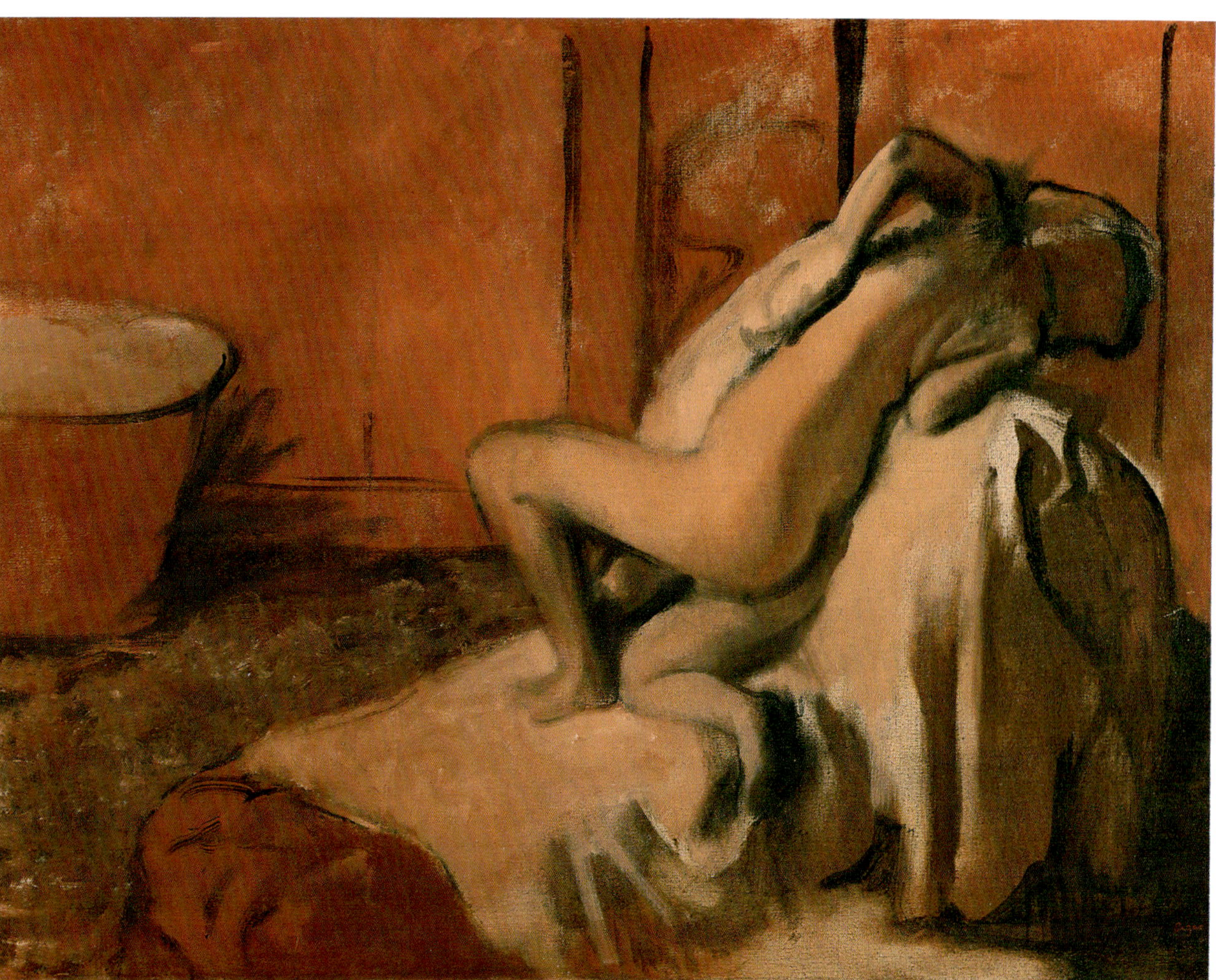

resolve these conflicting claims, a struggle that leaves its imprint on Degas's late, haunting, yet uneasy nudes (fig. 18) and on Cézanne's powerful interpretations of the subject.

"To my mind," Cézanne observed, "one does not put oneself in place of the past, one only adds a new link."[63] Like all the revolutions of modern art, Impressionism looked to the past as well as to the future. The Impressionists rejected, assimilated, and quoted the past in an infinite variety of ways as they sought to make an art for their own time. These radical spirits of the 1870s have themselves long since become guardians of tradition and have taken their place in the canon of great artists enshrined in museums throughout the world.

Notes

1. Baudelaire 1964.

2. Reff, "Louvre" 1964, pp. 552–53.

3. Francis Haskell's *Rediscoveries in Art* (1976, 1980) was a pioneering study in the history of taste and early old master exhibitions. Other studies on individual artists and their responses to earlier art, notably by Michael Fried on Manet (Fried 1969, 1996), by Theodore Reff on Manet ("Manet's Sources" 1969, 1970), Degas (Reff 1963, "Copies" 1964), and Cézanne (Reff, "Reproductions" 1960, and "Cézanne and Poussin" 1960), and by Richard Thomson (Manchester 1987) and Richard Kendall on Degas (London 1996), have enormously enriched our understanding of the way these artists worked. A number of exhibitions have explored different dimensions of this theme. Richard Verdi's *Cézanne and Poussin: The Classical Vision of Landscape* (Edinburgh 1990) examined Cézanne's debt to his great seventeenth-century antecedent. In 1993 *Copier, créer: De Turner à Picasso, 300 oeuvres inspirées par les maîtres du Louvre*, shown at the Musée du Louvre (Paris 1993), was a fascinating survey of how artists from the eighteenth century to the twentieth copied and interpreted works in the Louvre, a subject taken up by the National Gallery, London, in the exhibition *Encounters: New Art from Old* (London, *Encounters* 2000), which invited contemporary artists to produce works inspired by the gallery's collection. Richard Brettell's book *Impression: Painting Quickly in France, 1860–1890* (London, *Impression* 2000), which accompanied an exhibition shown at the National Gallery, London, the Van Gogh Museum, Amsterdam, and the Sterling and Francine Clark Art Institute, Williamstown, Massachusetts, in 2000–2001, drew illuminating parallels between Impressionist technique and the bravura painting of earlier artists from Rubens to Fragonard. More recently, the splendid exhibition *Manet/Velazquez*, mounted in 2002–3 at the Musée d'Orsay in Paris and the Metropolitan Museum of Art, New York (New York 2003), enlarged our knowledge of the impact of the art of seventeenth-century Spain on nineteenth-century French painting.

4. Rosenblum 2000, p. 8.

5. Cuzin 1993, p. 33. See also Boime 1964.

6. Haskell 1980, p. 166.

7. Duro 1985. In analyzing the contents of the Musée des Copies, Duro discovered that the largest number of copies were after Raphael and the second largest group after Velázquez.

8. Paris 1993, p. 33.

9. The chapters on individual artists had been published separately beginning in 1849, with about half appearing before 1860.

10. Laurent 1863.

11. Quoted in Vollard 1938, p. 48.

12. The identification of Mary Cassatt is not certain. See London, *Impression* 2000, p. 208.

13. Letter to Émile Bernard, October 23, 1905, in Cézanne 1941, p. 250.

14. For an extensive discussion of Manet's copies after Italian art, see Meller 2002.

15. Quoted in Vollard 1924, p. 64.

16. Reff 1963, p. 242.

17. "L'air qu'on voit dans les tableaux des maîtres n'est pas de l'air respirable." Cited in Paris 1993, p. 34.

18. Brame and Reff 1984, no. 144.

19. "chercher l'esprit et l'amour [?] de / Mantegna avec la verve / et la coloration de Véronèse." Reff, *Notebooks* 1976, vol. 1, Notebook 15, p. 40.

20. Reff 1963, p. 247.

21. South Hadley 1987, p. 18.

22. Cited in Haskell 1980, p. 166.

23. Haskell 1980, pp. 171–72.

24. The Musée Espagnole was disbanded when Louis-Philippe was dethroned after the 1848 Revolution.

25. Letter to Fantin-Latour dated September 3, 1865, cited in New York 2003, p. 516.

26. This discussion of Manet's *The Little Cavaliers, Copy after Velázquez* is based on Juliet Wilson-Bareau's excellent analysis of this work in New York 2003, pp. 206–7 and 455–56, cat. 77. It has recently been shown that the work is a fragment of a large painting. See catalogue entry by Wilson-Bareau in New York 2003, p. 484, cat. 129.

27. Vollard 1925, p. 60.

28. Boston 1984, p. 43, cat. 16.

29. Annibale Carracci, *Hunting*, c. 1585–88, and *Fishing*, c. 1585–88, both Musée du Louvre, Paris. The works by Rubens is *Landscape with Rainbow* in the Louvre and *The Park of the Château of Steen* from the Kunsthistorisches Museum, Vienna, which Manet knew from reproductions in the chapter on Rubens in Charles Blanc's *Histoire des peintres de toutes les écoles;* see Reff 1970, pp. 456–57.

30. "It is now clear, for example, that most of the important pictures of the 1860s depend either wholly or in part on works by Velázquez, Goya, Rubens, Van Dyck, Raphael, Titian, Giorgione, Veronese, Le Nain, Watteau, Chardin, Courbet. . . . This by itself is an extraordinary fact, one that must be accounted for if Manet's enterprise is to be made intelligible." See Fried 1996, p. 23.

31. This evocative phrase borrows the title of Holly 1996.

32. Lilla Cabot Perry, "Reminiscences of Claude Monet from 1889–1909," reprinted in Washington 1990, p. 116.

33. See note 13.

34. Émile Zola, "Salon," published in *L'Evénement*, April–May 1866, reprinted in Zola 1991, p. 81.

35. See Isaacson 1994 for a thoughtful analysis of the whole issue of the Impressionists' remembering and forgetting the past.

36. Duranty 1986, p. 40.

37. Mallarmé 1986, p. 29.

38. I am indebted to observations made by Professor Hilton Brown, Harriet T. Baily Professor of Art, Art Conservation, Art History and Museum Studies, University of Delaware, for this information on artists' materials.

39. Quoted in Moore 1890, p. 423.

40. Goncourt, entry for February 13, 1874, cited in Herbert 1988, p. 121.

41. Herbert 1988, p. 121.

42. See Manchester 1987, pp. 56–60.

43. Collins 2005.

44. Manet 1979, p. 83.

45. Ph[illipe] Burty, *La République Française*, April 10, 1880, quoted in San Francisco 1986, p. 326.

46. Monet to Bazille, July 15, 1864, Wildenstein 1974, p. 420, letter 8, translated in Rewald 1973, p. 111.

47. Herbert 1988, p. 176.

48. Monet signed the visitors' book at the Trippenhuis. He also signed the register at the Frans Halsmuseum, Haarlem, in 1871. See Frances Jowell's essay in this catalogue.

49. This statement was reported in various forms by various commentators who spoke to Cézanne near the end of his life—Ambroise Vollard, Joachim Gasquet, and Émile Bernard. See Reff, "Cézanne and Poussin" 1960, p. 151. The statement in its most familiar form derives from a conversation with Émile Bernard published as "Une Conversation avec Cézanne," *Mercure de France*, no. 148 (June 1, 1921): 372–97, reprinted in Bernard 1925, pp. 98–135.

50. See Reff, "Cézanne and Poussin" 1960 and Reff 1963; Shiff 1984, pp. 180–83; Edinburgh 1990; and Kendall 1993.

51. Reff, "Cézanne and Poussin" 1960, p. 171.

52. Reff, "Reproductions" 1960, p. 307.

53. See Isaacson 1994, p. 449.

54. See House 1993, p. 149.

55. Gasquet 1926, p. 191.

56. "'J'ai voulu faire de l'impressionisme quelque chose de solide et de durable comme l'art des musées," reported by Maurice Denis in "Cézanne," *L'Occident*, September 1907, reprinted in Denis 1913, p. 250.

57. Vollard 1925, p. 56.

58. See Barter 1998, pp. 77–80, for a discussion of Cassatt's visits to Italy and her exposure to Italian art assembled by such Paris collectors as Gustave Dreyfus, Charles Ephrussi, Émile Gavet, and Jean-Léon Gérôme.

59. Meier-Graefe 1929, p. 318, cited in Bailey 1997, p. 256.

60. Walter Pach, "Pierre Auguste Renoir," *Scribner's Magazine* 51 (1912): 613, cited in Bailey 1997, p. 254.

61. Quoted in Vollard 1925, p. 53.

62. Quoted in Vollard 1938, p. 222.

63. Cézanne to Roger Marx, January 23, 1905, in Cézanne 1937, p. 273.

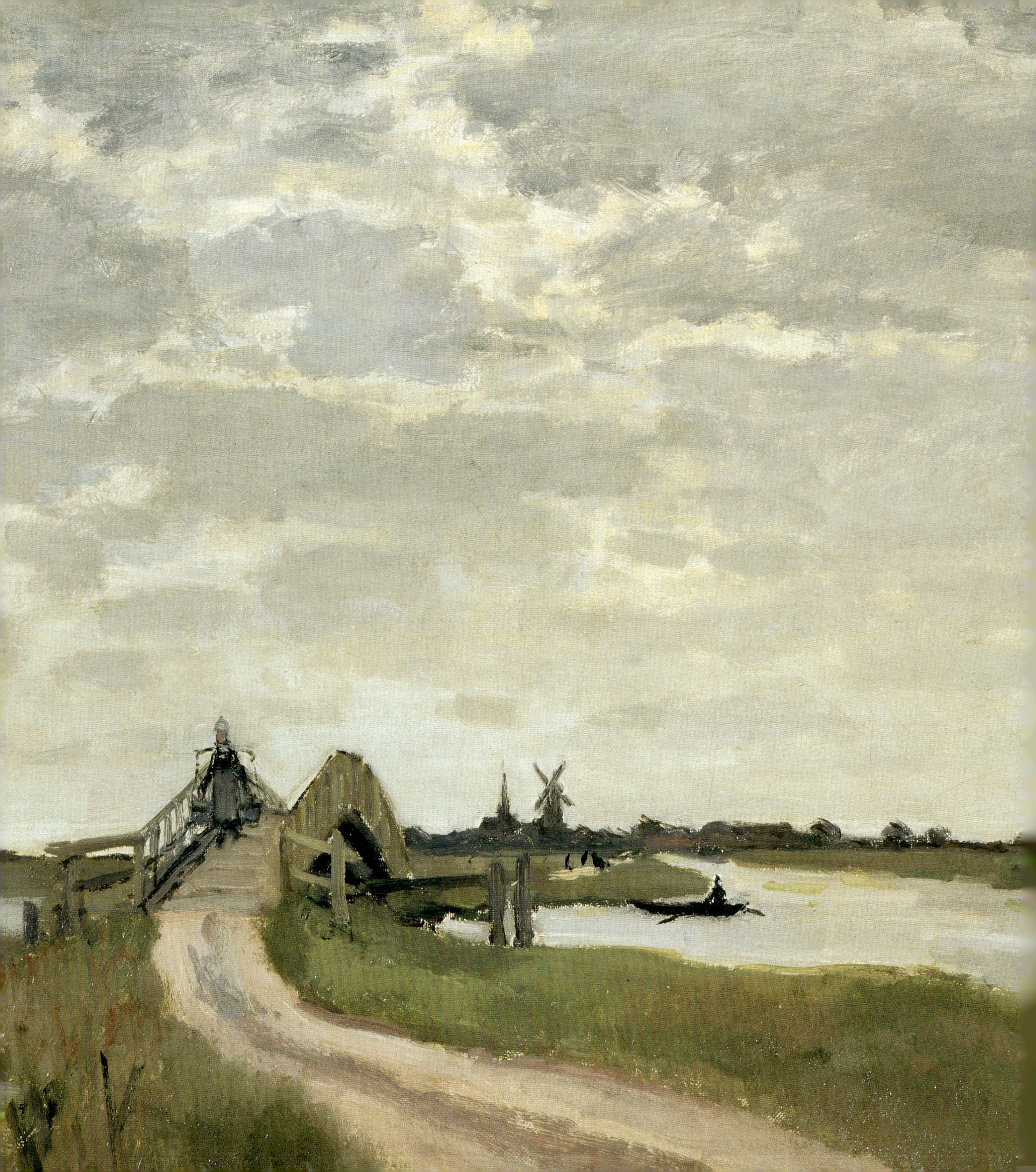

Frances Suzman Jowell

Impressionism

and the Golden Age of Dutch Art

And yet wouldn't it be interesting later on to have portraits of those who are managing the city now! When we go to Amsterdam, the painting of the *Syndics* [fig. 19] stops us in our tracks. Why? Because it is the true impression of something seen.

—Édouard Manet

These Dutch paintings representing the contemporary life of the artists naturally make one dream of the art of our time. . . . For a start, what happens today will be history tomorrow. . . . Who prevents one from making a masterpiece of a meeting of diplomats around a table—just as Rembrandt created a masterpiece of the *Syndics of the Drapers' Company*? Of an orator at a parliamentary rostrum, a teacher surrounded by young people; of a scene at the races, an outing to the opera, a stroll in the Champs Élysées; or simply men working at anything, or women enjoying anything.[1]

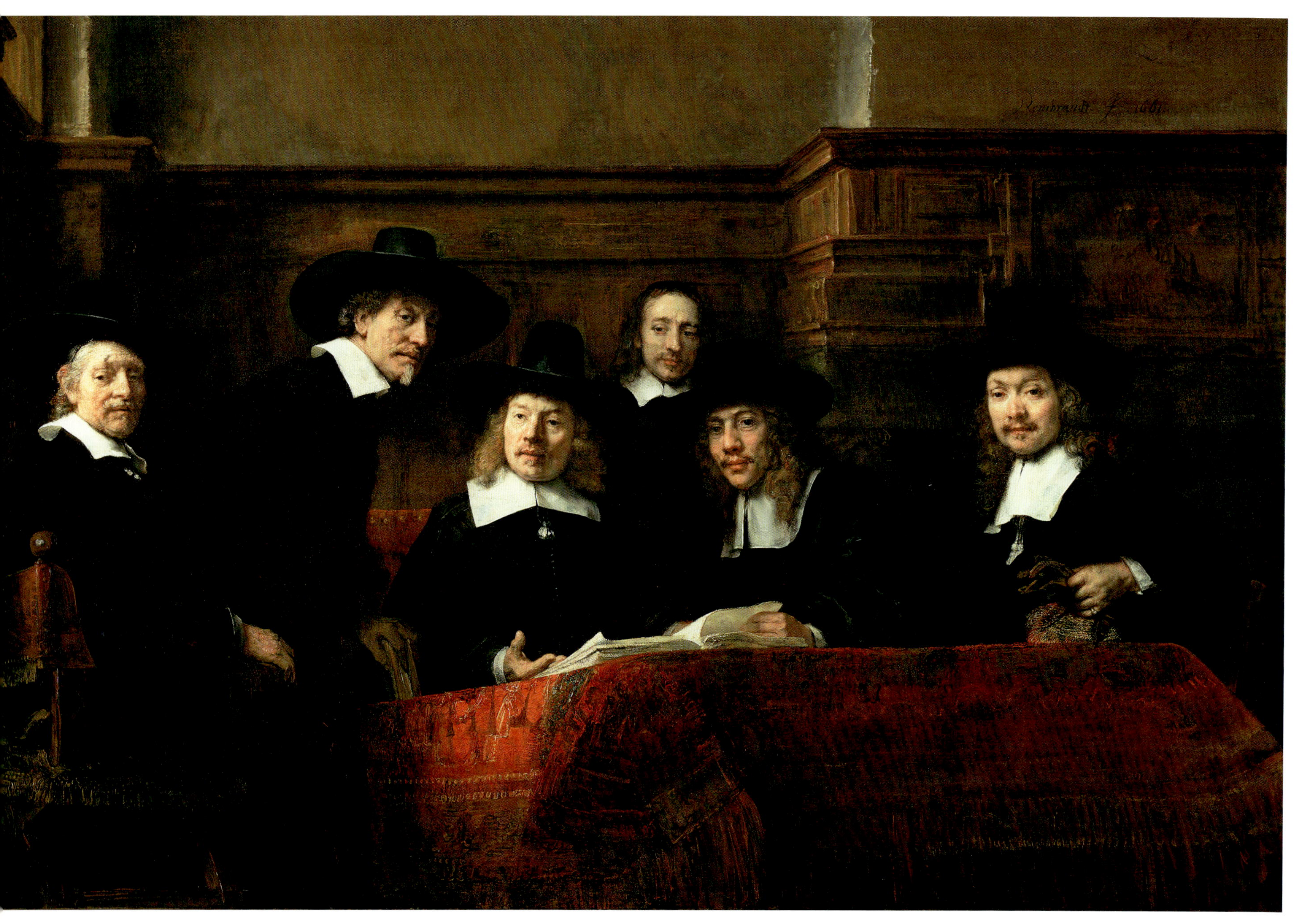

Fig. 19
Rembrandt Harmensz van Rijn
(1606–1669)
Syndics (The Sampling Officials), 1662
Oil on canvas, 75⅜ × 109⅞ in. (191.5 × 279 cm)
Collectie Rijksmuseum Amsterdam, SK-C-6

This passage by the renowned French critic and art historian Théophile Thoré (writing under his pseudonym, W. Bürger[2]) is taken from his pioneering study on Frans Hals published in 1868. Thoré could not have known the extent to which his dreams for the art of his time were to be realized during the following decades by the Impressionist painters whose most consistent hallmark would be their depiction of contemporary life as viewed and experienced: scenes of everyday leisure and work life of Paris and its suburbs; views of cities, towns, villages, and countryside; portraits and still lifes—all familiar, accessible, secular pictures with minimal reference to the traditional iconography or procedures of earlier European art.

Manet and the younger Impressionists surely knew of Thoré's contention that the legitimate ancestors of modern art were those old masters who themselves had depicted the life of their own times—most notably the seventeenth-century Dutch School, which Thoré characterized in the first of his two groundbreaking guides to the Dutch museums in 1858 as

> Life, *living life,* man—his customs, his occupations, his pleasures, his caprices. Some [artists] chose the citizen active in public life . . . ; others chose families at home, or in their outdoor recreations; here the upper classes, there the working classes, or outcasts. Others represented the environment of social life—the sea and beaches, with the maritime events so dear to the country; or the countryside and the forests, with laborers who till the earth or care for animals; rustic and hunting scenes; canals and streams, with mills, boats, fishermen; the towns, squares, and streets where the population circulated in all its variety. Everywhere animation, contemporary life, which is also eternal life—the history of the people and of the country.
>
> A true history . . . in luminous and faithful images; a kind of photography of their great Seventeenth Century, men and things, feelings and customs—the actions and gestures of a whole nation.[3]

Thoré attributed the emergence of this original school of painting in the seventeenth-century Dutch republic to its hard-won political and religious freedom and to the independence and energy of its citizens. Not only had they secured their land from the threatening sea, they had "by a spontaneous outburst of national genius"[4] re-created their society and their moral and intellectual world. Unlike their Flemish neighbors, they threw off the yoke of Catholic Spain and set up a democratic Protestant republic, and rejected the arcane religious, classical, and mythological subject matter of Italianate Renaissance art that served rulers and church. Instead, their new art, naturalism, served the entire society and was "art for mankind" (l'art pour l'homme).[5] As the first school to renounce the past and turn toward the new, it was the beginning of modern art.[6]

Thoré-Bürger was not the first (or last) writer to characterize Dutch art in these terms.[7] However, his two guides to the Dutch museums, *Musées de la Hollande,* which inaugurated a new era in the historiography of this school, gave wide currency to these ideas.[8] This, together with his argument for the special historical role of the Dutch School (as he defined it) for modern art, made Thoré a key figure in establishing the terms in which the seventeenth-century Dutch School was understood in France from the 1860s on. With varying emphasis, both the political context and the originality of descriptive naturalism as the essential quality of Dutch art of the Golden Age are reasserted by other French writers on Dutch art at the time.[9]

One of the best-known critics was Charles Blanc,[10] founder of the *Gazette des Beaux-Arts* (1859) and famous for his monumental project *Histoire des peintres de toutes les écoles,* which became an important resource for Manet and the younger Impressionists.[11] Blanc played a major role in the dissemination of knowledge of Dutch art both through his publications on Rembrandt and his installments on individual Dutch painters. These were published intermittently from 1849 before being collected in two volumes in 1861. Blanc's introductory essay explained the naturalism of the great Dutch School in the context of national independence, democracy, and Protestantism.[12]

Another French writer known to the Impressionists, Henry Havard,[13] in whose company Claude Monet visited the Rijksmuseum (then in the Trippenhuis) in 1871, insisted that only after the Dutch nation "had taken possession of itself" could its own original art flourish, and he ceded to Dutch landscapists the "inextinguishable glory" of having been "the first among the moderns to understand and interpret nature."[14] He stressed the "extériorité" (externality) of their art (excepting only Rembrandt, whose sublimity was generally agreed on)[15] and especially commended Dutch genre painting for representing the varied aspects of current life and catering to the wide range of tastes and domestic circumstances of their citizen-patrons.[16] Havard also emphasized that artists of the Dutch republic were the first to portray and celebrate their own cities, as had several artists of republican France, whose civic affection for Paris was evident in their paintings of "all aspects of our great city."[17]

From a different perspective, the painter and critic Eugène Fromentin, in his lively account of his visit to the Netherlands, *Les Maîtres d'autrefois* of 1876, characterized the essential aim of the "free and national" Dutch art as "the portrait of Holland, its exterior image, faithful, exact, complete and like, with no embellishment. Portraits of men and places, citizen habits, squares, streets, country places, the sea and sky, . . . In appearance nothing can be more simple than the discovery of this art of earthly aim."[18] While grumpily noting ways in which certain contemporary painters were currently availing (or misavailing) themselves of the Dutch old masters, he also reminded his readers of the salutary "influence of Holland" on French landscape in recent decades.[19]

The example of Dutch landscape had indeed been important to the Barbizon painters and was frequently invoked in the critical debates of the 1830s and 1840s in which Thoré had participated.[20] In the wake of the 1848 Revolution, Dutch painting continued to be an important historical resource for Gustave Courbet and the Realist movement, particularly in civic group portraiture and genre painting.[21] The exiled Thoré could not contribute directly to the critical debates about Realism, but instead, as "W. Bürger," he turned his attention to the art of the past, especially the innovative naturalism of certain old masters of the seventeenth and eighteenth centuries.[22] The artists he singled out included (among others) Diego Rodríguez de Silva y Velázquez, Jean-Antoine Watteau, Jean-Honoré Fragonard, Jean-Siméon Chardin—but above all the Dutch School in general as "the most determined, the most original, the most varied, the most revolutionary, the most natural and the most human at the same time: it is definitely the [school] which is most liberated from the past, which sticks closest to nature, and thereby best indicates one of the directions of future art."[23] In his *Salons* of the 1860s W. Bürger frequently alluded to the originality and technical skills of Dutch naturalism as instructive for contemporary artists. During these years he wielded a double authority, both as W. Bürger, the leading scholar and connoisseur of seventeenth-century Dutch art, and as Théophile Thoré, the veteran republican critic whose earlier judgments had been vindicated.[24] His views were known not only through his publications but also through personal contacts with artists, collectors, and critics. He frequented studios of contemporary artists and played an active role in the art market—especially in drawing to the attention of collectors, critics, and artists his favored old masters.[25] Most significantly, his general championship of the seventeenth-century Dutch School and his reshaping of the canon coincided with Manet's most intense and complex involvement with the art of the past and with the crucial formative years of the younger artists later to be termed the Impressionists.

Thoré's criteria for both contemporary and past art concerned subject matter or formal qualities—or both. Thus decorative, smoothly painted mythological or historical scenes by such artists as Adriaen van der Werff and Gerard de Lairesse were castigated as decadent in subject and treatment; the formerly popular Italianate landscapists such as Nicolaes Berchem and Jan Both were banished as "pseudo-Italians" or "de-naturalized Dutchmen";[26] and Gerrit Dou and the other *fijnschilders* were reproved for overmeticulous industrious finish and contrived artificial light effects on the grounds that "true art never has these futile preoccupations. Art is more spontaneous in its response, more frank in its results."[27] As will be seen, while effectively sending these artists offstage, he ushered others into the limelight, appealing to criteria that were consistent with some values of the contemporary avant-garde.

Naturalism, according to Thoré-Bürger, did not rest only on subject matter (the what) but also on the execution (the how). The crux of his argument was that seemingly trivial, familiar subjects could be imbued with as much significance and *poésie* as the most elevated themes of religious, historical, or mythological narrative through what he considered the essential means of painting—color, light, and chiaroscuro (rather than the linear or sculptural draftsmanship of *dessinateurs*). He valued spontaneous, rapidly executed paintings—from which he inferred attributes of sincerity, truth, and originality of artistic response—and he belittled "finishers" (*finisseurs*). Thus in 1868 he defended Johan Barthold Jongkind's controversial sketchy manner as preferable to the "patient knitters of lengthily ruminated images," insisting that "true" artists painted quickly and *d'impression.* And he cited, among other "glorious" earlier examples, Dutch artists such as Hals, Rembrandt, and Jan van Goyen.[28] He lauded paintings that conveyed the artist's personal response and a heightened sense of life and nature—especially the sense of all-enveloping air and natural light, of which he found abundant examples in Dutch art.

But were such Dutch works readily accessible to Manet and the young Impressionists? Although Thoré urged painters to visit the Dutch museums, even devising a fortnight's itinerary for impecunious artists,[29] Paris too provided ample opportunities for artists to study Dutch painting. By the 1860s the Musée du Louvre held (among others) well-known works by Rembrandt, Meindert Hobbema, Jacob van Ruisdael, Nicolaes Berchem, Van Goyen, Aelbert Cuyp, Willem van de Velde, Gabriel Metsu, Gerard Terborch, Adriaen van Ostade, Jan Davidsz de Heem, and Willem Claesz Heda.[30] In 1869 the collection was amplified by approximately fifty Dutch paintings from the La Caze bequest—including Rembrandt's *Bathsheba*, Hals's *The Gypsy* (fig. 23), Terborch's *Reading Lesson*, and Maes's *Benediction*. In 1870 the museum acquired its first Vermeer—*The Lace Maker* (fig. 20). Fromentin could reasonably claim in the mid-1870s that, except for the group civic portraits in Holland, a visit to the Louvre provided a "just idea of Dutch art," of "its spirit, its character, its perfections, the diversity of its styles."[31]

However, besides the Louvre, it is especially relevant that during the 1860s and 1870s artists in Paris were witness to the high profile of Dutch paintings on the flourishing art market. A series of spectacular public sales and occasional exhibitions of old masters from well-known private collections served to publicize increasingly valuable Dutch paintings. In his chapter on private collections in Paris written for the *Paris-Guide* of 1867 (the year of the Exposition Universelle), Thoré took the reader on a lively, whirlwind tour of the most famous private galleries in the city, commenting in passing that "it's not my fault, if, in all the collections, the Dutch outdo all!"[32]

This disclaimer was somewhat disingenuous, for Thoré, more than any other, had been instrumental in making known and promoting his favored Dutch artists to collectors, critics, and artists. In fact, in 1874 (the year of the first Impressionist exhibition and just five years after his death) a major exhibition from private collections held at the Palais Bourbon included among the much-vaunted paintings works by two Dutch artists whose prominence owed much to Thoré: Frans Hals and Johannes Vermeer ("van der Meer").[33]

Both these painters, one rescued from notoriety and the other from obscurity, were of special interest to Manet and his circle. While the patchy, perceptible brushwork, bright color, apparent spontaneity, and lively activity of the paint surface that would come to characterize Impressionism is not comparable to the palette and procedures of seventeenth-century Dutch painting, aspects of Hals and Vermeer were seen as having "modern" relevance. In Hals's case his bold, gestural brushwork, his suggestive areas of "unfinish," and the informal naturalness of his figures were instructive. In Vermeer's works, the luminous nuances of natural light and air were admired, whether achieved by harmonies of color, blurred, unfocused areas, overlapping contours, or occasional distinctive *pointillé* highlights. In both, of course, the primacy of visual experience was crucial.

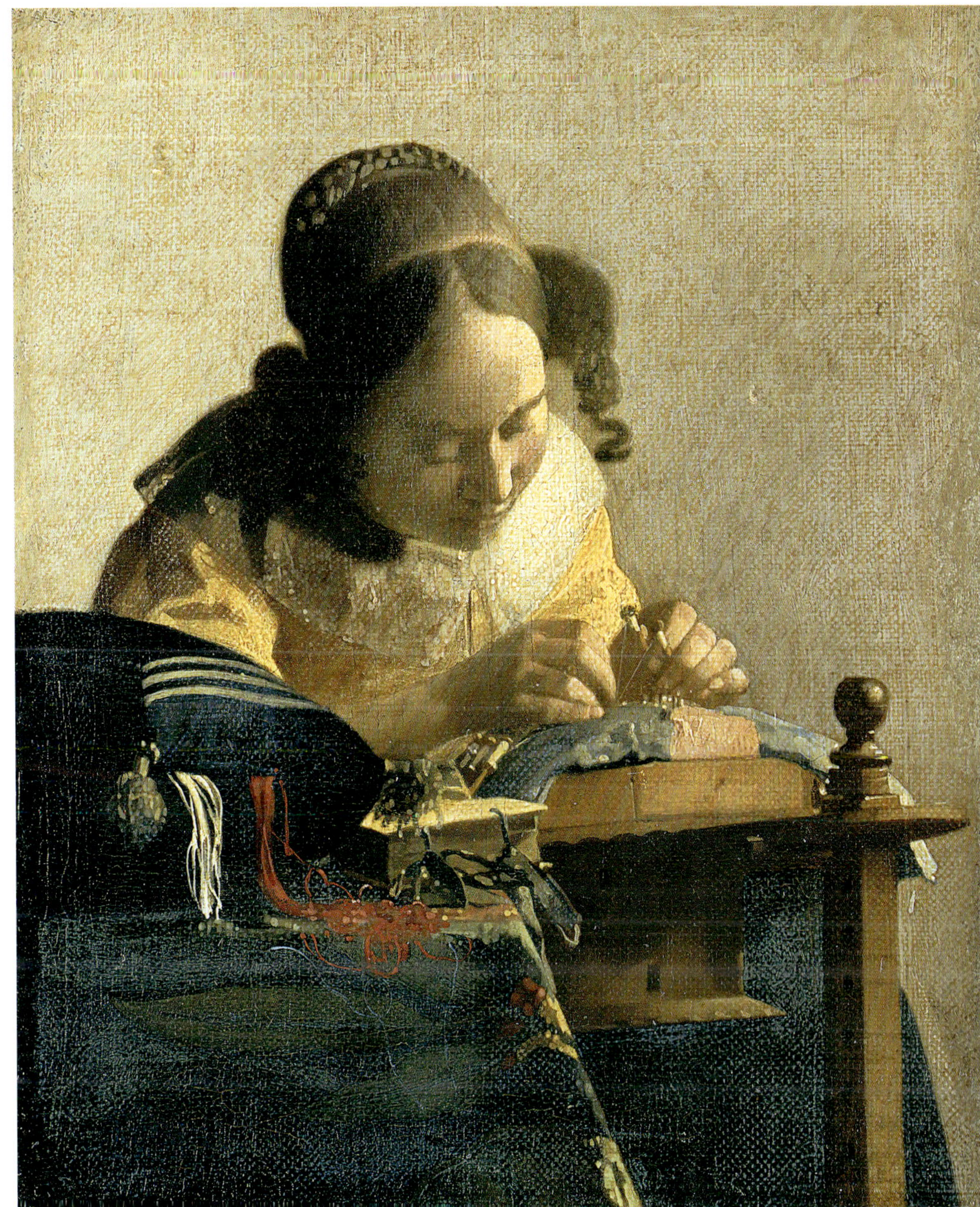

Fig. 20
Johannes Vermeer (van Delft)
(1632–1675)
The Lace Maker, 1669–70
Oil on canvas laid down on wood,
12¼ x 9½ in. (31 x 24 cm)
Musée du Louvre, Paris, France

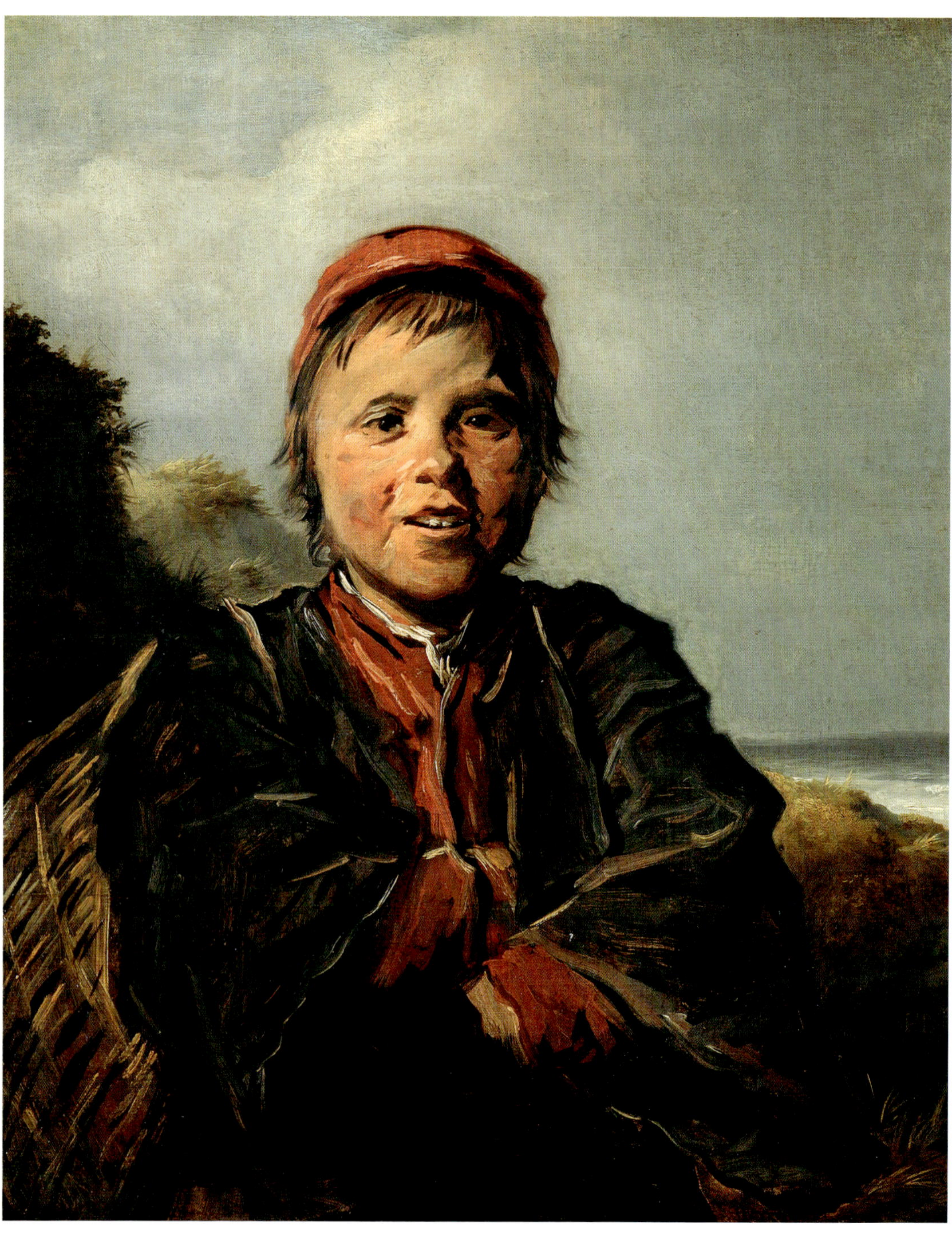

Cat. 42
Frans Hals
Fisher Boy, 1630–32

Hals's works had for the past century generally languished on the art market, often dismissed as slapdash and unfinished, the work of a talented but uneven artist whose feckless debauchery was legend.[34] Hals's construed impetuosity had been censured in the eighteenth century by the painter-academician Sir Joshua Reynolds and lamented by prominent dealers, who warned contemporary painters to avoid his vice of painting too quickly.[35]

Thoré, by contrast, was an enthusiastic advocate for Hals's much maligned procedure:

> He painted so much! He painted so quickly—and so well! Even the slightest painting by him is attractive and offers a lesson to artists. All aspects of his work are instructive, his faults as well as his strengths—for his faults are always those of a great practitioner. In his exaggerated brusqueness, his risky contrasts, his informal carelessness, there is always the hand of a bountifully talented painter, and even the sign of a certain kind of genius—somewhat superficial, it is true, and inspired by the external appearances of things, by movement, style, color, and effect, by whatever moves and glitters, rather than by the secret and inner spiritual side of life, even somewhat vulgar, if one can so refer to genius—but frank and bold, as irresistible as instinct.[36]

Hals's *Singing Boy with Flute* (fig. 21), then in the Suermondt collection, is described as

> [a] lively study, slashed on in one go. He never did otherwise. All his brushstrokes stand out, aimed exactly and wittily where they should. One could say that Frans Hals painted as if fencing, and that he flicked his brush as if it were a foil . . . such beautiful passes. Sometimes a little reckless to be sure, but as skillful as he is bold.[37]

Not many of Hals's works were readily available in public collections at that time. In 1860 the Louvre had one work attributed to Hals—a portrait of Descartes.[38] For those who traveled to Holland, there were a few paintings in Dutch museums, such as the so-called *Portrait of the Artist and His Wife* and *The Merry Drinker* (fig. 25) in Amsterdam, but most of his civic group portraits remained in relatively inaccessible municipal buildings in Haarlem.[39] However, this situation changed dramatically after the establishment of the Frans Halsmuseum in Haarlem in 1862, when eight great civic group portraits (eighty-four figures in all) were displayed together, celebrating not only the original commissioning bodies but also the artist.[40] Henceforth, a journey to visit the Dutch museums invariably included the new Haarlem museum, as can be seen by the visitors' registers.[41] The signatures of Monet and Manet appear, respectively, in 1871 and 1872, and in 1873 Mary Cassatt visited the museum, where she made a much-treasured copy of part of one of Hals's *Officers and Sergeants of the Saint Hadrian Civic Guard*.[42] A different response was later recorded by Berthe Morisot, who noted somewhat petulantly that she preferred Hals's paintings in the La Caze collection.[43]

It was indeed in Paris, the center of the European art market, that several of the finest of Hals's dispersed paintings first surfaced during the 1860s—to the acclaim of his new audiences. By 1864 the Pereire collection could boast of Hals's *Portrait of a Woman* (fig. 22), which was recommended by Thoré as exemplary for modern artists—especially the "marvelous" depiction of her clasped hands "achieved by a . . . few bold strokes which precisely show up the form and movement."[44] In 1865 an elegant *Portrait of a Man* (later dubbed *The Laughing Cavalier*) was acquired by Lord Hertford for an unprecedented sum at auction, and the following year the disappointed underbidder, Baron James de Rothschild, expensively acquired the small, informal *Portrait of Van Heythuysen,* in which the sitter is tilting back his chair.[45] In 1866 the famous *Exposition Rétrospective* of old masters from private collections, held in a gallery next to the contemporary Salon, displayed Hals's *Portrait of a Woman* from the Pereire collection and the alluring *Jeune paysanne souriante* (also known as *La Bohémienne [Gypsy]*) from the La Caze collection (fig. 23),[46] painted, in Thoré's words, "in tones of gold, with the wildness of his

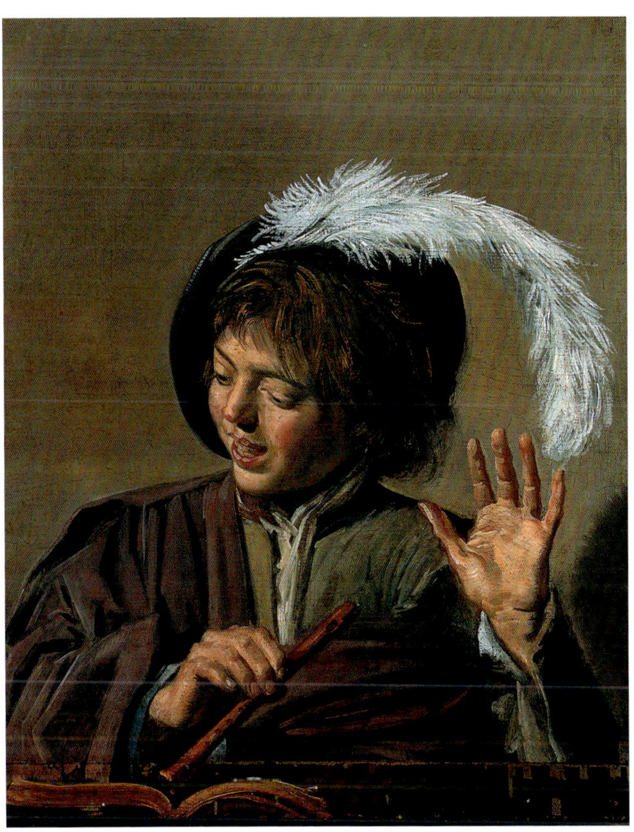

Fig. 21
Frans Hals
Singing Boy with Flute, c. 1623/25
Oil on canvas, 27⅛ × 21¾ in.
(68.8 × 55.2 cm)
Gemäldegalerie, Staatliche Museen zu Berlin, Berlin, Germany

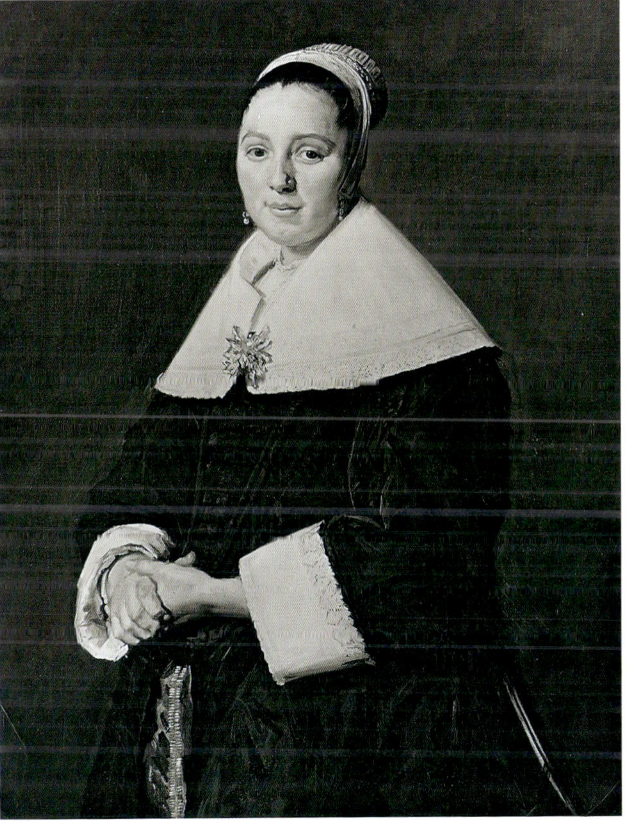

Fig. 22
Frans Hals
Portrait of a Woman
Oil on canvas
Location unknown

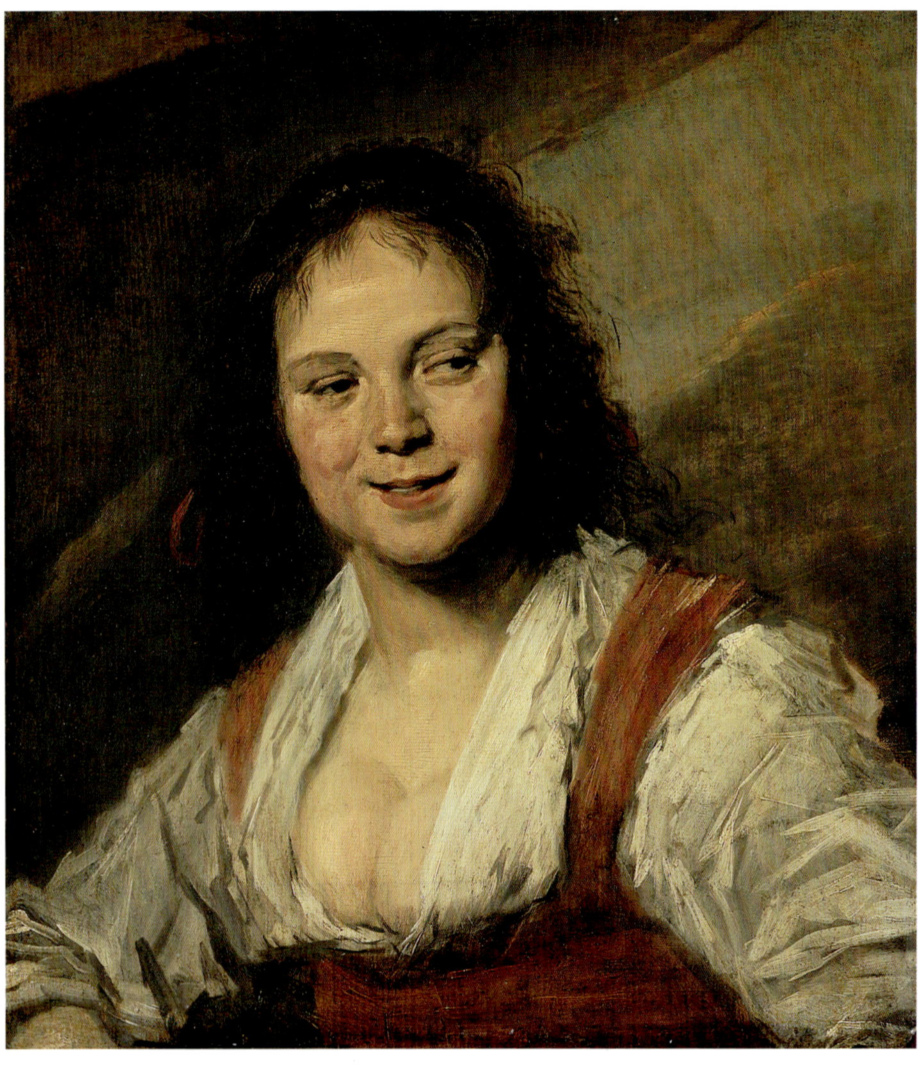

Fig. 23
Frans Hals
The Gypsy, 1628–30
Oil on wood, 22⅞ × 20½ in. (58 × 52 cm)
Musée du Louvre, Paris, France

Cat. 53
Édouard Manet
Gypsy with a Cigarette, c. 1862

early style: a masterpiece improvised in a few hours of bright light and good humor."[47] In 1867 Thoré rhetorically applauded Hals's pride of place in the most celebrated collections in Paris: "May one of the most valiant portraitists in the world, may Frans Hals reclaim his legitimate place!"[48] By the following year, in his pioneering study of Hals, he located approximately thirty of his paintings in Paris.[49]

Hals's special resonance for the contemporary avant-garde was explained in 1866 by Manet's friend and champion Zacharie Astruc in his review of the *Exposition Rétrospective:*

> The reputation of this master will owe much to the modern school which particularly takes to him and celebrates him as an inspiration. The truth is that he represents a healthy and invigorating approach, that he is true to his vision, and that it is now or never that the sincere path must be followed if we wish the domain of French art to strengthen and grow.[50]

Hals's art was not only construed as expressing the boldness, optimism, and liveliness of the new freedom-loving republic, it was also increasingly associated with modern aesthetic values.[51] Hals's apparent spontaneity and gestural brushwork, which both animated his figures and brought the painting process to the fore, were now viewed as a brilliant example of improvisatory painting *en premier coup* (painting directly onto the canvas without preparation), and the immediacy and freedom of his procedure were praised for their prophetic modernism.

While Hals became an inspiring example to a wide variety of artists in the late nineteenth century, his works were particularly instructive to Manet and the young Impressionists—and to their audiences. Manet's contemporaries frequently commented on presumed allusions or similarities to Hals in his works, particularly after his third visit to Holland in 1872. His well-received *Le Bon Bock* (fig. 24) in the Salon of 1873 was generally considered to be a Halsian paraphrase of such works as the *Merry Drinker* (fig. 25) then in the Amsterdam museum.[52] Théodore Duret later commented that it was Hals who inspired Manet to paint Émile Belot with a beer mug "en souvenir."[53] Elsewhere Paul Mantz referred to the presence of "Hals, that great swashbuckler, [in] the way the paint is applied to the canvas,"[54] while Edgar Degas reportedly quipped, somewhat facetiously, that Manet "did not paint fingernails because Frans Hals did not depict them."[55] In a decidedly hostile vein, Fromentin commented, "all of Manet is already in Hals, but that the Frenchman has copied the weaknesses of Hals, the results of his senility."[56] Most significant, however, is Antonin

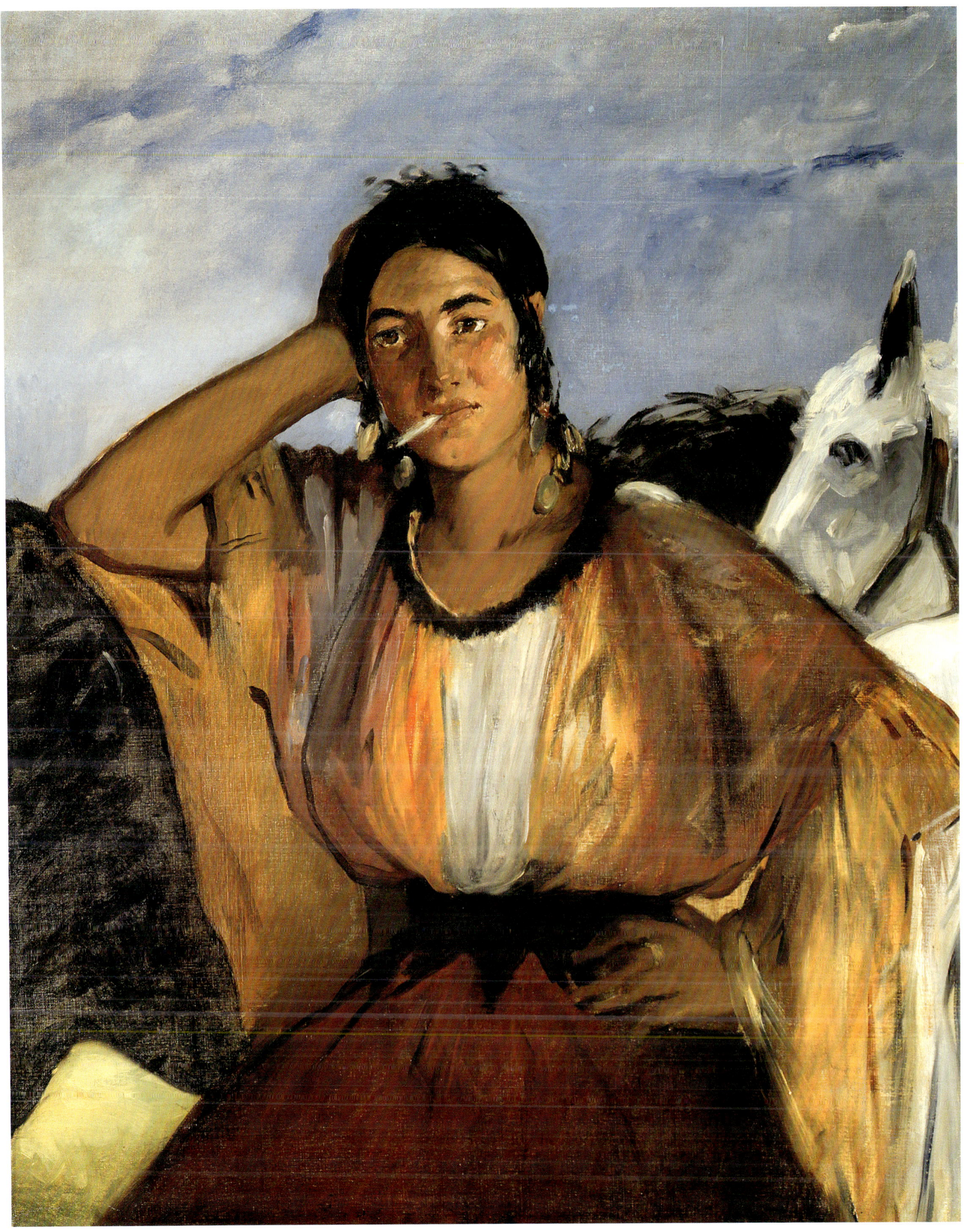

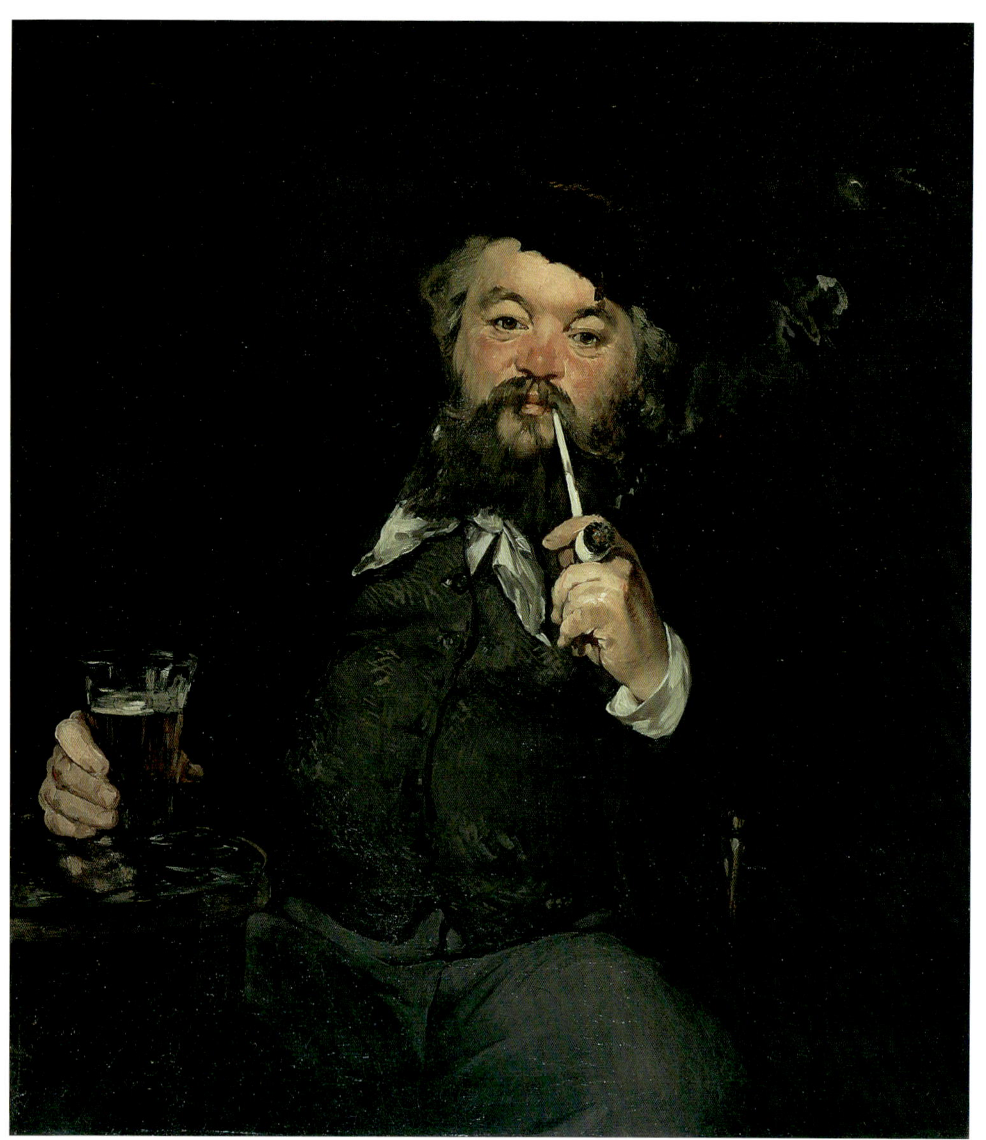

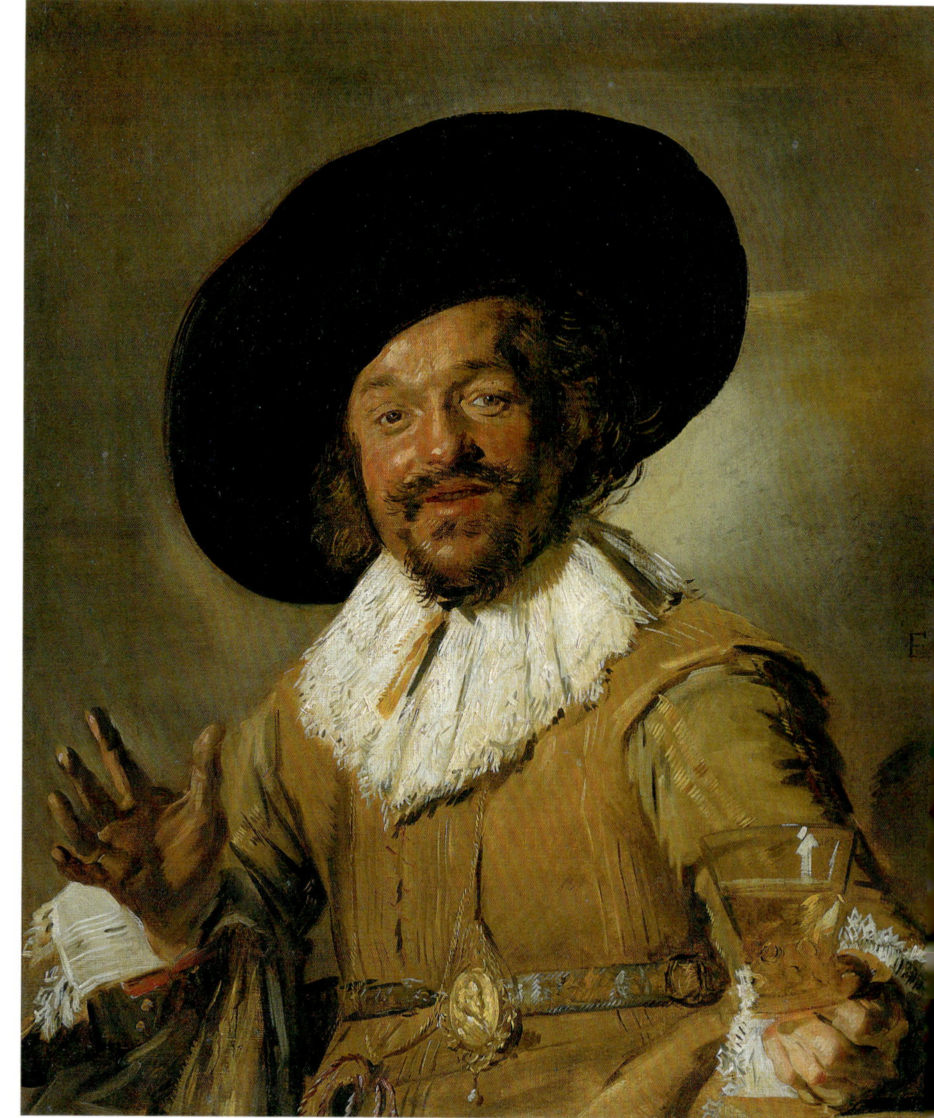

Fig. 24
Édouard Manet
Le Bon Bock, 1873
Oil on canvas, 37¼ × 32¾ in.
(94.6 × 83.3 cm)
Philadelphia Museum of Art,
The Mr. and Mrs. Carroll S. Tyson, Jr.,
Collection, 1963

Fig. 25
Frans Hals
Merry Drinker, 1628–30
Oil on canvas, 31⅞ × 26⅛ in.
(81 × 66.5 cm)
Collectie Rijksmuseum Amsterdam,
SK-A-135

Proust's suggestion that it was Hals who inspired Manet's ambition to paint the Paris of his own time: "the boldness of Frans Hals's own style made such an impression on him [Manet] in Holland that back in Paris, armed with all those memories, he decided to tackle frankly the diverse aspects of Parisian life."[57]

Hals's paintings remained firmly in the public eye in Paris—whether in exhibitions, sales of major collections, or through publications. In 1874 an exhibition at the Palais Bourbon of works from private collections[58] included, among the many Dutch paintings, more than ten works attributed to Hals, and his popularity was attested to in subsequent exhibitions. In 1883 the avant-garde Belgian journal *L'Art Moderne* published the article "Le Modernisme de Frans Hals," asserting that Hals's works expressed the current preoccupations of contemporary painters: "Frans Hals is a modern [painter]. His aesthetic, his color, his draftsmanship, his procedures, belong to our time."[59] Contemporary art thus cast a retrospective modernity on the old master—bearing out Michael Baxandall's comment: "Arts are positional games and each time an artist is influenced he rewrites his art's history a little."[60]

Whereas Hals's widespread popularity from the 1860s on was reflected in studios, sale rooms, and private and public collections, interest in the rare Vermeer was initially limited to a smaller circle of artists and amateurs. The Parisian public had its first sight of the unknown Vermeer at the famous *Exposition Rétrospective* of 1866, which displayed some eleven putative works by him: four figures in interiors (e.g., fig. 26) (the only paintings to retain their attribution), three landscapes (fig. 27), two "interiors of towns" (fig. 28), and two scenes of beguinages (untraced).

Vermeer's presence was entirely owing to Thoré's determination to publicize his "rediscovery" of the obscure Vermeer, who had been mainly known by three works in Holland: the *View of Delft* (fig. 29) on view in the Mauritshuis and two works then in the Six collection in Amsterdam, *Woman Pouring Milk* and the *Little Street* (both now in the Rijksmuseum). Thoré's indefatigable researches, which began only during the last years of his exile,[61] now culminated with the publication of his critical study and catalogue raisonné a few months after the exhibition.[62] Reviewers responded enthusiastically to their first view of Vermeer's works. Manet's friend Astruc, for example, marveled that this hitherto neglected artist, now brought to light,

> pleased, astonished, seduced; his gallant style, the fine qualities of his observations, his concise and sparing manner,

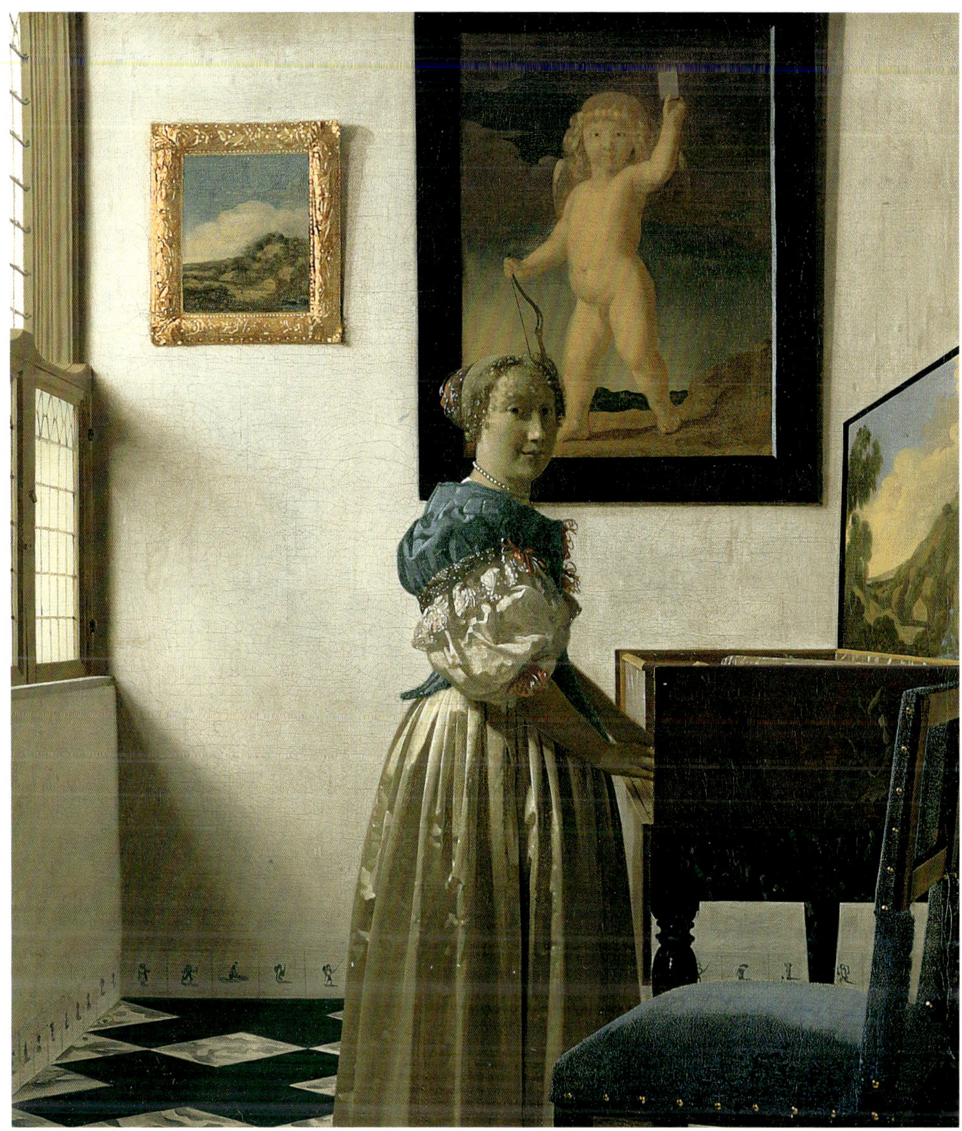

Fig. 26
Johannes Vermeer (van Delft)
(1632–1675)
A Young Woman Standing at a Virginal, c. 1670–72
Oil on canvas, 20⅜ × 17¾ in. (51.7 × 45.2 cm)
The National Gallery, London

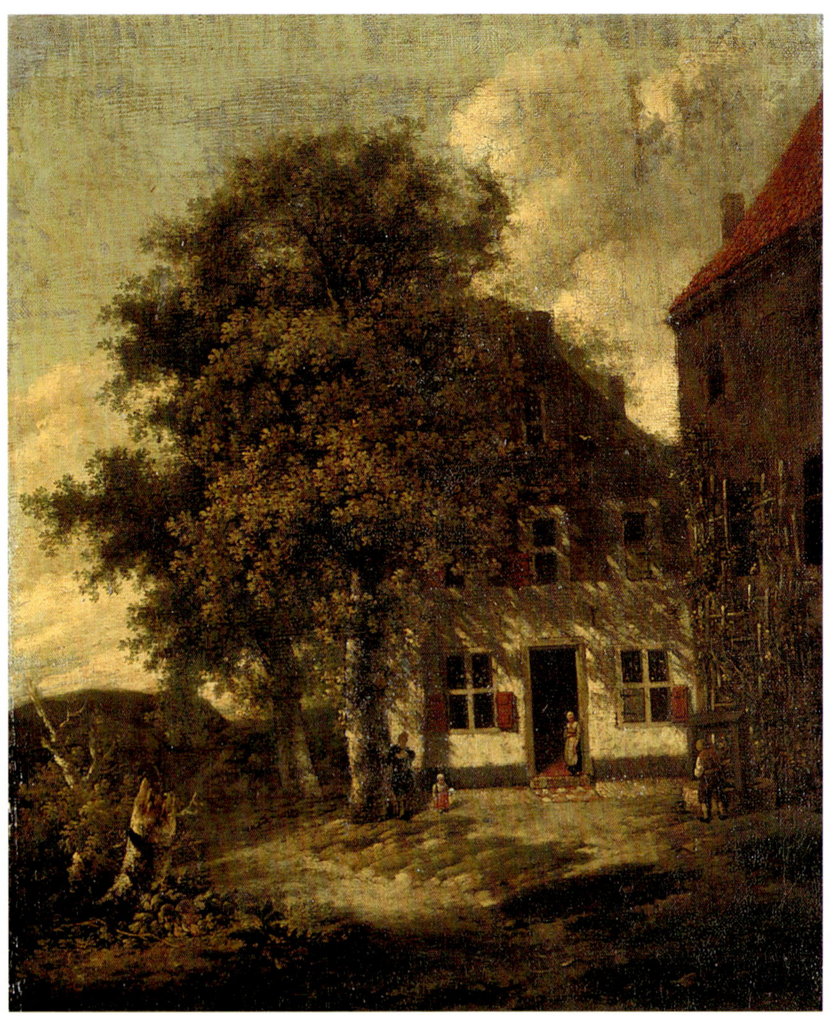

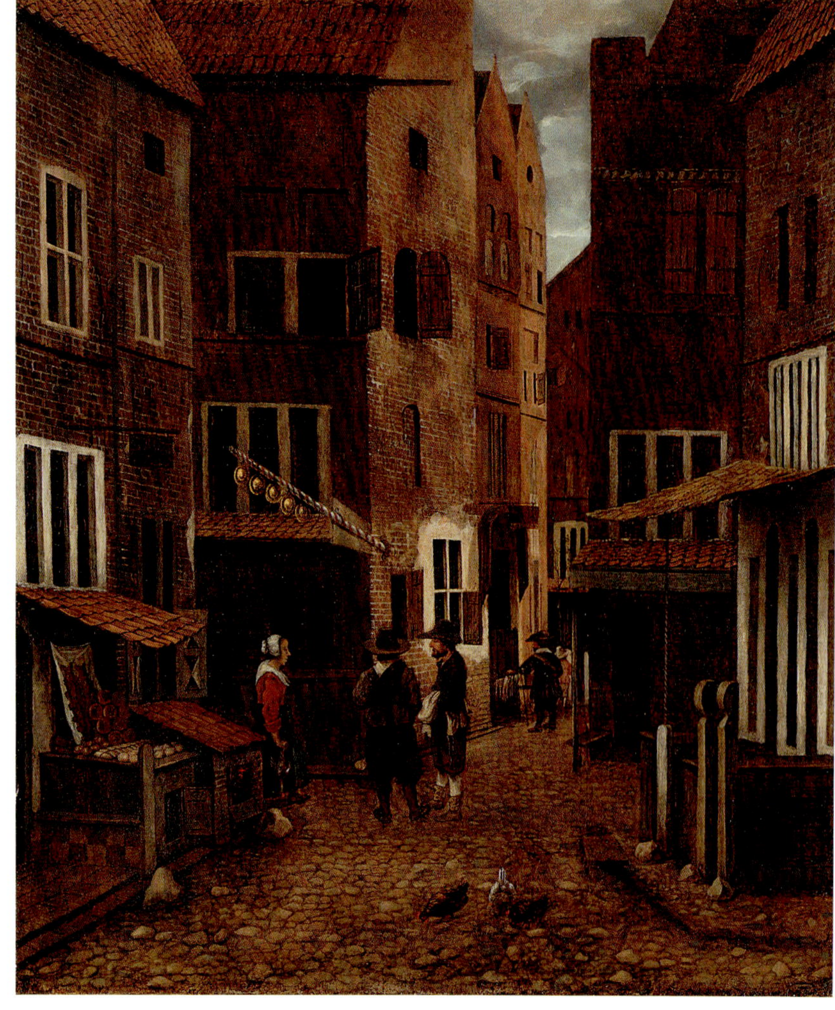

Fig. 27
Dirk Jan van der Laen
(1759–1829)
The House in the Country
Oil on canvas, 19½ × 16¼ in.
(49.5 × 41.4 cm)
Gemäldegalerie, Staatliche Museen
zu Berlin, Berlin, Germany

Fig. 28
Jacobus Vrel (act. 1654–62)
Street Scene, c. 1654–62
Oil on panel, 16¼ × 13½ in.
(41.3 × 34.3 cm)
The J. Paul Getty Museum, Los Angeles,
California, Gift of J. Paul Getty

OPPOSITE:
Fig. 29
Johannes Vermeer (van Delft)
(1632–1675)
View of Delft, c. 1660–61
Oil on canvas, 38 × 45½ in.
(96.5 × 115.7 cm)
Royal Cabinet of Paintings Mauritshuis
The Hague

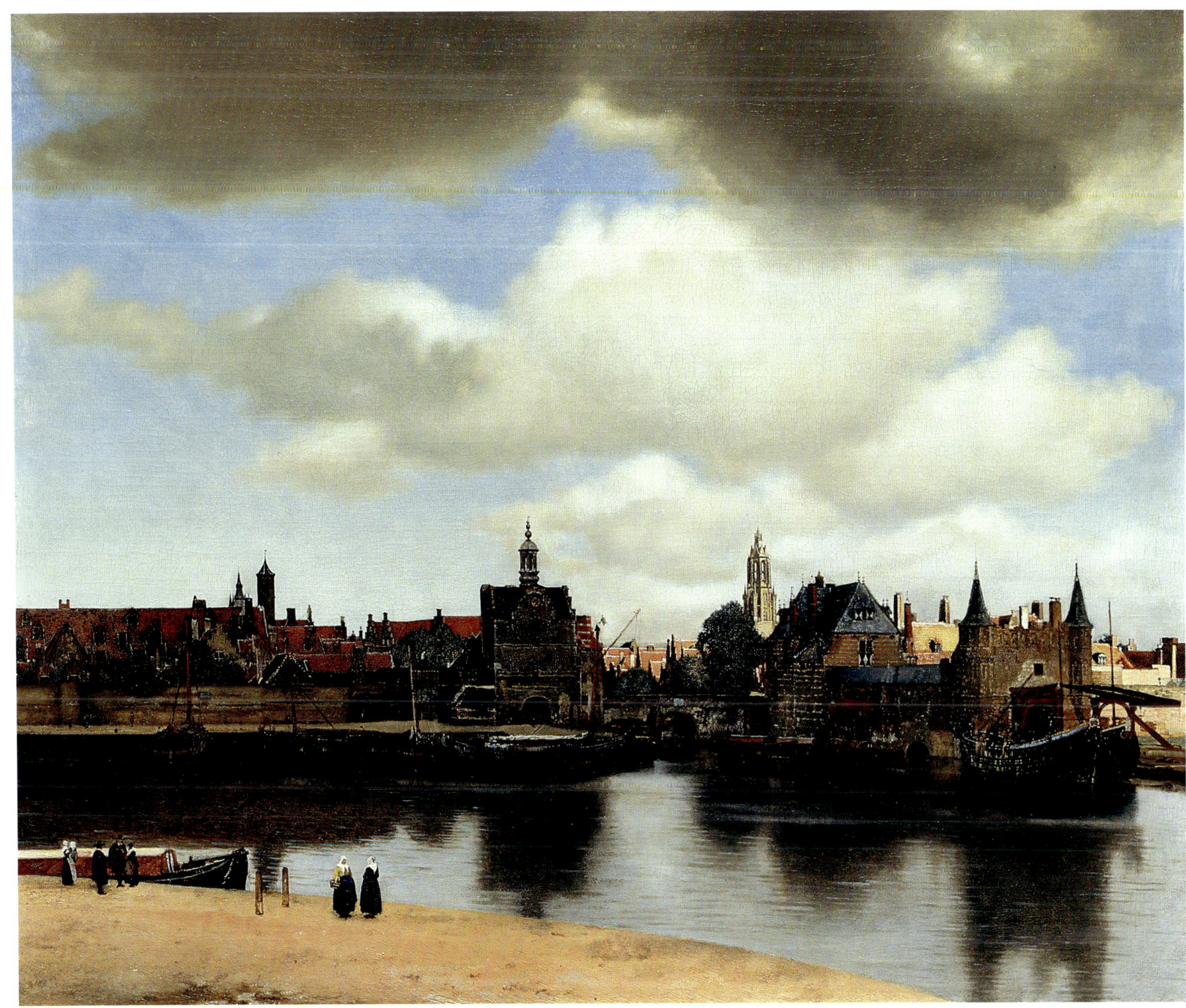

> the fervor of his brush, his delicate and fluid harmonies, his understanding of the overall effect [*effet*], and the concentration on the essential parts of the subject—all this strikes at first view, and further study only reinforces this first favorable impression. From now on all the world will celebrate the interesting Meer.[63]

Vermeer's new appreciative audience was undeterred by the diversity of the works displayed. The interiors were praised for revealing his versatile skill in the depiction of light filtering through windowpanes, spreading across surfaces, highlighting, shimmering, sparkling, enveloping.[64] Of the landscapes, *The House in the Country* (fig. 27) (now attributed to Dirk Jan van der Laen) was reportedly especially popular among artists who were entranced by the golden rays filtering through trees onto white cottage walls. A townscape—or "intérieur de ville" (fig. 28) (now attributed to Jacobus Vrel)—was admired for its casual simplicity of subject matter and its transparency and harmony of color.[65] All commentators, like Thoré, stressed the luminosity, color, and space depicted in Vermeer's paintings.[66]

As in the case of Hals, it seems that Manet was the first to acknowledge Vermeer in his own paintings. It has been convincingly argued that Manet's *Luncheon in the Studio* of 1868 (fig. 30), a genre scene of figures in a domestic interior, was in part an attempt to incorporate the recently "rediscovered" Vermeer into his work, as seen in the quality of natural light, the foreground chair and still life, the disposition of the figures, and the suggestion of a map on the back wall.[67]

Unlike Hals, Vermeer's popularity during the 1860s was limited to a relatively small circle. During his lifetime Thoré placed a few important paintings in private collections but was unable to persuade any

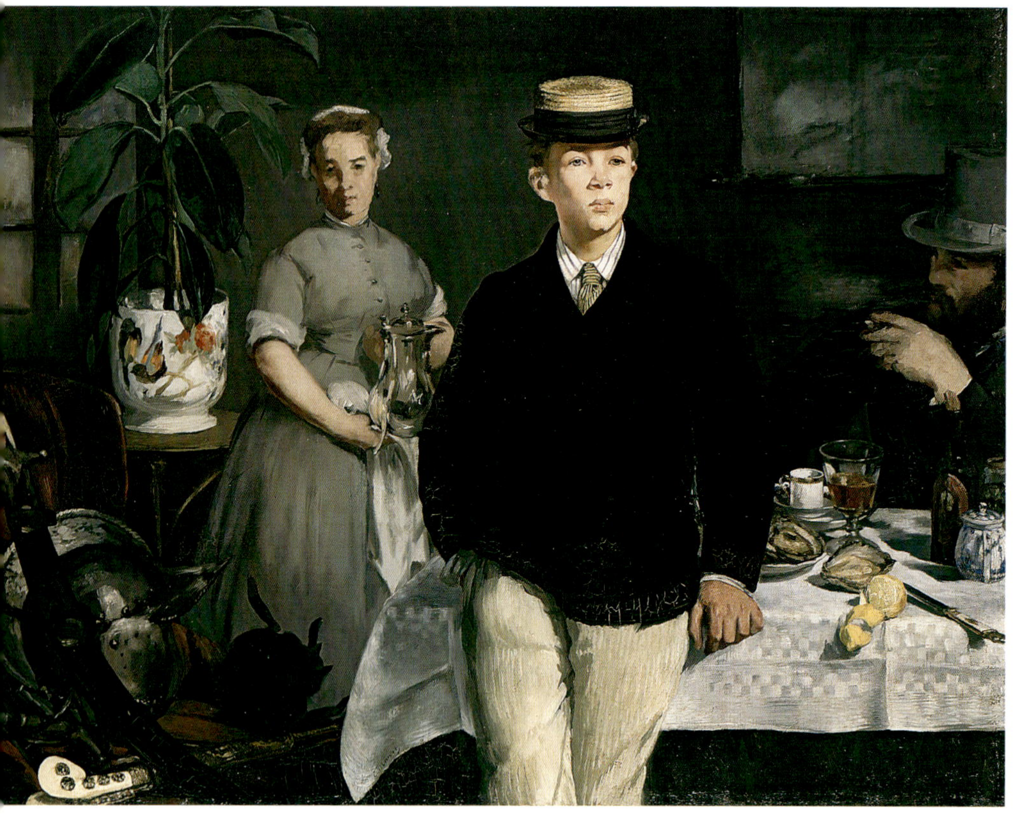

Fig. 30
Édouard Manet
Luncheon in the Studio, 1868
Oil on canvas, 46½ × 60⅝ in.
(118 × 154 cm)
Bayerische Staatsgemäldesammlungen,
Neue Pinakothek, Munich

public museum to acquire a Vermeer—despite Vermeer's relatively low prices.[68] However, a year after Thoré's death in 1869, the Louvre acquired the *The Lace Maker* (fig. 20), the "delicious little painting" he had introduced ten years earlier.[69]

The Lace Maker, remarkable for its intimacy, diffused forms, informal, close-up pose, gentle light, varied textures of paint, and *pointillé* highlights, was reportedly Pierre-Auguste Renoir's favorite painting. According to Jeanne Baudot, who accompanied Renoir to the Louvre in the mid-1890s, "Renoir was sensitive to the sincerity with which the Dutch and Flemish painters expressed the charms of everyday life. He particularly liked Terborch and [Pieter] de Hooch. But his favorite was *The Lace Maker* by Vermeer."[70] Renoir might have had in mind the quiet concentration of the lace maker when chosing such subjects as *Christine Lerolle Embroidering* (cat. 87, p. 53) or the well-known close-up *Woman Reading* (Musée d'Orsay, Paris).

During the 1870s and 1880s Vermeer's other paintings were only occasionally on public view.[71] However, in 1872, *Little Street* and *Woman Pouring Milk* were in an exhibition in Amsterdam of Dutch art from private collections, where they were probably viewed by Manet—who might also have read Havard's enthusiastic review in the *Gazette des Beaux-Arts*.[72] Havard later wrote a book on Vermeer in which he characterized Vermeer's style in primarily formal, almost abstract, terms—describing *taches* as "agreeable notes in an adorable concert of fine, delicate, melting, enveloping tonalities . . . ; each local tone has its own accent . . . and in it they play an important role in this melodious symphony, it is by 'la tache' made and not by the idea expressed."[73]

Vermeer's *View of Delft* became his most celebrated painting—with its astonishing luminosity, diffused highlights, and varied textures—and, like paintings by Hals, acquired a kind of retrospective modernity that continued into the twentieth century.[74] His magisterial view of Delft as well as the more modest townscapes were exemplary precedents for the cityscapes and intimate street scenes by Camille Pissarro, Alfred Sisley, and Monet.

Typically Dutch themes of windmills, water mills, canals, ports, and seascapes under huge expanses of sky (cat. 1, p. 94) are frequent subjects in Impressionist paintings (cat. 57, p. 95). The recent exhibition *Manet and the Sea* vividly demonstrated Manet's awareness of traditional marine painting in which the Dutch specialized.[75] His *Moonlight over Boulogne Harbor* (1868; Musée d'Orsay, Paris), recalls nocturnal landscapes and moonlit marines of Dutch paintings, one of which Manet owned.[76]

Although Monet's interest in harbors and working waterways—sail and steam craft—presumably had to do with his growing up in Le Havre, his awareness of the picturesque possibilities of these marines may have been stimulated by earlier Dutch art, to which he would have been introduced by Eugène Boudin and the Dutch painter Jongkind before the first of his three visits to Holland in 1871, when he took refuge after fleeing the Franco-Prussian War.[77] Monet's name was recorded in the visitors' registers of the Rijksmuseum on June 22 (in the company of Henry Havard and the painter Henri Michel-Levy) and of the Frans Halsmuseum in Haarlem in October.[78] It is tempting to speculate that he may also have traveled with Bürger's *Musées,* especially since the older (now deceased) critic had warmly and cheerfully commended the young Monet's two paintings in his *Salon* of 1866.[79]

During his stay in the village of Zaandam, Monet painted several scenes of windmills such as *Windmill and Boats near Zaandam, Holland* (cat. 60, p. 96), in which the massive mill on the bank, set against the huge sky and skudding clouds, recall Ruisdael's famous *Windmill at Wijk* (fig. 31), then in the Van der Hoop collection in Amsterdam. Monet also created his own brightly colored version of traditional Dutch town portraiture in his several views of Zaandam (cat. 61, p. 97).[80] Monet made at least two more visits to Holland, in 1874 and 1886, resuming his interest in Dutch town and canal views—as in his *The Zuiderkerk, Amsterdam (Looking up the Groenburgwal)* of 1874 (cat. 64, p. 60).

That Monet may have emulated the harmonious and luminous tonalities found in popular Dutch landscapes was implied by Alfred de Lostalot, a perceptive and sympathetic critic, who commented that certain of Monet's landscapes were probably more to the public's liking than the artist's. He describes a particular *View of Rouen* (fig. 32), as "painted in a discreet light, muted by a mist-laden sky, intercepting the violet radiation . . . with a faded, deep amber sky which seems cut out from a picture by Cuyp" (fig. 33).[81]

Hobbema is frequently cited in relation to Impressionist landscapes—especially his famous *The Avenue at Middelharnis* (fig. 34), famous for its boldly receding central road. Both Sisley and Pissarro, whose compositions frequently used a receding road to lead the eye and to create the compositional space, would have been familiar with this work from their London visits.[82]

Although Dutch still life seems on the whole to have been less important to the Impressionists than French or Spanish precedents,[83] Thoré's eloquent commentary on the oxymoronic French term *nature morte* in the second of his *Musées* serves as an apt introduction to the typically vibrant Impressionist still lifes:

> We still do not know how to replace it [*nature morte*] by a term that would include, at the same time, dead game birds, animals and birds, fish . . . flowers and bouquets, fruit, vases and utensils, arms and musical instruments, jewelry and diverse ornaments, drapery and costumes, and the thousand objects that can be grouped together to create a pretext for a pleasing colored representation under the effect of light. "Nature morte" is absurd.
>
> Aren't flowers alive? They have their breath and their health; they are gay and brilliant, or sad and dull; they are in constant motion, although almost imperceptibly, while turning toward the light, separate to allow importunate branches to pass, droop in response to thirst, swell and spread in the caress of a ray of light. Flowers are not "nature morte"; . . . There is no such thing as "nature morte."[84]

It is interesting that the flower painting that Manet presented to Thoré, *Peonies with Secateurs* (Musée d'Orsay, Paris) is strangely reminiscent of a game still-life.

Of all the Impressionists, Manet's references to Dutch art are the most complex and varied. His early copies of Dutch paintings were obviously learning experiences.[85] Yet his *Surprised Nymph* (fig. 35), once suggested as having been prompted by Rembrandt's *Susannah* (fig. 36), has since been shown to have a more complex, sometimes indirect, range of sources.[86] By contrast, *Madame Manet at the Piano* (fig. 37) refers directly to Metsu's *Woman Playing the Harpsichord* (fig. 38), which Manet probably knew through the engraved reproduction entitled *Hollandaise au clavecin* (*Dutch Woman at the Harpsichord*) in Blanc's *Histoire des peintres* (fig. 39).[87] The painting could be understood as an affectionate, even humorous, transposition of the earlier image into his own domestic world—Manet's Dutch wife now the subject of the painting. Furthermore, his frequent inclusion of identifiably Dutch motifs, such as a peeled lemon, a half-balanced knife, or oysters, were quotations from the traditional vocabulary of Dutch still life.[88]

Other reminders of Dutch portraiture include Renoir's portrait of Alfred Sisley (fig. 40), which recalls the informal pose of leaning over the back of the chair frequently used by Hals, as in his *Portrait of a Seated Man* (fig. 41),[89] and Degas's *Portrait of Edmond and Thérèse Morbilli* (c. 1865; Museum of Fine Arts, Boston), which may allude to Rembrandt's etched *Self-Portrait with His Wife*.[90] Dutch genre in all its variety was well known to the Impressionists—from staid bourgeois interiors to suggestive *conversations,* from placid productive rustic life to bawdy tavern scenes. Thus, although Pissarro's paintings of local markets were based on his firsthand experience, he would also have been familiar with a work such as Metsu's famous *Vegetable Market* (Musée du Louvre, Paris). Likewise, Manet's *Chez le Père Lathuille* (1879; Musée des Beaux-Arts, Tournai) and his other modern café paintings have, as Robert L. Herbert has suggested, "many

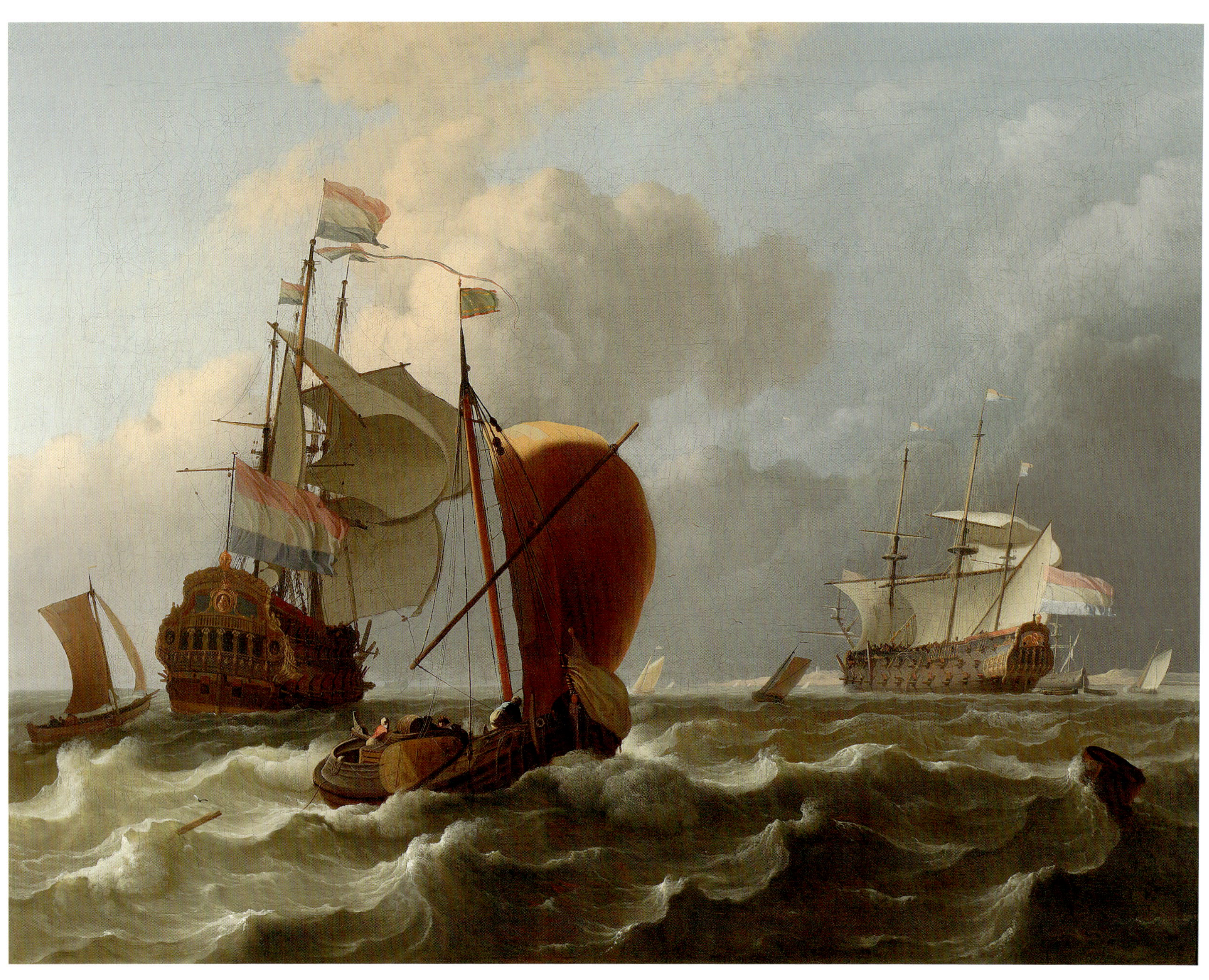

Cat. 1
Ludolf Backhuysen
The "Koning Willem III" and Other Ships in the Sea-lanes off Texel, c. 1690

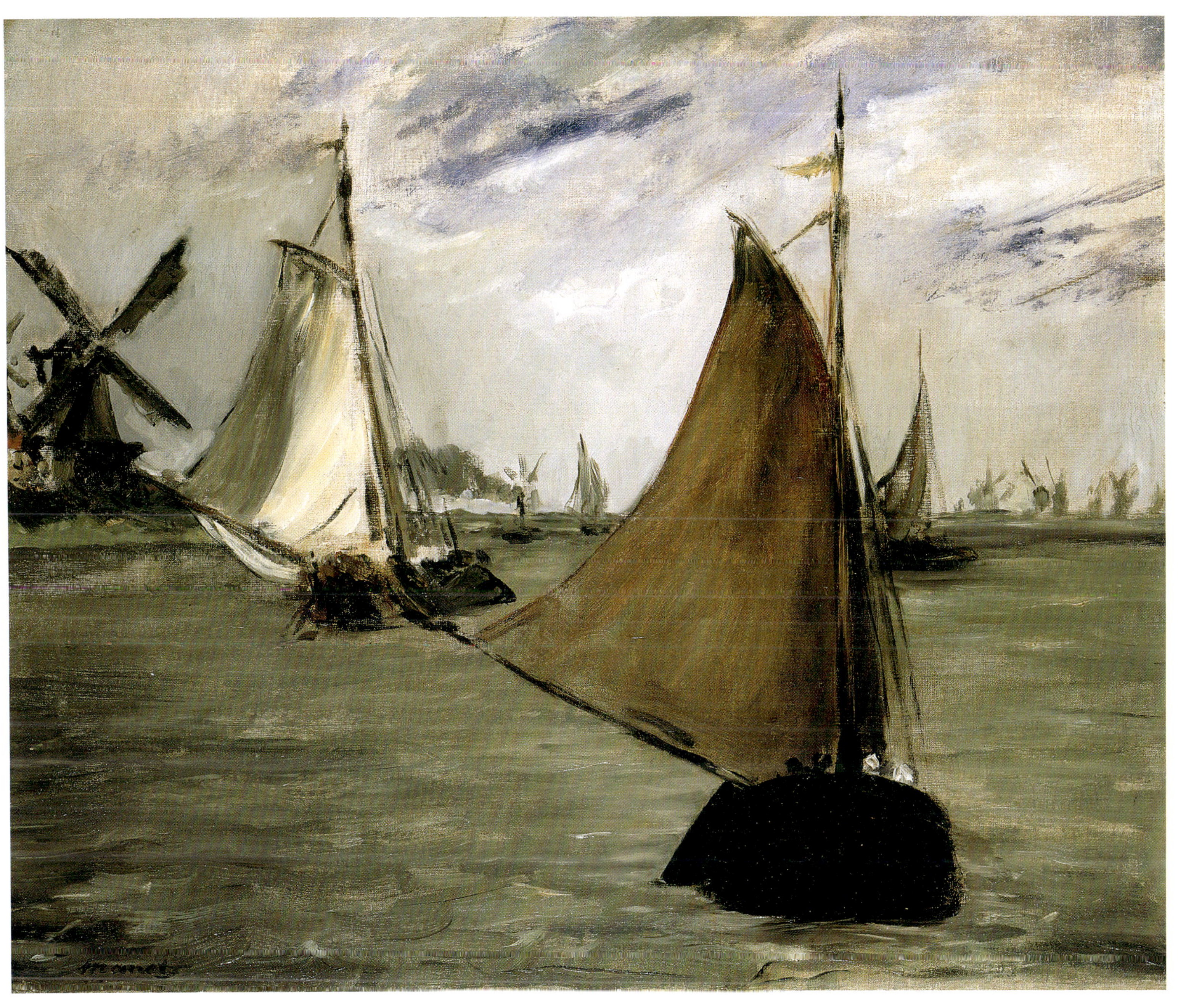

Cat. 57
Edouard Manet
Marine in Holland, 1872

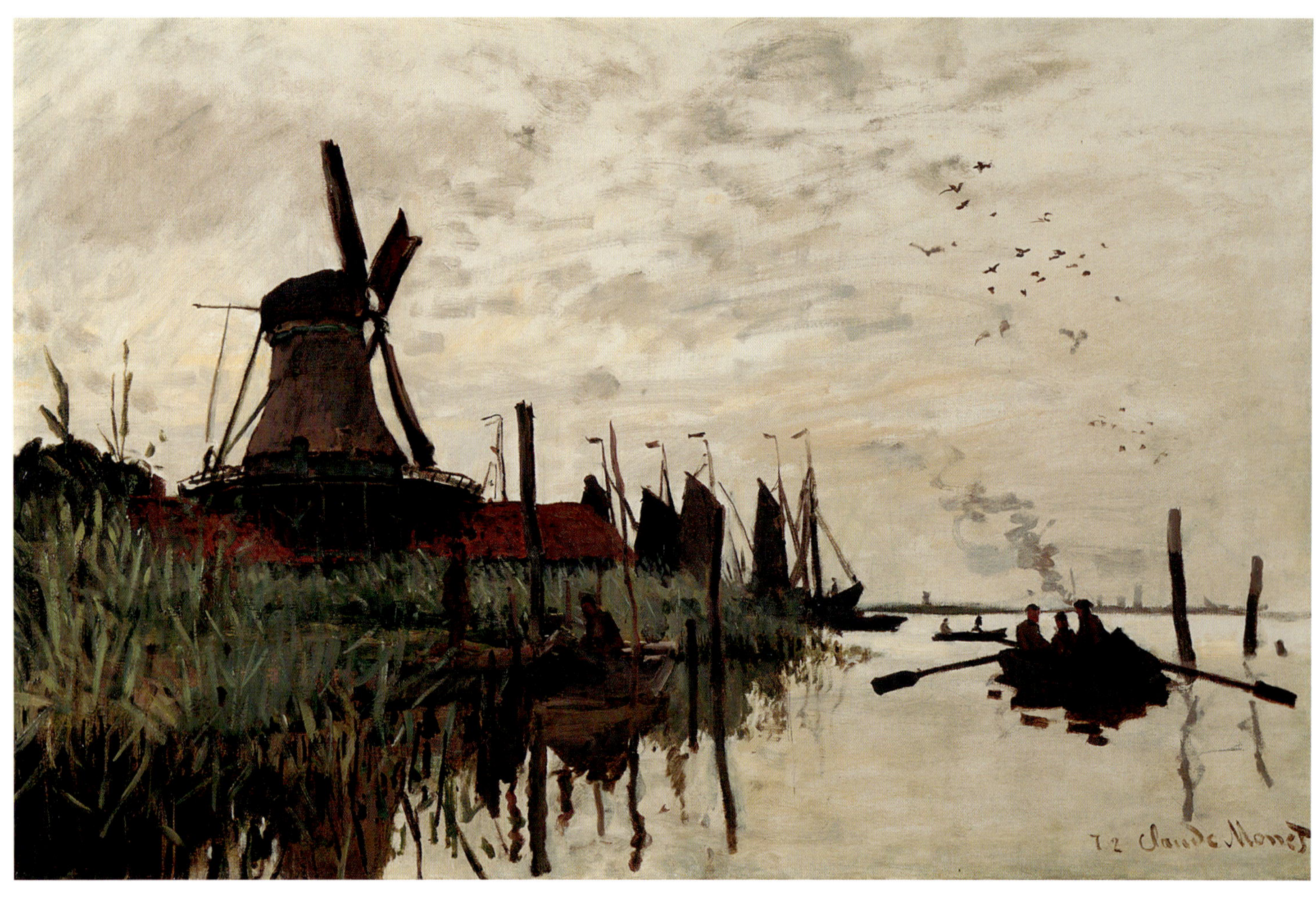

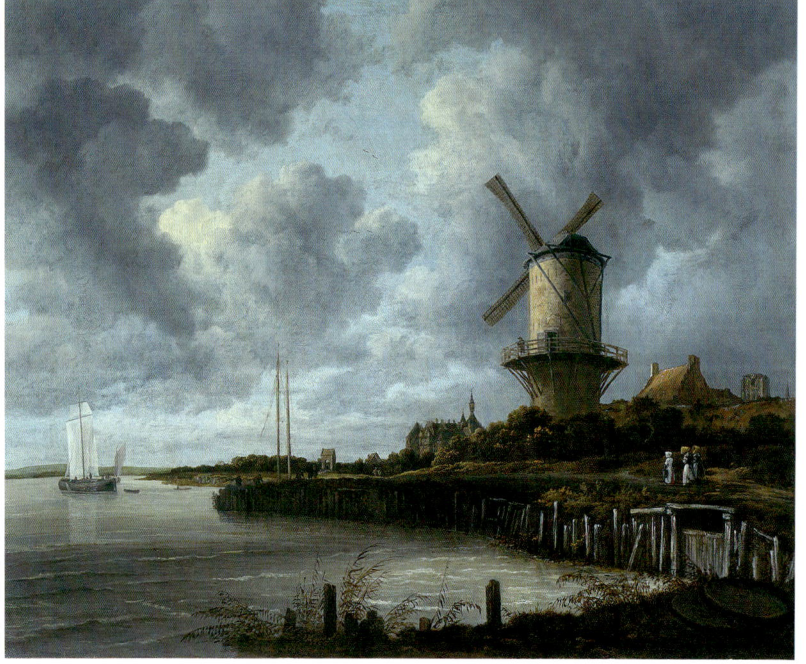

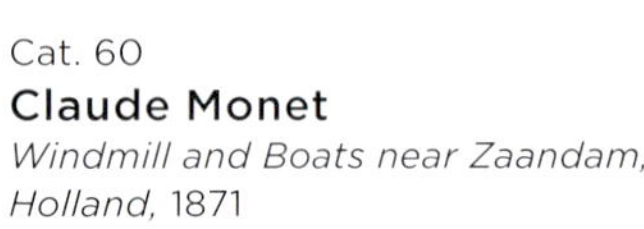
Cat. 60
Claude Monet
Windmill and Boats near Zaandam, Holland, 1871

Fig. 31
Jacob Isaacksz van Ruisdael (1628–1682)
Windmill at Wijk, 1668–70
Oil on canvas, 32⅝ × 39¾ in. (83 × 101 cm)
Collectie Rijksmuseum Amsterdam, SK-C-211

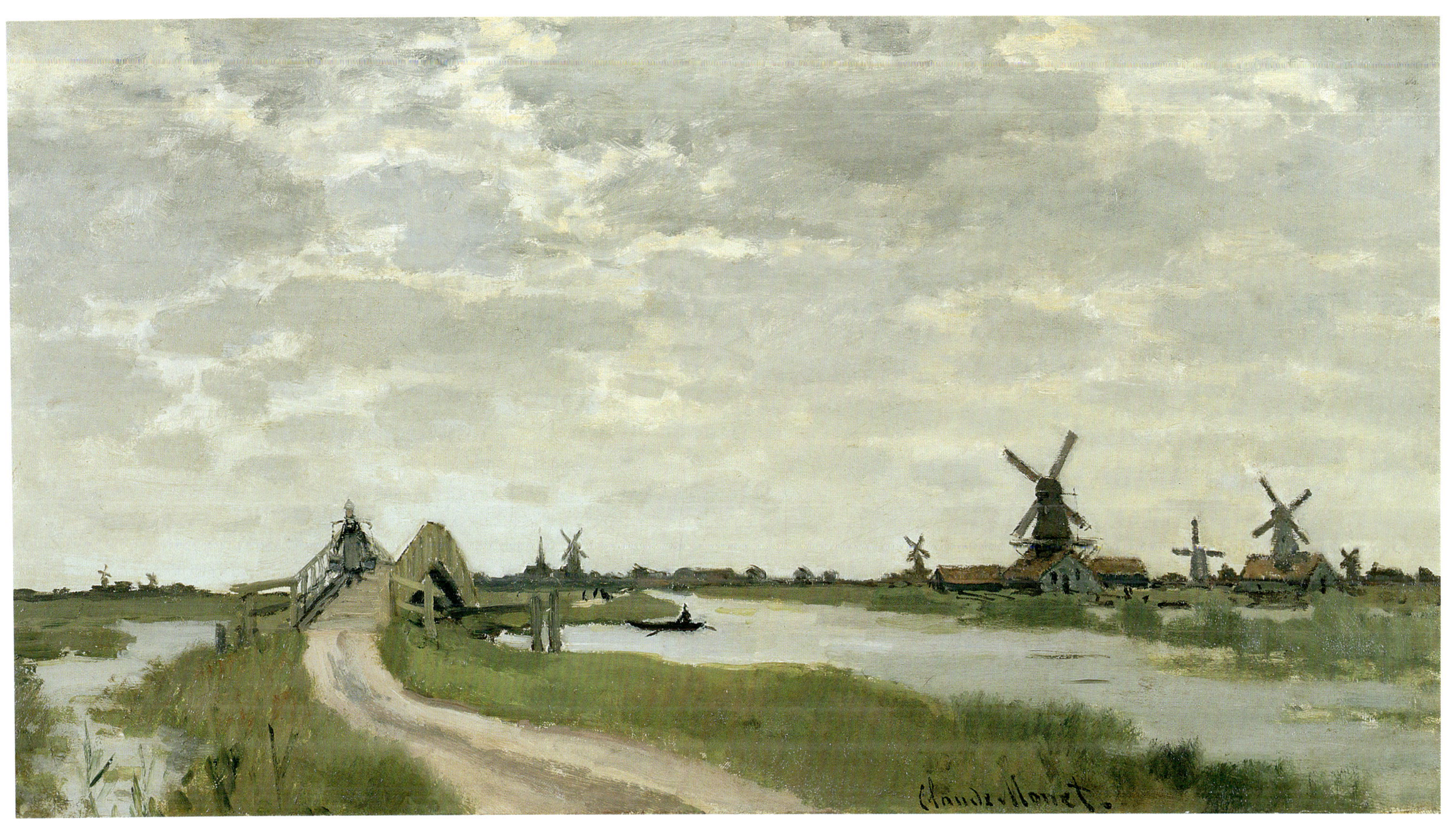

Cat. 61
Claude Monet
Windmills near Zaandam, 1871

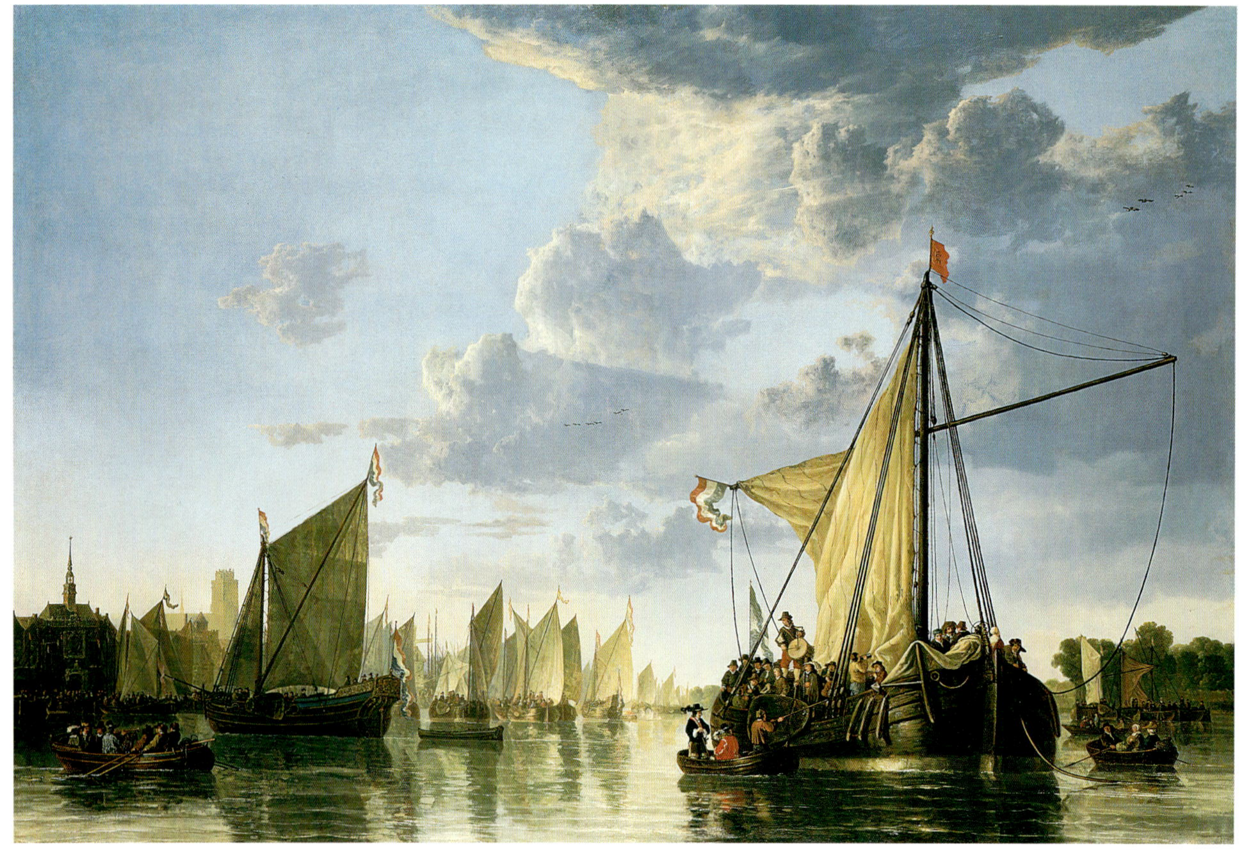

Fig. 33
Aelbert Cuyp (1620–1691)
The Maas at Dordrecht, c. 1650
Oil on canvas, 45¼ × 67 in.
(114.9 × 170.2 cm)
National Gallery of Art, Washington,
Andrew W. Mellon Collection, 1940.2.1

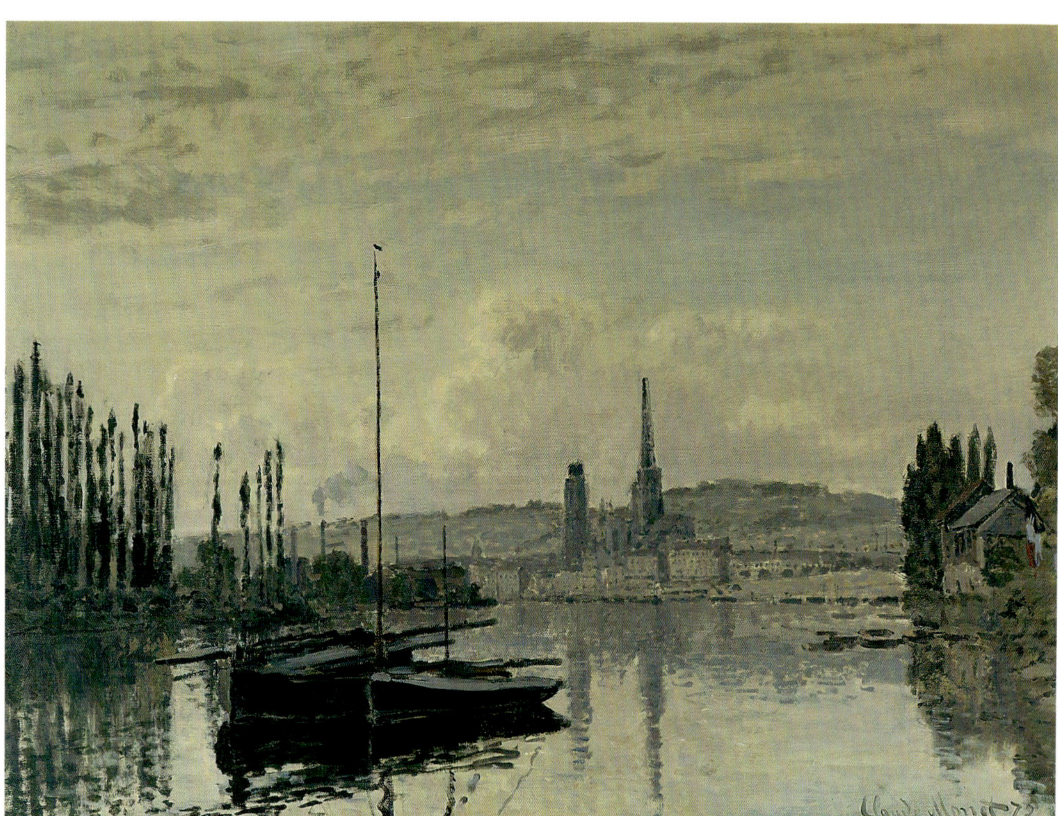

Fig. 32
Claude Monet
View of Rouen, 1872
Oil on canvas, 21¼ × 28⅞ in.
(54 × 73.3 cm)
Private collection, courtesy
of Pyms Gallery, London

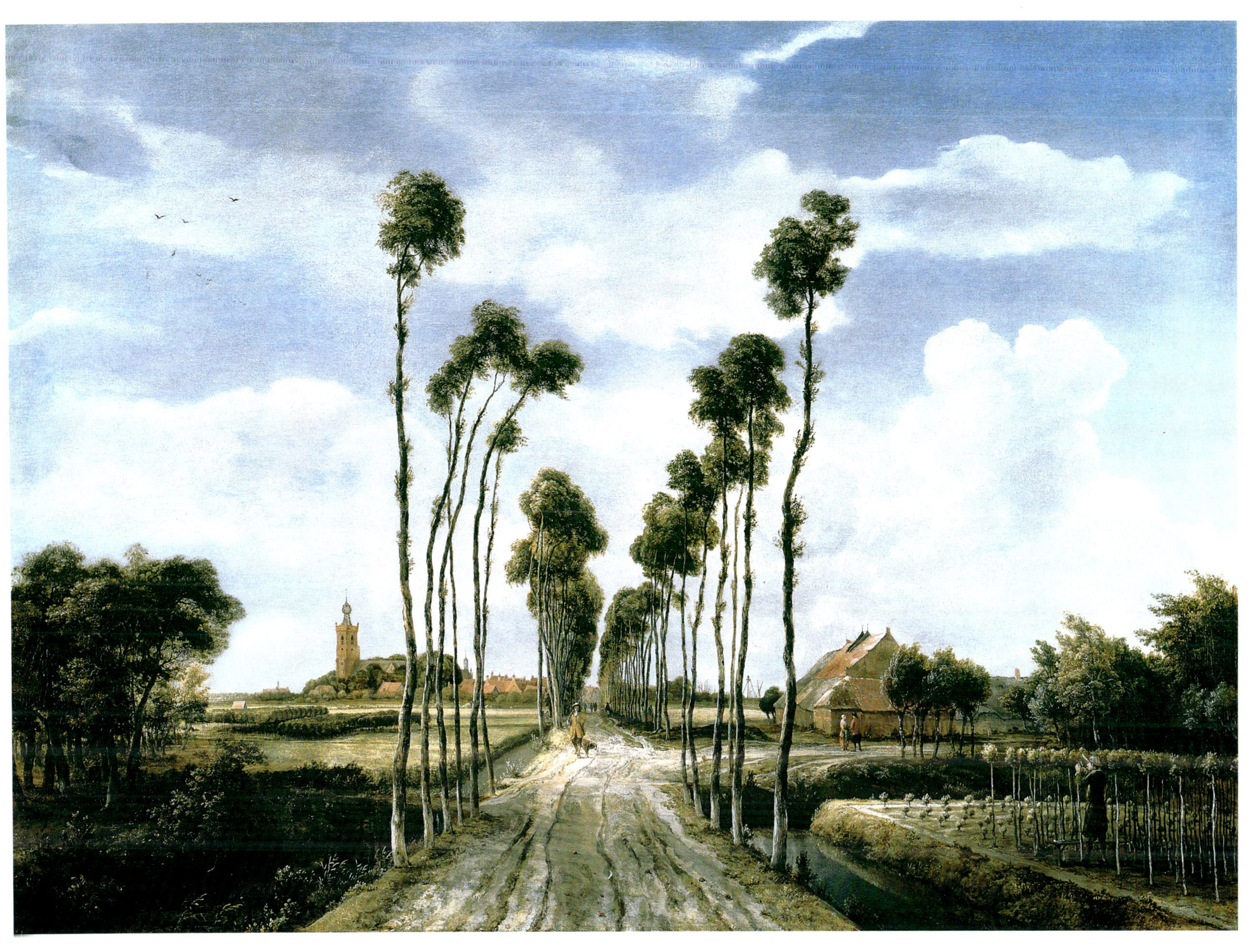

Fig. 34
Meindert Hobbema
The Avenue at Middelharnis, 1689
Oil (identified) on canvas,
40¾ × 55½ in. (103.5 × 141 cm)
The National Gallery, London

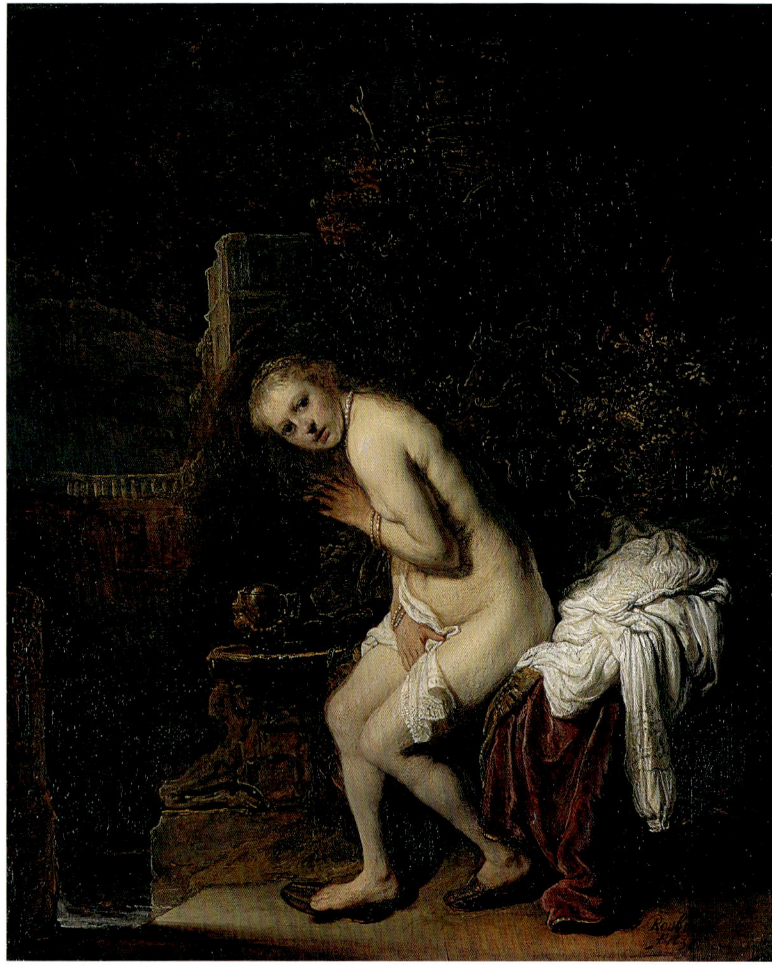

Fig. 36
Rembrandt Harmensz van Rijn
(1606–1669)
Susanna, 1636
Oil on panel, 18⅝ × 15¼ in. (47.4 × 38.6 cm)
Royal Cabinet of Paintings Mauritshuis
The Hague

forebears among the taverns and cafés of seventeenth-century painting," with their themes of courtship and seduction.[91]

A familiar topic in accounts of Dutch art in the second half of the nineteenth century is how certain Dutch painters "discovered" particular beauties in nature and invented ways of depicting them. Thus, Van Goyen, reputed to have roamed the countryside, sketching directly from nature, was praised as the first to reveal the poetic possibilities of luminous harmonies in low horizons of water under vast skies in his rapidly and freely painted transparent oil washes;[92] Jan Wynants was deemed the first to realize the picturesque possibilities of casually or accidentally discovered sites in his native Holland,[93] while Hals, as has been shown, was viewed as the first to animate his figures by wielding his brush with such freedom and bravura.

The Impressionists' debt to the old masters of the Golden Age of Dutch painting (as then understood) took many forms. However, whether explicit or implicit, whether by specific quotation or compositional borrowings, whether by emulation or transposition, it was never in the spirit of imitation of the earlier artists. As Pissarro insisted, their kinship served rather to enhance the originality of the Impressionists, for they too looked "with their own eyes." He explained this in a letter to his son, written after he had visited Amsterdam to see the great exhibition of Rembrandt in 1898:

> I haven't had time to write about what I felt when I looked at Rembrandt's masterpieces: they're admirable, and the thought that struck me after I had seen not only the Rembrandts, but the works of Frans Hals, Vermeer, and so many other great artists, was that we modern painters, we are unassailably correct to seek, or rather to feel differently, since different we are, and that for the rest their art is so definitely of their time that it would be absurd to try to follow in their path. Also, as I have often told you, I am suspicious of those adroit painters who know how to pastiche the old masters. I have not as much respect for these adroit ones as I have for those who, even without making masterpieces, yet look with their own eyes! But how can I describe Rembrandt's portraits to you? The paintings by Hals, and the *Canal* [*View of Delft*] by Vermeer, a masterpiece akin to the works of the impressionists; I returned from Holland more than ever an admirer of Monet, Degas, Renoir, Sisley. . . . Happy are those artists who see and love nature![94]

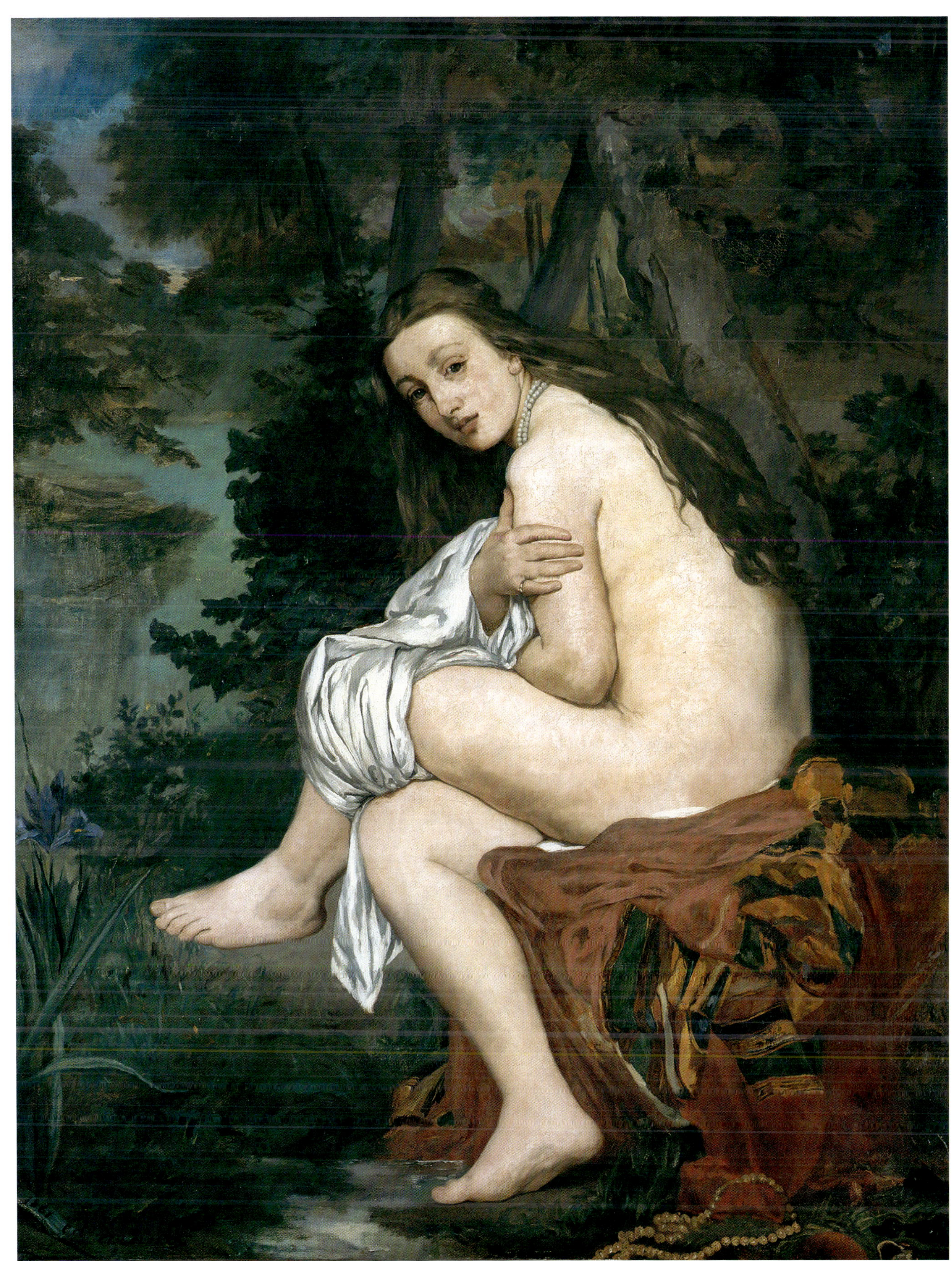

Fig. 35
Édouard Manet
The Surprised Nymph, 1861
Oil on canvas, 56⅞ × 44¼ in.
(144.5 cm × 112.5 cm)
Museo Nacional de Bellas Artes,
Buenos Aires

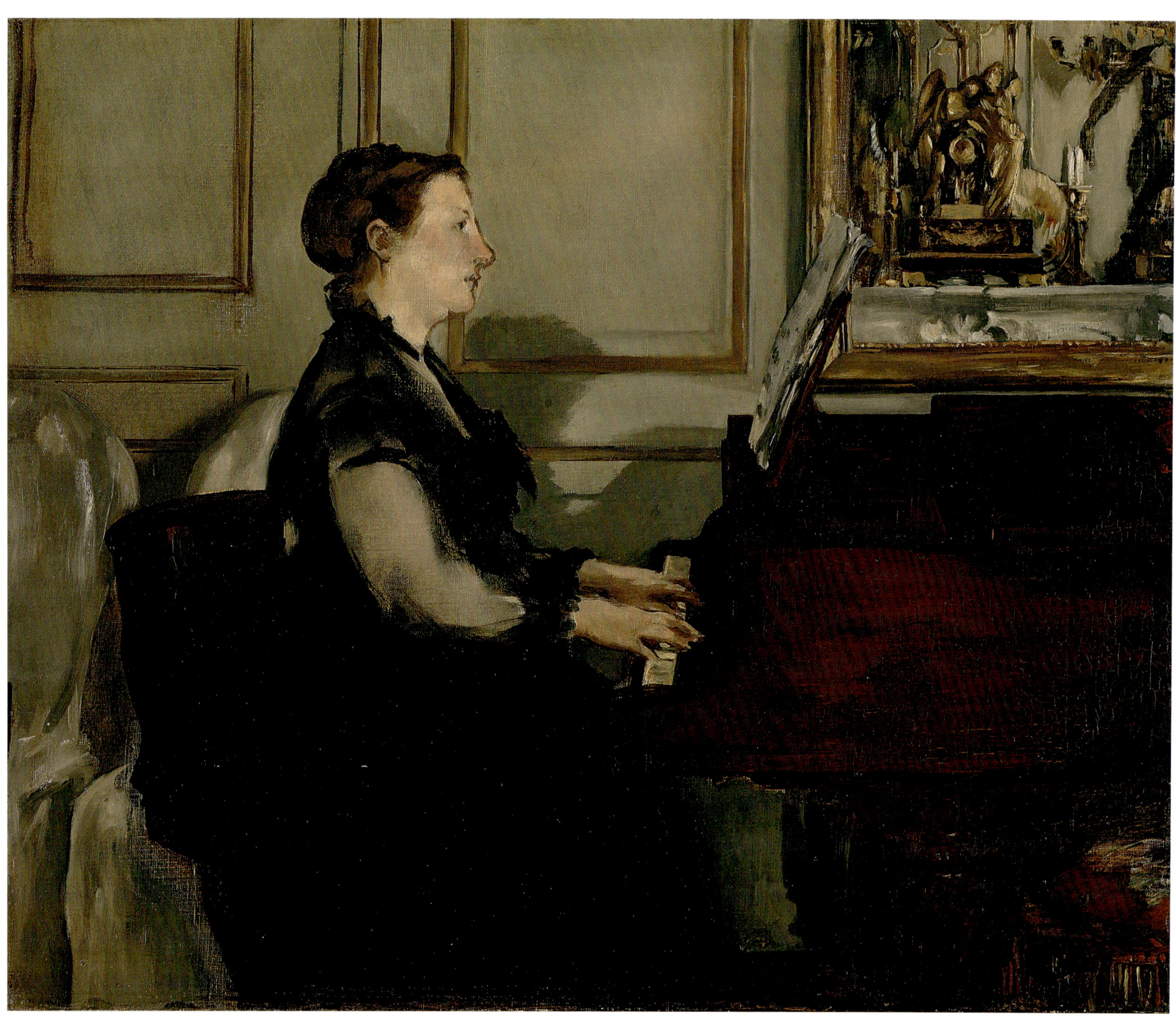

Fig. 37
Édouard Manet
Madame Manet at the Piano, 1868
Oil on canvas, 15 × 18¼ in. (38 × 46.5 cm)
Musée d'Orsay, Paris, France

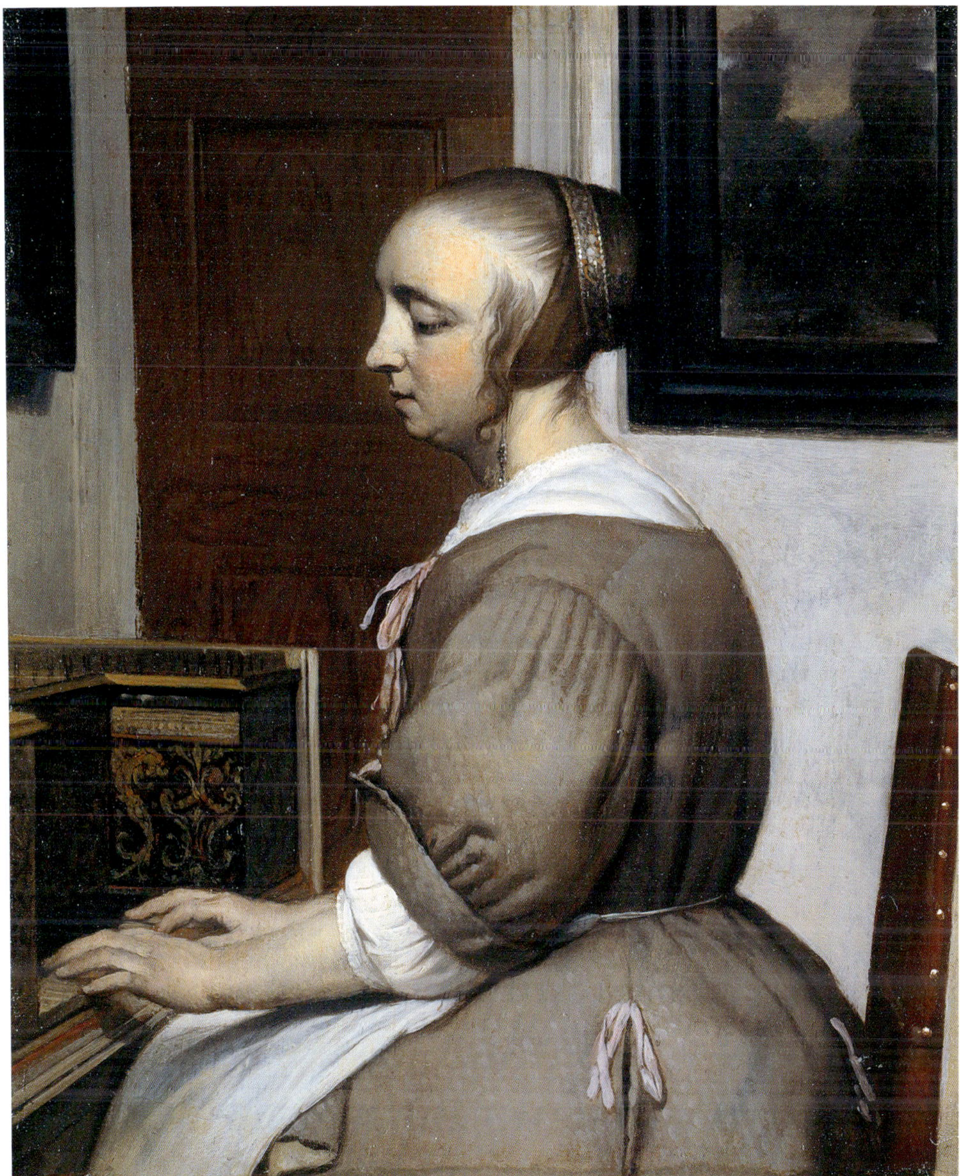

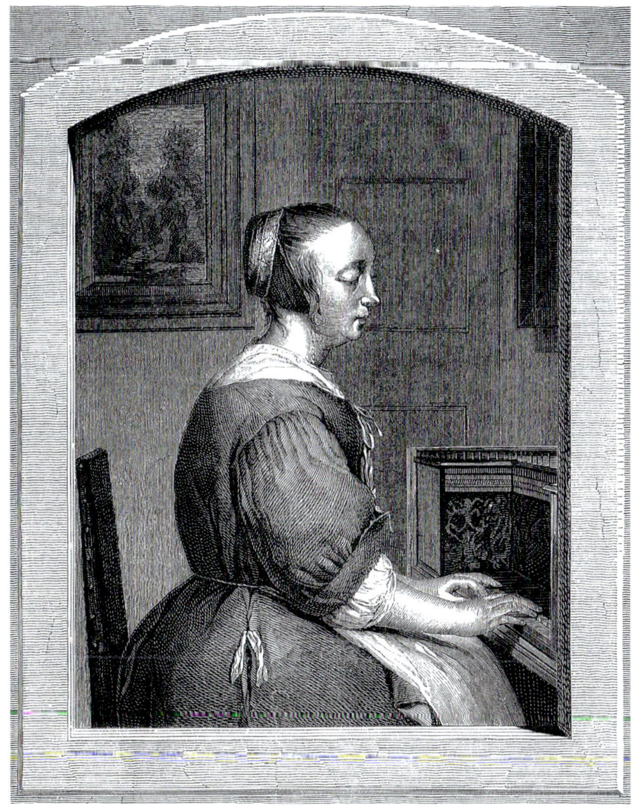

Fig. 38
Gabriel Metsu (1629–1667)
Woman Playing the Harpsichord
Oil on wood, 9⅜ × 7⅞ in. (23.9 × 19.9 cm)
Petit Palais, Musée des Beaux-Arts de la Ville de Paris

Fig. 39
Engraving after Metsu, *Dutch Woman at the Harpsichord*. From Blanc, *Histoire de peintres de toutes les écoles, École hollandaise*

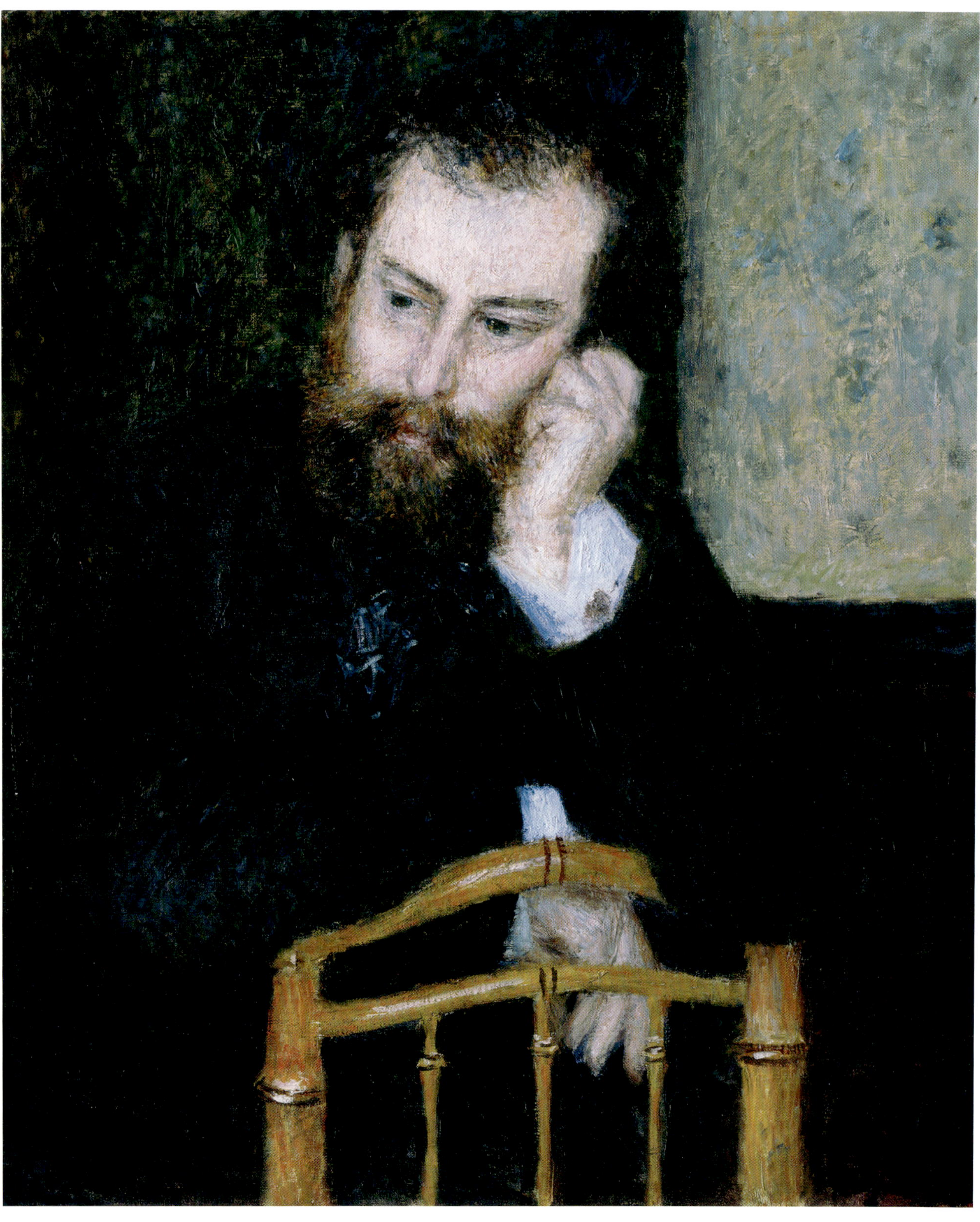

Fig. 40
Pierre-Auguste Renoir
Alfred Sisley, 1875–76
Oil on canvas mounted on composition board, 26⅛ × 21⅝ in. (66.4 × 54.8 cm)
Mr. and Mrs. Lewis Larned Coburn Memorial Collection, 1933.453, The Art Institute of Chicago

Fig. 41
Frans Hals
Portrait of a Seated Man, c. 1645
Oil on oak, 16¾ × 13 in. (42.4 × 33 cm)
National Gallery of Canada, Ottawa,
Purchased 1969

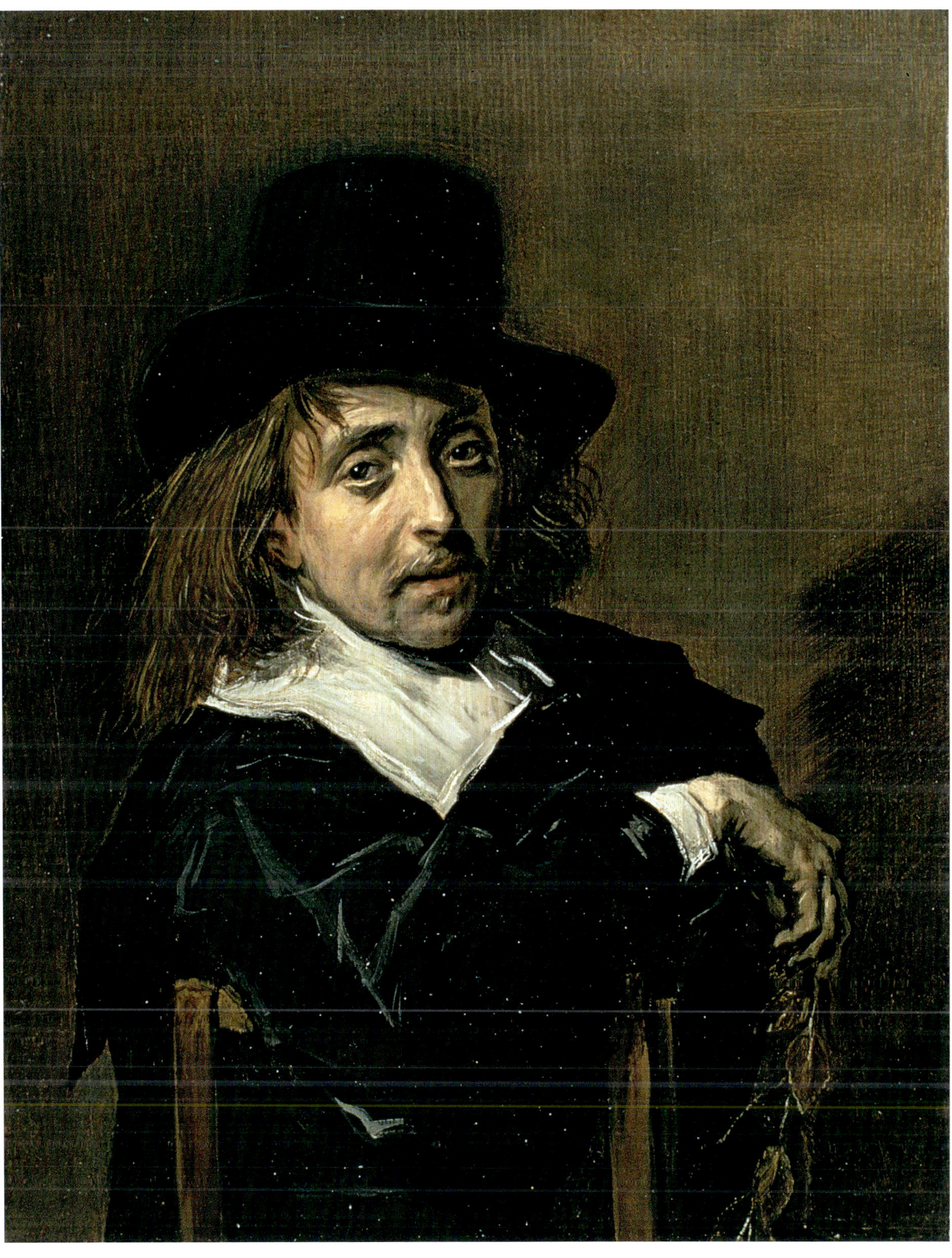

Notes

Epigraph: "Et cependant quel intérêt n'auraient pas plus tard les portraits des hommes qui gèrent actuellement de la ville! Lorsque nous allons à Amsterdam, le tableau des *Syndics* nous empoigne. Pourquoi? Parce que c'est l'impression vraie d'une chose vue." Proust 1913, p. 95.

1. "Ces tableaux hollandais représentant la vie contemporaine des artistes font songer aussi très-naturellement à l'art de notre époque, . . . D'abord, ce qui est aujourd'hui sera de l'histoire demain; . . . Qui empêche de faire un chef d'oeuvre avec une assemblée de diplomates assis autour d'une table, de même que Rembrandt à fait un chef-d'oeuvre avec les *Syndics* de la corporation des drapiers? Avec un orateur à la tribune des deputés, un professeur au milieu de la jeunesse; avec une scène des courses, une sortie de l'Opéra, une promenade aux Champs-Elysées; ou simplement avec des hommes qui travaillent à n'importe quoi, des femme qui s'amusent à n'importe quoi." Bürger 1868, p. 436.

2. Théophile Thoré (1807–1869), known posthumously as Thoré-Bürger, was the prominent French art critic exiled for his radical republican activities after the 1848 Revolution. He used the pseudonym W. Bürger (John Citizen) from 1855 for publications on the art of the past and retained it after his return to France in 1860 for both art historical writings and art criticism. I will refer to him as "Thoré," while noting the authorship of W. Bürger where appropriate. For studies of his work, see, for example, Chaumelin 1867; Marguery 1926; Heppner 1938; Meltzoff, "Vermeer" 1942; Rebeyrol 1952; Grate 1959; and Jowell 1977, "Art Market" 1996, 1998, 2001, 2003.

3. "La vie, *la vie vivante,* l'homme, ses moeurs, ses occupations, ses joies, ses caprices. Les uns ont pris le citoyen en action pour la chose publique . . . ; les autres ont pris les familles chez elles, ou dans leurs distractions extérieures; ceux-ci les classes distinguées, ceux-là les classes laborieuses, où les classes excentriques. D'autres ont représenté le milieu où s'agite la vie commune, les mers et les plages, avec les episodes de l'existence maritime, si chère au pays; les campagnes et les forêts, avec les dompteurs de la terre et les dompteurs des animaux; scenes agrestes et scenes de chasse; les canaux et les ruisseaux, avec des moulins, des barques, des pêcheurs; les villes, places et rues, où la population circule avec toute sa variété. Partout l'animation, la vie présente, qui est aussi la vie éternelle,—l'histoire du people et du pays. Véritable histoire . . .

en images lumineuses et justes, une sorte de photographie de leur grand XVII siècle, hommes et choses, sentiments et habitudes,—les faits et gestes de toute une nation." Bürger 1858, pp. 322–23. (Thanks to Tim Ades for advice on the translation of this passage.)

4. "par un élan spontané du génie national." Bürger 1858, p. x.

5. Ibid., p. 326. This motto, coined in the 1840s, was derived from Pierre Leroux's quasi-religion *l'Humanité,* a democratic socialist doctrine that preached the fraternal future of mankind. On Leroux and Thoré, see Grate 1959; Jowell 1977, esp. pp. 23–92, 144–68; and MacWilliam 1993, esp. pp. 181–87.

6. "l'art hollandais est le premier qui ait renoncé à toute imitation du passé, et qui se soit tourné vers du neuf." Bürger, *Musées* 1860, p. xv.

7. There is a considerable literature on the historiographical sources of these ideas, some of which can be traced to Hegel. See Demetz 1963, pp. 97–115; or the summary in Chu 1974, esp. chap. 2. The frequent confusion of Flemish and Dutch Schools by French critics is damned by Thoré as "historical heresy," a phrase quoted from the Dutch author Westrheene 1857; see Bürger 1858, pp. 319–20.

8. On Thoré-Bürger's pivotal role in the changing canon of Dutch art, see Hecht 1998, pp. 169–73; and Jowell 2001, pp. 45–60.

9. Nineteenth-century appreciation of Dutch naturalism was undisturbed by theories of visual perception or iconographic research into allegorical meanings that later complicated and enriched the interpretation of Dutch art. On current controversies, see de Jongh 2000; and Franits 1997.

10. Charles Blanc (1813–1882) had a distinguished career as art historian, theoretician, critic, editor; he was twice appointed Director of Administration of Fine Arts and professor at the Collège de France.

11. On the importance of this publication, see Reff 1970.

12. Blanc 1861, vol. 1, pp. 18–19.

13. Henry Havard (1838–1921) was for a while an expatriate in Holland, where he worked as a journalist and art critic. His publications on seventeenth-century Dutch art included exhibition reviews and articles for the *Gazette des Beaux-Arts* as well as volumes on the school in general. Havard 1879–81, 1882. For more on Havard, see Bakker 1986, pp. 29–32; Pickvance 1986, pp. 99–100, 135; and Hertel 1996, esp. pp. 85–92.

14. "c'est pour les Hollandais un titre de gloire impérissable que d'avoir été les premiers, parmi les modernes, à comprendre et à interpreter la nature." Havard 1872–73, p. 394; and Havard 1882, p. 190.

15. Havard 1882, p. 18.

16. Ibid., pp. 119–20.

17. Havard 1879–81, vol. 3, pp. 2–3. Havard argues that it was only in the Dutch and Venetian republics that the citizens' love and loyalty toward their own cities resulted in the portrayal of all aspects of urban scenes. "Par ordre d'émancipation, c'est donc en Hollande que cette peinture civique, urbaine, ou pour parler un langage plus courant, cette peinture de ville, a vu le jour tout d'abord. Nous l'y trouvons dès l'aurore de la liberté, c'est à dire, dès le commencement du XVIIè siècle."

18. Fromentin 1963, p. 131.

19. On Fromentin, see Meyer Schapiro's introduction to Fromentin 1963, pp. ix–xliv. Schapiro comments, pp. xxxvi–xxxvii: "In the defense of Impressionism (as of Realism in the generation before) the example of the Dutch painters had been a powerful argument. The art of the 1860's and 70's renewed a tradition of bourgeois painting that had been interrupted by the authoritative grand style of the seventeenth and eighteenth centuries. The painter Boudin wrote that the people and the landscape of his own century were no less worthy subjects of painting than had been the Hollanders and Holland of the seventeenth. The actuality of color and brushstroke, light and atmosphere, outdoor painting and direct vision in the most recent art made the old works seem almost contemporary. It would have been impossible at this time to write about the Flemish and Dutch masters without hinting at the modern school."

20. van der Tuin 1948, pp. 79–116; see also Grate 1959, pp. 188–220; Jowell 1977, pp. 144–68; and Chu 1974, pp. 18–31. On the role of Dutch painting in the development of Barbizon artists, see Robert L. Herbert in Boston 1962, esp. pp. 18–19.

21. Chu 1974, esp. chaps. 4 and 5.

22. While some of these ideas are found in Thoré's earlier writings, he developed them further after seeing the great Manchester Art Treasures Exhibition in 1857; see Bürger 1857.

23. "la plus deliberée, la plus originale, la plus varieé, la plus revolutionnaire, la plus naturelle, et la plus humain à la fois; c'est assurément celle qui est la plus degagé du passé, qui adhere la plus à la nature, et qui par là signale le mieux une des tendances de l'art à venir." Bürger 1861, p. 258. These ideas, from his little known *Salon* of 1861, are taken from an earlier essay, "Nouvelles Tendances de l'art" of 1857, first published in 1862 in the *Revue Germanique* (Bürger 1862) but more prominently in 1868 as the preface to the republication of his earlier *Salons;* see Thoré-Bürger 1868. It is worth mentioning that although especially renowned for his advocacy and elucidation of the Dutch School, Thoré's writings on the French, Spanish, and English Schools were also well known and influential. On the significance of his writings to Manet, see Fried 1996.

24. Paul Mantz, reviewing the republication of Thoré's *Salons* (see note 23 above), recalled how Thoré supported innovators, courageously celebrated the boldness of the new school, and believed in "the insulted Delacroix, the unknown Decamps, the prohibited Rousseau" (à Delacroix insulté, à Decamps méconnu, à Rousseau proscrit). Mantz 1868, p. 401.

25. See Jowell 1995, "Art Market" 1996, 2003. He once resorted to sending a resplendent fish still life by the then little-known Abraham Hendricksz van Beyeren for exhibition in the studio of the restorer-dealer Étienne François Haro (1827–1897), where it could be seen and admired by artists and amateurs. See Bürger 1864, pp. 312–13.

26. He found comparable villains in contemporary art, and his opposition to Italianate or Neoclassical landscape had been an issue in his art criticism of the 1840s, when he condemned the pernicious authority of Italianate art in French art. See Jowell 1977, esp. chap. 6, "French Art and the Italianate Tradition," pp. 117–43; and Jowell, "Géricault" 1996.

27. "mais l'art véritable n'a point de ces préoccupations futiles. L'art est plus spontané d'impression, plus franc dans ses resultants." Bürger 1858, pp. 82–83. For recent discussion of Thoré's role in "Dou's slide into obscurity," see Wheelock 2000, pp. 15–16. The reputations of these artists, demoted for various artistic vices, did not recover until well into the next century.

28. "les patient tricoteurs d'images longuement ruminées." See Thoré-Bürger 1870, vol. 2, pp. 514–15. As cogently argued by Jane Mayo Roos, a general connotation of the term *impression,* or painting *d'impression,* was well established by the 1870s, but she omits Thoré's significant contribution to the earlier critical debate with Blanc in the 1860s. See Roos 1996, pp. 162–64. More surprising is the absence of any reference to contemporary critical commentary about "the Old Master precedent for the extraordinary flowering of rapid painting in France during the second half of the nineteenth century" in the otherwise excellent essay by Richard R. Brettell in London, *Impression* 2000, p. 29.

29. Written soon after his return from exile, it included practical information about major public and private collections, not unexpectedly recommending his recently published *Musées* as the most reliable and informative guides to the Dutch School. See Bürger, "Petit Guide" 1860.

30. Rembrandt (*Slaughtered Ox*), Hobbema (*Watermill*), Ruisdael (*The Bush*, *Tempest*), Metsu (*Vegetable Market*, *The Virginal Lesson*), Van Goyen (*View of Dordrecht*), Van Ostade (*Family Portrait*), De Heem (*The Dessert*). For information on the mid-nineteenth-century holdings in the Louvre, see Villot 1853; see also Brejon de Lavergnée, Foucart, and Reynaud 1979, esp. Index 8, Provenances, pp. 188–97, for dates of acquisitions.

31. Fromentin 1963, p. 168.

32. "c'est ne pas ma faute si, dans toutes les collections, les hollandaise priment tout." Bürger 1867, p. 541. Two years later he commented on the increased commercial value on the art market of Dutch pictures of familiar, simple scenes. Bürger 1869, p. 6; see also Jowell, "Art Market" 1996, p. 124.

33. Paris 1874. On this important exhibition, see Mantz 1874.

34. See Jowell 1974; and Jowell 1989.

35. Such as Jean-Baptiste-Pierre Lebrun: "His works would sell for higher prices had he not produced so much, or painted so quickly; for a painting to fetch a high price, it is not sufficient that it bear the mark of genius, it must also be properly finished; or else, I must concede that that which has been quickly executed is similarly regarded and paid for. Advice to contemporary artists who do not base their reputations firmly on finished works and precious study" (Ses productions se seraient vendues beaucoup plus cher s'il avait pas tant produit, ni peint si vite: car, pour qu'un tableau soit payé fort cher, il ne suffit pas qu'on appercoive l'empreinte du génie, il faut encore qu'il soit finit: autrement, j'admets que cequi a été fait vite se regarde et se paie de meme. Avis aux artistes modernes, lorsqu'ils n'asseoient pas leurs reputations sur des ouvrages achevés et précieux d'étude). Lebrun 1792–96, vol. 1, pp. 71, quoted in Jowell 1974, p. 104.

36. "Il a tant peint! Il peignait si vite—et si bien! Il n'y a pas la moindre peinture de lui qui ne soit attirante pour les artistes et qui ne leur offer des enseignements. De lui, tout est instructif, ses défauts autant que ses qualités; car ses défauts sont toujours d'un grand praticien. Dans ses brusqueries exagérées, dans ses contrastes hasardés, dans ses négligences trop sans façon, il y a toujours la main d'un peintre généreusement doué, et même le signe d'un certain genie, assez superficiel il est vrai, et provoqué par l'aspect extérieur des choses, par le mouvement, la tournure, la couleur, l'effet, par ce qui remue et brille, plus que par les caractères secret et intimes de la vie,—assez vulgaire même, si l'on peut parler ainsi du génie,—mais franc et brave, irrésistible comme l'instinct." Bürger, *Études* 1860, p. 13.

37. "Vive étude, sabré de premier coup,—il n'en fait jamais d'autres. Tous ses coups de brosse marquent, lancés justement et spirituellement où il faut. On dirait que Frans Hals peignait comme on fait de l'escrime et qu'il faisait fouetter son pinceau comme un fleuret. Oh l'adroit bretteur . . . ! Parfois un peu téméraire sans doute, mais aussi savant qu'il est hardi." Ibid., pp. 13–14.

38. *Portrait of Descartes,* now considered a copy of small portrait in Copenhagen, see Slive 1970–74, vol. 1, pp. 164–65.

39. Bürger 1858 and *Musées* 1860.

40. See Chu 1987 for a fascinating account of the museum as a place of artistic pilgrimage.

41. Ibid., pp. 112–14, 130–41.

42. Private collection: illustrated in ibid., p. 124, fig. 7.8. See Sweet 1966, p. 27: "Mary Cassatt also visited Holland at this time, being chiefly interested in the works of Frans Hals. In Haarlem she copied his Meeting of the Officers of the *Cluveniers-Doelen*, of 1633, and managed to achieve the spirit and freshness of the original, without slavish imitation of each brushstroke. In later years she was proud of this copy and used to show it to young art students, assuring them that such an exercise was essential for their development." See also ibid., p. 195, for Cassatt's later advocacy of studying after Hals.

43. Morisot 1950, p. 127.

44. "Les deux mains unies ensemble sont merveilleuses. . . . On ne sait trop comment c'est fait, par quelques touches hardies qui accusent juste la forme et le mouvement." Bürger 1864, p. 299.

45. 50,000 francs at the Pourtalès sale in 1864 and 35,000 francs at the van Brienen sale in 1865, respectively. The latter is now considered to be replica; see Slive 1970–74, vol. 3, pp. 65–66, no. 123.

46. See Paris 1866. Both works were subsequently reproduced in the *Gazette des Beaux-Arts:* the *Portrait of a Woman* in 1868 (Bürger 1868, 231) and *The Gypsy* in 1870, soon after it had entered the Louvre; see Mantz 1870, p. 396, where it is accompanied by a eulogistic description.

47. "dans les tons d'or, avec la sauvagerie de la première manière: un chef-d'oeuvre improvisé en quelques heures de vive lumière et de bonne humeur." Bürger 1868, pp. 435–37.

48. "Qu'un des plus vaillants portraitistes du monde, que Frans Hals reprenne sa place légitime!" Bürger 1867, pp. 536–51. Comte Mniszech owned approximately a dozen paintings attributed to Hals, eight of which are presently identifiable. Other collectors included Lord Hertford, Baron James de Rothschild, the Pereires, Oudry, Double, La Caze, and Lavalard.

49. Bürger 1868, pp. 444–47.

50. "La reputation de ce maitre devra beaucoup à l'école moderne qui le prise singulièrement et lui fait partout fête comme à un inspirateur. La vérité est qu'il représente un côté d'étude sain et fortifiant, qu'il ne ment point à sa vision, et que c'est le moment où jamais de suivre les voies sincères si l'on veut que la domaine de l'art français se fortifie pour s'aggrandir." Astruc 1866; first cited in Flescher 1978, p. 299.

51. The introduction to a large portfolio of reproductive etchings published in 1873 attributed Hals's popularity to the modern preference for "original creations marked by strong individuality" to more "considered and finished works, fruits of a more advanced culture, perhaps, but by the same token less spontaneous and less natural. The more a work of art reveals its initial inspiration, the more it springs freshly and vibrantly from the brain of the artist, the more it awakens our interest and sympathy" (les créations originales et frappés au coin d'une forte individualité bien audessus des oeuvres plus réflechies, plus travaillées, fruit d'une culture plus avancées, peut-etre, mais par la meme moins spontanées et moins naturelles. Plus ses productions trahissent l'inspiration première, plus fraiche et vibrante elle jaillessent du cerveau de l'artiste, et plus elle éveillent chez nous d'intéret et de sympathie." Vosmaer 1873, pp. 28–29. Vosmaer's text was translated into French, German, and English.

52. The critic Albert Wolff's complaint that Manet had put "water in his beer" provoked the painter Alfred Stevens to reply that it was "pure Haarlem beer." Quoted in Hamilton 1986, pp. 166–67.

53. Duret 1902, pp. 82–84. Belot was a habitué of the Café Guerbois; see Hamilton 1986, p. 165. Duret insisted that only the pose was reminiscent of Hals.

54. Courthion and Cailler 1960, p. 170.

55. From Degas's table talk at Berthe Morisot's, as recorded in a notebook and reprinted in Valéry 1989, pp. 81–83.

56. Fromentin is an interesting witness, since he was hostile to the Impressionists and occasionally criticized Hals as too "fashionable" or overly witty and showy, with too much "hand." See Jowell 1989, pp. 73–74.

57. "la hardiesse des parties pris de Franz Hals lui causa, en Hollande, une telle impression que, revenue à Paris, armé des tous ces souvenirs, il se décida à aborder franchement les divers aspects de la vie parisienne." Proust 1996, p. 88. Some years later (c. 1879) Manet wrote to the authorities offering to decorate the rebuilt Hôtel de Ville (destroyed during the Commune) with scenes of Paris, which would include such subjects as "Paris-Markets, Paris-Railways, Paris-Port, Paris-Underground, Paris-Races, and Parks" and a gallery around the ceiling with appropriate portrayals of "living men who in the civil realm have contributed or are contributing to the grandeur and richness of Paris" (J'aurais Paris-Halles, Paris-Chemins de fer, Paris-Pont, Paris-Souterrain, Paris-Courses et Jardins. Pour le plafond, une galerie autour de laquelle circuleraient dans les mouvements appropriés tous les hommes vivants qui, dans l'élément civil, ont contribué ou contribuent à la grandeur et à la richesse de Paris). It was signed Édouard Manet, "Artist painter, born in Paris" (Artiste peintre, né à Paris). Proust 1913, p. 94.

58. *Exposition aux Palais Bourbon aux profit des Alsaciens-Lorrains*, reviewed by Paul Mantz in Mantz 1874.

59. "Frans Hals est un moderne. Son esthétique, son coloris, son dessin, ses procédés, appartiennent à notre époque." The writer added that nothing could be more precious for young modern artists seeking to learn from the experience of a great master than a visit to the museum at Haarlem; such a pilgrimage would be "among artistic excursions one of the most fertile in observation, the most fruitful in instruction, the most attractive that we know" (l'une des excursions artistiques les plus fertiles en observation, les plus fécondes en enseignements, les plus attrayantes que nous connaissions"). Anon. 1883, p. 302.

60. Baxandall 1985, p. 60.

61. Although his claim to have been struck by Vermeer's *View of Delft* in 1842 is usually taken at face value, it seems to me to be wishful retrospective thinking. There is no evidence dating from those years, and in 1858 he was somewhat critical of the painting. See Jowell 1998.

62. Bürger 1866; republished in Blum 1946. Further on Thoré's "rediscovery" of Vermeer, see Meltzoff, "Vermeer" 1942; Jowell 1995; and Jowell 1998.

63. "l'artiste a plu, étonné, séduit; sa crane allure, les fines qualités de son observations, sa manière concise et sobre, sa chaleur de pinceau, ses harmonies délicates et souples,—cette entente de l'effet qui concentre tout l'intérêt sur les parties essentielles au sujet,—tout cela a frappé à première vue, et l'étude n'a fait que fortifier cette première impression si favourable. Tout le monde fêtera désormais l'intéressant Meer." Astruc 1866, quoted in Jowell 1998, pp. 37–38, 51 n. 9.

64. The four figure paintings were *Soldier with Laughing Girl* (The Frick Collection, New York), then in the Double collection; two works owned by Thoré, *Woman with a Pearl Necklace* (Gemäldegalerie, Berlin) and *A Young Woman Standing at a Virginal* (The National Gallery, London; fig. 26); and *The Geographer* (Städelsches Kunstinstitut, Frankfurt).

65. These paintings—some of which remained in the hands of Thoré-Bürger's heirs (see Jowell 2003)—were included in the summary catalogue in Havard 1888.

66. Countering Francis Haskell's view of Thoré's attitude to Vermeer (in Haskell 1976, pp. 89–90), Henri Zerner and Charles Rosen have shown how Thoré compared aspects of Vermeer's handling to the contemporary avant-garde—such as the exaggerated impasto in the *View of Delft* or the prodigious light and bold color in the *Little Street*—"Nothing but a wall, and a few casements without the least ornament, But what color!" (Rien qu'un mur, et quelques ouvertures sans la moindre ornamentation. Mais quelle couleur!). Bürger 1866, p. 463; see Rosen and Zerner 1984, esp. pp. 192–202.

67. Fried 1996, pp. 105 and 497 n. 169. It has also been suggested that Degas may in part owe his use of the pictorial device of a picture within a picture

to Vermeer's example. Reff, *The Artist's Mind* 1976, pp. 91–94.

68. Jowell 1998, pp. 49–50.

69. Bürger, *Musées* 1860, pp. 70–72. For an interesting discussion of this painting, see Liedtke 2000, pp. 256–57.

70. "Il etait sensible au charme de la vie quotidienne exprimé avec tant de ferveur par les Flamands et les Hollandais. Il aimait tout particulièrement Terburg, de Hoog et surtout *la Dentellière* de Vermeer." Baudot 1949, p. 29, quoted in Ottawa 1997, p. 228. It is interesting that in his *Salon* of 1868, Thoré's recommendation of the skillful depiction of impalpable air around figures achieved by seventeenth-century Dutch artists is immediately followed by lyrical praise for Renoir's *Lise* (Folkwang Museum, Essen)—for its interplay of colored shadows: "The dress of white gauze, enriched at the waist by a black ribbon whose ends reach to the ground, is in full light, but with a slight greenish cast from the reflections of the foliage. The head and neck are held in a delicate half-shadow under the shade of a parasol. The effect is so natural and so true that one might very well find it false, because one is accustomed to nature represented in the conventional colors of bad painting. Does not color depend on the surrounding environment?" (La robe de gaze blanche, ceinte à la taille par un ruban noir dont les bouts tombent jusqu'à la terre, est en pleine lumière, mais légèrement verdacée par les reflets du feuillage. La tête et le cou sont tenus dans une delicate pénombre à l'abri d'un parasol. L'effet est si naturel et si vrai, qu'on doit le trouver faux, car on est habitué à se représenter la nature sous les couleurs conventionnelles de la mauvaise peinture. Est-ce que la couleur ne depend pas du milieu qui l'enveloppe?"). Thoré-Bürger 1870, p. 531.

71. The few Vermeers in Paris collections were dispersed in sales, while the three major figure paintings in Thoré-Bürger's own collection remained in the hands of his heirs until 1892. On Thoré-Bürger's collection, see Jowell 2003.

72. Havard 1872–73.

73. "Beaucoup d'entre ces personnages ne figurent là, en effet, que comme des taches heureuses. Ce sont des notes agréables dans un concert adorable de tonalités fines, délicates, fondues, enveloppées. Ils ne commandent pas le reste; rien ne leur est subordonné; chaque ton local, au contraire, a sa valeur propre et son accent voulu, et, s'ils jouent un rôle important dans cette mélodieuse symphonie, c'est par la tache qu'ils font, et non par l'idée qu'ils expriment." Havard 1883, pp. 213–14; and Havard 1888, p. 20.

74. By the twentieth century it was possible to mount an exhibition in which a wide range of paintings by subsequent artists were, as it were, bathed in Vermeer's light. See Paris 1966.

75. See esp. DeWitt 2003, pp. 1–14, where the composition of Manet's *Battle of Kearsage and Alabama* (1864; Philadelphia Museum of Art) is compared with Ludolf Backhuyzen's *Vessels on a Stormy Sea* (Musée du Louvre, Paris) and considered in the context of the Dutch marine tradition.

76. A moonlit schene by Aert van der Neer, which he evidently tried to sell in 1867. There was a thriving market for nocturnal views: between 1860 and 1880 approximately fifty were sold in Paris. See Paris 1983, cat. 118, esp. pp. 311–12; and Philadelphia 2003, p. 2.

77. Boudin copied Dutch art in 1849 in Paris and Belgium; Jongkind published etchings of *Six Views of Holland*, 1862; see Bakker 1986, pp. 25–26.

78. See Bakker 1986, pp. 22, 35 n. 29; and Huussen 1986, pp. 41–42, figs. 26, 27.

79. Bürger admired the "opulent painting" that had been finished in four days and predicted that it would confer immortality on its model, Camille. He described the *Road in Fontainebleau Forest* as "a superb sketch . . . effect of evening with the sun illuminating the great trees. A true painter can do just what he wants" (une ébauche superbe . . . effet de soir, avec le soleil illuminant les grands arbres. Quand on est vraiment peintre on fait tout ce qu'on veut). Thoré-Bürger 1870, pp. 325, 285–86.

80. Christiane Hertel interestingly associates these with Havard's complex evocation of a Venetian-like colorfulness of contemporary Netherlands, later evolving into the innate, vigorous colorism of the Golden Age of Dutch art. Hertel 1996, pp. 88–92. See also Pickvance, in Amsterdam 1986, p. 135, cat. 19, who points out that the small vertical canvas *Footbridge* (Musée municipal des Ursulines, Macon) is dedicated to Henry Havard and caters to his friend's taste for traditional seventeenth-century Dutch painting.

81. "Il est des tableaux ou M. Monet arrive à contenter tout le monde, sauf lui-même peut-être; ce sont ceux qui ont été peints sous un jour discret, tamisé par un ciel chargé de vapeurs, interceptant en grande partie les radiations violettes: telles, cette *Vue prise à Rouen,* au ciel ambre, fondu, profond, qui semble détaché d'un tableau de Cuyp." Lostalot 1883, p. 346 (see drawing by artist on p. 345). Cuyp was much admired; see, for example, Mantz 1874, p. 294, on the impressive Cuyp landscapes exhibited at the Palais Bourbon.

82. See London 1992, pp. 94, 120, 162; and Lloyd 1981, p. 44.

83. However, there are some specific comparisons: De Heem's sumptuous *Still Life with Fruit* (fig. 84) is specifically cited in connection with Cézanne's still lifes of the 1880s and 1890s (see Shackelford 2001, p. 27), and Dutch still-life vocabulary is frequently incorporated by Manet in genre or portraiture. On the comparable rendering of material texture and shine in seventeenth-century Dutch art, see Pryzyblski 2001, p. 31.

84. "[N]ous ne savons, jusqu'ici, comment la remplacer par un terme qui comprenne à la fois le gibier mort, animaux et oiseau, le poisson, . . . les fleurs et bouquets, les fruits, les vases et ustensiles, armes et instruments de musique, bijoux et ornaments divers, draperies et costumes, et les milles objets qu'on peut grouper pour en faire le prétexte d'une représentation colorée, amusante, sous le coup de la lumière. Nature morte est absurde. Est-ce que les fleurs ne vivent pas? Elles ont leur respiration et leur santé; elles sont gaies et brillantes, ou tristes et ternes; elles s'agitent sans cesse, quoi que presque imperceptiblement, se tournent vers la lumière, s'écartent pour laisser passer des branches perfides, s'infléchissent sous l'influence de la sécheresse, se gonflent et s'épanouissent sous la caresse d'un rayon. Les fleurs ne sont pas de la nature morte! Il n'y a point de nature morte." Bürger, *Musées* 1860, pp. 317–18. The notion of the unity of all things is derived from Pierre Leroux's philosophy *l'Humanité* (not from Franciscan thought, as improbably suggested in Baltimore 2000, p. 37).

85. Such as Rembrandt's *Anatomy Lesson* (Mauritshuis, The Hague) and Joos van Craesbeeck's *Smoker* (Musée du Louvre, then attributed to Adriaen Brouwer); see Chu 1974, pp. 42–43, figs. 71, 72.

86. See Krauss 1967; Paris 1983, no. 19; and Fried 1996, p. 147.

87. The painting, now in the Petit Palais, Paris, was then in a private collection in Rouen.

88. One example being the still life at the side of *Luncheon in the Studio* (fig. 30).

89. Suggested in Ottawa 1997, cat. 26.

90. Chu 1974, p. 60. On Degas's early copies of Rembrandt, see ibid., pp. 76–77; and Reff, "Copies" 1964, p. 251. It has also been suggested that the sense of momentary interruption in Degas's *Sulking: The Banker* (1869–71; The Metropolitan Museum of Art, New York) may have been inspired by Rembrandt's *Syndics;* see Reff, *The Artist's Mind* 1976, p. 118. Paul Poujard later recalled Degas's comment, "In our beginnings, Fantin, Whistler and I we were all on the same road, the road from Holland"; see Degas 1947, p. 236.

91. Herbert 1988, pp. 66–69.

92. Havard 1882, pp. 191–92. Since the La Caze bequest (1869) the Louvre possessed four works by Van Goyen, and his works were increasingly sought after by collectors. On Van Goyen's rising reputation during the 1870s, see Mantz 1875, pp. 138–43.

93. "Wynants was the first, or one of the first to realize that any landscape, come across by chance, could inspire the painter, especially when it is a bit of his own country" (Wynants fut le premier ou un des premiers à s'apercevoir qu'une campagne quelconque, parcourue au hazard, peut inspirer le peintre, surtout quand cette campagne est une portion de sa patrie." Blanc 1869, p. 119; see also Havard 1882, pp. 197–98.

94. "Je n'ai pas eu le temps de t'écrire ce que j'ai éprouvé en voyant les chefs d'oeuvre de Rembrandt: c'est admirable, et a réflexion qui m'est venue après avoir vu non seulement les Rembrandt, mais les Frans Hals, les Van der Meer, et tant d'autres grands artistes, c'est que nous, modernes, nous avons raison de chercher, ou plutôt de sentir autrement, puisque nous somme autres et que et que du reste c'est un art tellement particulier d'une époque que c'est absurde d'essayer de marcher dans cette voie. Aussi, comme je te l'ai dit souvent, je me méfie des peintres adroits qui savant pasticher les vieux maîtres, je n'ai certainement pas la meme en ne faisant pas de chefs-d'oeuvre, regardent avec leurs yeux à eux. Comment te decrire les portraits de Rembrandt, les Hals et ce *Canal* de Van der Meer, chef d'oeuvre qui se rapproche des impressionistes; je suis revenue de Hollande plus que jamais admirateur des Monet, Degas, Renoir, Sisley. . . . Heureux les artistes qui voient et aiment la nature!" Pissarro 1989, p. 520.

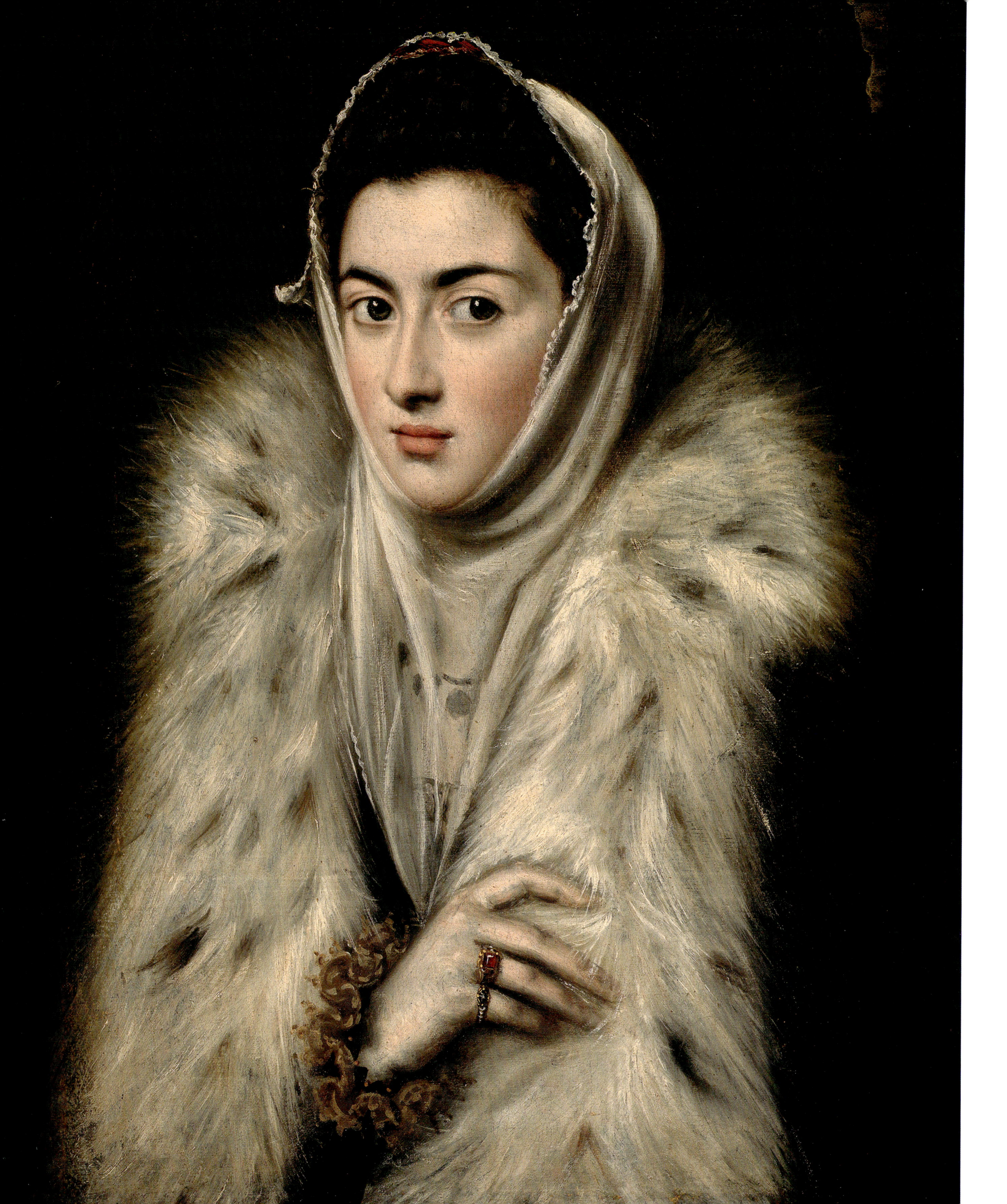

Xavier Bray

The Spanish Old Masters and the French Impressionists

Sketches of Spain

In August 1865 Édouard Manet wrote to his friend Zacharie Astruc announcing that he was leaving for Spain "immediately, the day after tomorrow perhaps; I am extremely eager to see so many beautiful things and to ask the advice of Master Velázquez."[1] Later that month, Manet took the train from Paris, crossing the French-Spanish border at Irún, arriving finally in Madrid on August 31, where he checked in, appropriately, at the Grand Hôtel de Paris on the Puerta del Sol. During the seven days that he spent there, he visited the Museo del Prado, saw a bullfight on Sunday afternoon, and visited the cathedral town of Toledo. The only blight on his trip was, he remarked, the appalling Spanish food, or "sale cuisine," as he later described it to Astruc.[2]

This was Manet's first and only trip to Spain, and yet he had already been producing paintings in Paris with a strong Spanish flavor for some six years. Since Napoleon's invasion of the Spanish peninsula in 1808, Parisian culture had been dominated by all things Spanish. Old master paintings by Diego Rodríguez de Silva y Velázquez, Bartolomé Esteban Murillo, Francisco de Zurbarán, Jusepe de Ribera,

Cat. 40
El Greco (1541–1614) (detail)
Lady in a Fur Wrap, 1577–80

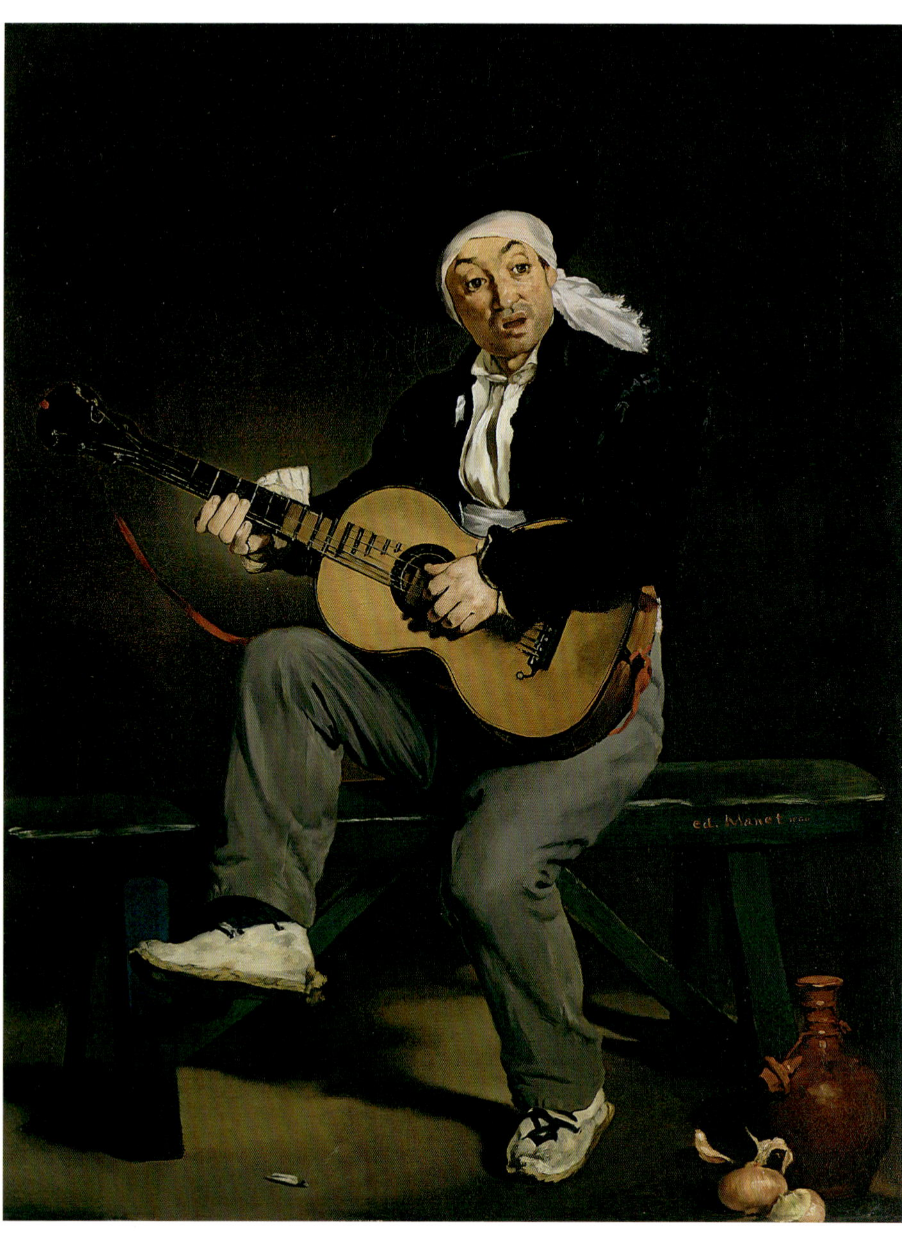

Fig. 42
Édouard Manet
The Spanish Singer, 1860
Oil on canvas, 58 × 45 in.
(147.3 × 114.3 cm)
The Metropolitan Museum of Art,
Gift of William Church Osborn, 1949
(49.58.2)

and Francisco de Goya had flooded into Paris, as did such colorful Hispanic customs as flamenco dancing and bullfighting. This extraordinary phenomenon had a profound effect on a generation of artists that included Manet, Edgar Degas, Paul Cézanne, Pierre-Auguste Renoir, Mary Cassatt, and Berthe Morisot.

Although a number of these artists—namely Astruc, Manet, Degas, Renoir, Cassatt, and Morisot—did eventually visit Spain in person, they did so as a result of having already acquired a taste for Spanish art in Paris. Ironically, what these artists had seen of Spain in Paris prompted them to produce some of the most celebrated paintings of the second half of the nineteenth century, including Manet's iconic *The Spanish Singer* (fig. 42). As important as Spanish subject matter was to the French painters, perhaps more important was the technique of the Spanish old masters—be it the dark and somber palette of Ribera or the loose, almost magical, brushwork of Velázquez.

Artists were not the only ones affected by the vogue for Spanish culture. The writer Prosper Mérimée had traveled to Spain in 1830, returning with romantic tales that he recounted in his widely read *Lettres d'Espagne* (1830–33). His novel *Carmen* was adapted by the composer Georges Bizet in 1875 into what is still today the quintessentially Spanish opera. Spanish dance companies visited the capital and were hugely popular. Like most fashions, however, this *Espagnolisme,* as the movement came to be known, was in fact a romanticized and watered-down version of the real Spain. Even today, purists in Spain, particularly in the world of flamenco singing, will shout as an insult when dissatisfied with the performance, "vete a Paris" (go to Paris).

For those in the nineteenth century in search of the authentic Spain, painting and sculpture offered the truest insight into the culture of the Iberian Peninsula, particularly that which was produced during its cultural heyday known as the Spanish Golden Age, between the sixteenth and eighteenth centuries. Artists such as Velázquez, Zurbarán, Ribera, and Murillo invested in a kind of realism, a truth to nature, in which the dignity of the individual or religious subject was treated as naturalistically as possible. This veracity appealed to Manet and to some of the Impressionists whose own artistic aims included depicting nature truthfully and recording life as spontaneously as possible. Furthermore, the painterly technique of the Spanish old masters, especially Velázquez, whose quick touches of the brush seem to be able to capture the moment, offered the nineteenth-century painters an invaluable tool with which to record everyday life in Paris.

During the first half of the nineteenth century a huge number of Spanish paintings poured into France. When Napoleon invaded the Iberian Peninsula in 1808, he installed his brother Joseph Bonaparte as king of Spain. Led by unscrupulous greed, Joseph and his generals, particularly the infamous Marshal Jean de Dieu Soult, general of the Imperial Guard, pillaged some of the greatest masterpieces of Spanish paintings from churches, convents, and the royal collection in Madrid. Literally hundreds of paintings by the great names of the Spanish Golden Age, Velázquez, Murillo, and Zurbarán, left Spain during this period and were taken to France. In 1810 Marshal Soult seized 999 paintings from Seville's churches and convents, sending the best of them to Paris, where Dominique Vivant-Denon, director of the Musée Napoléon, was busy amassing art taken from all over Europe to create the ideal "museum" that would reflect the glories of the newly created French Empire. However, Napoleon's defeat at Waterloo in 1815 meant that many of the paintings seized by force, such as the vast *Apotheosis of Saint Thomas Aquinas* by Zurbarán, the altarpiece of the College of the Dominican friars in Seville, were returned to their rightful owners. But already Spanish art had attracted the attention of the French public, who were stunned by Spanish artists' indifference to the academic ideals that were so much a part of their own native, French, school.

The best collection of Spanish art to remain in Paris following Napoleon's defeat was that of Marshal Soult. Housed in his mansion in the rue de l'Université, it could be viewed by appointment. One of his most celebrated paintings was the *Immaculate Conception* by Murillo, taken in 1813 from the Hospital de los Venerables Sacerdotes, Seville (fig. 43). The French had a particular fondness for Murillo's sweet and serene images of the Virgin and Christ Child or of Saint John the Baptist as a young boy. Executed with a light, feathery touch that creates a vaporous effect, together with saccharine colors and tearful eyes looking up toward heaven, Murillo's paintings may have reminded French viewers of the portraits of young maidens by the eighteenth-century French painter Jean-Baptiste Greuze.

When part of Soult's collection was sold after his death in 1853, his *Immaculate Conception* fetched 615,300 francs, the highest price ever paid up to that date for a picture. It was acquired by the French State for the Musée du Louvre, where it would undoubtedly have been seen by Manet and the Impressionists hanging in the Salon Carré. However, it was not this strand of sentimental Spanish art that interested them, though it was much admired by the French public. Rather, the artists were attracted by the art of Ribera and

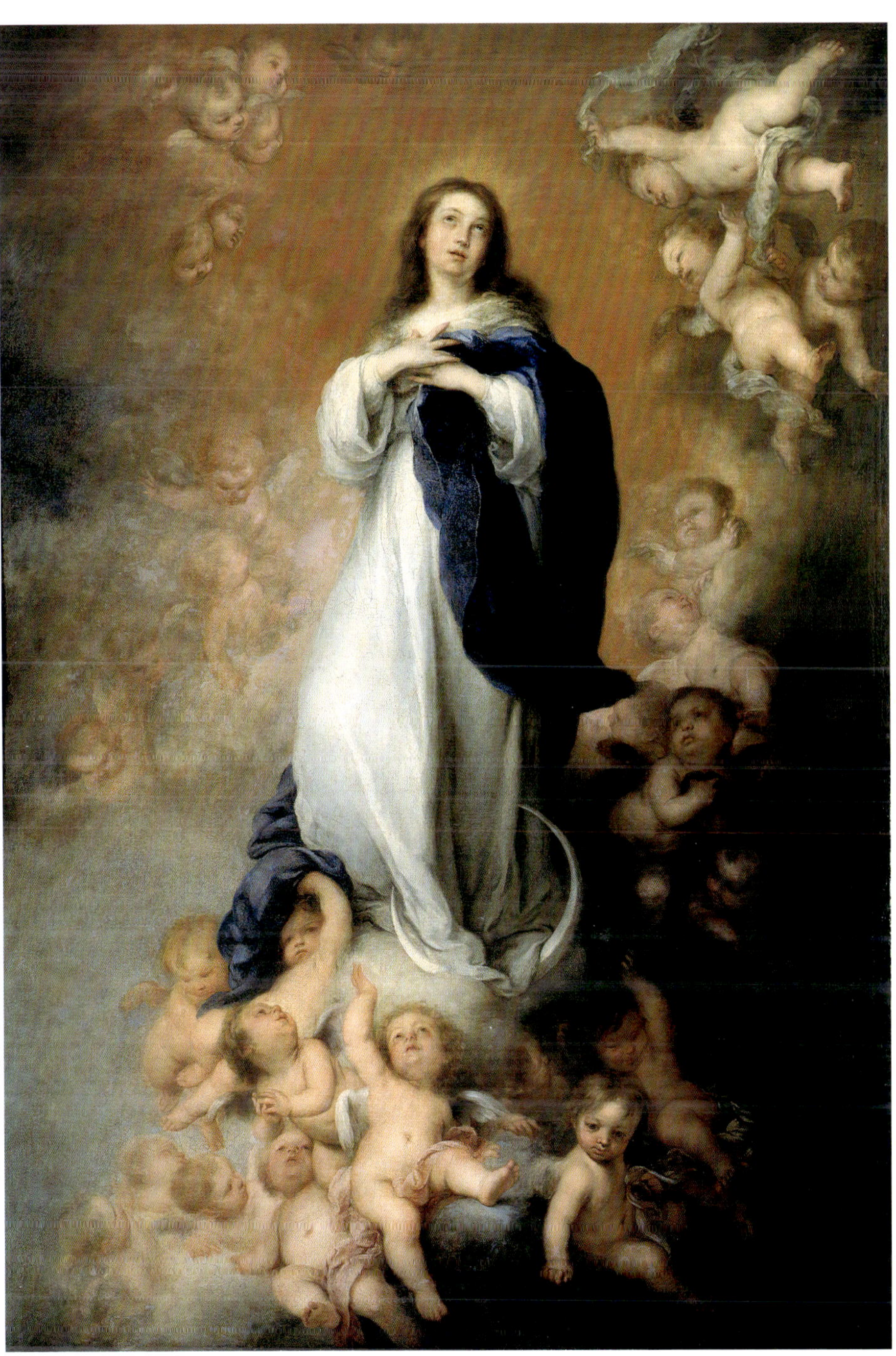

Fig. 43
Bartolomé Esteban Murillo
"Soult" Immaculate Conception, c. 1678
Oil on canvas, 107⅞ × 74¾ in. (274 × 190 cm)
Museo del Prado, Madrid

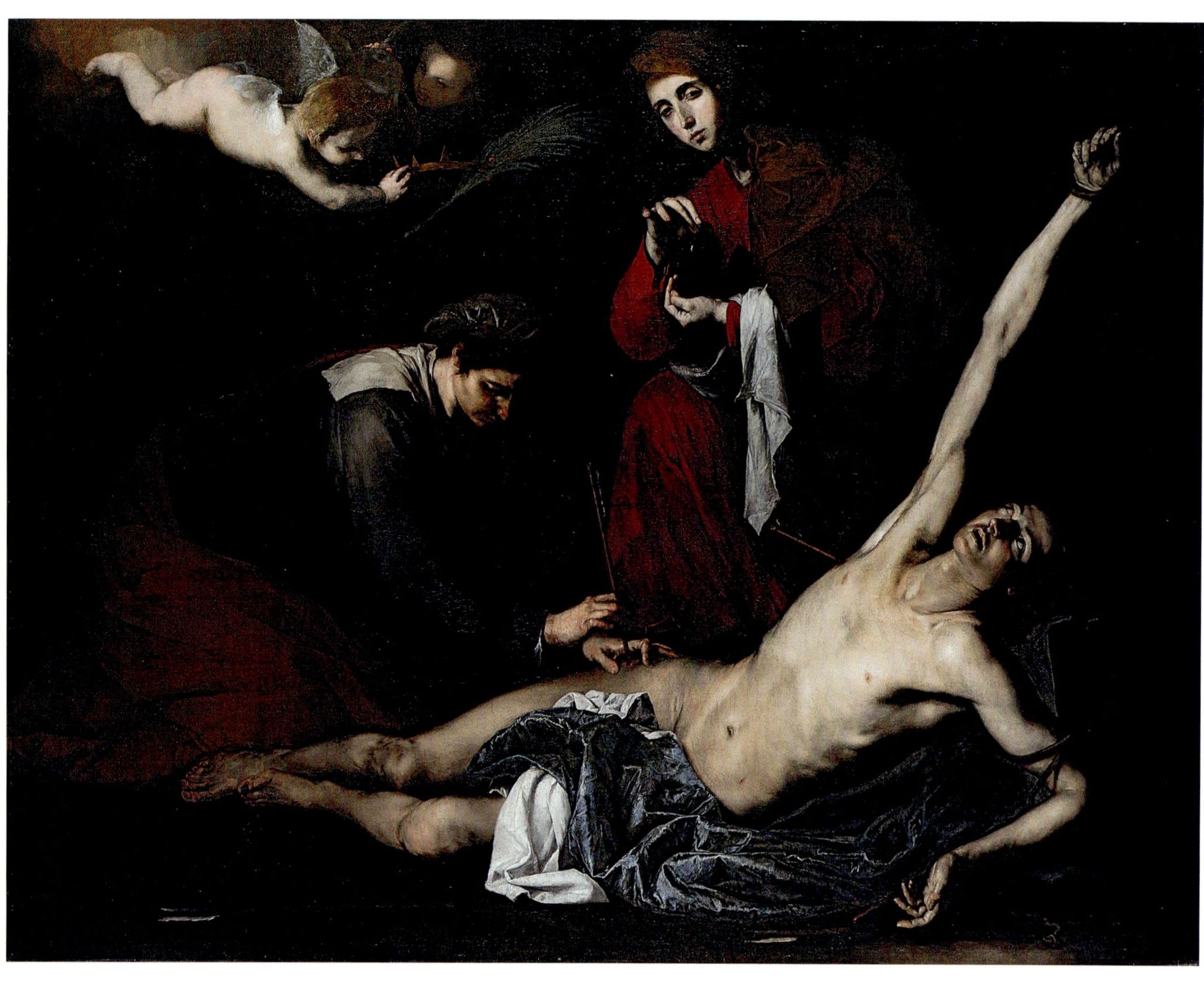

Fig. 44
Jusepe de Ribera (1591–1652)
Saint Sebastian Cured by the Holy Women, 1621
Oil on canvas, 71 × 91⅛ in. (180.3 × 231.6 cm)
Museo de Bellas Artes de Bilbao

Zurbarán. Their paintings, together, of course, with those of the legendary Velázquez, epitomized Spanish art at its most brutal and realistic.

French painters would likely have been familiar with Soult's *Saint Sebastian Cured by the Holy Women* (fig. 44) by Ribera, which was eventually put up for auction in Paris by Soult's family in 1867.[3] The dark, gloomy atmosphere of this painting and the manner in which Ribera "carves" the figures out from the darkness by selectively lighting the scene, as well as his use of the color black, certainly must have impressed both Manet and his less well-known contemporary Théodule Ribot, who painted his own very successful version of this painting, almost a pastiche, for the Salon of 1865.[4] Ribera shows Saint Sebastian's naked body stretched diagonally across the composition, every sinew and muscle reproduced with exactitude. One of the women who attend him, possibly Saint Irene, removes the arrow while the other is about to apply ointment from a jar.

Although the angels at the top left remind us that this is an episode of Christian martyrdom, Ribera has based his visual representation on real life. We could be witnessing a scene in a seventeenth-century hospital. Such realistic depictions of tortured Christian martyrs fascinated French viewers, and although some were repelled by the violent nature of Spanish Catholicism, the Spanish artist's skill at picturing this naturalism kept them looking. The poet Théophile Gautier, who had seen Ribera's paintings during his voyage to Spain in 1840 and devoted an entire poem to him in 1845, captures this curious fascination for physical agony: "As another seeks the beautiful, you look for what shocks: / Martyrs, executioners, gypsies, beggars / Displaying an open sore beside a rag."[5]

The dissolution in 1835 of religious institutions in Spain offered the French authorities an ideal opportunity to buy paintings legitimately. King Louis-Philippe dispatched Baron Isidore Taylor with the instruction to buy whatever he could. Taylor returned from Spain with 450 paintings, including 81 by Zurbarán, 39 by Murillo, 28 by Ribera, 23 by Alonso Cano, 19 by Velázquez, and 11 by Goya.[6] This time, it was Ribera's contemporary, the Sevillian-born Zurbarán, who caused the greatest stir when his work was put on display in the Louvre in the Galerie Espagnole that opened to the public on January 7, 1838.

Having spent most of his career working for Seville's monastic orders, Zurbarán was nicknamed by the French press the "painter of monks." His pictures were stark, minimalist, and deeply spiritual. By removing artifice and focusing on the essential aspects of a narrative, often isolating figures in space, he gave his compositions a potent visual impact. Zurbarán's paintings were considered the perfect reflection of religious Spain, a country in love with death and penitence.[7] One critic wrote that Zurbarán's "monks [are] surrendered to all the agonies of the cloister, to all the macerations of the monastery, to all the anguish that can tear apart martyrs. . . . This is really horrible to see, it will make you shiver."[8] The obsession for Zurbarán's images of monks almost became a vogue in itself, inspiring particularly the literary set in Paris, among them Gautier, who wrote:

> Monks of Zurbarán, white Carthusians who in the shadow,
> Slide silently on the flagstones of death,
> Murmuring Our Father and Hail Mary without end,
> For what crime do you atone with such great remorse?[9]

Of all Zurbarán's paintings, his *Saint Francis in Meditation* (fig. 45) was most commented on. Wearing a rough, worn habit, Saint Francis kneels in a neutral space that could almost be an extension of our

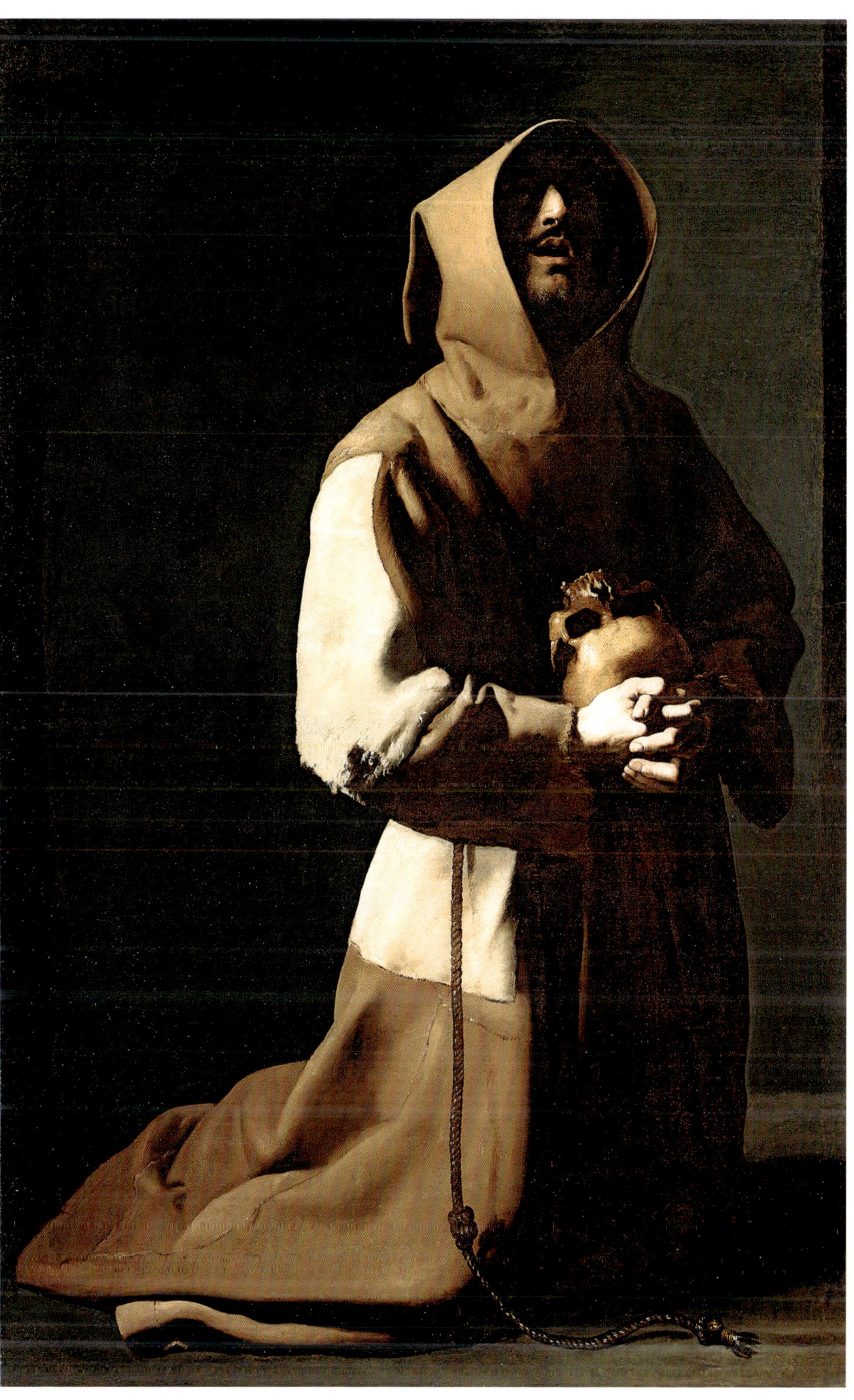

Fig. 45
Francisco de Zurbarán
(1598–1664)
Saint Francis in Meditation, 1635–39
Oil (identified) on canvas, 59⅞ × 39 in. (152 × 99 cm)
The National Gallery, London

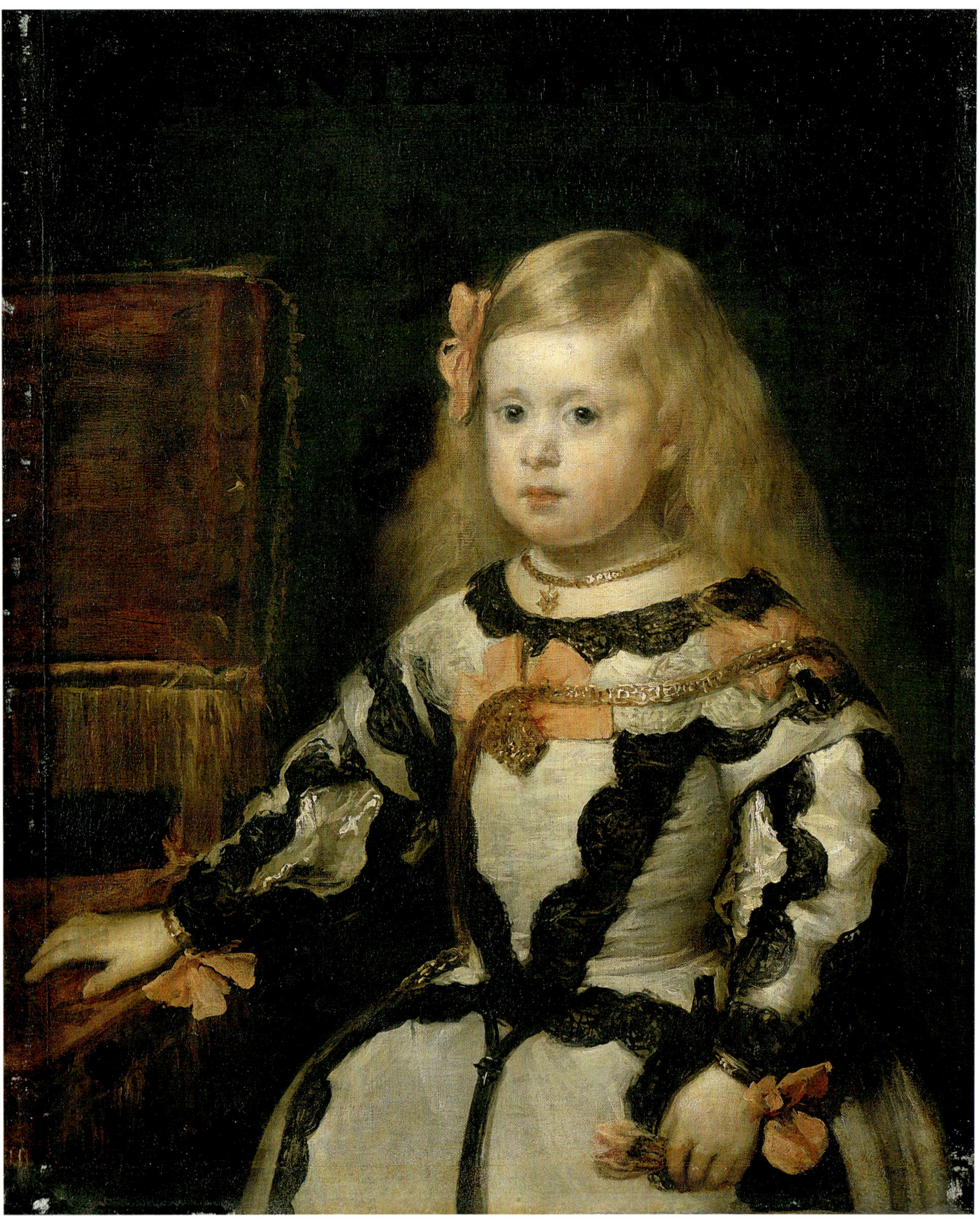

Fig. 46
Diego Rodríguez de Silva y Velázquez
Portrait of the Infanta Margarita, Daughter of Philip IV, King of Spain, 1661–73
Oil on canvas, 27½ × 22⅞ in. (70 × 58 cm)
Musée du Louvre, Paris, France

Cat. 52
Édouard Manet
Infanta Margarita, after Diego Rodríguez de Silva y Velázquez, 1862

Cat. 34
Edgar Degas
Infanta Margarita, Copy after Velázquez, 1861–62

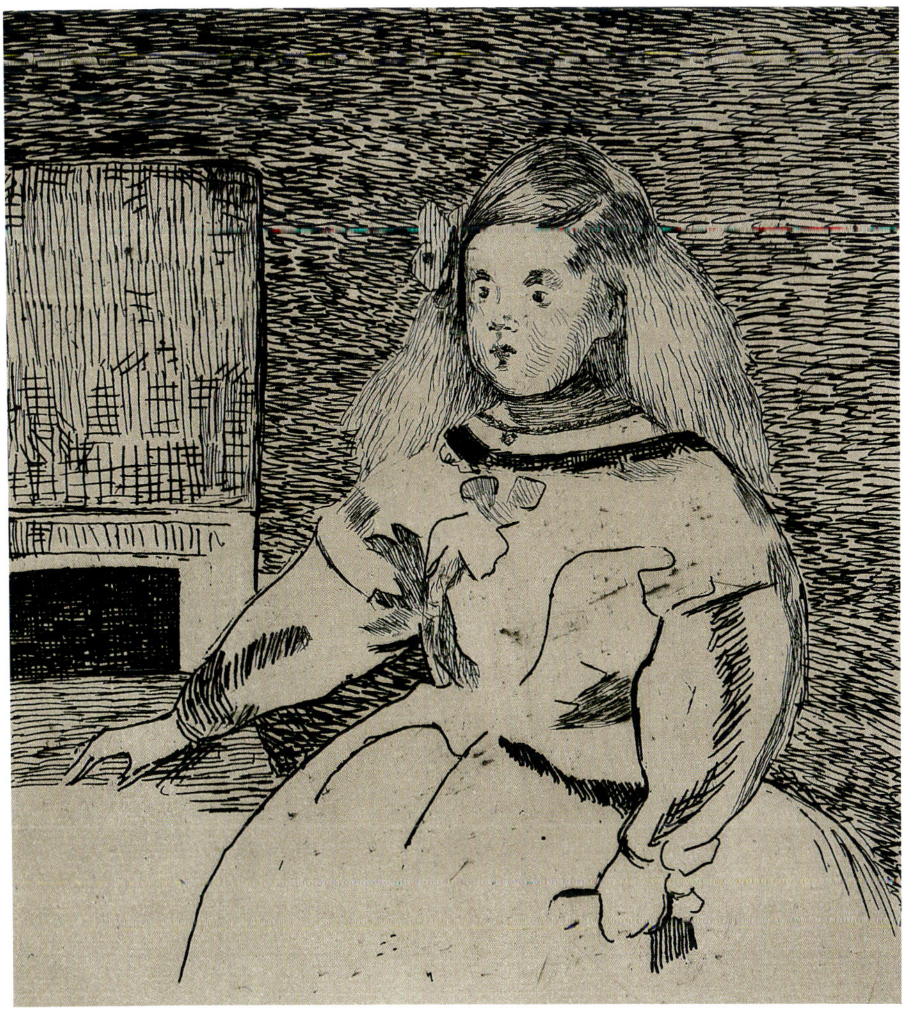

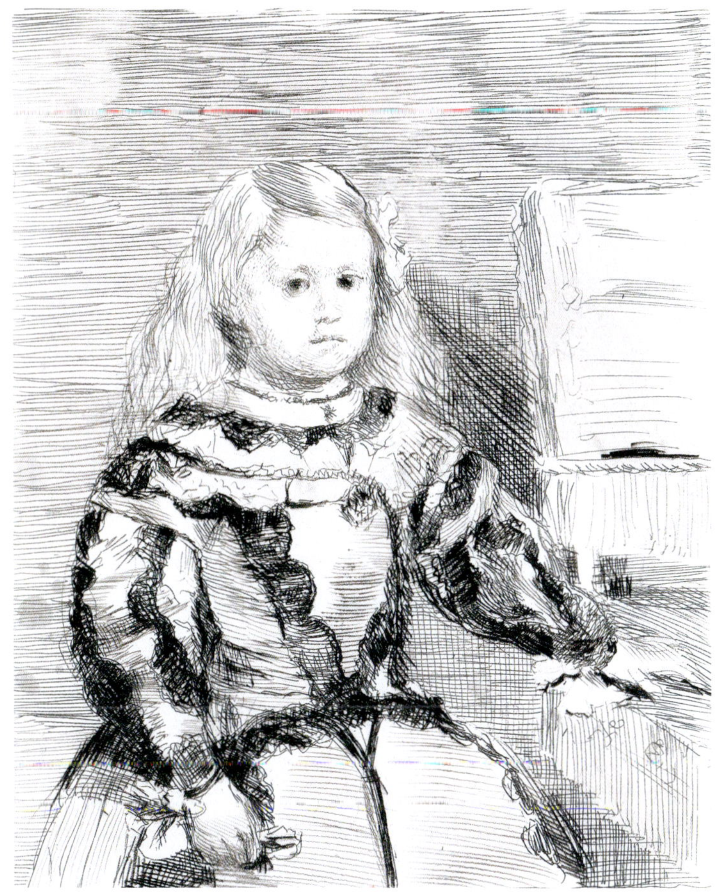

own; our gaze is obliged to focus on him, joining him in his ecstatic communion with God. His cupped hand holds a skull, a stark reminder of the brevity of life, and his head leans back to look up into the heavens. Only after the viewer's eye has adjusted to the dark cavity beneath the hood can one see Saint Francis's eyes. So strong was the impact of this picture that the art critic Charles Blanc found "all of Spain . . . epitomized in this passionate, devout and somber painting, at once mystical and harsh."[10] Several engravings after it were printed in art journals, and even Camille Corot, known primarily for his landscapes, painted a kneeling Saint Francis about 1840–45 (Musée du Louvre, Paris).[11]

In 1841 the British diplomat Frank Hall Standish gave Louis-Philippe his collection of Spanish paintings that he had amassed while he was ambassador in Seville, which further enriched the Louvre's holdings. Suddenly, Paris was the place to visit for anyone wishing to see the crème de la crème of Spanish art. However, the dramatic events surrounding the 1848 Revolution and the subsequent dethroning of Louis-Philippe had as a side effect the disbanding of the Galerie Espagnole, to widespread dismay. Astonishingly, the new regime decided the paintings were the ex-king's private collection and were allowed to follow Louis-Philippe to England, where he spent the last years of his life in exile. His collection was eventually sold in 1853 at Christie's in London, in what was one of the greatest sales of the century. When Manet and the young future members of the Impressionist movement were emerging on the Parisian art scene, France had already lost its remarkable stronghold of Spanish art.

Without the Galerie Espagnole, the Louvre's collection of Spanish painting was seriously depleted. Only a small group remained: those previously in the French royal collection together with a handful of later acquisitions. Yet remarkably, this small and in some cases undistinguished group of Spanish paintings, many of them today not even considered autograph works by the great Spanish masters, was enough to give the young avant-garde French painters a vital injection of *Espagnolisme* that would alter the direction of their work and shift the very course of nineteenth-century French painting.[12]

It was in the Louvre, in front of a small painting of the Infanta Margarita (fig. 46), then considered an autograph work by Velázquez, that the young Degas and Manet met for the first time.[13] The painting had been sent to France in 1654 by Philip IV, king of Spain, as a diplomatic gift to Louis XIV. Degas, who had registered to copy in the Louvre in September 1861 and again in January 1862, was making an etching after it when Manet found him, who reputedly expressed astonishment at seeing Degas working directly on a copperplate.[14] Manet made a very sensitive drawing directly from the original and then an etching of it soon after, concentrating on blocking in the composition with thick etched lines, whereas Degas's etching respected the femininity and youth of the sitter in a more detailed and subtle rendering (see cat. 52, p. 117; cat. 34, p. 117). The individuality of their two responses is telling and this would remain a factor of the Impressionists' response to Spanish painting.

Degas's and Manet's decision to make an etching after the painting reflects the contemporary view that Velázquez's *Infanta* was not easy to replicate in color. Indeed, the British art historian Sir William Stirling-Maxwell, who published one of the first catalogues of Velázquez's oeuvre, observed, it was "one of the most popular pictures in the gallery, and a bone of contention for the copyists."[15] Mérimée had tried to copy it earlier, in 1831, but declared himself incapable of finishing the task because of the chromatic complexity of the painting.[16] Yet, ultimately it was precisely the extraordinary skill and lightness with which Velázquez manipulated the brush that the Impressionists sought to emulate. Renoir later famously remarked that the pink ribbon in the Infanta's hair was executed with such confidence that "All of the art of painting is in it."[17]

Renoir paid homage to Velázquez's portrait in *La Loge* (fig. 47), which he exhibited in the first Impressionist exhibition in 1874. He transformed the Infanta into a young lady, the model Nini from Montmartre, sitting in a theater box. Rather than a bow, in her hair is a pink rose. Like the Infanta, she wears a white dress patterned with broad black stripes. Though she is perhaps twenty years older, she has a similarly sweet expression as she looks out obliquely at the viewer. Renoir has paid particular attention to the folds and creases of the dress material around her elbows and to the way it bunches into her lap, in the same way that Velázquez's workshop suggests the puffiness of the young Infanta's sleeves in contrast to the tightness of the bodice around her waist. Renoir's painting is a marvelous but subtle updating of Velázquez's image, a recognizable homage that retains his own artistic individuality.

With Manet, there is always a much stronger sense of his wish to update the Spanish old masters into a modern idiom. In about 1859–60 Manet made a direct copy after a painting then considered to be by Velázquez, *Meeting of Thirteen People* (or *The Little Cavaliers*, as Manet called them), which had been acquired by the Louvre in 1851 (cat. 100, p. 28; cat. 48, p. 29).[18] Compositionally, Manet changed nothing, though one can see his conscious attempt to loosen up his style in emulation of Velázquez. The Spanish painter concentrated on representing the space around the figures rather than the outlines of the figures themselves, whereas Manet, who uses more black, particularly around the figures, brings a very different kind of clarity to the composition.

Underlying Manet's fascination with the picture was the contemporary belief that the group of men on the left represented Velázquez in conversation with Murillo and other artists. For Manet, whose chief aim was to be a painter of modern life, Velázquez served as a real source of inspiration and helped him in his quest to achieve this. Manet's copy of the *Meeting of Thirteen People* was followed a few years later with one of his greatest masterpieces—*Music in the Tuileries Gardens* (fig. 48). In one of his finest studies of contemporary life, he showed himself in conversation with fellow artists, literary figures, and composers.

In August 1862 a troupe of Spanish dancers from Madrid, directed by Don Mariano Camprubi of the Teatro Real, came to Paris and performed at the Hippodrome for three months (August 12–November 2). This gave Manet an ideal opportunity to capture a taste of real Spain in paint. He is said to have persuaded the whole troupe to pose for him in the studio of the Belgian artist Alfred Stevens, because it was much larger than his own. The result of this "sitting" is seen in *Spanish Ballet* (1862; The Phillips Collection, Washington, D.C.), which he structured very much along the lines of *The Little Cavaliers*. Dancers and musicians are spaced across the canvas without any indication of a defined space or setting. Manet also made individual portraits of dancers, such as *Lola de Valence* (1862–63; Musée d'Orsay, Paris) and *Don Mariano Camprubi* (1862–63; private collection, United States). Although these are among Manet's most successful Spanish-style paintings, the manner in which he conceived them—in a studio, with

Fig. 47
Pierre-Auguste Renoir
La Loge (Theatre Box), 1874
Oil on canvas, 31½ × 25 in.
(80 × 63.5 cm)
Courtauld Institute of Art Gallery, London, Samuel Courtauld; Bequest, 1948

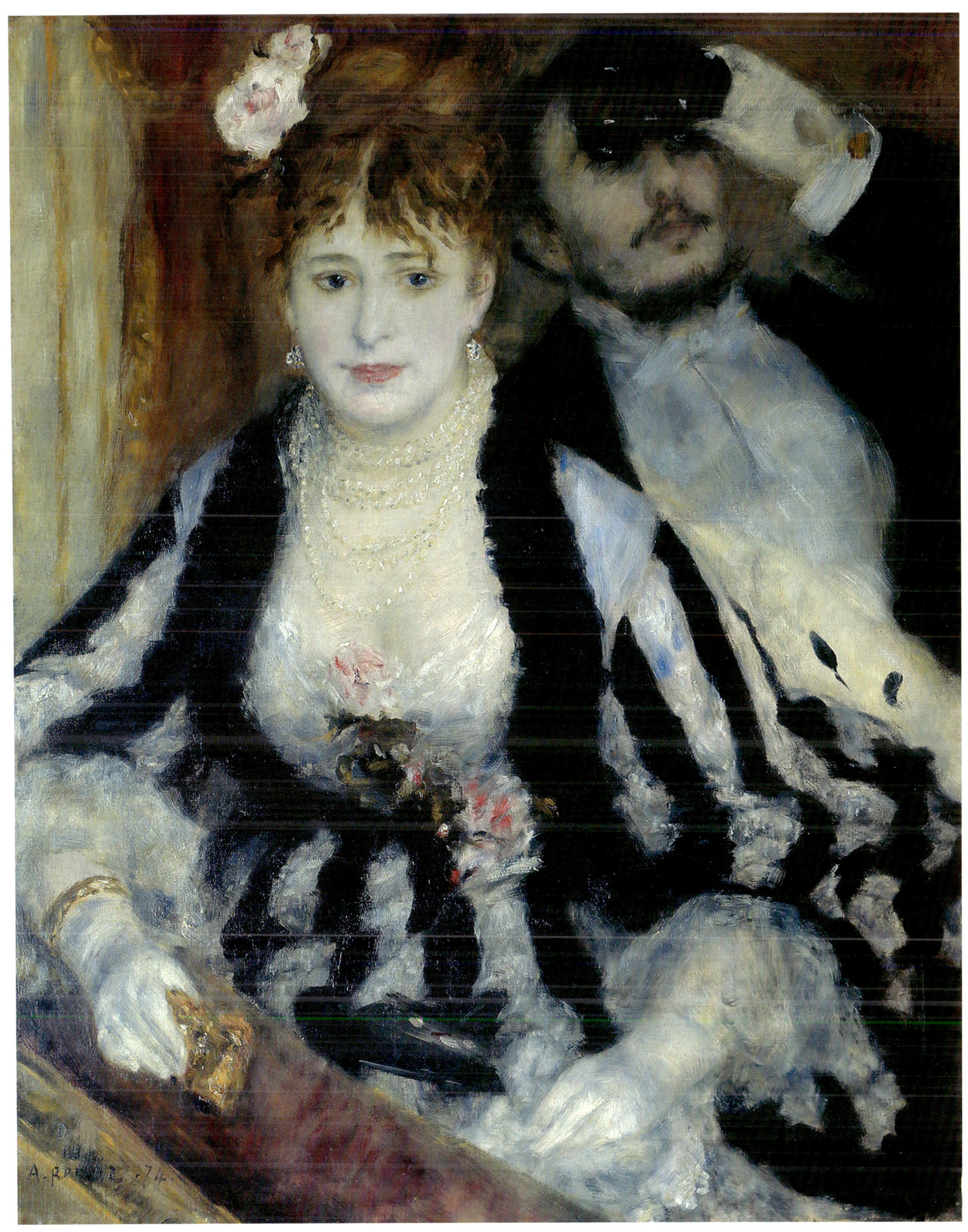

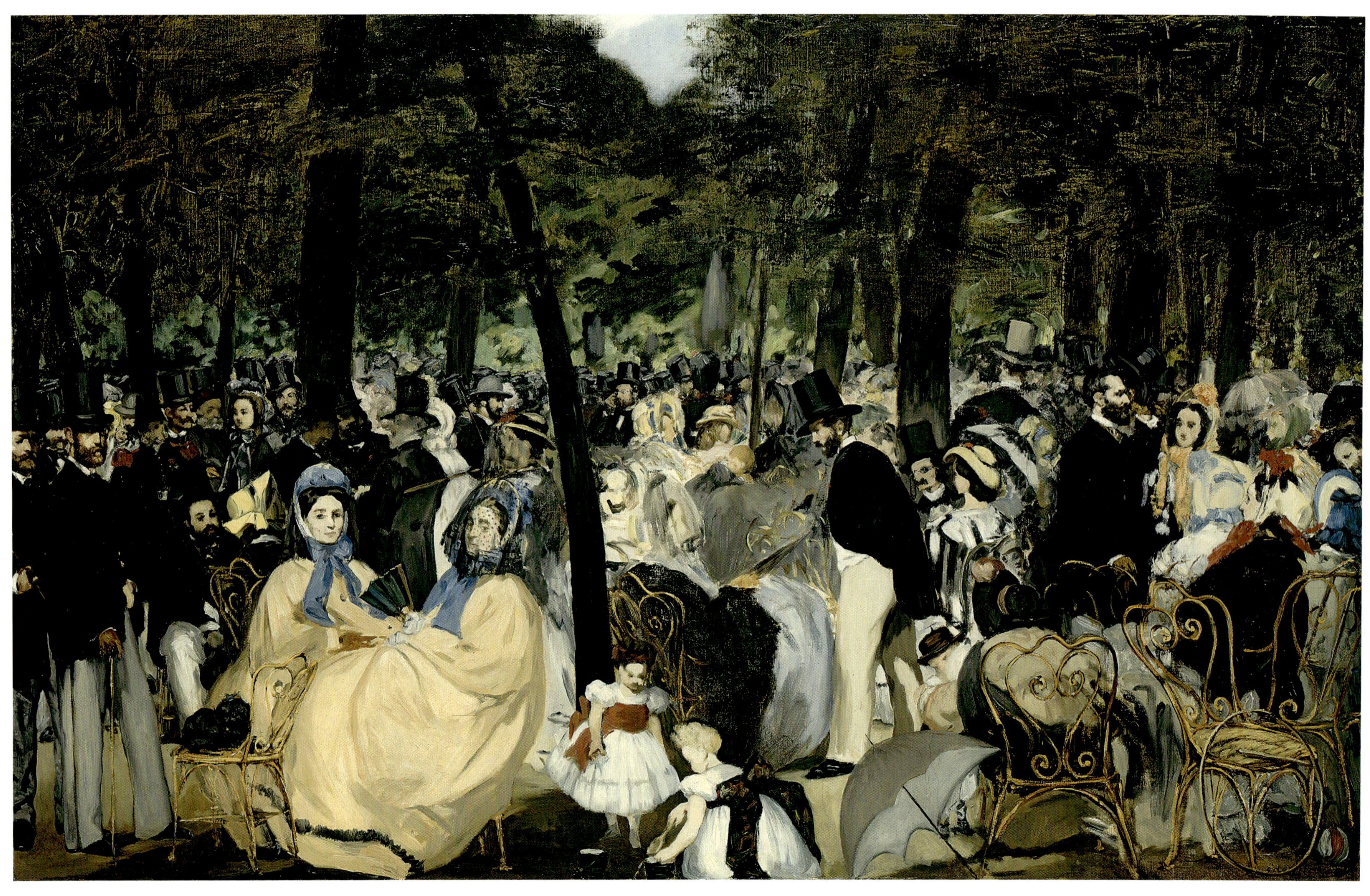

Fig. 48
Édouard Manet
Music in the Tuileries Gardens, 1862
Oil (identified) on canvas, 30 × 46½ in.
(76.2 × 118.1 cm)
The National Gallery, London,
Sir Hugh Lane Bequest, 1917, NG3260

Fig. 49
Édouard Manet
Monk in Prayer, 1865
Oil on canvas, 57⅝ × 45¼ in.
(146.4 × 115 cm)
Museum of Fine Arts, Boston,
Anna Mitchell Richards Fund, 35.67

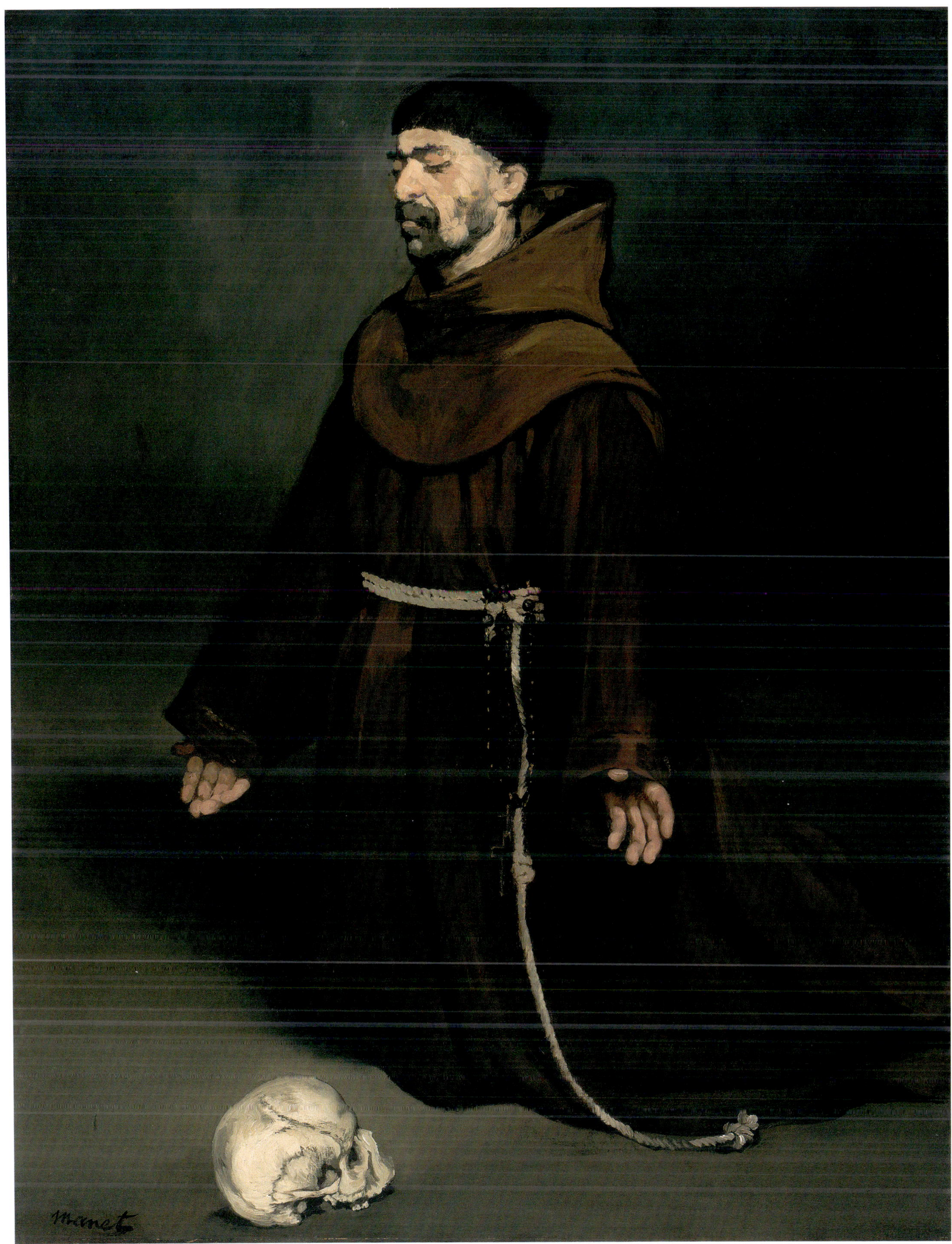
manet

Fig. 50
Italian
A Dead Soldier, 17th century
Oil on canvas, 41¼ × 65¾ in.
(104.8 × 167 cm)
The National Gallery, London

Fig. 51
Édouard Manet
The Dead Toreador, probably 1864
Oil on canvas, 29⅞ × 60⅜ in.
(75.9 × 153.3 cm)
National Gallery of Art, Washington,
Widener Collection, 1942.9.40

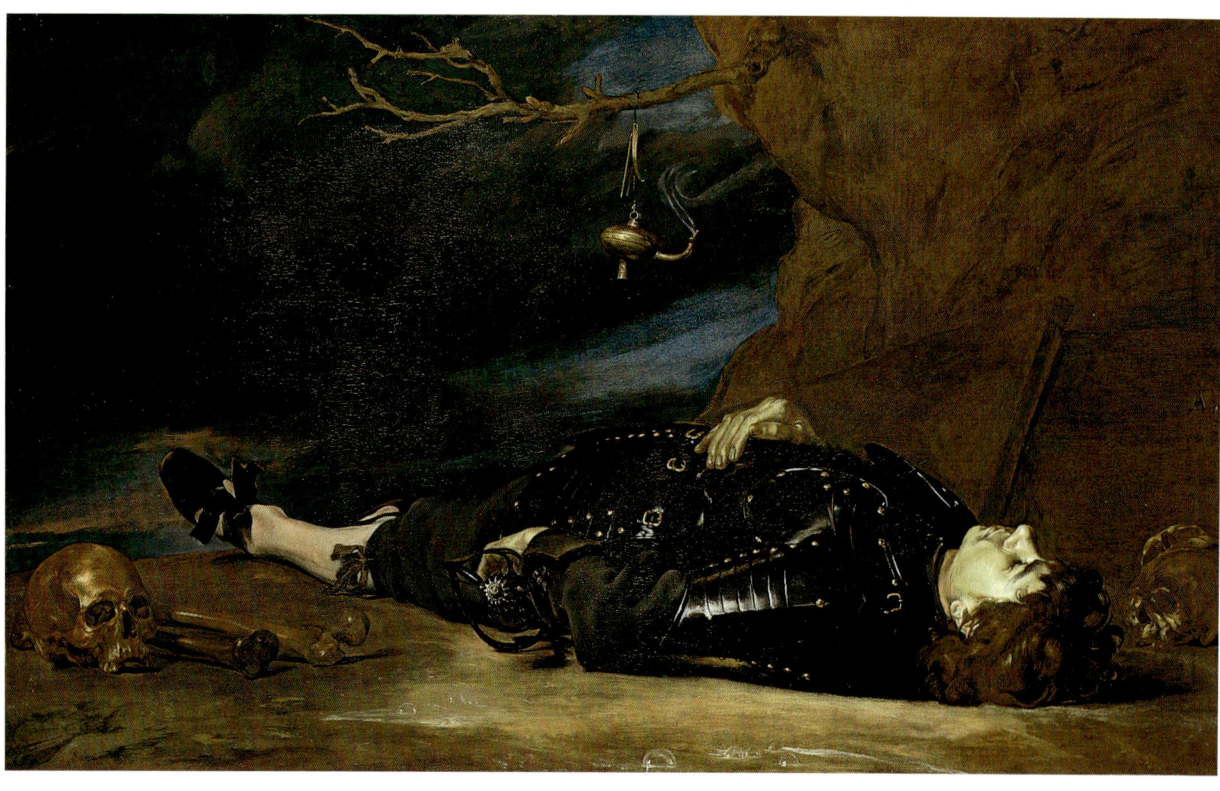

props, costumes, and models in order to create the Hispanic picture he had in mind[19]—went in every way against what would become the tenets of the Impressionist movement, which advocated painting out of doors and capturing the fleeting effects of light.

Yet at this point in the 1860s, Manet had no interest in this type of plein air painting. Instead, he wanted to become a modern painter, and to do this he would make use of the old masters. For Manet, the strong and clear compositions set against neutral grounds of Velázquez or Zurbarán were perfect models. Adapting and modernizing these techniques, Manet could paint pictures that would stand out and catch the eye, ideal for attracting attention at the Salon, where pictures were crammed on top of each other. His *Monk in Prayer* (fig. 49), painted in 1865, is a moving reworking of Zurbarán's *Saint Francis in Meditation,* with which he was familiar through prints. Later, in 1868, he might have seen it in the original when he traveled to London, where the painting was at the time. Zurbarán's achievement in stripping away artifice to capture the essence of man's mortality inspired Manet to do the same—but in a different way. Manet removes the monastic hood to reveal the model's face. His eyes are closed and hands are spread out so as to open himself to the divine. Manet's monk is an up-to-date rendition of a Capuchin monk in prayer; Spanish mysticism has been turned into a more universal interpretation of man's mortality.

Manet's dependence on Spanish precedents could go against him, however. In 1864 he submitted to the Salon *Incident at a Bullfight* (*Episode d'une course de taureaux*). The picture attracted protest and hilarity from both critics and the public, who criticized its implausible perspective—the bull was too small and the torero too large. It was obvious that Manet at this date had never actually seen a bullfight. For the main figure of his complex composition, the dead toreador, he used a celebrated painting, then attributed to Velázquez, the so-called *Dead Soldier* in the Portalès collection, Paris (fig. 50). Manet was fascinated by the corpse of this youthful warrior in black silk, lying surrounded by skulls, rendered in a limited palette and with macabre realism. The transformation from the old to the new was not entirely successful this time, and he produced a painting that as a whole did not have the impact he wished for. Conscious of this, Manet cut up the canvas and reworked *The Dead Toreador,* or *L'Homme Mort,* as he called it, as a single-figure picture (fig. 51).[20]

Today, this work is regarded as one of his supreme masterpieces, yet at the time Manet realized that his uncut picture was flawed. It was time to go to Spain and seek advice from Maître Velázquez

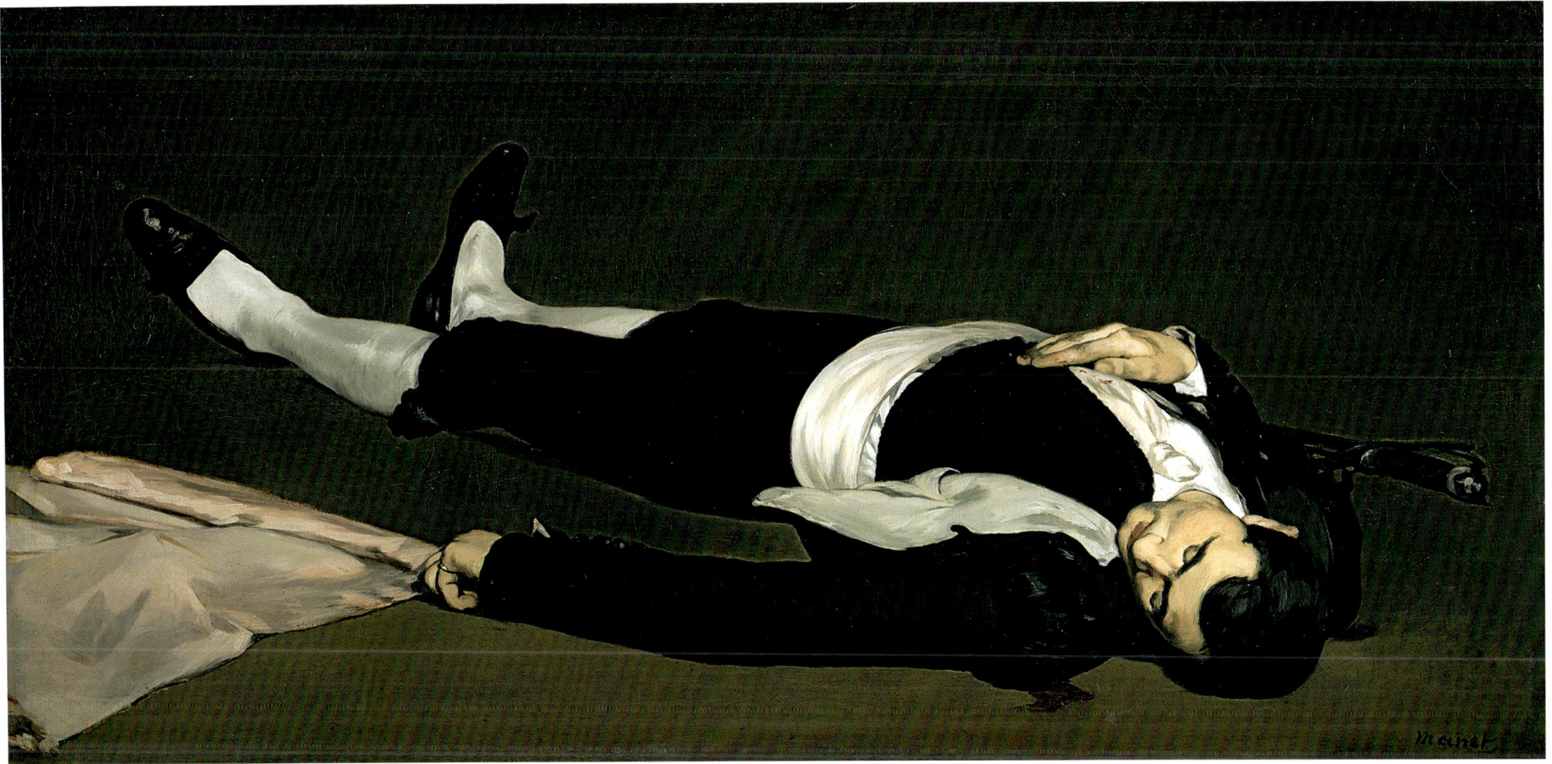

and see a bullfight. Arriving in Madrid at the end of August 1865, he met the cognac merchant and future champion of the Impressionists, Théodore Duret, who was to become his traveling companion. (Later he would paint Duret's portrait à la Velázquez [cat. 56, p. 221].) After the experience of seeing paintings by Velázquez at the Prado, Manet wrote enthusiastically to his friend the painter Henri Fantin-Latour: it is "Velázquez who all by himself makes the journey worthwhile. . . . He is the supreme artist; he didn't surprise me, he enchanted me."[21] Manet describes Velázquez's masterpieces such as *Las Meninas* (fig. 58) and the dwarf and philosopher portraits as "amazing pieces. Still, the portrait of the actor Pablo de Valladolid (fig. 52) particularly excited him; he claimed that it was "the most extraordinary piece of painting that has ever been done . . . the background disappears, there's nothing but air surrounding the fellow, who is all in black and appears alive."[22]

After his return to Paris, Manet made use of this picture on several occasions. His *The Tragic Actor (Rouvière as Hamlet)* (fig. 53) and *The Fifer* (1866; Musée d'Orsay, Paris) employ the same neutral beige background to bring the figures into our space. Manet submitted both to the Salon of 1866, but both were rejected, possibly because of their stark simplicity. By contrast, the bullfight he saw in Madrid was to serve him well. *Bullring in Madrid* (1865–67; Musée d'Orsay, Paris), *Bullfight* (The Art Institute of Chicago), and *The Saluting Torero* (1865; The Metropolitan Museum of Art, New York) were based on quick pencil sketches made on the spot. As a result, they are infinitely more atmospheric and genuine than his earlier attempt to render a bullfight. In doing so, Manet was unconsciously allying himself with what would become during the following decade the chief aim of the Impressionists, that of capturing the impression of a moment. To avoid being rejected by the Salon jury in 1867, Manet organized his own solo exhibition, held in a pavilion near the grounds of the great Exposition Universelle. Almost half of the fifty-three works exhibited were of Spanish or Spanish-related subjects. Referring to *The Fifer* and *The Tragic Actor,* one critic described Manet as the "*Velasquez of the boulevards* or a Spaniard of Paris."[23] Manet had at last succeeded in his aim of becoming a painter of modern life through his updating of Spanish precedents.

Meanwhile, Cézanne, who was at the outset of his career, was making use of the Spanish old masters in an entirely different way. Among his first canvases, many of which show a fascination for violent imagery, is a macabre painting—*The Autopsy (Preparation for the Funeral)* (fig. 54)—which is an extraordinary translation of Ribera.

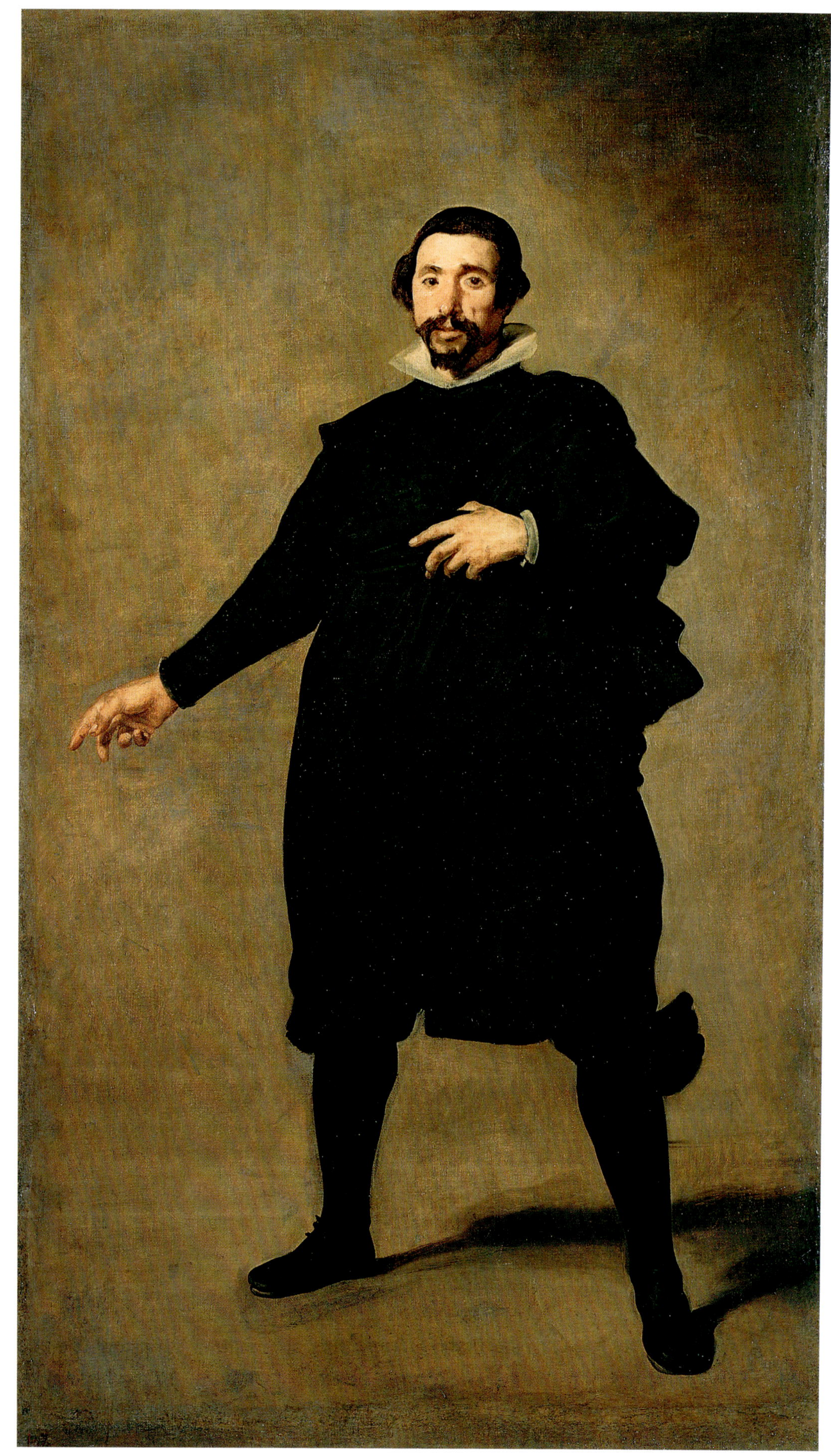

Fig. 52
Diego Rodríguez de Silva y Velázquez
The Jester Pablo de Valladolid,
ca. 1632–35
Oil on canvas, 84 × 49½ in.
(213.4 × 125.7 cm)
Museo Nacional del Prado, Madrid

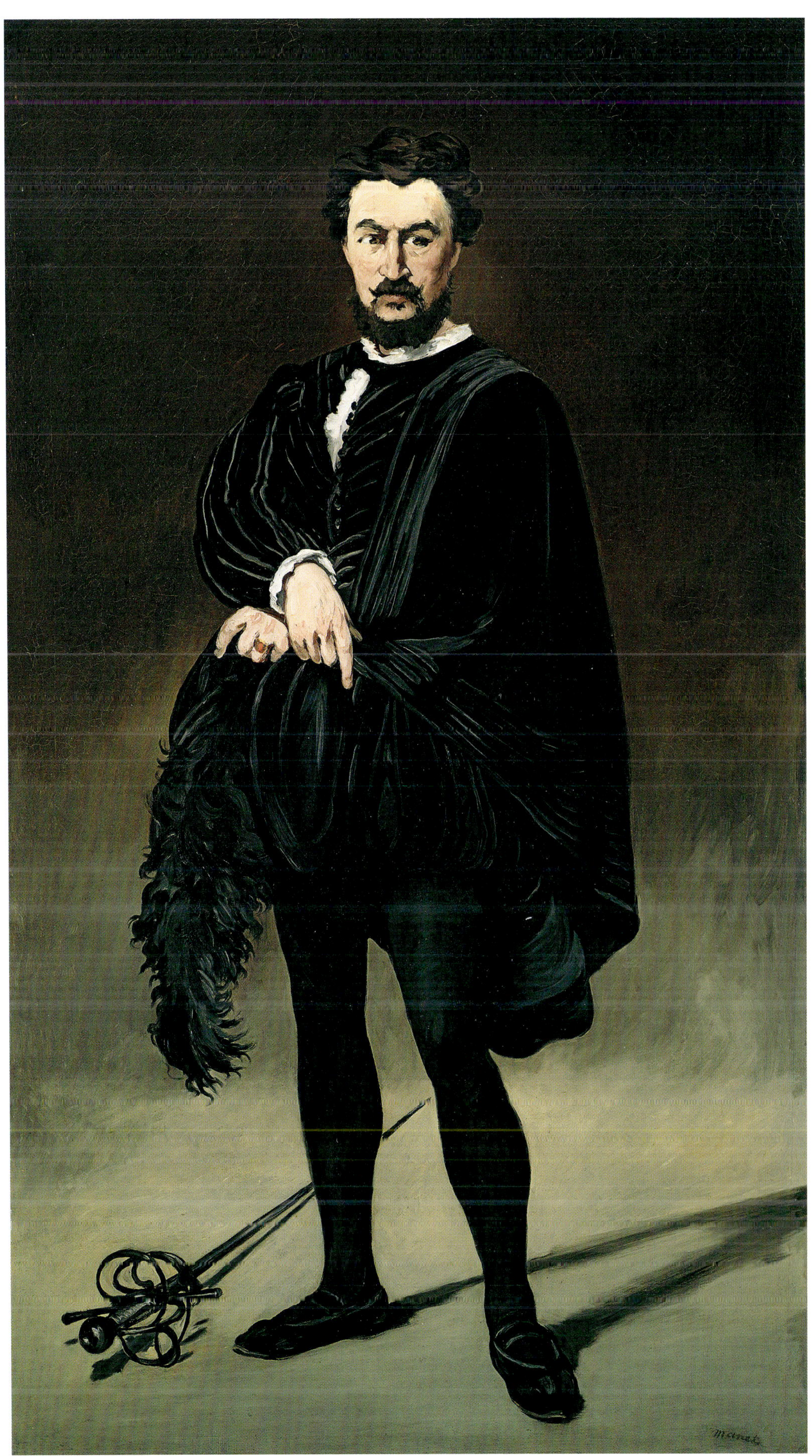

Fig. 53
Édouard Manet
The Tragic Actor (Rouvière as Hamlet), 1866
Oil on canvas, 73¾ × 42½ in. (187.2 × 108.1 cm)
National Gallery of Art, Washington, Gift of Edith Stuyvesant Gerry, 1959.3.1

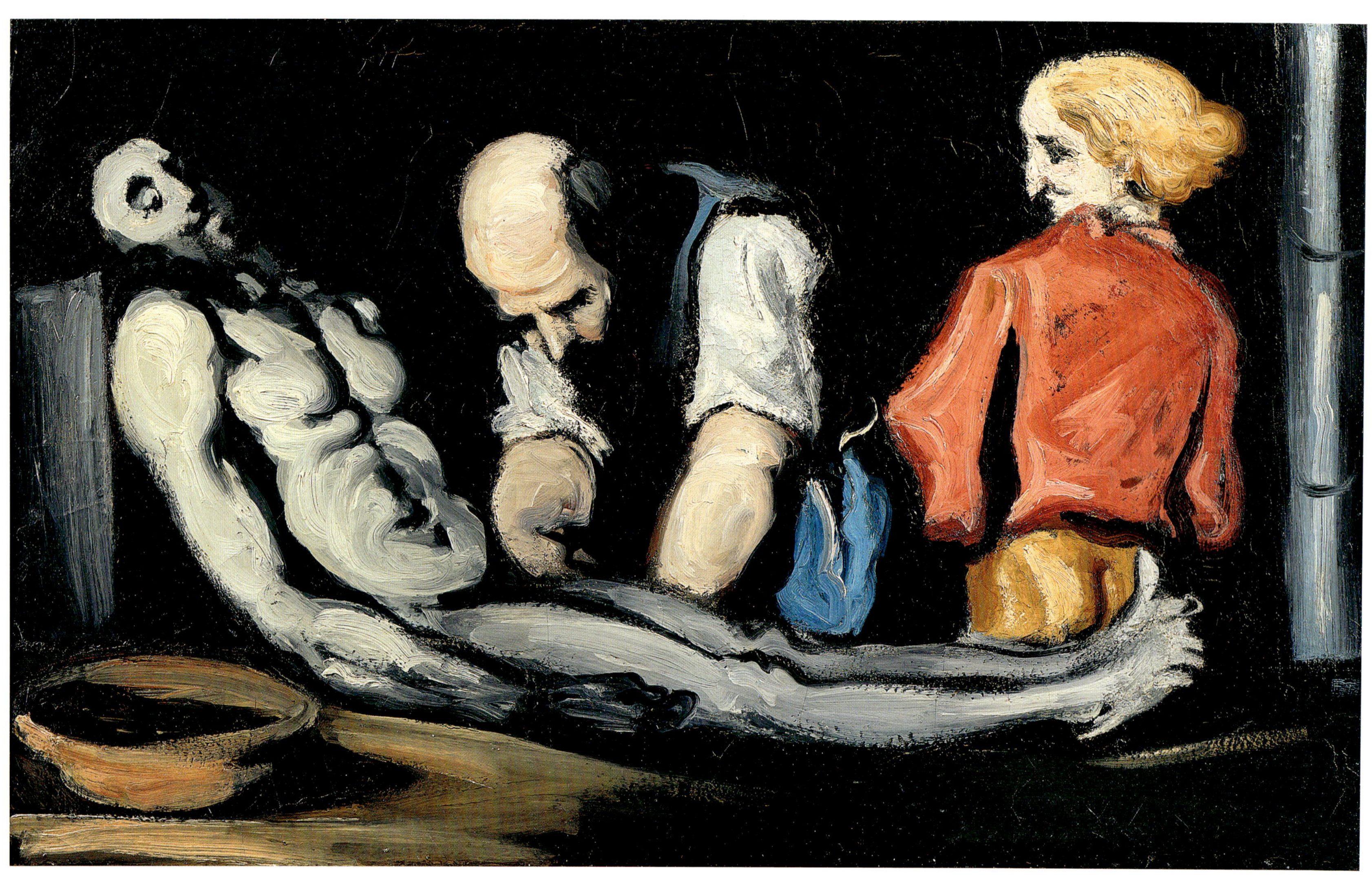

Fig. 54
Paul Cézanne
The Autopsy (Preparation for the Funeral), 1869
Oil on canvas, 19½ × 31⅝ in. (49.5 × 80.5 cm)
Private collection, courtesy of Pyms Gallery, London

In 1868 the Louvre had acquired Ribera's *Entombment,* in which the body of Christ, heavy and monumental, is being lifted into his tomb.[24] Cézanne transformed Ribera's dramatic staging of the New Testament subject into a secular meditation on death. A cadaver lies on a table, its rigid body roughly propped up against an upturned crate. A middle-aged woman and a bald, bearded man, whose features resemble Cézanne's own, attend the corpse, perhaps washing it in preparation for burial. The somber scene is crudely lit with an intense chiaroscuro that enhances its emotive power. The raw intensity of Ribera's painting is emulated by Cézanne, although nowadays it is Cézanne's turbulent inner personal life that is more often cited as its cause.[25]

Far less well known as an artist than either Cézanne or Manet was the latter's great friend Zacharie Astruc. Astruc was a painter, critic, sculptor, poet, and collector of Spanish art, who exhibited at the first Impressionist exhibition in 1874 and had traveled to Spain between February and May 1864.[26] The trip was the result of a long and passionate involvement with Spanish culture, initially inspired by childhood reading of Victor Hugo and Alfred de Musset. Perhaps because of his intimate knowledge of the Hispanic world, Astruc became fascinated with a medium that few appreciated—that of Golden Age polychrome sculpture.

On his return to Spain in 1872, Astruc made an exact replica of a small painted wood sculpture, *Saint Francis Standing,* then attributed to Alonso Cano and displayed in the sacristy of the Cathedral of Toledo but today recognized as by Pedro de Mena (fig. 55).[27] Although something of a forgotten medium today, in the nineteenth century this small piece of sculpture was esteemed as an extremely precious object. The art of polychromy was one of remarkable refinement, and this sculpture rendered the dead but standing Saint Francis with terrifying truth that transfixed viewers. It was considered "a masterpiece of cadaverous ecstatic sentiment"[28] and so jealously guarded by the canons of the cathedral that they refused to let the king of Brazil see it in 1869. Astruc had to wait three months before permission was given to make his copy, which had been commissioned by the president of the French Republic, Louis Thiers, for his Musée des Copies.[29]

Astruc's copy perfectly captures the psychological presence of this celebrated piece. French critics hailed it as a sensation, praising its "réalisme farouche," when it was brought back to Paris in 1874.[30] It was seen and acclaimed privately by Astruc's friends, including Manet and Alfred Stevens, and then exhibited by the dealer Goupil in

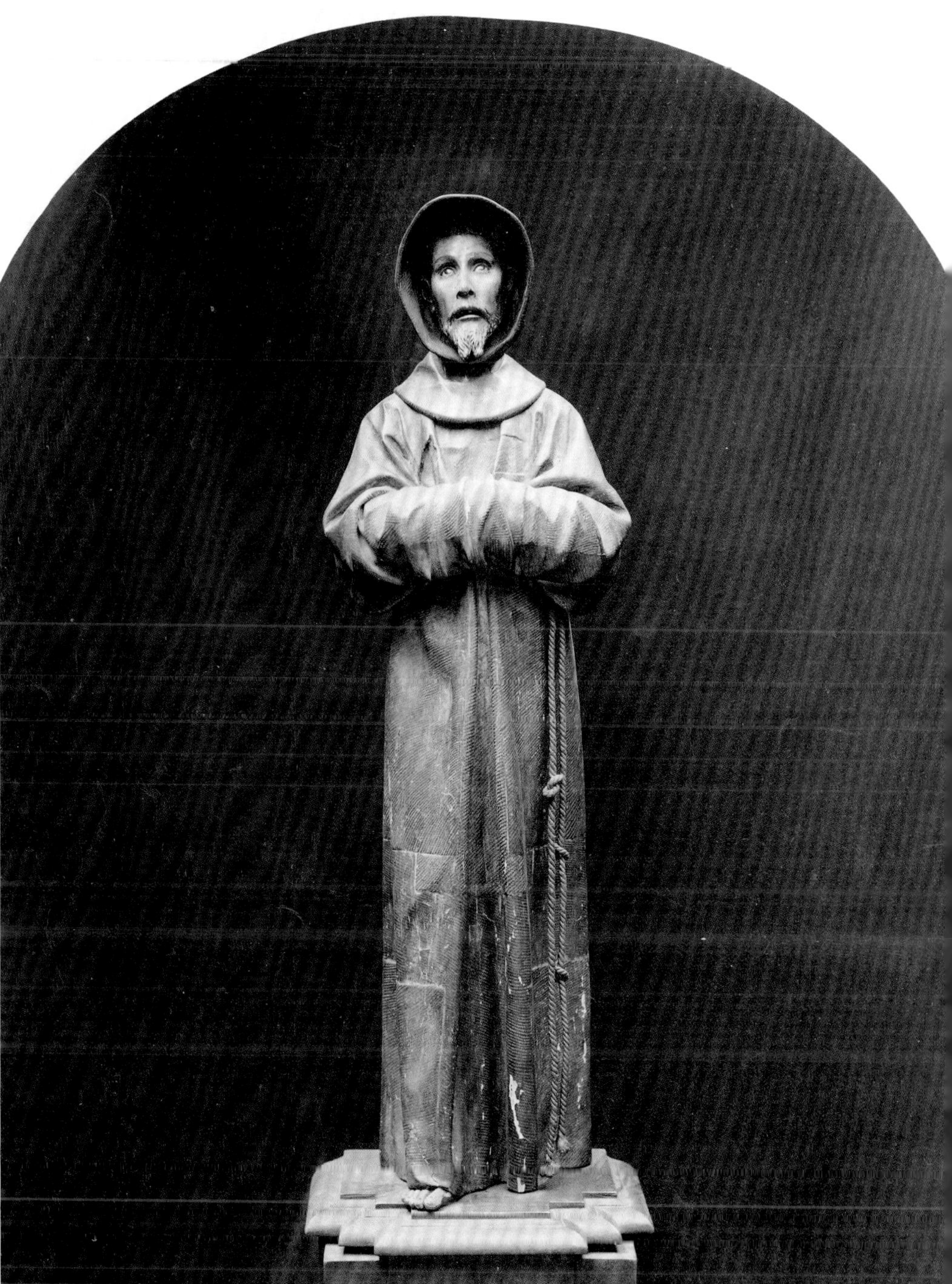

Fig. 55
Zacharie Astruc, after the original by Pedro de Mena in the Sacristy of Toledo Cathedral
Saint Francis Standing, 1872–73
Polychromed wood, 34¼ in. (87 cm)
Ny Carlsberg Glyptotek, Copenhagen

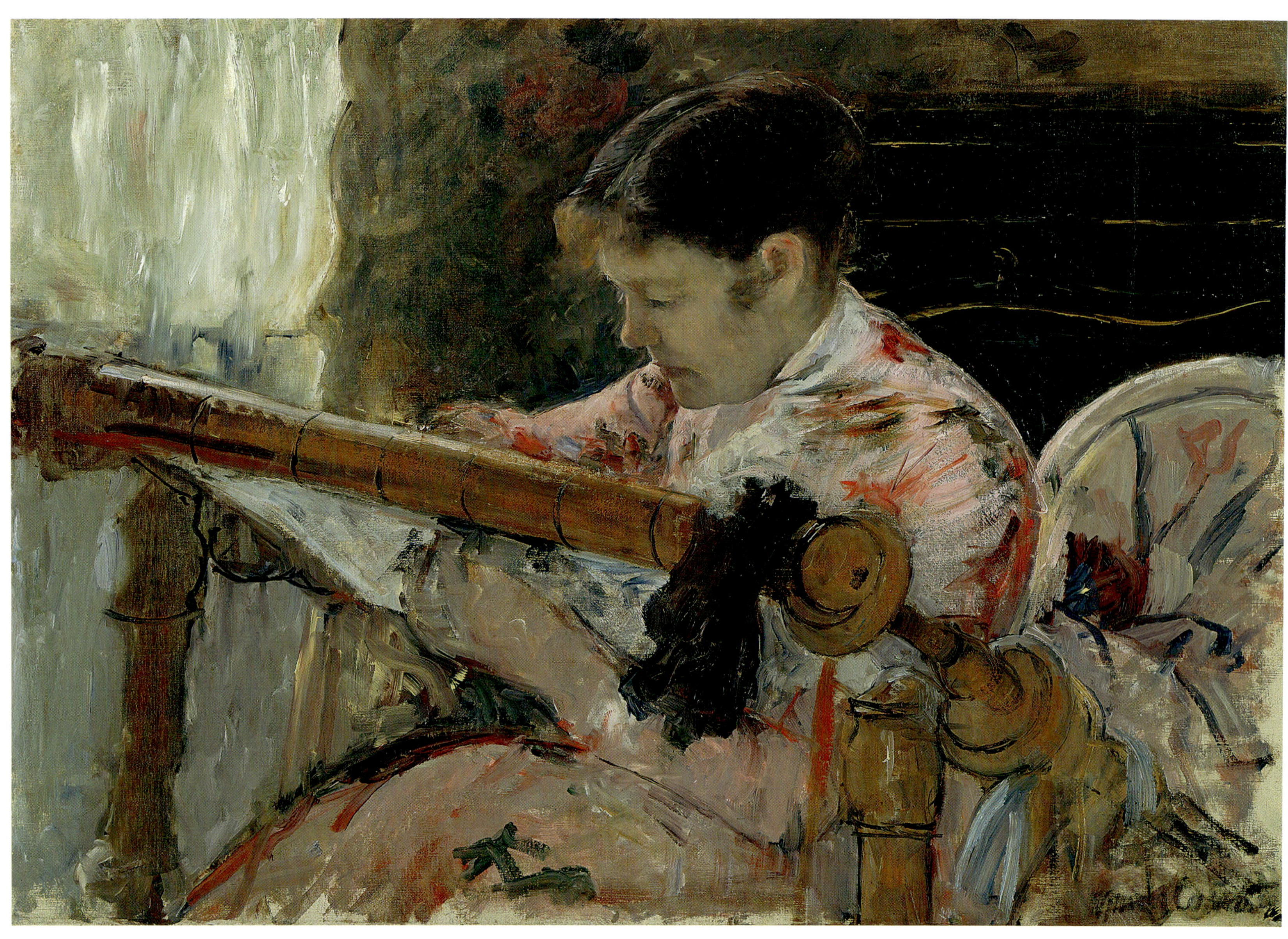

Fig. 56
Mary Cassatt
Lydia at a Tapestry Frame, c. 1881
Oil on canvas, 24⅝ × 36¾ in. (65.5 × 92 cm)
Flint Institute of Arts, Michigan, 1967.32

his shop window, where it was seen and commended by a writer for the newspaper *Le Figaro*.[31] The following year, Astruc's copy, together with a bronze and marble reproduction by Christofle & Compagnie, were displayed at the *Exposition des Arts Industriels de l'Union Central* at the Palais de l'Industrie.[32] Such was the critical acclaim that a book containing nothing but excerpts of press reviews was printed.[33] Astruc's sculpture was subsequently mass-produced in bronze and marble, and in 1889 he was asked to produce a larger version, which was placed in the newly completed Cathedral of the Sacré Coeur in Paris. The extraordinary public response to this sculpture shows how this type of Spanish Catholic art struck a chord with the French people at this date.

It seems also to have struck a particular chord with one member of the Impressionist group, Degas, who in 1881 exhibited the only sculpture he would ever show in public at the sixth Impressionist exhibition, *The Little Fourteen-Year-Old Dancer*. Degas's *Little Dancer* was made of tinted wax and had real black hair that was tied back with a ribbon. Wearing a tulle and gauze skirt, she stands with her legs in a relaxed fourth position, hands clasped behind her back, with her small face tilted upward, in a manner not at all dissimilar to the way Astruc's copy of Pedro de Mena's *Saint Francis* lifts his chin and peers out of his monastic cowl. This was an attempt at a new type of realism for Degas and it seemed in many respects to recall the realism of Spanish sculpture. Indeed, the critic Jules Claretie commented that she is "of a strangely attractive, disturbing, and unique Naturalism, which recalls with a very Parisian and polished note the Realism of Spanish polychromed sculpture."[34]

However, Degas's *Little Dancer,* which interestingly stands almost at the same height as the *Saint Francis* (39 in. versus 34¼ in.), met with fierce disapproval from the critics. One wrote, "If he wants to show us a statuette of a dancer, he chooses her from among the most odiously ugly. . . . And, yes, certainly among the dregs of the dance schools are poor girls who look like this young monster. . . . but what is the use of these things in the art of sculpture? Put them in a museum of zoology, anthropology, or physiology, fine; but in a museum of art, forget it!"[35] This hostility was, however, very much to the point, as Degas was clearly using the sculpture to question accepted ideas of art. Joris-Karl Huysmans, a generally more sympathetic critic, observed: "The terrible realism of this statuette makes the public distinctly uneasy, all its ideas about sculpture, about cold, lifeless whiteness, about those memorable formulas copied again and again for centuries, are demolished. The fact is that on the first blow, M. Degas has knocked over the traditions of sculpture."[36]

From the Impressionist's perspective, however, the abiding legacy of the Spanish old masters would remain the free and magical touch of Velázquez's brushwork. The seemingly contradictory effect of his technique—from close up his brushwork looked loose and disparate but as one stepped back it came into sharp focus—fascinated those interested in optical effects. From the 1870s onward several figures who would become the Impressionists made pilgrimages to Madrid in search of something better than the weak examples of Velázquez's work in the Louvre, to experience what Manet had in 1865. Morisot traveled to Madrid in the summer of 1872, staying with Astruc and closely studying Velázquez and Goya at the Prado. Although we know little of her reactions, her spirited brushwork is surely testimony to the influence of Velázquez. Certainly Cassatt, who on October 5 that same year registered as a copyist at the Prado and made sketches after Velázquez's *Spinners* (1658; Museo del Prado, Madrid), was amazed by Velázquez's "freedom of touch"[37] and wrote to a friend saying, "I think that one learns how to paint here, Velasquez's manner is so fine and so simple."[38] The lessons she learned from Velázquez's *Spinners* are echoed in her *Lydia at a Tapestry Frame* (fig. 56), one of her finest meditations on the art of representing movement through brushwork.[39] By 1879 Velázquez was officially regarded as the precursor of Impressionism. Paul Lefort, in his essay "Velazquez" published that year in the *Gazette des Beaux-Arts*, recognized the modernity of his technique, which, according to him, "our Impressionists, that young avant-garde school, have only just begun to imitate."[40]

Degas, too, visited Madrid in 1889,[41] but it was Renoir's sojourn in May–June 1892 that represents the climax of the Impressionist interest in Velázquez. His dealer and friend Ambroise Vollard reported that Renoir said of his trip:

> If it hadn't been for the Prado, I should have turned round and come right home the same day. But I couldn't miss Velasquez. . . . What I love so much is that aristocratic quality that you find over and over again in Velasquez. . . . I know that the critics find fault . . . for his too great facility. . . . Only the painter, who knows his business thoroughly, can create the impression that a picture was done at one stroke.[42]

Soon after his return to Paris, Renoir painted one of his masterpieces, *The Artist's Family* (fig. 57), based on Velázquez's *Las Meninas*

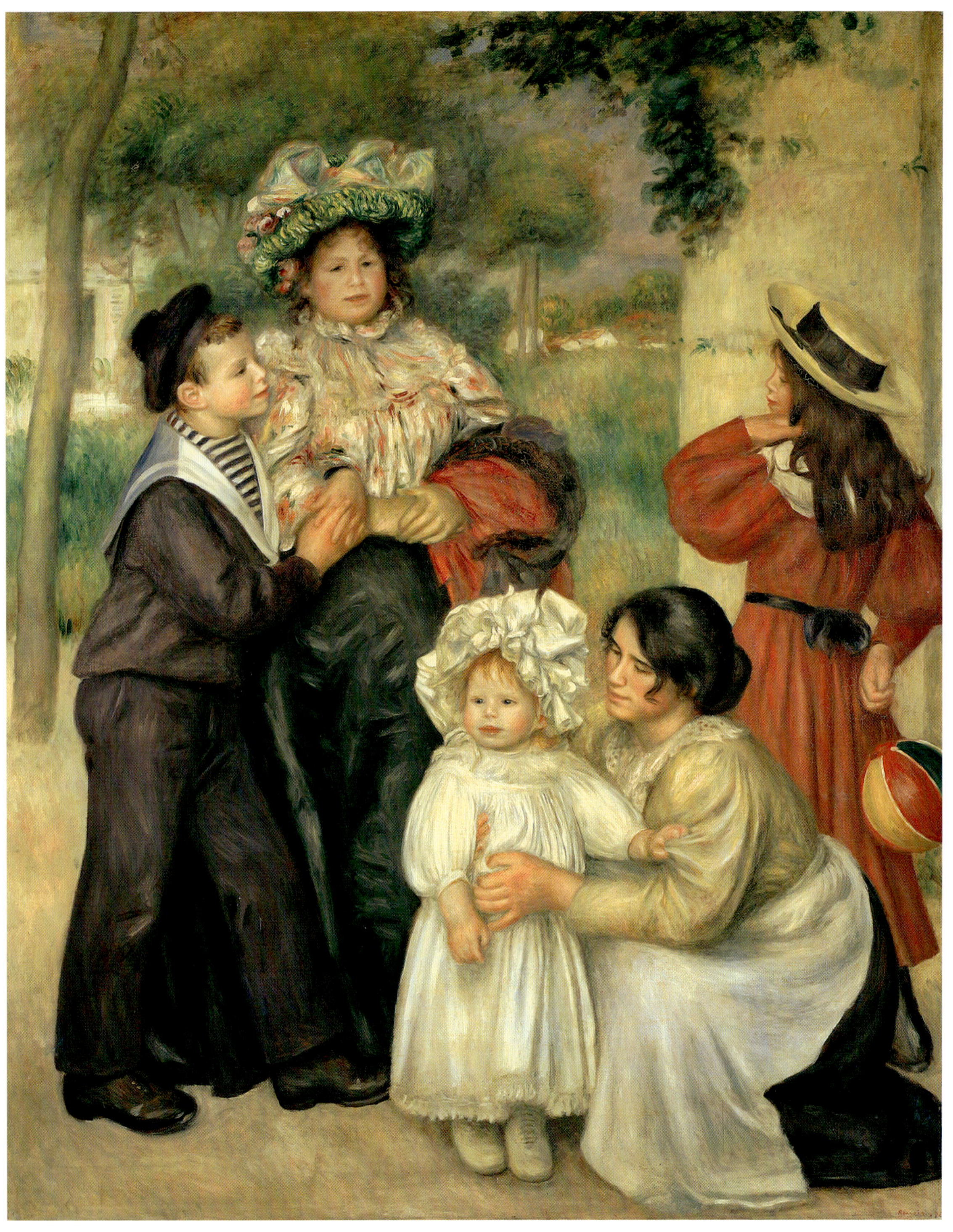

Fig. 57
Pierre-Auguste Renoir
The Artist's Family, 1896
Oil on canvas, 68 × 54 in.
(172.7 × 137.2 cm)
The Barnes Foundation, BF819

Fig. 58
Diego Rodríguez de Silva y Velázquez
Las Meninas, 1656
Oil on canvas, 125⅛ × 108⅝ in.
(318 × 276 cm)
Museo Nacional del Prado, Madrid

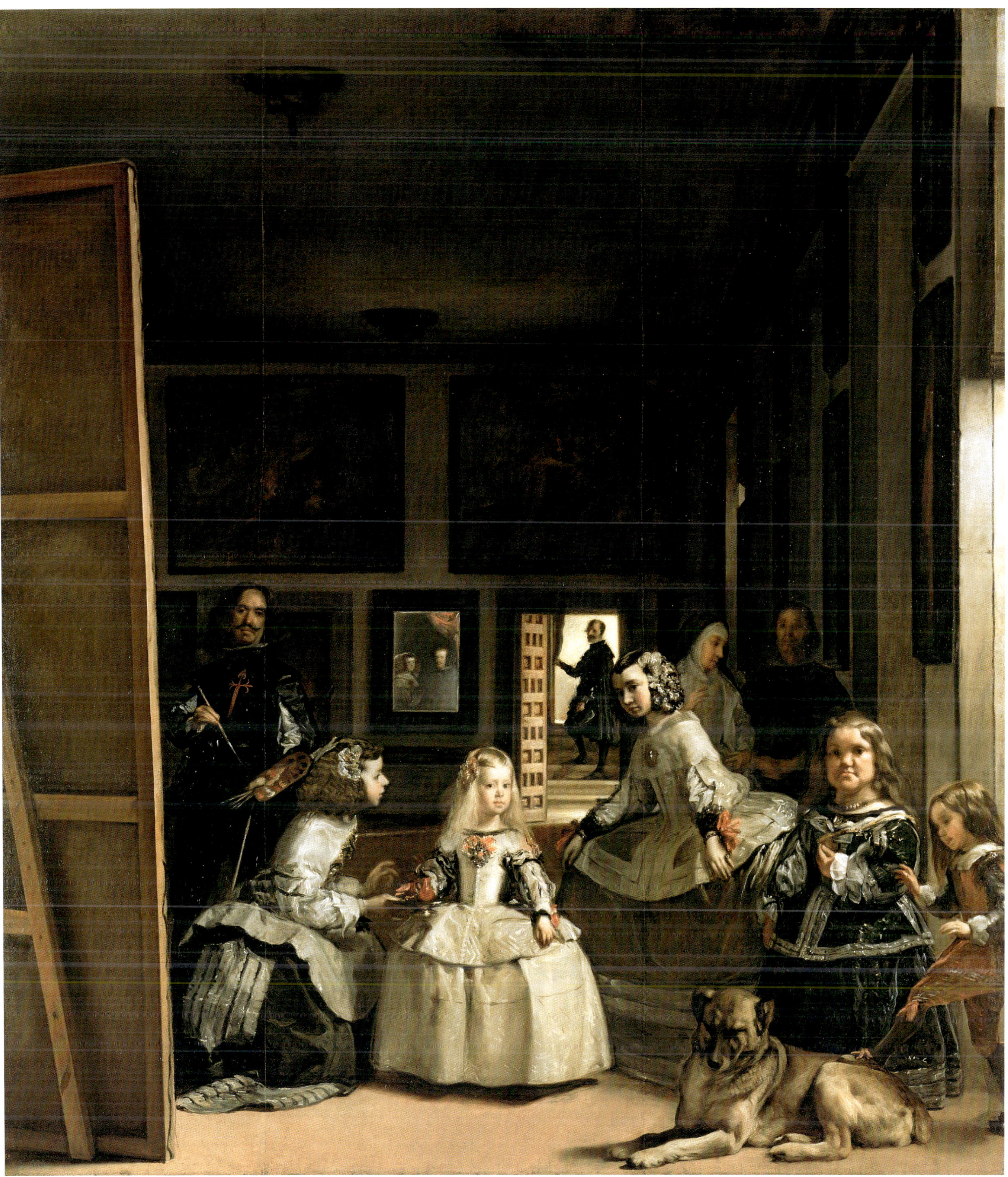

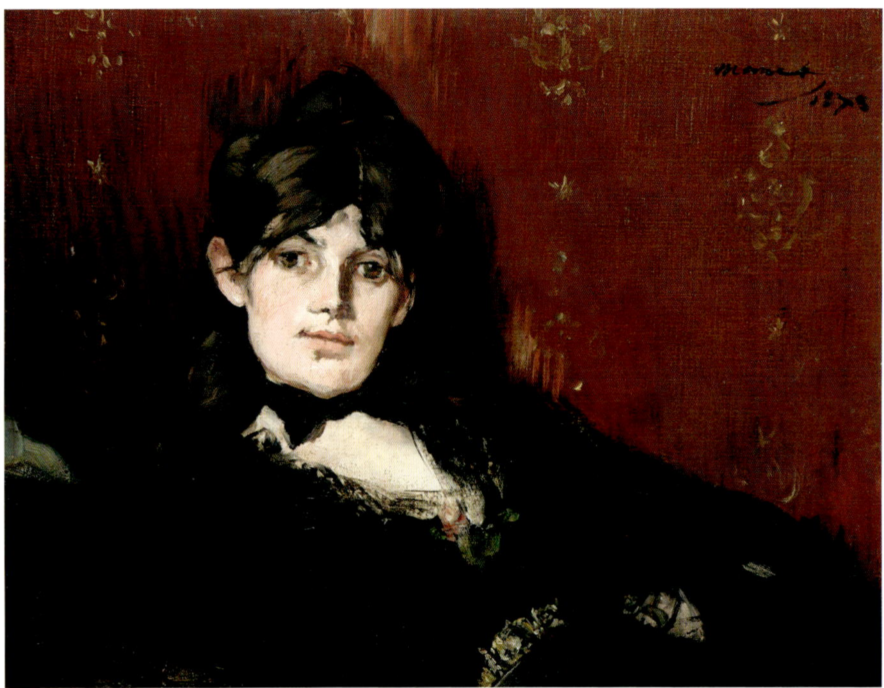

Cat. 57a
Édouard Manet
Portrait of Berthe Morisot (1841–95) Reclining, 1873

(fig. 58), the Spanish master's celebrated portrait of the Spanish royal family. In it, the Infanta Margarita, dressed in silvery white, stands in the foreground of the composition accompanied by her retinue, watching the artist at work. In Renoir's painting, his youngest child, the not-yet-two-year-old Jean, who is also dressed in white and accompanied by a kneeling maid, imitates the pose of one of the Infanta's maids of honor in *Las Meninas*. Behind, stands his elder son, Pierre, holding the arm of his mother, Aline, while he looks across to a young girl, said to be the neighbor's daughter who plays flirtatiously with her hair.[43]

Renoir's family is dressed in their Sunday best and captured, not in a studio like Velázquez's group, but in the open air, in the garden of the château des Brouillards at 13, rue Girardon, Montmartre. In Renoir's hands, *Espagnolisme,* and specifically Velázquez, has metamorphosed into an altogether different French idiom of its own. *Las Meninas* has been updated into an intimate portrait of Renoir's family. When Dr. Albert Barnes first tried to buy the picture from Renoir in 1915, his dealer Durand-Ruel replied that the painter "has always refused to part with it. I believe he wants to give it to the Louvre after his death."[44] Renoir saw *The Artist's Family* as the ideal representative of his art, exemplary of the debt he owed Velázquez.

And yet the artist who was to become the forerunner of twentieth-century art, Cézanne, who was at this time living a solitary existence in Aix-en-Provence far from public view, believed it was fundamental to step away from the old masters. Writing to his friend Charles Camoin on September 13, 1903, Cézanne explains how influential Thomas Couture's lesson had been about learning from the old master painters: *"Keep good company, that is: go to the Louvre,"* but how important it was that "after having seen the great masters who repose there, we must hurry out and, by contact with nature, revive within ourselves the instincts, the artistic sensation which lives within us."[45]

Cézanne's attitude enabled him to form a visual language that was ultimately more revolutionary than that of any of his contemporaries. In spirit, the artist with whom Cézanne shares this approach to artistic representation is the sixteenth-century Greek-born but Spanish-adopted painter, El Greco, rediscovered in the late nineteenth century and hailed by many as a protomodernist. Born on the island of Crete, El Greco lived in the cathedral town of Toledo for thirty-seven years and worked in complete artistic isolation, creating one of the most original styles in art history. His elongated figures and abstraction of real space have a strong affinity with Cézanne's motifs, whether painting the landscape of Provence or figures, particularly his series of *Bathers* (The National Gallery, London). When Pablo Picasso explained the origins of Cubism, he asserted that "we should look for Spanish influence in Cézanne. . . . Observe El Greco's influence on him. A Venetian painter, but he is Cubist in construction."[46]

Ultimately, whether it was the truth of Velázquez or the abstract quality of El Greco, the richness of the legacy of the Spanish old masters gave Manet and the Impressionists fresh impetus in their quest to paint modern life. The lessons they learned from the Spanish masters were invaluable and remain a key to understanding the new style that they created.

Notes

1. Quoted in Manet 1988, p. 15.

2. Manet to Astruc, September 17, 1865, in ibid., p. 50.

3. The painting was relatively well known through an engraving after it, which was published in Reveil 1828–34.

4. The picture, which was bought by the French State, is now in the Musée d'Orsay. See New York 2003, p. 516.

5. Gautier 1890, vol. 2, p. 115.

6. Baticle and Marinas 1981.

7. Thoré 1835.

8. Jubinal 1837, pp. 28–29.

9. "Moines de Zurbarán, blancs chartreux qui dans l'ombre / Glissez silencieux sur les dalles des morts / Murmurant des *Paters* et des *Aves* sans nombre. / Quel crime expiez-vous par de si grands remords." Gautier 1929.

10. Blanc et al. 1869, no. 122 (Zurbarán issue), n.p.

11. For Corot, see New York 2003, p. 470, cat. 97. Zurbarán's *Saint Francis in Meditation* was made into a print on several occasions and would have been well known to artists such as Manet: a lithograph by Eugène Forest was made for *L'Artiste* in 1839; and in 1849 Alphonse Masson made an etching that he exhibited at the 1855 Salon.

12. For Goya and France, see Wilson-Bareau, "Goya and France" 2003.

13. Delteil 1919, no. 12.

14. Reff 1963; Reff, "Louvre" 1964, pp. 555–56; and Boston 1985, p. 43, cat. 16.

15. Stirling-Maxwell 1999, p. 278.

16. Lipschutz 1988, pp. 138–39.

17. "tout l'art de la peinture est là dedans!" quoted in Vollard 1920, p. 146.

18. Manet also made an etching after the painting, which appears in Renoir's *Still Life with Bouquet*, 1871 (see cat. 79, p. 31).

19. One gets a glimpse of Manet's own studio and the props he used in *Still Life with Spanish Hat and Guitar* (1862, Musée Calvet, Avignon).

20. See New York 1999.

21. Cited in New York 2003, p. 231.

22. Ibid.

23. "C'est un *Velasquez* boulevardier, soit, un Espagnol de Paris." Claretie 1867, p. 2.

24. See London 2006, p. 74, cat. 8.

25. See New York 1997, pp. 44–47, lot 113.

26. For a full account on Astruc and Spain, see Flescher 1978.

27. See Anderson 1998, pp. 79–81, no. 9.

28. Ford 1966, vol. 3, p. 1259.

29. Astruc was approached by Joseph Tourny, an artist commissioned by Louis Thiers to copy works of art in Spain. See Flescher 1978, p. 55. It was Charles Blanc, founder of the *Gazette des Beaux-Arts,* who was behind this enterprise. See Boime 1964; and Alvarez Lopera and Naverrete Martínez 1990, pp. 37–40.

30. Demény 1874.

31. Gille 1874.

32. Flescher 1978, pp. 56–57.

33. Silvestre 1875. Astruc's copy was so popular that it was even reviewed in a British magazine: *The Art Monthly Review and Photographic Portfolio* 1, no. 4 (April 29, 1876): 48.

34. Jules Claretie, "La Vie à Paris: Les Artistes indépendants," *Le Temps,* April 5, 1881, cited and translated in Wissman 1986, p. 341. Interestingly, the connection between Degas and polychrome religious sculpture was also made by Nina de Villars in *Le Courrier du Soir,* April 23, 1881 (cited and translated in San Francisco 1986, p. 362): "When I saw in village churches these virgins, these saints of polychromed woods, covered with ornaments, fabrics, and jewelry, I told myself—why does a great artist not have the idea to apply these techniques, so naïve and so charming, to a modern and powerful work, and it is a true joy to find my idea realized here."

35. Henry Trianon, *Le Constitutionel*, April 24, 1881, cited and translated in San Francisco 1986 p. 362.

36. Joris-Karl Huysmans, "L'Exposition des indépendants en 1881," *L'Art Moderne* (Paris: G. Charpentier, 1883), pp. 226–27, cited and translated in Washington 1984, pp. 66–67.

37. Quoted in Mathews 1984, p. 103.

38. Quoted in ibid., pp. 107–8.

39. Bilboa 2002, p. 118, no. 38.

40. "que nos impressionnistes, cette jeune avant-garde de l'école, commencent à peine encore à la balbutier." Lefort 1879, 419.

41. See Reff 1963, p. 251, for Degas's copying of Velázquez's *Menippus*.

42. Vollard 1920, pp. 146–47. English translation is from Vollard 1934, pp. 126–30.

43. For identification of the models, see Christopher Riopelle, catalogue entry, in New York 1993, pp. 76–79.

44. Cited in ibid., p. 79.

45. "*Ayez de bonnes frequentations,* soit: *Allez au Louvre.* Mais après avoir vu les grands maîtres qui y reposent, il faut se hâter d'en sortir et vivifier en soi, au contact de la nature, les instincts, les sensations d'art qui resident en nous." Cézanne 1937, p. 255, letter 163.

46. Cited in Richardson 1991, p. 430.

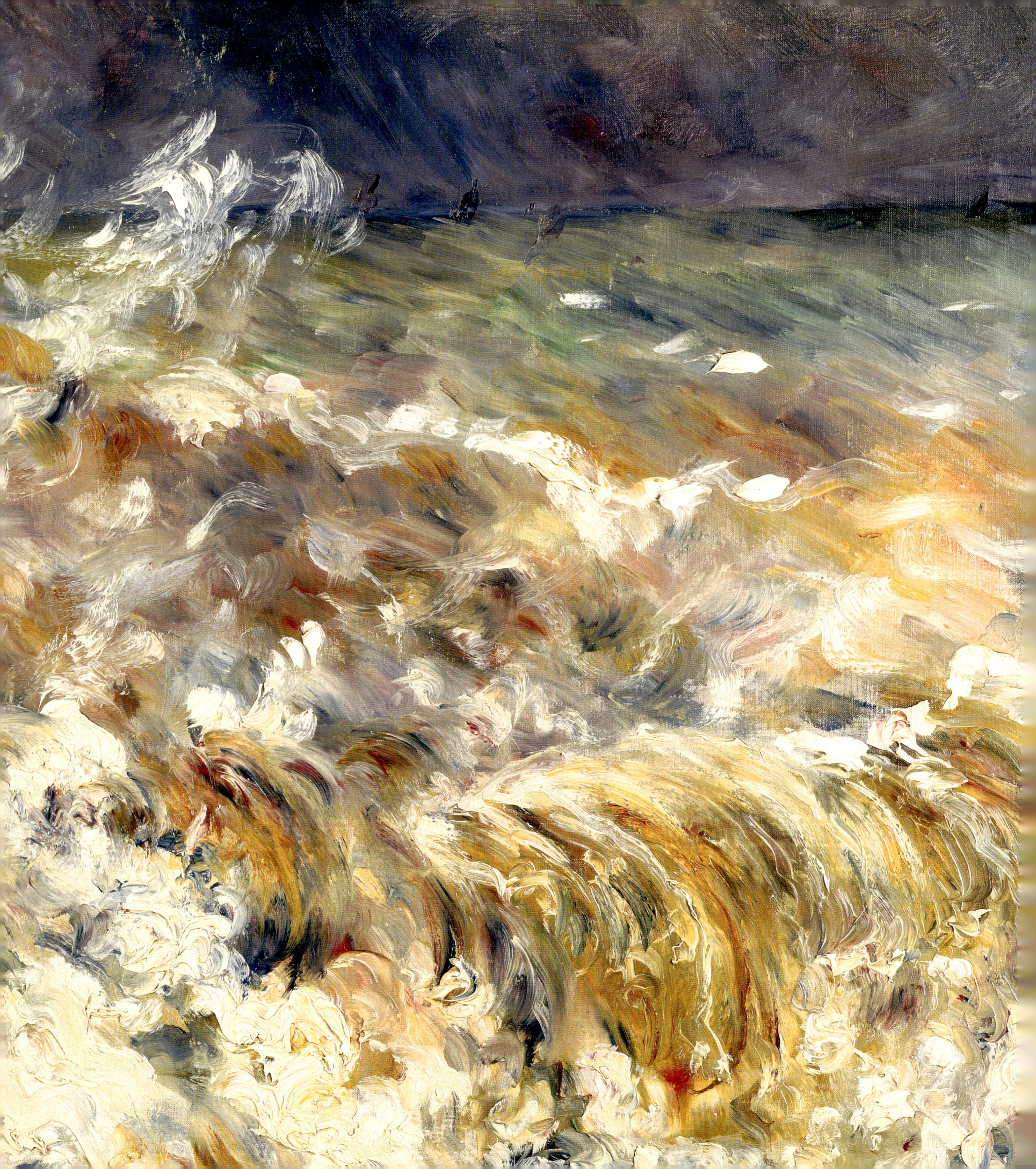

Richard Rand

Impressionism and Eighteenth-Century French Art

Painted in an Hour

At the third independent group exhibition of Impressionist painters, held in the rue le Peletier in Paris in April 1877, Pierre-Auguste Renoir displayed an informal portrait of one of his favorite sitters, the actress Jeanne Samary (fig. 59).[1] Modest in size, the painting features the deftness of touch that during these years characterized Renoir's technique and Impressionism generally. Despite the presence of the now-famous *Ball at the Moulin de la Galette* (fig. 12)—which indeed captured the most attention—among the twenty works exhibited by the artist, the portrait of Samary epitomized Renoir's art for many critics, for better or for worse. For most observers, Renoir's portrayal of the famous actress encapsulated both the positive and the negative aspects of Impressionism; since the sitter was well known and often represented, observers could judge the success of Renoir's portrait as both a work of art and a telling likeness.

The range of responses was correspondingly broad: "It's really just an *impression,* nothing but, or nothing less than, a smile captured on the canvas." "Mlle Samary is altogether adorable . . . like a vaporous apparition on a cloud at twilight." Conversely, "Mlle Samary is

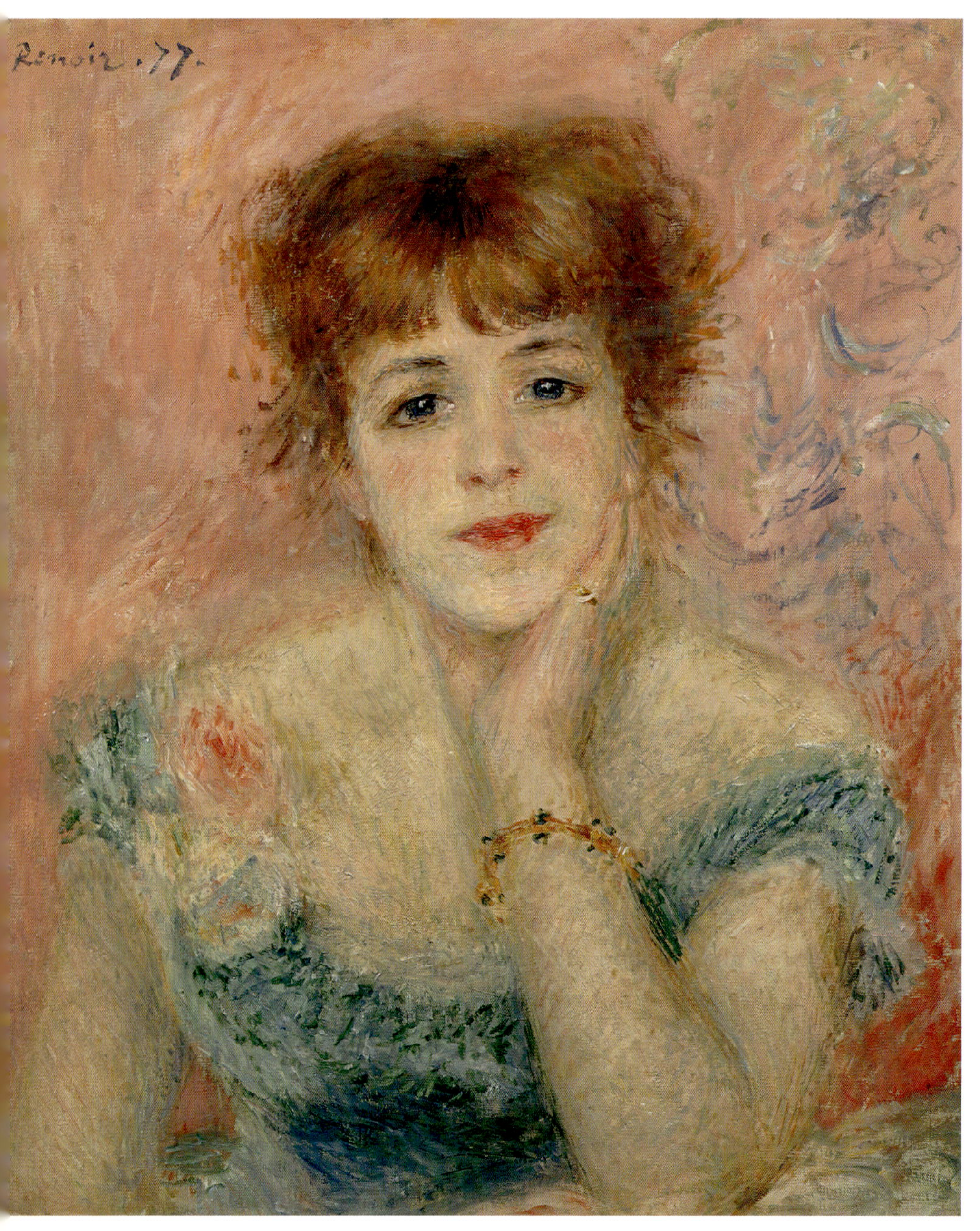

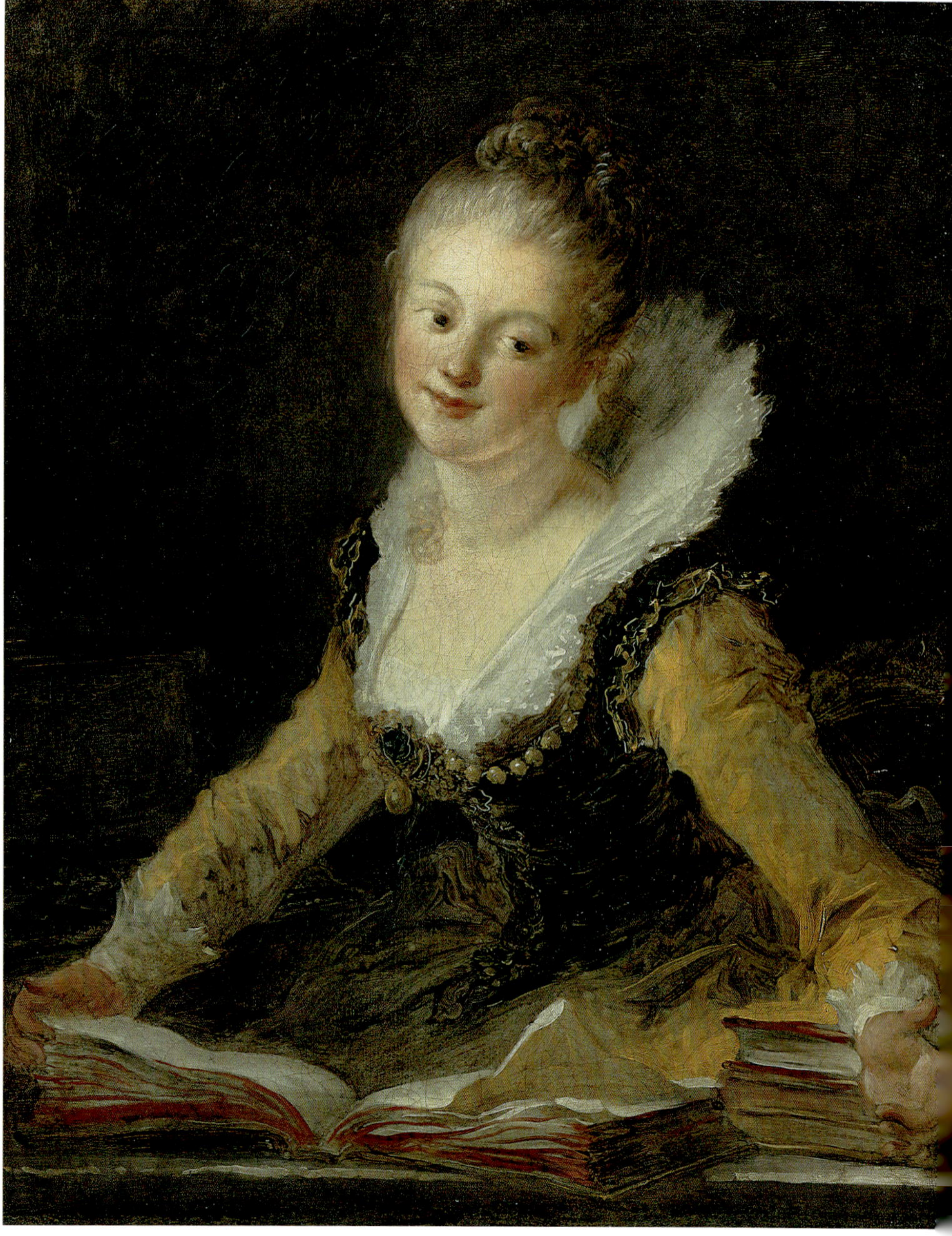

Fig. 59
Pierre-Auguste Renoir
Portrait of Jeanne Samary (La Rêverie), 1877
Oil on canvas, 22 × 18½ in. (56 × 47 cm)
The State Pushkin Museum of Fine Arts, Moscow

Fig. 60
Jean-Honoré Fragonard
Study, c. 1769
Oil on canvas, 31⅞ × 25⅝ in. (81 × 65 cm)
Musée du Louvre, Paris, France

represented as a woman horribly made-up [*platrée*]."[2] All the critics were attentive to the extraordinary technical means Renoir brought to the portrait: "We have no idea what strange process the painter used for the portrait of Mlle S***: on a pink background covered with dots of blue strokes, he dimly blurred a figure without contours, her hair changing from Prussian blue to deep red."[3] For most these aesthetic qualities were unprecedented, representing a new direction in painting decidedly apart from accepted academic practice. But for others Renoir's brushwork and color brought to mind an earlier period of art that in recent decades had enjoyed a revival in the cultural life of Paris: the Rococo painting of eighteenth-century France. This allusion surfaced as a general feeling among some critics: with its bright colors and dancing brushwork the painting "awakens a memory of certain Beauvais tapestries. It's a decorative portrait more than a serious painting."[4] For the prominent critic Philippe Burty it suggested a more specific source and elicited a more positive response: "One would have to go back to the lively sketches [*vives pochades*] of Fragonard to discover a similar sort of portrait painting, not only for a comparable technique, but for a temperament that is so quintessentially French."[5]

In referring to Jean-Honoré Fragonard, Burty may have had in mind a work like *Study,* one of the painter's so-called *portraits de fantaisie* that hung in the Musée du Louvre (fig. 60). To be sure, the earlier work is more highly resolved and maintains a traditional hierarchy of finish—the figure is more resolved than the ground—whereas Renoir's brushwork is "democratic," in that it treats the main subject and background with a similar touch. But both pictures share a fluid and delicate brushwork appropriate to the charms of the women, with red, smiling lips and a coquettish tilt of the head. The identity of Fragonard's subject is unknown, although already in 1860 the painting had acquired the allegorical label of "study." Even though the name of Renoir's sitter was known, the portrait early on acquired its own poetic title, *La Rêverie*.

The consequences of these statements for our understanding of Impressionism's relation to the art of the past are obviously profound, not only because they suggest yet another way of grounding the innovations of Impressionism in tradition—with the implication that it grew out of an appreciation of past art as much as it heralded a new approach—but also in that for some Impressionism needed to be understood as a "quintessentially French" phenomenon. If the first of these notions—specifically, what relation may be drawn between the formal aspects of Impressionism and eighteenth-century French painting—is the topic of this essay, the latter concern will not be entirely ignored.

The "Rediscovery" of Eighteenth-Century French Art in the 1860s

By the late 1870s an allusion to eighteenth-century French art would not have struck many as particularly surprising. Over the previous twenty years appreciation of Rococo painting had been growing, part of an overall reassessment of pre-Revolutionary French history and culture that had begun in earnest during the Second Republic. Starting in the 1840s, certain enterprising collectors took advantage of deflated values to assemble impressive holdings of Rococo art. François Marcille (1790–1856) and Laurent Laperlier (1805–1878), for example, were assiduous collectors of the works of Jean-Siméon Chardin, among other eighteenth-century masters.[6] Two others, François Hippolyte Walferdin and Louis La Caze, marked the apogee of this trend. Walferdin (1795–1880), a physicist and customs officer, was a voracious collector of eighteenth-century art, in particular works by Fragonard. He shared a hometown—Langres—with Denis Diderot (in fact, Walferdin would edit the complete works of the great Enlightenment *philosophe* and art critic), a happenstance that no doubt encouraged his fascination with ancien régime culture. Concerned that the Louvre was able to exhibit only a single work by his favorite artist, and a rather uncharacteristic one at that (the monumental *Coresus and Callirhoe,* the artist's reception piece to the Royal Academy of Painting and Sculpture), Walferdin donated in 1849 Fragonard's *The Music Lesson,* a more intimate high-life scene in the manner of François Boucher (fig. 61). This was shortly after he had been elected to the National Assembly in the early days of the Second Republic, and he stipulated that it was "to the Republic that I make this gift," a gift that could be rescinded if the government were to change.[7] No doubt the picture's appeal for him lay in the free improvisation of its handling—a potential signifier of liberty and Enlightenment—rather than its subject matter—an uncomfortably celebratory paean to pre-Revolutionary aristocratic leisure. In any case, when the Second Republic collapsed in 1852, Walferdin did not demand the return of the painting. Such was his love for the artist's works that when he died in 1880, a public auction of his collection—so vast that it took place over ten days—dedicated an entire catalogue to his paintings and drawings attributed to Fragonard.[8]

Walferdin's taste for art was obsessive in its focus. Broader in scope and more significant for the cultural life of France was the extraordinary collection assembled by Louis La Caze (1798–1869), a physician celebrated for his ministrations to the poor.[9] In his later life he devoted nearly all his energies to art. He served on the Salon jury but primarily focused on his personal collecting. He roamed Paris in search of paintings, dividing the city into sectors that he methodically scoured, never neglecting even the most humble *marchand*. The result was an assemblage of more than six hundred paintings (such was his single-mindedness that an inventory of his house in 1869 found a desk, a bed, two sofas, and two chairs as his sole furnishings). The masterpieces that he acquired—from Rembrandt van Rijn's *Bathsheba* to Frans Hals's *The Gypsy* to Jusepe de Ribera's *Club-footed Boy*—are still incredible to contemplate. But French painting, above all eighteenth-century French painting, proved his greatest passion. Again the list is staggering: Jean-Antoine Watteau's *Gilles* (among eight works by the artist), Chardin's *The Brioche* (one of thirteen), and ten masterpieces by Fragonard. Like Walferdin, La Caze focused on those aspects of eighteenth-century French painting that maintain their appeal and critical focus today: not the continuation of the *grande manière* by such painters of historical subjects as Carle Van Loo, Gabriel François Doyen, or Jean-Baptiste-Marie Pierre—the artists who were most esteemed (at least officially) in the ancien régime itself—but in the painters of the *petits genres* who represented the intimate and seductive side of aristocratic life: Boucher, Chardin, and Fragonard especially. In 1869 La Caze bequeathed his collection to the nation, with the greatest works going to the Louvre and others sent to museums in the provinces. The impact of the La Caze bequest on the museum was profound—indeed, it continues to resonate to this day. In 1920–21, when Édouard Vuillard was commissioned to paint a series of decorative panels for the Swiss industrialist Camille Bauer, he chose as one of his subjects the La Caze gallery in the recently reopened Louvre (private collection, Switzerland).[10] The focused view, with its intent artists copying the masterpieces, zeroes in on several of the collection's highlights of eighteenth-century French painting, including Nicolas de Largillière's *Portrait of a Man,* Watteau's *Jupiter and Antiope,* Chardin's *The Jar of Olives,* and—cut off at the lower left—Fragonard's *Study*.

By the time Renoir painted Samary in 1877 he would have known Fragonard's *Study* well, probably having first seen it in 1860, when it was displayed at an extraordinary exhibition primarily of eighteenth-century French painting held at the Galerie Martinet on the boulevard des Italiens. Organized by Philippe Burty himself, and drawing heavily from several of the most important private collectors of the day—among them Laperlier, Marcille, and Walferdin, as well as La Caze—the exhibition helped to reintroduce Parisians to art of the ancien régime. The exhibition at Martinet's sparked a wholesale reappraisal of eighteenth-century French art among critics, who were not averse to making comparisons to contemporary developments. These two events—the 1860 exhibition at the Galerie Martinet and the bequest of the La Caze collection in 1869—precipitated a rediscovery (or, perhaps it is best to call it a reinterpretation) of eighteenth-century French painting that has remained extraordinarily resilient, not to say seductive, until recent years. The emergence into public discourse of these collectors' particular tastes in Rococo painting would be taken up by such writers as Thoré-Bürger, Théophile Gautier, Charles Blanc, the Goncourt brothers, and others to construct a reading of eighteenth-century art that emphasized its inherent Frenchness and, in particular, its formal qualities.

Eighteenth-Century Painting and the Impressionists

The reappearance of great examples of eighteenth-century French painting did not escape the attention of contemporary artists. This was acknowledged as early as 1849 on the occasion of Walferdin's donation to the Louvre of Fragonard's *Music Lesson*. The director of the national museums, Philippe Auguste Jeanron, himself a painter, noted in his acceptance letter "the worth of Honoré Fragonard, who was without doubt one of the glories of our national school in an era which many have hastened to decry but to which some of our talented painters are returning."[11] Rococo painting was currently out of fashion because it "reflects in a regrettable manner the false elegance and the frivolity of its age." Some eighteenth-century practitioners, Fragonard among them, were nevertheless "full of spirit in our national manner, lovers of nature and followers in the best traditions, [and] have made their marks in it to the honor of our national tradition." Jeanron's derision of the ancien régime in tandem with an appeal to present-day nationalist sentiment signal the political climate of the first years of the Second Republic. In fact, when looking at a Rococo painting, nineteenth-century critics sometimes could not help but appreciate the older art in contemporary terms. To cite but one example, in a review of the Galerie Martinet exhibition in 1860, Gautier noted that in such paintings as Fragonard's *The Storm,* from the La Caze collection (fig. 62), the artist "understands landscape as we do today: his trees, skies, rocks, and hills would be right at home in a modern exhibition, next to canvases by [Louis] Cabat, [Théodore]

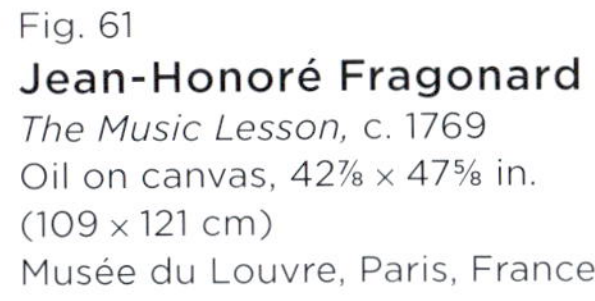

Fig. 61
Jean-Honoré Fragonard
The Music Lesson, c. 1769
Oil on canvas, 42⅞ × 47⅝ in.
(109 × 121 cm)
Musée du Louvre, Paris, France

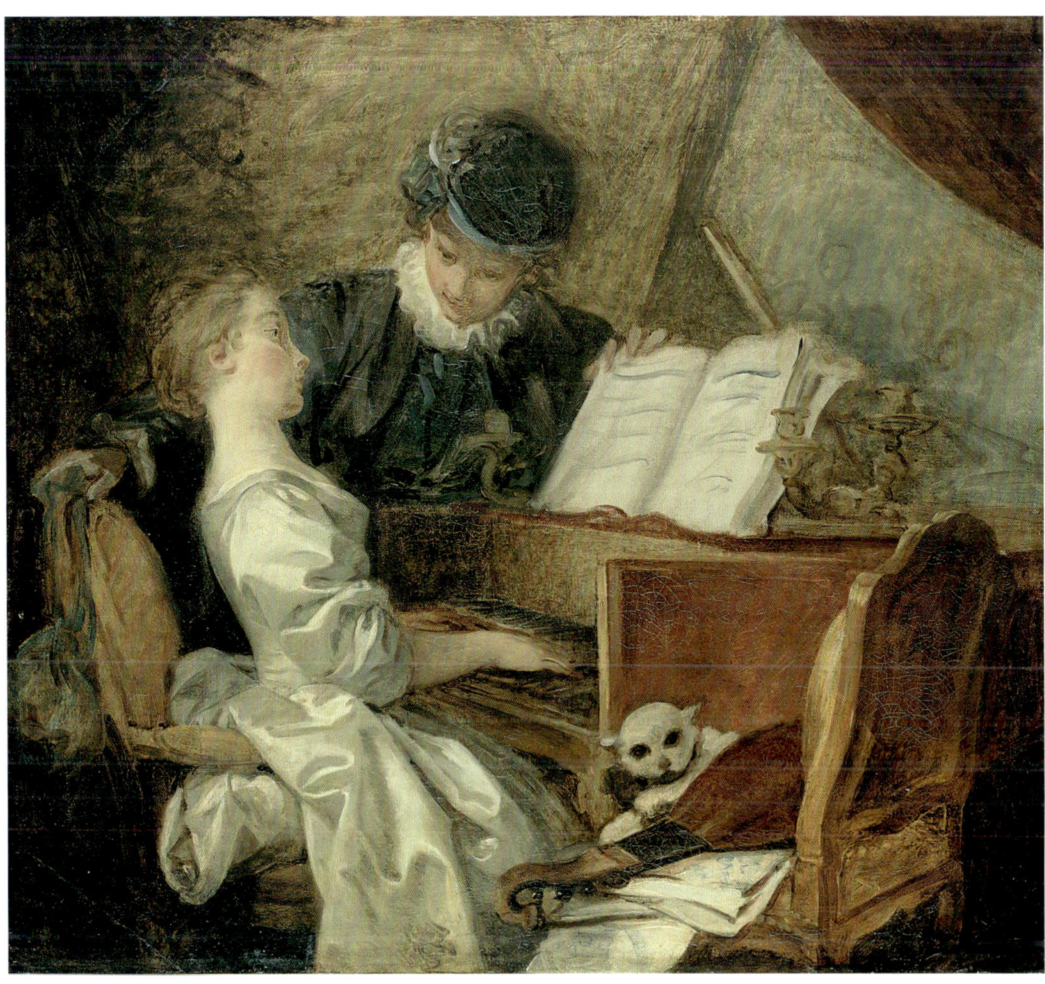

Rousseau, [Camille] Corot, and [Charles-François] Daubigny, without creating dissonance."[12]

It is worth recalling that Rococo painting—like seventeenth-century Dutch art—was reemerging into public discourse during the very period the Impressionists were learning their craft, and just before Édouard Manet introduced his most innovative paintings to a scandalized public. We will return to Manet at the end of this essay, but suffice it to cite two key Impressionists—Renoir and Berthe Morisot—for whom the discovery of eighteenth-century art had a profound impact. In 1858 and 1860 respectively, Morisot and Renoir had registered in the Louvre as copyists, an indication of their interest in studying older art.[13] As Renoir later told Ambroise Vollard: "I will say, to be absolutely precise, that Boucher's *Diana at the Bath* [fig. 16] is the first picture that struck me, and I have continued to love it all my life, as one loves his first loves, more so even if one never fails to tell me he was nothing but a decorator."[14] Renoir went on to say, however, that it was Morisot, of all the artists of his generation, who loved Rococo art: "And what another anomaly to see emerge in our age of realism a painter so imbued with the grace and finesse of the eighteenth century, in a word, the last elegant and 'feminine' artist that we have had since Fragonard, never mind the 'virginal' quality that Madame Morisot had in abundance throughout her art."[15]

Renoir's gendering of Rococo painting as feminine, opposed to realism, which he no doubt would have characterized as masculine, has had a long life in the literature.[16] Be that as it may, Morisot retained a fascination for eighteenth-century painting throughout her career, to judge from two copies after works by Boucher, produced in 1884 and 1892: the latter, painted on an autumn trip to Tours, replicates the lower left corner of Boucher's *Apollo Revealing His Divinity to the Shepherdess Isse* (1750) in the local Musée des Beaux-Arts; the earlier, included in this exhibition along with Boucher's sketch of the

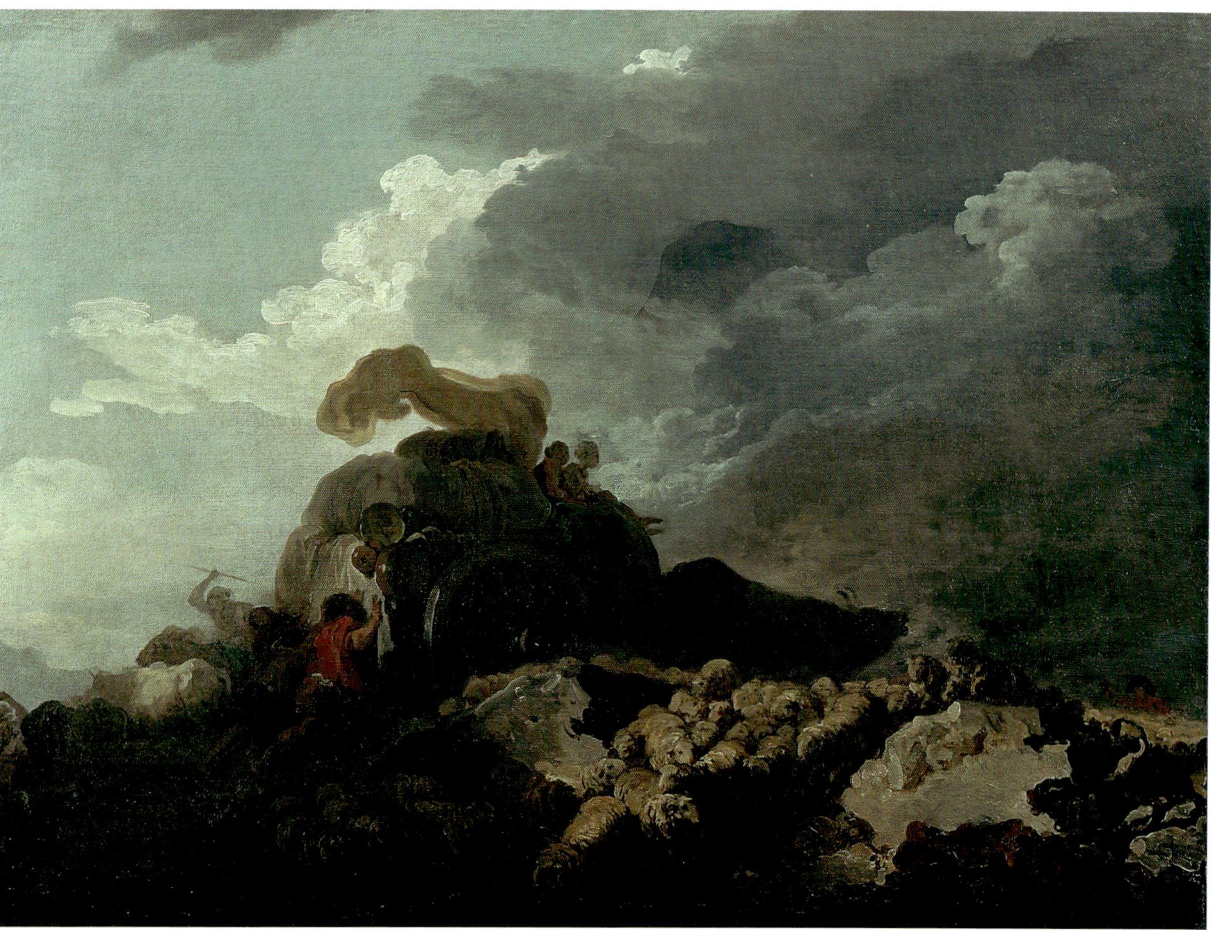

Fig. 62
Jean-Honoré Fragonard
The Storm (The Stuck Cart), 1759
Oil on canvas, 28¾ × 38⅛ in.
(73 × 97 cm)
Musée du Louvre, Paris, France

composition, was based on *Vulcan Presenting to Venus the Arms for Aeneas* in the Louvre (cat. 9, p. 143; cat. 67, p. 142).[17] The copy of the painting in the Louvre was made specifically to hang above the chimney in the Salon Blanc of Morisot's house on the rue de Villejust in Paris.[18] Significantly, in both paintings she focused on subsidiary figures, showing little interest in Boucher's accomplishments as a designer of grand *tableaux* (the *Vulcan and Venus* in the Louvre was made as a design for a Gobelins tapestry).[19] Rather, the particulars of Boucher's handling of paint—especially as it described the forms of the twinned nymphs, interpreted at the time as Graces, and cooing doves in the upper right quadrant of the background of his vast canvas (the foreground figures having been brought to a higher degree of finish)—appear to have appealed to her most. In Morisot's hand the brushwork assumed an even more audacious fluency, energizing the composition despite an extremely circumscribed range of pale tones: blues, pinks, and white, the latter the most predominant, as befitting the main decoration of the Salon Blanc.

In her original productions as well, the world of the ancien régime cabinet picture hovers constantly. We feel its spirit in intimate paintings of domestic life like *Getting Out of Bed* of 1886, in which the seventeen-year-old Isabelle Lambert, one of Morisot's favored models in these years, rises from her bed and steps into her slippers (private collection, Paris).[20] The picture was painted in one of the bedrooms of the Villejust house, with its furnishings fully in the Louis XVI style, but the theme and, above all, the rapid calligraphy of the informal brushwork call to mind works by the Rococo masters, in this case Fragonard. The direct inspiration might have been his now iconic if euphemistically titled *Girl Playing with Her Dog* from about 1770–75, which Morisot might have seen when it sold in Paris in 1880 as part of the Walferdin collection (fig. 63). Edmond and Jules de Goncourt had characterized the picture as "a flower of eroticism, full of freshness and completely French."[21] Morisot toned down considerably the *outré* playfulness of Fragonard's gamine, relying on her model's delicately shaped ankle and the seemingly casual slip of the white shift off her

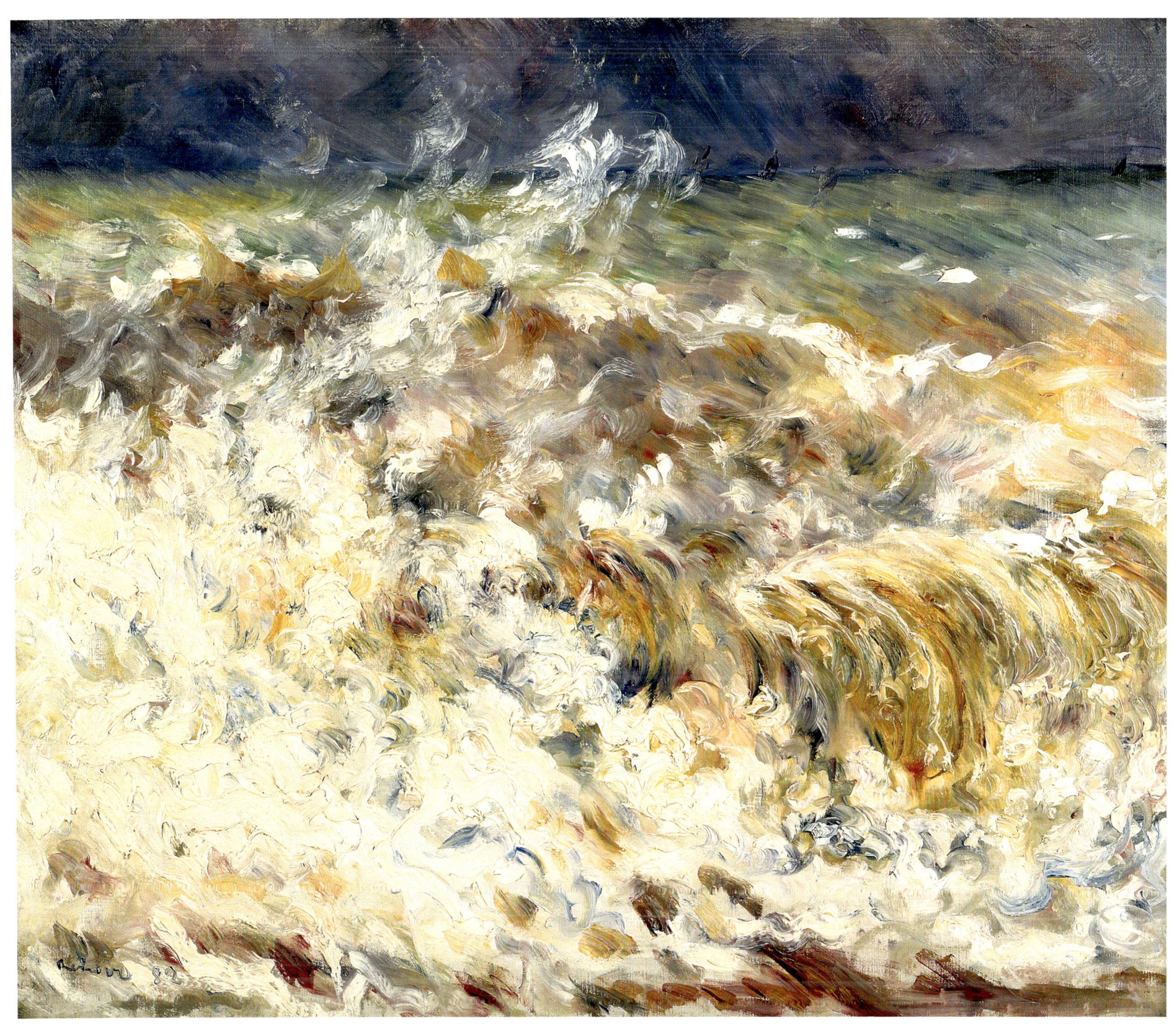

Cat. 84
Pierre-Auguste Renoir
The Wave, 1882

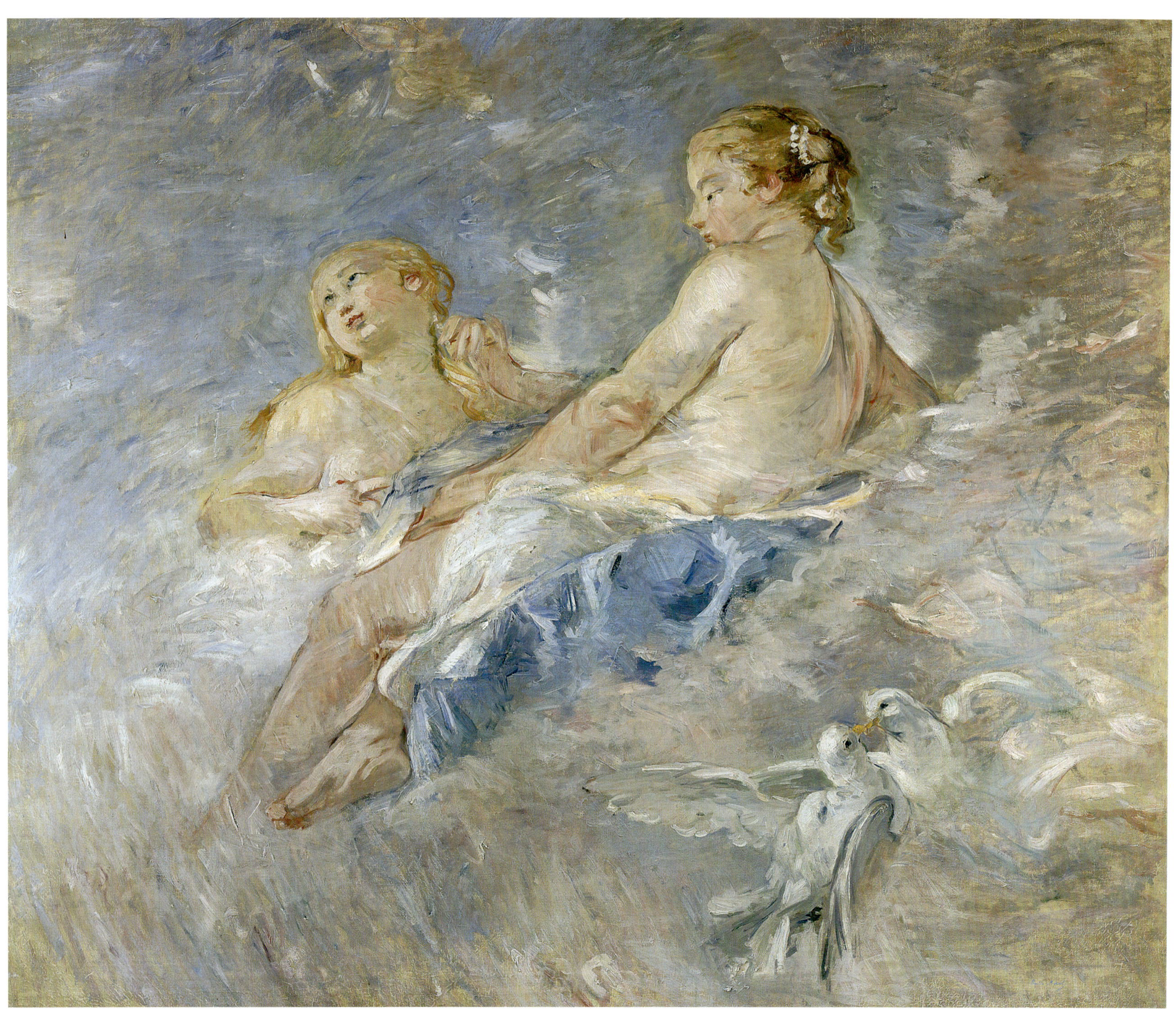

Cat. 67
Berthe Morisot
Venus Asking Vulcan for Arms
(after the 1757 original by Boucher in the Louvre), 1884

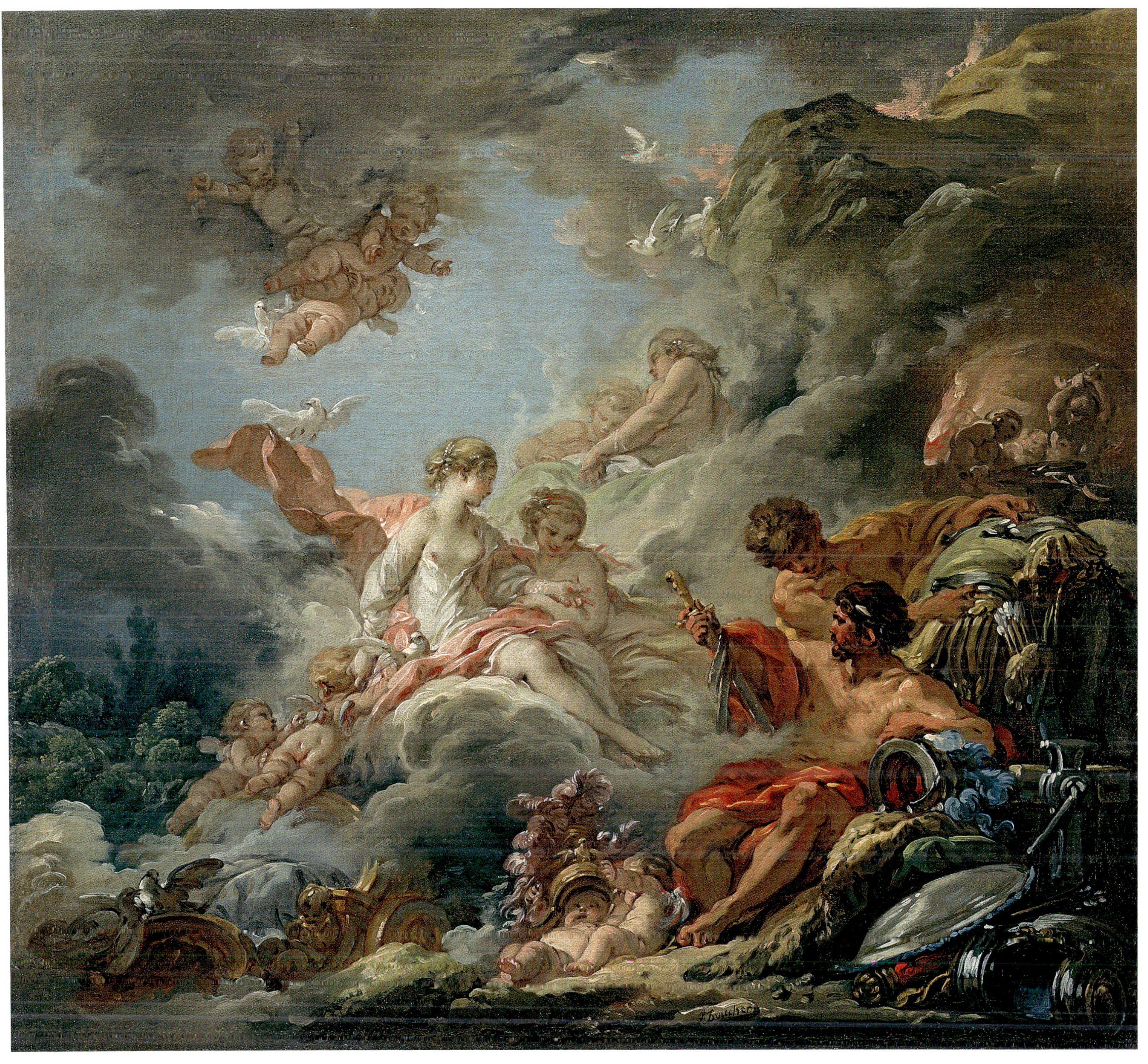

Cat. 9
François Boucher
Vulcan Presenting Arms to Venus for Aeneas, 1756

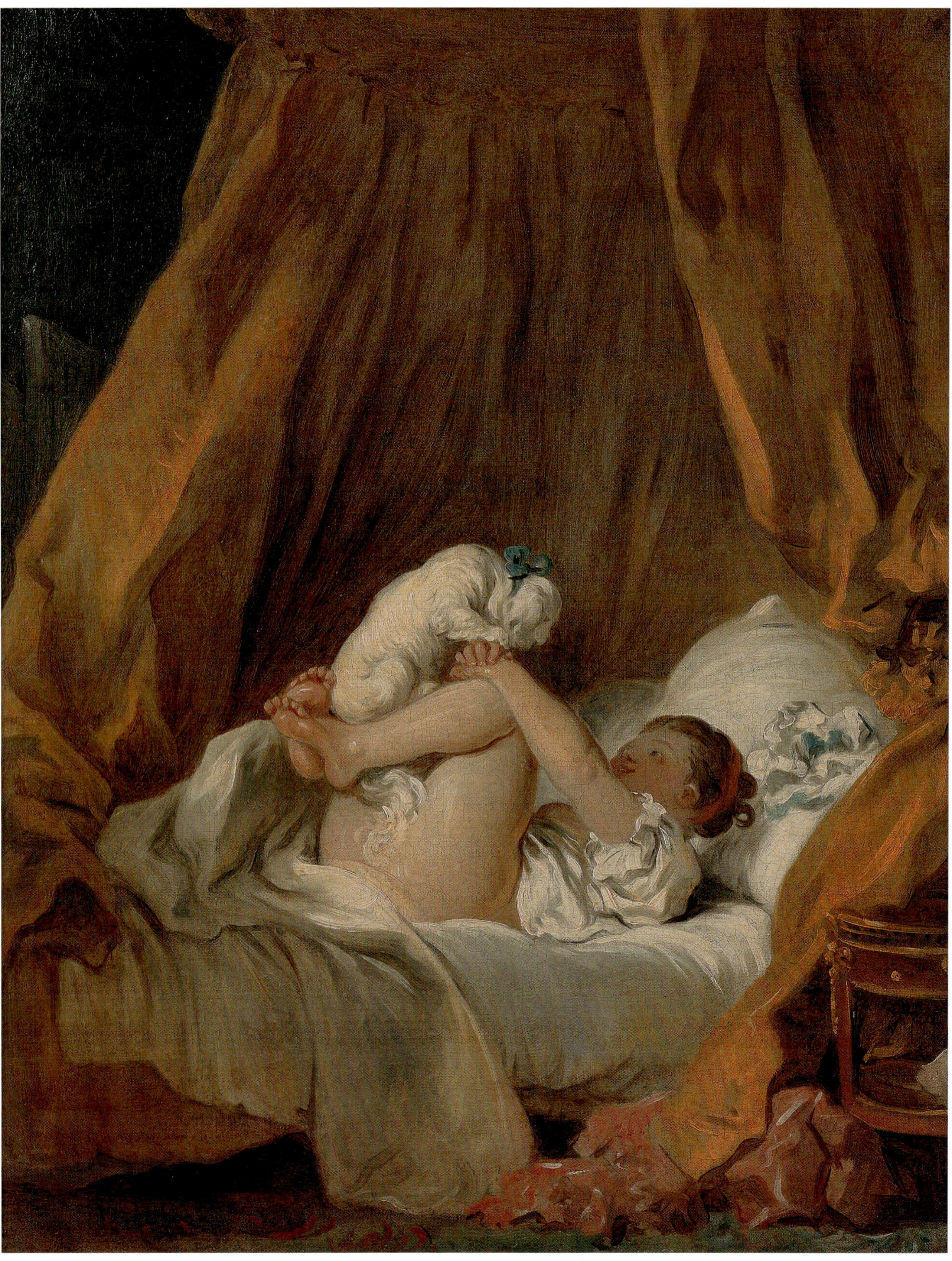

Fig. 63
Jean-Honoré Fragonard
Girl Playing with Her Dog (La Gimblette), c. 1770
Oil on canvas, 35 × 27½ in. (89 × 70 cm)
Bayerische Staatsgemäldesammlungen, Alte Pinakothek, Munich, Collection of the Bayerische Hypotheken- und Wechsel Bank

left shoulder to carry any erotic charge. But if anything she extended the dynamic fluidity of Fragonard's brushwork, here as in many of her pictures creating forms out of bold slashes of the brush.

Painted in an Hour: Fragonard and the Sketch Aesthetic

The thematic connection between Impressionist art and Rococo painting is obvious from a number of the works in the current exhibition. Yet the subjects from modern life that form the primary repertoire of Impressionism have just as convincing roots in Dutch art of the seventeenth century, which was undergoing its own reevaluation during these years. Rather, it was at the level of technique that eighteenth-century French art arguably had the most to offer the burgeoning independent artists of the New Painting. Whatever appeal there was in the everyday subjects of Dutch painting, its style, particularly the somber range of tones favored by most Golden Age artists, was a more appropriate model for realist artists. The young Impressionists, who preferred a highly keyed palette, saw the pastel colors favored by the Rococo painters as more suitable for emulation. Moreover, the penchant for a rapid, seemingly spontaneous—or at least informal—brushwork, while characteristic of certain Dutch painters like Frans Hals, found its truest exponents in the Rococo. Here Fragonard quickly emerged as the exemplary prototype.

Until the 1860s Fragonard had remained in a kind of critical oblivion, little studied and relatively undervalued except for a handful of connoisseurs like La Caze and Walferdin. Moreover, his paintings were not readily available for the general public, including artists, to study. Until the La Caze bequest in 1869, only two major works by the artist were in the Louvre: his grand historical painting *Coresus and Callirhoe* and *The Music Lesson,* from the Walferdin collection, the type of small-scale amorous subject that would increasingly dominate his production (and his posthumous reputation). For critics of the 1860s, the two paintings neatly summed up Fragonard's career: the brilliant up-and-coming history painter who broke with the academy to produce small-scale gallant paintings for private patrons.

Most critics, like the Louvre's director, Jeanron, could overlook the distasteful association of Fragonard's art with the old order, recapturing his art for a contemporary audience at the level of technique. Rather than being pigeonholed as a latecomer in the tradition of Watteau—continuing in the pre-Revolutionary years to produce a kind of updated *fête galante* for an increasingly out-of-touch aristocracy, Fragonard could now be seen as precociously adopting the stance of the vanguard modern painter, beholden only to himself and supported by connoisseurs who well appreciated the formal values of his pictures. Many biographers—Charles Blanc and the Goncourts foremost among them, but others, such as Jules Renouvier in his 1863 biography—stressed Fragonard's independent nature, his reluctance to complete important commissions, his break with the academy to pursue a career apart from official sanction.[22] This formulation of his career, repeated in nearly all the accounts, must have made Fragonard a sympathetic model for the avant-garde artists of the 1860s and 1870s in their ongoing battles with a highly regulated art world. Like Fragonard, they sought to create an arena outside the constraints of the academy, appeal to private collectors, exhibit in alternative venues, and enlist the support of friendly critics.

In his landscapes—images like *The Storm* (fig. 62) or his large decorative paintings of gardens—Fragonard seemed to be searching for a visual vocabulary that would represent the contingencies of modern life, whether struggling over a mountain pass in an ox cart (a scene no doubt witnessed by the artist on his journeys to Italy) or a more enjoyable promenade through a garden. For the Goncourts, Fragonard's technique was a force of nature: "What passion, what a stormy brush in *The Storm,* that masterpiece owned by M. Lacaze! . . . everything is caught in movement, and the brush rolls with the wind throughout the scene."[23] But the imaginations of the writers were most captured by his figural works—the *portraits de fantaisie* in particular.

Fragonard's *Study* was one of four pictures in the La Caze collection that were referred to as "portraits de fantaisie." The other three represent men, including one identified—without much proof—as M. de la Bretèche, the brother of Fragonard's great patron the abbé de Saint-Non (fig. 64). Like *Study,* it was exhibited at the Galerie Martinet in 1860. In the century and a half since these first examples emerged in the mid-nineteenth century, at least fifteen have been associated with the group, among them the freely brushed and coyly intimate *A Young Girl Reading* in the current exhibition (cat. 38, p. 231). They are all of similar format and motif, each about 31½ by 25⅝ inches (80 by 65 cm) in size, and all datable to the years about 1770. They remain essentially mysterious; we know next to nothing about them, and art historians have spent a great deal of time trying to discover whom they represent, if anybody, for whom they might have been painted, whether they represent a series or if certain ones can be paired or placed into groups, and so on. They are generally taken as emblematic of Fragonard's uniqueness in the Rococo

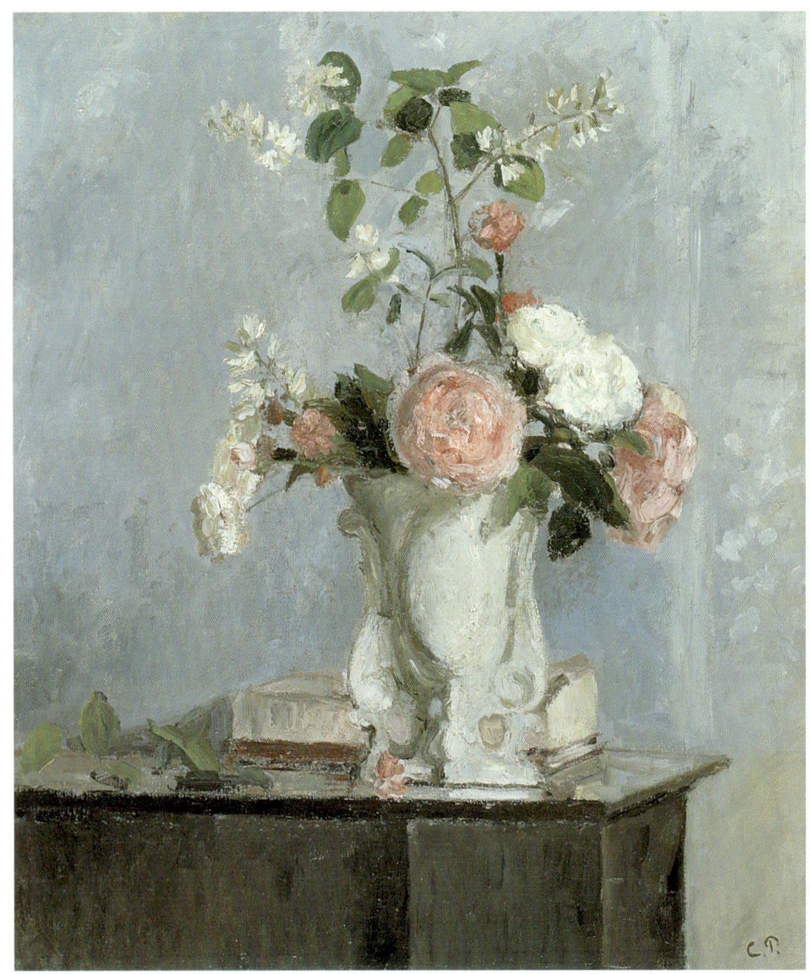

Cat. 74
Camille Pissarro
Bouquet of Flowers, c. 1873

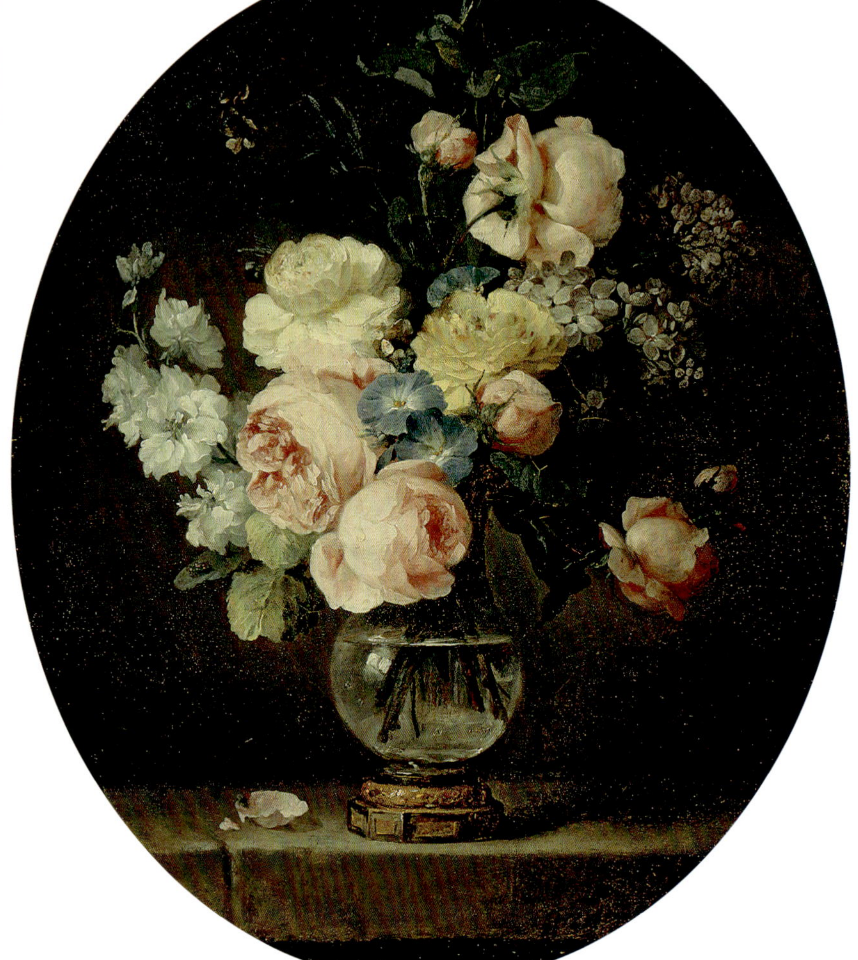

Cat. 98
Anne Vallayer-Coster
Vase of Flowers, 1775

tradition, personal works that display his amazing skills as a painter while forever keeping their secrets.[24]

Burty's catalogue entry on the presumed portrait of La Bretèche noted that it was "costumé à l'espagnole," a description that was repeated by all contemporary commentators. This was a reference to the theatrical dress worn by the figures, which were often described in the eighteenth century as being Spanish in style, although, as critics have more recently pointed out, the clothing owes more to seventeenth-century Flemish court attire than to anything Iberian. Nevertheless, Fragonard's evocation of Spanish costume—what the Goncourts referred to as "the trousseau of some Seville carnival"[25]—enhanced the essentially fantastic nature of the picture, giving it an exotic air that Fragonard's lively brushwork only increased. In fact, Fragonard's pictures seem to exist in a kind of fluid state between actual portraiture and fantasy. Early on several of them acquired allegorical titles, whether justified by the visual evidence or not: "inspiration," "study," or, as in the case of the so-called La Bretèche, perhaps more justifiably, "music." Here the painterly trace of the artist's hand serves to evoke, one might suggest, the music played on the guitar.

Yet the fantasy portraits are convincing as neither portraits nor allegories. The improvisational technique, in which the artist's conceptual process is played out before our eyes, gave vital expression to the painter's protean genius, as well as lending his mysterious subjects a metaphoric character far removed from any physiognomic specificity. These pictures, as Mary Sheriff has argued, are both representations of enlightened states of mind and self-portraits of the artist, in which the purported identity or métier of the sitter is subsumed under the painter's self-expressive brushwork.[26] This concept of enlightened genius retained its power in the late nineteenth century. Renouvier's 1863 biography, for example, celebrated Fragonard as the "supreme master of the sketch, in which he was able to retain in even his most finished works . . . the vivacity of his inspiration."[27]

Burty referred to Fragonard's portraits as "lively sketches," and for the critics of the 1860s the obvious speed and fluency with which they had been painted were the pictures' most remarkable features. The four fantasy portraits from the La Caze collection were singled out by all the critics as quintessential examples of Fragonard's fluid, dynamic style of painting. It is worth quoting the Goncourts at some length to give a sense of the impact of these works. This is from their essay of 1865, which has remained to this day an influential text:

> In the La Caze collection, there are four half-length, life-size portraits. On the back of one of them is inscribed—according to my opinion, in the painter's own hand—the following: "Portrait of M. de la Bretèche, painted by Fragonard in 1769, in the space of an hour." An hour! No more. An hour sufficed him to pose, dispatch and polish off, with swagger and confidence, these large portraits in which is set off and displayed all the Spanish fantasy with which painters of the time attired and ennobled their contemporaries. An hour to complete this canvas! He scarcely had time to apply his paint.

These pictures confirmed that "Fragonard had gone much farther than anyone else in this charming style who seized the impression of things and threw it onto the canvas like an instantaneous image."[28]

The obvious enthusiasm for Fragonard's rapid handling expressed by the Goncourts reflected a growing trend. Beginning in the 1840s, critics like Thoré and artists like Eugène Delacroix had recognized the aesthetic as much as the practical value of oil sketches, along with the benefits of a "lack of finish" in studio paintings, especially landscapes.[29] A glance back to 1849 and the donation of *The Music Lesson* to the Louvre finds the director, Jeanron, writing to Walferdin about a potentially disturbing aspect of the work: "the picture that you have sent us, though it bears the marks of rapid workmanship and, besides, may not be very elaborate in its finish, is a good one and has a pleasant look." He went on: "Pictures in this state are very useful to the galleries where Art is studied because they often reveal the secrets of a master and a school better than highly finished works."[30] For Jeanron the picture's fluid brushwork was instructive to young artists, but only as it revealed the master's secrets, that is, as it demonstrated an intermediate step toward a more complete canvas, not unlike the traditional role played by an *esquisse* or *étude* in academic painting.[31] Just a few years later, in 1853, Delacroix would have no qualms. Writing in his journal, he cautioned, "When we finish a picture, we always spoil it a little. The final touches which are supposed to draw the parts together detract from its freshness."[32]

By 1860 critics were more accepting of looser brushwork and lack of finish as appropriate and even desirable in an exhibition picture. Théophile Gautier, in his review of the 1860 Martinet exhibition, was exuberant in his praise of Fragonard's facility: "The passion of his brush, the frankness of the tones laid down with a rare brilliance, and the transparency of the nervously rubbed shadows suggest the rapidity of the most cursory sketch." He makes the witty suggestion

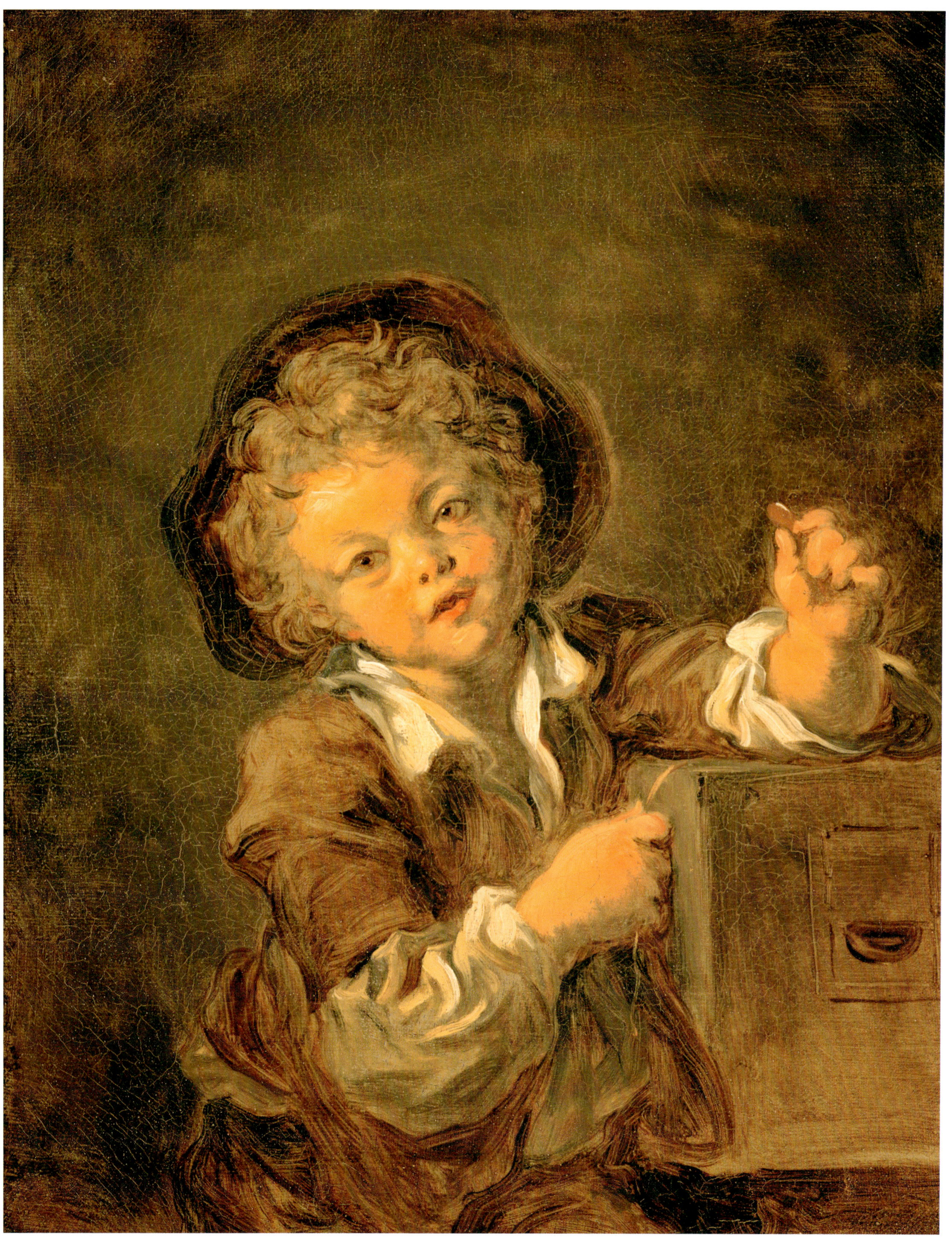

Cat. 37
Jean-Honoré Fragonard
Boy with a Peep Show, c. 1780

Fig. 64
Jean-Honoré Fragonard
Music: Portrait of M. de la Breteche, Brother of L'Abbé de Saint-Non, c. 1769
Oil on canvas, 31½ × 25½ in. (80 × 65 cm)
Musée du Louvre, Paris, France

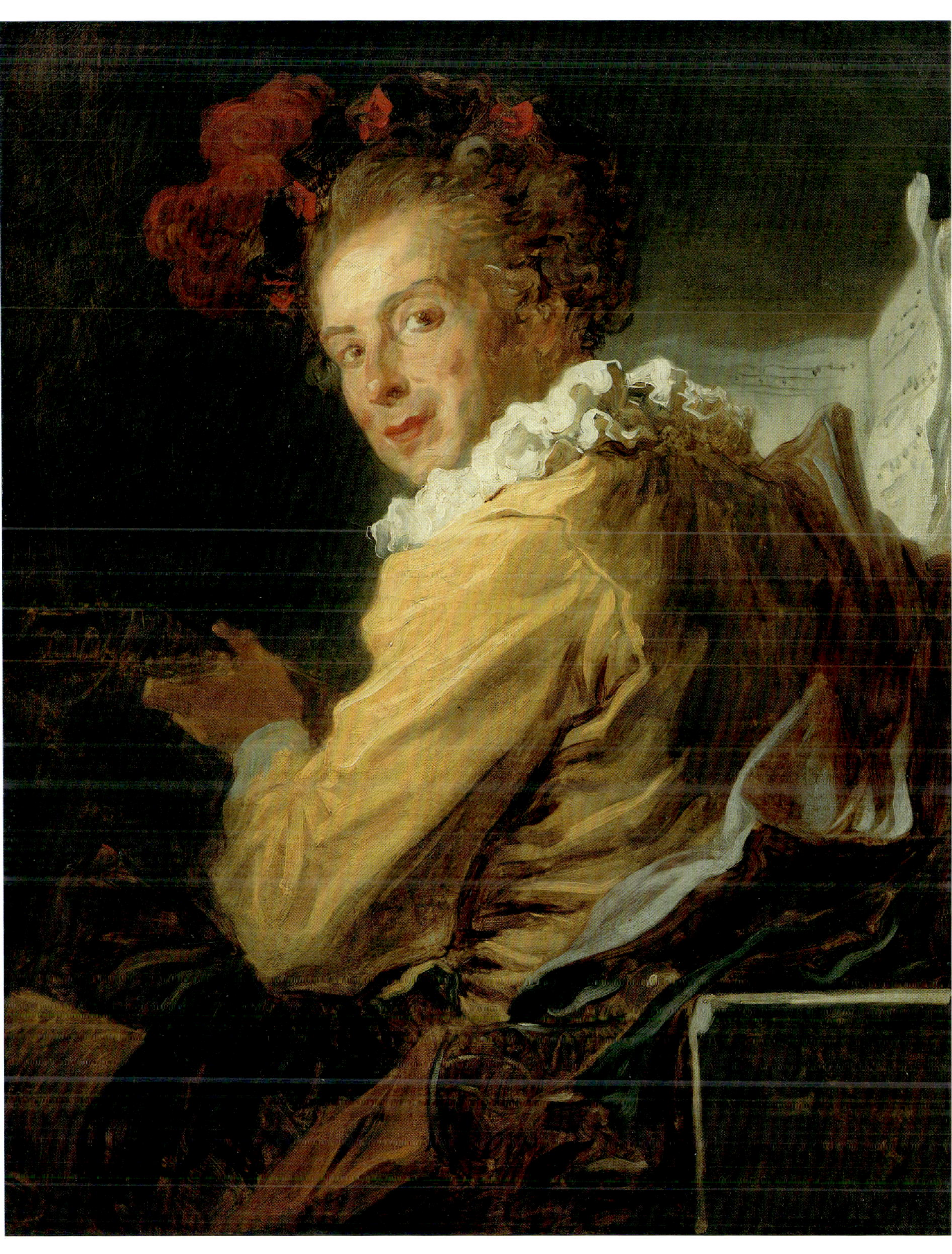

that the shortened signature, "frago," visible at the lower right, indicates that the painter "didn't have the time to paint the last syllable of his name."[33] Thoré wrote that "with three scumbled brushstrokes, he [Fragonard] created the texture of satin better than the Dutch [*les Mieris*]: with one sweep of the hand, this conjurer gave life to the sitter." He concluded that "true masters have never taken long to produce their masterpieces."[34]

The *Non-fini* and the *Pochade:* Chardin and Fragonard

It was easy for critics to believe the tradition that Fragonard's fantasy portraits were painted in an hour, so compelling was the physical evidence of the pictures themselves. (Although it is worth noting parenthetically that in his 1865 biography Charles Blanc inadvertently doubled the time to two hours).[35] By this time Fragonard's protean abilities as a manipulator of paint were already legendary. To the critics of the 1860s, his art was the antithesis of Chardin's, his contemporary and early master. In the Goncourts' reductivist characterization, Fragonard's ebullient paintings were the luxury products of a leisured aristocracy, while Chardin's gave sober expression to bourgeois values. (This kind of dichotomy, of course, still persists today, despite what we now know about the true nature of Chardin's clientele.) The apparent difference in style reinforced this fundamental opposition: Chardin's painstaking technique seemed the inverse of Fragonard's impetuous improvisations. Chardin's care and exactitude are obvious on the surfaces of his canvases, with their mottled, tacky impasto and deliberate, systematic brushwork, in their own way perfectly in sync with his subjects. It was easy to associate this technique with the craft-guild traditions from which Chardin emerged, and by extension with an art suitable to the *Tiers état*.[36] The subject of the appealing *Child with a Spinning Top* (fig. 65), exhibited in 1860 at Martinet's, concentrates on the spinning top with the same patience and absorption we imagine the artist employed in painting the boy.

We should recall—as did all the biographers who recounted the details of his life in their publications of the 1860s—that Fragonard had spent time as a student in Chardin's studio. There he learned, we are told, the "mere rudiments of his craft," but not much else, before moving on to study with Boucher. Nevertheless, Fragonard must have remembered several of Chardin's half-length genre scenes when painting his fantasy portraits. A number of these, like *Child with a Spinning Top,* were disguised portraits (in this case of Auguste-Gabriel Godefroy, the future controller general of the French navy).[37] Surrounded by attributes and every bit as mysterious in their thoughts, they formed, arguably, powerful thematic precedents for Fragonard's own imaginary character studies. And while to us the means of expression differs radically—Fragonard's brushwork is like a great exhalation of energy and verve; Chardin, one suspects, must have held his breath with each stroke of the brush—the critics of the 1860s and ensuing decades acknowledged some striking similarities. Blanc, in his 1865 biography, admired his straightforward technique: "[Chardin] abbreviates, simplifies, and eliminates details. He takes great care not to tell everything, so that the viewer may add something of his own and complete the painter's thought."[38] Vincent van Gogh picked up on this notion of the *non-fini* two decades later, writing enthusiastically to his brother Theo about the Goncourts' biography:

> I enjoyed immensely what he says about Chardin's technique. I am more convinced than ever that the true painters did not finish their things in the way which is used only too often, namely correct when one scrutinizes it closely. The best pictures, and, from a technical point of view the most complete, seen from near by, are but patches of color side by side, and only make an effect at a certain distance.[39]

While Fragonard revealed all in his broadly painted canvases, allowing the viewer into a vicarious participation in his creative process, Chardin concealed his method. The viewer cannot penetrate the surfaces of his dense and viscous impasto; the congealed surfaces betray no trace of the underlying structure. His method was notoriously secretive; indeed, eighteenth-century critics like Diderot marveled at the "magic" of his technique.

The distinction between what was seen as Fragonard's informal and quick brushwork and Chardin's elimination of details and avoidance of careful finish brought into play technical concerns that animated contemporary debate on the proper stages of painting. Terms like *esquisse, étude,* or *pochade,* whose shades of meaning are difficult to translate into English, are often used interchangeably now, but in their time each was distinct.[40] In identifying Fragonard as a model for Renoir's *Portrait of Jeanne Samary,* Burty referred to the former artist's "vives pochades," for which the translation "lively sketches" is hardly adequate. A *pochade* was an informally but boldly painted canvas that may have begun life as an oil sketch (*esquisse*) but which the artist decided was a complete work in its own right. Claude Monet, for example, often exhibited *pochades,* sometimes

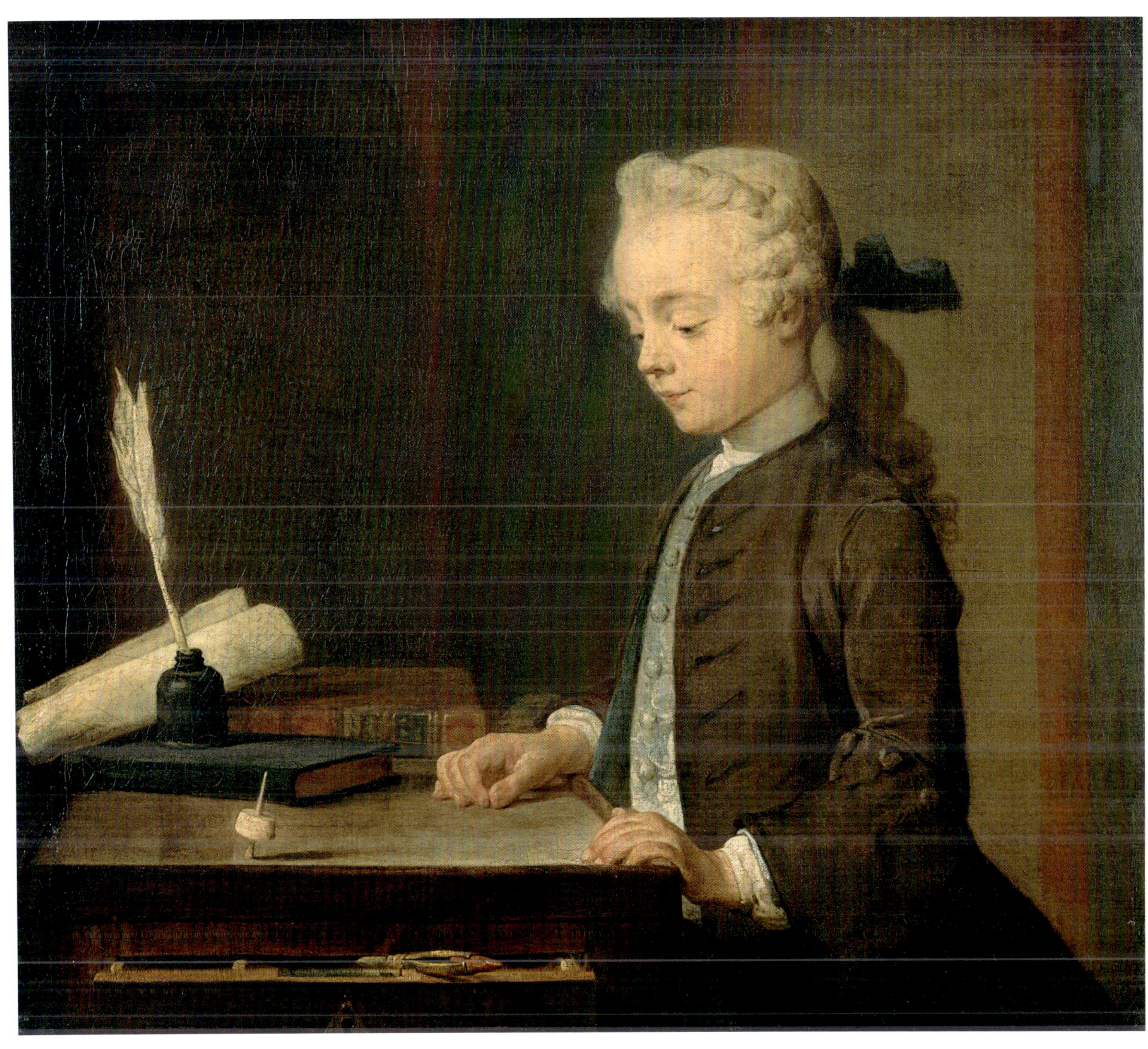

Fig. 65
Jean-Siméon Chardin
Child with a Spinning Top (Auguste Gabriel Godefroy), 1737–38
Oil on canvas, 26⅜ × 29⅞ in. (67 × 76 cm)
Musée du Louvre, Paris, France

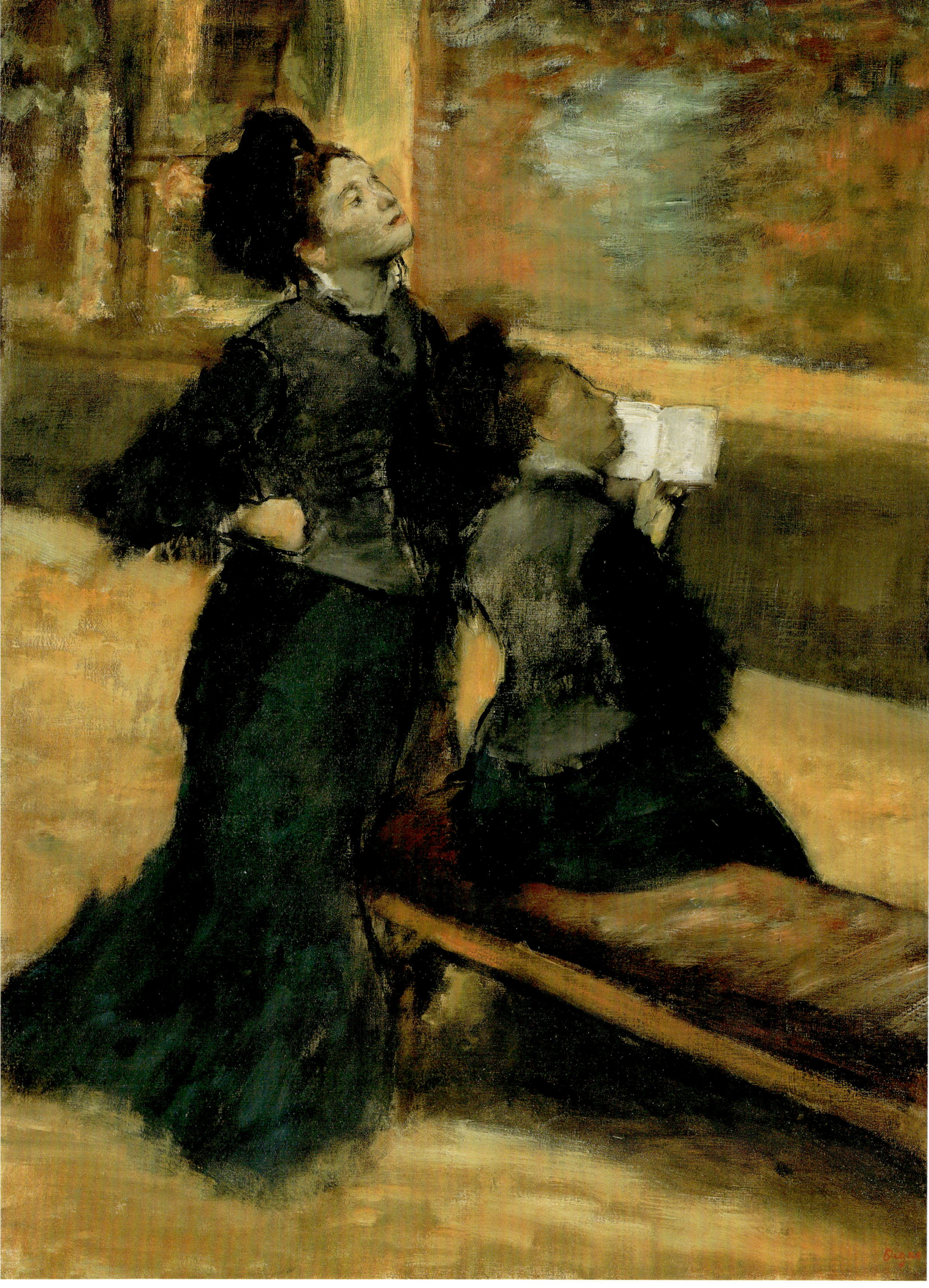

Cat. 35
Edgar Degas
Visit to a Museum, c. 1879–90

referring to them as "impressions" if they were primarily concerned with representing an atmospheric effect. Most famously, at the 1874 Impressionist exhibition he showed the celebrated canvas of the harbor at Le Havre with the title *Impression, Sunrise,* indicating that he did not consider it a finished *tableau* in the usual sense. (Indeed, he gave a second view of Le Havre, much more elaborately worked up, the more formal title of *Le Havre, Fishing Boats Leaving the Port*). As John House has noted, Monet assigned relative value to his paintings in his own mind, charging buyers more for "finished" pictures (*tableaux*) than for *pochades* or *impressions*.[41] Yet he clearly valued his most successful *pochades,* writing, for example, to a friend in 1884, "I am very proud of myself, because, in a free hour, I did a successful *pochade*, better than many of the things on which I've toiled for fifteen sessions."[42] Thus, when Burty referred to Renoir's *Portrait of Jeanne Samary* in light of Fragonard's "vives pochades," he was bringing into play a term that was very much up for negotiation. The Impressionists' propensity to exhibit and sell works that could be seen as unfinished or having been accomplished rapidly and with little evident effort was a mark of their modernity. Yet, paradoxically, by turning to earlier French artists like Fragonard and, to a lesser degree, Chardin, artists recently celebrated by critics, art historians, and collectors, the Impressionists could justify their radical moves by appealing to tradition.

That numerous examples of such earlier works were now fully integrated into the French galleries of the Louvre, providing the young artists with a distinguished pedigree in rapid gestural painting, is no better emblematized than in Edgar Degas's enigmatic *Visit to a Museum* of about 1879–90 (cat. 35, p. 152). Here two women clad in black—sometimes thought to be Mary Cassatt and her sister—admire the installations in the Louvre (one would like to think they are in the Galerie La Caze itself, although that is doubtful).[43] In all probability the picture is simply unfinished—an *ébauche* (that is, the underpainting of an incomplete composition) rather than a *pochade*—but it nevertheless vibrates with a vital energy as Degas's brush dances around the figures. The framed old master paintings lining the wall become a blur of color and abstract forms made from the same marks that represent the two women. In this instance, at least, the contingencies of modern life are rendered indistinguishable from the world of past art.

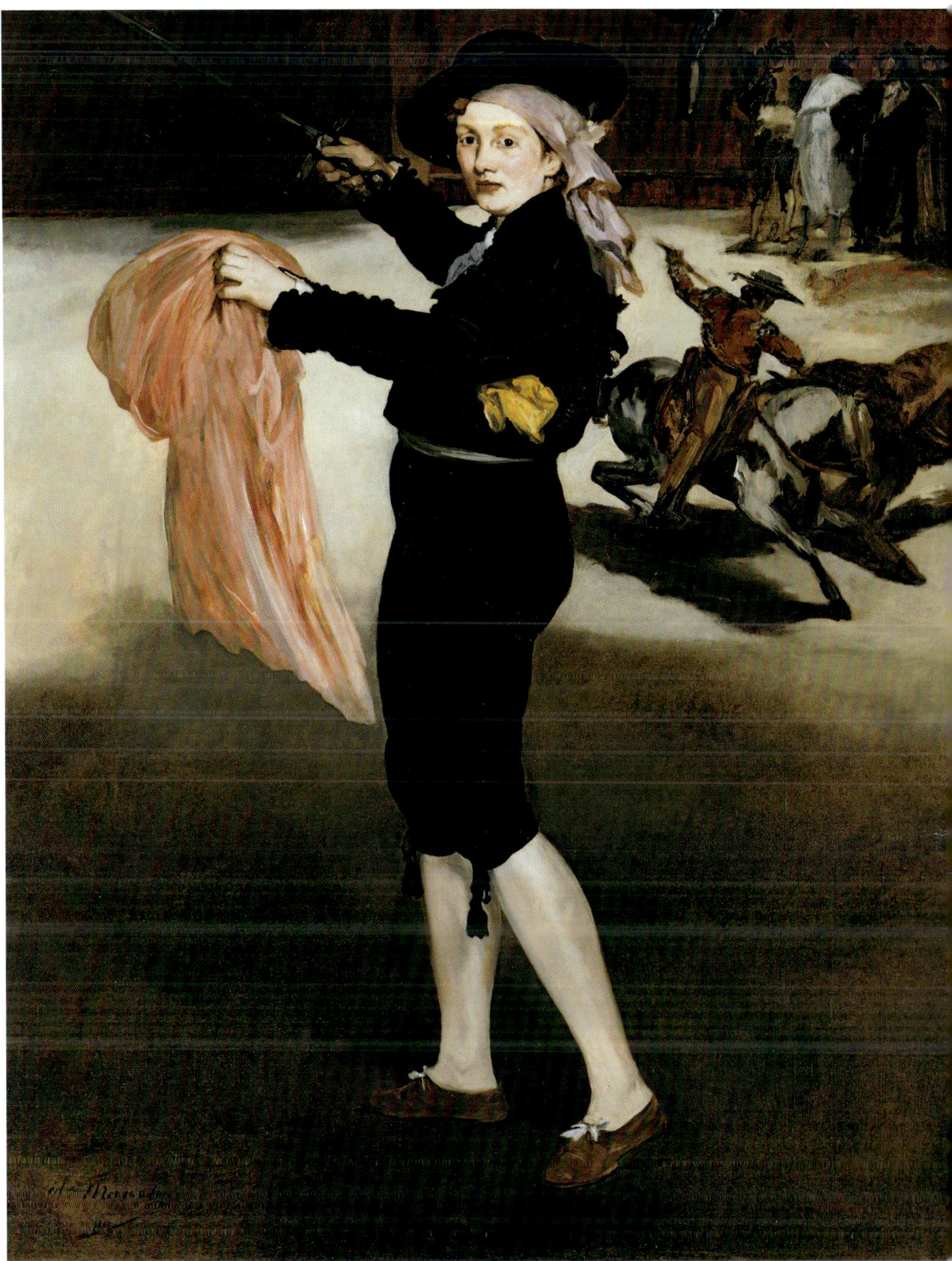

Fig. 66
Édouard Manet
Mademoiselle V . . . in the Costume of an Espada, 1862
Oil on canvas, 65 × 50¼ in. (165.1 × 127.6 cm)
The Metropolitan Museum of Art, New York, H.O. Havemeyer Collection, Bequest of Mrs. H. O. Havemeyer, 1929 (29.100.53)

Manet and Fragonard: Beyond the Sketch

Of all the proponents of the New Painting, Manet arguably possessed the greatest facility in emulating Fragonard's elegance and ease of brushwork. He alone seems to have completely appreciated the experimental character of Fragonard's fantasy portraits as early as the 1860s—not only their technical performative brilliance but also their sophisticated play with sources, their exotic costuming, and their blurring of genre categories. The obvious comparisons are, of course, Manet's series of Spanish subjects of the early 1860s, such as *The Spanish Singer,* shown at the Salon of 1861 but probably painted in late 1860 (fig. 42), shortly after Fragonard's fantasy portrait of the guitarist La Bretèche "in Spanish costume" was shown at the Galerie Martinet exhibition. And while we are certainly not in need of yet another source for Manet's image—the artist himself cited both Hals and Diego Rodríguez de Silva y Velázquez—Fragonard's guitar player turned in an unstable manner might have served Manet as a point of departure. Manet worked over his image with some deliberation, repainting the neck of the guitar some three times. Yet he was able to bring a bravura handling and speed to key parts of the picture; as he boasted to Antonin Proust, "Just think, I painted the head in one go. After working for two hours, I looked at it in my little black mirror, and it was all right. I never added another stroke."[44]

The ultimate tribute to the fantasy portraits is, perhaps, Manet's *Mademoiselle V . . . in the Costume of an Espada,* exhibited at the Salon des Refusés in 1863 (fig. 66). Manet's ambivalent early experience with the Salon jury made him a particularly apropos heir to Fragonard's fiercely held independence. Manet's enigmatic masterpiece raises all the questions posed by Fragonard a hundred years before: it confounds conventions of portraiture by dressing the French sitter in exotic, Spanish, garb; the actions and expressions of the protagonist are elusive in the extreme; the figure is placed in an ambiguous setting—though Fragonard's figure leans on a desk, the obscured background of Manet's picture defies a clear reading of the space; and the flattened stage drop behind Victorine Meurent negates traditional perspective. Manet appropriated past art in all kinds of ways, as Michael Fried, Theodore Reff, and others have well established, from ancient sculpture and Renaissance prints for the figure of Victorine to the lithographs by Francisco de Goya that make up the background bullfight scene, knitting these sources together to create an altogether original conception.[45] But while the pastichelike composition and awkward perspective continue to startle today, it was Manet's extraordinary technical performance in *Mademoiselle V* that most provoked commentators in his own time. Jules Castagnary, for example, saw the picture as a "good sketch" (*ébauche*): "There's a certain life in the color, a certain directness in the touch that are in no way vulgar. But then what? Is this drawing? Is this painting?"[46] Thoré linked Manet's "free and spirited touch" to Goya, but Fragonard's so-called *La Bretèche* would have been just as suitable a model. Turned sideways from the picture plane, Victorine catches the viewer's eye with a disconcerting glance over her shoulder that has no precedent in Goya but parallels remarkably the effect of the Fragonard. And while the blacks and deep reds do signal Manet's passion for Spanish art, the "too vivid color" (Thoré) of the crimson cape, boldly stroked on the canvas wet into wet, are straight off the palette of the Rococo painters who were so much the rage in the early 1860s. Finally, the very indeterminacy of Fragonard's fantasy portraits—were they actual portraits, allegories of genius or the arts, or "mere" sketches?—undermined the Enlightenment notion that art should have a moral purpose and social utility. Rather, the canvas becomes the site for a self-referential display of artistry, a site confounding to the pedant but liberating to the refined insider who could vicariously participate in the artistic process and revel in the detached irony of the subject. It is in Fragonard that Manet, the most urbane and sophisticated painter of his generation, found his true model.

Notes

1. For a full discussion of Renoir's numerous portraits of Samary, see Ottawa 1997, pp. 155–60, 292–95. This essay is developed from a presentation given at a symposium at the National Gallery, London, in November 2000 held in conjunction with the exhibition *Impression: Painting Quickly in France, 1860–1890,* curated by Richard R. Brettell. I would like to thank Kathleen Adler for inviting me to participate in the symposium.

2. "C'est bien là une *impression,* rien, moins que rien, un sourire fixé sur la toile." Ch. Flor O'Squarr, *Le Courrier de France,* in Berson 1996, vol. 1, p. 172. "Mlle Samary, est tout simplement adorable . . . comme une apparition vaporeuse sur un nuage crépusculaire." Jacques, *L'Homme Libre,* in ibid., vol. 1, p. 156. "Mlle Samary est représentée en femme horriblement plâtrée." Baron Grimm, *Le Figaro,* in ibid., vol. 1, p. 151.

3. "On n'a pas d'idée des procédés estranges employés par le peintre pour le portrait de Mlle S***: sur un fond rose tout pointillé de traits bleus, s'estompe vaguement une figure sans contours, avec des cheveux qui passent du bleu de Prusse au carmine foncé." A. Descubes, *Gazette des Letters, des Sciences et des Arts,* in ibid., vol. 1, pp. 143–44.

4. "L'aspect tendre en éveille le souvenir de certaines tapisseries de Beauvais. C'est un portrait de decoration plutôt qu'une sérieuse peinture." Léon de Lora, *Le Gaulois,* in ibid., vol. 1, p. 162.

5. "Il faut remonter aux vives pochades de Fragonard pour rencontrer, non pas des points de comparaison matérielle, mais des analogies de temperament français s'appliquant à la peinture de portrait." Ph. B., *La République Française,* in ibid., vol. 1, p. 124.

6. Cleveland 1979, esp. pp. 34–39.

7. "C'est à la République que je fais ce don . . . Si jamais la forme du Gouvernement proclamé le 4 mail 1848 par l'Assemblée Nationale dont je fais partie avait le malheur d'être changée en France. Il serait par cela seul complètement annulé." Rosenberg 1989, p. 119. On Walferdin and his donation, see Wildenstein 1960, pp. 38–39.

8. Paris 1880, over April 12–16. The other sales of his collection, including paintings, drawings, prints, miniatures, and terra cotta sculptures, as well as his vast library, took place on April 5–9.

9. Béguin and Constans 1969.

10. On the commission, including images of the other panels, see Washington 2003, pp. 336–41, cats. 284–88.

11. Wildenstein 1960, p. 38.

12. "Fragonard entend le paysage comme on le fait aujourd'hui: ses arbres, ses ceils, ses rochers, ses collines pourraient prendre rang dans une exposition moderne à côté de toiles de Cabat, de Rousseau, de Corot, de Daubigny, sans faire dissonance." Gautier 1860.

13. London 1990, p. 207.

14. "Je dirai, avec plus de precision, que la *Diane au Bain* de Boucher est le premier tableau qui m'ait empoigné, et j'ai continue toute ma vie à l'aimer, comme on aime ses premières amours, encore que l'on ne se soit pas fait faute de me dire que ce n'était qu'un décorateur." Vollard 1920, p. 19.

15. "Et quelle autre anomalie, de voir apparaître, dans notre âge de réalisme, un peintre si imprégné de la grace et de la finesse du XVIIIe siècle; en un mot, le dernier artiste elegant et 'fémini' que l'on ait eu depuis Fragonard, sans compter ce quelque chose de 'virginal' que Madame Morisot avait à un si haut degree dans toute sa peinture." Vollard 1920, p. 166.

16. See, for example, the discussion in Sherriff 1990, pp. 26–29. For a gendered reading of Impressionism, see Broude 1991.

17. For the copy after *Apollo and Issé,* see Clairet, Montalant, and Rouart 1997, p. 185, no. 145, and p. 272, no. 324.

18. See Lille 2002, pp. 267–69, cat. 74.

19. Her choice of detail may have been prompted by Henri Fantin-Latour, who made a copy of just this section, now in the Musée Magnin, Dijon. See Lille 2002, p. 269, fig. 2.

20. Clairet, Montalant, and Rouart 1997, p. 210, no. 195. For a good recent discussion, including a photograph of the bed depicted in the painting, see Lille 2002, pp. 324–27, cat. 99 (entry by Hugues Wilhelm).

21. "Une fleur d'érotisme toute fraîche, toute française." Goncourt 1882, vol. 2, p. 333.

22. Blanc 1865, "Fragonard," p. 8; and Renouvier 1863, pp. 166–70.

23. "Quelle fougue, quelle tempête de pinceau dans *L'Orage*, ce chef-d'oeuvre possédé par M. Lacaze! tout est saisi dans le movement, et la brose roule dans toute la scène avec le vent qui y passé." Goncourt 1882, vol. 2, p. 337.

24. For a good overview, see New York, *Fragonard* 1988, pp. 255–93, cats. 125–41.

25. Goncourt 1882, vol. 2, p. 337.

26. Sheriff 1987.

27. "Maître supreme dans l'esquisse, à qui il fut donné de garder dans ses ouvrages les plus finis, et jusque dans la miniature, la vivacité de l'inspiration." Renouvier 1863, p. 167. On the nineteenth-century equation of quick painting and inspiration, see Boime 1971, pp. 176–78.

28. "Fragonard a été plus loin que personne dans cette peinture enlevée qui saisit l'impression des choses et en jette sur la toile comme une image instantanée." Goncourt 1882, vol. 2, p. 337.

29. Boime 1971, pp. 92–96.

30. Wildenstein 1960, pp. 38–39.

31. For a full discussion of the role of the oil sketch in academic training, see Boime 1971, pp. 79–121, 166–84.

32. Quoted in ibid., p. 93.

33. "La fougue de la brosse, la franchise des teintes posees avec une rare maestria, la transparence des ombres nerveusement frottées, dénotent les rapidités de l'esquisse la plus cursive" and "Ce portrait et signé *Frago*, 1769, comme si le peintre n'avait pas eu le temps d'écrire la dernière syllable de son nom pour rester dans les limites de la gageure." Gautier 1860.

34. Bürger, "Exposition" 1860, p. 347.

35. Blanc 1865, "Fragonard," p. 12.

36. As suggested by Vincent van Gogh "*Tiers état,* Corot-like as to bonhomie—with more sorrow and adversity in his life." See Van Gogh 1958, vol. 2, p. 431.

37. For a recent discussion of the painting, see London, *Impression* 2000, pp. 224–25, cat. 50.

38. Blanc 1865, "Chardin," p. 9.

39. Van Gogh 1958, vol. 2, p. 431.

40. See, for example, the discussion in Boime 1971, pp. 92–96. A good discussion of these terms, especially as it refers to Monet, is House 1986, pp. 157–66. In addition, see Richard R. Brettell in London, *Impression* 2000, pp. 35–36.

41. House, *Impressionism* 2004, pp. 46–47; for a full discussion of these issues, see chap. 2, "Sketch and Finished Painting," and chap. 5, "Making a Mark: The Impressionist Brushstroke."

42. Quoted in House 1986, p. 162.

43. Brettell (in London, *Impression* 2000, p. 209) has plausibly identified the setting as the large Italian gallery, with a corner of Veronese's vast *Marriage at Cana* visible at the upper right.

44. Quoted in New York 1983, p. 64. The pose of Manet's guitar player has been linked to Greuze's *Mandolin Player* (Muzeum Narodowe, Warsaw); cf. New York 1983, p. 64, fig. a.

45. For the fullest discussion, see Fried 1969; reprinted, with the addition of "Manet's Sources Reconsidered," in Fried 1996. See also Reff, "Manet's Sources" 1969.

46. For a good overview of the critical response, see Charles Moffett's entry on the painting in New York 1983, pp. 110–14, cat. 33; Castagnary at p. 112.

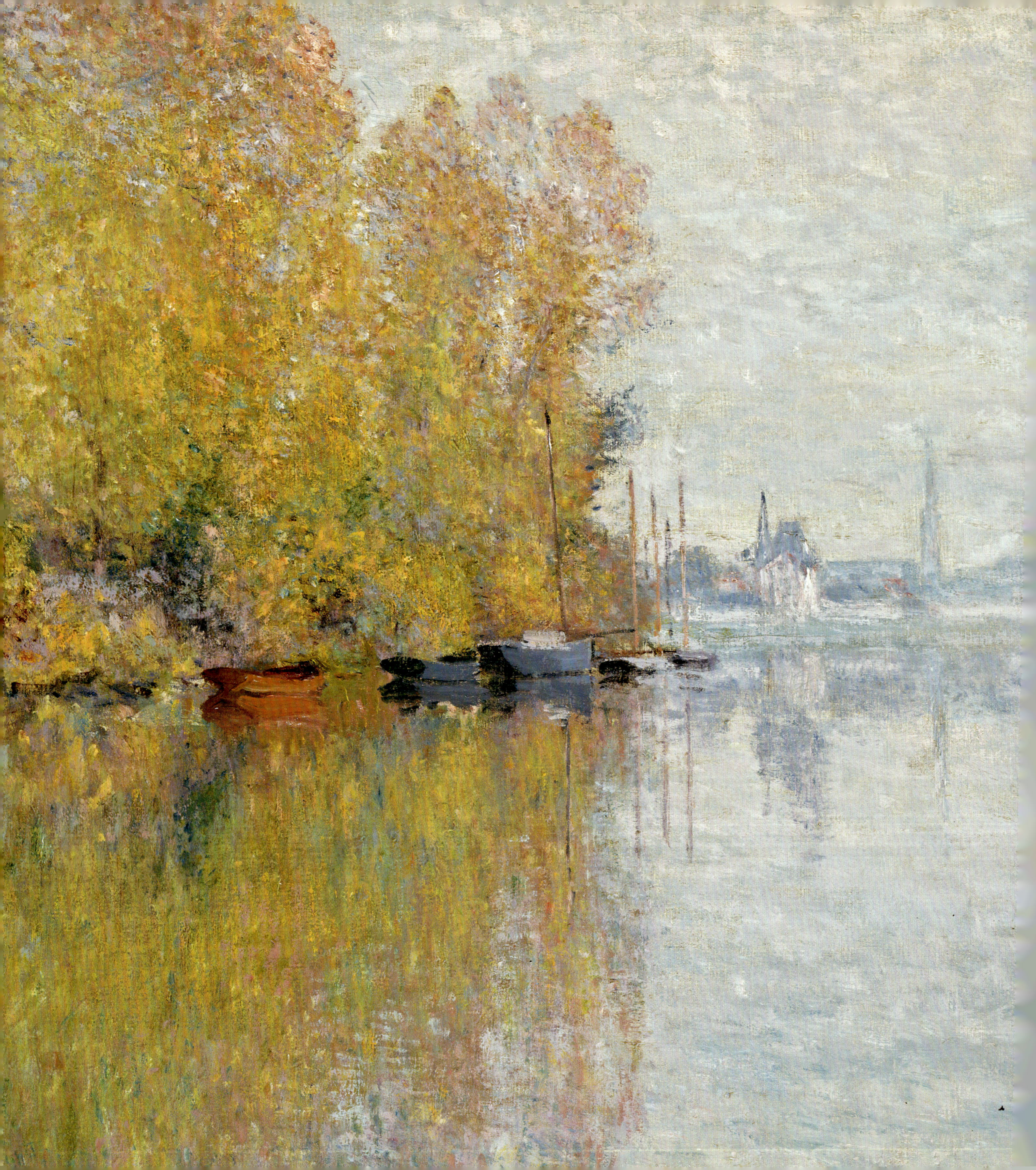

Michael Clarke

The Landscape Tradition

Impressions of Old Masters

> That Corot comes from Lorrain and reflects him is evident, but it is also clear to what degree he transformed what he took, in this lies all his genius; his figures are as modern as you please. In short, it is only here [in France] that artists are faithful to the tradition of the masters, *without robbing them*.
>
> —Camille Pissarro, letter to his son Lucien, March 23, 1898

This intriguing observation of the elderly Pissarro, namely that the nineteenth-century painter Camille Corot was in effect the artistic heir of his seventeenth-century predecessor Claude Lorrain, the so-called father of classical landscape, upholds the truism that artists in the latter part of their careers often reflect on the complexities and implications of artistic tradition. When they are young—and this was certainly the case with the Impressionists—they do not want to be seen as dwelling on the past and instead promote themselves as offering something new, a radical break with what has gone before. Lionello Venturi, *archiviste* of Impressionism, later recalled that

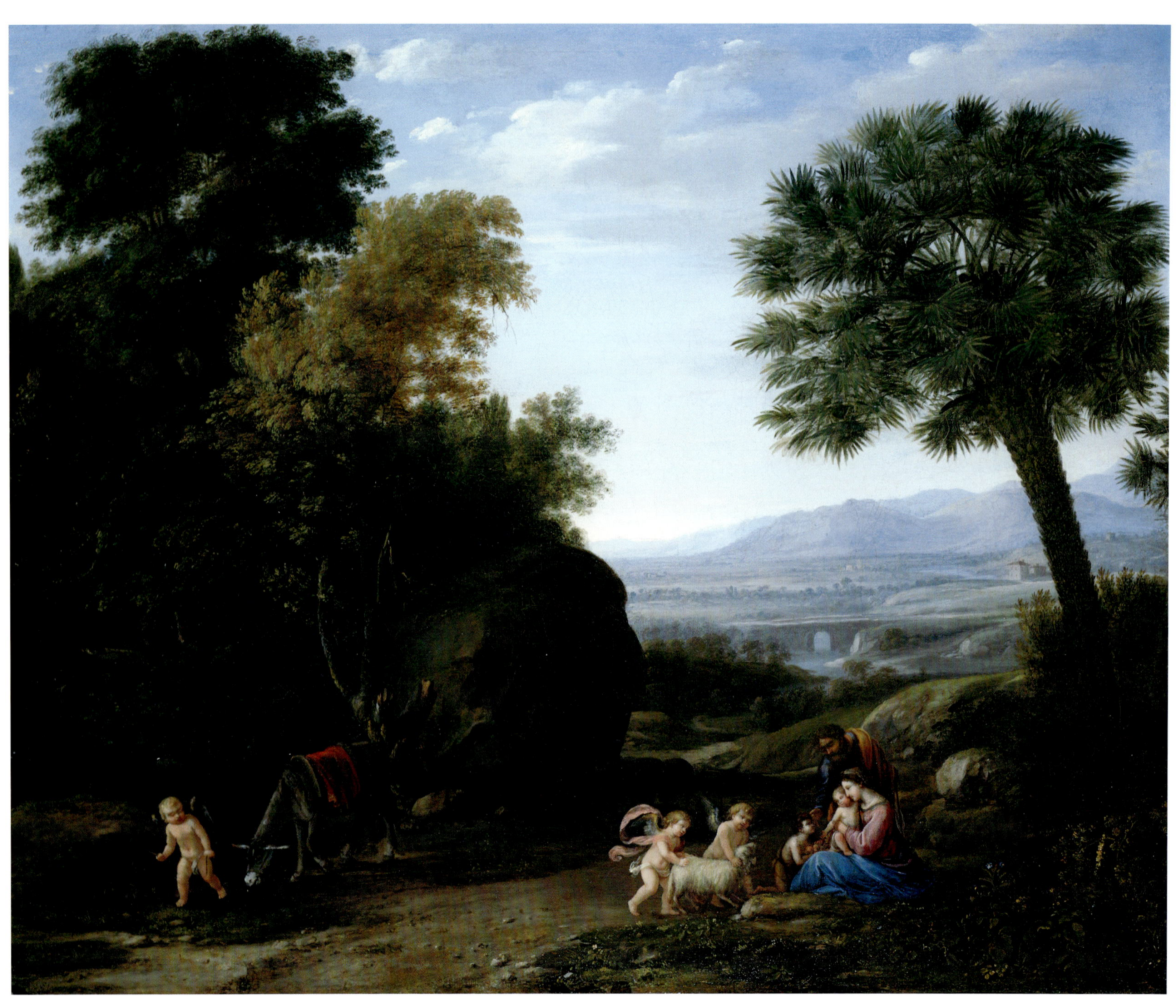

Cat. 46
Claude Lorrain
The Rest on the Flight into Egypt,
c. 1640

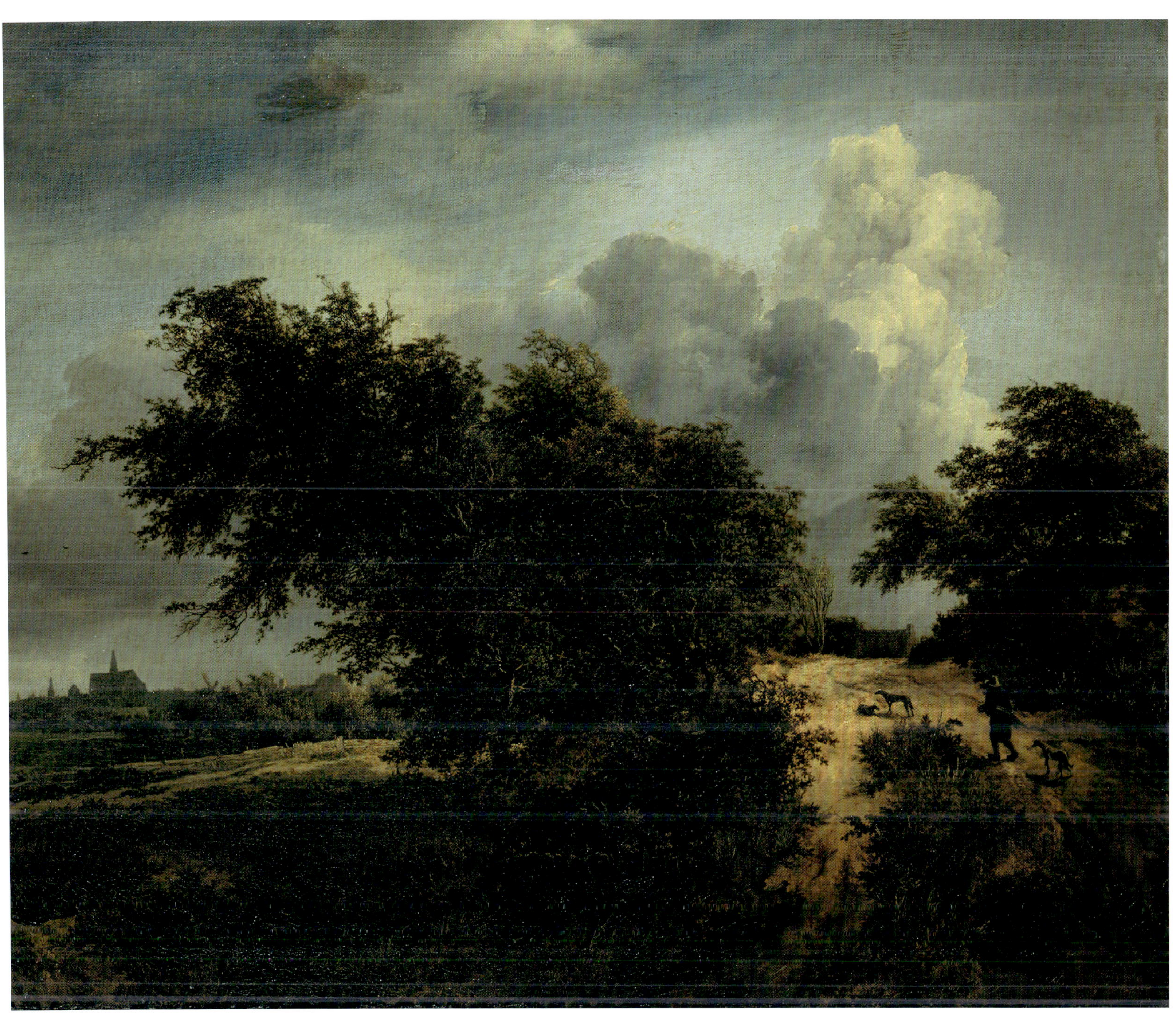

Fig. 67
Jacob Isaacksz van Ruisdael
(1628–1682)
The Bush, c. 1650–80
Oil on canvas, 26¾ × 32¼ in.
(68 × 82 cm)
Musée du Louvre, Paris, France

Pierre-Auguste Renoir exhibited a "superb indifferent insolence of his youth, disdainful of museums whose doors remained closed, smitten only by the open air."[1] Later, of course, Renoir would become a great admirer of the old masters and of the eighteenth century in particular. With maturity, and a measure of success, artists often seek a historical context for their achievements. After his return from a trip to Holland in 1898, Pissarro wrote to Lucien of Johannes Vermeer's celebrated *View of Delft* (fig. 29): it was "a masterpiece which comes close to the Impressionists; I have returned from Holland an even greater admirer of Monet, Degas, Renoir, Sisley."[2] Vermeer's great painting therefore reinforced Pissarro's admiration for his fellow Impressionists, but he was firmly against any kind of pastiche of the achievements of his great Dutch predecessors, since "it is an art that is so much of its particular time that it is absurd to try to follow this path."[3]

The Impressionists certainly developed a manner of painting that broke radically with what had gone before and in many respects were as "modern as you please," yet their links with the past should not be overlooked. In the genre of landscape it can be demonstrated that they did indeed look at the "tradition of the masters," although their various approaches differed in many respects from those of their more conservative contemporaries practicing in that category. Furthermore, the subtlety required of any evaluation of possible links between Impressionism and the past is underlined by our also having to take into account the contribution of the generation immediately preceding them, the so-called School of 1830. Masters such as the aforesaid Corot and Théodore Rousseau made no secret of their debts to their predecessors, to figures in the great French classical tradition such as Claude and Nicolas Poussin, and to the Dutch landscape school of the seventeenth century as represented by Jacob Isaacksz van Ruisdael (fig. 67) and Meindert Hobbema, among others. Although largely overlooked in the earlier parts of their careers, by the 1860s Corot, Rousseau, and other members of the Barbizon School were enjoying considerable critical and commercial success. Their renown was reinforced in the 1870s by several factors: a number of commemorative exhibitions were held following the deaths of many of these artists, and many dealers began to promote Barbizon landscapes. Chief among them was Paul Durand-Ruel, who in 1878 mounted a major retrospective of the School of 1830 to coincide with the Exposition Universelle held that year. Their work was therefore never absent from public scrutiny, and elsewhere I have proposed that Claude Monet's reversion to a more traditional type of landscape painting during the years he spent at the relatively isolated little town of Vétheuil from 1878 to 1881 was dependent on his close predecessors.[4]

Recent publications and exhibitions have established that the debt the Impressionists owed to Corot and his contemporaries was more extensive than many commentators have previously been prepared to admit.[5] Corot's sylvan mists pervaded both the early hoarfrosts of Pissarro and Monet's *Morning on the Seine* series of the 1890s (fig. 68). One can posit an ultimate inspiration from Claude (figs. 69, 70), either directly or via Corot. Similarly, Rousseau's depictions of the great oaks of the Forest of Fontainebleau undoubtedly stimulated the young Impressionists in the early to mid-1860s on their visits to Chailly on the edge of the forest, as illustrated in a canvas such as Monet's *Pavé de Chailly (Forest of Fontainebleau)* (fig. 71). There they may well have been inspired by the example of Rousseau, who had recently been described as "Le Ruysdael de la forêt de Fontainebleau."[6] A particularly striking example of early Impressionist interest in the forest tradition as represented by both the Dutch old masters and the nineteenth-century painters of Barbizon is Alfred Sisley's *The Avenue of Chestnut Trees near La Celle-Saint-Cloud* (fig. 72), shown at the Salon of 1868, in which the centralized composition harks back to the forest scenes of Hobbema, for example *The Oak Forest* (fig. 73), albeit mediated by knowledge of Corot, Rousseau, Gustave Courbet, and others. It can reasonably be suggested, therefore, that the generation of Corot and Rousseau served for the Impressionists as a sort of filter of the old master tradition. This secondhand experience must be borne in mind as one searches for possible links between the Impressionists and the old masters in the genre of landscape. And one should remember the last phrase of Pissarro's remark, quoted as the epigraph to this essay; the existence of a historical continuum in French landscape that he acknowledged ("artists are faithful to the tradition of the masters") did not encompass direct quotation or, as he put it, "robbing."

Perhaps Pissarro would be pleased, therefore, to learn that one recent commentator has placed him squarely "in the ideal landscape tradition." In his pioneering study *Pissarro and Pontoise: The Painter in a Landscape*,[7] Richard Brettell has been at the forefront of the development of an iconographic approach to Impressionism, convincingly arguing that Pissarro's development of a peopled landscape at Pontoise in the 1860s and 1870s resulted in "an awkwardly modern Arcadia," a remark that by definition invokes the shade of Poussin. In a similar vein, Brettell maintained: "Most of Pissarro's paintings have a sizable population of figures, nearly as many as

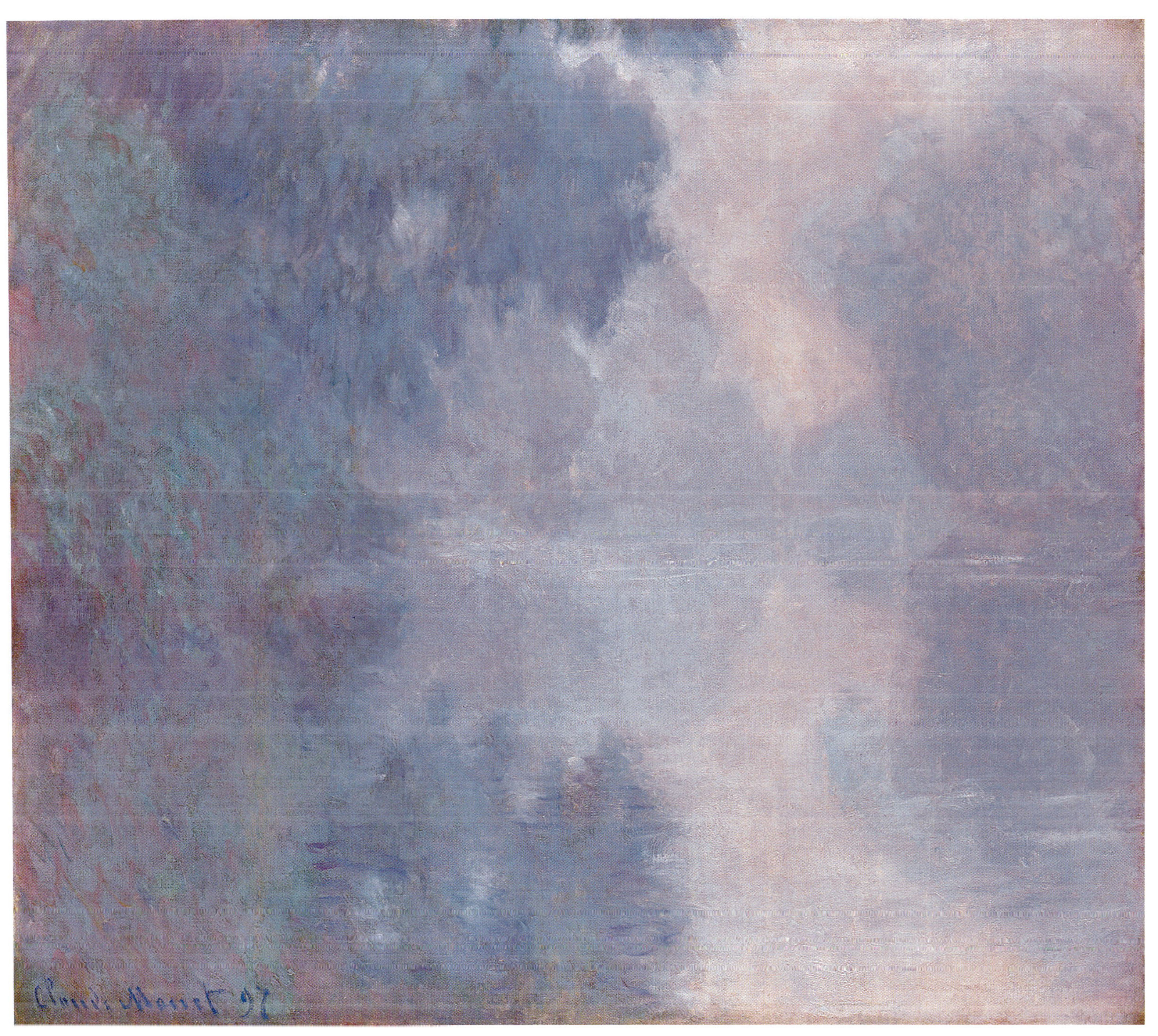

Fig. 68
Claude Monet
Morning on the Seine, Giverny, 1897
Oil on canvas, 32¼ × 36¾ in. (81.9 × 93.4 cm)
Mead Art Museum, Amherst College, Amherst, Massachusetts, Bequest of Susan Dwight Bliss, AC 1966.48

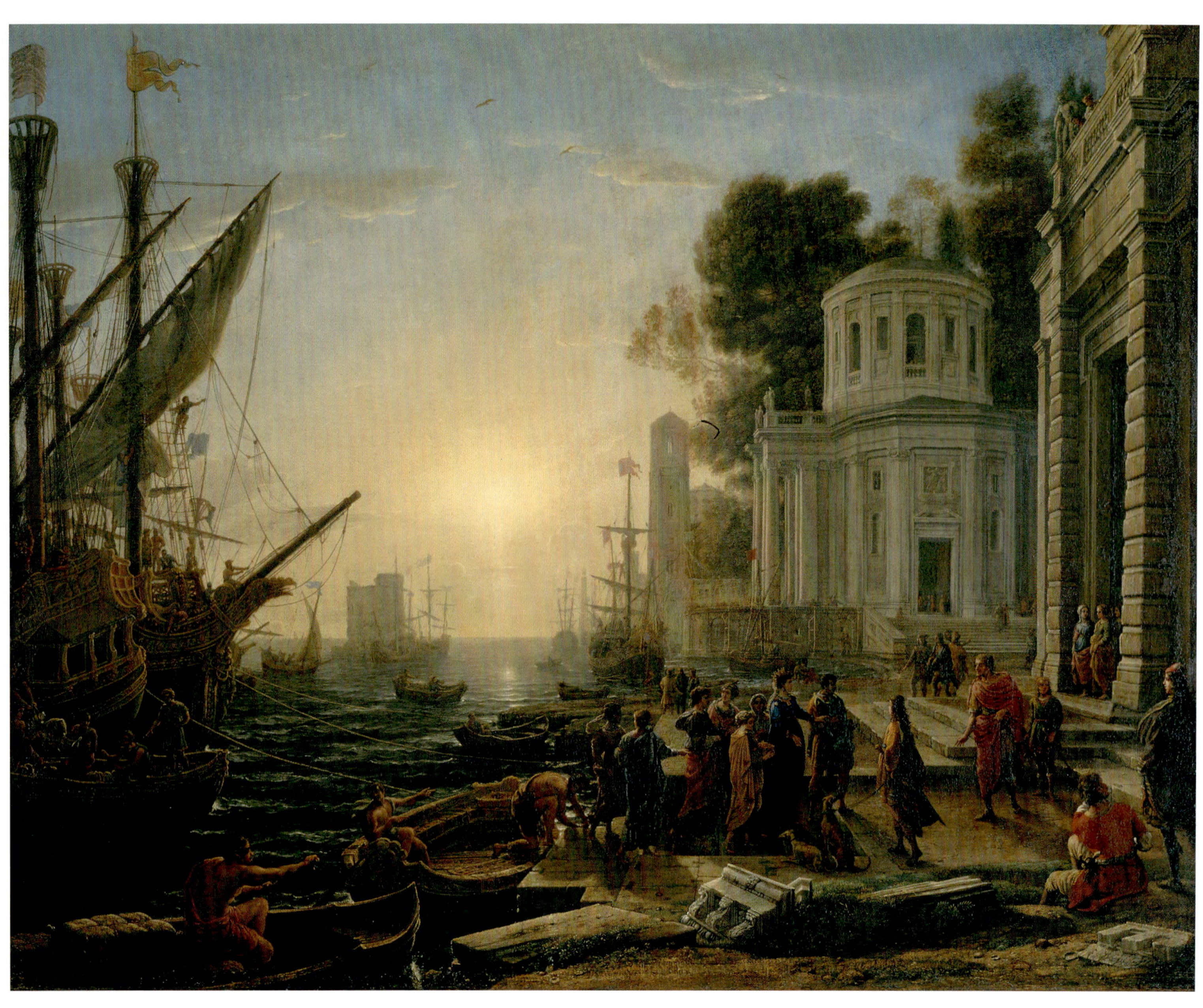

Fig. 69
Claude Lorrain
The Disembarkation of Cleopatra at Tarsus, 1642–43
Oil on canvas, 46⅞ × 66⅞ in.
(119 × 170 cm)
Musée du Louvre, Paris, France

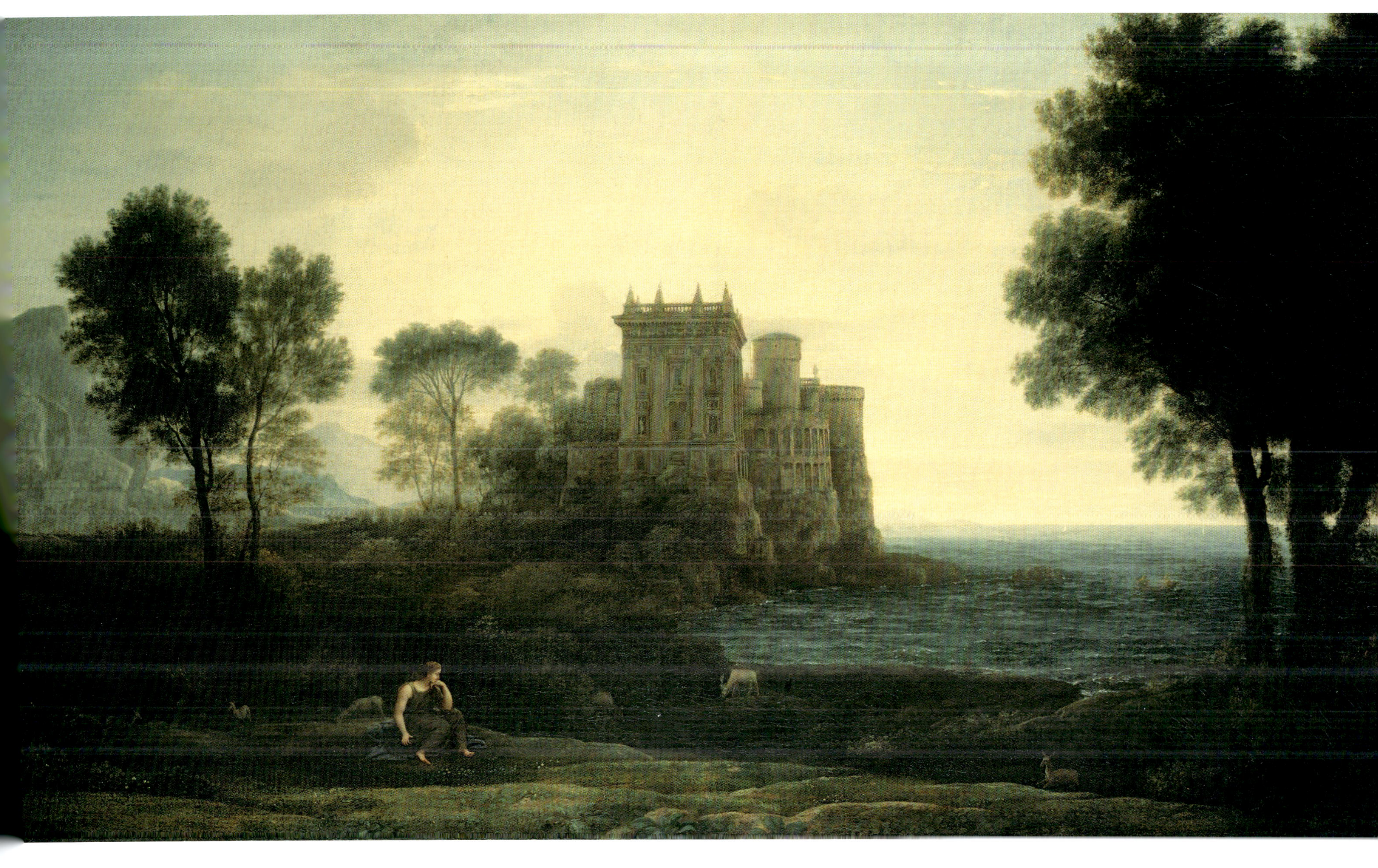

Fig. 70
Claude Lorrain
Landscape with Psyche outside the Palace of Cupid ("The Enchanted Castle")
Oil on canvas, 34¼ × 59½ in. (87.1 × 151.3 cm)
The National Gallery, London, Bought with contribution from the National Heritage Memorial Fund and the National Art Collections, 1981

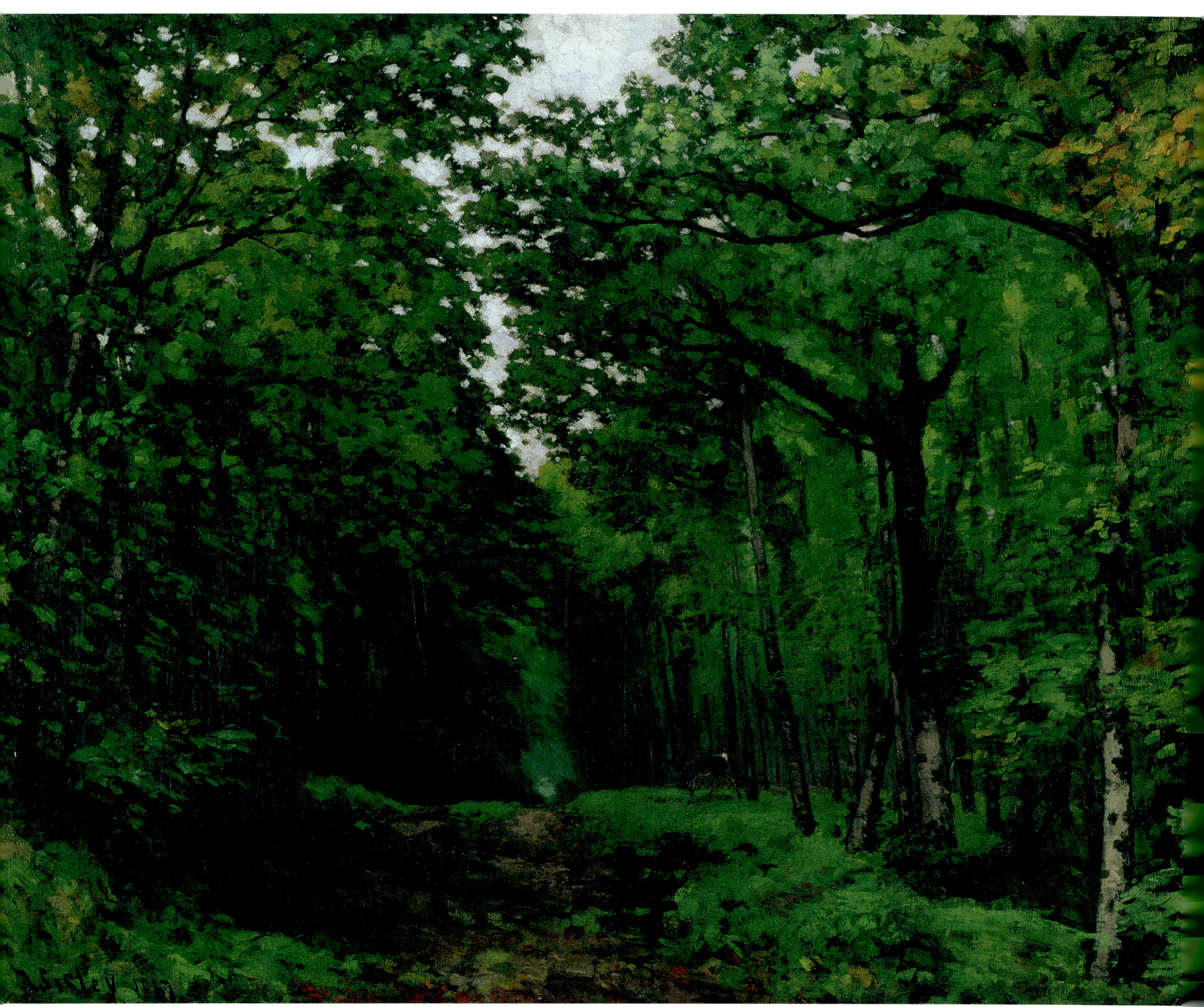

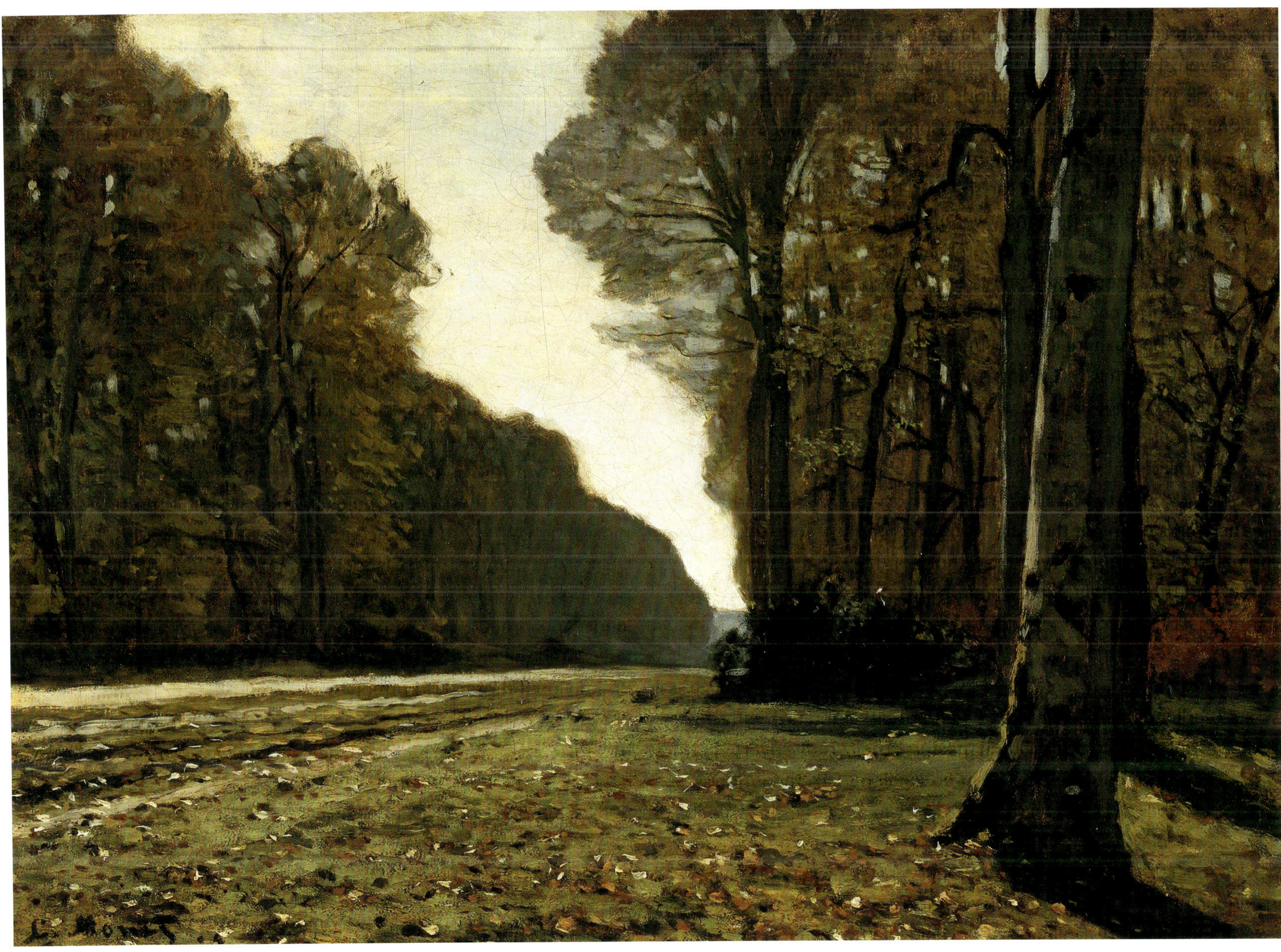

Fig. 72
Alfred Sisley
The Avenue of Chestnut Trees near La Celle-Saint-Cloud, 1867
Oil on canvas, 37½ × 48⅛ in. (95.5 × 122.2 cm)
Southampton City Art Gallery, Hampshire

Fig. 71
Claude Monet
The Road to Chailly (Forest of Fontainebleau), c. 1865
Oil on canvas, 17⅛ × 23¼ in. (43.5 × 59 cm)
Musée d'Orsay, Paris, France

there are in seventeenth-century landscapes. They speak of Claude, Van Goyen, Hobbema, and, of course, Poussin."[8] Indeed, Pissarro undertook in 1872–73 an ambitious series of four paintings of the seasons (private collection, Madrid). Conceptually if not stylistically, these acknowledged the older master's famous depiction of that subject, painted in 1660–64 for the duc de Richelieu. Acquired by Louis XIV in 1665, the paintings were on full public view in the nineteenth century in the newly created Musée du Louvre, where Pissarro could have seen them. In his broad panoramic canvases of the seasons, Pissarro celebrated the agricultural plenitude of the raised farmland of the Vexin plateau just north of Pontoise. Pissarro's paintings fall both within the great tradition of sets of the seasons, as exemplified by Poussin, and without it, in the sense that they concentrate on an utterly contemporary, albeit rural, depiction of their chosen subjects.

Now, of course, Pissarro's paintings do not "look" particularly like the works of any of their distinguished predecessors—his facture and palette were far removed from those of the seventeenth-century Dutch, and the broadly applied, relatively unmixed colors of Impressionism bespeak a totally different technical approach from the finely brushed glazes of the older masters. If any superficial comparison is to be drawn with his scenes of peasant labor in the countryside, it is surely (earlier remarks quoted by him notwithstanding) with those of the seventeenth-century Dutch masters. Their "rediscovery" in the mid-nineteenth century was due in no small part to the writings of Thoré-Bürger. He aptly described their art as providing a "true history, . . . a kind of photography of their great seventeenth century."[9] In retrospect, it could be said that France, and Paris in particular, was experiencing a "great nineteenth century," with obvious parallels to seventeenth-century Holland in the field of the visual arts—artists wished to celebrate national achievement, prosperity, and the beauty of their native land.

The debt to Dutch art could be seen more obviously in the works of Pissarro's more orthodox contemporaries—such as the Barbizon artists Narcisse Diaz de la Peña, Jules Dupré, and Rousseau—but rather too slavishly. As Charles Blanc observed of the 1866 Salon, "The Dutch, who have been the preferred masters of the modern school, and from whom proceed our genre and landscape painters, have been much more varied in their execution than their descendants."[10] This complaint of monotony and lack of variety is encountered frequently in the criticism of mainstream French landscape painters at the Salon during the early Impressionist era.

In addition to the Dutch, from the early years of his career Pissarro had demonstrated an awareness of the French academic tradition in landscape, itself founded on a profound appreciation of the worth of the old masters. Academic teaching decreed that large pictures intended for exhibition be preceded by a compositional sketch. Pissarro adhered to this practice for certain of his more ambitious pieces intended for the Salons of the 1860s, for example the so-called *Towpath* (Glasgow City Council [Museums]) of 1864, the sketch or *esquisse* for which survives at the Fitzwilliam Museum, Cambridge. In another of his many and highly informative letters to his son Lucien, he reveals his knowledge of the major treatise of French Neoclassical landscape painting, Pierre-Henri de Valenciennes's *Elémens de Perspective. . . .* , first published in 1800: "In the box [that Pissarro has sent to Lucien] you will find a book which has been separated into several parts for greater convenience; [Armand] Guillaumin sends it to you. It is by the famous Valenciennes, it is still the best and the most practical, try to take account of its basic principles."[11] As Peter Galassi has demonstrated, Neoclassical landscape theory unwittingly provided a crucial bridge between the old masters and "modern" landscape practice. In its pursuit of the *beau idéal,* Neoclassicism advocated the *étude* or study *sur le motif,* that is, directly from nature, of individual motifs and effects that could be incorporated into the final, essentially classical, composition produced in the studio. Thus the fresh, open-air oil sketches of Valenciennes, Corot, and others are now taken as direct harbingers of Impressionism, under the assumption that Impressionist paintings were produced almost entirely in the open air. However, Galassi neatly subverted this prevailing orthodoxy in one of his closing remarks:

> The same is true generally of modern landscape painting in France. By treating outdoor painting in isolation it is possible to construct a continuous tradition from Valenciennes to [Paul] Cézanne. Such a continuity is implied when historians note, as they often now do, that Pissarro advised his son to consult Valenciennes's treatise. But the key to the French tradition is precisely that outdoor painting was not isolated from the grand ideals of the studio. Impressionism is inaccurately described as a triumph of outdoor painting over studio routine, of empiricism over stale convention. Rather the triumph consisted in investing the fresh opportunity of open-air work with the venerable ambitions of the studio.[12]

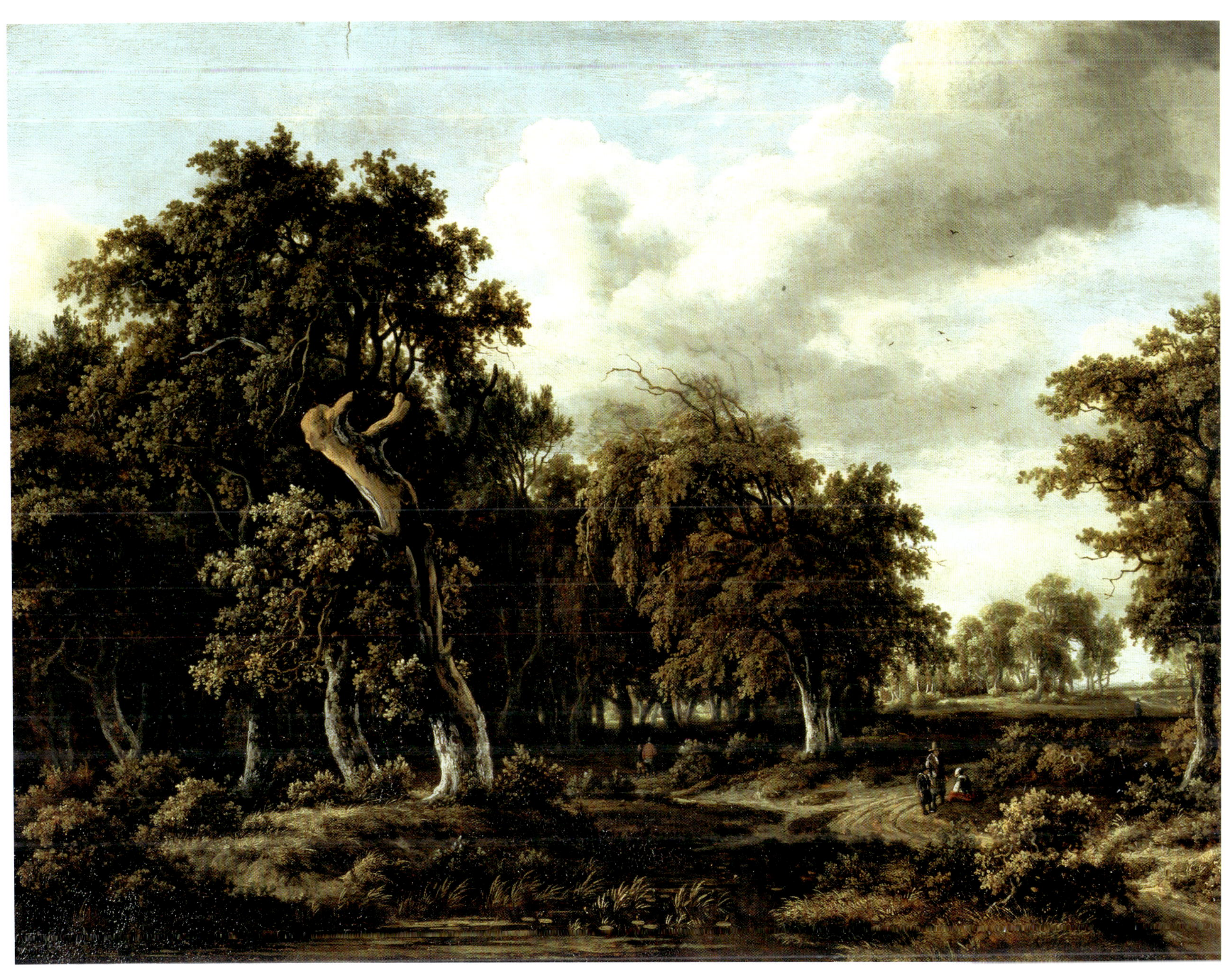

Fig. 73
Meindert Hobbema
The Oak Forest
Oil on wood, 23⅝ × 31½ in. (60 × 80 cm)
Musée du Louvre, Paris, France

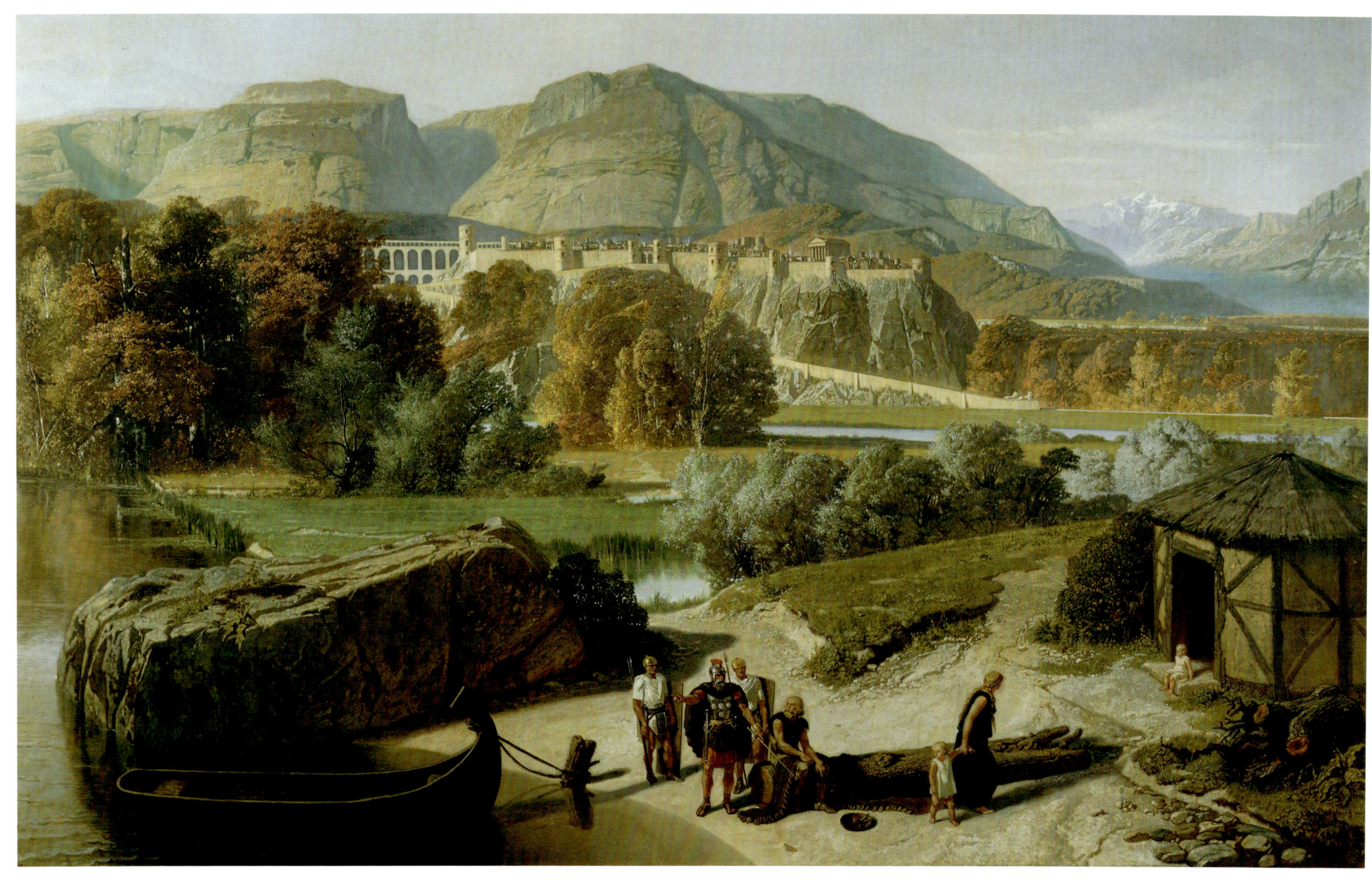

Fig. 74
Octave Penguilly l'Haridon
(1811–1870)
Roman City in the Alps, Shortly after the Conquest of Gaul, 1870
Oil on canvas, 51½ × 81⅞ in.
(131 × 208 cm)
Musée d'Orsay, Paris, France

As Galassi correctly observed, the Impressionists never abandoned those "venerable ambitions." Frequent references in their surviving correspondence and detailed technical examinations of their works attest to the fact that much of their work was completed in the studio, and on rare occasions begun there. This was particularly true of Monet in the 1860s, though by about 1870 he was more firmly committed to open-air painting. Nevertheless, he continued to paint large studio compositions from time to time and never wholly renounced the practice of studio reworking; his correspondence with his dealer Durand-Ruel contains frequent references to studio retouchings. By the latter part of his career the practicalities of advancing years made the use of the studio an increasing necessity, and the constant expectation that he paint in the "open air" clearly irritated him. Witness the following remark from a letter of 1905: "whether my Cathedrals, my Londons and other canvases are painted from nature or not, that is nobody's business and is of no importance. I know so many painters who paint from nature and create nothing but horrors."[13]

By that date Impressionism and its main practitioners had acquired considerable celebrity, and, as we shall see, certain writers were already attempting to place it and them within the context of the long tradition of landscape painting in France. Understandably, these observers made little reference to the somewhat *retardataire* "classical" landscapes that were still being produced as late as the 1870s, such as Octave Penguilly l'Haridon's extraordinary *Roman City in the Alps, Shortly after the Conquest of Gaul* (fig. 74), a painting in the grand style that makes conscious reference to France's Roman past. As John House has observed, the picture is a curious hybrid, partly Neoclassical and partly related to the historical genre paintings of Jean-Léon Gérôme, which had recently become popular.[14] The predominant visual language is that of the *paysage historique* or *paysage composé*, ultimately based on Poussin and Claude and for which a quadrennial Prix de Rome had been established as long ago as 1816.[15] By the 1860s, this category had been deemed redundant; it was officially discontinued in 1863. The last Prix de Rome for landscape was awarded in 1861 to Paul-Albert Girard for his *The Triumph of Silenus* (fig. 75), a subject that had been depicted in Western art since classical times. Such landscapes had become nothing more than repetitive pastiches. A more viable approach to the classical tradition was practiced by Corot in such diaphanous pastorales as *Memory of Mortefontaine (Oise)* (fig. 76) of 1864, though Émile Zola, in a famous review of the 1866 Salon, urged Corot to kick over the final traces of this heritage: "If M. Corot would agree to kill off once and for all the nymphs with which he populates his woods, and replace them with peasant women, I would love him beyond measure."[16]

Two years later, in his Salon review for 1868, Zola produced a piece of critical writing that is of fundamental importance to our discussion. In the section "Les Paysagistes," he began with the ringing declaration, "Our landscape painters have clearly broken with tradition." He continued: "Classical landscape is dead, killed off by life and truth. Nobody would dare to say today that nature needs to be idealized, that the skies and waters are vulgar, and that it is necessary to render harmonious and correct horizons if one wishes to make beautiful works." Only the Dutch School, in its particular setting, had, according to Zola, hitherto interrogated and understood nature. By contrast, nature in Poussin's France had been so unattractive in reality that it had to be reinvented: "The landscape painter composed a landscape as one builds an edifice. The trees represented the columns, the sky was the dome of the temple. There was not the least sympathy for pearly dawns, for blood red sunsets, not the least concern for truth and life. A simple need for grandeur, an ideal of majestic architecture."[17] Acknowledging the large number of artists working in this category, Zola went on, however, to deplore their sameness, their lack of personality, of artistic temperament. These painters—and it is worth remembering that Zola was writing about Salon rather than Impressionist landscape—constituted the great flock of painters who migrated each summer to the countryside, easels at the ready, to depict the trees, thickets, and mists that half a century of French Romantic poetry—the verses of Alfred de Musset, Gérard de Nerval, Alphonse de Lamartine, and others—had predisposed the French public to admire. These were the sort of painters, modeled very much on the figure of Charles-François Daubigny, who had been celebrated in Frédéric Henriet's *Le Paysagiste aux champs* of 1866.[18] This popular text aptly described the generation of midcentury landscape painters, memorably dismissed by Charles Baudelaire as "too herbivorous in their diet."[19] As Zola described it:

> Our landscape painters leave at dawn, [paint] boxes on their backs, happy as hunters who love the open air. They go to sit themselves down it matters not where, there by the edge of the forest, here at the water's edge, scarcely choosing their motifs, finding everywhere a living horizon with a human interest, as it were. All, the minor and the great, the excellent

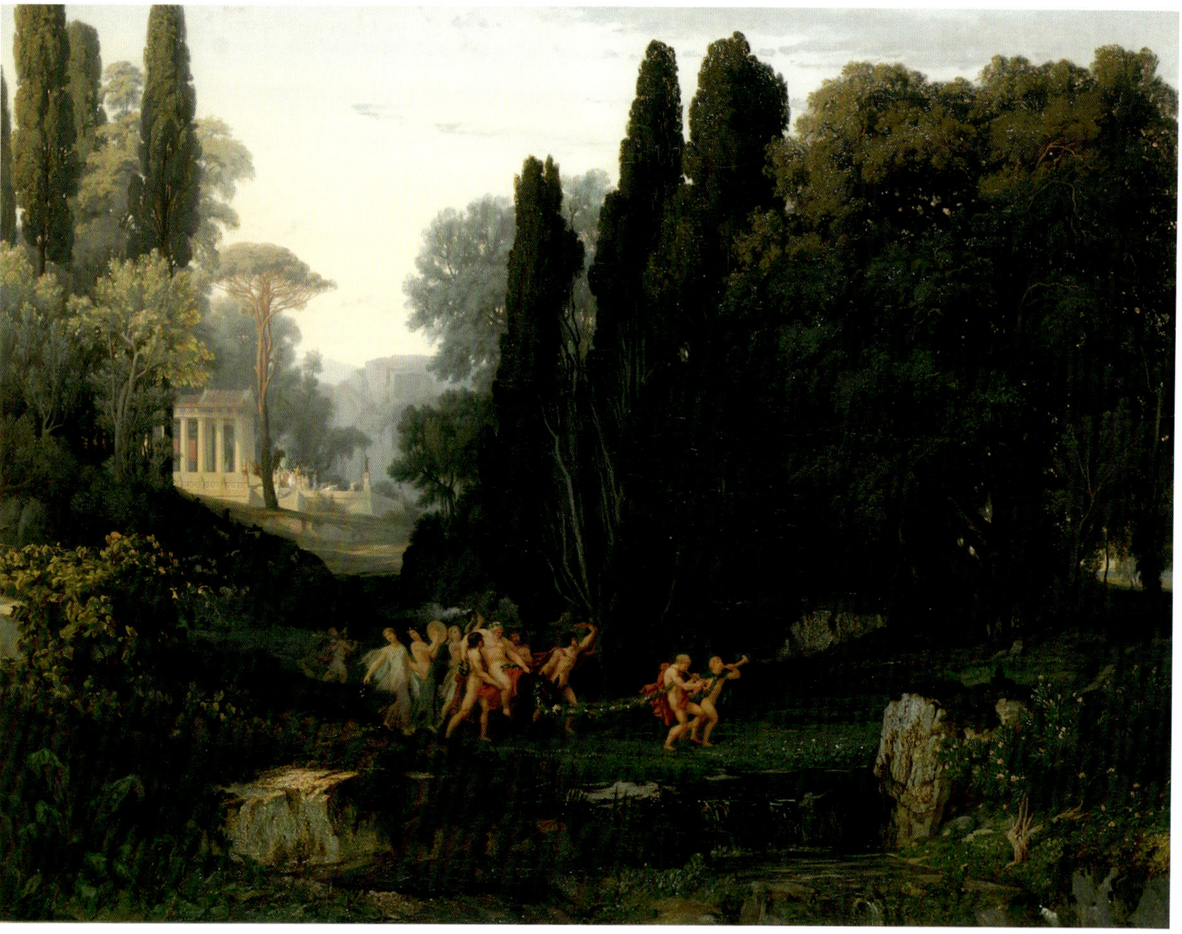

Fig. 75
Paul-Albert Girard (1839–1920)
The Triumph of Silenus, 1861
Oil on canvas, 44½ × 57⅞ in.
(113 × 147 cm)
École Nationale Supérieure des Beaux-Arts, Paris

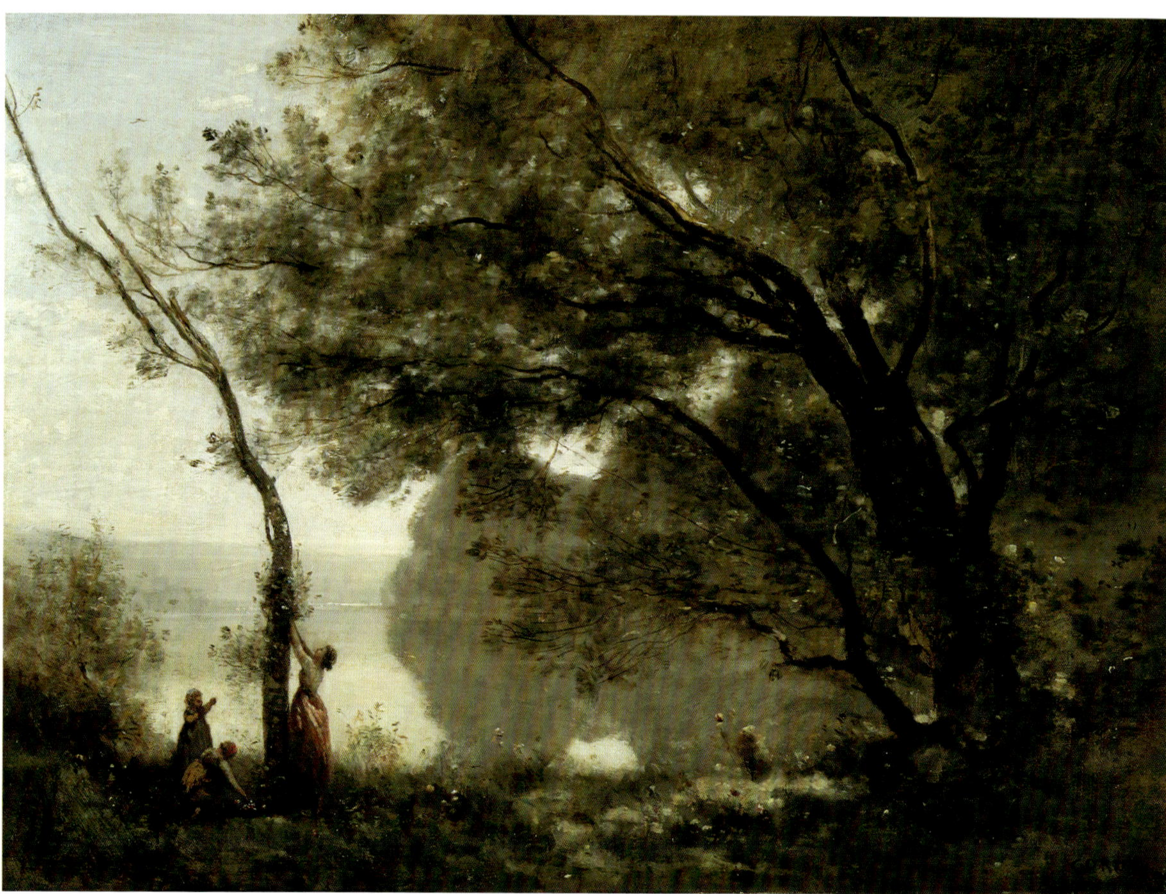

Fig. 76
Jean-Baptiste Camille Corot (1796–1875)
Memory of Mortefontaine (Oise), 1864
Oil on canvas, 25½ × 35 in. (65 × 89 cm)
Musée du Louvre, Paris, France

and the mediocre, follow the same footpaths, obey the same instinct which leads them into the countryside and tells them to interpret it such as it is.[20]

Such mindless repetition was countered, in Zola's view, by a category that, tellingly, he labeled not "paysagiste" but "actualiste." These were the painters of "sujets modernes," who had perceived that "la peinture classique" made the public yawn and had accordingly dispensed with it. At the top of this category came Monet:

> He loves the horizons of our towns, the gray and white dots made by houses in the clear sky, he loves, in the streets, busy people who run in thick cardigans; he loves racecourses, aristocratic promenades with the din of carriages; he loves our women, with their umbrellas, their gloves, their fabrics, even their false hair and their face powder, everything which makes them women of our civilization.
>
> In the fields Claude Monet will prefer an English park to a corner of a forest. He likes to find the trace of man everywhere, he always wishes to live in our midst. Like a true Parisian he takes Paris to the countryside, he cannot paint a landscape without placing in it dressed-up gentlemen and ladies. Nature would appear to lose interest for him as soon as it does not bear the imprint of our social habits.[21]

Monet's great manifesto along these lines was to have been his *Luncheon on the Grass,* an extremely large, fifteen-by-twenty-foot canvas destined for the Salon of 1866 but never completed. Two fragments survive in the Musée d'Orsay, Paris. The original compositional sketch, now in the Pushkin Museum, Moscow (fig. 77), provides further proof of how the young Impressionists followed academic practice in some of their early exhibition projects. In this gathering on the edge of the Forest of Fontainebleau, contemporary Paris, in the form of Monet and a company of his friends, has gone to the countryside, bringing with it the trappings of modern fashion and the urbanite's love of a picnic. The Forest of Fontainebleau, directly accessible by train from Paris since 1849, was an extremely popular tourist spot, as well known as the gardens of the Tuileries or the various bathing spots and *guinguettes* (an open-air café or dance hall) on the great loops of the Seine to the west of Paris that were frequented by the rapidly increasing bourgeoisie of the Second Empire. Contemporary mores were thus richly observed in Monet's hugely ambitious project, a large-scale celebration of modern leisure. But the debt to the old master tradition was considerable. Initially, of course, there was the inspiration of Edouard Manet's infamous, and far more ambiguous, *Luncheon on the Grass* (fig. 3) of 1863, shown at the Salon des Refusés that year. Manet's mixture of modern clothed male and nude and partially clothed female figures was much more deliberately provocative, though it was "clothed," as it were, in Manet's stated desire to redo Titian's *Le Concert champêtre* (fig. 4) and in his very obvious compositional borrowing from the Renaissance engraver Marcantonio Raimondi's print after Raphael's *Judgment of Paris* (fig. 5). Old master prints also played a crucial role in the strange *Fishing* (cat. 51, p. 36), dated 1861–63, in which Manet drew on landscapes by Annibale Carracci and Peter Paul Rubens as sources of inspiration (figs. 8–10). In the right foreground he portrays himself and his mistress Suzanne Leenhoff in the manner and costume of Rubens and his second wife, Hélène Fourment. What matters in the context of this essay is the ease with which Manet quoted from, and in this instance comfortably pastiched, the old master tradition, perhaps as a private gesture. As Belinda Thomson has tellingly observed, Manet "was undoubtedly a catalyst and rallying figure for the rising generation."[22] He never participated in any of the Impressionist group shows, however, and his more obvious imbibing of the old masters set him somewhat apart from his colleagues.

Monet's lineage was less marked but nevertheless discernible. His *Luncheon on the Grass*[23] can clearly be located within the great French tradition of parkland scenes in which the sexes gather to eat (the eighteenth-century hunting picnics of Carle Van Loo, for example) or for dalliance. In the latter context one thinks particularly of the early-eighteenth-century *fêtes galantes* of Jean-Antoine Watteau such as his *Assembly in a Park* (fig. 78), a number of which were on public view, and of the works of his follower Jean-Baptiste-Joseph Pater (cat. 71, p. 173).

Even in what might be termed the decade of High Impressionism, the 1870s, echoes of the old masters can be found in a variety of Impressionist compositions. Inevitably, certain of Monet's Dutch landscapes of 1871, undertaken during his exile from France during the Franco-Prussian War, call to mind those of his seventeenth-century forebears. The extensive views, low horizons, and soaring skies that were depicted by artists such as Salomon van Ruysdael are found again in certain canvases by Monet (cat. 94, p. 176; cat. 60, p. 96). In some instances there is an almost uncanny correspondence in the placement of the canal or riverbank, the depiction of a rowboat. Monet's approach to composition in these pictures, matters

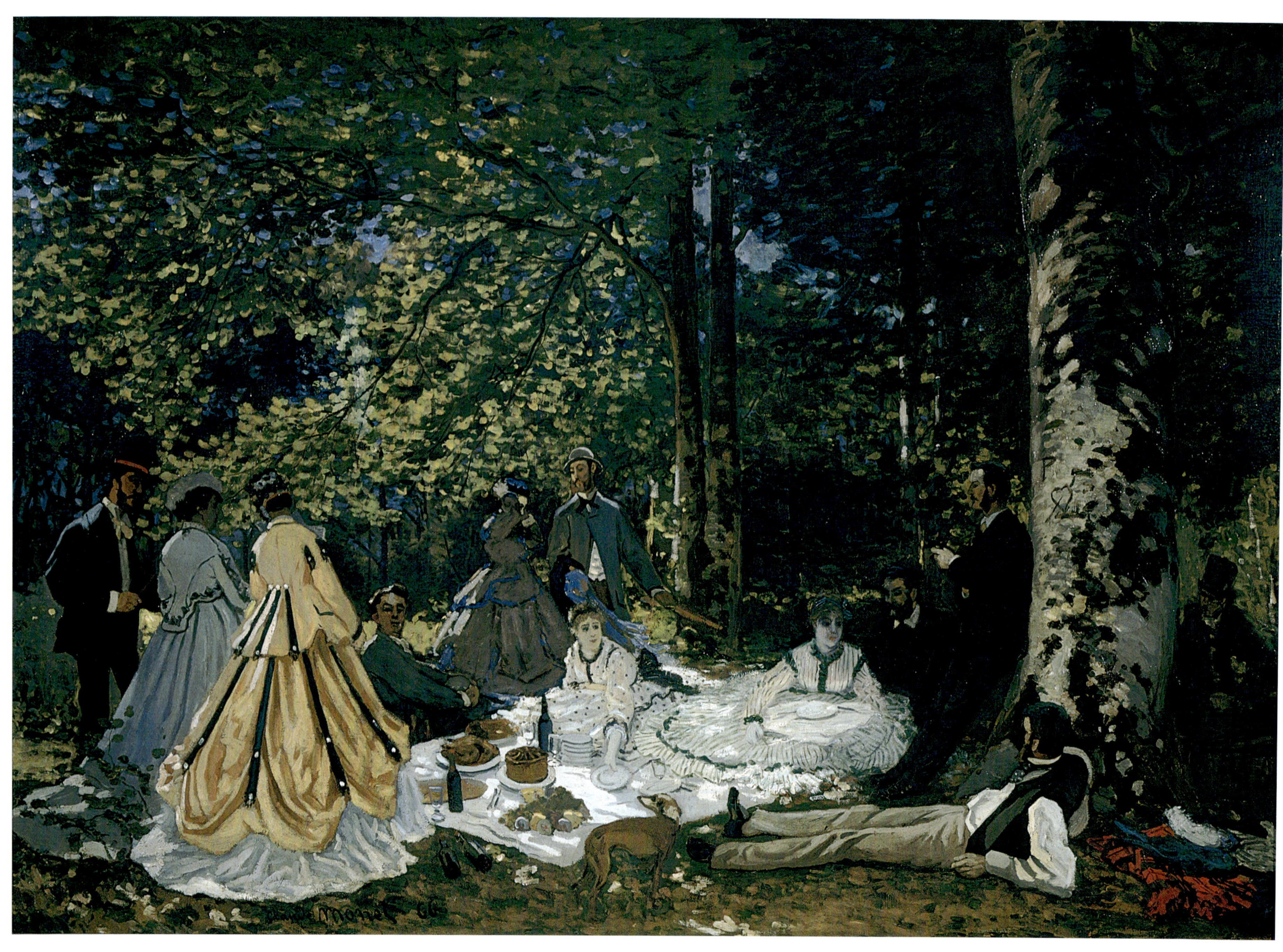

Fig. 77
Claude Monet
Luncheon on the Grass, 1866
Oil on canvas, 51⅛ × 71¼ in.
(130 × 181 cm)
The State Pushkin Museum
of Fine Arts, Moscow

Fig. 78
Jean-Antoine Watteau
Assembly in a Park
Oil on wood, 12½ × 18⅛ in. (32 × 46 cm)
Musée du Louvre, Paris, Francevv

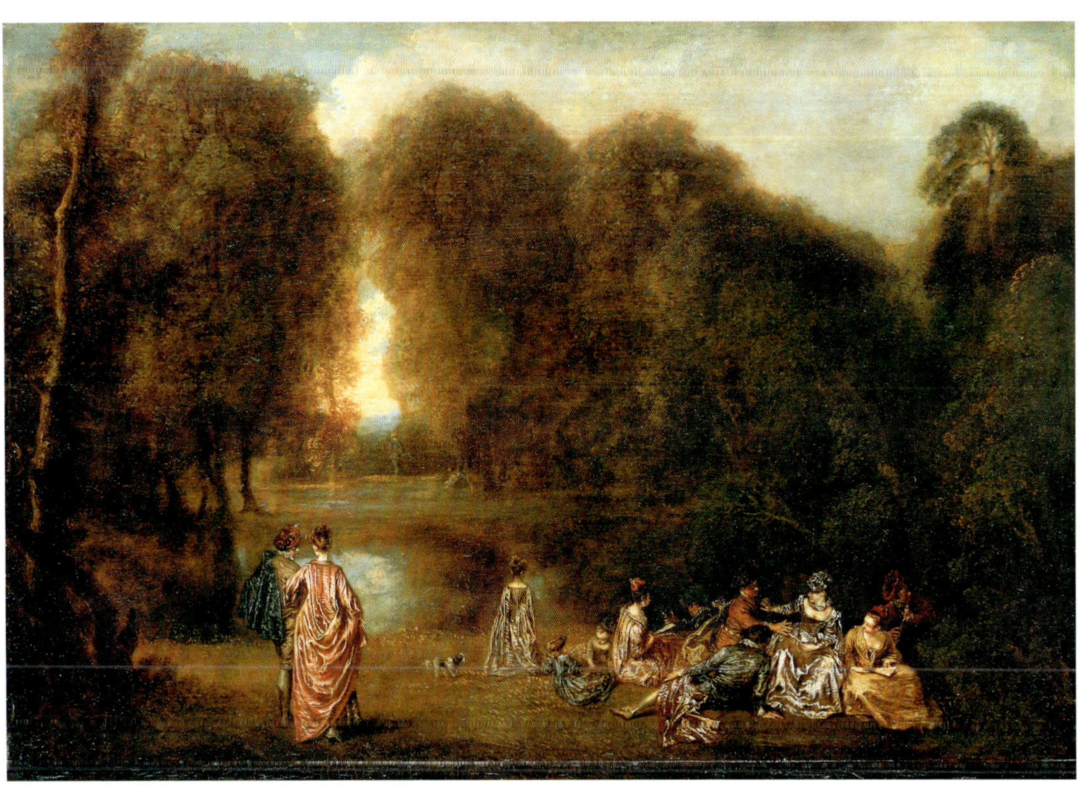

Cat. 71
Jean-Baptiste-Joseph Pater
Country Party, 18th century

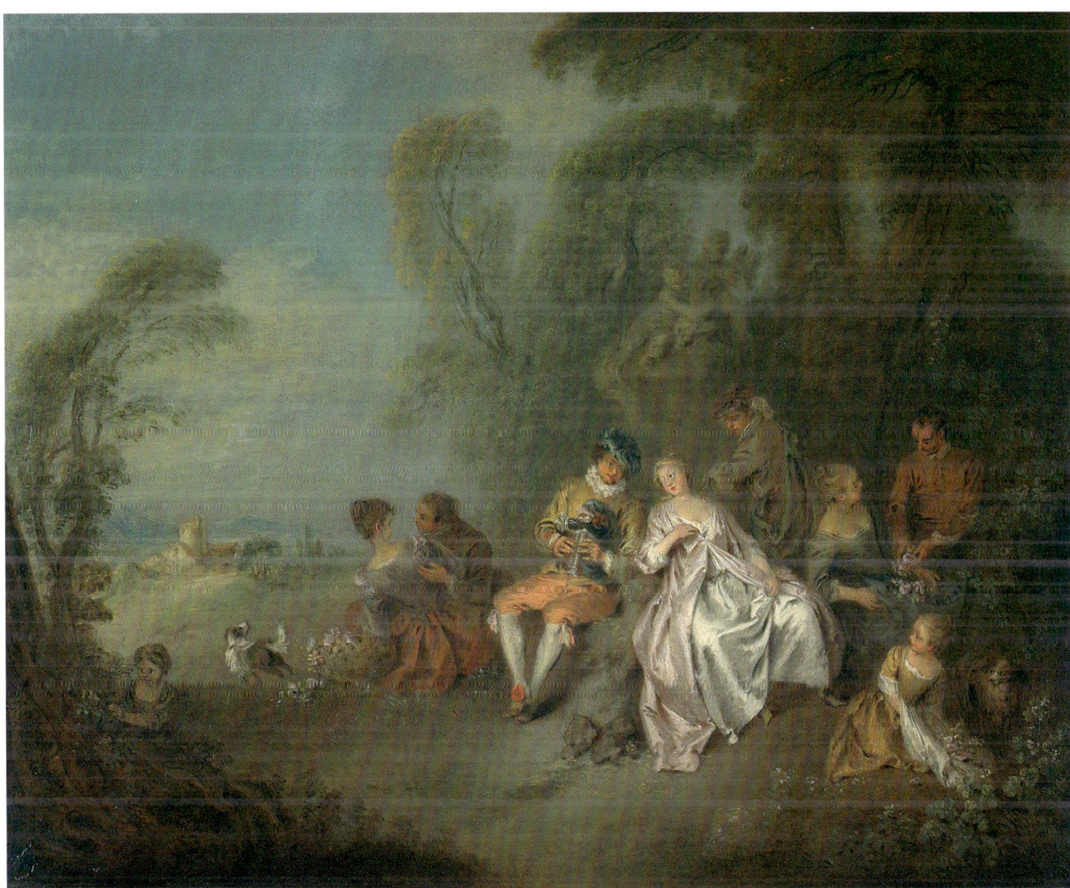

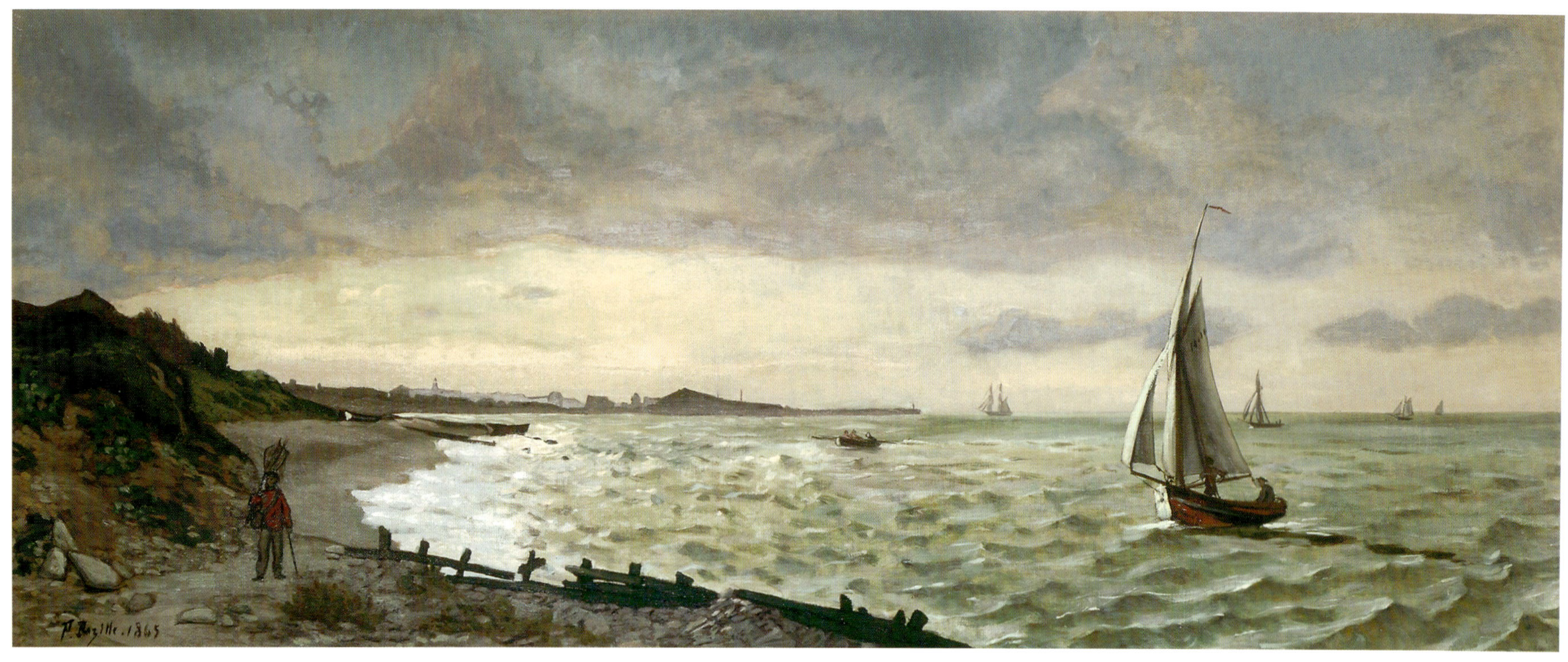

Cat. 2
Frédéric Bazille
The Beach at Sainte-Adresse, 1865

of color and facture notwithstanding, suggests more than a passing acquaintance with Dutch art, a subject that had been of increasing interest to French artists in the nineteenth century, many of whom are recorded in the visitors' book to the Trippenhuis, which housed the Rijksmuseum's collection until 1885 and which Monet visited with his friends Henry Havard and Henri Michel-Lévy on June 22, 1871.[24]

The most instructive comparison between the old masters and the Impressionists can be found in the complex and much discussed case of Paul Cézanne, an artist whose involvement with the Impressionists was short-lived, as he spent the majority of his later career in his native Aix-en-Provence, far removed from the Parisian mainstream. Although there is no reliable record in his own lifetime of Cézanne's remark that he wished to "re-do Poussin over again according to nature,"[25] it recurs sufficiently frequently in posthumous reminiscences of the artist for its veracity to be credible. As Richard Verdi has convincingly demonstrated, a deep artistic affinity between the two men can be seen in their ordered approach to landscape,[26] even though very few specific landscape compositions by Poussin can be shown to have directly influenced Cézanne. Indeed, although Cézanne's letters are littered with references to such old masters as Rubens and Tintoretto, he never mentions Poussin.

Nevertheless, the mighty structures that underlie Cézanne's heroic examination over several decades of the Mont Sainte-Victoire (cat. 13, p. 178; cat. 19, p. 178) find their only true predecessors in Poussin's rigidly ordered compositions of the late 1640s, such as the Phocion landscapes (fig. 79 and Walker Art Gallery, Liverpool) and the *Landscape with Buildings* (c. 1640–50; Museo del Prado, Madrid). Intriguingly, the only tangible evidence of a link with the classical tradition is provided by the existence in Cézanne's studio effects of two engravings after Jean-Victor Bertin,[27] one of the major, if unremarkable, exponents of the Neoclassical landscape manner that perpetuated the tradition of Poussin. Again, one is struck by the Impressionists' indirect knowledge of and appropriation from the old masters. Commentators after Cézanne's death were quick to place him in a direct line of descent, however, with Maurice Denis referring to him as "the Poussin of Impressionism,"[28] and Émile Bernard describing him as "a bridge . . . which brings Impressionism back to the Louvre."[29] Cézanne himself probably put it best in a letter of 1905 to Roger Marx: "To my mind one does not put oneself in place of the past, one only adds a new link."[30] Rather than direct imitation, we register an awareness on Cézanne's part of what has gone before together with a desire to add to the past in the spirit of development therefrom.

By the close of the nineteenth century many critical knives were being sharpened as far as Impressionism was concerned. Just as pictures painted in its idiom began to achieve widespread commercial success in both Europe and the United States, so in France it was perceived not as the fresh pursuit of modern subjects that had so enthralled Zola but as the betrayal of the great French tradition, as an art of materialism disfigured by what one writer, Raymond Bouyer, criticized as its pursuit of "optical accidents of the prism." Bouyer occupies an interesting fin de siècle position. In a series of six articles entitled "Le Paysage dans l'art," which appeared in the conservative journal *L'Artiste* in 1893, he attempted a review of the subject. Underlying his series was his proposal for a historical and comparative museum devoted to landscape. Just as, Bouyer claimed, the history of music could be traced from Giovanni Palestrina through Ludwig van Beethoven to Richard Wagner, so could landscape be followed from its beginnings in Flanders, on to Ruisdael and finally to the modern school. Bouyer's proposal was doubtless stimulated in part by a number of exhibitions that had recently been held in which the landscape masters of the past had been juxtaposed with those of the nineteenth century:

> we shall recall the *Cent chefs d'oeuvre* of 1883, where *The Forest* of old Meindert Hobbema demonstrated its robustness by the side of the antique poems of Corot, the modern poems of Rousseau and Millet, in the face of the fugitive poems of Diaz: we shall cite the May collection (Georges Petit gallery, 3 June 1890),[31] where ancient landscapes, romantic ones, indeed Impressionist ones were side by side: Berchem and Van Arthois, very dark, at the beginning; at the end, Sisley, Camille Pissarro, Claude Monet, multicolored; at the center, the divine Corot.[32]

Thus, at a surprisingly early date, Impressionism had been admitted into the "history" of landscape.

Monet's work was frequently exhibited in the first decade of the twentieth century, and it, and Impressionism in general, was increasingly assessed against the art of the past. Instead of being lauded for its own merits, it was sometimes found wanting in such a context. Reviewing an exhibition of Monet and Renoir at Durand-Ruel in 1908, Pierre Hepp observed: "Indeed, comparing it [Impressionism] to the landscape painters of the great epochs, one judges it to be too passive, letting itself be too split in two by spectacles, scarcely intervening intellectually except in practical execution."[33] In other words, compared to the art of the past, Impressionism was all technique but no intellectual content. The same exhibition led another critic, J. F. Schnerb, to go even further, contrasting Monet unfavorably with former masters of landscape, including Rembrandt, Claude, J.M.W. Turner, and John Constable: "He has not admitted *repoussoirs,* shaded foregrounds contrasted with luminous distances, he has not condensed the light on an object which forms the center, around which luminous intensity wanes accordingly."[34] He had not, in effect, created a classical landscape or *paysage composé* in the manner of Claude Lorrain. Such strictures notwithstanding, Monet's work generally received ever-increasing acclaim, particularly the later series of *Water Lilies*.

This critical evaluation of Impressionism in a historical context continued until the advent of World War II. In his *Traité du paysage* of 1939, the late Cubist painter André Lhote discerned two great families of landscape painters: the one concerned with tone and developing from Rembrandt; the other devoted to color, originating in Pieter Breughel and leading to the Impressionists. He also compared the Impressionists with Rubens: "Like Rubens the Impressionist pays homage to the nascent freshness of the world." Intriguingly,

Cat. 95
Alfred Sisley
View of Saint Mammès, 1880

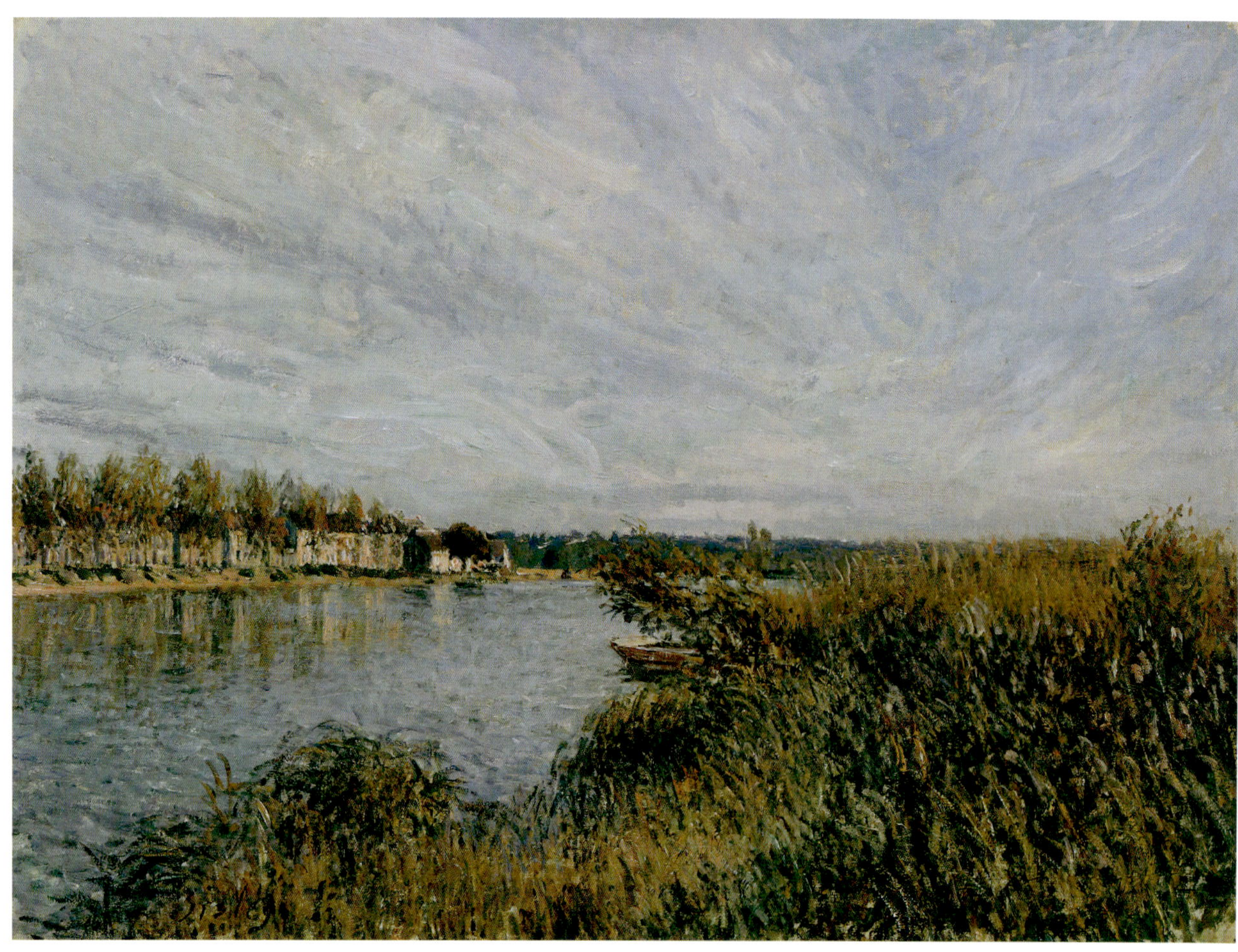

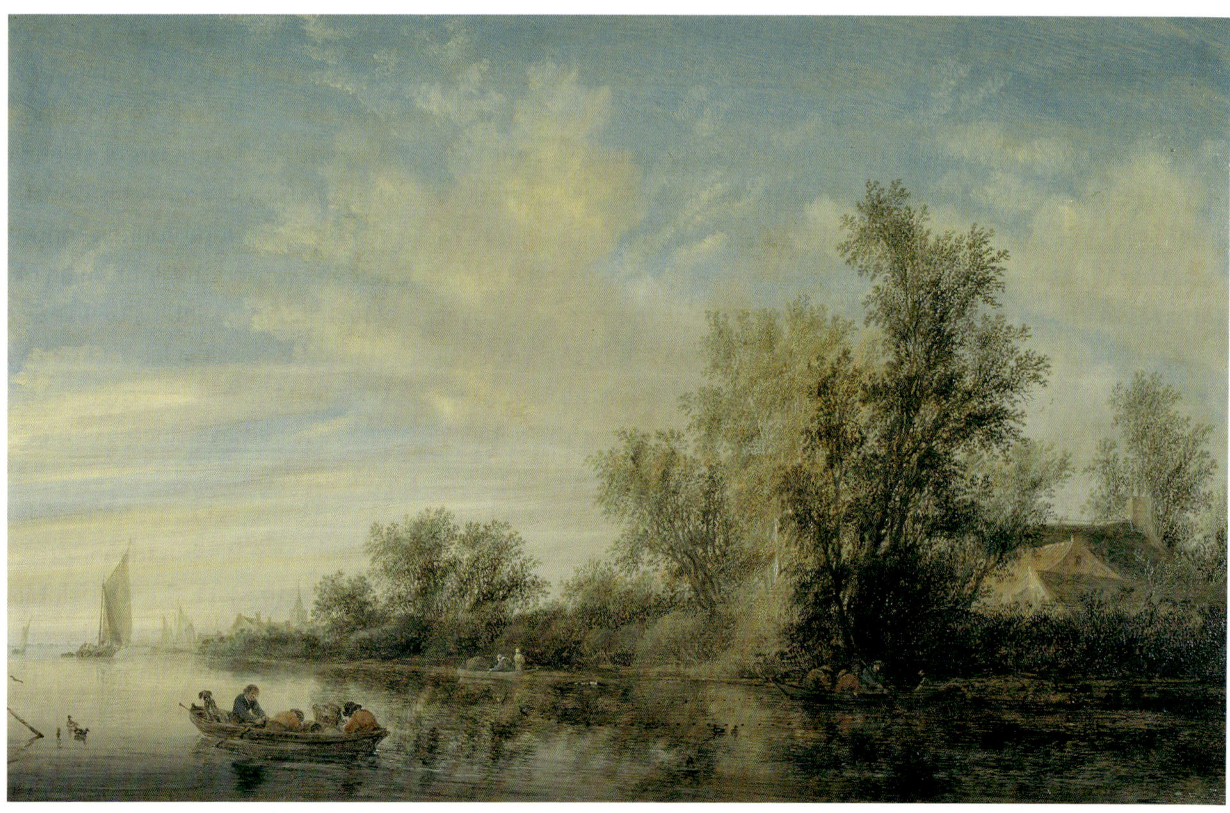

Cat. 94
Salomon van Ruysdael
River Landscape, 1644

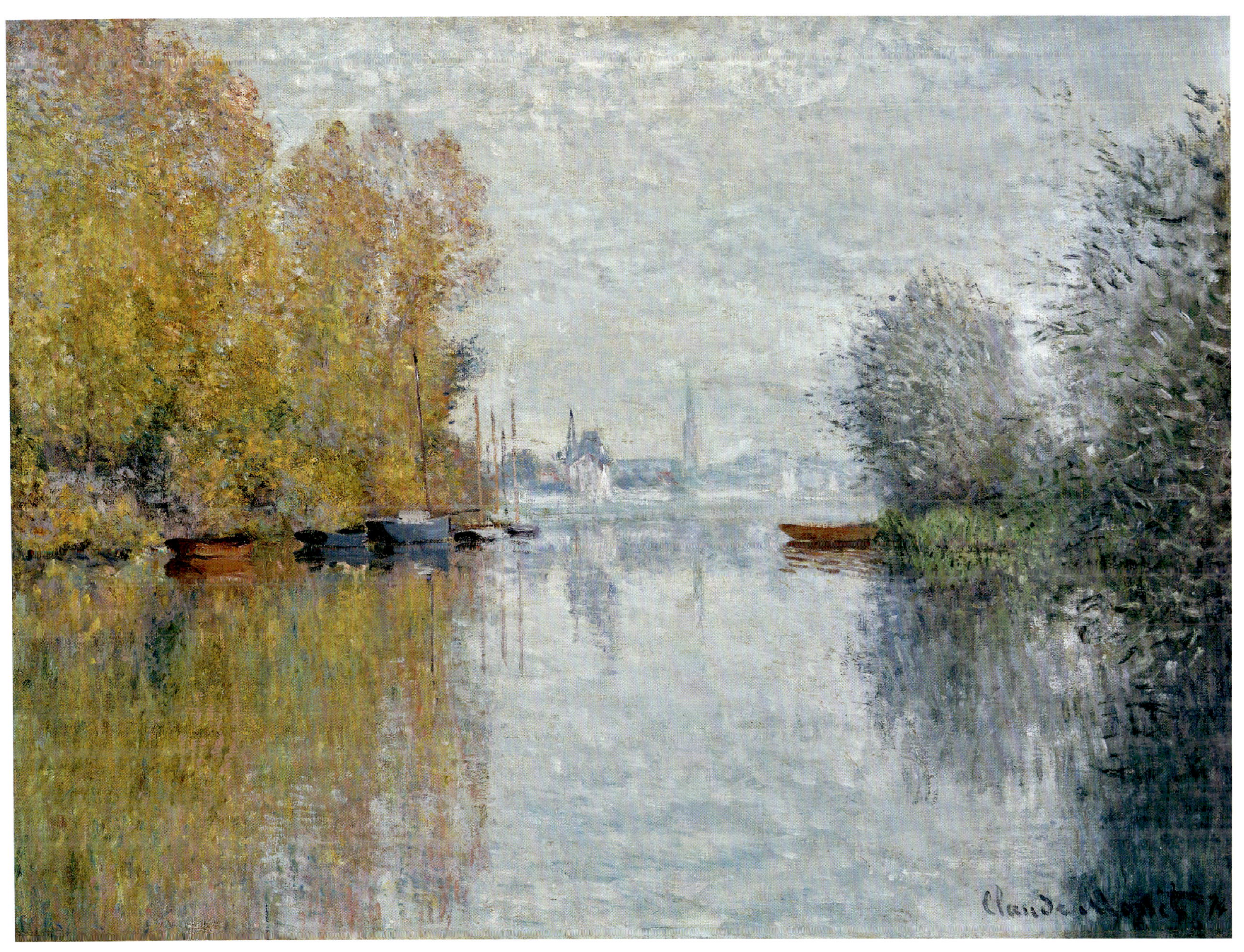

Cat. 62
Claude Monet
Autumn on the Seine, Argenteuil, 1873

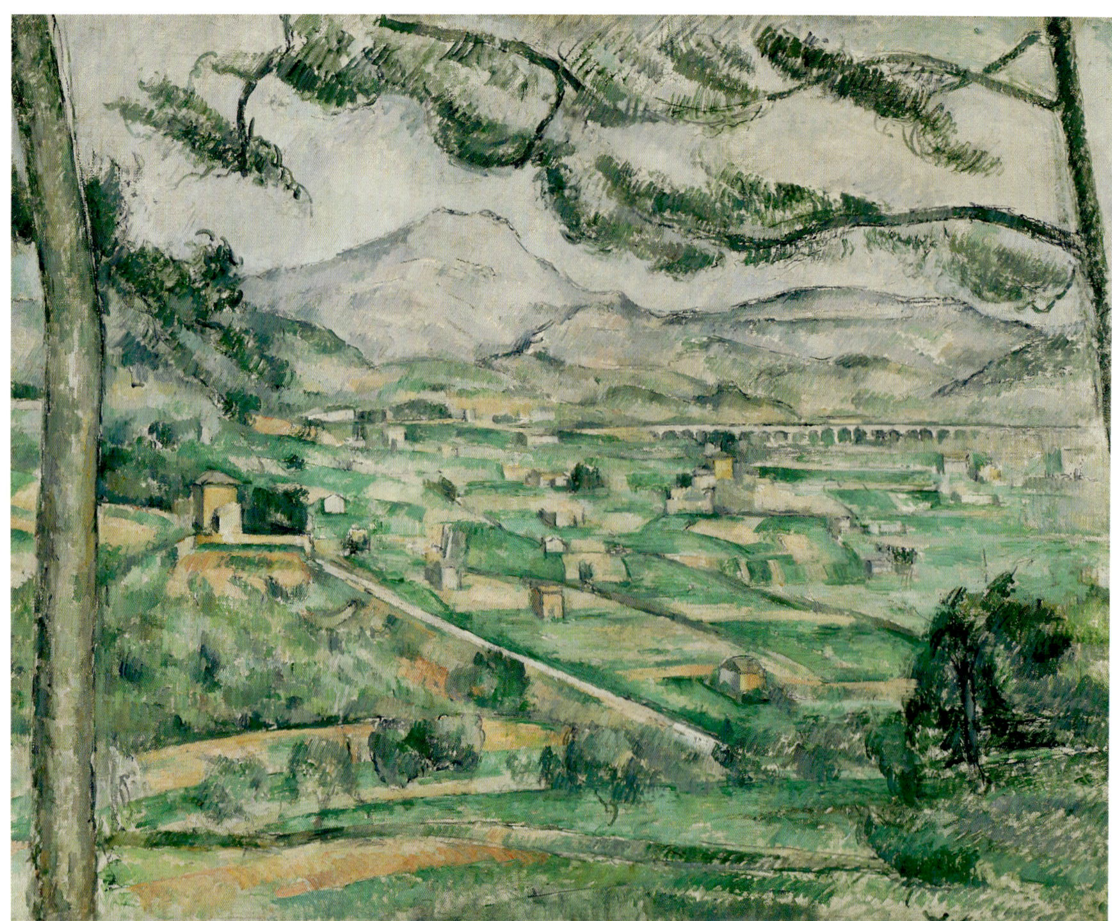

Cat. 13
Paul Cézanne
Mont Sainte-Victoire, 1886–87

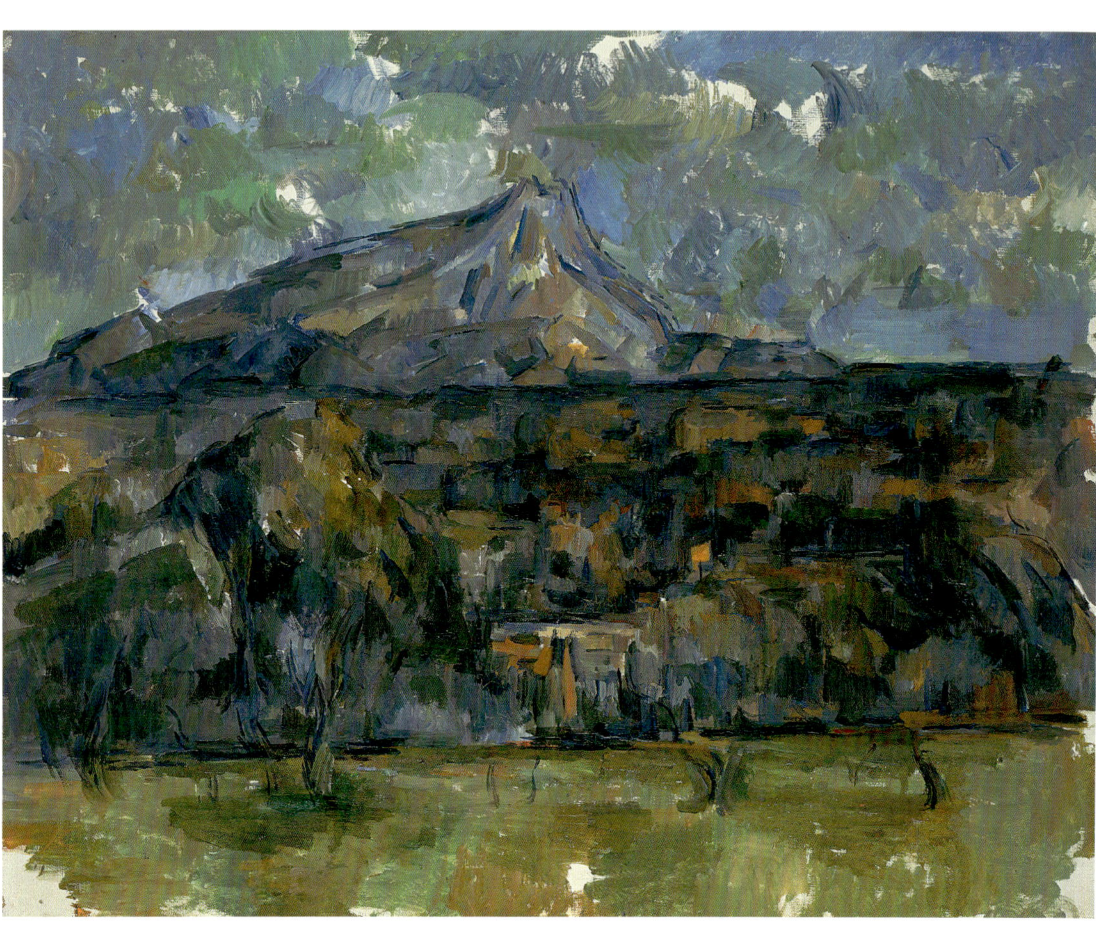

Cat. 19
Paul Cézanne
Mont Sainte-Victoire, 1902–6

Fig. 79
Nicolas Poussin (1594–1665)
Landscape with Burial of Phocion
Collection Earl of Plymouth, Oakley Park, Great Britain

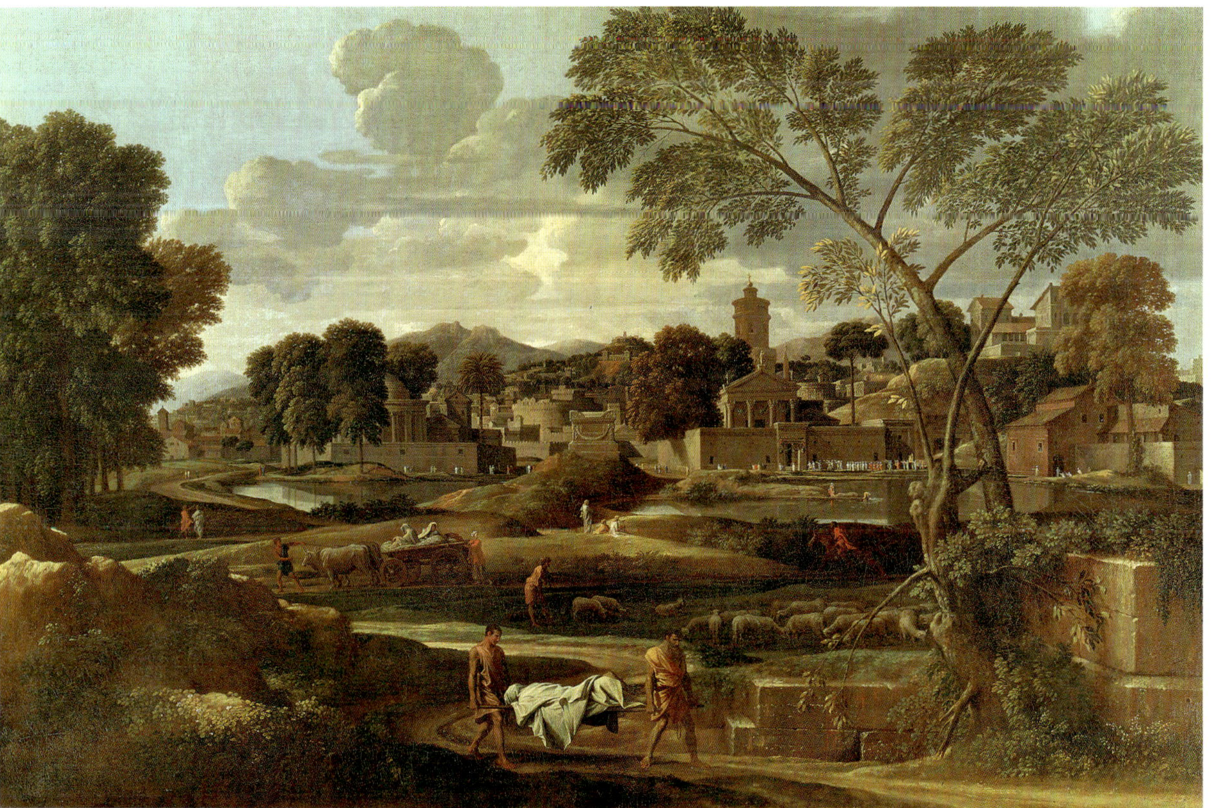

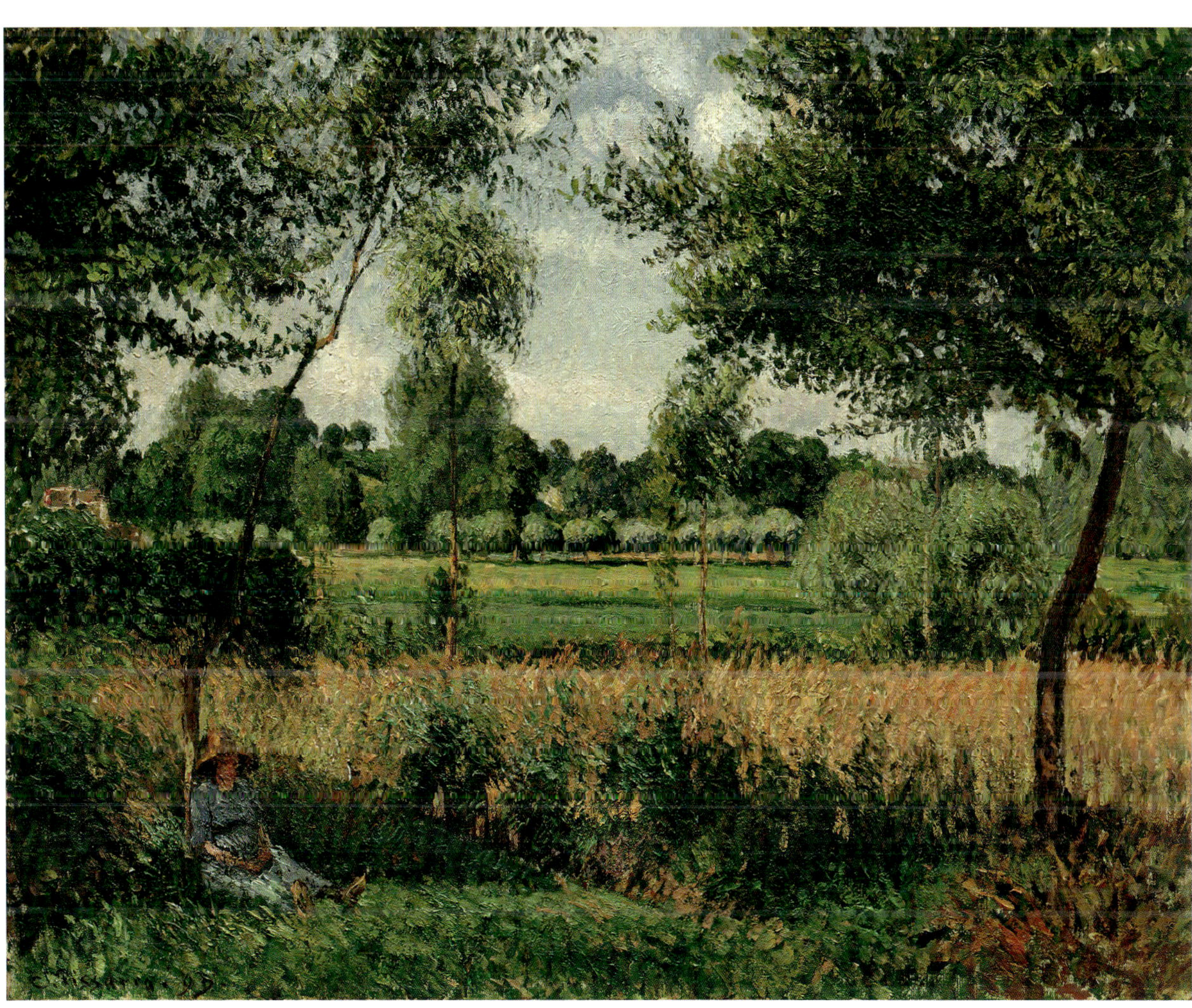

Cat. 76
Camille Pissarro
Morning, Sunlight Effect, Éragny, 1899

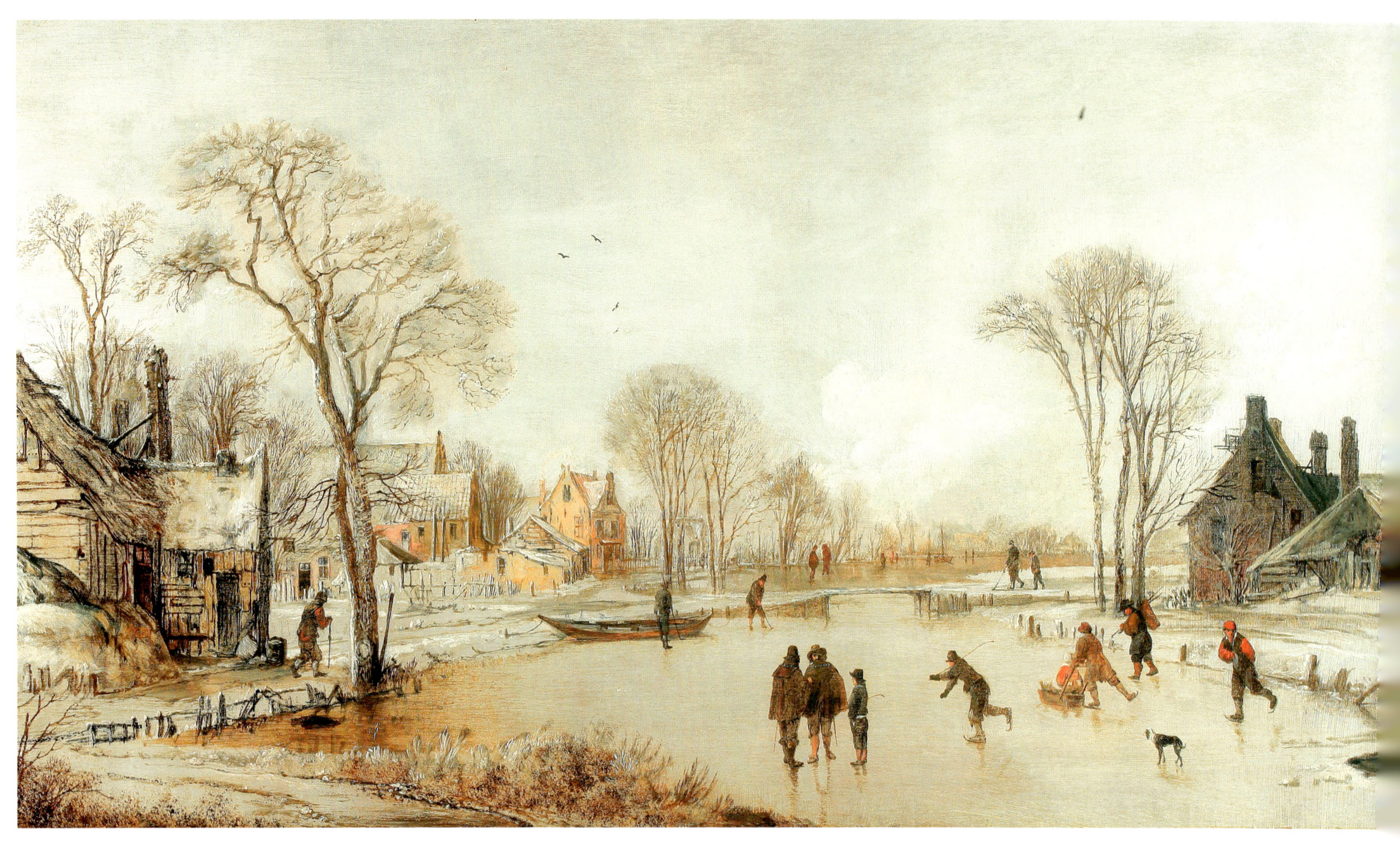

Cat. 70
Aert van der Neer
Skaters on a Frozen Canal by a Village

he also compared the great *Bathers* (The National Gallery, London) and *Sunday Afternoon on the Island of La Grande Jatte* (The Art Institute of Chicago) of the Neo-Impressionist Georges Seurat to the work of Piero della Francesca with its "architectural humans."[35] As far as the *paysage composé* was concerned, this had, according to Lhote, been taken up again by the Cubists in 1911–14, thereby having effectively bypassed Impressionism.

Although this is not the place to enter into a full critical history of Impressionism, it is worth noting that after World War II, and particularly in the major history of the movement published by John Rewald,[36] Impressionism was presented as a phenomenon that had broken fundamentally with the past, of which it bore little or no trace. Its undoubted originality, particularly with regard to technique, was constantly stressed. With the studies of Robert L. Herbert and others its subject matter was reassessed, and a different, and highly valid, originality was claimed. It was brilliantly demonstrated that Impressionism, far from representing just the unthinking depiction of the everyday, modern world, was a far more considered affair, which, literally, gave painting a new iconography. For Herbert, too, though, there was an element of the tabula rasa to Impressionism:

> Denial of memory meant denial of history, a pervasive consequence of the Impressionists' orientation. "History" was not simply the discarded subjects of earlier painting, but the means by which they were rendered, particularly the structure of light and dark that gave conventional painting the satisfactory illusion of three dimensions. The exaltation of bright color and patchy brushwork was the Impressionists' way of presenting what one could see, without recourse to what one "knows" by virtue of traditional artistic training.[37]

Whereas such a view is hard to gainsay in many respects, there are sufficient instances of a resonance with the past to claim that artistic "history" was not altogether forgotten, particularly in the fascinating but problematic category of landscape, with all its complex accompanying historical baggage. The great French old master–inspired tradition of landscape never died out, though it was partially circumvented by the Impressionists, only to be openly acknowledged by many of them in their later careers. In retrospect they can be placed in this long line of descent from the masters, but with due acknowledgment of their often startling originality, which ensured they could never be accused, in Pissarro's words, of "robbing" them.

Notes

Epigraph: Pissarro, *Lucien* 1980, p. 323.

1. Venturi 1939, vol. 1, p. 104.
2. Pissarro 1989, p. 520.
3. Ibid.
4. Clarke 2003.
5. For example, Paris 1994.
6. M. Stevens, *Impressions d'une femme au Salon de 1859* (Paris, 1859), p. 123, quoted in Schulman 1999, p. 24.
7. Brettell 1990.
8. Ibid., p. 122.
9. Bürger, *Musées* 1860, p. 12, quoted in Chu 1974, p. 12.
10. Blanc 1866, p. 36.
11. Pissarro 1980, p. 260.
12. Galassi 1991, p. 226.
13. House 1986, p. 151, gives an excellent account of Monet's changing attitude to "finish" and working out of doors over the years. Letter quoted from Wildenstein 1985, no. 1764.
14. London 1995, no. 23.
15. See Grunchec 1983.
16. Zola 1974, p. 73.
17. Ibid., p. 115.
18. Henriet 1876.
19. Baudelaire 1965, p. 201.
20. Zola 1974, p. 116.
21. Ibid., p. 111.
22. Thomson 2000, p. 49.
23. Isaacson 1972.
24. Verbeek 1958, pp. 64–65. Monet's initial enthusiasm had been for the Dutch landscape itself, and he revealed in a letter of June 17, 1871, to Pissarro: "I have not had time to visit the museums, I wish to work first of all and I'll treat myself to that later." Wildenstein 1974, p. 428. Five days later he did.
25. See Shiff 1984, pp. 180–83.
26. Edinburgh 1990.
27. Reff, "Reproductions" 1960, p. 304.
28. Maurice Denis, "Cézanne," *L'Occident*, September 1907, quoted in Edinburgh 1990, p. 58.
29. Émile Bernard, "Souvenirs sur Paul Cézanne et lettres inédites," *Mercure de France* October 1 and 16, p. 627, quoted in ibid., p. 35.
30. Quoted in ibid., p. 35.
31. Ernest May (1845–1925), Parisian financier; see Distel 1989, pp. 223–30.
32. *L'Artiste* 6 (August 1893): 99–126.
33. P. Hepp, "Exposition de paysages par Claude Monet et Renoir (Galerie Durand-Ruel)," *Chronique des Arts*, May 30, 1908, pp. 214–15, quoted in Levine 1976, p. 293; translation by Clarke.
34. J. F. Schnerb, "Paysages par Claude Monet et Renoir, Galeries Durand-Ruel," *La Grande Revue* 49 (June 10, 1908): 395, quoted in ibid., p. 294; translation by Clarke.
35. Lhote 1939, p. 55.
36. Rewald 1946.
37. Herbert 2002, p. 93.

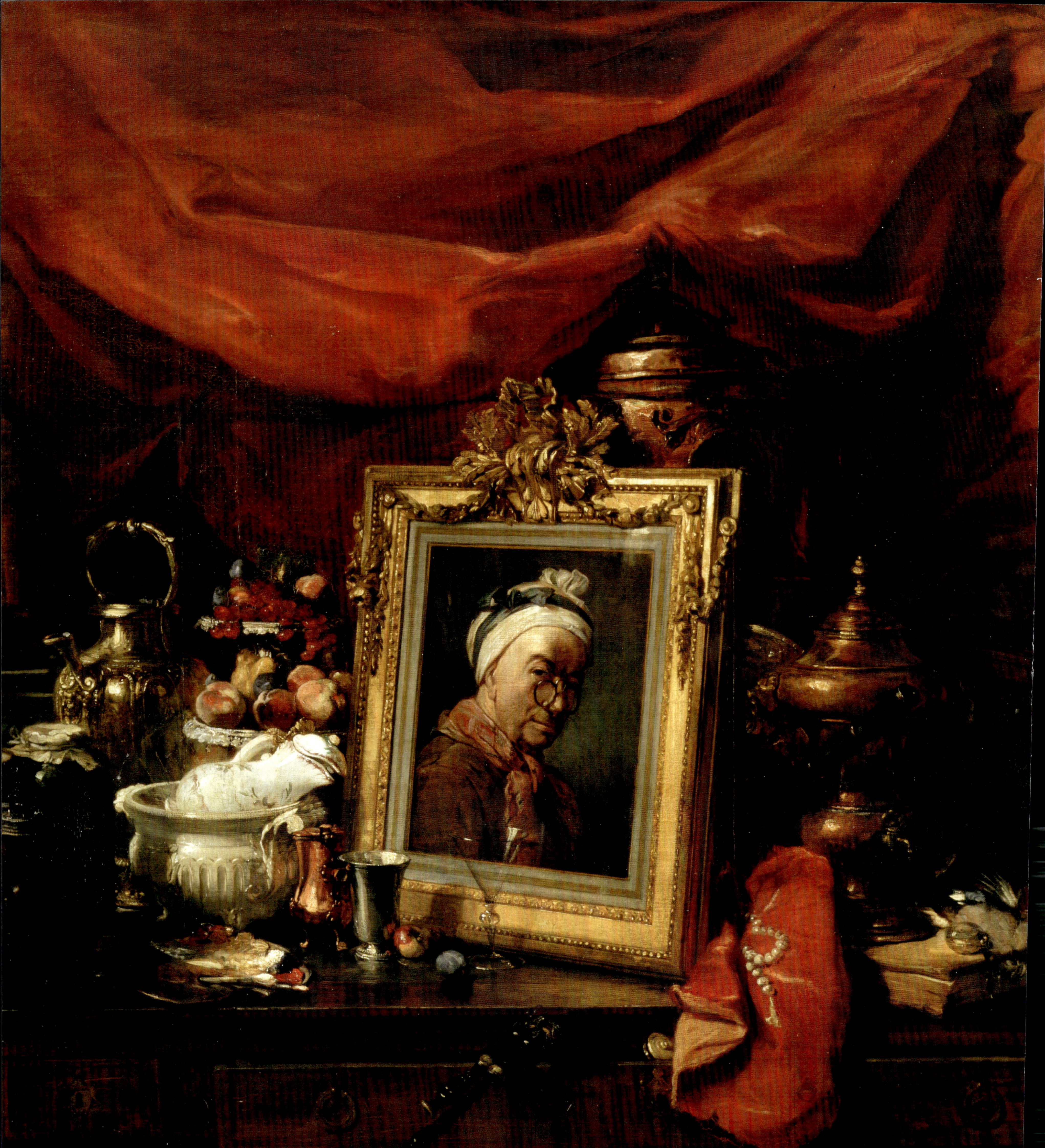

Lesley Stevenson

In Search of the Past

The Case of Still Life

During the second half of the nineteenth century, the genre of still life occupied an equivocal position in the official art world. It seemed to be less firmly rooted in the past than the more prestigious genres of history painting, portraiture, landscape painting, and genre painting. By the 1860s and 1870s, the position of still life was being reassessed, and the supposedly debased subject matter and informal handling of this, the lowest of the genres, were finally enjoying some success at the Paris Salons.

However, some of the old prejudices remained. Not only had still life not been written about widely in academic treatises, but the very framework within which it was discussed was much less strictly codified than that for other genres. Indeed, academic texts often omitted it altogether, because of its perceived irrelevance. The principle enshrined in academic doctrine by such theorists as André Félibien, Charles Le Brun, and Roger de Piles—for painting to rival the other liberal arts it must aspire to the condition of literature and distance itself from any associations with the artisanal—meant that still life was often overlooked in the construction of a hierarchy or

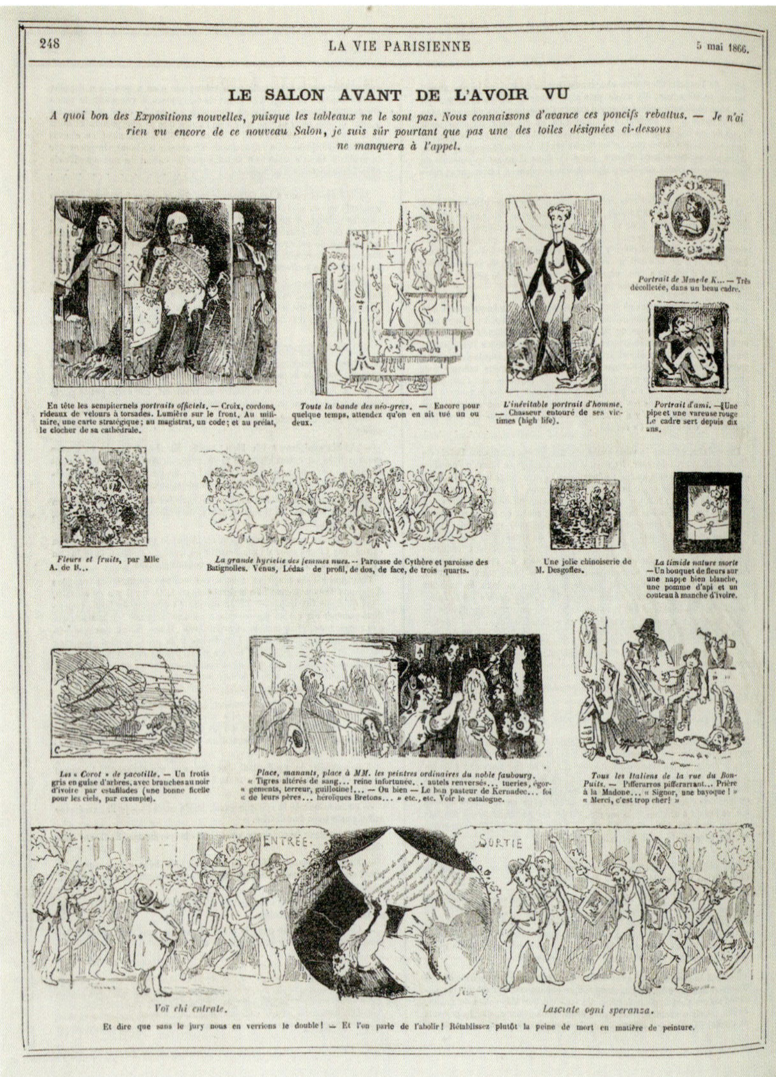

248 LA VIE PARISIENNE 5 mai 1866.

LE SALON AVANT DE L'AVOIR VU

A quoi bon des Expositions nouvelles, puisque les tableaux ne le sont pas. Nous connaissons d'avance ces poncifs rebattus. — Je n'ai rien vu encore de ce nouveau Salon, je suis sûr pourtant que pas une des toiles désignées ci-dessous ne manquera à l'appel.

Portrait de Mme de K... — Très décolletée, dans un beau cadre.

En tête les sempiternels *portraits officiels*. — Croix, cordons, rideaux de velours à torsades. Lumière sur le front. Au militaire, une carte stratégique; au magistrat, un code; et au prélat, le clocher de sa cathédrale.

Toute la bande des néo-grecs. — Encore pour quelque temps, attendez qu'on en ait tué un ou deux.

L'inévitable portrait d'homme. — Chasseur entouré de ses victimes (high life).

Portrait d'ami. — Une pipe et une vareuse rouge Le cadre sert depuis dix ans.

Fleurs et fruits, par Mlle A. de B...

La grande hyrielie des femmes nues. — Paroisse de Cythère et paroisse des Batignolles. Vénus, Lédas de profil, de dos, de face, de trois quarts.

Une jolie chinoiserie de M. Desgoffes.

La timide nature morte — Un bouquet de fleurs sur une nappe bien blanche, une pomme d'api et un couteau à manche d'ivoire.

Les « Corot » de pacotille. — Un frotis gris en guise d'arbres, avec branches au noir d'ivoire par estafilades (une bonne ficelle pour les ciels, par exemple).

Place, manants, place à MM. les peintres ordinaires du noble faubourg. « Tigres altérés de sang... reine infortunée.. autels renversés... tueries, égorgements, terreur, guillotine!... — Ou bien — Le bon pasteur de Kernadec... foi de leurs pères... héroïques Bretons... » etc., etc. Voir le catalogue.

Tous les Italiens de la rue du Bon-Puits. — Pifferarros pifferarrant... Prière à la Madone... « Signor, une bayoque! » « Merci, c'est trop cher! »

Voï chi entrate. *Lasciate ogni speranza.*

Et dire que sans le jury nous en verrions le double! — Et l'on parle de l'abolir! Rétablissez plutôt la peine de mort en matière de peinture.

Fig. 80
The Diffident Still Life, from
La Vie Parisienne, May 5, 1866
British Library, London

simply treated as a subset of genre.[1] The attempt to elevate painting to the level of the other liberal arts effectively undermined the position of still life, which was dismissed as mechanical copying, devoid of any literary pretensions.

André Félibien's *De l'origine de la peinture* (1660) attempted a systematic classification of painting according to subject matter, and this was further formulated in the preface to his *Conférences de l'Académie royale de peinture et de sculpture pendant l'année 1667* (1669), in which the lowest category of painters were said to depict "things that are dead and do not move" and "fruit[s], flowers, or shells."[2] In his *Cours de peinture par principes* (1708), Roger de Piles demonstrated that the hierarchy of the genres was more than simply a taxonomy of subject matter; it depended on a commensurate ranking of technique: "if the painter finds himself undertaking a humble subject, it is necessary that he endeavor to make it grand by the extraordinary manner with which he treats it."[3] Only by developing a superior technique could a painter hope to transcend the limitations of the minor genres. This question—what was the appropriate handling for a specific genre—continued to animate practitioners and theorists well into the nineteenth century. While history painting demanded a suitably elevated technique to complement the grandeur of its theme, it was deemed excusable, even necessary, for still life's method to acknowledge the humble nature of its subject matter. But as de Piles's injunction made clear, the question of treatment was significant. For still life, its lowly status was usually reinforced by intimacies of scale, predicated on notions of difficulty and laboriousness, which lingered far into the nineteenth century. The caricatural preview of the Salon of 1866 in *La Vie Parisienne* included a postage-stamp-size sketch of a still life, *La Timide Nature morte (The Diffident Still Life)* (fig. 80), in which an uncluttered and simple composition has been reduced to the formulaic and far from heroic. However, the relative absence of academic dogma about the still life meant it could not be codified in the same way as the other genres, allowing practitioners some flexibility. While in theory still life was shunned as insufficiently intellectual, in practice some painters attempted to work around the constraints.

The foundation of the Royal Academy of Painting and Sculpture in 1648 had a demonstrable effect on the way in which still life was perceived. Before that date a tradition of still-life painting had flourished in the Saint-Germain-des-Prés district of Paris, which from the beginning of the seventeenth century had been a center for Protestant painters from the Low Countries seeking refuge from religious

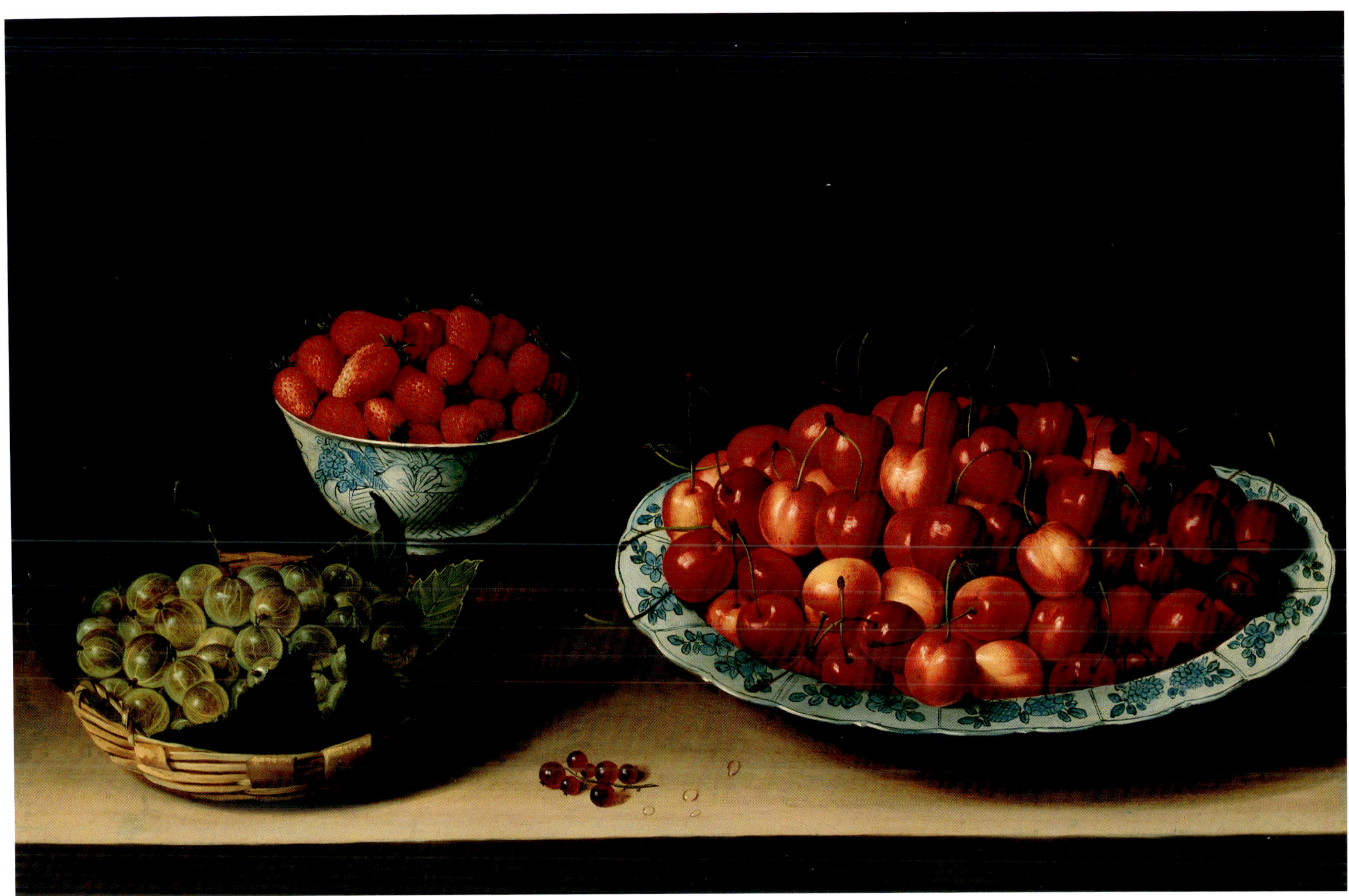

persecution, and these artists had a formative influence on native French painting. *Still Life with Cherries, Strawberries, and Gooseberries* (fig. 81) by Louise Moillon adopts a directness of approach to the humble subject coupled with a simplicity of composition that owes something to Flemish antecedents. A comparison with Jean-Baptiste Monnoyer's *morceau de réception* (the painting he submitted to be admitted to the academy), *Still Life of Flowers and Fruit* (fig. 82) demonstrates the kind of compromises the painter of still life had to make to gain acceptability within academic circles. While observing the limitations of the genre (Monnoyer makes no attempt to be literary), this large, elaborately composed work was nonetheless injected with quasi-narrative touches: pseudoclassical sculptures, painter's brush and palette, drapery, artlessly arranged flowers and

Fig. 81
Louise Moillon (1610–1696)
Still Life with Cherries, Strawberries, and Gooseberries, 1630
Oil on panel, 12⅝ × 19⅛ in. (32.1 × 48.6 cm)
The Norton Simon Foundation

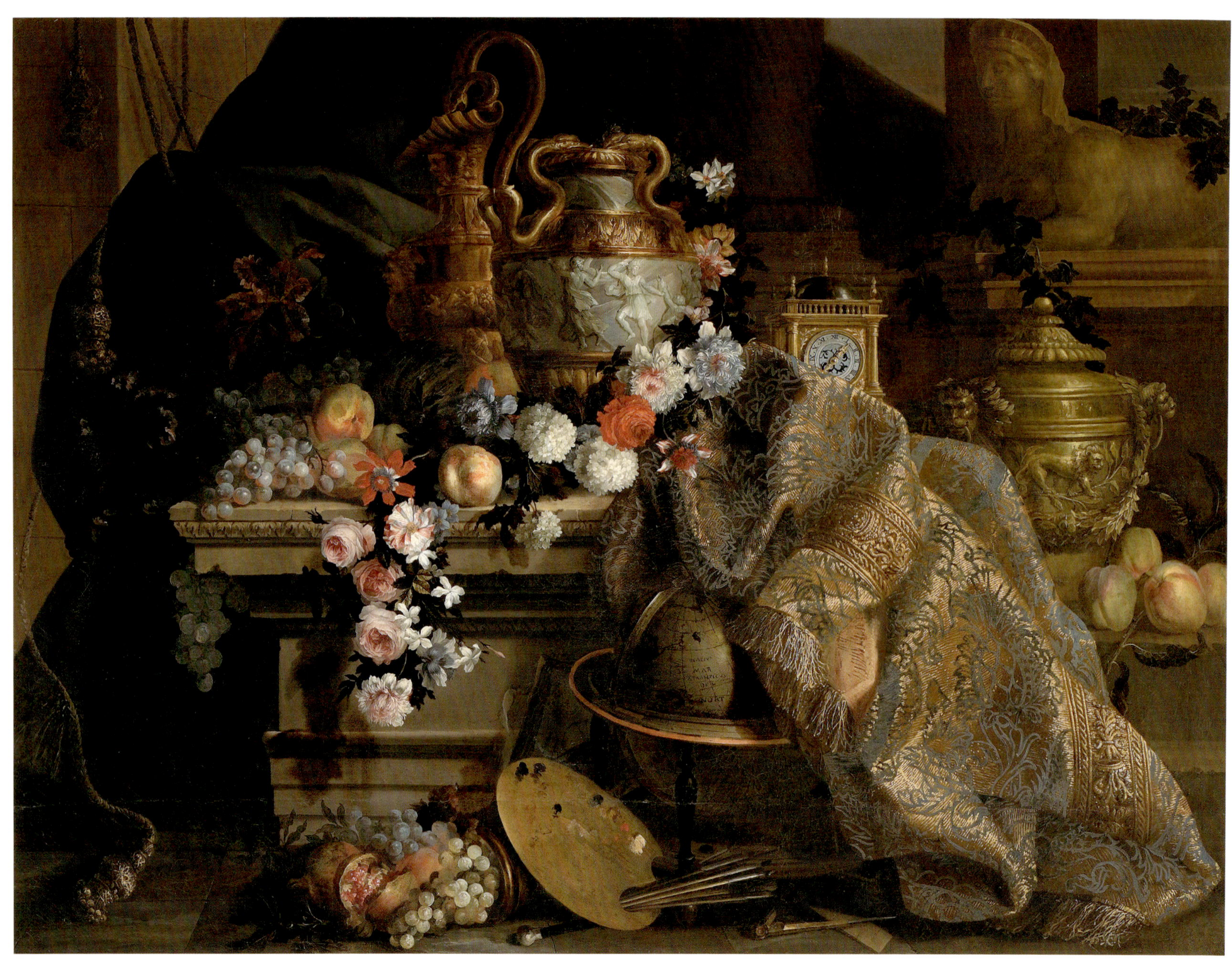

Fig. 82
Jean-Baptiste Monnoyer
Still Life of Flowers and Fruits, 1665
Oil on canvas, 55⅞ × 72⅜ in. (142 × 184 cm)
Musée Fabre, Montpellier Agglomération

fruits. In attempting to circumvent some of the limitations of a rigidly hierarchical academic system, Monnoyer transformed the intimate still life from the earlier part of the century into a much more decorative, monumental genre with pretensions to greatness.

The ambivalent status of still life continued into the nineteenth century in part because of its persistent perception as a feminine genre. The financial and artistic success achieved by Moillon was exceptional; by the nineteenth century, the association of the genre with the accomplishment arts of the husband-hunting leisured classes and the inevitable association with craft dissuaded "serious" artists from too close an identification with still life. Henri Fantin-Latour wrote in exasperation to his English dealer Edwin Edwards in 1862 about the ease with which he could sell his flower pieces: "Ever since I have been able to get rid of them it has seemed to me like business, I have felt like an art dealer. . . . Never have I had more ideas about Art in my head, and yet I am forced to do flowers. While painting them—standing before the peonies and roses—I think of Michelangelo. This cannot go on."[4] Most painters enjoyed an ambivalent relationship with still life: although commercially useful, lingering prejudices ensured that it was never a favorite subject.

The principle that still-life painting was eminently suitable for women and girls had been codified in various pedagogical treatises. Jean-Jacques Rousseau's *Émile* (1762) was one of the most influential in prescribing gender-specific roles in child-rearing. Rousseau stressed the importance of drawing for girls:

> for this art is not unimportant when it comes to dressing tastefully, but I would certainly not want them to apply themselves to landscape, even less to the figure. Leaves, fruit, flowers, draperies, everything which is useful in conveying an elegant line to arrangements, and for making an embroidery pattern for oneself when one cannot find any to one's taste, that is enough for them.[5]

In particular, Rousseau emphasized the importance of coquetry in the young woman's arsenal.

Édouard Manet's portrait of Eva Gonzalès (fig. 106) of 1870 is a realization of some of these ideas. Seated at an easel in a drawing room, wearing an impractical costume, gazing into the middle distance while putting the finishing touches to an already framed still life of peonies, Gonzalès is much closer to eighteenth-century prototypes like Adélaïde Labille-Guiard's *Self-Portrait with Two Pupils* (1785; The Metropolitan Museum of Art, New York) than Pierre-Auguste Renoir's *Portrait of Frédéric Bazille (1841–1870) Painting "The Heron with Wings Unfurled"* of 1867 (fig. 83), which represents a modern male artist hunched in concentration over a still sketchy still life. Manet's portrait served a different purpose—it was a Salon painting rather than an intimate portrayal of a fellow artist—but this does not diminish the inherent prescriptiveness of the representation. Gonzalès's femininity is made explicit through the vehicle of the floral still life propped on the easel. That work has never been identified, and indeed Gonzalès is not known to have painted still lifes at this date. It is probably fictional and serves as a foil to her feminine charms. Bazille's still life, however, has been identified as belonging to the much more "masculine" genre of the game piece and owes something to Dutch precedents, and indeed to Jean-Siméon Chardin, in handling and coloration as much as in choice of subject (cat. 3, p. 191; cat. 21, p. 190).[6]

It is often pointed out that only two women—Berthe Morisot and Mary Cassatt—exhibited at the Impressionist shows, but there was a third, now forgotten, figure whose work was admired at the second Impressionist exhibition of 1876. That year, a British publication, the *Academy*, carried a review of the exhibition, noting that in the third room there were some still lifes "by a woman of society who adopts the pseudonym of Jacques François. She has a harmonious palette, and uses grays and free tints with remarkable skill."[7] The mysterious society woman has never been identified, nor have any of the works that she exhibited: she has been rendered invisible not only by both her caste and gender but also by the fact that the genre she practiced was still largely regarded as insignificant by the Impressionists themselves. For while individuals sometimes painted still lifes, as a genre it was underrepresented at the eight Impressionist shows.

At the first exhibition in 1874, of the chief members of the group, only Renoir exhibited a flower piece. At the following show, in 1876, none of the key Impressionists showed still lifes, although Jacques François's works were on display. In 1877, however, Paul Cézanne had a series of paintings on show, including three *natures mortes* and two *études de fleurs*, as well as a watercolor of flowers. The reviewer in *L'Impressionniste* singled out Cézanne's paintings, praising them for their tonal harmony: "his still lifes so beautiful, so exact in the relation of tones, have something solemn in their truthfulness."[8] That same year, both Renoir and Claude Monet exhibited a bouquet of dahlias and an additional flower piece. At the next exhibition, in 1879, Monet exhibited another painting of flowers, and in 1880 both Gustave Caillebotte and Paul Gauguin were represented by a *nature morte*. But in 1882 the largest number of still lifes were exhibited, with Monet, Renoir, Caillebotte, Gauguin, and Camille Pissarro including examples of the genre in their submissions. However, this was very much the exception, and for those painters who exhibited at the Impressionist shows, only for Cézanne was the genre central to his oeuvre; at the group shows, the still life remained marginal.[9] The Impressionist idiom did not lend itself easily to the still life, with its heavily aestheticized environment manipulated by the artist; instead, landscape painting allowed the Impressionist painters most easily to display their interest in modern-life subject matter coupled with an immediacy of handling. This helps to explain the scarcity of still-life painting at the earlier exhibitions, but the relative neglect of the lowest of the genres was also—paradoxically—because of its association with the past.

Like other painters, members of the Impressionist group trawled the past for a variety of reasons. Of these, a deference to authority was key; the past offered a set of exemplars invested with a gravity that imbued the homage with a ready-made rigor. But this was seldom the case with still life—its history as a maligned genre meant that those references were negligible, and it was ill suited to the *pleinairiste*, modern-life aesthetic favored by many of the Impressionist painters. Still life, drawing on the quotidian, did not demand reference to the higher authority offered by the past. With its concerns close to hand, it was not imbued with the universality required of the higher genres. The implicit challenge of emulating the old masters felt by younger painters hardly carried the same weight in a genre that had traditionally been seen as largely inconsequential.

Charles Blanc's magisterial fourteen-volume, illustrated survey of European painting, *Histoire des peintres de toutes les écoles* (completed in 1876), for all its comprehensiveness, offered few illustrations of still lifes to copy.[10] The Dutch, Flemish, and German Schools were represented by still-life painters, but in the French School the section devoted to Jean-Siméon Chardin was illustrated by a single example, and the only other French painter whose still lifes were illustrated, Monnoyer, was represented by four fairly modest paintings of single bouquets of mixed flowers seen at eye level. There were no other illustrations of still lifes in the *Histoire*.[11] For those countries with strong academic traditions, still life was still marginalized, and even the native contribution, represented by Chardin, appeared to be negligible.

On their trips to foreign museums, individual painters made copies of old master works, but no examples of still lifes are recorded.[12] Nor did a readily available set of precedents in Paris lead painters toward a study of the genre; indeed, until 1870, there were only a few still-life paintings in the Louvre. Of these, Jan Davidsz de Heem's *A Table of Desserts* (fig. 84), a sumptuous large-scale banquet piece, occupied a key position in the national collection. Combining a Dutch interest in realism in the dissectionist's precision in revealing the fruits' fleshy interiors and the artisanal attention to detail with a Flemish taste for closely massed forms heaped on the tabletop, the seventeenth-century painting resurfaced in the series of big Baroque still lifes that Cézanne completed toward the end of his life, when he was working in Aix-en-Provence, far from the Louvre. *Still Life with Apples and Oranges* (cat. 17, p. 192) relies on the crumpled white linen in which the fruits nestle, the rich colors and the complex stagings of Dutch banquet pieces such as Abraham van Beyeren's *Banquet Still Life* (cat. 6, p. 189). But Cézanne's late still lifes drew on vestigial memories of the sumptuousness of the De Heem rather than being a copy or a quotation from the old master.

For, when it came to still-life painting, the "past" was still largely awaiting construction, and the work of Chardin, the sole French pretender to the claim of genius, was only gradually being recognized. After the popular Revolution of 1848, the administration of the Louvre had given greater prominence to the minor genres, but there remained very few still lifes on display. The unearthing of the Le Nain brothers' work in particular has been read as a republican gesture,[13] a reclamation of humble subject matter, which might have provided an intellectual rationale for a revival in interest in still-life painting, but that was not to be reflected in the Louvre's display for another generation. The catalogue for the Louvre, published as late as 1881, divided the Western canon into three "schools."[14] The "Italian School" included only one still life, and there were no Spanish still-life paintings.[15] Only "Germany and the Low Countries" boasted several old master still lifes, and the "French School" included a number of Chardin still lifes, several Monnoyers, individual examples by painters like Anne Vallayer-Coster and Henri-Horace Roland de la Porte, and some by Jean-Baptiste Belin de Fontenay. Other eighteenth-century still-life painters were scarce, and examples from pre-academic painters and members of the Saint-Germain-des-Prés school of still-life painting were not included in the collection until the twentieth century. The "French tradition" was largely represented by Monnoyer and, above all, Chardin, whose work may be upheld as the single biggest influence in a revival of interest in the neglected genre of still life by the mid-nineteenth century.

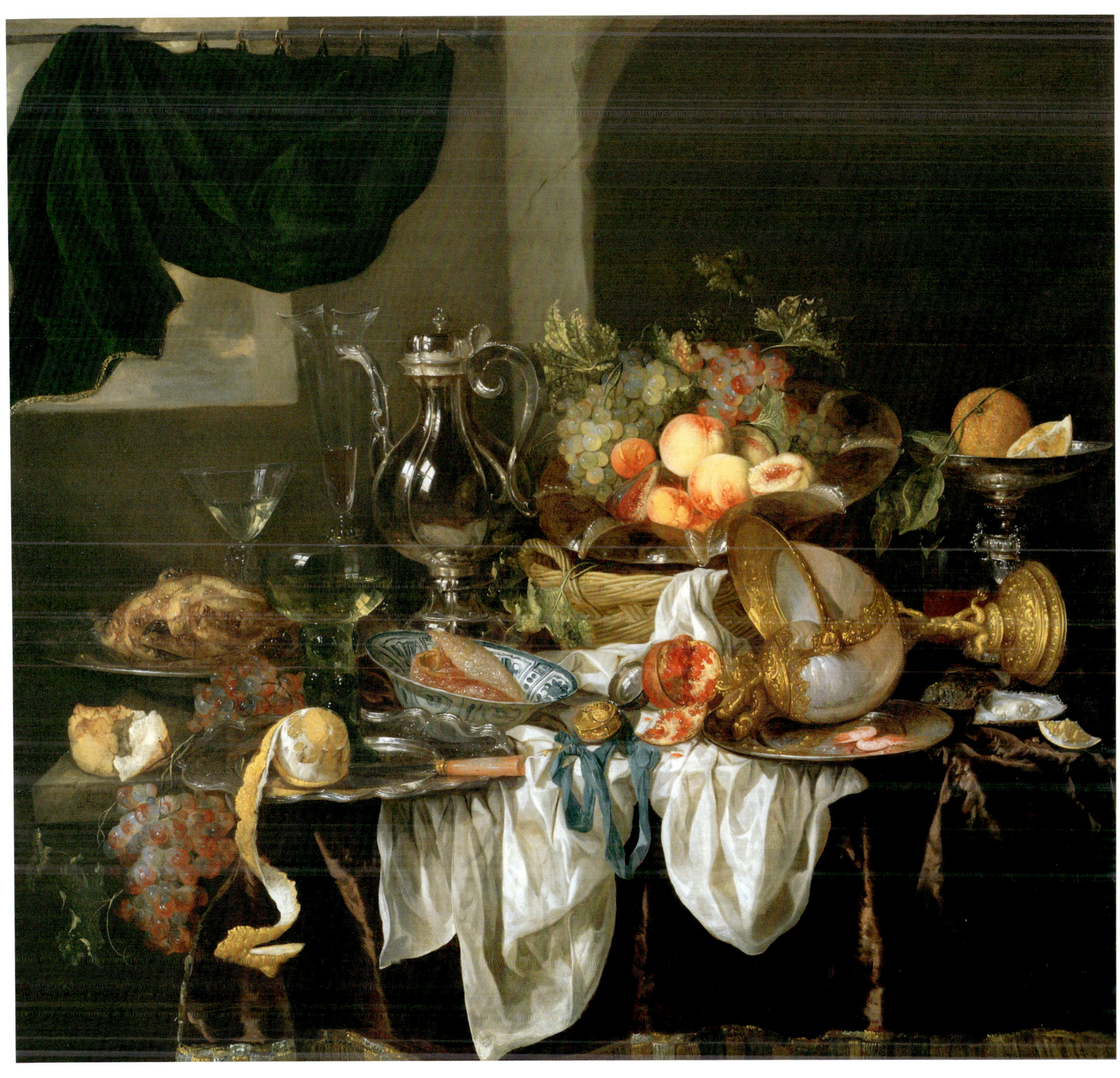

Cat. 6
Abraham Hendricksz van Beyeren
Banquet Still Life, c. 1653–55

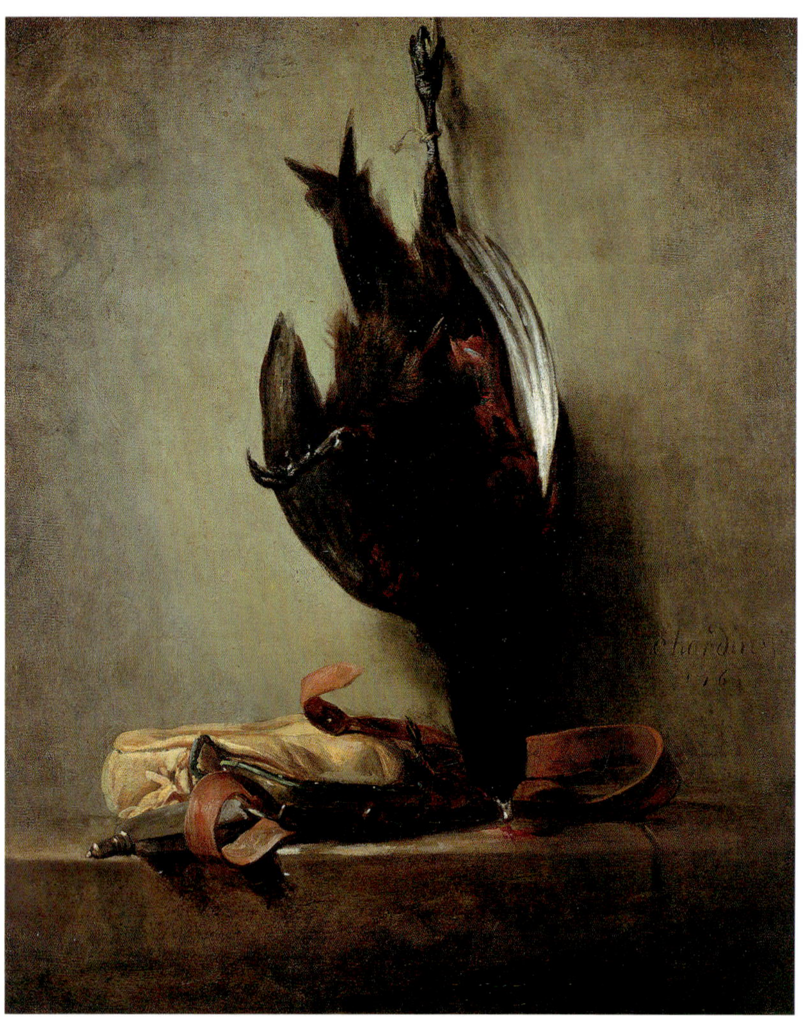

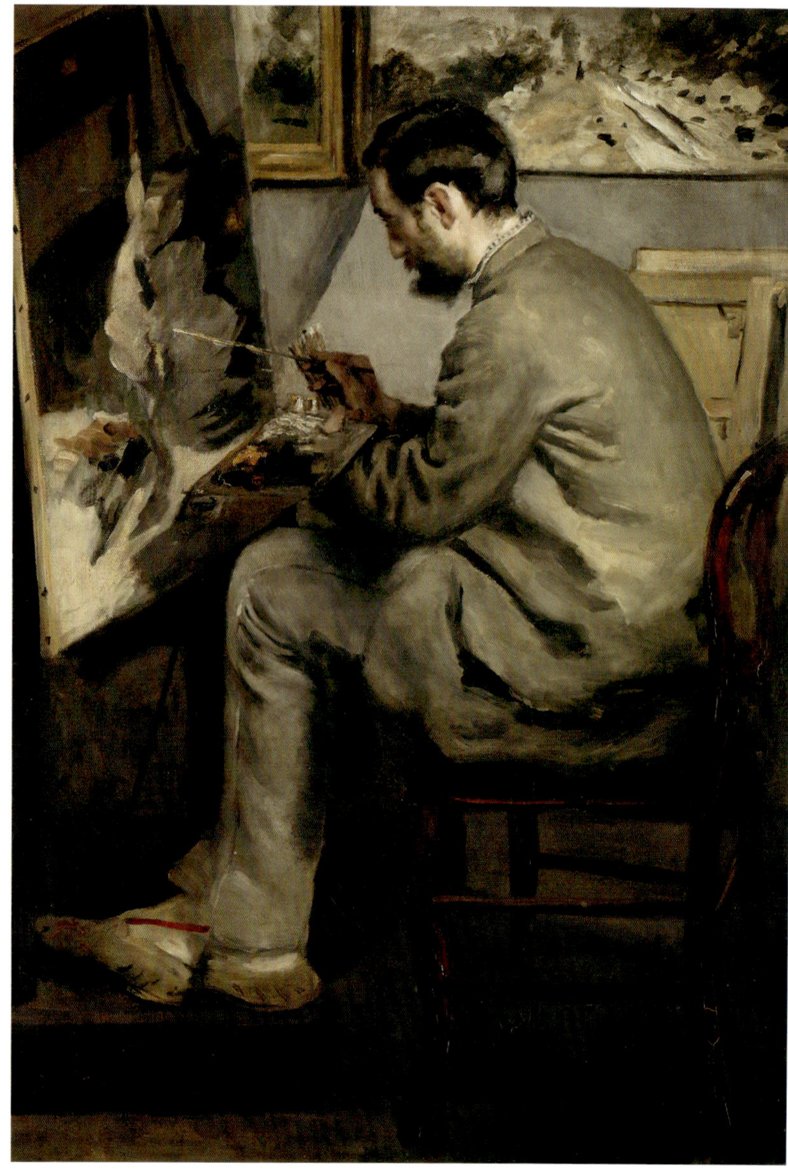

Cat. 21
Jean-Siméon Chardin
Still Life with Dead Pheasant and Hunting Bag, 1760

Fig. 83
Pierre-Auguste Renoir
Portrait of Frédéric Bazille (1841–1870) Painting "The Heron with Wings Unfurled," 1867
Oil on canvas, 41⅜ × 28⅞ in.
(105 × 73.5 cm)
Musée d'Orsay, Paris, France

Cat. 3
Frédéric Bazille
The Heron, 1867

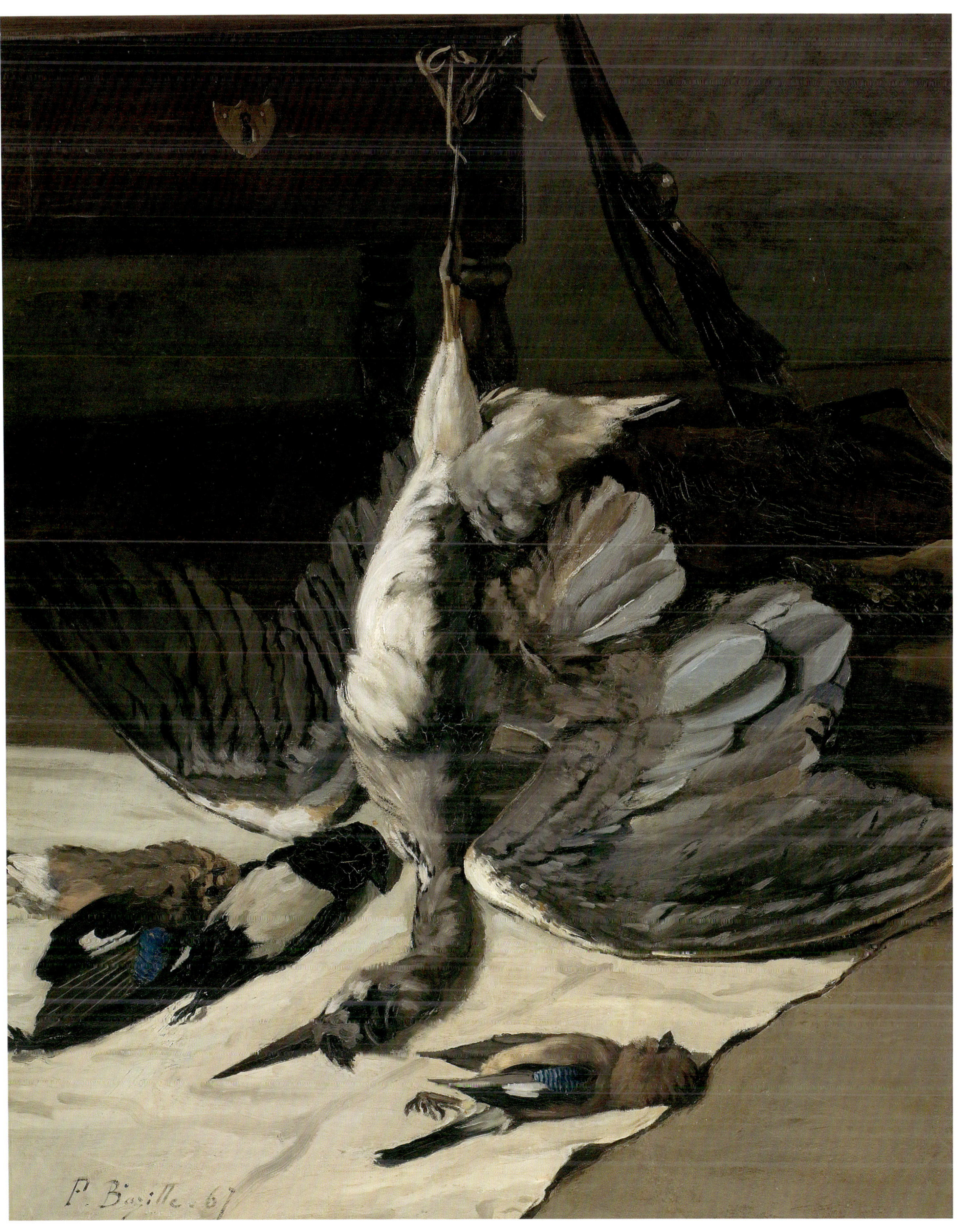
F. Bazille. 67

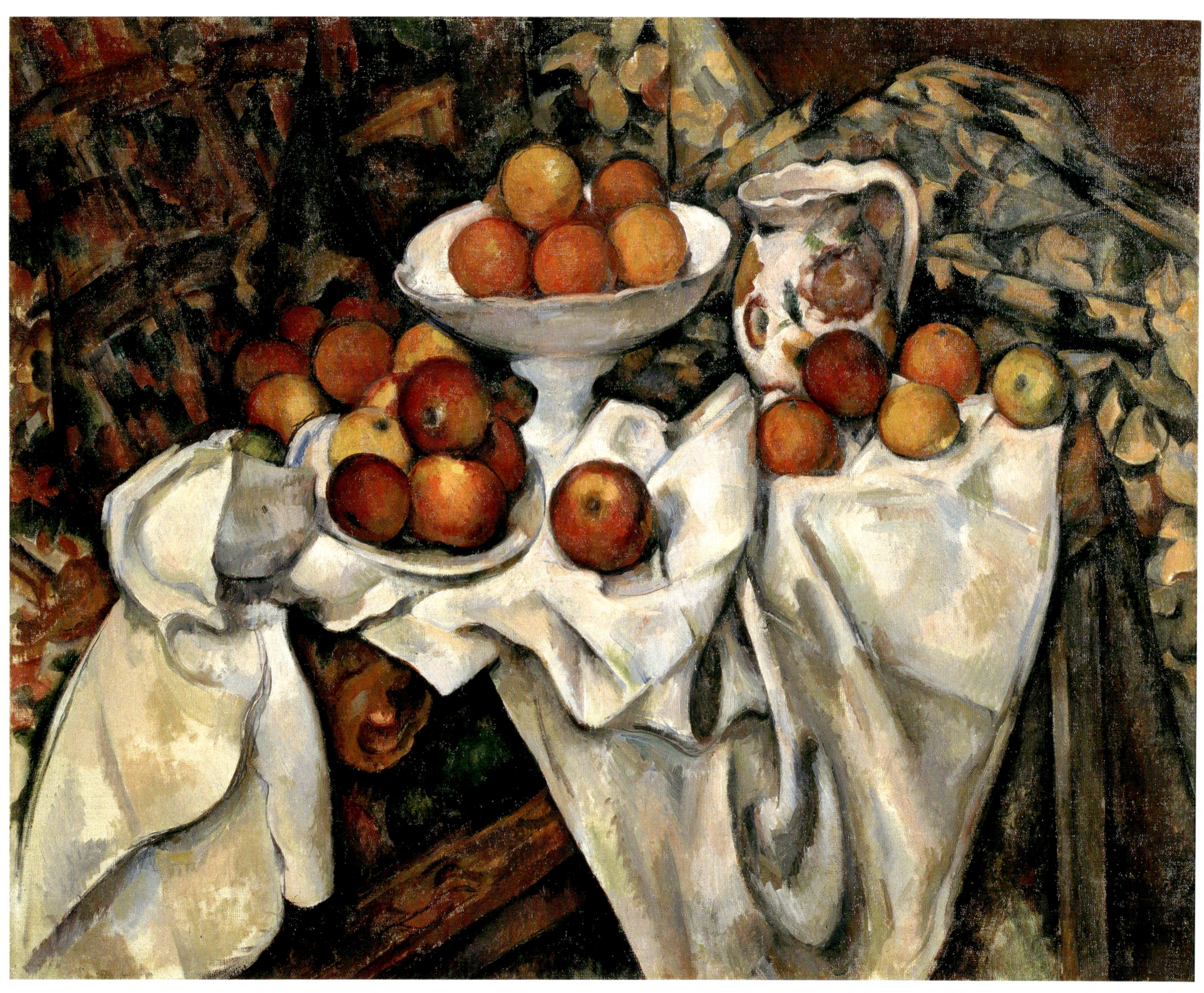

Cat. 17
Paul Cézanne
Still Life with Apples and Oranges,
ca. 1895–1900

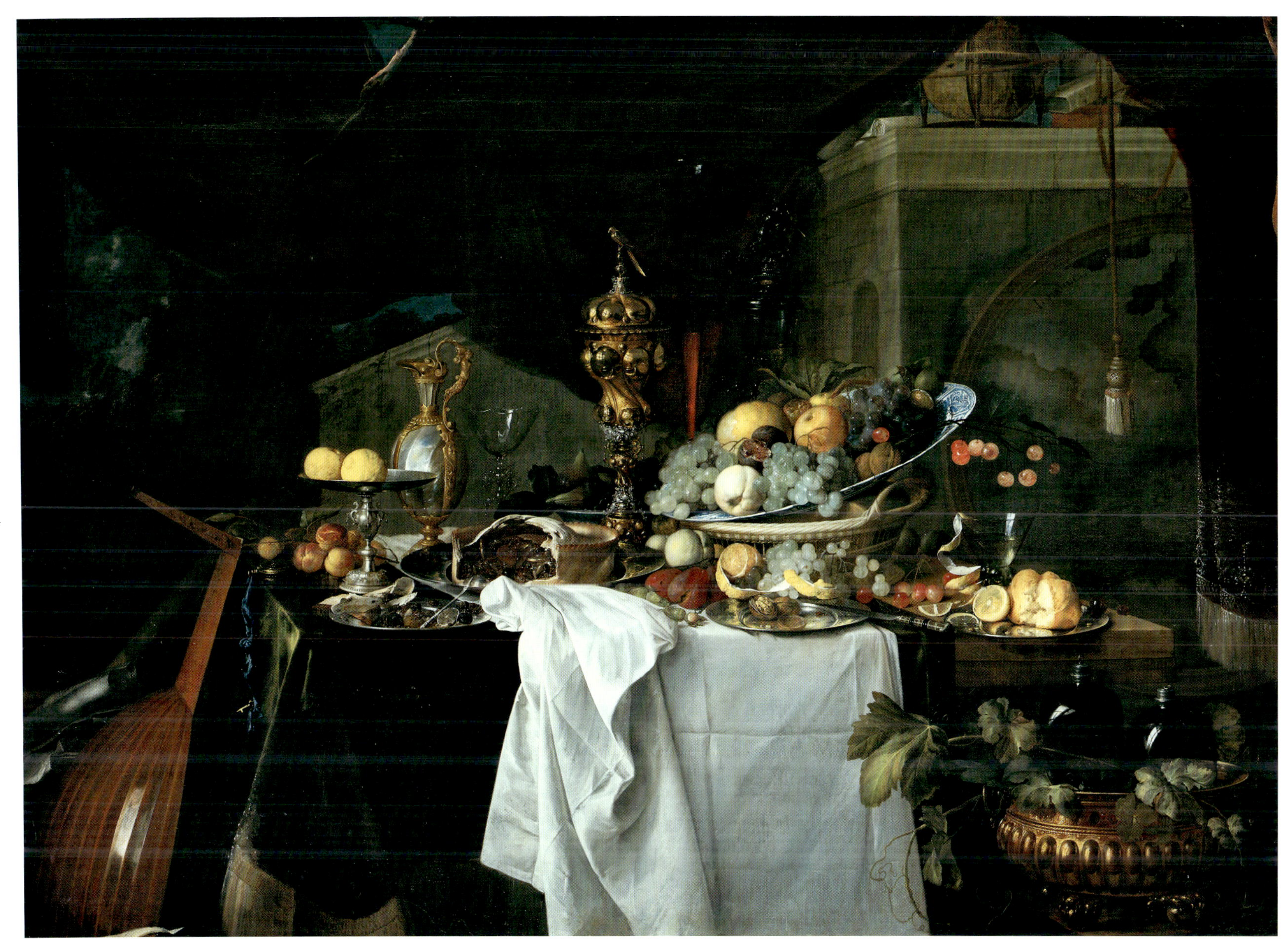

Fig. 84
Jan Davidsz de Heem
(1606–1683)
A Table of Desserts, 1640
Oil on canvas, 58½ × 80 in.
(149 × 203 cm)
Musée du Louvre, Paris, France

In 1845 Champfleury could complain that "Chardin was represented by only a single still life,"[16] but that same year, the sale of the collection of Casimir Perrin, marquis de Cypierre, on March 10, has been singled out as the start of a rediscovery of interest in the eighteenth-century master,[17] although none of the five Chardins in the catalogue was a still life.[18] The following year, Pierre Hédouin in his articles on Chardin published in the *Bulletin des Arts* of November 10 and December 10 included a biography and a rudimentary catalogue raisonné. Ten years later, at the sale of the collection of the famous opera singer Paul Barroilhet,[19] some of his unidentifiable *natures mortes* fetched about three hundred francs apiece, but *The Silver Goblet* was sold for two thousand francs. The introduction to the Barroilhet sale catalogue was written by Théophile Gautier, who invoked the Salon criticism of Denis Diderot in describing Chardin's still lifes and made explicit the connections between the eighteenth-century French painter on the one hand and his Dutch and Flemish predecessors on the other:

> Diderot, the founder of picturesque criticism in France, admired Chardin greatly, and with reason, although perhaps he was more sensitive, as was his habit, to the choice of subject than to the actual worth of the painter. . . . The still life known as *The Silver Goblet,* in M. Barroilhet's collection, is a marvel of composition and color; the Flemish and Dutch masters never produced anything more real, more sincere, or better expressed.[20]

Gautier recognized the importance of Dutch and Flemish painting for Chardin and the contribution of popular subject matter in explaining his appeal after 1848. Writing in 1873, René Ménard looked back at the revival of Chardin in the 1840s:

> The still life was greatly in favor with the young generation, who completely neglected the study of the nude, considering instead man in his relations with the external world, and attempted to represent that with the peasant's clogs, the worker's blouse, and citizen's overcoat. . . . Chardin therefore became the idol of a whole generation of artists who adopted him as a kind of patron.[21]

Like a number of painters who made reference to Chardin's still lifes in their work at this time, Ménard reduced Chardin's work to the most formulaic, in which objects are used metonymically to stand for a kind of authenticity and populist values. Already by 1873, if not before, a significant myth had developed around the figure of Chardin.

The exhibition held at Louis Martinet's gallery in the boulevard des Italiens in 1860 brought the work of Chardin to a wider audience than had previously been possible;[22] twenty-seven still lifes by him were on display.[23] The introduction to the catalogue had been written by Francis Petit, but the catalogue raisonné with biographical data, provenances, and descriptions of the works had been researched and written by Philippe Burty, who also relied on Diderot's criticism to invest his opinions with authority, quoting at length and verbatim from Diderot's 1763 description of *The Jar of Olives* (fig. 86).[24]

The articles on French eighteenth-century painters in the *Gazette des Beaux-Arts* in 1863 and 1864 by the Goncourt brothers brought Chardin to the attention of the general public. Still life they regarded as

> the specialty of Chardin's genius. He raised this secondary branch of painting to the highest level of art. And never, perhaps, has the material fascination of painting dealing with objects of no intrinsic interest and transfiguring them by the magic of handling been developed so far. Who has given our eyes such a sensation of the actual presence of things? Chardin penetrates like a ray of sunlight into the beautiful but somber little kitchen of Wilhem Kalf. He wields a magic beside which all else pales, all others fade away. Van Huysum with his herbals and dry flowers, de Heem and his airless fruit, Abraham Mignon and his poor bouquets, meager, cut out, metallic.[25]

Finally, in 1870, the genre achieved greater prominence in the Louvre when the La Caze collection went on display.[26] Two long articles on the bequest appeared in the *Gazette des Beaux-Arts,* written by Paul Mantz who, like Ménard, emphasized the centrality of the genre of still life to Chardin's genius, which he too regarded as celebrating the values of unpretentious people, as expressed through their objects:

> These qualities are found in the still lifes where he groups together the objects from an honest household. . . . M. La Caze had found a dozen of these intimate Chardins: the best are *The Jar of Olives, The Brioche,* and *The Water Cistern*. . . . Here is an art that is healthy and sturdy, and the serenity with

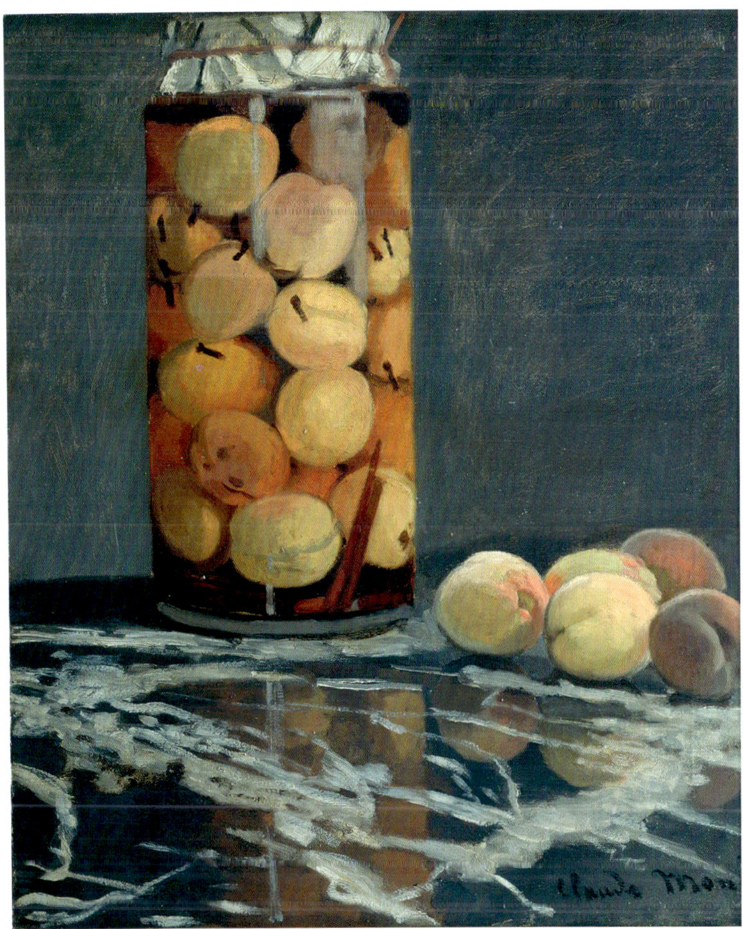

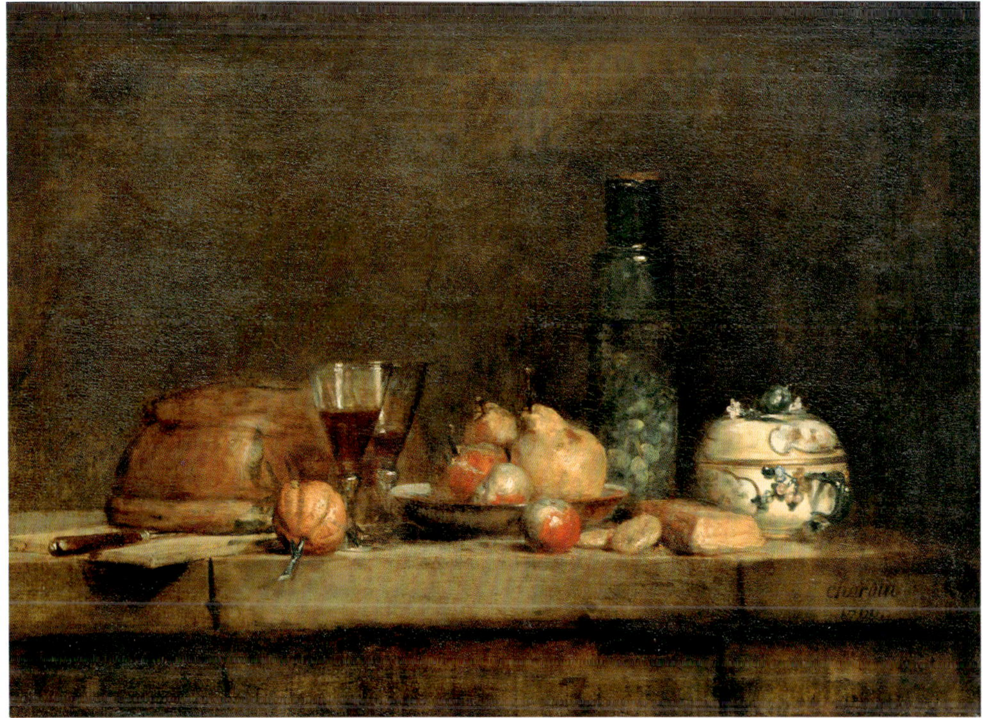

which the objects are arranged and painted awakens the idea of a society in which daily life is unassuming and hard.[27]

Yet again, Diderot's role in the promotion of Chardin was emphasized by Mantz: "Diderot loved to distraction these desserts of Chardin."[28]

Both Monet and Manet responded to those still lifes singled out by Mantz as especially noteworthy. Monet's *Jar of Peaches* (c. 1866; fig. 85) pays homage to the central object in Chardin's *The Jar of Olives* (fig. 86), which he could have seen when La Caze opened his home to the public. Manet's *The Brioche* of 1870 (fig. 87) and the later version of 1876 (Dallas Museum of Art) similarly both focus on a quotation from Chardin's *The Brioche* (fig. 88). Although the painting by Monet is formally daring in its isolation of the bottled peaches rather than surrounding it with the accoutrements of the bourgeois home, the subject matter and composition of Manet's canvas are much closer to Chardin's original. The grouping of objects with the balancing of large and small, the plain background, the trompe l'oeil effect of the silver knife overhanging the table edge had all been mercilessly ridiculed as formulaic in *La Timide Nature morte* (fig. 80) four years earlier. But it was the palpably timeless subject matter that fixed Manet into a French tradition; this was the closest he ever came to imitating a painting by Chardin. George Mauner claims that Manet never copied a painting by Chardin. He had no need to, as the objects were the same.[29] Mauner's implication is clear: when it came to still life, direct quotations from the past had none of the authority of those from the higher genres.[30] If Manet reworked those objects, it was still within fairly tight formal constraints. Yet at the same time, by playing into that French tradition at this point in Manet's painting the political reverberations rise to the surface.

These works by Monet and Manet are relatively unusual, however, in providing substantial quotations from an old master. It was much more common to find a less overt homage, with Chardin as the source, but filtered through additional layers of reference. By this

Fig. 85
Claude Monet
Jar of Peaches, c. 1866
Oil on canvas, 21⅞ × 18⅛ in.
(55.5 × 46 cm)
Galerie Neue Meister, Staatliche Kunstsammlungen Dresden

Fig. 86
Jean-Siméon Chardin
The Jar of Olives, 1760
Oil on canvas, 28 × 38⅝ in.
(71 × 98 cm)
Musée du Louvre, Paris, France

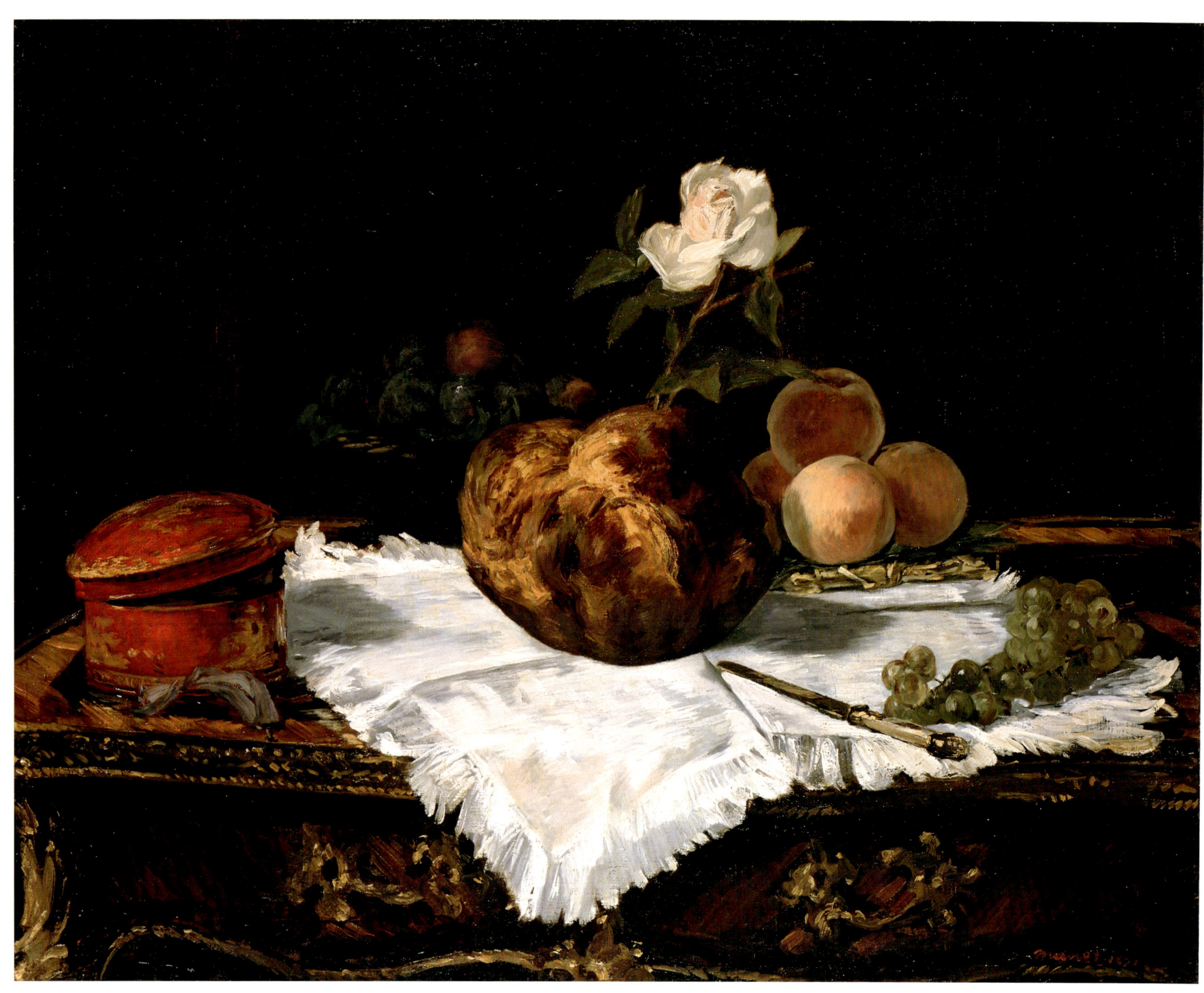

Fig. 87
Édouard Manet
The Brioche, 1870
Oil on canvas, 25⅝ × 31⅞ in.
(65.1 × 81 cm)
The Metropolitan Museum of Art,
Partial and Promised Gift of
Anonymous Donor, 1991 (1991.287)

Fig. 88
Jean-Siméon Chardin
The Brioche, 1763
Oil on canvas, 18½ × 22 in. (47 × 56 cm)
Musée du Louvre, Paris, France

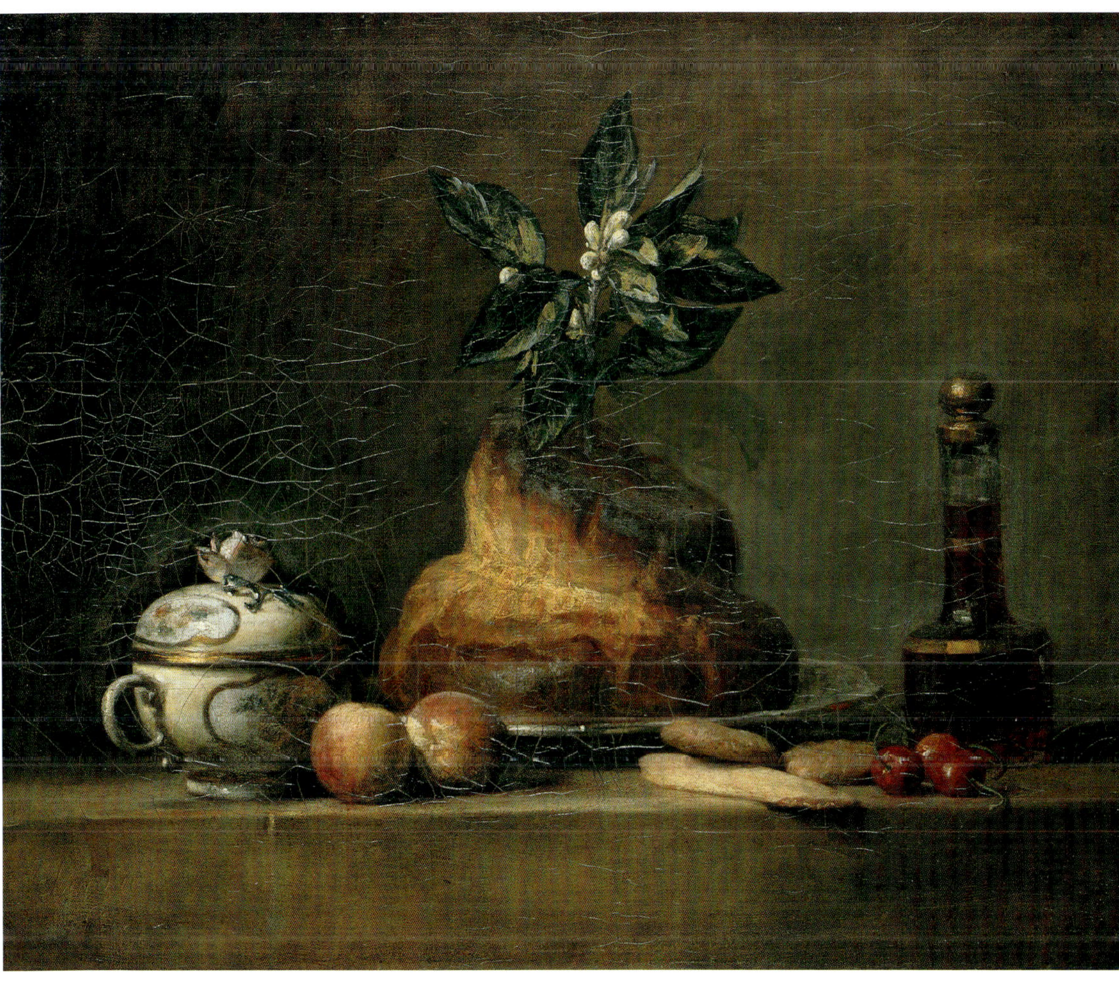

date, a number of artists were painting in a Chardinesque manner, but often their work was a derivative travesty of the simplicity of the eighteenth-century painter's still lifes. In particular, Philippe Rousseau's overambitious, hugely inflated *Chardin and His Models* (fig. 89), shown at the Salon of 1867, subsequently acquired by the State, and reproduced in both the *Gazette des Beaux Arts* and the *Album Autographique,* attempted to assemble a series of sources from Chardin's paintings into a meaningful whole. The work demonstrates the kind of legitimacy Rousseau was able to wring out of a minor genre by leaden references to a collection of old master prototypes.

The scarcity of direct citations to old master still-life paintings by the Impressionist group may to a certain extent be explained by the way in which an approach to the past was heavily mediated by the work of the previous generation of still-life painters, especially the Realist group around François Bonvin, including Philippe Rousseau, Antoine Vollon, and Théodule Ribot. In many cases it was these artists who provided a means of accessing the past for the Impressionist generation, but in doing so they seem to have exhausted its possibilities.[31] Frédéric Bazille's *The Heron* (cat. 3, p. 191) of 1867 derives ultimately from seventeenth-century Dutch and eighteenth-century French game pieces like Chardin's *Still Life with Dead Pheasant and Hunting Bag* (cat. 21, p. 190), but the placing of the dead bird on the floor, allowing its wings to fan out, is compositionally closer to a work like Bonvin's *The Crow* (1849; Burrell Collection, Glasgow).

After the Martinet show, a number of critics acknowledged the debt that the young generation of Realists owed to the art of the past. Thoré-Bürger wrote in 1861: "[Bonvin] is also a master, with his unambitious genre. He takes his place alongside the Le Nain brothers, Chardin, and the Dutch."[32] The role of critics in helping to produce a climate in which still lifes became increasingly acceptable cannot be overestimated. Petra ten-Doesschate Chu, in particular, has emphasized the revival of interest in different kinds of genre, which

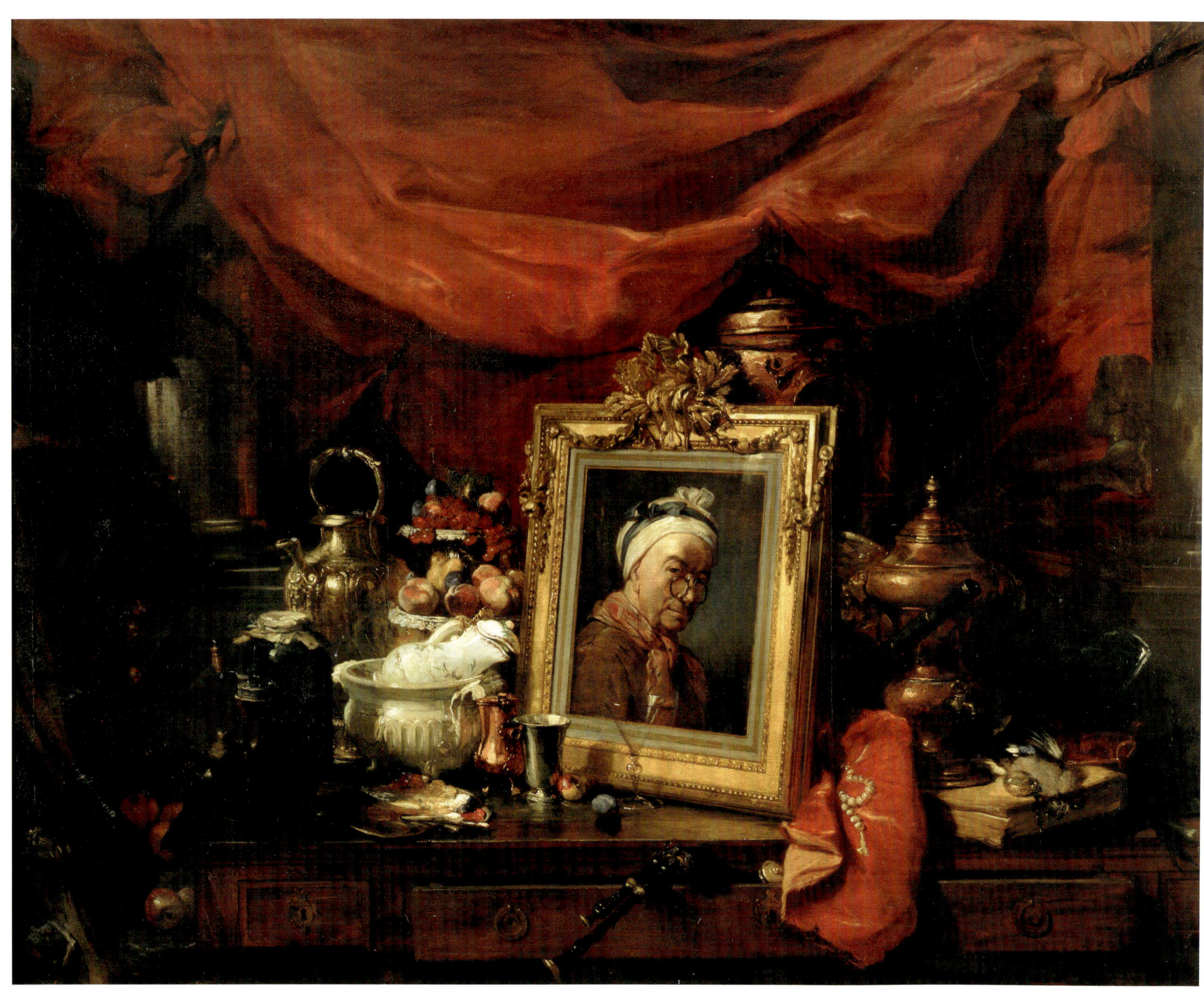

Fig. 89
Philippe Rousseau (1816–1887)
Chardin and His Models, 1867
Oil on canvas, 69⅞ × 89 in. (177.5 × 226 cm)
Musée d'Orsay, Paris, France

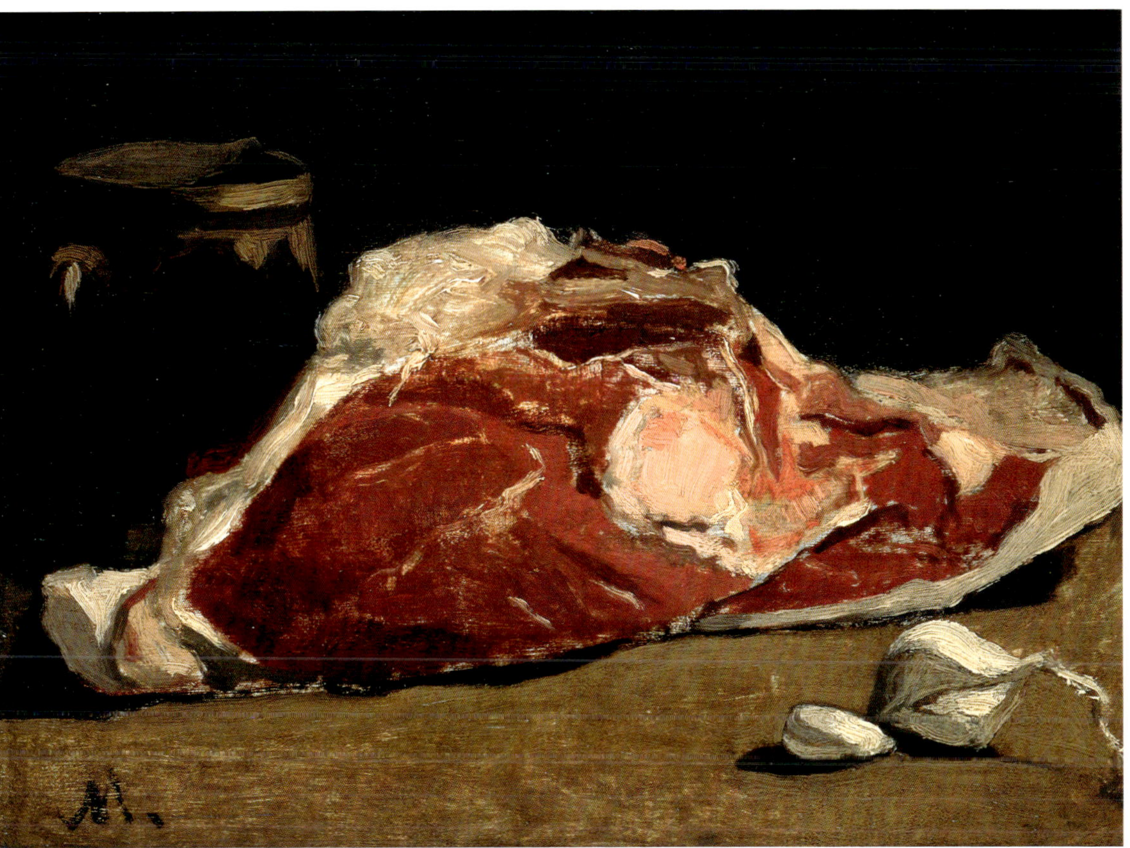

Fig. 90
Claude Monet
Still Life: A Quarter of Beef, 1864
Oil on canvas, 9½ × 13 in. (24 × 33 cm)
Musée d' Orsay, Paris, France

she believes was "mainly due to the efforts of literary men (Théophile Gautier, Champfleury, Thoré)."[33] These critics invoked Chardin's name to confer an authority onto neglected genres, especially still life. As early as 1849 (before all of Diderot's *Salons* were available in print), Champfleury wrote in *La Silhouette* about the still lifes by his friend: "François Bonvin . . . [who] deserves an enthusiastic Diderot of his own. For him, a pot, a jug, a vase, a cup are all subjects more complicated and more mysterious than a man."[34] Linking the Realist still-life painters to Chardin, as seen through the writing of Diderot, was to place the eighteenth-century painter at the inception of a demonstrably French tradition, which endured through the use and representation of everyday objects. Monet's *Still Life: A Quarter of Beef* (fig. 90), for instance, reworks the still lifes of Chardin, Jean-Baptiste Oudry, and Alexandre François Desportes, and reaches back through the eighteenth-century French painters to the Dutch seventeenth-century masters but as seen through Realist eyes. In the 1860s Monet's still lifes owed a great deal to the art of the past, but with weighty interventions from more contemporary painters like Bonvin and Eugène Boudin.

After the Revolution of 1848, Dutch art had acquired a reputation for republican values and was supported by a number of left-wing critics, especially Thoré-Bürger, who published his *Musées de la Hollande* in 1858 and 1860. Moreover, Dutch painting validated a craft tradition, unconstrained by academic precepts, in which still life enjoyed a considerable reputation. Even the artistically conservative Charles Blanc acknowledged this in his *École hollandaise* when he suggested: "If one wanted to provide a definition of art, one would find it just as readily in a kitchen piece by Kalf as in a heroic subject by Poussin."[35]

However, although the Louvre had a comprehensive collection of Dutch paintings—with the exception of any by Johannes Vermeer—from as early as 1830, still lifes were not well represented. Only with the La Caze bequest was this rectified; then about fifty northern still lifes entered the national collection. Chu points out that Dutch still life was not as popular in nineteenth-century Paris as it had been in the eighteenth century; French eighteenth-century masters—Desportes, Oudry, Chardin—were preferred, but, of course, their work was rooted in the Dutch practice.[36] In tying still life to an enduring Frenchness,

Fig. 91
Gustave Caillebotte (1848–1894)
Fruit Displayed on a Stand, c. 1881–82
Oil on canvas, 30⅛ × 39⅝ in. (76.5 × 100.6 cm)
Museum of Fine Arts, Boston: Fanny P. Mason Fund in memory of Alice Thevin, 1979.196

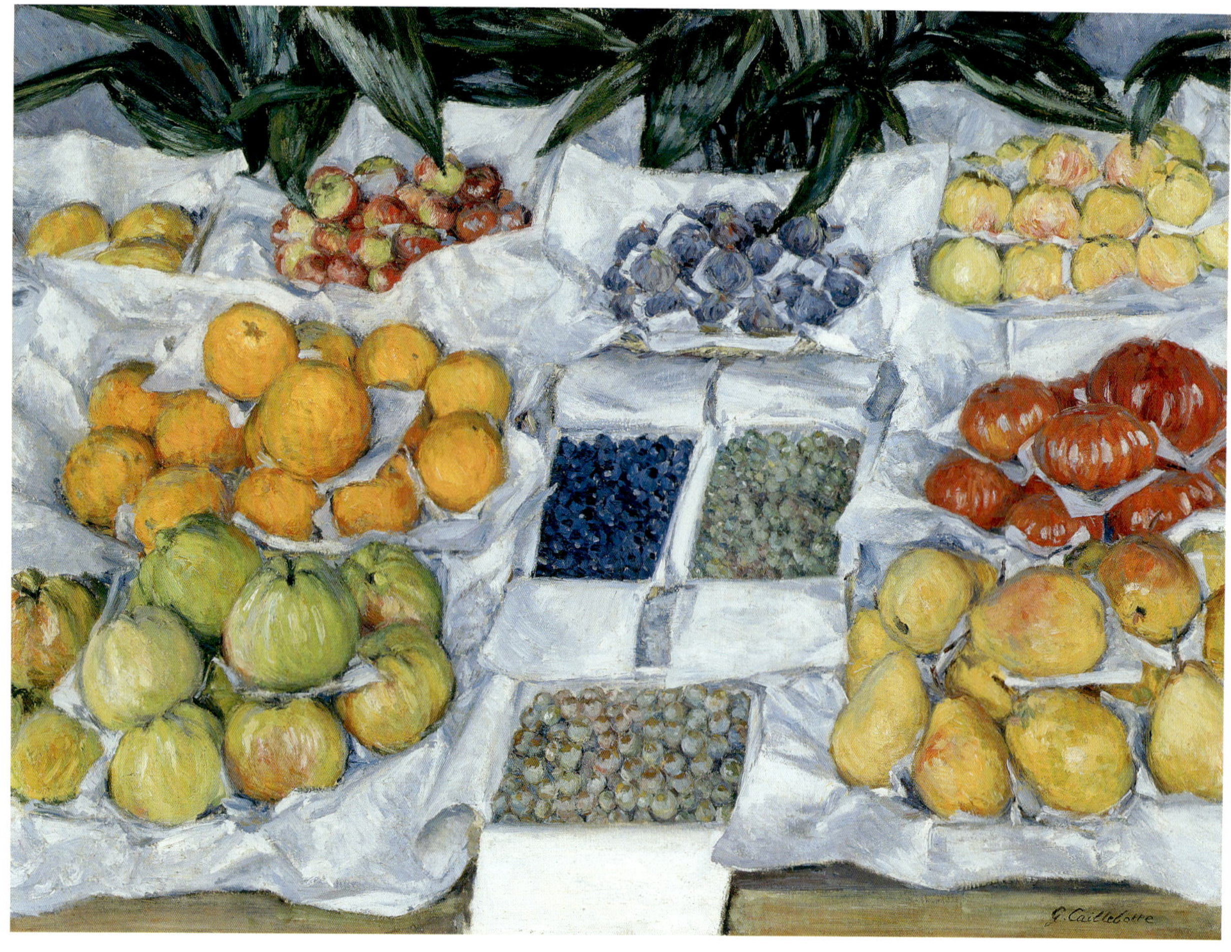

which gained its populist support through the representation of commonplace objects, which had not changed since Chardin's time, those critics who supported still life and the Realist painters who practiced it allowed little room for the genre to develop: still life was immediately rooted in a ready-made tradition by virtue of its subject matter. This timelessness, which might have lent it a universalizing appeal, instead prevented its proper flourishing. By the late 1860s Manet may have begun locating his still lifes in the drawing room rather than the kitchen,[37] but it was still the bourgeois setting of Chardin's *The Brioche* (fig. 88) rather than a depiction of the urban *vie moderne* that could be found in his paintings of other genres by this date.

Not until the 1880s did Gustave Caillebotte begin painting still lifes that grappled with the subject of the modern city and raised questions about the role of objects in contemporary society. His *Fruit Displayed on a Stand* (fig. 91) leaves the domestic behind and enters into a candid celebration of the commodity form, invested with all of the allure of the urban spectacle. Superficially *Fruit Displayed on a Stand* treats the same theme as Moillon's *Still Life with Cherries, Strawberries, and Gooseberries* (fig. 81); those fruits, however, were intended for domestic consumption, but with Caillebotte they are laid out on the altar table of a quite different order of consumption.

By this time, the humble still life was no longer constrained by academic prejudices, produced by ambivalent artists who could hope to sell only to a small circle of amateurs; in breaking so decisively with the past, the genre was finally able to be exploited fully. A case in point is Cézanne's *Still Life with Statuette* (cat. 16, p. 63). In the timelessness of the objects depicted, the inclusion of the cast of the putto, and in the sumptuous assembling of the whole, it manages to nod to the past. At the same time its complex composition and its use of multiple viewpoints render it defiantly modern, finally evading constricting taxonomic constraints in the pursuit of an invigorated tradition.

Notes

1. Although the term *still-leven* had appeared in Dutch inventories from about 1650, its French equivalent, *nature morte*, was not coined until the middle of the eighteenth century and then only in theoretical writings.

2. "des choses mortes et sans mouvement" and "des fruits, des fleurs ou des coquilles." Félibien 1705, preface, n.p.

3. "si le Peintre se trouve engagé dans un petit sujet, il faut qu'il tâche de le rendre grand par la maniere [*sic*] extraordinaire dont il le traitera." Piles 1708, pp. 70–71.

4. Fantin-Latour to Edwin Edwards, May 15, 1862, quoted in Ottawa 1983, p. 113.

5. "car cet art n'est pas indifférent à celui de se metter avec goût: mais je ne voudrois point qu'on les appliquât au paysage, encore moins à la figure. Des feuillages, des fruits, des fleurs, des draperies, tout ce qui peut servir à donner un contour élégant aux ajustemens, et à faire soi-même un patron de broderie quand on n'en trouve pas à son gré, celà leur suffit." Rousseau 1762, vol. 4, book 5, pp. 41–42.

6. Alfred Sisley also treated the same subject at the same time as Bazille (Musée Fabre, Montpellier, on deposit from the Musée d'Orsay, Paris). Although the subject matter was traditionally Dutch, it is much more likely that both painters were referring to later French precedents, such as Chardin's *Still Life with Dead Pheasant and Hunting Bag* (cat. 21, p. 190) and Oudry's *The Dead Crane* (Staatliches Museum, Schwerin).

7. Burty 1876, p. 364.

8. "ses natures mortes si belles, si exactes dans les rapports des tons, ont quelque chose de solennel dans leur vérité." Rivière, "L'Exposition" 1877, p. 1.

9. For full listings and identifications of these works, see San Francisco 1986; Berson 1996, vol. 2.

10. Reff 1970, pp. 456–58.

11. The German School had a flower piece by Abraham Mignon; the Flemish included Frans Snyders's *The Game Dealer,* two examples of flowers by Daniel Seghers, and a game piece and a still life of fish by Adriaen van Utrecht. The Dutch School included examples by Jan Davidsz de Heem, Jan Weenix, Willem Kalf, Melchior de Hondecoeter, Pieter van Slingelandt, and five flower pieces by Jan van Huysum. The French School included illustrations of several flower pieces by Monnoyer, but both Alexandre-François Desportes and Jean-Baptiste Oudry were represented

by hunting scenes rather than still lifes. Chardin's oeuvre was mainly illustrated by genre scenes and by a single still life: *Preparations for a Meal*. The impression given to a nineteenth-century reader was that the still life was largely a northern genre and certainly not one practiced by either the Spanish or Italians.

12. Reff, "Louvre" 1964.

13. Haskell 1980, pp. 115–16, discusses the reassessment of French eighteenth-century art, which was spearheaded by the political left: after 1848 Chardin was one of a number of ancien régime painters who enjoyed popularity. See also Meltzoff, "Le Nains" 1942.

14. Published in 1881, *Musée national du Louvre, Notice des tableaux exposés dans les galeries* (Paris: Charles de Mourgues Frères) has to be treated with caution: it included only those still lifes by Chardin that were part of the collection in 1855 when the introduction to the catalogue had been written: two others were included in a supplement. However, Emmanuel Bocher's third volume of *Les Graveurs françaises du XVIIIe siècle*, dedicated to Chardin and published in 1876, is a more reliable source and included the most recent additions to the Louvre collection of his work. Bocher listed a dozen still lifes then attributed to Chardin that had formed part of the La Caze bequest and were by then on display in the Louvre.

15. A still life by Francisco de Goya did not enter the Louvre until 1937. For information on Goya's still lifes, see Vischer 1997.

16. "Chardin n'était représenté que par une simple nature morte." Champfleury, "Les Nouveaux Tableaux du musée," *L'Artiste*, July 1845, pp. 8–9, in Lacambre and Lacambre 1973, p. 46. This was *The Ray*, which had entered the Louvre as Chardin's *morceau de reception* in 1728.

17. Paris 1979, p. 85.

18. Simches 1964 points to Cypierre as one of the first to collect eighteenth-century works at the start of the nineteenth century.

19. Gautier 1856, n.p. The copy of the catalogue in London, Victoria and Albert Museum, National Art Library, includes prices written in pencil.

20. "Diderot, l'instaurateur de la critique pittoresque en France admirait fort Chardin, et il avait raison, quoique peut-être il fût plus sensible, selon son habitude, au choix des sujets qu'au mérite même du peintre. . . . La nature morte désignée sous le nom du *Gobelet d'argent*, dans la collection de M. Barroilhet, est une merveille de composition et de couleur, les maîtres de Flandre et de Hollande n'ont rien fait de plus réel, de plus sincère et de mieux rendu." Ibid.

21. "La nature morte fut très en honneur parmi la jeune génération, qui négligeait complètement l'étude du nu, envisageait l'homme dans ses rapports avec la nature extérieure, et tentait de la rendre avec les sabots du paysan, la blouse de l'ouvrier, le paletot du citadin. . . . Chardin devint alors l'idole de toute une génération d'artistes qui le prit en quelque sort pour patron." Ménard 1873, p. 180.

22. Louis Martinet (1810–1894) had trained with Baron Antoine-Jean Gros and painted flowers and landscapes. See also Tourneux 1907, p. 391.

23. McCoubrey 1964 gives a total of twenty-five still lifes by Chardin on display. There were in fact twenty-seven.

24. Burty 1860, cat. 105. Diderot's Salon of 1763 had been published only in 1857. Diderot's name recurred in Thoré's introduction to his Salon of 1845, the year that *L'Artiste* republished Diderot's first short Salon of 1759 (it had first appeared in print in 1813). At the beginning of the Second Republic, *L'Artiste* published a series of six articles reviewing the Salon of 1849 signed "feu Diderot."

25. "la spécialité du génie de Chardin. Il a élevé ce genre secondaire aux plus hautes commes aux plus merveilleuses conditions de l'art. Et jamais peut-être l'enchantement de la peinture matérielle, touchant aux choses sans intérêt, les transfigurant par la magie du rendu, ne fut poussé plus loin que chez lui. Qui a donné aux yeux une pareille sensation de présence réelle des objets? Chardin semble entrer, comme le soleil, dans la belle et sombre petite cuisine de Willem Kalf. C'est une magie à côté de laquelle tout pâlit et tous faiblissent. Van Huysum et ses herbiers de fleurs sèches, de Heem et ses fruits sans air, Abraham Mignon et ses pauvres bouquets, minces, découpés, métalliques." Goncourt 1873, pp. 89–90. Translation from Goncourt 1948, pp. 114–15.

26. The collection had been bequeathed in 1869 but did not go on display until 1870. See Béguin and Constans 1969. See also Chennevières 1888–89.

27. "Ces qualités se retrouvent dans les tableaux de *still-life* où il groupe les ustensiles d'un ménage honnête, . . . M. La Caze avait trouvé une douzaine de ces Chardins intimes: les meilleurs sont le *Bocal d'olives*, *la Brioche* et la *Fontaine*. . . . C'est là un art sain et robuste, et la sérénité avec laquelle ces choses sont composées et peintes éveille l'idée d'un milieu social où la vie quotidienne est modeste et laborieuse." Mantz 1870, pp. 17–18.

28. "Diderot aimait à l'adoration ces desserts de Chardin." Ibid.

29. Baltimore 2000, p. 39.

30. However, see Mathey 1963 for examples of Manet's debt to the eighteenth-century master.

31. McCoubrey 1964; and Cleveland 1979. The case of Bonvin should be used with caution. His presence at the Salon by the 1860s, where other artists could have seen his work, was as a painter of genre rather than still life. Although he painted many still lifes in that period, these had entered private collections.

32. "[Bonvin] est maître aussi, dans son genre peu ambitieux. Il tient aussi des frères Lenain, de Chardin et des Hollandais." "Salon de 1861," in Thoré-Bürger 1870, p. 114.

33. Chu 1974, p. 34.

34. "François Bonvin . . . [qui] mérite un Diderot enthousiaste. Pour lui, un pot, une cruche, un vase, une tasse sont des sujets aussi compliqués et aussi mystérieux qu'un homme." Champfleury, *La Silhouette*, July 8, 1849, quoted in Moreau-Nélaton 1927, pp. 30–31.

35. "si l'on voulait donner une definition de l'art, on la trouverait aussi bien dans une cuisine de Kalf que dans tel sujet héroïque du Poussin." Blanc 1861, vol. 2, p. 1.

36. Chu 1974, p. 12. She notes that after the invasion of Holland and Belgium by General Pichegru in 1794–95, the Louvre temporarily acquired paintings from those countries, but that these were still largely regarded as an inferior art; only after about 1820 were they accorded more respect. Chu, p. II, suggests that although Dutch still life was not as popular as it had been in the eighteenth century, "Kalf, however, was much admired, less now for his early kitchen interiors than for his later classic compositions of costly dishes, goblets and food." Dutch painting was widely seen in Paris after La Caze bequeathed a number of northern still-life paintings to the Louvre in 1869. These are listed in the catalogue by Claire Constans in Béguin and Constans 1969.

37. As suggested by Hanson 1977.

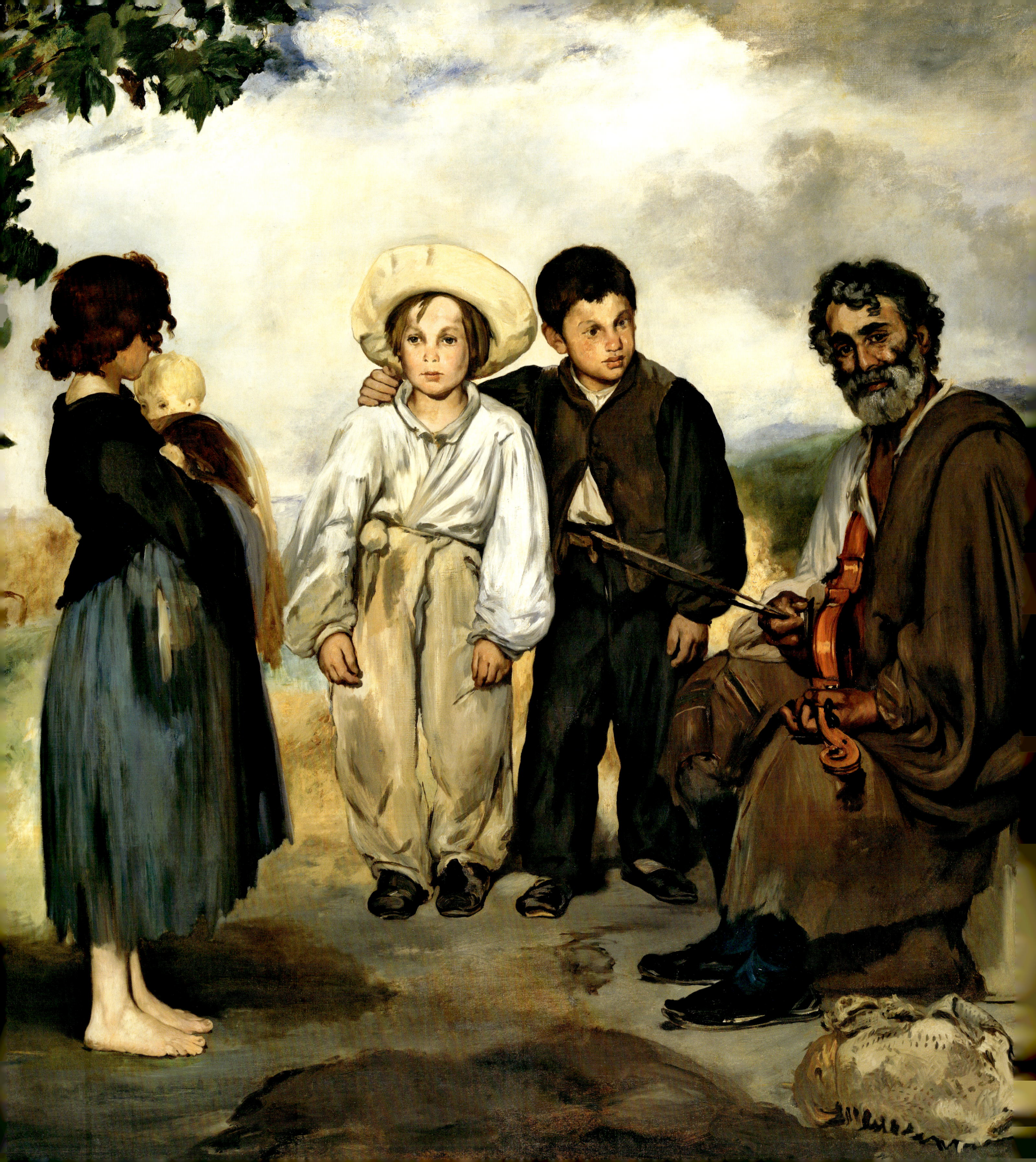

John House

Painting without a Subject? Genre

In the eyes of many commentators, genre painting became the dominant force in French painting in the years after 1850. For critics who supported the teaching of the École des Beaux-Arts, its focus on everyday scenes and seemingly trivial details was a betrayal of the elevated values for which traditional history painting was meant to stand.[1] By contrast, the protagonists of the painting of modern life saw this newfound prominence as a triumph. Marius Chaumelin wrote in 1868: "We can be proud of the importance that genre painting . . . has assumed in recent years. Do not these images of domestic life, these sketches of customs and characters, tell us the history of man himself? And is not this history as worthy of interest and as rich in lessons as the representation of empires bloodstained by war?"[2]

Indeed, in the 1860s it seemed that genre painting had invaded the bastions of history painting. Jean-Léon Gérôme, widely seen as having debased classical history painting to the level of genre, was appointed by the government as a professor at the École des Beaux-Arts in 1864. At the Paris Exposition Universelle of 1867 genre painters took virtually all the top medals, with the highest number of

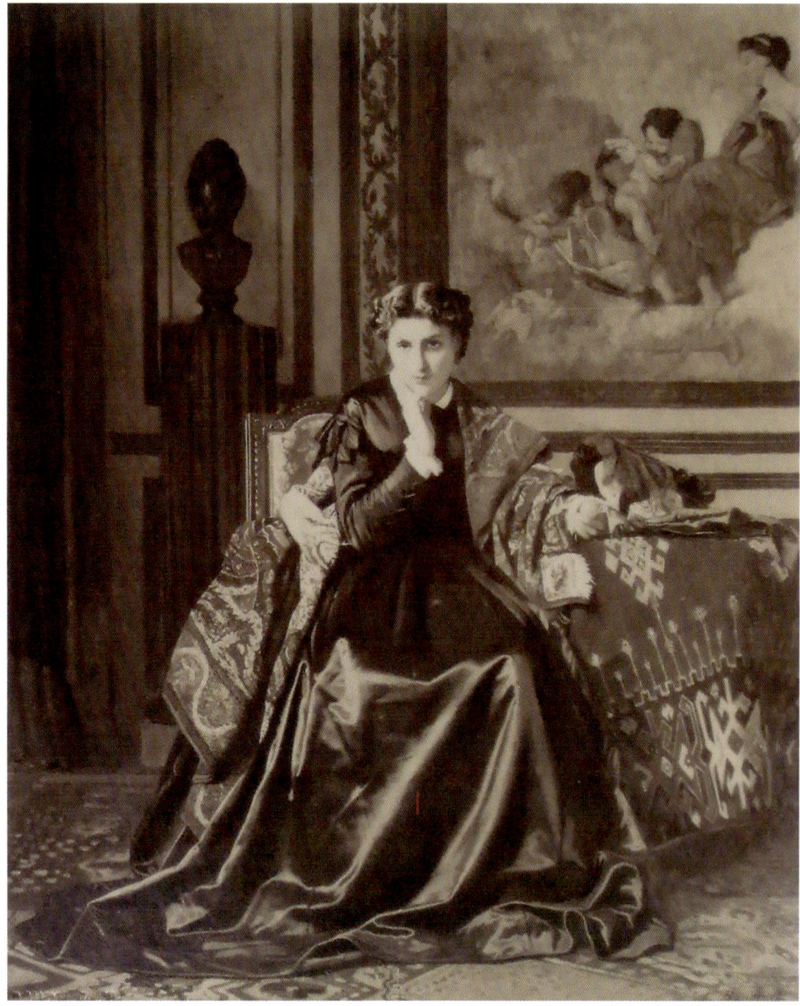

Fig. 92
Charles Baugniet (1814–1886)
Troubled Conscience, 1864
Location unknown

votes going to Jean-Louis-Ernest Meissonier, renowned for his tiny but exquisitely crafted historical genre scenes, depicting the quotidian existence of characters in seventeenth- and eighteenth-century dress.[3]

Reports of the death of history painting were exaggerated; new forms of historical and allegorical painting flourished under the Third Republic after 1870. In the repressive decade of the 1870s, before the republic was securely established, the government sought to reinstate traditional history painting at the top of the hierarchy of subject matter, and later in the century the authorities sponsored many major decorative schemes in public buildings—projects ranged from the depiction of the religious history of Paris in the Panthéon to the decorations, both allegorical and historical, in museums and town halls across the country.

However, throughout these years, paintings of everyday life flourished, in a great diversity of forms. Meissonier's historical genre scenes evolved—or degenerated—into the ubiquitous "cardinals and cavaliers" of the late nineteenth century;[4] military scenes increasingly focused on the experiences and sufferings of ordinary soldiers; meticulously painted fashionable bourgeois interiors, often deeply indebted to seventeenth-century Dutch painting, were the stock-in-trade of dealers such as Adolphe Goupil (e.g., fig. 92); and bourgeois recreation, in Paris's parks (see cat. 78, p. 214), on and beside the river Seine, and on the fashionable beaches of Normandy, became increasingly popular as a subject for fine art.

This was the immediate context of the Impressionists' explorations of themes from contemporary life, and these were the paintings in relation to which their canvases were judged. There was, though, another dimension to their modern-life subject painting. They, like their contemporaries, were engaging in a dialogue with the arts of the past; more specifically, they were part of a wholesale reassessment of the history of painting that challenged academic values and the primacy of Raphael, and in their place constructed—or invented—a "Realist tradition" in the history of art.[5] This involved the reassessment—or "rediscovery"—of certain artists from the past, such as the Le Nain brothers, Johannes Vermeer, and Jean-Siméon Chardin.[6] But, more important, artists and writers used their reexamination of these and other past artists as a means of articulating a new aesthetic, a set of values that they saw as integral to the creation of a genuinely modern art for the nineteenth century.

We can glean the essentials of this aesthetic from a number of texts. There were two crucial strands to the writers' arguments: the rejection of the conventions of post-Renaissance academic art; and a challenge to the primacy of the "subject" in painting. Writing in 1860, Champfleury saw the Le Nains as the "fathers of current experiments" because of their "antiacademic" compositional methods, the fact that they did not "bother to group their figures."[7] Writing about the Dutch painters of the seventeenth century, Charles Blanc stressed their adherence to "the principle of pure imitation" and praised their rejection of "Italian conventions" and of the temptation of "style."[8] In 1857 Théophile Thoré was more explicit in his hope that a new art for the future could emerge from the lessons of the "naturalist schools" of the seventeenth century, an art that would mark the final death of the lineage of the arts of antiquity and the Renaissance.[9]

Eugène Fromentin in 1876 focused on the question of the "subject." In this context, of course, the challenge was not to the notion of representational art but rather an insistence that painting should function in purely visual terms, without invoking narratives, associations, and emotions that were extraneous to the direct visual experience of the image itself. He noted the truthfulness and sincerity of Dutch art and stressed the absence of the "subject" in Dutch genre painting. This was in contrast to the lineage of French genre painting that descended from Jean-Baptiste Greuze, with its preoccupation with moralizing and sentimental anecdotes.[10] Scholarship since the 1960s has reassessed this reading of Dutch art, arguing that there was indeed a moral dimension to Dutch genre painting for its original viewers. For our purposes, though, it is vital to note that nineteenth-century viewers and critics did not see it in these terms. Fromentin put this very succinctly: "What reason does a Dutch painter have for painting a picture? None; and note that nobody ever asks him for one."[11]

Rejection of compositional formulas, rejection of the generalization and idealization associated with "style," rejection of the whole heritage of the Italian Renaissance, and rejection of the literary, emotional, and anecdotal dimensions of painting: taken together, these amounted to a wholesale repudiation of all the values for which the Académie and the École des Beaux-Arts stood. But there was a further dimension to these texts. All of them associated Dutch art with notions of "independence," "freedom," and democracy. As the French between the 1850s and the 1870s saw it, the emergence of the new painting in Holland in the seventeenth century depended on social and political preconditions. Likewise, commentators saw the hardworking bourgeoisie depicted by Chardin as untainted by the values of the ancien régime court,[12] and Charles Blanc described the peasants represented by the Le Nains as "silently preparing their future emancipation."[13] Pressures of censorship prevented these writers from stating their message too explicitly: the nineteenth century would only find its "New Painting" in conditions of political freedom.

There were no geographic or national boundaries to this newly invented "realist" tradition. Its canonical artists embraced Diego Rodríguez de Silva y Velázquez, the Dutch painters of the seventeenth century, and in France the Le Nain brothers from the seventeenth and Chardin from the eighteenth century. However, at this point one must emphasize another form of limit on this process of historical reevaluation: the simple question of access to the works of art. In our age of the *musée imaginaire,* when on the walls of a single room you can find high-quality photographic reproductions of countless thousands of celebrated works of art from across the whole world, it is easy to forget just how different the situation was in the mid-nineteenth century. Artists on their travels could see only what was displayed in museums. In Paris, the Musée du Louvre's holdings of the art of this "realist tradition" were transformed by the arrival of the bequest of Louis La Caze, but that did not happen until 1869. Old master exhibitions were few and far between. The Manchester Art Treasures Exhibition of 1857, drawn from British private collections, was the first occasion on which a genuinely synoptic, comparative display of the arts of the past was mounted.[14] It marked the public debut of Velázquez's strikingly antiacademic *"Rokeby" Venus*[15] and was visited by many artists and critics, among them James McNeill Whistler. The limitations were still greater for those unable to see the original works. Engraved reproductions were either very expensive or very poor in quality (e.g., fig. 93); only later in the century did monochrome photographs of art become commonplace.

With these broader issues in mind, we can examine the ways in which the artists of the 1860s and 1870s explored the art of the past and used what they found in it for their own purposes. It is misleading to describe this relation as one of "influence," since this implies the impetus came from the source exerting the influence. Rather, we should see the engagement with past art in terms of creative adaptation and transformation and analyze how the nineteenth-century artists used it in their own overall artistic projects, within the context of the politics of the art world in these decades.

Late in his life, Edgar Degas is reported to have said: "At the beginning of our career, Fantin [Henri Fantin-Latour], Whistler and I, we were all on the same road, the road from Holland."[16] However, we must ask what Degas meant by this comment, how did he see his links with Dutch art? Did he view it primarily in formal terms or as a sanction for painting contemporary subjects? Or is this a false distinction? The nineteenth-century commentators suggested that form and content be considered together. Their accounts move seamlessly between discussion of the everyday-life subject matter of the genre painters of the past and their adoption of antiacademic, anticlassical formal languages. Both their choice of subjects and the ways in which they treated them marked their jettisoning the lineage of post-antique, post-Renaissance art. At the same time these antiacademic ways of composing pictures were the most appropriate way of evoking the painter's experiences of his or her daily environment.

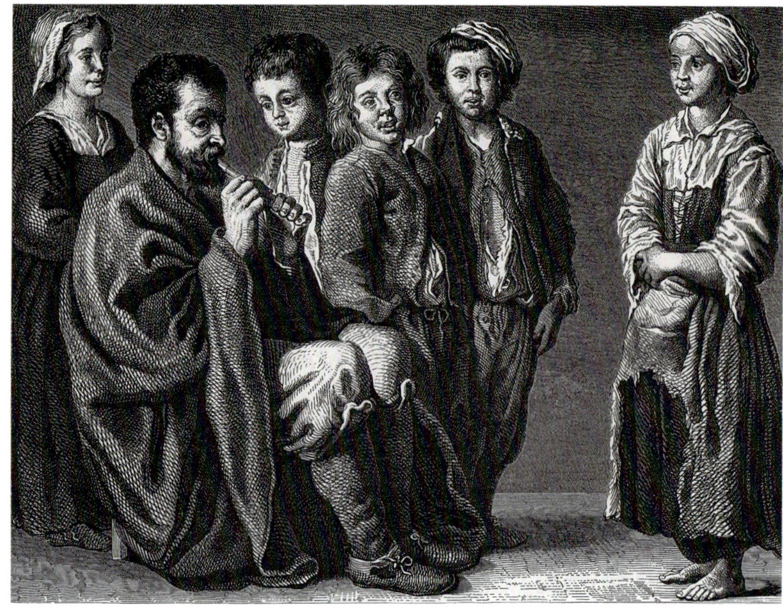

Fig. 93
Engraving after Louis Le Nain, *The Old Fife Player.* From Blanc, *Histoire des peintres de toutes les écoles, École française* (1862)

The crucial dimension of this language of the everyday was its rejection of hierarchies. Compositionally, the paintings repudiated the centered, focused modes of pictorial ordering that led the eye effortlessly to the key elements in the scene; instead, the canvases incorporated multiple points of interest and focus. Champfleury's comments on the Le Nains are the most explicit statement of this antiacademic approach to pictorial composition, but the same arguments lie behind the recurrent iteration in other texts of the rejection of post-Renaissance values. These nonhierarchical modes of pictorial organization were inseparable from the subjects depicted: ordinary people in their everyday surroundings. Clearly, there were aesthetic preferences at play, too, and in a work like Whistler's portrait of the painter's mother of 1871 (fig. 94) the overt references to Dutch compositional conventions are part of an overall aesthetic project that led Whistler to present the picture at the Royal Academy of Arts in London in 1872 with the primary title *Arrangement in Gray and Black,* relegating the painting's ostensible subject to a subtitle. Here, a comparison with the spareness of a canvas such as Caspar Netscher's *The Lace Maker* (fig. 95) seems particularly relevant, though we cannot be sure that Whistler knew this picture. However, even in Whistler's case the choice of subject matter remained highly significant, and in Paris the painters of the Impressionist circle were all, in these years, committed to a "painting of modern life" that encompassed both form and content.

The formal language of the canvases, as well as their subjects, could be seen in broadly political terms, as a democratic art that considered every aspect of everyday life as equally worthy of depiction. This political dimension had a particular relevance in the years under discussion—during Napoleon III's Second Empire and, most of all, during the first highly repressive years of the Third Republic, between 1871 and 1879. It is no coincidence that it was in these years that the Impressionist group set up its own exhibitions, exhibitions that propagated an informal "painting of modern life" that defied the government's attempts to reinstate a hierarchical "high art" form of history painting at the summit of the hierarchy of the genres.

Painters demonstrated their engagement with past genre painting in various ways. Édouard Manet explicitly synthesized the French with the Spanish in *The Old Musician* of 1862 (fig. 96), his first major multifigure genre painting, which included specific references to Velázquez's *The Drinkers* in a composition whose staccato structure carries clear echoes of the Le Nains (e.g., fig. 93);[17] these particular allusions were especially relevant in this canvas of a "low-life" subject. On other occasions, Manet made generic references to Dutch painting. Such is the case in *Repose* of about 1870 (Rhode Island School

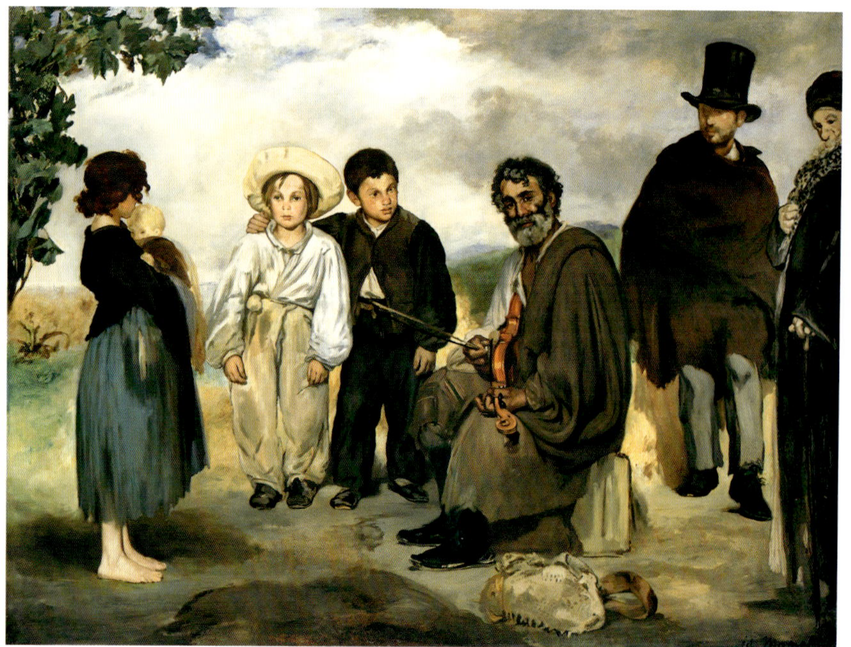

Fig. 96
Édouard Manet
The Old Musician, 1862
Oil on canvas, 73¾ × 98 in.
(187.4 × 248.2 cm)
National Gallery of Art, Washington,
Chester Dale Collection, 1963.10.162

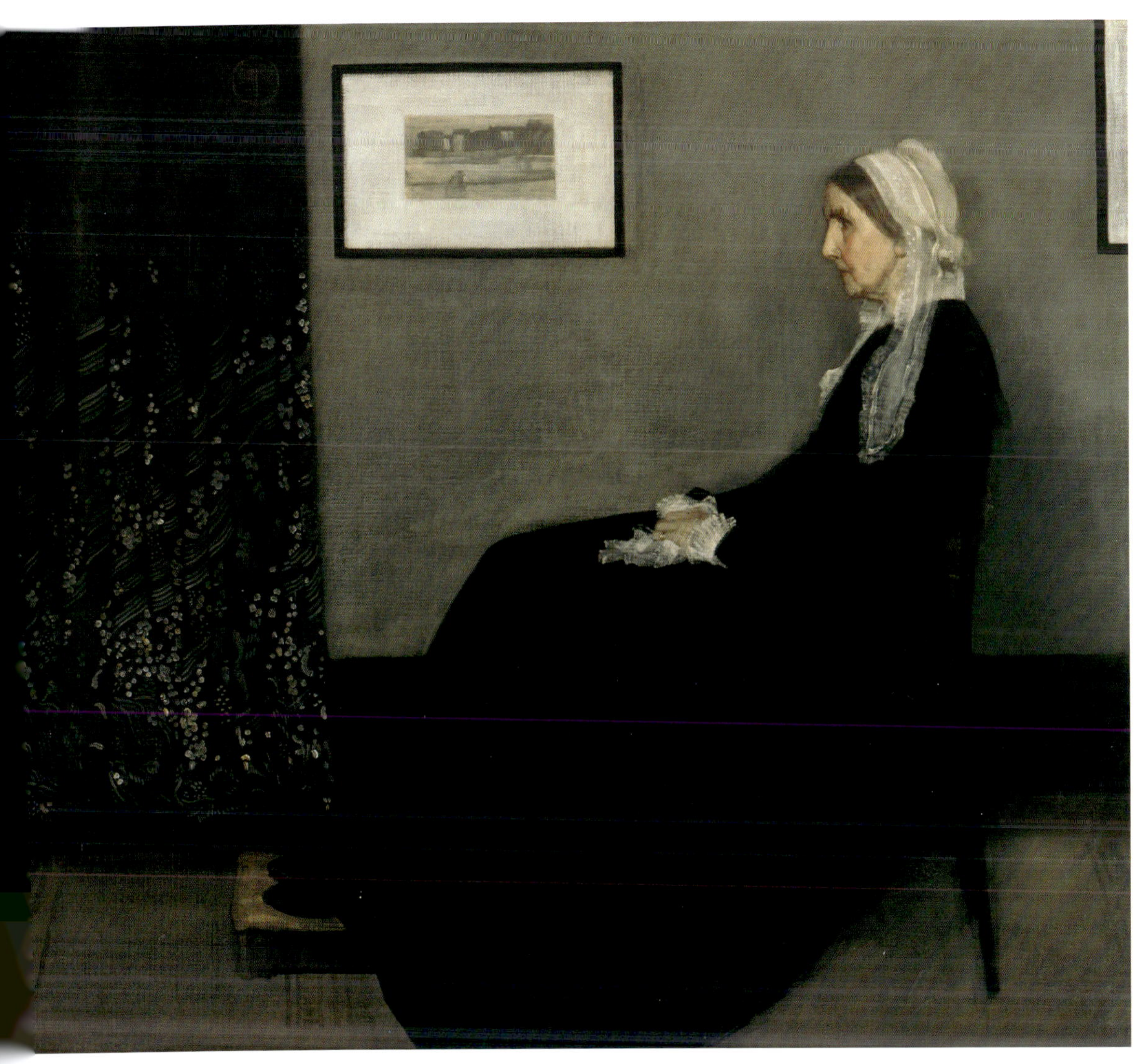

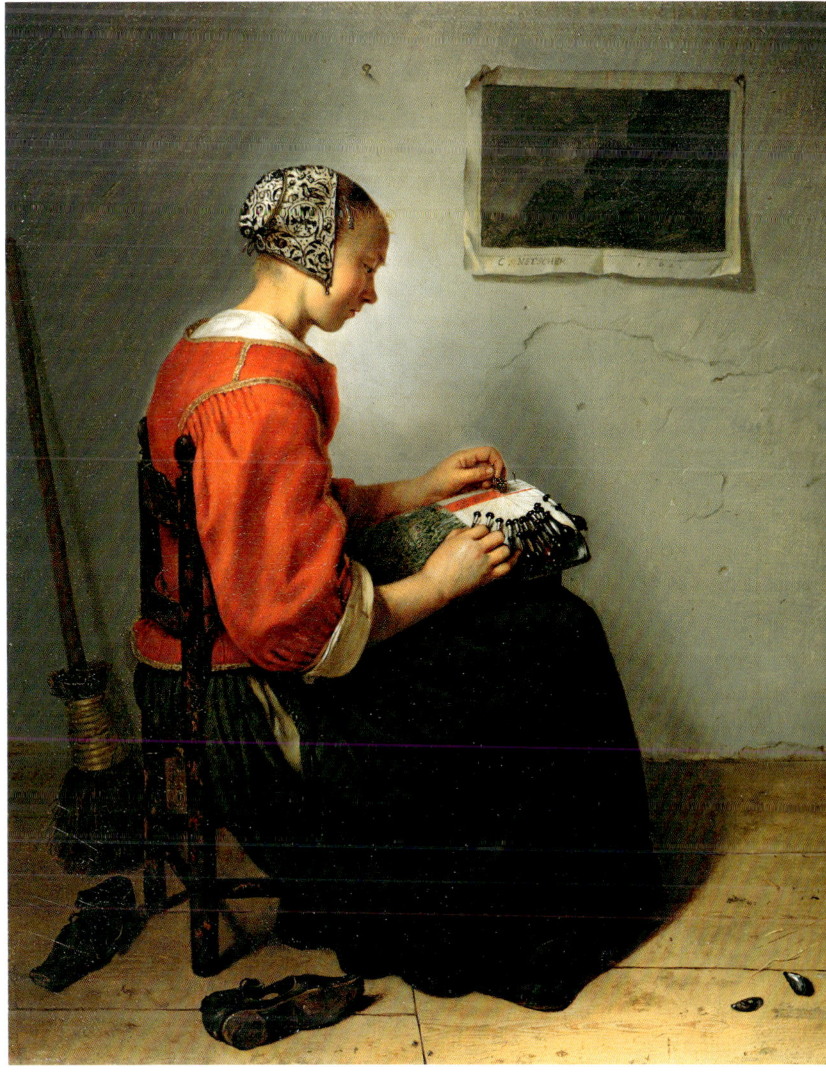

Fig. 94
James McNeill Whistler (1834–1903)
Arrangement in Gray and Black No. 1 or *The Artist's Mother*, 1871
Oil on canvas, 56⅞ × 64 in. (144.3 × 162.5 cm)
Musée d' Orsay, Paris, France

Fig. 95
Caspar Netscher (1639–1684)
The Lace Maker, 1662
Oil on canvas, 13 × 10⅝ in. (33 × 27 cm)
By kind permission of the Trustees of the Wallace Collection, London

Fig. 97
Pierre-Auguste Renoir
Madame Claude Monet Reading, c. 1872
Oil on canvas, 24 × 19¾ in.
(61.2 × 50.3 cm)
Sterling and Francine Clark Art Institute, Williamstown, Massachusetts

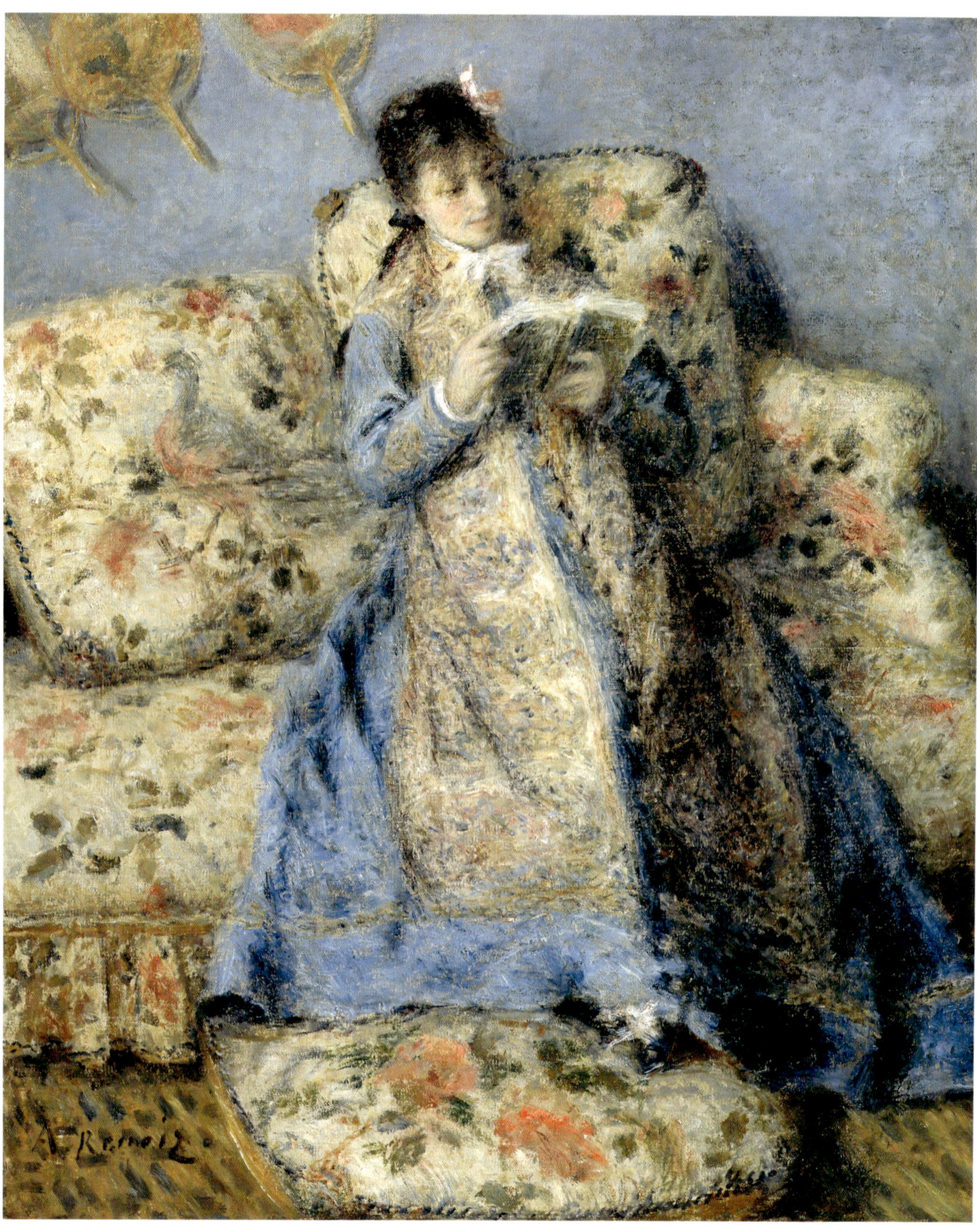

of Design, Providence), with its seated figure silhouetted against a wall on which a picture hangs whose upper edge is cut by the actual picture frame. Again, the reference is appropriate to the subject—a domestic interior with a bourgeois female figure.

Degas revealed his own "road from Holland" most directly in the compositional formats of canvases such as *The Bellelli Family* of about 1858–67 (fig. 103) and *Portrait of Madame Camus* of 1870 (National Gallery of Art, Washington, D.C.). By contrast, the complex interplay of figures and interior spaces in his ballet rehearsal scenes of the early 1870s suggests a rather more oblique affinity with the interiors of painters such as Pieter de Hooch, again appropriately, since both Degas and De Hooch were fascinated by the intersection of figures and settings that gave meaning to their movements and gestures.

Pierre-Auguste Renoir's art in these years is a salutary reminder that we should not seek single, specific "sources" for the genre paintings of the period. *Madame Claude Monet Reading* (fig. 97) retains something of the Dutch echoes of Manet's *Repose*, a canvas to which it presumably refers directly. However, the execution of the painting reveals fluent, painterly qualities more comparable to those of

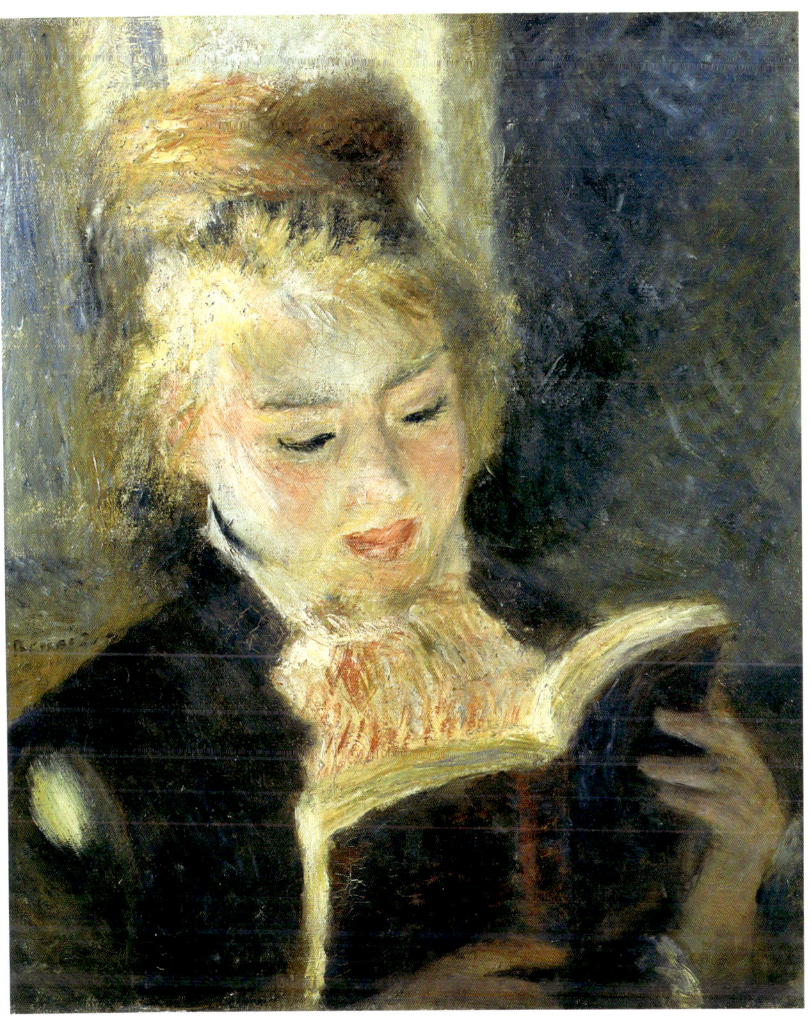

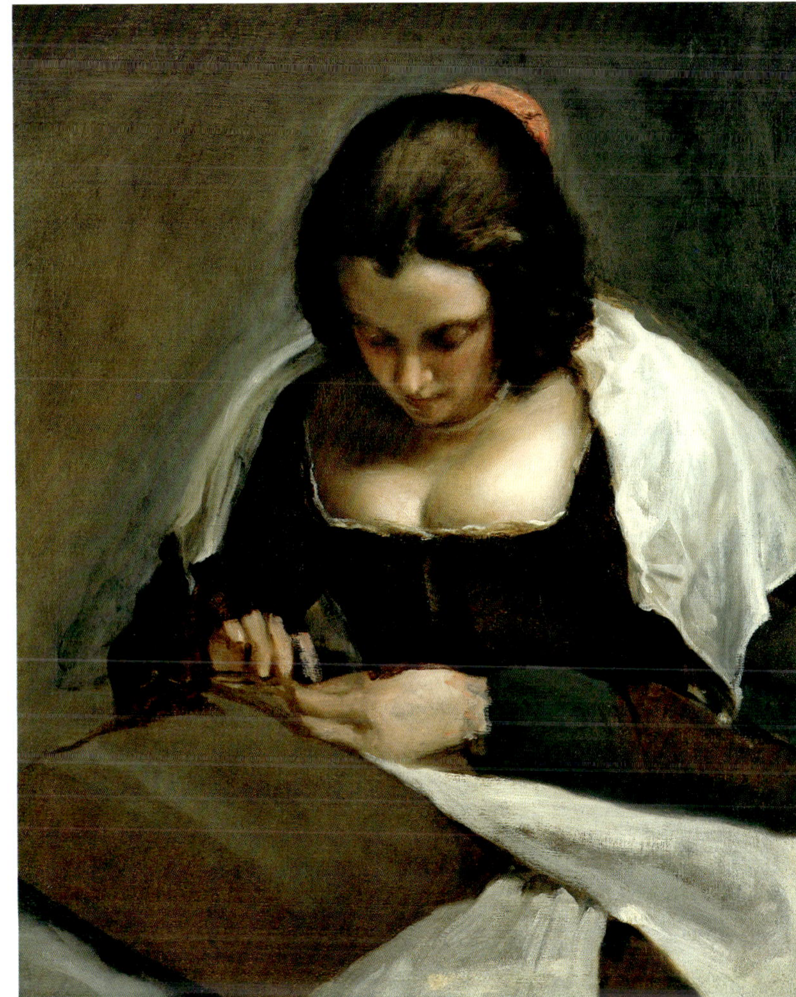

Jean-Honoré Fragonard. Likewise, Renoir's *La Loge* of 1874 (fig. 47) can be seen as a loose synthesis of Titian and Fragonard,[18] while *The Reader* of about 1874–76 (fig. 98) can equally readily be compared with Fragonard's *A Young Girl Reading* (cat. 38, p. 231) or Velázquez's *Needlewoman* (fig. 99), or indeed with Vermeer's *The Lace Maker* (fig. 20), a canvas that entered the Louvre in 1869.

At the same time, Renoir was seeking to rework another genre "tradition," that of the fête champêtre. Canvases such as *La Promenade* of 1870 (J. Paul Getty Museum, Los Angeles) and *The Swing* of 1876 (fig. 100) can be seen as drawing on this type of painting. Indeed, Renoir's close friend Georges Rivière made an explicit comparison between *The Swing* and works by Antoine Watteau in his retrospective review of the third Impressionist group exhibition.[19] Watteau's *Harlequin and Columbine* (fig. 101), a canvas that Renoir could have seen in an exhibition in Paris in 1860,[20] can stand as an

Fig. 98
Pierre-Auguste Renoir
The Reader, c. 1874–76
Oil on canvas, 18¼ × 15⅛ in.
(46.5 × 38.5 cm)
Musée d'Orsay, Paris, France

Fig. 99
Diego Rodríguez de Silva y Velázquez
Needlewoman, c. 1640/1650
Oil on canvas, 29⅛ × 23⅝ in.
(74 × 60 cm)
National Gallery of Art, Washington, Andrew W. Mellon Collection, 1937.1.81

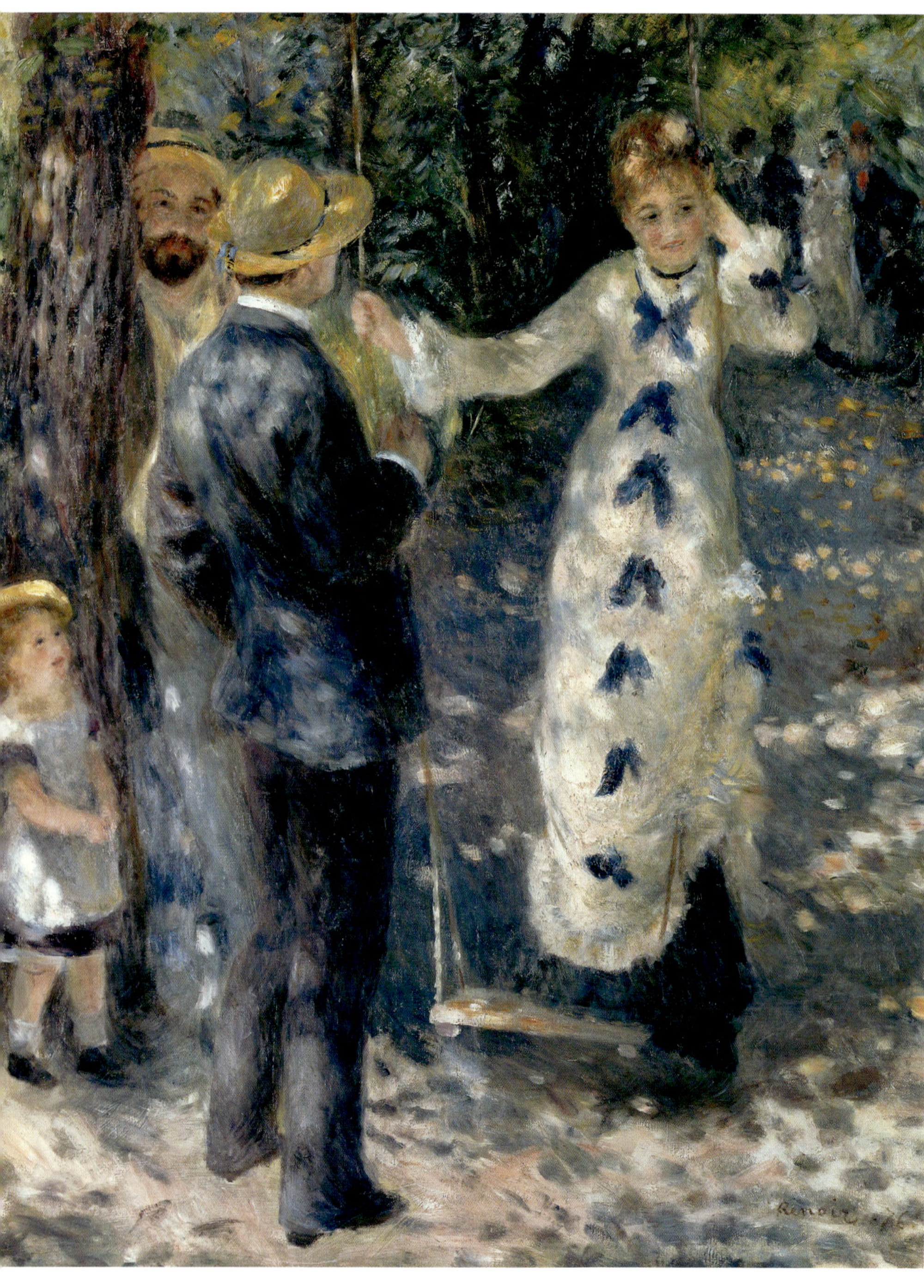

Fig. 100
Pierre-Auguste Renoir
The Swing, 1876
Oil on canvas, 36¼ × 28¾ in.
(92 × 73 cm)
Musée d'Orsay, Paris, France

example, though again one-to-one comparisons are less relevant than generic similarities. The reference to the fête champêtre was especially appropriate for these paintings because Renoir was looking for pictorial form to depict decorous images of modern courtship.

The crucial issue in relation to the Impressionists' modern-life genre paintings of the 1870s is the status of their subject matter. As many scholars have argued in recent years, they must unequivocally be seen as paintings of modern life, and as paintings that engaged directly with certain key aspects of the social worlds of Paris and its surroundings.[21] However, at the same time, these were paintings that in Fromentin's terms were devoid of subject. This emerges most vividly by comparison with the fashionable genre paintings of the period—the paintings that formed the stock-in-trade of the dealer Adolphe Goupil (e.g., fig. 92). In these, gestures and facial expressions invite anecdotal readings, and the titles act as cues to the "correct" interpretation. By contrast, the Impressionists' genre paintings consistently deny the possibility of legible narrative. In Manet's case, the gestures and details in his major exhibition canvases often actively work against the possibilities of such interpretation, as, for instance, in *The Balcony* (Musée d'Orsay, Paris) and *Luncheon in the Studio* (fig. 30), exhibited together at the 1869 Salon.[22] Renoir also set up scenarios that eluded specific interpretation, as in *The Swing*, but without so blatantly transgressing accepted compositional conventions. Both artists gave their canvases very nonspecific titles that merely defined the location or the theme in the most general terms.

There was a political dimension to the subjectlessness of these paintings. For the authorities during the Second Empire, and especially in the repressive climate of the early Third Republic during the 1870s, legibility and classification formed a fundamental weapon of social control. Social types and social situations that could be clearly interpreted might in turn be adjudged in relation to the authorities' very restrictive codes of behavior and, if necessary, be suppressed. The illegibility of the subjectless picture marked a rejection of narrative closure, but it also posed a challenge to these wider frameworks of surveillance.[23]

As argued above, the immediate context for the Impressionists' pictorial experiments was the work of their contemporaries, in relation to which their canvases were viewed and judged. However, a text such as Fromentin's is evidently relevant to their experiments, containing as it does a sustained critique of the obsession with the "subject" in the French genre painting of the past century: "In France, every painting that does not have a title and which therefore does not

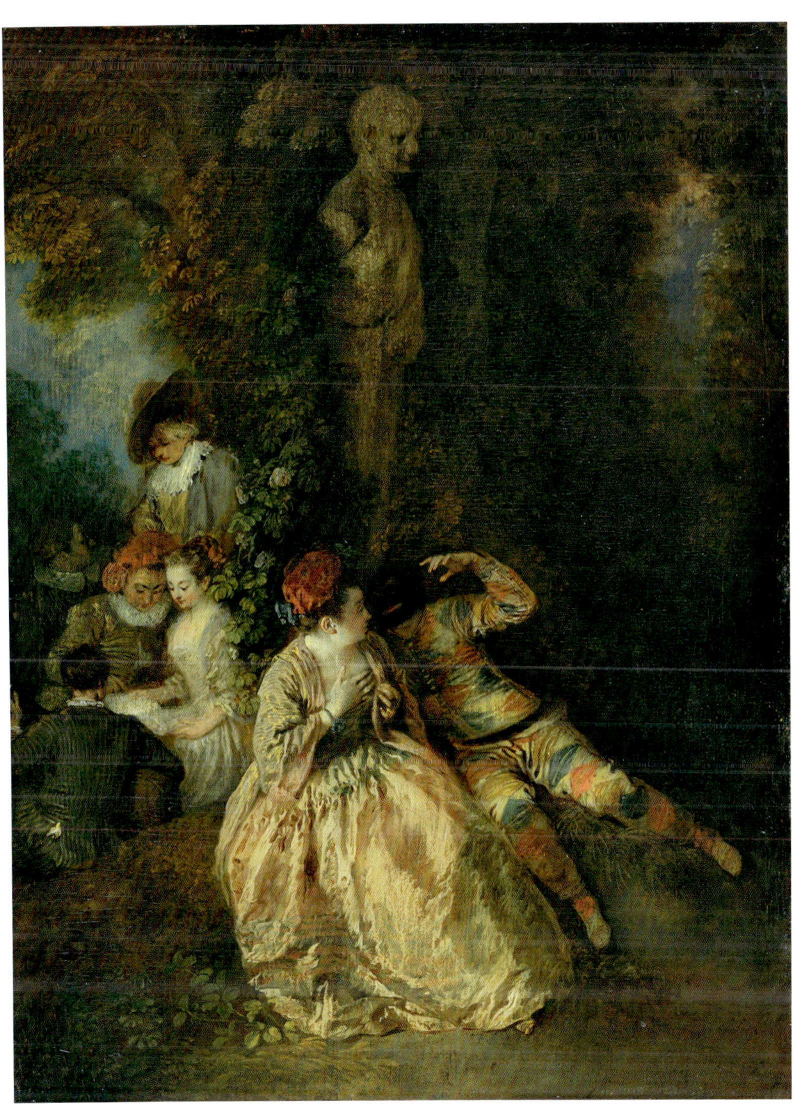

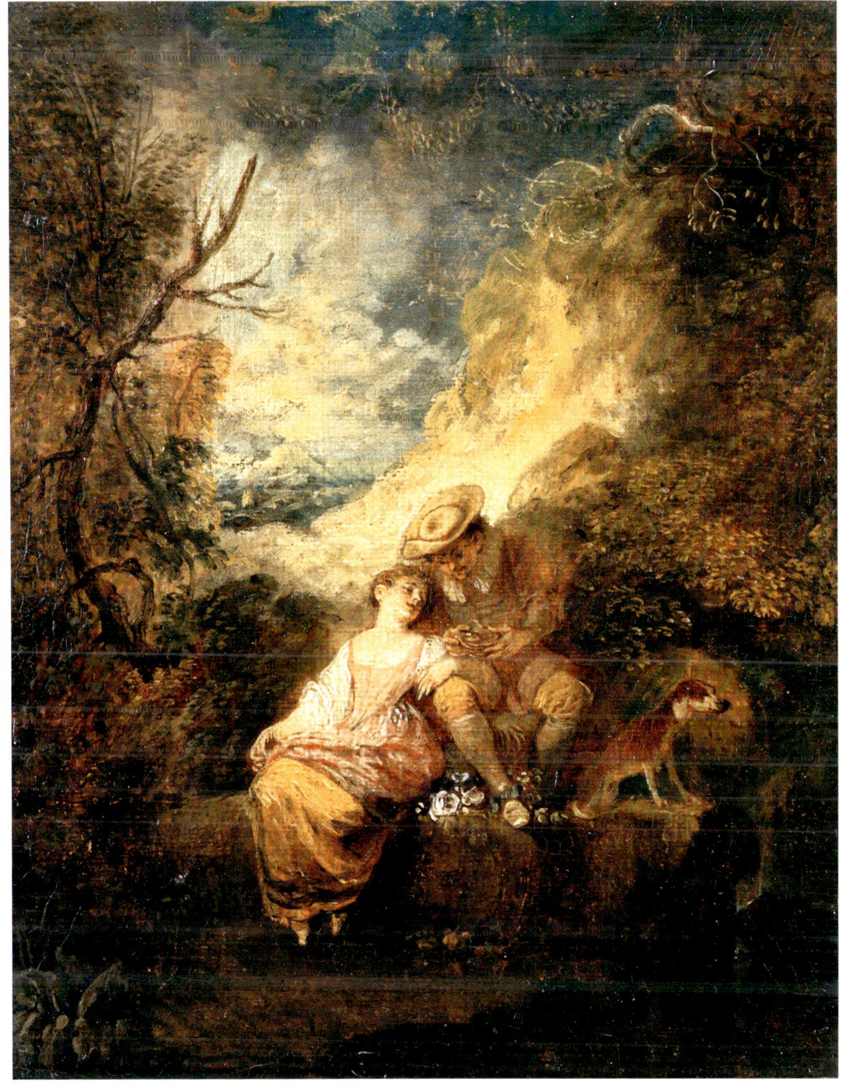

Fig. 101
Jean-Antoine Watteau
Harlequin and Columbine, c. 1716–18
Oil on oak panel, 14⅛ × 9¾ in.
(36 × 24.9 cm), made up to 14⅛ × 10¼ in.
(36 × 25.9 cm)
By kind permission of the Trustees
of the Wallace Collection, London

Cat. 101
Jean-Antoine Watteau
The Robber of the Sparrow's Nest,
c. 1712

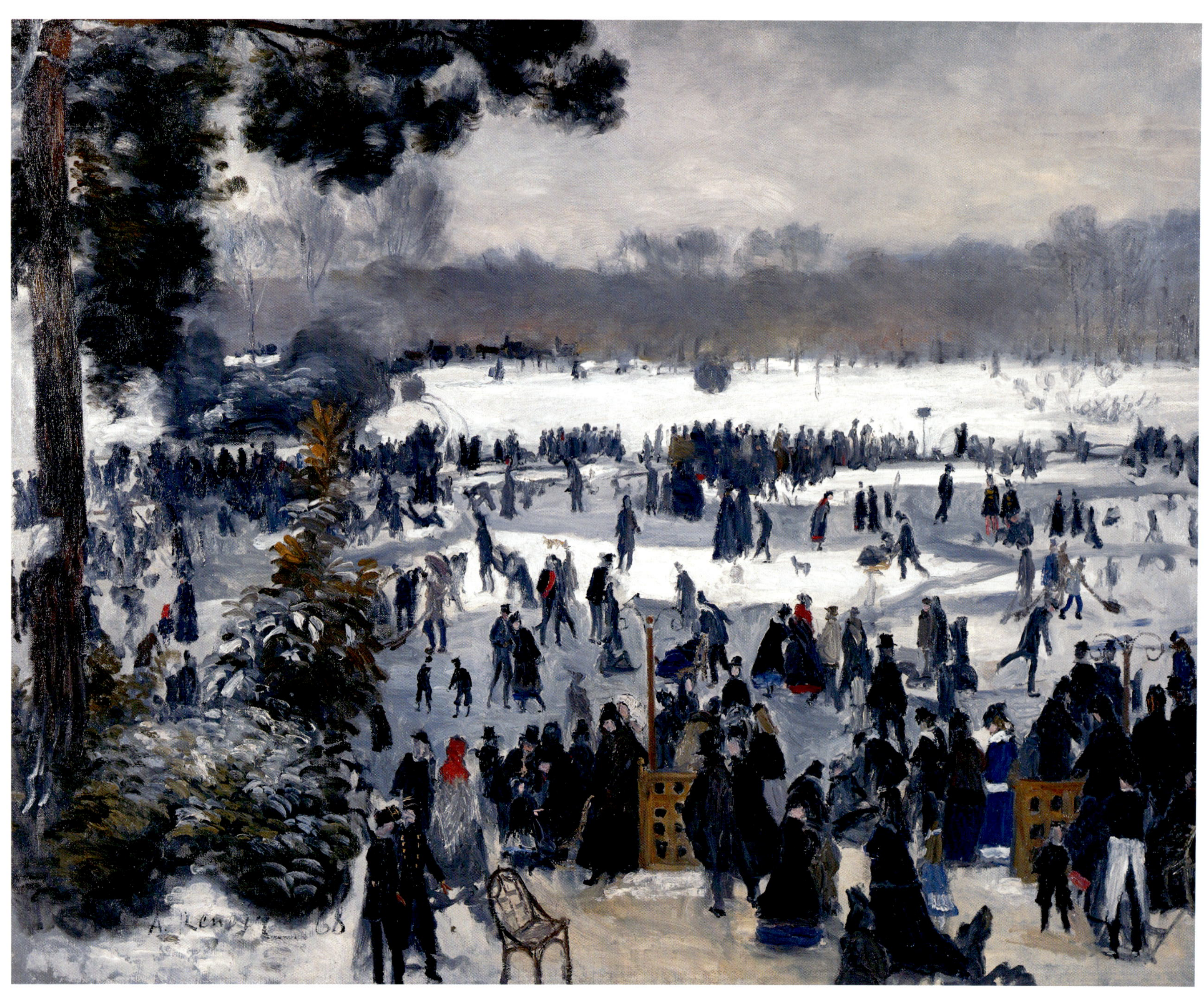

Cat. 78
Pierre-Auguste Renoir
Skaters in the Bois de Boulogne, 1868

contain a subject, runs a great risk of not being treated as a serious or carefully conceived work."[24] Fromentin's promotion of the genre painting of the Dutch seventeenth century offered a powerful sanction for a genre painting without "subject." Indeed, it is very likely that the members of the Impressionist group were well aware of this passage in his text, since other passages from his book were cited (not uncritically) in Edmond Duranty's pamphlet *La Nouvelle Peinture,* published to accompany the second group exhibition in 1876.

There are many ways of contextualizing the Impressionists' paintings, many historical frames that may legitimately be deployed to make sense of their projects. Their relation to the arts of the past is one of these. My argument here is that this should not be viewed in terms of identifying "sources" for their art, or in positing one-to-one correspondences between their canvases and works from the past. Rather, their art needs to be seen in a wider framework, in the context of the wholesale reevaluation of past art that formed part of the "realist" project of painters and writers alike. It was their particular form of engagement with the antiacademic and the subjectless in the art of the past that made their own art so distinctively modern.

Notes

1. See, for example, Merson 1861, pp. 229–30, quoted in House 1997, p. 6.

2. Chaumelin 1868, quoted more extensively in House 1997, p. 6.

3. On the triumph of genre at the 1867 exhibition, see Mainardi 1987, pp. 123–93.

4. See Cincinnati 1992.

5. I take the notion of the "invention of tradition" from Hobsbawm and Ranger 1983.

6. See Meltzoff, "Vermeer" 1942; Meltzoff, "Le Nains" 1942; McCoubrey 1964; Jowell 1998; and, for a broader discussion, Haskell 1976.

7. Champfleury 1860, pp. 179–80.

8. Blanc 1863, pp. 4, 17; on Blanc's *Histoire des peintres,* a publication of central importance in the art historiography of the nineteenth century, see Reff 1970.

9. Bürger, *Trésors* 1860, pp. 320–21.

10. Fromentin 1910, pp. 181, 186–92.

11. Ibid., p. 191.

12. Blanc, "Chardin," 1862, p. 5; Mantz 1870, pp. 17–18.

13. Blanc, "Le Nain," 1862, p. 4.

14. On the Manchester exhibition, see, most recently, Haskell 2000, pp. 82–89.

15. Eloquently described by Thoré (Bürger, *Trésors* 1860, pp. 120–22), who regretted that it was hung so high on the wall—perhaps, he speculated, as a result of "English prudery."

16. Letter from Paul Poujaud to Marcel Guérin, July 11, 1936, recalling Degas's comment, in Degas 1945, p. 256.

17. I emphasize the crucial role played by references to Velázquez in this canvas, in contrast to Michael Fried's insistence on the primacy of French "sources" in Manet's art of the early 1860s. Fried 1996, pp. 23–184.

18. For a comparison with Titian, see House, *Impressionism* 2004, pp. 129–31.

19. Rivière, "Les Intransigeants" 1877, reprinted in Berson 1996, vol. 1, p. 186.

20. Richard Wallace lent it to *Tableaux de l'École Française*, the major loan exhibition organized by Louis Martinet in Paris in 1860, with the title *L'Amour badin* (cat. 272).

21. See, e.g., Clark 1984; Herbert 1988; House, *Impressionism* 2004.

22. For discussion of these canvases in these terms, see House, *Impressionism* 2004; and House, "Face to Face" 2004.

23. These issues are discussed in detail in House, *Impressionism* 2004, chaps. 1 and 4.

24. Fromentin 1910, p. 188.

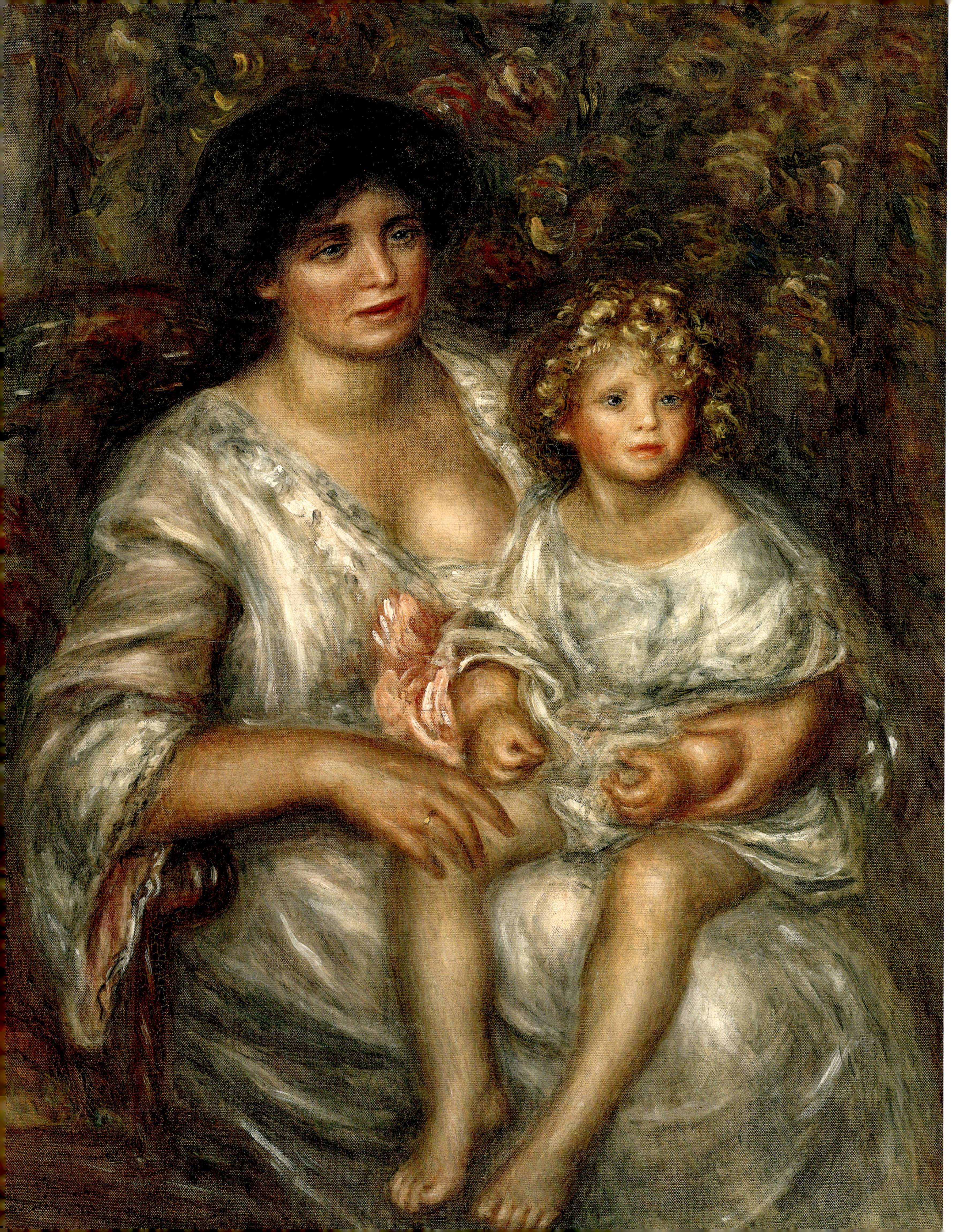

John Collins

An Elegant Alliance

Impressionist Portraiture and the Art of the Past

Introduction

With the exception of Alfred Sisley, who remained a committed landscapist, all the Impressionists painted portraits. Despite the formal constraints of portrait painting—the functional requirement to convey a true likeness, the need to highlight the sitter's personality and achievements—it remained central to Impressionist subject matter. While Camille Pissarro and Claude Monet preferred landscapes, their Impressionist colleagues Mary Cassatt, Berthe Morisot, Édouard Manet, Edgar Degas, Paul Cézanne, and Pierre-Auguste Renoir have left a body of work in portraiture that is sustained in depth over their entire careers. These artists adopted historical traditions while emphatically transforming portraiture through a contemporary painterly vision. Within the broader context of contested territory and rivalry with the Salon and the academic establishment, in which both sides considered the old masters as allies, the Impressionists' referencing of the portraiture of the past became a critical strategy in their attempts to forge a genuinely expressive, modern identity.[1]

Although considered to be a secondary genre to history painting and mythology within the academic hierarchy of subject matter, portraiture had been a staple of the Salon exhibitions since their inception in 1699. In the nineteenth century the portrait gained in prominence at the Salon proportionately with the financial means of image-conscious middle classes. During the 1840s, for example, portraits accounted for a quarter to a third of the paintings exhibited at the Salon.[2] Critics often discussed portraits separately from other categories and intensely debated whether likenesses truly conveyed modern identity. Charles Baudelaire was among the first to address the issue seriously. His writings about portraiture express the need to get beyond appearances and the falseness of social decorum; a desire to reinvigorate the portrait as an art form by making it relevant to contemporary experience. In an essay entitled "The Painter of Modern Life," written in 1859–60 but not published until 1863, he claimed the best portraitists of the past had succeeded because they were able to capture the character of their epoch:

> By "modernity" I mean the ephemeral, the fugitive, the contingent, the half of art whose other half is the eternal and the immutable. Every old master has had his own modernity; the great majority of fine portraits that have come down to us from the former generations are clothed in the costume of their own period. They are perfectly harmonious because everything from costume and coiffure down to gesture, glance and smile (for each age has a deportment, a glance and a smile of its own)—everything, I say, combines to form a completely viable whole.[3]

The 1850s and 1860s

Like the majority of young artists of their generation, the Impressionists first encountered old master portraiture at the Musée du Louvre. While working as a porcelain painter in the 1850s, Renoir ran to the Louvre during his lunch breaks to study the old masters. In the early 1860s he copied Peter Paul Rubens's *Hélène Fourment and Her Children,* which would frequently serve him as a source for later portrait paintings.[4] Before Paul Cézanne arrived in Paris in April 1861 from his hometown of Aix-en-Provence, his boyhood friend Émile Zola suggested a study routine centered on copying masterworks.[5] Degas and Manet first met at the Louvre in late 1861 or early 1862 while Degas was etching a copy of Diego Rodríguez de Silva y Velázquez's *Infanta Margarita* (cat. 34, p. 117), an authoritative image of childhood, now assigned to a workshop copy.[6]

Another source for the portrait painting of the early Impressionists was the interest shown by critics, historians, and collectors in old masters who pioneered techniques to portray in more truthful ways the individuals of their own time. Manet, for example, often borrowed from the engraved reproductions in Charles Blanc's *Histoire des peintres de toutes les écoles,* a series of artists' biographies published from 1861 until 1876.[7] Among the sources that have been suggested for the somber portrait of Manet's parents of 1860 (fig. 102) are Rembrandt's etching of a bearded man and paintings by Frans Hals and the brothers Le Nain—all artists who were rediscovered in the nineteenth century.[8] However, when it was first exhibited at the Salon of 1861, the portrait was labeled derogatorily as "Realist" for bearing those qualities of verisimilitude for which the past masters are now appreciated. The critic of the conservative *Gazette des Beaux-Arts* described the artist as "merciless," for whom "nothing is sacred."[9] A friend of the family later compared Manet's parents to a "couple of concierges."[10] Certainly, there is little to indicate Auguste Manet's successful career as a judge, though his seated pose and clenched fist may be explained by a recent paralysis.[11] A *Légion d'Honneur* lapel pin is just a touch of color in a sea of black, and the mother's gesture of a hand in her embroidery basket is an endearing domestic touch inconsistent with portraiture's conventional role of communicating social status. Rather, the cooler palette and stoic humility borrowed from the seventeenth-century genre scenes of the brothers Le Nain suggest Manet wanted to portray his parents in one of the intimate moments with which he was most familiar.

The sketchlike finish of Manet's *Victorine Meurent* (cat. 54, p. 220), appears indebted to the tactile surfaces and quickly applied brushwork of Frans Hals. Charles Blanc highlighted Hals's reputation for rapid painting that captures fleeting effects and character with a minimum of finish in the first of his volumes of *Histoire des peintres*.[12] Meurent, of course, would become Manet's favorite model, whose nude pose in *Luncheon on the Grass* (fig. 3) caused such a scandal at the Salon des Refusés in 1863, but in this portrait she seems demure, with a pensive turn of head, not unlike Hals's young Dutch patroness (cat. 43, p. 220). At once responsive to Italian and Dutch masters, Manet would also be strongly attracted by such Spanish sources as Francisco de Goya and Velázquez. Both Spanish masters have been discussed in connection with the full-length portrait of the critic Théodore Duret of 1868 (cat. 56, p. 221), whom Manet met

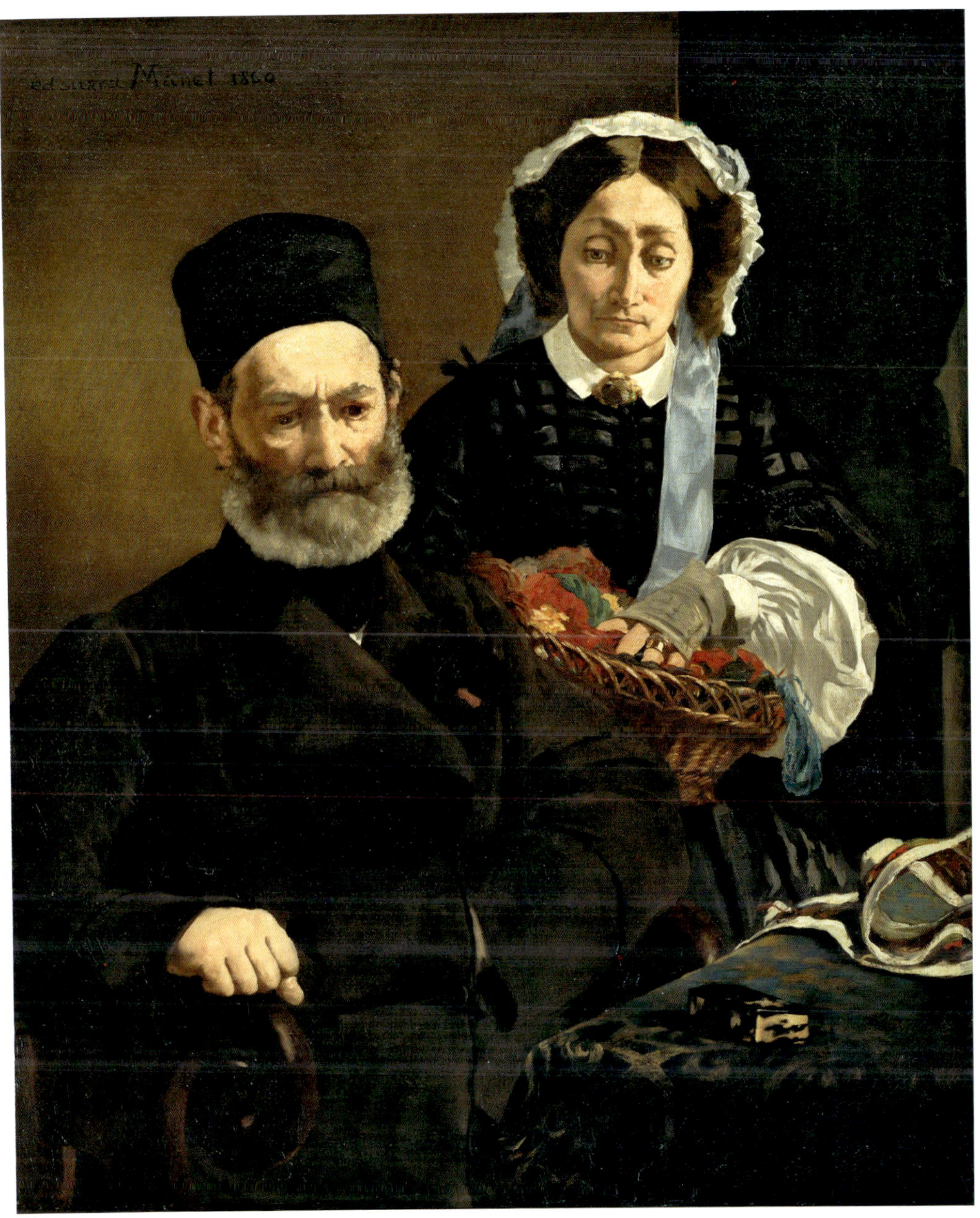

Fig. 102
Édouard Manet
M. and Mme Auguste Manet, Parents of the Artist, 1860
Oil on canvas, 43⅞ × 35⅞ in. (111.5 × 91 cm)
Musée d'Orsay, Paris, France

in Madrid when he visited there in 1865.[13] However, the relatively diminutive size of the Duret portrait belies the traditional grand scale of aristocratic full-length portraiture, which Manet studied in Madrid at the Museo del Prado. This element of parody, also evident in *Luncheon on the Grass,* as a strategy of challenging academic authority, is likewise a characteristic of Cézanne's early portraiture. For example, the way he seats his artist friend, the dwarf Achille Emperaire (1869–70; Musée d'Orsay, Paris) in a tall-backed chair recalls Jean-Auguste-Dominique Ingres's *Napoleon I* (1806; Musée de l'Armée, Paris), which in turn alludes to images of enthroned kings dating from age of Charlemagne.

Degas's careful study of old masters, in the Louvre and on his travels, accounts for his ability to capture effectively the human image in everyday situations with a startling psychological insight that transcends time and place yet remains disturbingly vivid even today.[14] At the beginning of Degas's career his father astutely predicted that portraiture would be the "finest jewel in [his] crown."[15] Indeed, portraits are central to an understanding of Degas's oeuvre and account for as much as 45 percent of his production between 1855 and 1876.[16] His study of the old masters was not simply a reflection of his romantic nostalgia for the past but important to his exploration of how portrait painting could express modern identity through commonalities of sentiment and emotion between past and present, what Carol Armstrong aptly termed the "recuperative spirit" of past traditions.[17]

Degas's interest in physiognomy emerges in his drawings of the 1850s and 1860s after the old masters. He often isolated facial features that intrigued him in religious paintings or portraits in a way, blurring their historical character so that, out of context, the face would be mistaken for that of a contemporary Parisian.[18] Conversely, in his sketches preparatory for portraits of friends or family he might cast the sitter in the style of one of his beloved pantheon of old masters (cat. 28, p. 222), such as the study

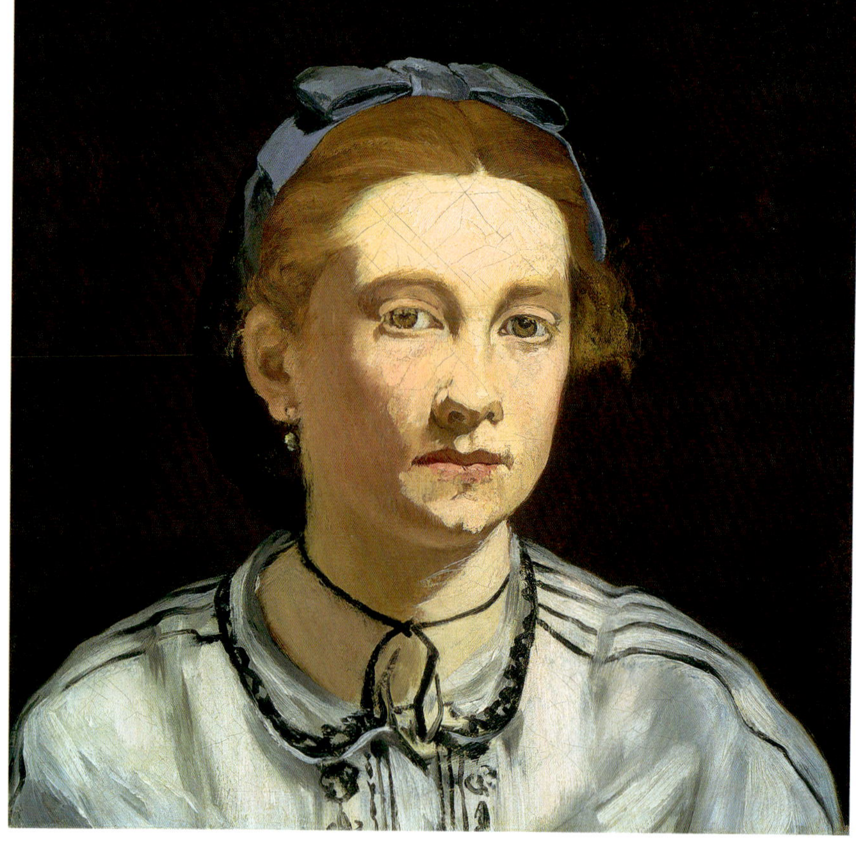

Cat. 54
Édouard Manet
Victorine Meurent, c. 1862

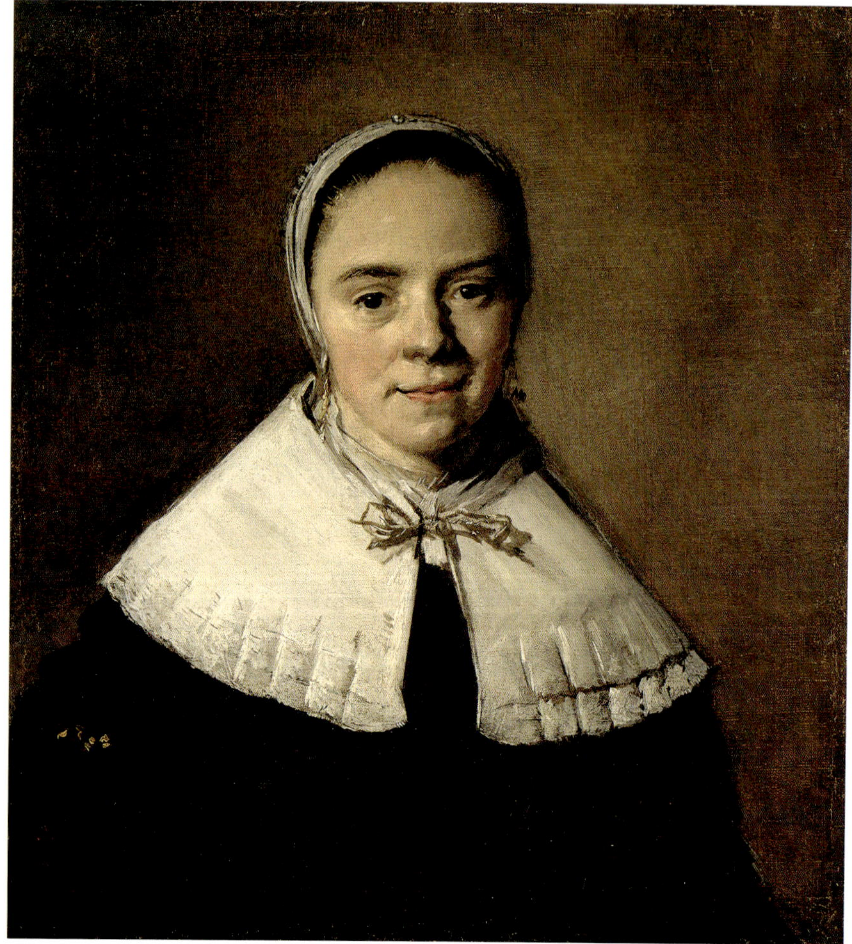

Cat. 43
Frans Hals
Portrait of a Young Woman, c. 1655–60

OPPOSITE:
Cat. 56
Édouard Manet
Portrait of Théodore Duret, 1868

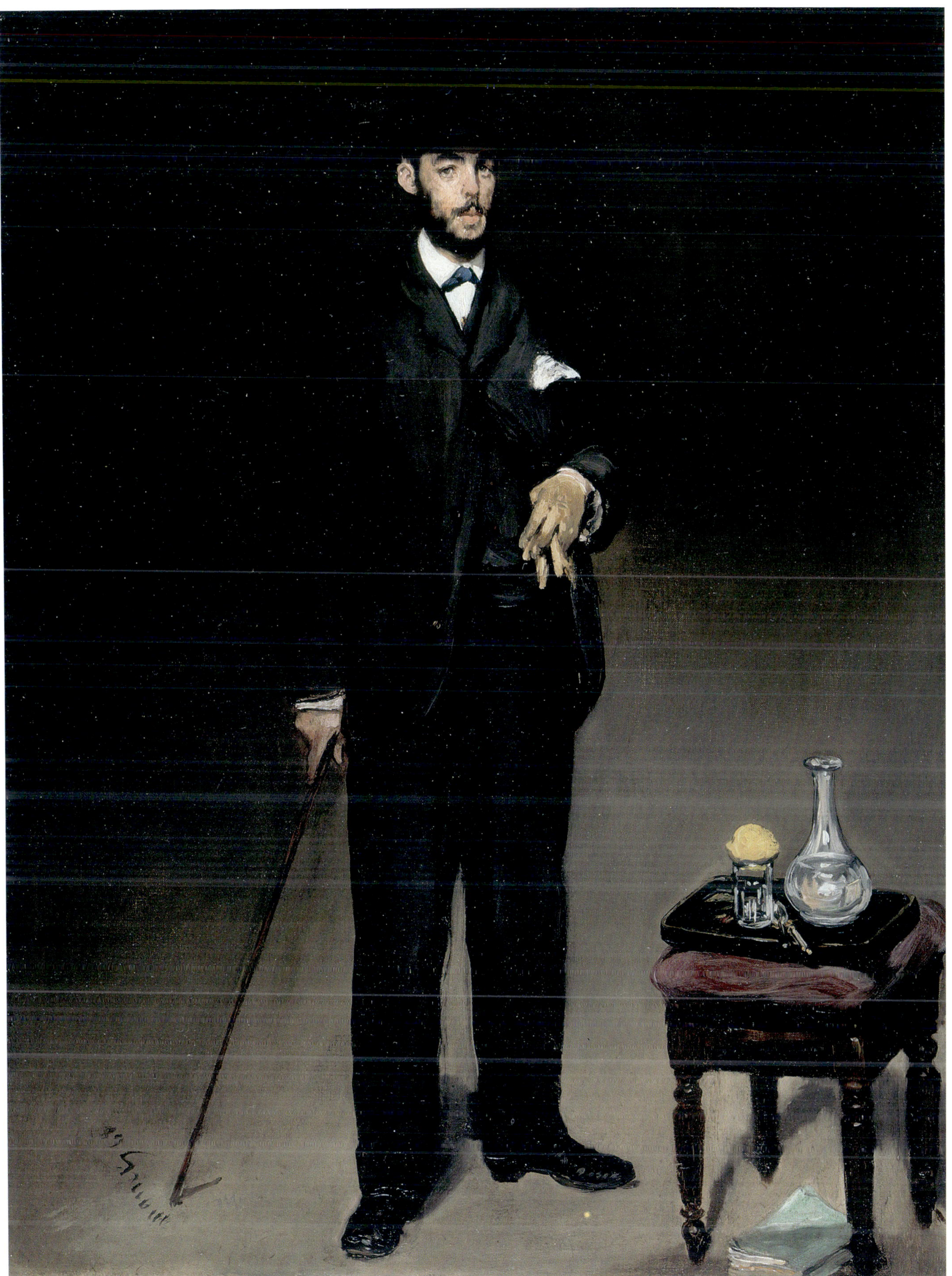

Cat. 28
Edgar Degas
Self-Portrait in the Style of Filippino Lippi, c. 1858

for a portrait of his sister Marguerite Degas, which bears a distinctive Pontormoesque allure.[19] As Theodore Reff has suggested, "[Degas] conceives of the portrait not only as a likeness of an individual, but as a means of representing an emotion, hence as a modern equivalent of the noble subjects and idealized portraits in which such emotions had traditionally been shown."[20]

Degas's important early portrait, the brooding, psychological study of his aunt's family, *The Bellelli Family* (fig. 103), is the largest painting he would ever undertake; he undoubtedly intended it for the Paris Salon when he began it in 1858.[21] At the time he was immersed in the study of Italian Renaissance masters in Florence. However, we know from correspondence that he aspired to emulate the grace and nobility of a wide variety of old master sources, including Anthony Van Dyck, Giorgione, Sandro Botticelli, Andrea Mantegna, and Rembrandt van Rijn.[22] When the work finally emerged in the Degas studio sale of 1918, after languishing in storage for almost fifty years, it was immediately praised as a "modern primitive" and inspired comparisons to Flemish painting, the donors of the fifteenth-century *Pietà of Avignon* at the Louvre, as well as Hans Holbein and Ingres.[23] The adoringly demure features of his cousin Giovanna could easily be mistaken as having been painted by Holbein, while her pose under the protective arm of her mother recalls Goya's *Family of Charles IV* (Museo Nacional del Prado, Madrid), resulting in an eclectic mix of sources.[24] Theodore Reff has further suggested that the inclusion of Degas's own drawing of his grandfather Hilaire Degas in the gilded frame behind his aunt makes reference to a portrait tradition dating from the Renaissance, that of including effigies of deceased family members.[25]

Degas's study of old masters at the Louvre in the 1850s emerges in subtly reinterpreted ways in his later portraiture. The Venetian Renaissance double portrait of two noblemen, once thought to be by Giovanni Bellini but now attributed to Giovanni Cariani, held a special attraction for Degas about 1858–60 when he made a copy of it in oil (fig. 104).[26] The Renaissance work is striking for the emotional detachment and self-absorption of the two individuals portrayed. It is just this enigmatic quality of two juxtaposed, yet disinterested models that Degas returns to in the portrait of his cousins Giovanna and Giuliana Bellelli, painted in 1865–66 (fig. 105). The artist intensifies the sense of alienation of the Venetian double portrait in posing the two girls facing away from one another, eliminating their interaction and suggesting sibling tension or moodiness brought on by the recent death of their father.[27]

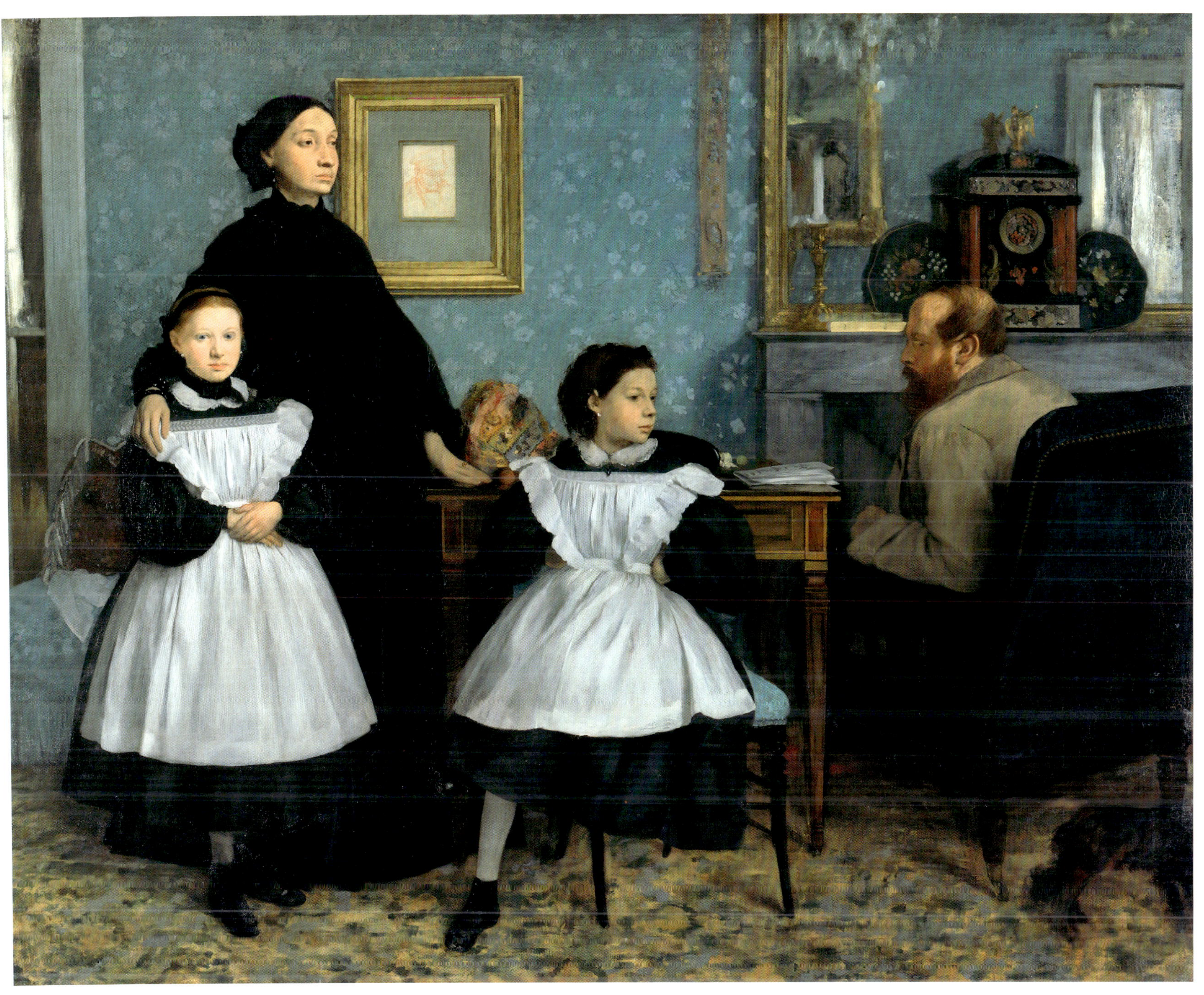

Fig. 103
Edgar Degas
The Bellelli Family, 1858–67
Oil on canvas, 78¾ × 98⅜ in.
(200 × 250 cm)
Musée d'Orsay, Paris, France

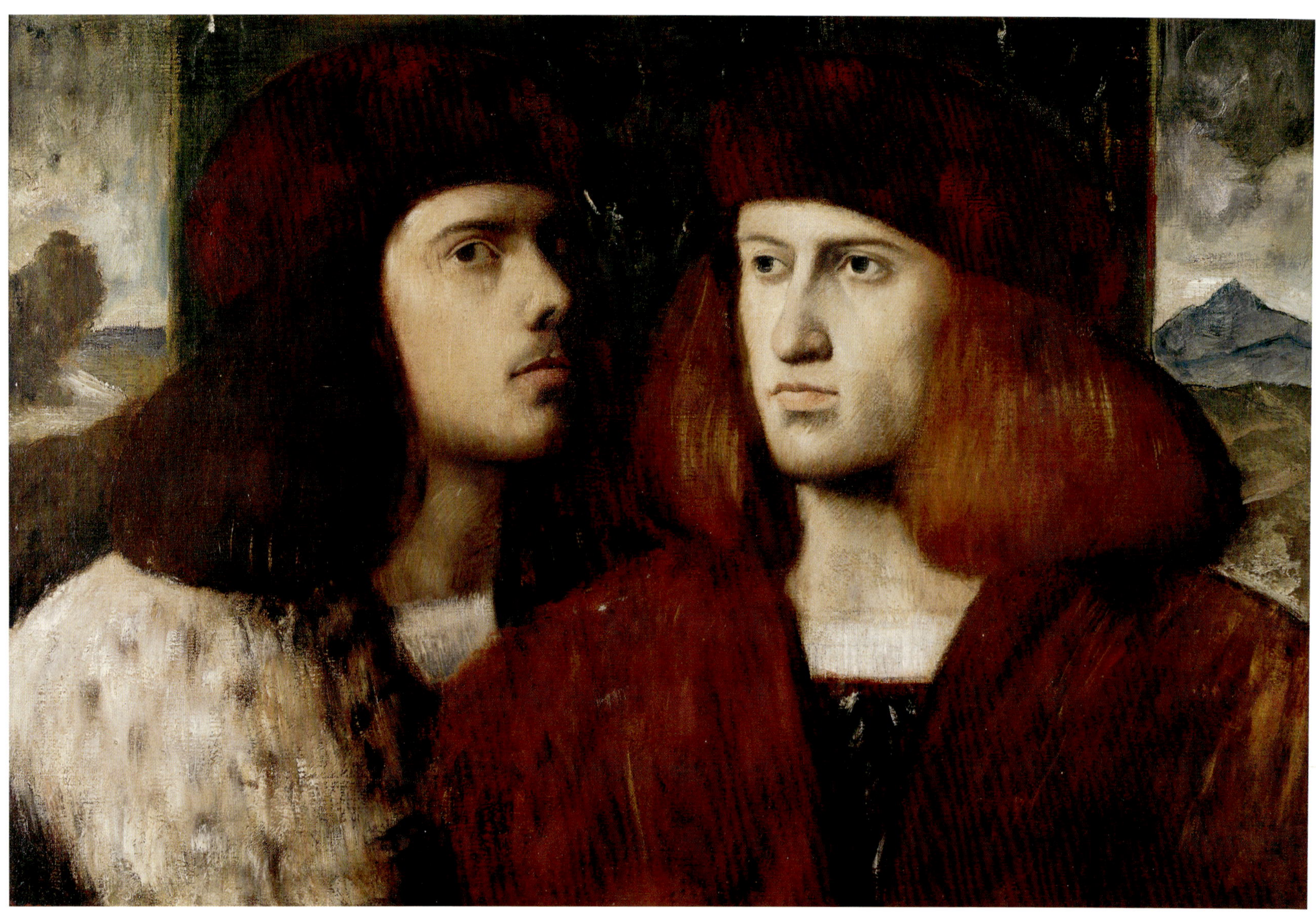

Fig. 104
Edgar Degas
Double Portrait, after Giovanni Cariani, 1858–60
Oil on canvas, 16⅞ × 24¾ in. (43 × 63 cm)
The Clark Family Collection, Saltwood Castle, United Kingdom

Fig. 105
Edgar Degas
The Bellelli Sisters (Giovanna and Giuliana Bellelli), 1865–66
Oil on canvas, 36¼ × 28½ in.
(92.1 × 72.4 cm)
Los Angeles County Museum of Art,
Mr. and Mrs. George Gard De Sylva Collection

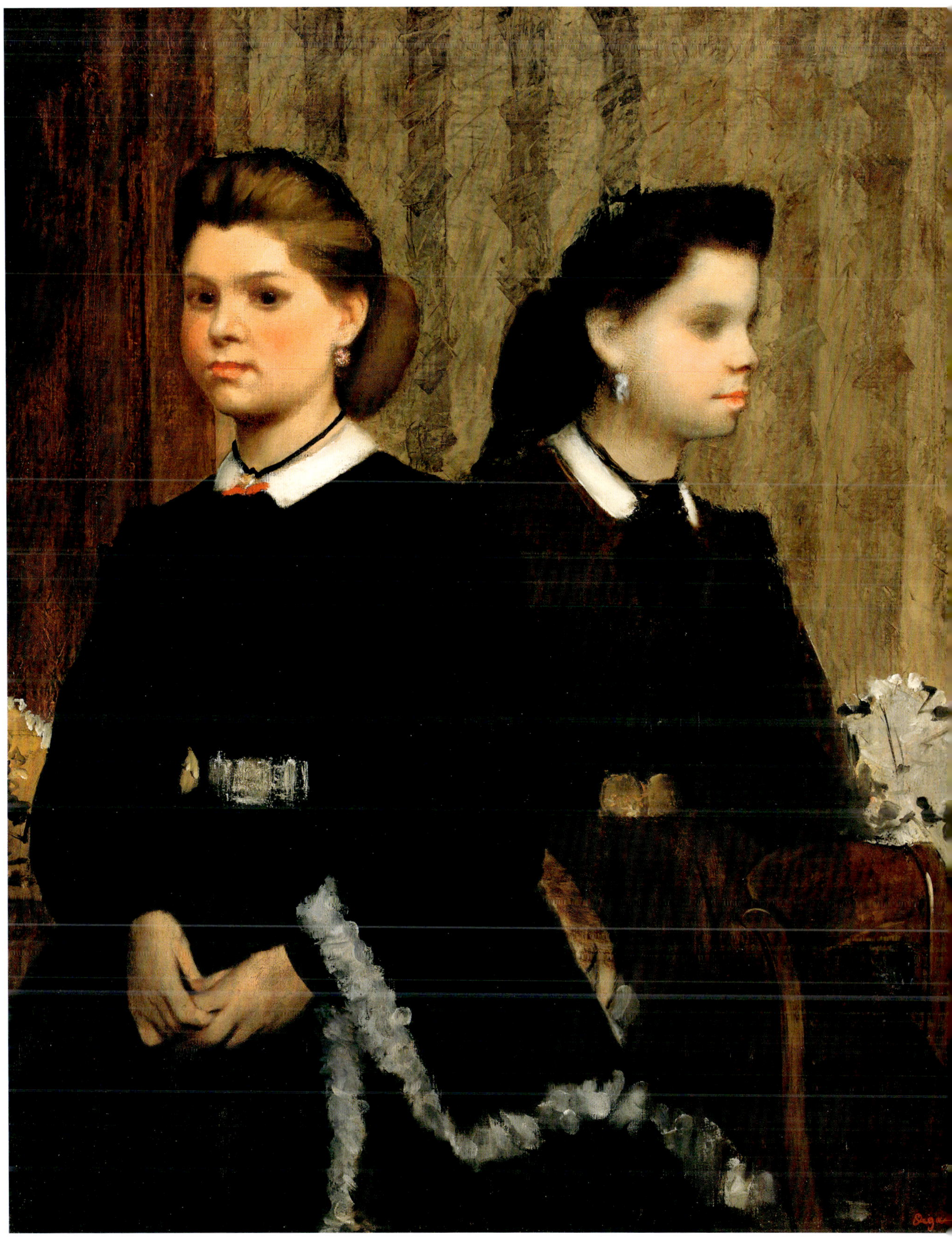

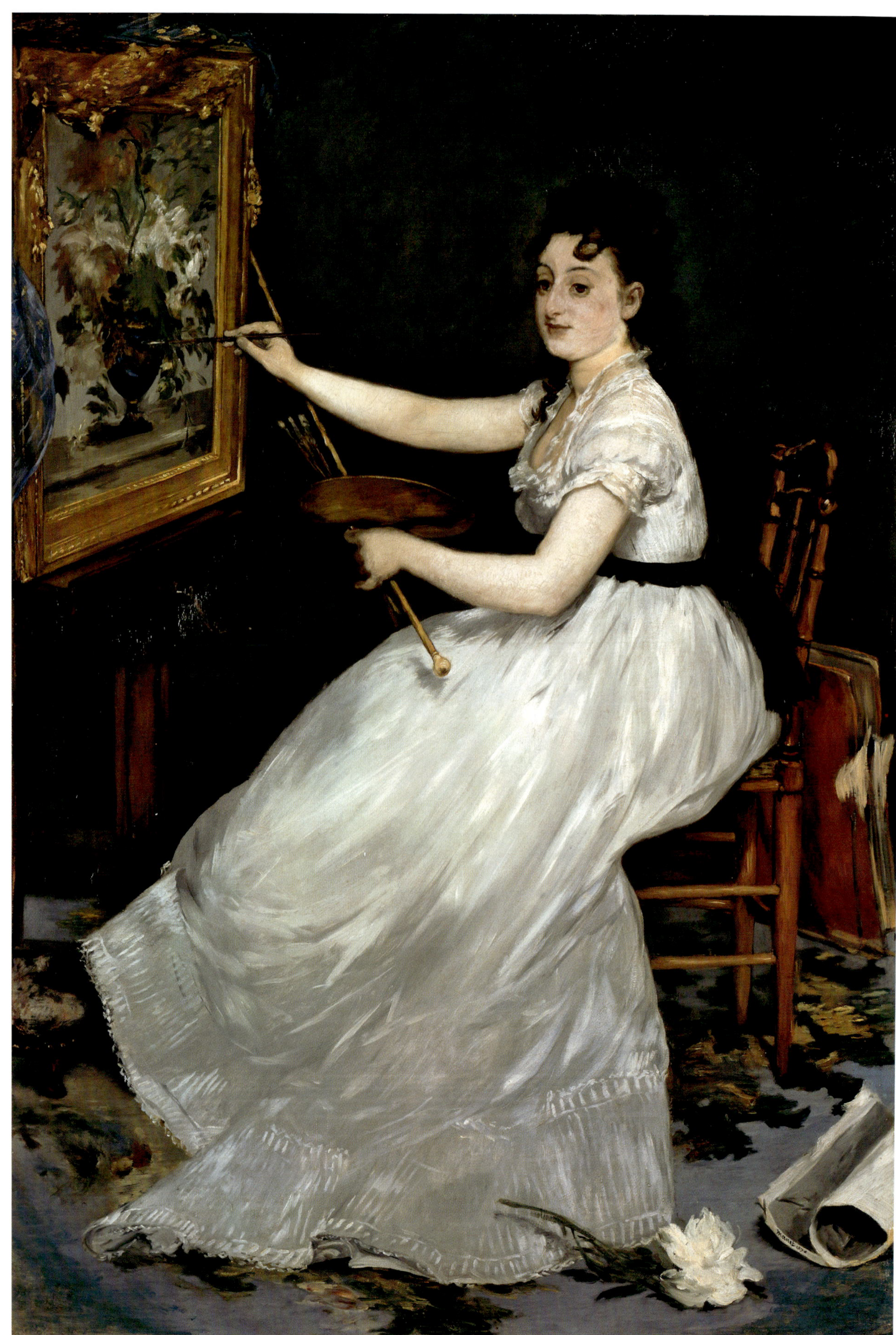

Fig. 106
Édouard Manet
Eva Gonzalès, 1869–70
Oil on canvas, 75¼ × 52½ in.
(191.1 × 133.4 cm)
The National Gallery, London, Sir Hugh Lane Bequest, 1917; on loan to the Hugh Lane Municipal Gallery of Modern Art, Dublin, since 1979, NG3259

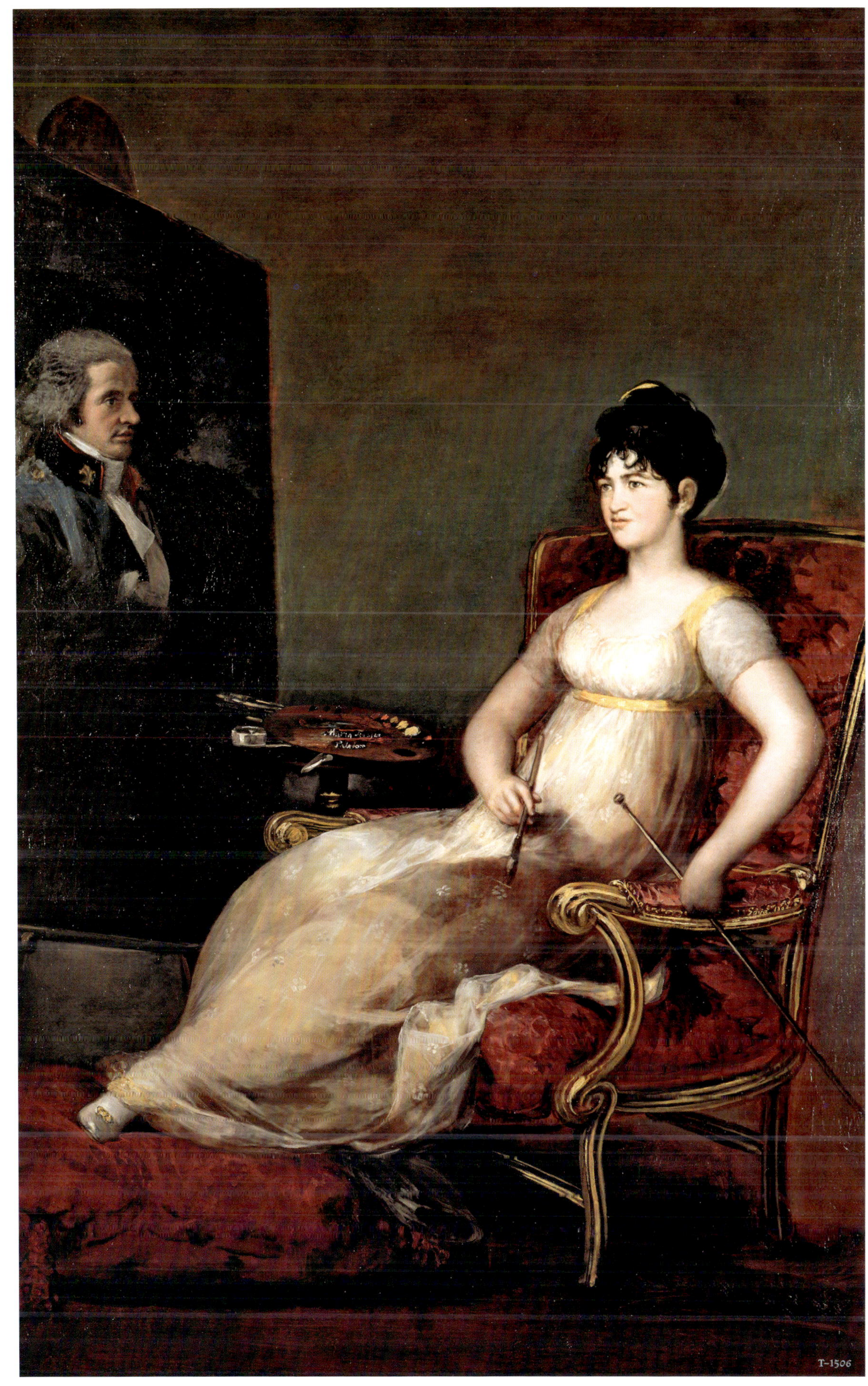

Fig. 107
Francisco de Goya
Doña María Tomasa de Palafox, Marquesa de Villafranca, 1804
Oil on canvas, 76¾ × 49⅝ in. (195 × 126 cm)
Museo del Prado, Madrid

At the same time, such works by Manet as *The Balcony* (1868–69; Musée d'Orsay, Paris) reveal that he remained under the strong influence of Goya. His *Eva Gonzalès* (fig. 106) portrays the woman who was his pupil from February 1869. Mahlstick and brush in hand, she is busy at her easel painting a still life. Manet's portrait of her appears to quote the Spanish master's *Doña María Tomasa de Palafox, Marquesa de Villafranca* (1804; fig. 107). The conspicuous display of a fashionable, loose-fitting, short-sleeved gown that falls about her legs seems a concession to decorum and the expectations of the Salon jury of 1870, which voted to include the portrait in the display. This suggestion of the *haute bourgeoise* in the portrayal of Gonzalès suits her as someone who followed Manet's example of exhibiting at the Salon and who took her unusual choice of profession seriously enough to provoke the professional jealousy of Berthe Morisot: "Manet is lecturing me, and holds up that eternal Mlle Gonzalès as an example. . . . she gets things done, whereas I accomplish nothing. Meanwhile, he's starting her portrait over again, for the twenty-fifth time. She sits every day, and in the evening her hair has to be washed with soft soap. What an inducement that is for people to pose for him."[28]

The 1870s and 1880s

When the future Impressionists exhibited portraits at the Salon in the 1860s, they were already seen as radical in their shift of emphasis from likeness to questions of identity.[29] This oppositional stance to academic practice and the Salon jury system became a primary motivation behind the formation of the Société anonyme coopérative d'artistes peintres, sculpteurs, etc. in December 1873.[30] If the group appeared to show a lack of interest in portrait painting in their first exhibition of 1874, the numbers of exhibited portraits would rise significantly in 1876 and 1877 among the works shown by Degas and Renoir. Gustave Caillebotte and Morisot regularly sent strong showings of portraits, as did Mary Cassatt when she began exhibiting with the group in 1879. Generally speaking, portraits ranged from 20 to 30 percent of the works exhibited in 1876, 1877, 1879, and 1880, dropping again in proportion in 1882 and 1886. According to Zola, portraits remained a ubiquitous presence at the Salon during the same period. In his review of the Salon of 1875, Zola complained that portraits were like a "rising tide" each year, but faulted contemporary portraitists for having lost their chance to define modern identity by being too idealistic and reliant on formulas established by the old masters.[31]

The Impressionist position on the art of the past and its relation to portrait painting was best articulated in a brochure entitled *The New Painting,* published on the occasion of the second Impressionist exhibition, in 1876, by the Realist art critic Edmond Duranty.[32] Thought to express the views of Degas, the essay dwells at length on the importance of those qualities crucial to the portraitist, the "special characteristics of the modern individual—in his clothing, in social situations, at home or on the street."[33] Revisiting Baudelaire's argument in "The Painter of Modern Life," Duranty states the Impressionists only emulated the strategies of the old masters before them: "The strength of Renaissance artists and the Pre-Renaissance primitives came from the fact that under the guise of Antiquity—or one should simply say the label of Antiquity—they described the customs, costumes, and decors of their own age, revealing their private lives and recording an era."[34] In Duranty's view, it seems, the Impressionists' relationship with the past could only be described as one of love-hate. They admired the old masters for their faith in naturalism and their ability to capture the timely essence of the individual, but they condemned prolonged reliance on the past as a hindrance to the acceptance of modern concepts of beauty and artistic vision.

Georges Rivière argued along the same lines as Duranty in the article "To the Wives," published in *L'Impressionniste,* a journal that appeared four times in April 1877 on the occasion of the third Impressionist exhibition.[35] Those who considered themselves progressive when it came to social and political matters, Rivière insisted, should also think progressively when selecting an artist for their portrait. The Impressionists dared take a different approach from the venerable Dubufe family of portrait painters who represented the aristocratic legacy of the Second Empire.[36] Again, what had to be dispensed with were preconceived notions of artistic excellence based on what could be compared favorably to Rembrandt, Titian, or Velázquez. In making his case for the new kind of beauty represented by the art of the Impressionists, Rivière appealed directly to the vanity of his reader in proposing that a wife who considered herself young and pretty should identify with the sun and joy of Impressionist paintings.

The perception by the majority of art critics and the art-viewing public that the Impressionists were entirely hostile toward art of the past likely discouraged any understanding that there were real affinities between the two groups of artists, that the real conflict was between the Impressionists and an outmoded canon of beauty perpetuated by the academic establishment.[37] However, there were exceptions; sympathetic critics could appreciate the relationship between Impressionist portraiture and the art of the past. For example, in 1876 Philippe Burty compared Degas's *Portraits in an*

Office (New Orleans) (1873; Musée municipal de Pau, France) to early Flemish painting, though this support is tempered by the fact that he admired the picture's unusual degree of finish.[38] The painting depicts the artist's uncle and cousins in the office of their New Orleans's cotton business. Recently Marilyn Brown has suggested that its resemblance to Dutch syndicate portraiture in the representation of business as a masculine preserve may have persuaded the Musée du Pau to acquire the work in 1878.[39] In the twentieth century it has drawn from commentators a range of old master comparisons, from Jean-Antoine Watteau's *Gersaint's Shop Sign* (1721; Charlottenburg Palace, Berlin), to Johannes Vermeer, Holbein, and Rembrandt (fig. 19).[40]

It was also Burty who in his review of the third Impressionist exhibition of 1877 compared Renoir's portrait of the actress Jeanne Samary, known as *La Rêverie* (fig. 59), to the "lively sketches" (*vives pochades*) of Jean-Honoré Fragonard—not from the point of view of handling (*matérielle*), but in how Renoir represented the French temperament in portrait painting.[41] Burty again seems to skirt the issue of finish, yet one can easily see a relation between the broken Impressionist brushwork of Renoir's portrait and Fragonard's rapidly painted *figures de fantaisie* (cat. 38, p. 231).[42] The bequest of the collection of Dr. Louis La Caze to the Louvre in 1869, at the dawn of the Impressionist decade, considerably extended the representation of Fragonard and eighteenth-century French artists.[43]

In 1865 Fragonard had been dubbed a "sketcher of genius" by Edmond de Goncourt and his brother Jules in their series of biographies known as *Eighteenth Century Painters*.[44] Perhaps Burty had Renoir's portrait in mind when he encouraged Edmond in 1877: "Go to see the portraits exhibited by the Impressionists at 6, rue Le Peletier. They are a little mad. But it's a madness that is deeply thought provoking."[45] Burty shared the Goncourts' love of the ancien régime and hence his comparisons of the Impressionists to the art of the past are highly significant, particularly given his close relationship with them.[46] He solicited artists to participate in the first Impressionist exhibition in 1874 and authored the introduction to the catalogue accompanying an auction of Impressionist paintings in 1875. In his role as art critic for *La République Française,* he played an important advocacy role for their cause.

Fragonard's name again emerges as a point of comparison in critical response to the portraits and figures Berthe Morisot exhibited at the fifth Impressionist exhibition of 1880, including *Summer* (1878; Musée Fabre, Montpellier). The light, feathery brushstrokes of these paintings, where foreground and background are treated with equal emphasis, recall Fragonard's *fa presto* technique that so struck the Goncourts.[47] It was Burty who was most emphatic in his admiration: "Since the eighteenth century, since Fragonard, no one at all has used clearer tones with such intelligent assurance."[48] Paul Mantz wrote of Morisot's "Fragonardian refinement," while Charles Ephrussi allied Morisot with a French Rococo tradition by highlighting her "distinction, elegance, gaiety and nonchalance. She loves painting that is joyous and lively."[49]

The brush technique and subject matter of *Mrs. Duffee Seated on a Striped Sofa, Reading* (cat. 10, p. 230) suggest that in the mid-1870s Mary Cassatt also fell under the influence of Fragonard's *figures de fantaisie*. The sitter's absorption in her reading evokes an air of informality, as do the brightly colored silks and hair ribbon, further recalling the Rococo taste of the *dix-huitième siècle*. As the painting was given to the model by the artist and remained in her family collection, it appears to have been intended primarily as a portrait.[50] Similarly, Manet's late *Portrait of Isabelle Lemonnier* (cat. 58, p. 232), shares an affinity with Fragonard in how the subject is as much about winter life in Paris as it is about the sitter: the Impressionists brilliantly adapted the eighteenth-century notion of the "genre-portrait." In this painting the lyrical silhouette of the coated model also evokes the *majas* of Goya's *Los Caprichos* and Manet's own Goyaesque etching *Exotic Flower,* of 1868. Moreover, the Spanish influence is not irrelevant to the sitter's identity, for Isabelle Lemonnier was named after her godmother, Queen Isabella of Spain, for whom her father was engaged as jeweler.[51]

Just how critical portraiture had become in the late nineteenth century to the broader debate over national schools and tradition is evident in the major exhibition *Portraits du Siècle (1783–1883),* which sought to establish a direct relation between contemporary portraiture and that of the past century.[52] During a two-month period, the exhibition raised for charity the stunning sum of more than one hundred thousand francs, and planning for a second exhibition in 1885 was already begun.[53] Among the members of the organizational committee were Paul Baudry, Léon Bonnat, Alexandre Cabanel, Carolus-Duran, and Charles Chaplin, all successful contemporary academic portraitists whose work was well represented in the category of living artists. In the historical section were portrayals by Jacques-Louis David, Jean-Baptiste Greuze, Ingres, Eugène Delacroix, and many others. That the Impressionists were represented at all was likely a result of the influence of Charles Ephrussi, who also sat on

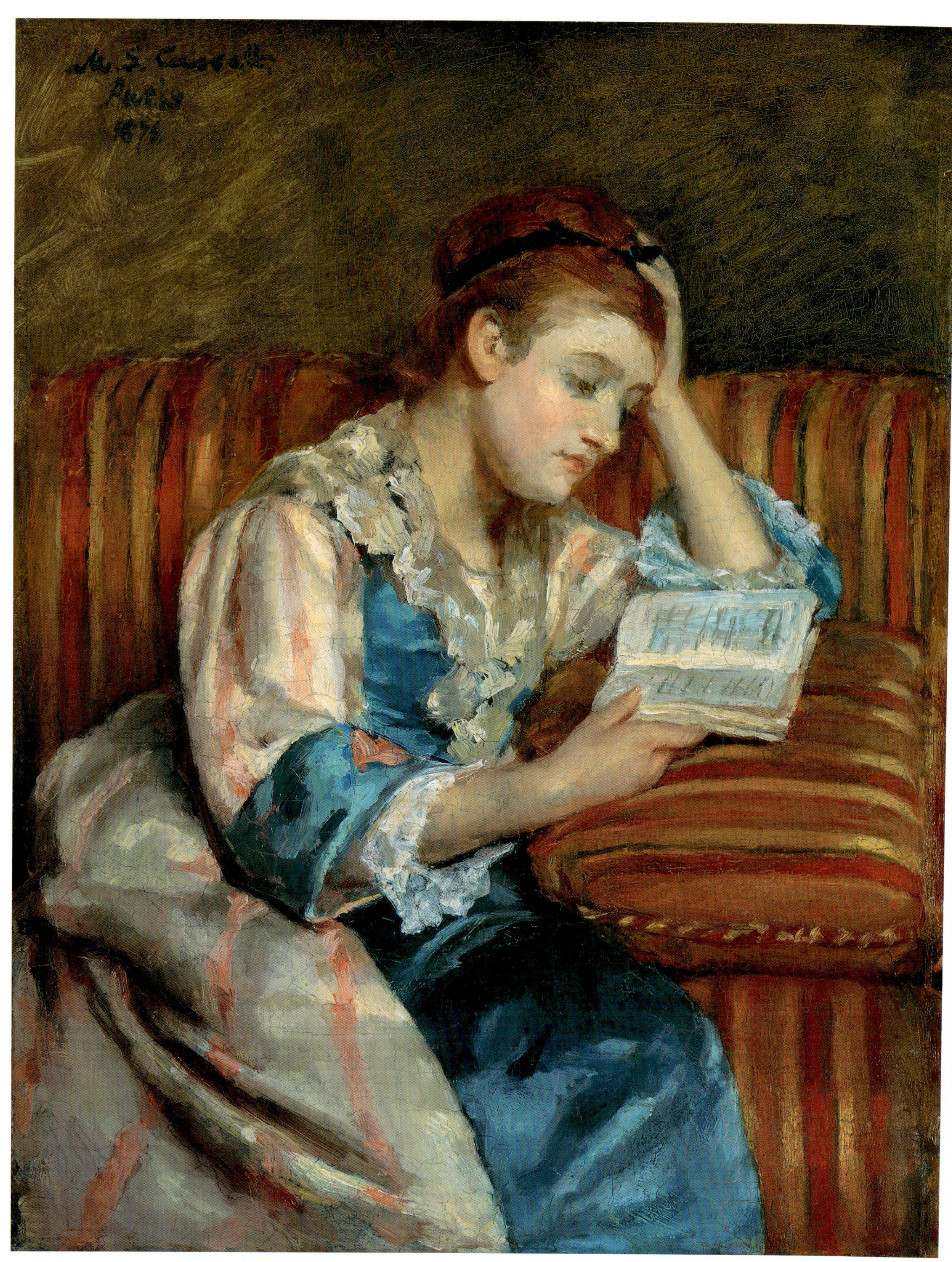

Cat. 10
Mary Cassatt
Mrs. Duffee Seated on a Striped Sofa, Reading, 1876

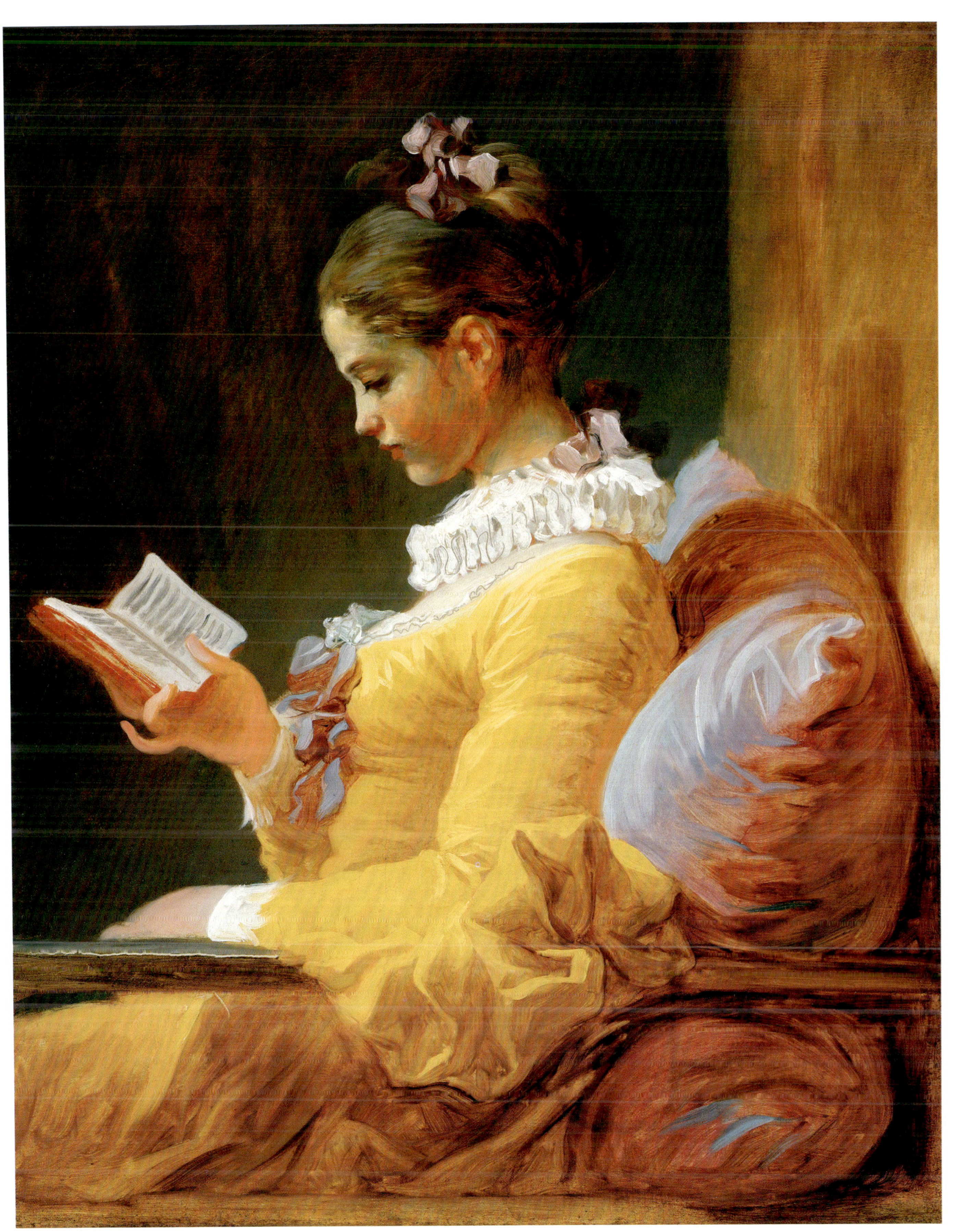

Cat. 38
Jean-Honoré Fragonard
A Young Girl Reading, c. 1776

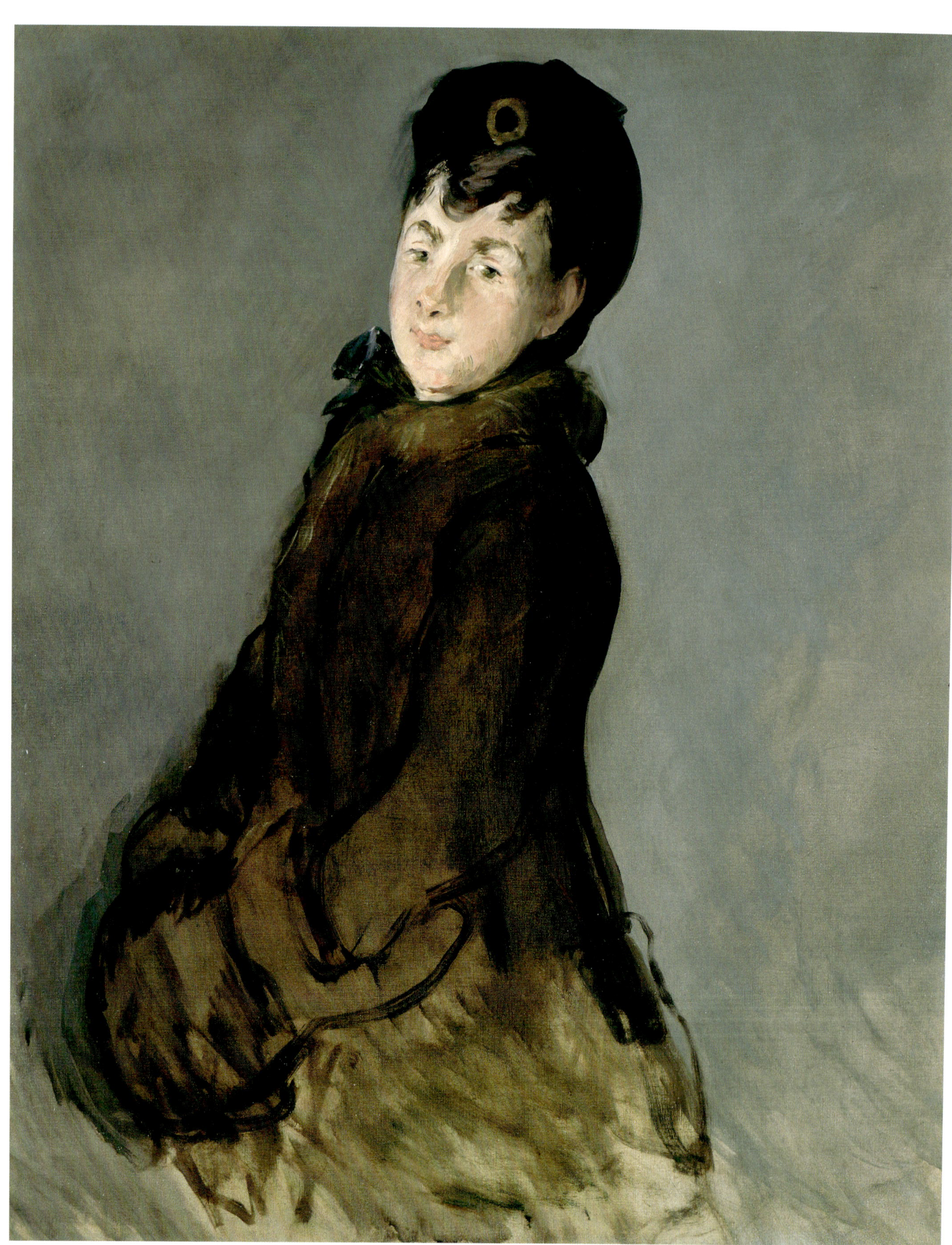

Cat. 58
Édouard Manet
Portrait of Isabelle Lemonnier, c. 1879

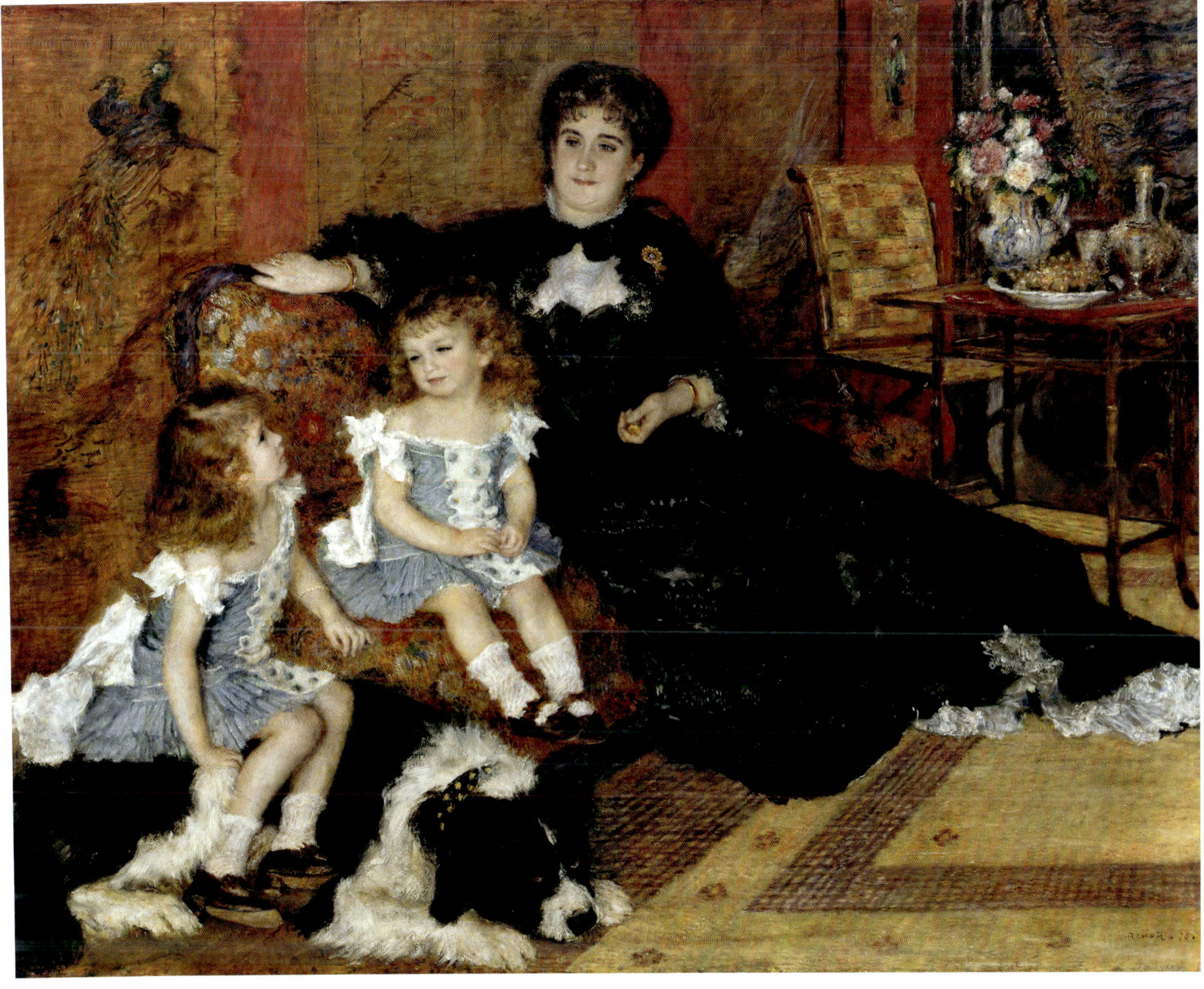

Fig. 108
Pierre-Auguste Renoir
Madame Georges Charpentier (Marguerite-Louis Lemonnier, 1848–1904) and Her Children, Georgete-Berthe (1872–1945) and Paul-Émile-Charles (1875–1895), 1878
Oil on canvas, 60½ x 74⅞ in. (153.7 x 190.2 cm)
The Metropolitan Museum of Art, Catharine Lorillard Wolfe Collection, Wolfe Fund, 1907 (07.122)

the organizing committee. The works shown included Manet's *M. and Mme Auguste Manet, Parents of the Artist,* discussed above, and his *Portrait of Émile Zola* (1868; Musée d'Orsay, Paris), criticized for its lack of modeling.[54] Renoir's *Portrait of Jeanne Samary (La Rêverie),* which Burty had remarked on in 1877, also proved a tendentious choice. Paul Gauguin recalled seeing the exhibition with a conservative friend who had become outraged by its presence.[55]

For Bonnat and Carolus-Duran portrait painting had become a lucrative specialty. Wealthy clients, aristocrats, theater personalities, and politicians actively sought them out and willingly parted with as much as fifteen thousand francs per commission.[56] The success of these artists inspired many imitators, who if they were lucky enough to be chosen to paint the portrait of an esteemed opera star became overnight sensations.[57] When Renoir declined to take part in the fourth Impressionist exhibition of 1879 and returned to the Salon with a portrait of the family of the publisher Georges Charpentier, *Madame Georges Charpentier and Her Children* (fig. 108), and the full-length portrait *Jeanne Samary* (1878; State Hermitage Museum, Saint Petersburg), by then a star actress of the Comédie Française, he did so as a participant in the cult of celebrity that had emerged around portrait painting. However, his fee of fifteen hundred francs for the Charpentier portrait suggests a much different relationship with the sitter than that of the *portraitiste mondain.*[58] Critics took Renoir to task for his past as a nonconformist, labeling him a "converted *intransigeant*" and welcoming him back into the "bosom of the church," while at the same time chastising his form and color.[59]

The magnificent portrait *Madame Georges Charpentier and Her Children* recalls the old masters through its commanding presence and a timeless elegance of presentation. Part of the charm of the painting derives from Renoir's genuine affection for the Charpentiers.[60] The

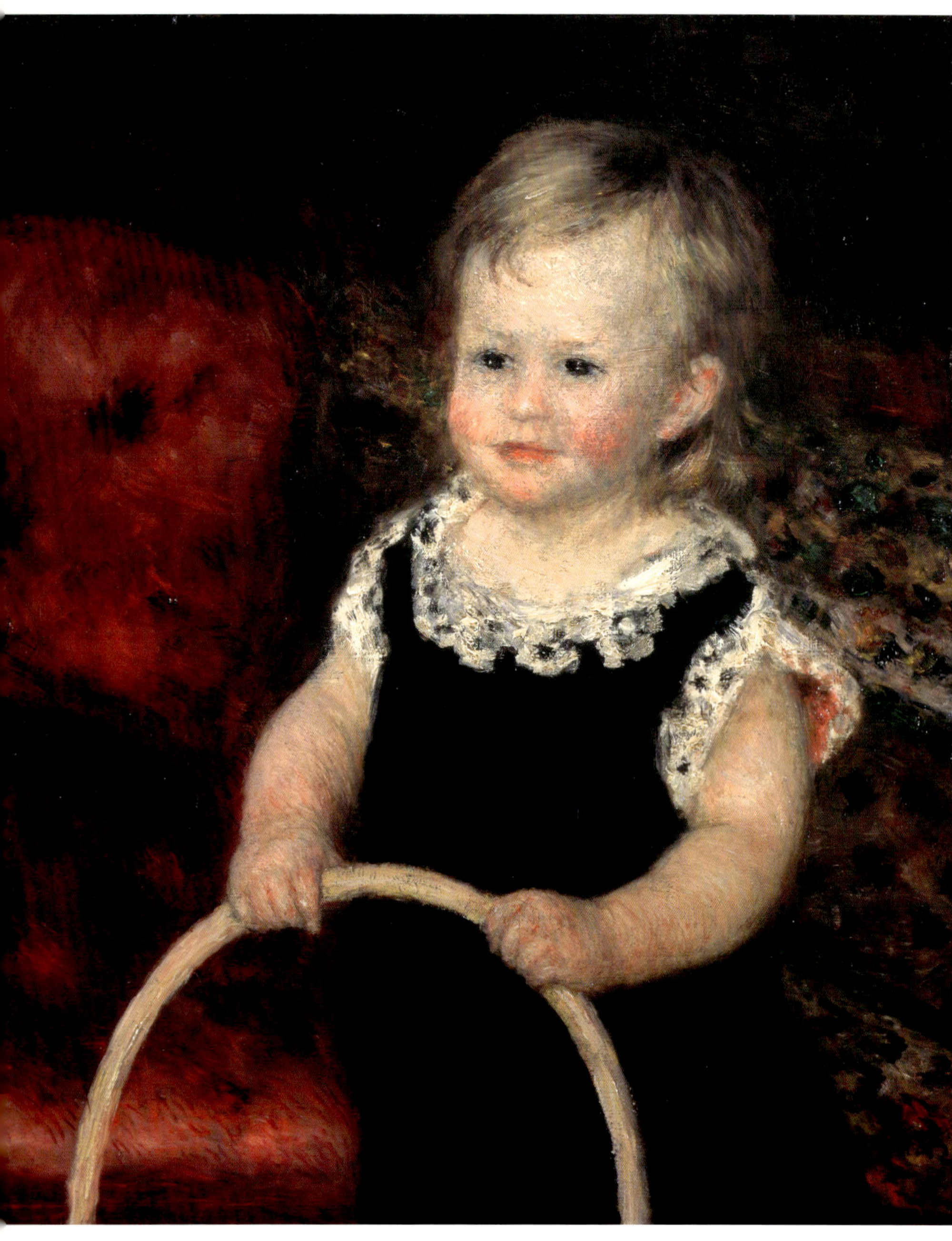

Cat. 81
Pierre-Auguste Renoir
Child with a Hoop, c. 1875

Cat. 23
Henri-Pierre Danloux
Portrait of a Little Girl, 2nd half 18th century

family contributed substantially to his income during the late 1870s, so much so that he referred to himself as the Charpentier *peintre ordinaire*, a term used in the ancien régime to describe a patronage appointment within the royal household.[61] Colin Bailey has provided a thorough account of the painting's various references to revered masterpieces that hung in the Louvre during Renoir's lifetime—Rubens's *Hélène Fourment and Her Children*, which he had copied at the Louvre in the 1860s, Van Dyck's *Children of Charles I*, now considered a copy, and Ingres's *Madame Rivière*.[62] Renoir's first biographer, Julius Meier-Graefe, commented how the painting rivaled the old masters in its arrangement.[63] Renoir is as careful in his construction of perspective as Albrecht Dürer or Tintoretto, ensuring that the orthogonal lines created by the carpet and Japanese wall hangings guide the eye and reinforce the pose of the figures. When *Madame Georges Charpentier and Her Children* was lent to a major Renoir retrospective at Bernheim Jeune in 1900, Thadée Natanson predicted that a place had been reserved for the painting "in a museum not far from Frans Hals and Velasquez," and indeed at the Charpentier sale of 1907 it was purchased by the Metropolitan Museum of Art, New York.[64]

Impressionist portraits of children, and particularly those of Renoir, are revealing of a crucial aspect of modern identity in nineteenth-century France—sensitivity to the nature of the family where the child played a central rather than a marginal role and an appreciation of the creativity of children (cat. 81).[65] From 1879 until 1884 Renoir painted at least one portrait of each of the four children of his devoted patron Paul Berard and in 1881 assembled them in an unusual composite portrait that also attests to his love of the eighteenth century (cat. 83, p. 236).[66] This portrait conveys a remarkable spontaneity of pose and handling, as sunlight cascades across the faces of the children, enlivening the highlights of their skin, clothes, and hair—one wonders how one-year-old Lucie could remain asleep under such intense luminosity. Yet for all its characteristic Impressionist handling, Renoir draws on a delightfully original eighteenth-century model in the inception of the portrait, specifically the drawings of heads by Watteau, in which one model is seen from multiple angles, each in a different mood. Although collectors in the eighteenth century considered Watteau's drawings of heads to be merely studies, the sheets were often highly finished in the artist's *trois crayons* technique.[67] By the 1870s such studies were recognized as among the artist's most original compositions and highly sought after by collectors. Renoir may very well have seen Watteau's *Studies*

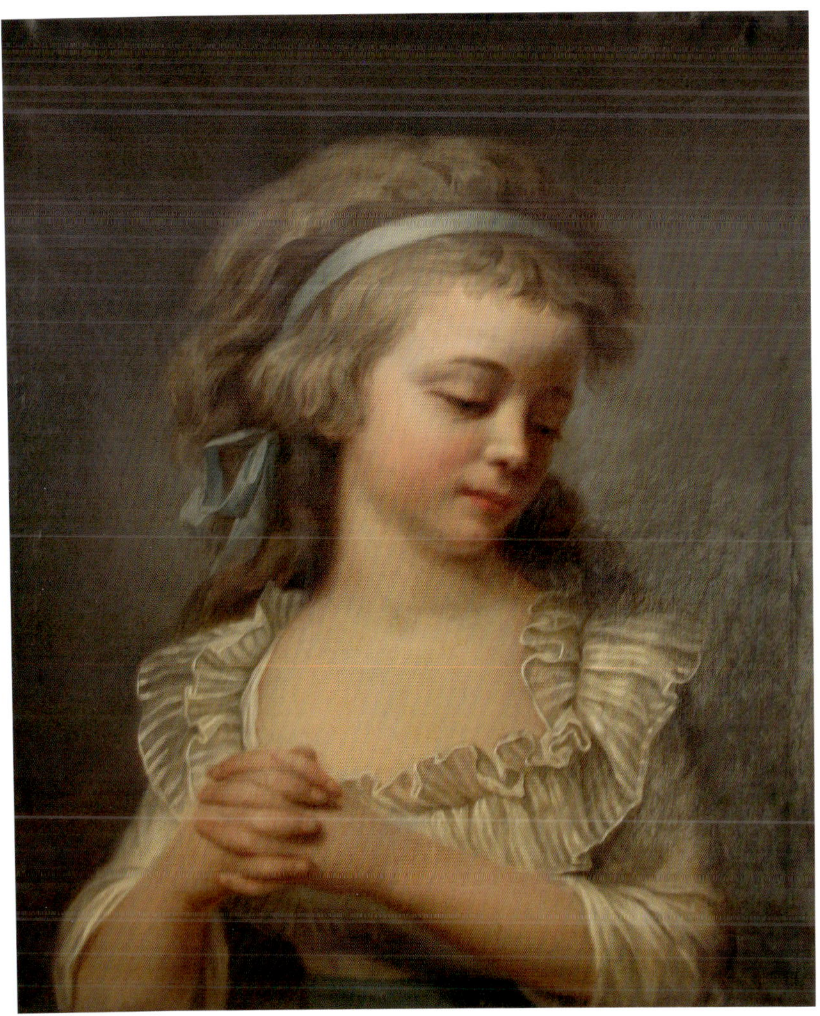

of *Nine Heads* (fig. 109) when it was exhibited in 1879 at the École des Beaux-Arts in Paris as part of an exhibition of early drawings organized by Ephrussi.[68]

While a trip to Italy to study old masters was frequently a part of an artist's early training—Manet and Degas had visited in the 1850s—Renoir's first visit to Italy took place only in 1881, relatively late in his career. In Rome he discovered Raphael and a new appreciation for museums, and in Naples the classic nobility of Antiquity. The experience proved profound, occasioning a personal crisis over his ability to draw. It ushered in his so-called dry style, intended to establish a renewed relationship with the past and the fresco technique by reducing the amount of oil he used to mix his paint. A painting such as Renoir's magisterial portrait of the Berard girls, *Children's Afternoon at Wargemont* (1884; Nationalgalerie, Berlin), reflects the influence of Italy in its absence of chiaroscuro, a firmer handling, attention to line, and sculptural form.[69] The deliberation that Renoir now brings to bear in the pose and activity of his sitters instills in them a calm, meditative quality that transcends the everyday and aspires to the condition of allegory.

Late Impressionism

Many of the Impressionists' late portraits continue to engage with old master traditions. Renoir's portrait *Christine Lerolle Embroidering* (cat. 87, p. 53), for example, places the daughter of the artist Henri Lerolle in a pose that recalls Vermeer's *The Lace Maker* (fig. 20). The Vermeer was a work close to Renoir's heart in the mid-1890s, when he was undertaking difficult negotiations with the Musée du Luxembourg to accept the Caillebotte collection of Impressionist paintings.[70] Renoir's late painting *Jean Renoir as a Huntsman* (fig. 110) can be seen as a direct reference to Velázquez's hunting portraits of the Spanish Hapsburgs, such as *Infante Don Baltasar Carlos in Hunting Costume* (fig. 111). It has little relevance to the leisure interests of the future filmmaker, who had a complete distaste for hunting. Rather, it was inspired by an ornate frame that Renoir purchased at an antique shop in Nice, believing it to be seventeenth-century Italian.[71] The Renoir family setter, Bob, stands in for the hunting hounds of Velázquez.

In the family portraits of Mary Cassatt, such as *Reine Lefebvre Holding a Nude Baby* (fig. 112), the child often takes on a role of symbolic virtue and innocence. While an intimate moment of domesticity is represented, the pose and the child's nudity suggest a traditional Christian iconography derived from the old masters. The theme appeared so frequently in the art of Cassatt that Georges Lecomte, one of the early historians of the Impressionist movement, referred to her as the painter of the "modern Holy Family."[72] Stylistically, the rhythmic outline of figures and firm modeling of this portrait recall the glazed terracottas of the Renaissance artist Luca della Robbia.[73] Judith Barter has drawn attention to the intersection of Cassatt's series of mother-and-child images with an interest in Italian Renaissance painting and sculpture among late-nineteenth-century collectors, such as the Havemeyers, who consulted Cassatt on their purchases.[74]

While Renoir remained less dependent on portrait commissions for the remainder of his career, he was frequently sought out by collectors, celebrities, and dealers to paint their portrait. In portraits after 1900 Renoir returns to the loose brushwork of the Impressionist years, though his technique now reveals a certain amount of reflection on old master techniques. As Colin Bailey suggests, Titian and Rubens may well have inspired the ribbonlike brushstrokes of his portrait *Madame Thurneyssen and Her Daughter,* painted while Renoir was on vacation near Munich in the summer of 1910 (cat. 89, p. 68).[75] To convey the intimacy of this scene of a mother and child,

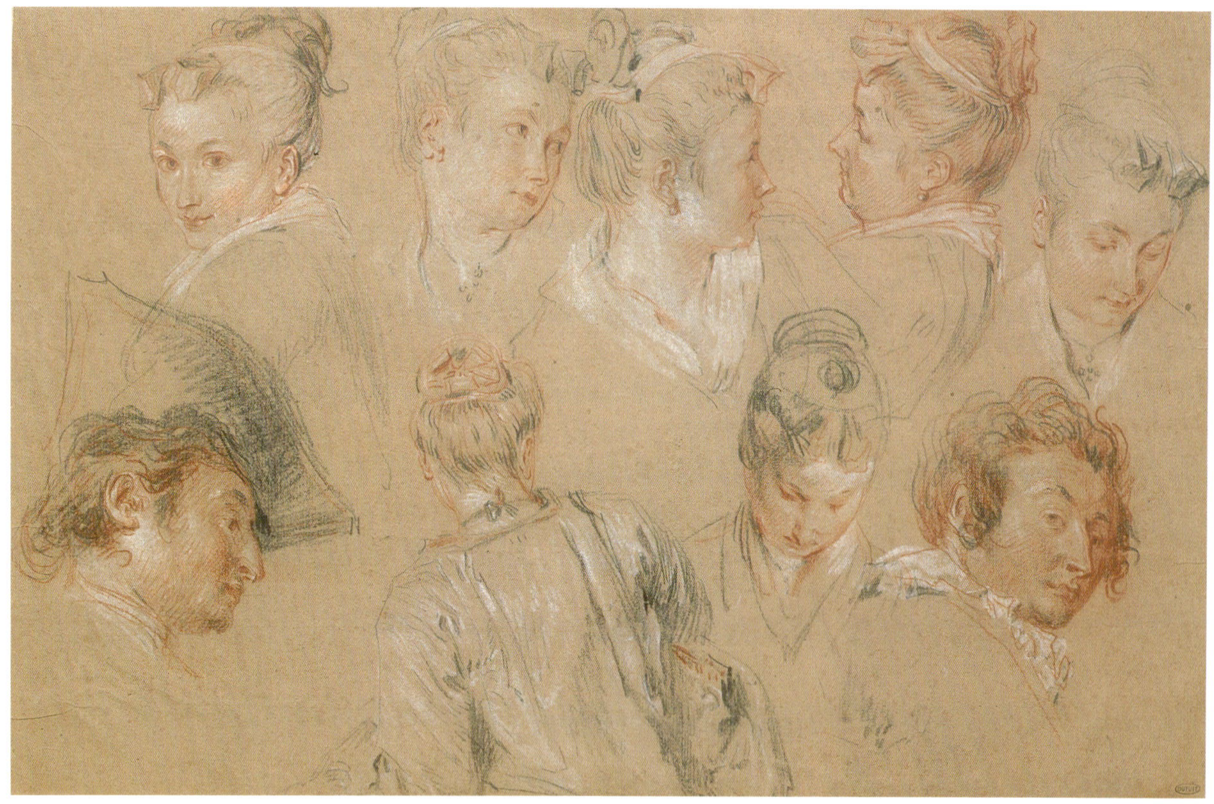

Fig. 109
Jean-Antoine Watteau
(1684–1721)
Studies of Nine Heads, c. 1715
Black and red chalk with white highlights on gray-brown paper, 10½ × 5¾ in. (26 × 14.6 cm)
Petit Palais, Musée des Beaux-Arts de la Ville de Paris

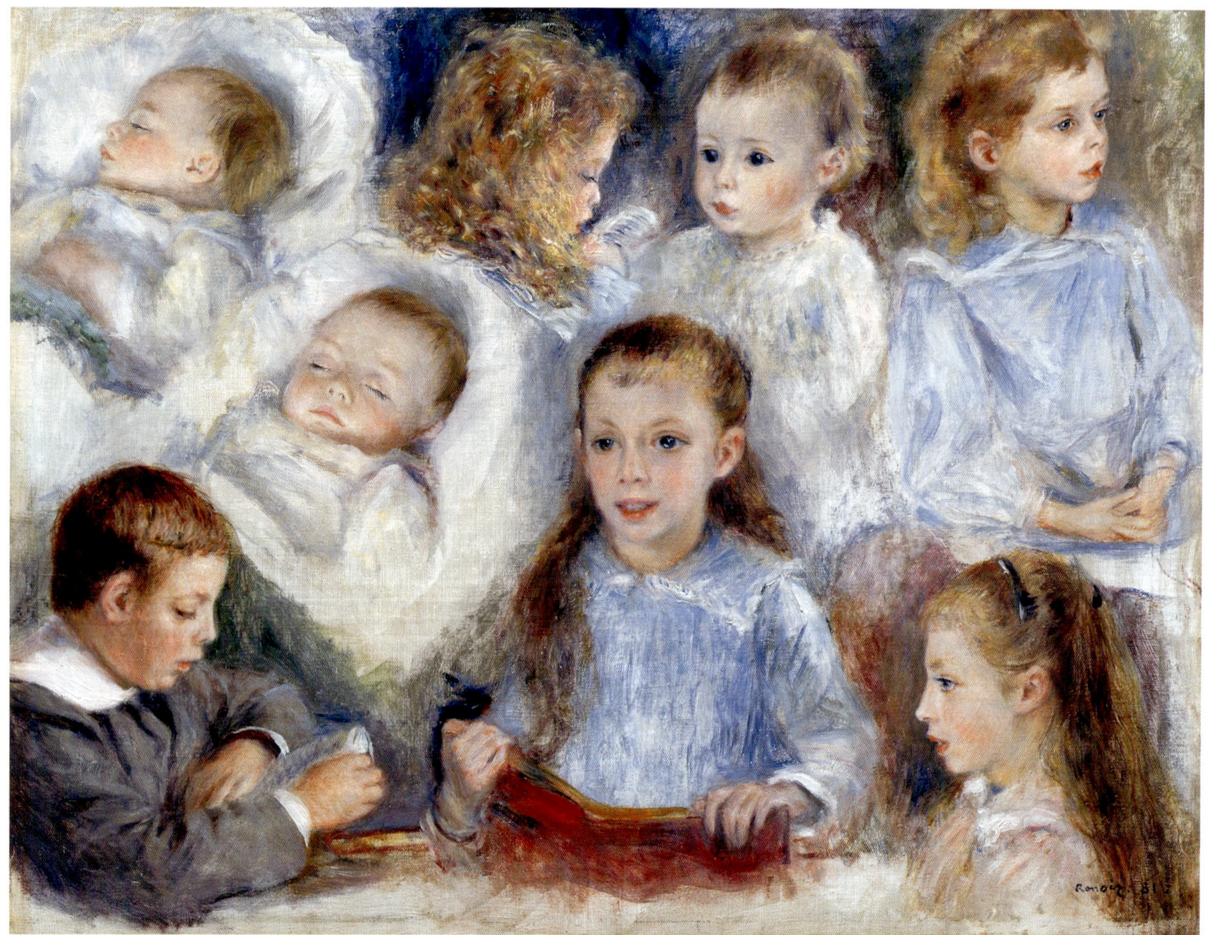

Cat. 83
Pierre-Auguste Renoir
Studies of the Berard Children, 1881

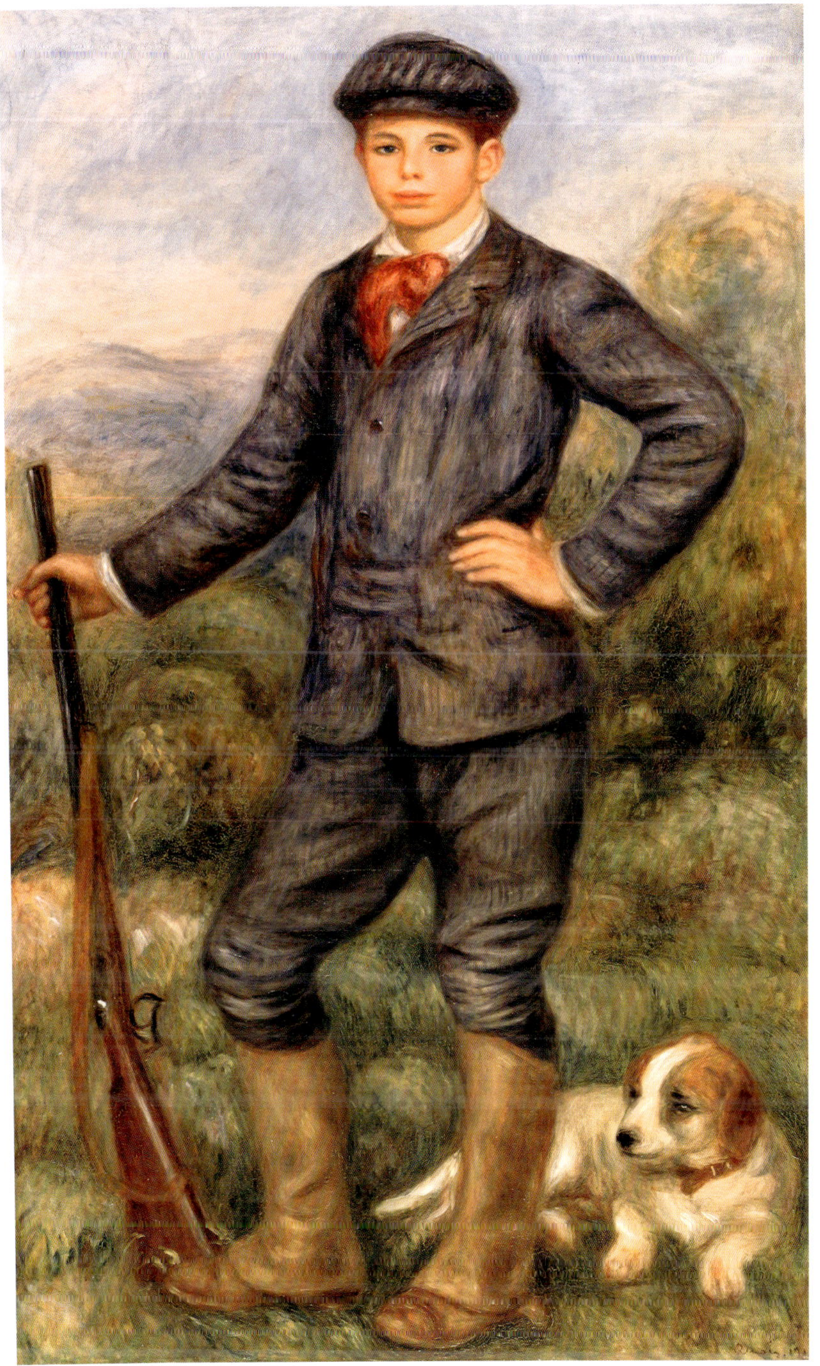

Fig. 110
Pierre-Auguste Renoir
Jean as a Huntsman, 1910
Oil on canvas, 68 × 35 in.
(172.7 × 88.9 cm)
Los Angeles County Museum of Art.
Gift of Jean Renoir and Dido Renoir

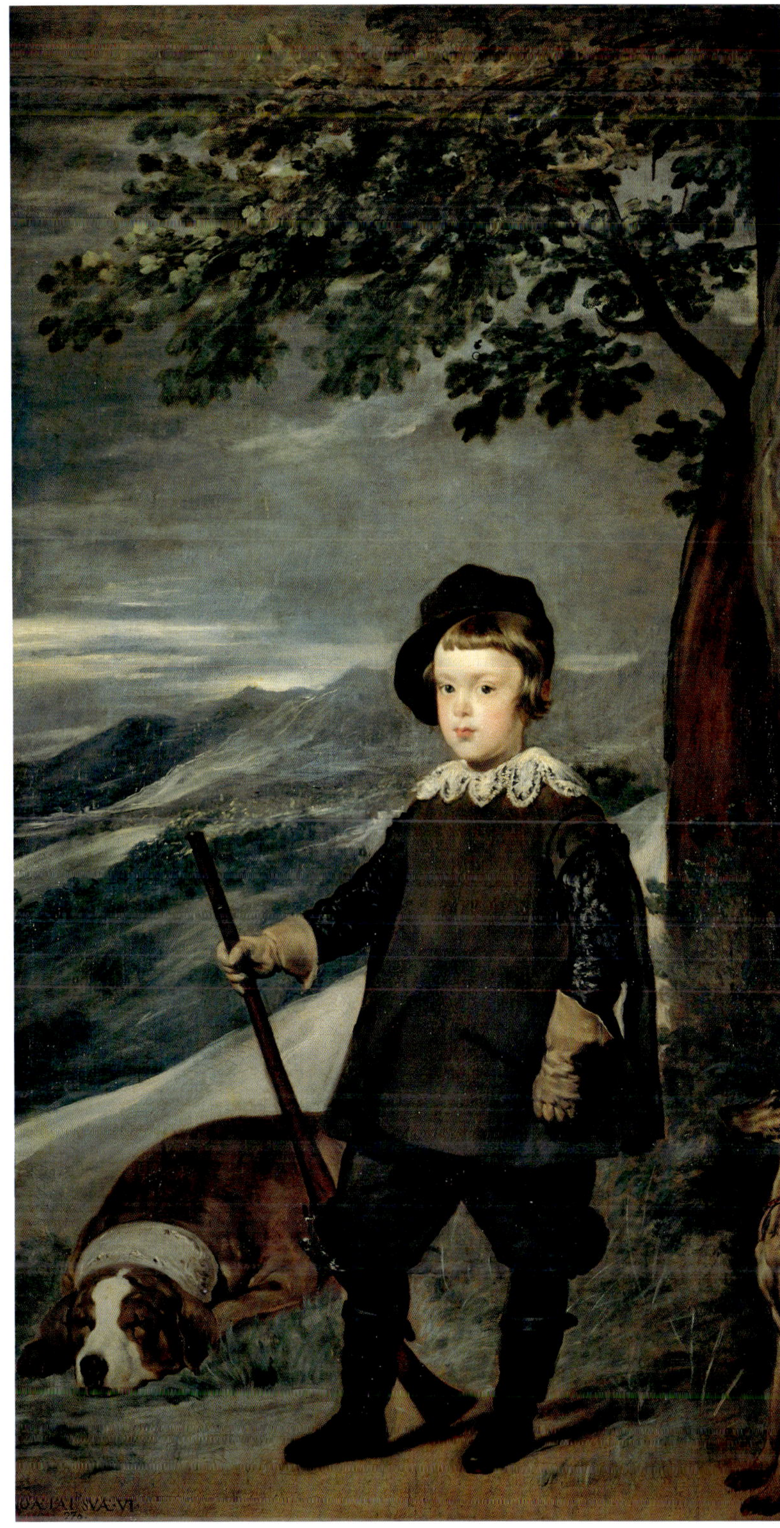

Fig. 111
Diego Rodríguez de Silva y Velázquez
Infante Don Baltasar Carlos in Hunting Costume, 1635–36
Oil on canvas, 75¼ × 40½ in.
(191 × 103 cm)
Museo Nacional del Prado, Madrid

Fig. 112
Mary Cassatt
Reine Lefebvre Holding a Nude Baby, 1902
Oil on canvas, 26¾ × 22½ in. (68 × 57 cm)
Worcester Art Museum, Worcester, Massachusetts, Museum purchase, 1909.15

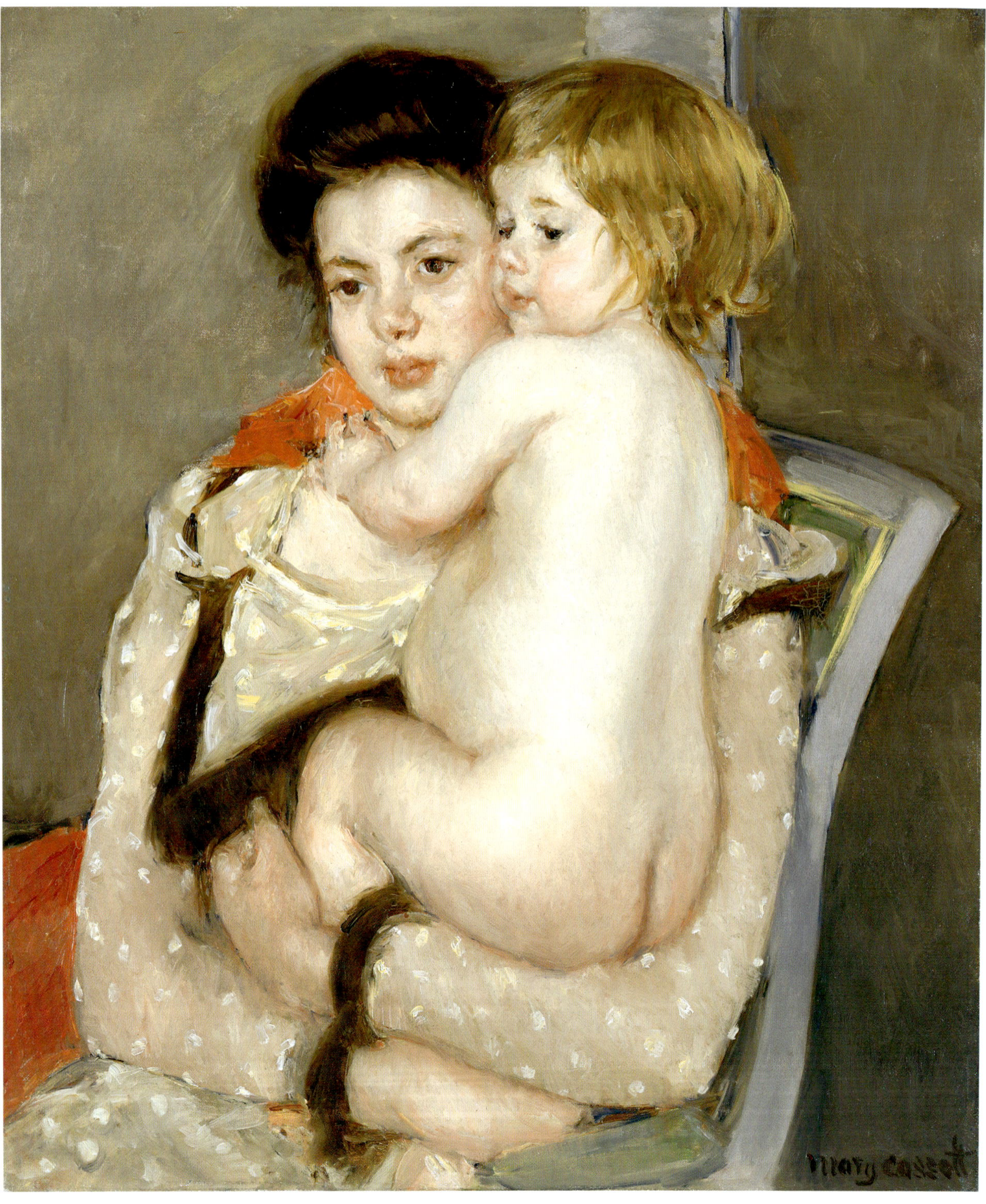

Renoir turned once again to Rubens's family portraits, this time to *Portrait of Hélène Fourment and Her Eldest Son Frans,* about 1635, in the Alte Pinakothek, Munich, a museum he visited during his stay with the Thurneyssens (fig. 14). A year later he spoke enthusiastically to an interviewer of Munich's outstanding collection of Rubens paintings: "There is the most glorious fullness and the most beautiful colour, and the layer of paint is very thin."[76] The partially bared breast of Madame Thurneyssen, apparently at the request of her husband, recalls the intimacy of the *maternités* that Renoir painted as a new father after 1885.[77]

Conclusion

Renoir's Thurneyssen portrait is a good example of how the lessons the Impressionists learned during the early stages of their careers, through close study of old master portraiture at museums and elsewhere, continued to play a role in later years. That several traditions can often be brought to bear on the discussion of any one Impressionist portrait is a testament to the painters' mastery of assimilation. Such internationalism, with its indiscriminate and coincident references to the past, remained an idiosyncrasy of Impressionist portraiture. Granted, certain preferences of school do emerge, such as Degas's identification with Italian Renaissance masters, Renoir's interest in eighteenth-century France, and Manet's taste for Spanish Baroque painting, yet they moved easily across national and school boundaries.[78] Of course, in all the examples discussed, the evident old master portrait traditions are transformed with exceptional originality together with an abundance of nineteenth-century influences, such as the descriptive realism of the novelist Honoré de Balzac, popular illustrated journals, and the exploration of color of Delacroix.

Impressionist painters frequently adopted references to the past in their portraiture to mitigate the radical nature of their work and to validate innovations that so notoriously undermined academic authority and inviolable standards of artistic excellence. Misunderstood during the nineteenth century, the allegiance of the Impressionists and old masters eventually came to be appreciated by the most demanding of critics. In his series of novels *Remembrance of Things Past,* Marcel Proust reveals himself a chronicler of the beau monde, that exclusive world of brilliant society whose members always turned to Carolus-Duran, Bonnat, and their followers to have their portraits painted. For Proust, portraiture was a practice closely associated with class. In the last book of the series, *Time Regained,* he concedes, somewhat disdainfully, that the Impressionists and those of a socially modest position who appeared in their portraits accurately represented modern identity in the late nineteenth century. These are the individuals, he says, who

> Are more within reach of the obscure artist's acquaintance, more likely to appreciate him, to invite him, to buy his pictures, than men and women of the aristocracy who, like the Pope and Heads of State, get themselves painted by academicians. Will not posterity, when it looks at our time, find the poetry of an elegant home and beautifully dressed women in the salon of the publisher Charpentier as painted by Renoir, rather than in the portraits of the Princesse de Sagan or the Comtesse de La Rochefoucauld by [Pierre-Auguste] Cot or [Charles] Chaplin?[79]

In suggesting that there had been no greater expression of elegance since the Renaissance than the Impressionist portrait *Madame Georges Charpentier and Her Children,* Proust affirms Baudelaire's maxim that the secret to achieving the renown of the old masters was to convey a new kind of beauty through a passionate engagement with the present.

Notes

I would like to thank Colin B. Bailey for his comments on this essay.

1. Impressionist portraiture and modern identity has been the subject of recent scholarship, including Ottawa 1997; Nochlin 1997; House 1999; and McPherson 2001.

2. Statistics recorded by Rosenthal 1987, p. 23. See also statistics recorded in Bailey 1997, p. 44 n. 12. On the impact of the Realist movement on the Salon, see Collins 2004, pp. 2–5.

3. Baudelaire 1964, p. 13. This essay was published in *Le Figaro* in 1863; see comments on the dating by Mayne, in Baudelaire 1964, p. xviii.

4. Vollard 1925, p. 23.

5. Zola to Cézanne, March 3, 1860, Cézanne 1976, p. 51.

6. See entry for Degas's etching by Gary Tinterow in New York 2003, pp. 473–74.

7. See, for example, *Fishing* based on engravings of Rubens's landscapes reproduced in Charles Blanc, *Histoire des peintres de toutes les écoles,* vol. 5, *École flamande* (Paris, 1864), pp. 7 and 19, as noted in Reff 1970, p. 457.

8. For an engaging account of this phenomenon, see Haskell 1976. The Le Nain were enjoying renewed interest among critics and supporters of the Realist movement as a result of the publications of Jules Champfleury and works in the La Caze collection such as *Peasants' Repast* (Musée du Louvre), attributed to Louis Le Nain, which Philippe Burty borrowed for his exhibition *Tableaux et dessins de l'École francaise* of 1860 at the École des Beaux-Arts, Paris. See Champfleury 1850. Michael Fried makes a comparison with Le Nain in Fried 1969, pp. 44–45, though Theodore Reff sees Rembrandt's etching as a source in Reff, "Manet's Sources" 1969, p. 42. For a comparison of the portrait to Hals, see Françoise Cachin's entry in New York 1983, p. 50. For interest in Hals, see Jowell 1974. On the Rembrandt revival, see McQueen 2003, esp. pp. 41ff.

9. L. Lagrange, "Salon de 1861," *Gazette des Beaux-Arts* 11 (July 1861): 52, as cited in New York 1983, p. 50.

10. Ibid., p. 48.

11. Auguste Manet's illness is well documented in Locke 2001, pp. 48ff.

12. See discussion in Reff 1970, pp. 456–58.

13. See Juliet Wilson Bareau's discussion of the portrait in New York 2003, p. 498.

14. Boggs 1994; as well as her earlier study Boggs 1962. See also Reff 1963; Reff, "Copies" 1964; and Reff 1971. See also Walker 1933; Tietze-Conrat 1944; and more recently Dumas 1988, pp. 33–34.

15. Auguste Degas to Edgar Degas, November 11, 1858, as cited in Boggs 1994, p. 18.

16. Loyrette 1989, p. 20.

17. Armstrong 1991, p. 110.

18. For example, Degas's drawing of the eerily present *Elisabeth of Valois, copy after Anthonis Mor,* 1865–70 (The Fitzwilliam Museum, Cambridge).

19. Note Boggs 1994, cat. 5, and discussion of the portrait, pp. 177ff. A decade later Marguerite posed in eighteenth-century costume, illustrated in Fevre 1949, opp. p. 80, inscribed "Portrait de ma soeur Marguerite coiffée en poudre pour un bal costumé, un an deux ans avant son mariage."

20. Reff, *Notebooks* 1976, vol. 1, p. 27.

21. See Nochlin 1992.

22. Degas to Gustave Moreau, Florence, November 27, 1858 (Musée Gustave Moreau, Paris): "Je voudrais une certaine grâce naturelle avec une noblesse que je ne sais comment qualifier. Van Dyck est un fameux artiste, Giorgion aussi, Botticelli aussi, Mantegna aussi, Rembrandt aussi, Carpaccio aussi," as cited in Reff, "More Unpublished Letters" 1969, p. 283.

23. See commentary in New York, *Degas* 1988, p. 82.

24. Gary Tinterow, in New York 2003, p. 55.

25. Reff, "Pictures" 1968, pp. 129–30. Degas's grandfather died August 31, 1858 (New York, *Degas* 1988, p. 51). An example of an earlier portrait within a portrait is Hans Eworth, *Mary Neville, Lady Dacre,* 1540, National Gallery of Canada (acc. no. 3337), which includes a portrait of the late Thomas Fiennes, Baron Dacre.

26. The copy in oil is catalogued by Lemoisne 1946–49, vol. 2, no. 59.

27. New York, *Degas* 1988, p. 120.

28. Berthe Morisot to her sister, August 13, 1870, as cited in New York 1983, p. 315.

29. Levine 1978, pp. 90–93.

30. See the discussion by Tucker 1986.

31. Zola wrote two separate reviews of the Salon of 1875. In "Le Salon de 1875," *Le Sémaphore de Marseille,* May 4, 1875, he wrote, "Les portraits montent chaque année comme une marée." Reprinted in Zola 1970, p. 212. In "Lettres de Paris. Exposition de tableaux à Paris," in *Le Messager de l'Europe,* June 1875: "Il [le peintre] désire peindre comme Rubens, Rembrandt, Raphael, ou Velasquez. Sa

tête est pleine d'un idéal lié au passé." Translated from the Russian and reprinted in Zola 1970, p. 235.

32. Edmond Duranty, *La Nouvelle Peinture*, 1876, reprinted in San Francisco 1986, pp. 477–84, translated, pp. 37–47.

33. As cited in ibid., pp. 43–44.

34. Ibid., p. 40; see also p. 39: "They [artists of the EBA] do not realize that it is by the flame of contemporary life that great artists and learned men illuminate these ancient things. Veronese's *Wedding at Cana* [Musée du Louvre, Paris] would have failed pathetically without his Venetian gentlemen."

35. Rivière, "Aux femmes" 1877, p. 2.

36. "Craignant les railleries de ses amis, il [votre mari] refuse malgré vos sollicitations de laisser faire votre portrait par un *novateur* qui se permet de ne pas marcher sur les traces vénérables de M. Dubuffe [*sic*]." Ibid., p. 2. On the Dubufe, see Bréon 1988.

37. See, for example, Paul de Charry's review of the fifth Impressionist exhibition in *Le Pays*, April 10, 1880. "Nous avouons, en toute vérité, au risque d'être honni et vilipendé, que notre contentement est plus grand devant un bon petit Wouwerman ou un joli Téniers que devant un sujet de M. Gauguin; nous avons le tort de préférer les perspectives données par Paul Véronèse à celles de M. Caillebotte." Cited in Berson 1996, vol. 1, p. 272.

38. "When he gives himself the time to complete and finish anything, he displays qualities which are analogous to those that distinguished the early Flemish painters." Philippe Burty, *The Academy*, London, April 15, 1876, in San Francisco 1986, p. 171.

39. Brown 1994, pp. 5–6.

40. Ibid., p. 5 n. 11.

41. "Le portrait de Mlle Samary rend si bien une jolie physionomie de soubrette éveillée et évoque si justement l'idée de l'atmosphère spéciale à la scène, qu'il faut remonter aux vives pochades de Fragonard pour rencontrer, non pas des points comparaison matérielle, mais des analogies de tempérament français s'appliquant à la peinture de portrait." Philippe Burty, "Exposition des impressionnistes," *La République Française*, April 25, 1877, p. 3, in Berson 1996, vol. I, p. 124.

42. Fragonard's *Portrait of M. de La Bretèche*, 1769, part of the La Caze collection given to the Musée du Louvre, has a period label on the back indicating it was painted in an hour, cited in New York, *Fragonard* 1988, p. 274.

43. Béguin and Constans 1969.

44. "Fragonard," in Goncourt 1981, pp. 288–91. First published as *Fragonard, étude contenant quatre dessins gravés à l'eau-forte* (Paris: E. Dentu, 1865).

45. "Allez donc voir les portraits, à la salle des Impressionnistes, rue Le Peletier 6. C'est un peu fou. Mais c'est d'une folie bien délicatement pénétrante." Undated letter from Burty to Edmond de Goncourt, although probably at the time of the exhibition of 1877, Bibliothèque nationale, Naf 22455, ff. 292–93, as cited in Weisberg 1993, p. 196.

46. Burty did much to revive interest in the ancien régime by organizing the exhibition *Tableaux de l'École française ancienne, tirés de collections d'amateurs,* held as a fund-raiser at the École des Beaux-Arts, Paris, in June 1860.

47. Goncourt 1981, p. 290.

48. Philippe Burty, *La République Française*, April 10, 1880, in San Francisco 1986, p. 326.

49. Paul Mantz, *Le Temps,* April 14, 1880, in ibid., p. 328; and Charles Ephrussi, *Gazette des Beaux-Arts,* May 1, 1880, in ibid., p. 327.

50. See the Museum of Fine Art's provenance line for the work at http://www.mfa.org/collections.

51. Information provided in the entry for *Madame Georges Charpentier and Her Children* in Ottawa 1997, p. 161. Madame Charpentier, née Marguerite Louise Lemonnier, was Isabelle's sister.

52. Paris 1883.

53. Lostalot 1883, p. 81.

54. Ibid., p. 91.

55. New York 1983, p. 51.

56. See Colin Bailey's excellent discussion of portrait patronage in Bailey 1997, pp. 17–20.

57. According to Émile Zola, "Il est de mode dans la bourgeoisie et la noblesse de commander son portrait à un artiste quelconque," from "Lettre de Paris Exposition de tableaux à Paris," *Le Messager de l'Europe*, June 1875, reprinted in Zola 1970, p. 236. At the Salon of 1875 Léon Bonnat exhibited the *Portrait of Madame Pasca*, celebrated actress, who is "à la mode actuellement," and the Russian Alexis Kharlamov became an immediate sensation with his portrait of opera singer Pauline Viardot. Ibid., p. 237.

58. Renoir's fee is given in Theodore Duret, *Renoir* (Paris: Bernheim Jeune, 1924), p. 66, as cited in Ottawa 1997, p. 297 n. 45. For celebrity portraits of Samary, see Ottawa 1997, pp. 155–60; and Collins 1998, pp. 323–25.

59. Albert Wolff, "Le Salon," *Le Figaro,* 11 May 1879, and Arthur Baignères, "Le Salon de 1879," *Gazette des Beaux-Arts,* XX, July 1879, p. 54, as cited in Ottawa 1997, p. 297 n. 51.

60. See Meyer Schapiro's comments about the decline of portraiture in the nineteenth century. "Portraits and accessories, schemata of compositions originally devised for the expression of rank and dignity, were applied to sitters who failed to win the admiration or respect of the artist, and became empty conventions." Schapiro 1997, p. 157.

61. Renoir signed a letter to Madame Charpentier "le plus dévoué des peintres ordinaires." Michel Florisoone, "Renoir et la famille Charpentier: Lettres inédites," *L'Amour de l'Art* 19 (February 1938): 35–38, as cited in Ottawa 1997, p. 297 n. 29.

62. Ibid., p. 184.

63. "Die Anordnung fordert die alten Meister in die Schranken." Meier-Graefe 1911, p. 66.

64. Natanson 1900, p. 371. See also provenance for the painting in Ottawa 1997, p. 296.

65. See Brown 2002; and Higonnet 1998.

66. Bailey 1997 discusses the portraits of the Berard children *Marthe* (1879; Museu de Arte de São Paulo), p. 18, *Margot* (1879; The Metropolitan Museum of Art, New York), p. 170, *André* (1879; private collection), pp. 38–39, *Studies of the Children of Paul Berard* (1881; Sterling and Francine Clark Art Institute, Williamstown, Mass.), p. 184, and *Lucie* (1883; The Art Insitute of Chicago), p. 204.

67. See Bailey 1998, esp. pp. 86–88.

68. First suggested in Ottawa 1997, p. 184. The drawing is reproduced in the fourth installment of Philippe de Chennevières's review, "Les Dessins des maîtres anciens exposés à l'École des Beaux-Arts," *Gazette des Beaux-Arts* 19 (September 1879): opp. 202.

69. See discussion of the painting in London 1985, p. 245, pointing out that Charles Ephrussi had donated two Botticelli frescoes to the Louvre in 1882; and Ottawa 1997, p. 210.

70. See Collins 2005.

71. Jean Renoir, "My Memories of Renoir," *Life* 32 (May 19, 1952): 98, as cited in Ottawa 1997, p. 246.

72. Georges Lecomte, *L'Art impressionniste d'après la collection privée de M. Durand-Ruel,* 1892, as quoted in Mathews 1996, p. 154.

73. For example, Luca della Robbia, *Madonna and Child in a Niche,* 1440–60, enameled terracotta, 48 cm high, The Metropolitan Museum of Art, New York, bequest of Susan Dwight Bliss, 1966.

74. Barter 1998, pp. 77–78; and Mathews 1994, pp. 257ff.

75. Ottawa 1997, pp. 254–58.

76. Walter Pach, "Pierre Auguste Renoir," *Scribner's Magazine* 51 (1912): 613, as cited in ibid., p. 254.

77. See for example *The Nursing Infant* (1886; private collection), with Renoir's first son, Pierre, and his wife, Aline Charigot.

78. On the occasion of the third Impressionist exhibition of 1877, Renoir's close friend and collaborator Georges Rivière wrote about *The Swing* (fig. 101), "On y reconnaît quelque chose du *Voyage à Cythère* avec une note particulière au XIXe siècle," referring to Watteau's *Embarkation for Cythera* (Musée du Louvre). Rivière, "Les Intransigeants" 1877, p. 299. The artist himself likely encouraged the linkage. See also the writings of Camille Mauclair, Mauclair 1905, pp. 35–47; and Mauclair 1921, p. 107. For Manet's and Degas's identification with past schools, see nn. 10 and 14 above.

79. Proust 2003, p. 45.

Angelica Daneo

Chronology
1849–1910

This chronology does not claim to be exhaustive but offers the most significant facts relating to the theme of the exhibition and, in particular, to the artists featured.

1849

June 12–13 The painting *Meeting of Thirteen People* (at the time attributed to Velázquez, cat. 100, p. 28) is sold at auction in Paris. The Musée du Louvre acquires it in 1851.
(Roldán 2003, p. 383.)

August Charles Blanc begins publishing in Paris the first chapters on individual artists that will become his *Histoire de peintres de toutes les écoles*. Planned as installments to appear one every two weeks, in reality they are published more irregularly. Once issued, all the chapters related to a national school are then republished in bound volumes.
(Reff 1970, pp. 457–58.)

1850

January 29 Édouard Manet registers to copy in the Louvre.
(Reff, "Louvre" 1964, p. 555.)

March 13 Sale of old master paintings from the collection of Mme Pinel Grandchamp at the Hôtel des Ventes, 42, rue des Jeuneurs. The preface draws attention to works by Philippe de Champaigne, Jean-Baptiste Oudry, and Jusepe de Ribera. The collection also includes a drawing by Jean-Honoré Fragonard and a landscape by Jacob van Ruisdael.

1851

The Louvre acquires the painting *Meeting of Thirteen People (Réunion de treize personnages),* then attributed to Diego Rodríguez de Silva y Velázquez.

1852

February 25 Manet begins copying François Boucher's *Diana at the Bath* at the Louvre.
(Reff, "Louvre" 1964, p. 556.)

May 19, 21–22 Sale of Marshal Jean de Dieu Soult's collection. The Spanish School is largely represented with works of art by Bartolomé Esteban Murillo, Francisco Zurbarán, Francisco de Herrera the Younger, and Alonso Cano.
(Rivero 2003, p. 110; Roldán 2003, p. 384.)

July 19 Manet travels to the Netherlands and visits the Rijksmuseum in Amsterdam.
(New York 1983, p. 505.)

Antonin Proust recalls: "I just talked about Manet's trips. He went to see the Rubens of Antwerp, the Rembrandts of Amsterdam, the Primitives [Early Netherlandish] of Brussels, the Hals of Harlem." (Je viens de parler des voyages de Manet. Il alla voir les Rubens d'Anvers, les Rembrandt d'Amsterdam, les primitifs de Bruxelles, les Hals de Harlem.)
(Proust 1913, p. 36.)

November 21 Louis-Napoleon proclaims himself emperor with the name of Napoleon III.

Louis Viardot's *Les Musées d'Espagne* published in Paris.

Frédéric Villot's *Notice des tableaux exposés dans les galeries du Musée National du Louvre par Frédéric Villot, conservateur de la peinture, 1re partie, écoles d'Italie et d'Espagne,* 2nd edition, published in Paris. For the Italian School is cited, among others, Gaspar Dughet, called Gaspar Poussin, *Paysage* (no. 186); for the Spanish School, Murillo, *Le Jeune Mendiant* (no. 551; cat. 69, p. 35) and Velázquez, *Portrait de l'infante Marguerite-Thérèse* (no. 555; fig. 46) and *Réunions de portraits* (no. 557; cat. 100, p. 28).

Villot's *Notice des tableaux exposés dans les galeries du Musée National du Louvre par Frédéric Villot, conservateur de la peinture, 2e partie, écoles allemande, flamande et hollandaise,* 1st edition, published in Paris. Peter Paul Rubens is included with *Portrait d'Hélène Fourment, seconde femme de Rubens, et de deux de ses enfants* (no. 460); Jacob van Ruisdael with six landscapes (nos. 470–75), but Salomon van Ruysdael is not represented.

1853

April 7 Edgar Degas registers to copy in the Louvre. On April 9 he also receives permission to copy at the Cabinet des Estampes of the Bibliothèque Impériale, where he copies engravings by Marcantonio Raimondi.
(Reff, "Louvre" 1964, pp. 555, 558–59.)

September–October Manet goes to Italy and visits Venice and Florence and, presumably, Rome.
(New York 1983, p. 505.)

Antonin Proust informs us that "In Italy he [Manet] appeared very much enamoured of the Titians, the Tintorets, little captivated by the Raphaels and the Michelangelos." (En Italie, il se montra très épris des Titien, des Tintoret, peu séduit par les Raphael et les Michel-Ange.)
(Proust 1913, p. 30.)

Among the works of art listed by Charles Blanc as appearing at the sale of Théophile Thoré's collection of antique and modern prints, we find Marcantonio Raimondi's *Le Jugement de Pâris:* "This beautiful print, the most perfect of Marc-Antoine, is engraved after an excellent composition of Raphael." (Cette belle estampe, la plus parfaite de Marc-Antoine, est gravée d'après une excellente composition de Raphael.)
(Blanc 1858, vol. 2, p. 497.)

1854

October 31 Degas starts copying Franciabigio's *Portrait de jeune homme* (at the time attributed to Raphael).
(Paris 1988, p. 48.)

Alfred Michiels's *Catalogue des tableaux et dessins de Rubens avec l'indication des endroits ou ils se trouvent* published in Paris.

Blanc's *Les peintres des fêtes galantes: Watteau, Lancret, Pater, Boucher par M. Charles Blanc, ancien directeur des beaux-arts* published in Paris.

1855

May–November Exposition Universelle on the Champs-Élysées. In anticipation of the vast audience expected for the fair, the Louvre opens its doors to the public every day of the week.
(Paris 1993, p. 45.)

July 7 Petition signed by 48 artists asking "His Majesty to allow the entry of the public in the Louvre, during the working hours, so as to facilitate the sale of their copies, which could not happen if the public is not admitted to visit the Palace at the same time as the artists are gathered there." (Sa Majesté de vouloir bien autoriser l'entrée des étrangers au Louvre, pendant les heures de travail, afin de faciliter ainsi la vente de leur copies; ce qui ne peut avoir lieu, si les étrangers ne sont admis a visiter le Palais, dans le temps même, ou les artistes s'y trouvent réunis.)
(Archives du Louvre, P18; Paris 1993, p. 45.)

Villot's *Notice des tableaux exposés dans les galeries du Musée Impérial du Louvre par Frédéric Villot, conservateur de la peinture, 3e partie, école française* published in Paris. Among the artists represented are Chardin (nos. 96–104), Jean-Baptiste Monnoyer (nos. 362–69, excluding the paintings designated as attributed), Oudry (nos. 384–91), and Nicolas Poussin (nos. 415–53).

J[ean] Duchesne's *Description des estampes exposées dans la galerie de la Bibliothèque Impériale formant un aperçu historique des productions de l'art et de la gravure, accompagnée de recherches sur l'origine, l'accroissement et la disposition méthodique de la collection* published in Paris. Twenty-three engravings by Marcantonio Raimondi are included; nos. 59 and 60 represent *Le Jugement de Pâris*.

1856

April 21–26, 28–29 Sale of M. H[is] de L[asalle]'s collection of old master prints at the Hôtel Drouot, Paris.

July 17 Degas arrives in Naples. He often visits the National Museum, to copy artworks from the collection.
(Paris 1988, p. 49.)

October 7 Degas visits Civitavecchia and Rome. He stays in Rome until the end of July 1857. There he attends the French Academy, copying from models as well as copying artworks in the Vatican museums and churches.
(Paris 1988, p. 49.)

La Revue Universelle des Arts (October 7, p. 383) reports that the artists who are copying in the museums welcome the presence of the public while they work in the galleries because "A certain number also, particularly notable for their good work, often meet rich foreigners who buy their works or even commission copies of the works that most impressed them. This permanent opening of our museums has therefore been fortunate for the artists, and at the same time a means of education for everyone." (Un certain nombre même, qui se font remarquer par de beaux travaux, rencontrent souvent la de riches étrangers qui leur achètent leurs ouvrages ou bien leur commandent des copies des œuvres qui les ont le plus impressionnés. Cette ouverture permanente de nos Musées a été ainsi une bonne fortune pour les artistes, en même temps qu'en moyen d'éducation pour tout le monde.)
(Paris 1993, p. 45.)

Alexandre-Charles Sauvageot donates to the Louvre his collection comprising 68 paintings, mainly sixteenth- and seventeenth-century portraits of the French, Flemish and Dutch, German, Spanish, and Italian schools. The *Catalogue du Musée Sauvageot* by A. Sauzay is published in 1861.
(*Donateurs* 1989, p. 317.)

1857

April 20–21 Sale of Théodore Patureau's collection of old master paintings, especially Flemish and Dutch, at the Hôtel Drouot. Blanc reports: "Also we can say that all Paris had participated in this grand occasion. The artists had come here to enjoy a museum that was to last for forty-eight hours." (Aussi peut-on dire que tout Paris s'était rendu à cette solennité. Les artistes y étaient venus pour jouir d'un musée qui devait durer quarante-huit heures.)
(Blanc 1858, vol. 2, p. 521.)

May 5 Manchester Art Treasures Exhibition, the first large, comprehensive display of old master paintings, opens in Manchester, England, and is

widely reviewed. W. Bürger's articles, commissioned by the Parisian newspaper *Le Siècle,* were published separately as *Trésors d'art exposés à Manchester en 1857,* and in later editions as *Trésors en Angleterre* (1860 and 1865). Blanc wrote *Les Trésors de l'art à Manchester*.
(Haskell 2000, p. 82; Jowell 1977, pp. 215–36; Jowell 2001, p. 54.)

August 21 Manet begins copying Rubens's *Portrait of Hélène Fourment and Her Children* at the Louvre.
(Reff, "Louvre" 1964, p. 556.)

October Degas copies at the Sistine Chapel, the Galleria Doria-Pamphilj, and the Galleria Capitolina in Rome.
(Paris 1988, p. 50.)

November 13 Degas visits the Galleria Corsini, where he sees Claude Lorrain's etchings.
(Paris 1988, p. 50.)

He records in his notebook: "Etchings by Claude Lorrain that I went to see / the 13th of Nov[ember 1857]—at the Corsini Gallery [Rome]." (Eaux fortes de Claude Lorrain que j'ai été voir / le 13 Nov[embre 1857]—à la Galerie Corsini [Rome].)
(Reff 1985, vol. 1, p. 66.)

November–December Manet goes to Italy. During this trip he copies Andrea del Sarto's frescoes in San Annunziata (Florence).
(New York 1983, p. 505.)

1858

March 19 Berthe Morisot registers to copy in the Louvre, particularly works by Titian and Veronese.
(Reff, "Louvre" 1964, p. 556; Clairet, Montalant, and Rouart 1997, p. 36.)

In 1860 she will complete her copy of *Le Calvaire,* after Veronese (cat. 66, p. 26).

July 24 Degas leaves Rome and moves to Florence, where he copies in the Uffizi. Between 1858 and 1859, he copies the *Portrait of a Young Woman,* a sanguine drawing then attributed to Leonardo da Vinci (now attributed to Bachiacca; cat. 30, p. 23).
(Paris 1988, pp. 51, 76.)

November 26 Manet registers to copy in the Cabinet des Estampes of the Bibliothèque Impériale.
(Reff, "Louvre" 1964, p. 559.)

The day before, November 25, he writes to the curator of the Bibliothèque Impériale asking for a student card that would allow him to use the print room.
(Manet 1991, p. 28.)

November 27 From Florence, Degas writes to Gustave Moreau: "[Jules-Élie] Delaunay has spoken to me at length about Venice, Carpaccio, you and a little bit about Veronese. . . . [Anthony] Van Dyck is a great artist, as are Giorgione, Botticelli, Mantegna, Rembrandt, Carpaccio." (Delaunay m'a longuement parle de Venise, de Carpaccio, de vous, et un tout petit peu de Véronèse. . . . Van Dyck est un fameux artiste, Giorgion aussi, Botticelli aussi, Mantegna aussi, Rembrandt aussi, Carpaccio aussi.)
(Reff, "More Unpublished Letters" 1969, p. 283.)

Publication in Paris of the first volume of W. Bürger's *Musées de la Hollande. Amsterdam et La Haye*.
(Bürger 1858.)

Le Livre de l'art ou traité de la peinture par Cennino Cennini, first French edition (translated by V. Mottez) of Cennino Cennini's *Il Libro dell'arte* published in Paris.

1859

April 26 Degas writes to Moreau about Genoa and expresses his admiration for the Van Dyck paintings at the Palazzo Rosso. He also mentions Turin and the museum there, where he saw a Veronese, a Velázquez, and a few Van Dycks.
(Reff, "More Unpublished Letters" 1969, p. 284.)

July 1 Manet registers again to copy in the Louvre. At this time, according to Theodore Reff, Manet copied *Meeting of Thirteen People* (cat. 48, p. 29; cat. 100, p. 28) and *Infanta Margarita* (both attributed to Velázquez at that time).
(Reff, "Louvre" 1964, p. 556.)

Blanc founds the *Gazette des Beaux-Arts* and publishes *L'Oeuvre de Rembrandt*.

1860

January 24 Pierre-Auguste Renoir registers to copy in the Louvre.
(London 1985, p. 294.)

March 3 Émile Zola writes to Paul Cézanne about the artist's expected trip to Paris: "Moreover, Paris offers you an advantage which you could find nowhere else: the museums, where from 11 o'clock in the morning until 4 in the afternoon, you can study the old masters. You could organize your time in the following way: from 6 in the morning until 11 o'clock you could paint from a living model in an art school studio, then take your lunch and from 12 until 4 in the afternoon you could copy a masterwork which attracts you, either in the Louvre or in the Luxembourg Museum." Zola also suggests that Cézanne could earn some money by selling copies: "On the other hand, you can make a little money on the side here! The studies made in the art schools, and especially copies made in the Louvre, are quite saleable."
(Cézanne 1976, pp. 51, 53.)

John Rewald, in his biography of Cézanne informs us that: "He [Cézanne] began to copy ancient and modern sculpture in the Louvre, especially the works of Puget. . . . He also copied plaster casts in the Trocadero Museum. Among the painters, Rubens and Poussin particularly attracted him, and Cézanne's sketchbooks are filled with drawings after Rubens, whose work, like Puget's, offered him subjects rich in color and movement."
(Rewald 1948, p. 172.)

March 24 Degas writes to his brother René from Naples that he is going to the museum there: "I have hardly the patience or the time to write for long—I am going to the Museum this morning." (Je n'ai guère la patience ni le temps de s'en écrire bien long.—Je vais aller au Musée ce matin.)
(Reff, "Unpublished Letters" 1968, p. 92.)

April 2–3 Sale of Paul Barroilhet's collection at the Hôtel des Ventes Mobilières (5, rue Drouot, salle 7). The collection includes paintings of old masters from the Italian, Spanish, Flemish, and French schools. Among the artists included are Francisco de Goya, Murillo, Velázquez, Rubens, Boucher, Chardin, Fragonard, and Greuze.

August 15 Valentin Carderera's "François Goya, sa vie, ses dessins et ses eaux-fortes," parts 1 and 2, is published in the *Gazette des Beaux-Arts*.

Exhibition of French old masters from private collections at the Galerie Martinet, 26, boulevard des Italiens. The eighteenth century is represented with works by, among others, Jean-Antoine Watteau, Jean-Baptiste-Joseph Pater, Chardin, Boucher, Fragonard, and Greuze.
(Burty 1860; Bürger, "Exposition" 1860.)

Georges de La Tour's *Portrait of a Man* is exhibited in Paris. Degas will copy it, although when he did so is not certain. Reff suggests sometime between 1860 and 1873, when the La Tour was sold at auction.
(Reff 1971, p. 539.)

A brief article, "La Fille du 'Greco,'" on El Greco's *Lady in a Fur Wrap* (cat. 40, p. 110), illustrated by a print, is published in Paris in *Le Magasin Pittoresque*; it explains that the portrait was once displayed in Louis-Philippe's Galerie Espagnole.

Auguste Marc-Bayeux's *Les Copistes du Louvre* published in Paris. Marc-Bayeux is concerned about the generosity of the ministry of fine arts

in commissioning copies, rather than sustaining and promoting living artists: "What the Ministry spends every year in commissioning copies and supporting copyists of the Louvre would certainly be enough to make the fortune of a dozen great and real painters. These little runts have nibbled the bread with which France would have nourished a Veronese or a Titian." (Ce que le Ministère dépense chaque année, en commandes de copies, et en encouragements au secours gratuits pour les copistes du Louvre, suffirait certainement a faire la fortune d'une douzaine de grands et vrais peintres. Ces avortons ont grignoté le pain dont la France aurait nourri un Véronèse ou un Titien.) His vivid account gives us a sense of the number of artists working in the galleries at the same time: "But the copyists! Here we are: those people have made of the Louvre their atelier. The copyist is male or female and rarely attractive. His presence reveals itself in the salons and the galleries, by an imposing spread of easels, knickknacks, odd stools, ladders, scaffoldings, crammed with canvases and paint boxes." (Mais les copistes! Nous y voici: ces-gens là ont fait du Louvre leur atelier. Le copiste est mâle ou femelle, et rarement séduisant d'aspect. Sa présence se manifeste dans les salons et les galeries, par un déploiement imposant de chevalets, de trucks, de tabourets fantasques, d'échelles, d'échafaudages, encombres de toiles et de boîtes de couleurs.) He distinguishes between the young artists, who copy in the Louvre to learn from the art of the past, and the mature painters, who copy to sell: "In fact, few young artists come to copy at the Louvre for study. Surely the study from nature is preferable and nourishes the qualities of originality, which are rapidly lost by copying the old masters. The few young people who come to study paint less than they draw; they are recognizable by their bored attitude; . . . The adult copyist, on the contrary, for whom the whole thing is a speculation, . . . is used to the practice of the house." (Dans le fait, peu de jeunes artistes viennent copier au Louvre, comme étude. Il est certain que l'étude d'après nature est préférable, et nourrit les qualités d'originalité, que l'on perd rapidement par la copie des maîtres. Les quelques jeunes gens qui viennent étudier, peignent moins qu'ils ne dessinent; ils se reconnaissent à leur attitude ennuyée; . . . Le copiste adulte, au contraire, celui pour qui la chose est une spéculation, . . . est rompu aux usages de la maison.) The article ends with a list of the most popular paintings copied since 1851 as well as the frequency with which they are copied. We learn from this that Murillo is the most copied artist and that his *Immaculate Conception* has been copied 197 times since 1851. Velázquez, Ribera, and Zurbarán are also very popular, and Marc-Bayeux reports that the *Infanta* of Velázquez has been copied 63 times. To his displeasure, Greuze is the most copied of the French artists: "I don't have anything against Greuze, but rather against those of our writers who had the unfortunate idea of exhuming the XVIII century and its painting." (Je n'en veux pas à Greuze, mais bien plutôt à ceux de nos écrivains qui ont eu la malheureuse idée d'exhumer le XVIII siècle et sa peinture.)
(Marc-Bayeux 1985, pp. 147, 148, 150.)

Publication of the second volume of W. Bürger's *Musées de la Hollande. Musée van der Hoop, à Amsterdam et Musée de Rotterdam.*
(Bürger, *Musées* 1860.)

1861

January 15 Antoine Claudet's article "La Photographie dans ses relations avec Beaux-Arts" published in the *Gazette des Beaux-Arts*.

March 5 Renoir registers to copy in the Louvre.
(Reff, "Louvre" 1964, p. 556.)

April 16 Camille Pissarro registers to copy in the Louvre.
(Reff, "Louvre" 1964, p. 556.)

June 4 In a letter to Joseph Huot, Cézanne writes: "I have seen, naïve thing to say, the Louvre and the Luxembourg and Versailles. . . . I have also seen the Salon."
(Cézanne 1976, p. 85.)

June 15 Louis Martinet, founder of the Société Nationale des Beaux-Arts, founds *Le Courrier Artistique,* a bimonthly periodical.

September 3 Degas registers to copy in the Louvre.
(Reff, "Louvre" 1964, p. 555.)

Degas's version of Mantegna's *Calvary* (cat. 33, p. 24) is executed during the last months of the year.
(Paris 1988, p. 88.)

November 8 The artist Charles Gleyre asks that Renoir be allowed to work in the department of prints of the Bibliothéque Imperiale.
(London 1985, p. 294.)

Blanc's two-volume *Histoire des peintres de toutes les écoles. École hollandaise* is published in Paris. The reproductions in the first volume include Gabriel Metsu's *Dutch Woman at the Harpsichord* (fig. 38) and Arent van der Neer's *The Skaters,* a winter scene of skaters on a lake. The second volume includes Pieter de Hooch's *Interior of a Dutch House*.

1862

January 14 Degas registers again to copy in the Louvre.
(Reff, "Louvre" 1964, p. 555.)

September–October Sometime during this period Manet meets Degas in the Louvre, while Degas is copying the *Infanta Margarita* (fig. 46), then attributed to Velázquez, directly onto a copperplate (cat. 34, p. 117).
(Roldán 2003, p. 389.)

Blanc's first edition of the three-volume *Histoire des peintres de toutes les écoles. École française* published in Paris and completed in 1863. The entry on Claude Lorraine (1865 ed., vol. 1, p. 14) comments: "The paintings of Claude, sought after throughout Europe, have become very rare; they have found a place, for the most part, either in the national galleries or in the noble collections of England. No gallery gathers a collection of paintings by Claude as large as the one of the Louvre." (Les tableaux de Claude, recherchés dans toute l'Europe, sont devenue de la plus grande rareté; ils sont pris place, pour la plupart, soit dans les galeries nationales, soit dans les collections seigneuriales d'Angleterre. Aucune galerie ne réunit une collection de tableaux de Claude aussi nombreuse que celle du Louvre.)

Monnoyer is included in the first volume with four reproductions of bouquets of flowers. According to Blanc (1865 ed., vol. 1, p. 8), Monnoyer's paintings can also be found "among dealers, among amateurs, in our museums, in the châteaux belonging to the State. . . . The Louvre owns a large number of paintings by this excellent artist." (chez les marchands, chez les amateurs, dans nos musées, dans les châteaux appartenant a l'État. . . . Le Louvre possède un grand nombre de tableaux de cet excellent artiste.)

Also included is the recently popular Pater (1865 ed., vol. 2, p. 8), painter of *fêtes galantes,* whose works "had fallen, during the time of the Empire and the Restoration, in such a discredit that the Louvre Museum does not own even one, or at least there is not one exhibited in the galleries devoted to the French School. Nowadays this painter, having regained a certain favor . . . he is again much sought after." (Étaient tombés, au temps de l'Empire et de la Restauration, dans un tel discrédit, que le Musée du Louvre n'en possède pas un seul, ou du moins il ne s'en trouve pas un d'exposé dans les galeries destinées à l'école française. Aujourd'hui ce peintre ayant repris quelques faveurs . . . il y est de nouveau fort recherché.) Chardin is included with reproductions of seven of his works. Regarding Greuze, Blanc informs us (1865 ed., vol. 2, p. 15) that the Musée Fabre in Montpellier possesses eleven paintings by him, including the study of "a head of a young boy sleeping" (une tête d'enfant endormi).

1863

April 9 Renoir receives permission to copy in the Louvre.
(Reff, "Louvre" 1964, p. 556.)

May 15 The artists who are rejected by the official Salon obtain permission to show their paintings separately; this will be known as Salon des Refusés.
(Rewald 1973, p. 80.)

Manet exhibits, among other works, the etching *Little Cavaliers*.
(Roldán 2003, p. 390.)

July 1 Blanc's "Velásquez à Madrid" published in the *Gazette des Beaux-Arts*.

November 20 Cézanne registers to copy in the Louvre.
(Reff, "Louvre" 1964, p. 555.)

November 26, 29, December 3 The newspaper *Le Figaro* publishes in three episodes "Le Peintre de la vie moderne" by Charles Baudelaire.

1864

June Letter from Baudelaire to Théophile Thoré, contesting the latter's suggestion in his Salon review that Manet pastiched Spanish masters, insisting that "M. Manet has never seen a Goya. M. Manet has never seen an El Greco. M. Manet has never seen the Pourtalès gallery."
(Roldán 2003, p. 391.)

Thoré's review of the extensive art collection of the brothers Émile and Isaac Pereire in Paris, published in the *Gazette des Beaux-Arts,* particularly praises the seventeenth-century Spanish and Dutch paintings.
(Bürger 1864.)

François-Anatole Gruyer's *Raphaël et l'antiquité* published in Paris.

Blanc's *Histoire des peintres de toutes les écoles, École flamande* published in Paris. Rubens is one of the most important artists portrayed. Among the reproductions included are *The Château Steen* (fig. 9) and *The Rainbow* (fig. 10).

1865

February 16 Morisot receives permission to copy in the Louvre.
(Reff, "Louvre" 1964, p. 556.)

March 27–April 4 Sale of the comte de Pourtalès-Gorgier's collection at 7, rue Tronchet. The Italian School of the fifteenth and sixteenth centuries is strongly represented.

May 31–June 3, 6–10, 12 Sale of the duc de Morny's collections of paintings at the Palais de la Présidence du Corps Législatif, 128, rue de l'Université. The collection includes paintings by old and modern masters. Some of the old masters represented are Rembrandt, Rubens, and Ruisdael; Chardin, Fragonard, and Greuze; Francesco Guardi; and Murillo and Velázquez.

August 20 In *La Chronique des Arts* the Louvre is said to be "less a place of study for the serious artists, the writers or for the audience than a laboratory for the producers of copies" (moins un lieu d'étude pour les artistes sérieux, pour les écrivains ou pour le public qu'un laboratoire pour les fabricants de copies).
(Paris 1993, p. 46.)

August 23[?] Replying to a letter from Zacharie Astruc, Manet expresses his desire to leave for his trip to Spain and "go ask master Vélasquez for advice" (aller demander conseil à maître Vélasquez).
(Manet 1988, p. 41.)

August 29[?] Manet leaves for Spain. On his way to Madrid, he stops in Burgos and Valladolid, where, he confides in a letter to Astruc, he admires the monuments of these two cities. Manet seems to have reached Madrid around September 1. There he meets Théodore Duret, with whom he starts exploring the city, visiting churches, museums, and, in particular, the Prado. They also organize a visit to Toledo.
(Manet 1988, pp. 16–18.)

September 3 Manet, while in Madrid, writes to Henri Fantin-Latour, reporting on his visit to the "Musée royale" (Prado) as well as informing him of his planned trip to Toledo, where he will see works by Goya and El Greco. At the Prado he sees a painting, similar in composition to the *Little Cavaliers* at the Louvre: "There is a huge painting here, full of little figures like those in the Louvre picture called the Cavaliers." (Il y a ici un tableau énorme rempli de petites figures comme celles qui se trouvent dans le tableau du Louvre intitulé les cavaliers.) And on Toledo: "Tomorrow I am going on an excursion to Toledo where I'm told I shall see both Greco and Goya very well represented." (Je vais demain faire une excursion à Tolède. Là je verrai Gréco et Goya très bien représentés, m'a-t-on dit.)
(Manet 1991, pp. 34–35; Manet 1988, pp. 43–44; Roldán 2003, p. 392.)

September 14 Manet writes to Baudelaire declaring his admiration for Velázquez: "I tell you he's the greatest artist there has ever been" and for some paintings by Goya, such as the portrait of the duchess of Alba: "I saw some interesting things by Goya, some of them very fine, including an incredibly charming portrait of the Duchess of Alba dressed as a *majo*."
(Manet 1991, p. 36; Manet 1988, pp. 47–48; Roldán 2003, p. 392.)

September 17 Manet writes to Astruc, once again praising Velázquez, in whom he declares to have found "the fulfillment of my own ideals in painting." He was disappointed in Ribera and Murillo, whom he sees as "second-rate artists."
(Manet 1991, p. 36; Manet 1988, p. 49; Roldán 2003, p. 392.)

October 13 Back in Paris, Manet writes to Duret, expressing confidence that Duret will write about Spain from an artistic and political point of view, especially on Velázquez, Goya, and El Greco.
(Manet 1991, p. 37; Manet 1988, p. 56; Roldán 2003, p. 393.)

October 26 Degas registers to copy in the Louvre.
(Reff, "Louvre" 1964, p. 555.)

He receives permission to copy Sebastiano del Piombo's *Holy Family* (at that time attributed to Giorgione).
(Paris 1988, p. 56.)

Émile Galichon's article "La Galerie Pourtalès" published in the *Gazette des Beaux-Arts*. Galichon describes the Italian paintings, while Paul Mantz, in an essay published the same year in the same journal, discusses the paintings of the Spanish, German, Dutch, Flemish, and French schools.

Edmond and Jules de Goncourt's essay on Fragonard published in the *Gazette des Beaux-Arts*. The essay will be revised and published again in 1873 for *L'Art du dix-huitième siècle*.

Léon Lagrange's essay on Pierre Puget published in the *Gazette des Beaux-Arts*.

Publication in Paris of Gustave Brunet's French translation of William Stirling-Maxwell's *Velázquez and His Works* (London: J. W. Parker and Son, 1855), which includes notes and a catalogue of Velázquez's paintings in European collections.

1866

February The Goncourts publish some excerpts from their journal under the title *Idées et sensations*.
(Goncourt 1989, vol. 1, p. LXXXIV.)

Starting in 1866 Aimé-Charles-Horace His de la Salle donates to the Louvre ten studies by Poussin for the series of the *Seven Sacraments*. Before dying in 1878 he makes another donation of about 300 drawings by, among others, Poussin, Théodore Géricault, Eugène Delacroix, Raphael, Leonardo da Vinci, Correggio, Rubens, and Rembrandt.
(*Donateurs* 1989, p. 232.)

An exhibition of old masters in private collections opens in Paris at the Palais des Champs-Élysées, in a gallery next to the Salon. Lagrange's "Exposition rétrospective de tableaux de maîtres" is published in the *Gazette des Beaux-Arts*.
(Jowell, "Art Market" 1996; Haskell 2000, pp. 89, 178 n. 23.)

W. Bürger's articles on Johannes Vermeer and his catalogue raisonné of Vermeer's paintings published in the *Gazette des Beaux-Arts*.
(Bürger 1866.)

Charles Clément's *Michel-Ange, Léonard de Vinci, Raphael; avec une étude sur l'art en Italie avant le XVIe siècle et des catalogues raisonnés historiques et bibliographiques* published in Paris.

1867

February 1 The Goncourts' article on Maurice Quentin de la Tour published in the *Gazette des Beaux-Arts*.

April 1–November 3 The Exposition Universelle is open for seven months with galleries on the Champ de Mars.

On this occasion Duret writes *Les Peintres français en 1867*. *Paris-Guide* includes an informative chapter by W. Bürger on private collections.
(Bürger 1867.)

April 11–13 Laurent Laperlier's collection of eighteenth-century French paintings and drawings, including works by Chardin, Boucher, and Greuze, is sold at the Hôtel Drouot.
(Eisler 1960, p. 211.)

May 15 Eliza Haldeman, in Paris with Mary Cassatt, writes to her mother and answers questions about Mary. "You asked me if Mary C. was accepted at the exposition, I thought I had told you we had both been refused though we have strong hopes for next year. . . . Mary wishes to be remembered to you, she laughed when I told her your message and said she wanted to paint *better* than the old masters."
(Mathews 1984, p. 46.)

June 3–6 Sale of the marquis de Salamanca's collection of old master paintings at 50, rue de la Victoire, Paris. The collection features in particular Spanish old masters of the sixteenth and seventeenth centuries with seventeen works by Velázquez and fourteen by Murillo. The Flemish, Dutch, and Italian schools are also represented.

Pierre Marcy's *Guide populaire dans le musées du Louvre* published in Paris. The first part includes a description of the artworks exhibited in the Grand Salon Carré, followed by a description of the paintings in the Petite Galerie des maîtres italiens and by those in the Grande Galerie. In the section dedicated to the Spanish School, Marcy explains: "Next to Velazquez is on display—number 551—a very popular canvas, the *Young Beggar* [the *Beggar Boy*] or, more colloquially, the *Flea-Ridden*—by Murillo." (A côté du Velazquez, est exposée—no. 551—une toile très-populaire, le "Jeune Mendiant" ou plus familièrement le "Pouilleux"—de Murillo.) Further: "Number 556 is a remarkable *Portrait of the cardinal Altamira*.—Nevertheless, this painting does not appear to us to combine all the great qualities of Velázquez, to whom it is attributed, qualities that are found to the fullest in the number 555, the *Portrait of the Infanta Marguerite-Thérèse,* daughter of Philip IV." (Le—no. 556—est un remarquable 'Portrait du cardinal Altamira'.—Cependant, cette peinture ne nous paraît pas réunir toutes les grandes qualités de Velasquez à qui on l'attribue, qualités que l'on retrouve entièrement dans le—no. 555—, 'Portrait de l'Infante Marguerite-Thérèse', fille de Philippe IV.) In the section dedicated to the Dutch School, Marcy praises Ruisdael, considered "one of the greatest landscape painters known." (Un des plus grands paysagistes connus.) In the Second Grand Salon de l'École Française, "number 25, *Venus Ordering Arms from Vulcan for Aeneas* introduces us to Boucher—the painter of gallant scenes, the famous decorator of eighteenth-century boudoirs." (no. 25—'Vénus commandant à Vulcain des armes pour Énée', va nous faire faire connaissance avec Boucher—le peintre des scènes galantes, le décorateur renommé des boudoirs du dix-huitième siècle.)

Alexis-François Rio's *Michel-Ange et Raphaël: avec un supplément sur la décadence de l'école Romaine* published in Paris.

Charles Yriarte's *Goya: Sa biographie, les fresques, les toiles, les tapisseries, les eaux-fortes et le catalogue de l'œuvre* published in Paris.

1868

February 13 Cézanne registers to copy in the Louvre.
(Reff, "Louvre" 1964, p. 555.)

March 13 Sale of F. de Villars's collection of old master paintings at the Hôtel Drouot. Boucher, Chardin, Fragonard, Goya, and Frans Hals are among the artists included.

March 26 For the last time Degas registers to copy in the Louvre.
(Reff, "Louvre" 1964, p. 555.)

April 18 Sale of twenty-three Dutch and Flemish paintings from the collection of Anatole Demidoff, prince of San Donato, in Paris.

May 8 Haldeman writes to her parents from Paris: "Miss Cassatt is with me as she has not yet decided where she will go for the summer. & we intend to draw from the pictures in the Louvre and from life."
(Mathews 1984, p. 52.)

Blanc's *Histoire des peintres de toutes les écoles, École vénitienne* published in Paris. Titian is included with a reproduction of the *Danaë*. Giorgione is represented with a reproduction of *Concert champêtre* (1884 ed.).

W. Bürger's study on Hals published in *Gazette des Beaux-Arts*.
(Bürger 1868.)

Lagrange's *Pierre Puget: peintre, sculpteur, architecte et décorateur de vaisseaux* published in Paris.

1869

March 1 The engraving of Pieter de Hooch's *Intérieur d'une chambre* appears in the *Gazette des Beaux-Arts,* following Blanc's article "La Galerie Delessert."
(Blanc 1869.)

March 15–18 Sale of the Delessert's collection, Paris.
(Jowell, "Art Market" 1996, p. 123.)

June 5 Sale in Paris of forty-three old master paintings belonging to the collection of the comte Kushelev-Bezborodko.

Bequest of Louis La Caze's collection to the Musée du Louvre. Among the artists represented are Van Dyck, Rubens, Hals (among the works *The Gypsy,* fig. 23), Ribera, Watteau (including *Assembly in a Park,* fig. 78), Fragonard (among the works *Study,* fig. 60), Chardin (including *The Jar of Olives,* fig. 86, and *The Brioche,* fig. 88), Boucher (including *The Forge of Vulcan*), Greuze, and Pater. The collection will go on display at the Musée du Louvre in 1870.
(*Donateurs* 1989, p. 244.)

Blanc's *Histoire des peintres de toutes les écoles, École espagnole* published in Paris. In this section Blanc includes El Greco, with a reproduction of *La Fille du Greco* (*Lady in a Fur Wrap,* cat. 40, p. 110). No paintings by El Greco are available at the Louvre, after the dispersal of the collection of King Louis-Philippe, but some examples of his art can be seen in private collections such as the ones of Pereire and Oudry. Velázquez is represented by a reproduction of *Little Cavaliers* (cat. 100, p. 28). Murillo is included with *Beggar Boy* (Musée du Louvre; see cat. 69, p. 35, for an anonymous copy).

1870

Early 1870 Cassatt travels to Rome, where she studies with the French artist Charles Bellay.
(Clement, Houzé, and Erbolato-Ramsey 2000, p. 22; and Chicago 1998, p. 331.)

February 26 Sale of the eighteenth-century French paintings from the collection of Anatole Demidoff, prince of San Donato, at the Galerie Martinet, 26, boulevard des Italiens. Among the artists represented are Boucher (11 paintings), Fragonard (1 painting), Greuze (19 paintings; no. 114, *L'Étude,* is illustrated by Éd. Hedouin in the *Gazette des Beaux-Arts*).

March 3–4 Sale of Spanish, Flemish, Italian, and German old master paintings from the collection of Anatole Demidoff, prince of San Donato, at the Galerie Martinet, 26, boulevard des Italiens.

March 14–15 Sale of the vicomte de Carvalhido's collection of old master and modern paintings at the Hôtel Drouot, Paris.

March 17–18 Sale of Prince Grégoire Soutzo's collection of old master prints, including works by Adriaen van Ostade, Albrecht Dürer, Van Dyck, Claude Lorrain, Marcantonio Raimondi, and Rembrandt. Degas knew Grégoire Soutzo and had access to his collection before the prince's death.
(Paris 1988, p. 71.)

July 19 Franco-Prussian War begins when France declares war on Prussia.

October Claude Monet and his family are in London.

December Pissarro and his family leave France for London.

Blanc's *Histoire des peintres de toutes les écoles, École ombrienne et romaine* published in Paris. Raphael is included with a reproduction of his *Judgment of Paris* (1884 ed., p. 19).

Mantz's article "La Collection La Caze au Musée du Louvre" published in the *Gazette des Beaux-Arts*.
(Mantz 1870.)

1871

January Pissarro meets Monet in London, and together the two artists start visiting galleries and museums, admiring paintings by J. M. W. Turner, John Constable, Thomas Gainsborough, Sir Thomas Lawrence, and Sir Joshua Reynolds.
(Pissarro and Durand-Ruel Snollaerts 2005, p. 130.)

March 18–May 27 Paris Commune.

May Monet and his family move to Holland. In June Monet reaches Zaandam, a town of canals and windmills, which inspires twenty-four paintings.
(Chicago 1995, p. 196.)

June 22 While in Amsterdam Monet visits the Rijksmuseum.
(Chicago 1995, p. 196.)

October While in Haarlem Monet visits the Frans Hals Museum.
(Chicago 1995, p. 196.)

October 26 Blanc presents a plan for a museum in Paris, Musée des Copies, which would display copies of important works of art owned by foreign museums. His plan is approved by the minister of fine arts, Jules Simon.
(Boime 1964, pp. 237, 238.)

October 27 In a letter to her friend Emily Sartain while in the United States, Cassatt talks about the lucrative prospect of making copies on commission: "I hear that Healy asked ($6000) dollars for a *copy of Van Dyke*!! & it was bought in Chicago. Of course that is absurd but still if one only gets one hundred dollars for a small copy it pays better than twice the sum for an original because you have to rent no models & no fire to pay while at work, & a *little copying* is good for one; not too much however."
(Mathews 1984, p. 77.)

Early December Cassatt leaves for Europe, and, with Sartain, she visits London, Paris, Turin, and Parma.
(Clement, Houzé, and Erbolato-Ramsey 2000, p. 23; Chicago 1995, p. 332.)

December 15 Sartain writes to her father about old masters seen in Parma (the letter is mailed from there on December 23): "The St. Jerome [Correggio's *Madonna and Child with Saint Jerome*] here is superb—Each time we see it, it seems more glowing and finer—Miss C. is delighted to copy it—The room it is in is warmed for copyists. . . . The Madonna of the Scodella [Correggio's *Madonna della Scodella*] is not done justice to in the copy our Academy has,—but I like it less than the St. Jerome."
(Mathews 1984, pp. 81–82.)

Duret leaves for London on his way to Japan and China.

F. Reiset's *Notice des tableaux légues au Musée National du Louvre par M. Louis La Caze* published in Paris.

1872

January Cassatt is in Parma, where she studies with Carlo Raimondi, professor of engraving at the Accademia. She admires in particular the paintings of Correggio and Parmigianino.
(Clement, Houzé, and Erbolato-Ramsey 2000, p. 23; Chicago 1998, p. 332.)

In a letter dated January 1, Sartain writes to her father: "Mary C. is now at work on a very large canvas, copying the 'Virgin Crowned', a copy by Annibale Carracci from Correggio—The original fresco was in the half dome off the chancel of San Giovanni. . . . Miss Cassatt thinks the Virgin's figure alone will do for an Assumption."
(Mathews 1984, p. 85.)

March 6–9 Sale of the MM. Pereires' collection at the Galerie Martinet, 26, boulevard des Italiens. The extensive collection includes paintings by old and modern masters. Among the old masters are works by Boucher, Fragonard, Greuze, and Pater; Goya, El Greco, Murillo, and Velázquez; Sandro Botticelli and Tintoretto; and Hals, Meindert Hobbema, de Hooch, and Ruisdael.

Summer Morisot visits Madrid, where she admires paintings by Velázquez and Goya.

June Manet travels to the Netherlands and visits the Frans Hals Museum in Haarlem and the Rijksmuseum in Amsterdam.
(New York 1983, p. 513.)

October 5 Cassatt arrives in Madrid and registers to copy in the Prado. In a letter to her friend Sartain, dated October 5, she writes: "I really never in my life experienced such delight in looking at pictures, no Titiens in Italy are finer, no Rafaelles either, . . . I don't hesitate to tell you that although I think now that Correggio is perhaps the greatest painter that ever lived, these Spaniards make a much greater impression *at first*. The men and women have a reality about them which exceed anything I ever supposed possible, Velasquez Spinners, good heavens, why you can walk into the picture. Such freedom of touch, to be sure he left plenty of things unfinished, as for Murillo he is a baby alongside of him."
(Mathews 1984, p. 103.)

October 13 Cassatt writes to Sartain from Madrid and again expresses her admiration for Velázquez and the Spanish School: "I am making a sketch

from the Velasquez at the gallery. . . . I sincerely think it is the most wonderful painting that ever was seen, this of the Spanish school. I have found a few French artists copying here, and all with one accord agree with me; I think that one learns *how to paint* here, Velasquez manner is so fine and so simple."
(Mathews 1984, pp. 107–8.)

October 26 Cassatt leaves for Seville. The next day she reports to Sartain her first impressions of the city. She will leave Seville in April 1873.
(Boone 1995, pp. 56, 70; Mathews 1984, pp. 109–10.)

1873

March 1 An engraving of Jacob de Ruisdael's *Le Pont de bois* (*The Wooden Bridge*) published in the *Gazette des Beaux-Arts*.

April 16 Blanc, then director of fine arts, opens the Musée des Copies to the public in the Palais de l'Industrie on the Champs-Élysées.
(Paris 1993, p. 33; Duro 1987, p. 54.)

It had been open to art critics and artists since November 1872.
(Boime 1964, p. 238.)

Louis Auvray's *Le Musée européen* was published in Paris in the occasion of the opening. The museum closes at the end of December.

May 15 The Salon des Refusés opens in Paris.

June Cassatt travels to The Hague and Antwerp, where she studies Rubens.
(Clement, Houzé, and Erbolato-Ramsey 2000, p. 23.)

In a letter of June 25 to Sartain, she admits to being "enchanted with the Rubens' here, especially the Adoration, but there is nothing else but the Rubens to admire, except one head of Rembrandt."
(Mathews 1984, p. 121.)

She also reaches Haarlem, where she studies Hals's work.

December 27 A group of artists, including Monet, Pissarro, and Renoir, found in Paris the Société anonyme coopérative d'artistes-peintres, sculpteurs, graveurs, et lithographes.

1874

February 13 The Goncourts record in their journal a visit to Degas's studio, where he shows them his pictures, mimicking the movements of his dancers and "speaking of Velásquez' 'soft muddiness' and the 'silhouetting' of Mantegna."
(Goncourt 1971, p. 134.)

March A selected number of works from the Musée des Copies (now closed) are transferred to the École des Beaux-Arts.

April 15–May 15 First Impressionist exhibition opens in the studio of the photographer Nadar, 35, boulevard des Capucines, Paris. Thirty participants: Astruc, Antoine-Ferdinand Attendu, Édouard Béliard, Eugène Boudin, Félix Bracquemond, Édouard-Emile Brandon, Pierre-Isidore Bureau, Adolphe-Felix Cals, Cézanne, Gustave Colin, Louis Debras, Degas, Jean-Baptiste-Armand Guillaumin, Louis Latouche, Ludovic-Napoléon Lépic, Stanislas Lépine, Jean-Baptiste-Leopold Levert, Alfred Meyer, Auguste de Molins, Monet, Morisot, Emilien Mulot-Durivage, Giuseppe de Nittis, Auguste-Louis-Marie Ottin, Léon-Auguste Ottin, Pissarro, Renoir, Léon-Paul Robert, Stanislas-Henri Rouart, Alfred Sisley (the comtesse de Luchaire does not appear in the catalogue, but is mentioned in the review by Marc de Montifaud).
(San Francisco 1986, pp. 118–23.)

Winter Manet travels to Venice and, as reported by Charles Toché, comments on Carpaccio, Titian, and Tintoretto: "I love the Carpaccios with their naïve charm . . . the Titians and Tintorettos in the Scuola di San Rocco are incomparable. . . . But in the end, you see, I always come back to Velasquez and Goya!"
(Manet 1991, p. 172.)

Exhibition of old masters from private collections at the Palais Bourbon, Paris.

Duret's *Voyage en Asie*, a recollection of his trip to Asia in 1871, published in Paris.

Blanc's *Histoire des peintres de toutes les écoles, École bolonaise* published in Paris.

1875

January 25–26 Sale of the marquis de Salamanca's collection at the Hôtel Drouot, Paris. Charles Pillet's *Collection Salamanca: tableaux anciens des écoles espagnole, italienne, flamande et hollandaise* published.
(Wilson Bareau, "Manet and Spain" 2003, p. 249 n. 122.)

March 24 Sale of paintings by Monet, Morisot, Renoir, and Sisley at the Hôtel Drouot, Paris.
(Distel 1990, p. 53; Bodelsen 1968, p. 331.)

August A new association of artists, called L'Union, is formed. The group includes Béliard, Cézanne, Guillaumin, Latouche, Meyer, and Pissarro.
(Rewald 1973, pp. 362–63.)

Edmond de Goncourt's *Catalogue raisonné de l'oeuvre peint, dessiné et gravé d'Antoine Watteau* published in Paris.

1876

March 6–7 Sale of paintings and drawings from the collection of Camille Marcille at the Hôtel Drouot. The eighteenth-century French School is predominant, with 5 paintings by Boucher, 10 by Chardin, 4 each by Fragonard and Greuze. Paul de Saint-Victor writes in the introduction to the catalogue (p. I): "We can say that Mr. Marcille was, together with Mr. Lacaze, Walferdin and Carrier, the restorer of the XVIII century French school in the taste and favour of the public." (On peut dire que M. Marcille fut, avec MM. Lacaze, Walferdin et Carrier, le restaurateur de l'école française du XVIII siècle, dans le goût et dans la faveur du public.)

March 30–April Second Impressionist exhibition opens at 11, rue le Peletier. Nineteen participants: Béliard, Bureau, Gustave Caillebotte, Cals, Degas, Marcellin Desboutin, Jacques François, Alphonse Legros, Lépic, Levert, Jean-Baptiste Millet, Monet, Morisot, Léon-Auguste Ottin, Pissarro, Renoir, Rouart, Sisley, Charles Tillot.
(San Francisco 1986, pp. 160–65.)

June 7 The Musée des Études, a study museum of casts, opens in the École des Beaux-Arts, Paris.
(Duro 1987, p. 55.)

Edmond Duranty's pamphlet entitled *La Nouvelle Peinture. À propos du groupe d'artistes qui exposent dans les galeries Durand-Ruel* published in Paris.

Blanc's *Histoire des peintres de toutes les écoles, École florentine* published in Paris.

Blanc's *Histoire des peintres de toutes les écoles, Écoles milanaise, lombarde, ferraraise, genoise et napolitaine* published in Paris.

Blanc's *Les artistes de mon temps* published in Paris.

G. Duplessis's "La Collection de M. Camille Marcille" published in the *Gazette des Beaux-Arts*.

Eugène Fromentin's *Les Maîtres d'autrefois* published in Paris. Fromentin discusses the influence of Dutch old masters, in particular Jacob van Ruisdael, and the Dutch landscape tradition on the French artists of the time.
(Boime 1976, p. 142.)

1877

February 15 L'Union organizes an exhibition. Cézanne, Guillaumin, and Pissarro resign and do not participate.
(Ann Arbor 1980, p. IX.)

April 4 Third Impressionist exhibition opens at 6, rue le Peletier. Eighteen participants: Caillebotte, Cals, Cézanne, Frédéric Cordey, Degas, Guillaumin,

Jacques-François (pseud.), Franc Lamy, Levert, Alphonse Maureau, Monet, Morisot, Ludovic Piette, Pissarro, Renoir, Rouart, Sisley, and Tillot.
(San Francisco 1986, pp. 203–7.)

May 28 Sale of paintings by Caillebotte, Pissarro, Renoir, and Sisley at the Hôtel Drouot, Paris.
(Bodelsen 1968, p. 331.)

Paul Lefort's *Francisco Goya: Étude biographique et critique, suivie de l'essai d'un catalogue raisonné de son oeuvre gravé et lithographié* published in Paris.

Alfred Michiels's *Rubens et l'école d'Anvers* published in Paris.

1878

April 11–12 Sale of paintings from the collection of Zacharie Astruc. Among the artworks included is Goya's *Still Life with Golden Bream* (cat. 39, p. 47).
(Roldán 2003, p. 398.)

May 1–November 10 The Exposition Universelle opens in Paris at the Palais de Trocadéro.

May Duret's *Les Peintres impressionnistes* published in Paris.

November 20 In a letter to Zola, Cézanne writes: "I bought a very curious book, it is a mass of observations of a subtlety that often escapes me, I feel, but what anecdotes and true facts! And people *comme il faut* call the author paradoxical. It is a book by Stendhal: *Histoire de la Peinture en Italie,* you have no doubt read it, if not, allow me to draw your attention to it."
(Cézanne 1976, p. 172.)

1879

February 17–18, 20–21 Sale of Laperlier's collection at the Hôtel Drouot. The eighteenth-century French School is well represented with 5 paintings by Chardin and 7 by Fragonard.

April 10–May 11 Fourth Impressionist exhibition opens at 28, avenue de L'Opéra. Fifteen participants: Félix Bracquemond, Marie Bracquemond, Caillebotte, Cals, Cassatt, Degas, Louis Forain, Paul Gauguin, Albert-Charles Lebourg, Monet, Piette (posthumously; not in cat.), Pissarro, Rouart, Henry Somm, Tillot, Federico Zandomeneghi.
(San Francisco 1986, pp. 266–71.)

April Georges Charpentier founds *La Vie Moderne,* a weekly periodical and an art gallery of the same name, where, in June, a show of Renoir's works launches a series of exhibitions.
(Distel 1990, p. 146.)

May 1 Lefort's article "Velazquez," in two parts, is published in the *Gazette des Beaux-Arts.* Lefort points to the modernism of Velázquez, who "is so ahead of his time that he seems to belong rather to ours." (Marque une telle avance sur son temps qu'il semble plutôt appartenir au nôtre.) An engraving of Velázquez's *L'Infante Marguerite* (Musée du Louvre) is included. Lefort praises Velázquez's artistic "language" by declaring: "And this language, firm, immutable, definite, complete, of Velázquez and already two centuries old, we seem to be able to say, without injustice, that our Impressionists, this young avant-garde of the school, barely start to stammer it out." (Et cette langue, ferme, arrêtée, définitive, complète, chez Velazquez, et déjà vieille de deux siècles, il nous semble pouvoir en dire, sans injustice, que nos impressionnistes, cette jeune avant-garde de l'école, commencent à peine encore à la balbutier.) Lefort acknowledges that it is increasingly easy for artists to visit Madrid and see Velázquez's artworks directly: "Since Spain became more accessible, our artists gladly cross the Pyrenees and go to Madrid in the attempt to pull from Velázquez his wonderful secrets of life." (Depuis que l'Espagne s'est faite plus accessible, nos artistes passent volontiers les Pyrénées et s'en vont à Madrid tenter d'arracher à Velazquez ses merveilleux secrets de vie.) A second article is published on September 1 with a print of *Réunion de portraits* (*Little Cavaliers,* attributed to Velázquez, in the Louvre), and a third article is published on November 1.

June 1 The first of five installments of the marquis de Chennevières's "Les Dessins de maîtres anciens exposés à l'école des beaux-arts" is published in the *Gazette des Beaux-Arts.* The second article (July 1) includes a print after Caspar Netscher's *Young Woman Playing the Mandoline.* The third article is published on August 1, and the fourth installment on September 1. It includes prints after Watteau's *Four Studies of a Woman* and *Studies of Heads* (collection of Mr. Rutter). The fifth and last article appears on October 1.

Fall Cassatt, in a letter to Morisot, talks about her summer travels: "This summer I didn't get anything done, we traveled for nearly four weeks, in Piedmont and then to Milan and returned through Switzerland by Lake Maggiore and the Simplon. I saw many things to admire, beautiful frescoes, really I don't see that the moderns have discovered anything about color. It seems to me that we haven't learned anything more about color or drawing."
(Mathews 1984, p. 149.)

Cassatt, Degas, and Pissarro discuss publishing a journal of prints, *Le Jour et la Nuit,* with Bracquemond, Jean-François Raffaëlli, and Desboutin.
(Ann Arbor 1980, p. X.)

1880

April 1–30 Fifth Impressionist exhibition opens at 10, rue des Pyramides. Nineteen participants: Félix Bracquemond, Marie Bracquemond, Caillebotte, Cassatt, Degas, Forain, Gauguin, Guillaumin, Lebourg, Levert, Morisot, Pissarro, Raffaëlli, Jean-Marius Raffaëlli, Rouart, Tillot, Eugène Vidal, Paul-Victor Vignon, Zandomeneghi.
(San Francisco 1986, pp. 310–14.)

April 12–16 Sale of François-Hippolyte Walferdin's collection of French paintings and drawings at the Hôtel Drouot. Two sections of the catalogue are dedicated to Fragonard. Other artists represented are Boucher, Chardin, Greuze, Poussin, and Watteau.

July 14 First celebration of this national holiday since 1794.
(Washington 1982, p. 246.)

Copies of artworks are no longer to be accepted at the Salon.
(Paris 1993, p. 47.)

The Goncourts' *L'Art du dix-huitième siècle* published in Paris between 1880 and 1882.

1881

Spring An exhibition of Renaissance sculpture opens at the Louvre.
(Chicago 1998, p. 77.)

April 2–May 1 Sixth Impressionist exhibition opens at 35, boulevard des Capucines. Thirteen participants: Cals (posthumously; not in cat.), Cassatt, Degas, Forain, Gauguin, Guillaumin, Morisot, Pissarro, Jean-François Raffaëlli, Rouart, Tillot, Vidal, Vignon, Zandomeneghi.
(San Francisco 1986, pp. 353–56.)

May 9–14, 16 Sale of baron de Beurnonville's collection of old master paintings at 3, rue Chaptal, including 21 paintings by Fragonard, 11 by Hals, 16 by Jacob van Ruisdael, and 5 by Salomon van Ruysdael.

October 1881–January 1882 Renoir travels to Italy. He visits Venice and, according to Ambroise Vollard, recalls: "My greatest surprise at Venice was the discovery of Carpaccio, with his fresh and gay colours. . . . One of his landscapes also interested me immensely, for it was neither more nor less than a view of Provence." He proceeds to Florence and Rome: "I did nothing at Florence, or at

Rome either, for that matter, but visit museums. I liked immensely Raphael's *Heliodorus Driven from the Temple* in the Vatican. . . . In the midst of the endless variety of masterpieces both at Florence and Rome, I must confess that my greatest joy was Raphael." He continues to Naples, where he admires Pompeii: "It was restful to find so much of the art of Pompeii and the Egyptians. I had begun to tire a little of Italian painting—for ever the same draperies and the same Virgins. . . . One picture in Naples which impressed me very much was the portrait of Pope Julius III by Titian."
(Vollard 1934, pp. 101, 102, 103.)

Winter Morisot visits Italy.
(Clement, Houzé, and Erbolato-Ramsey 2000, p. 113.)

She visits Genoa, Pisa and Florence.
(Clairet, Montalant, and Rouart 1997, p. 54.)

The French State abandons control of the Salon by giving it to the Société des Artistes Français.
(Ann Arbor 1980, p. X.)

Henry Havard's *L'Art et les artistes hollandaise* published in Paris.

1882

February Exhibition of the Société des Aquarellistes Français at the gallery of Georges Petit. Before this date it had been organized annually at the gallery of Durand-Ruel.
(Distel 1990, p. 38.)

March 1–April 2 Seventh Impressionist exhibition opens at 251, rue St. Honoré. Nine participants: Caillebotte, Gauguin, Guillaumin, Monet, Morisot, Pissarro, Renoir, Sisley, Vignon.
(San Francisco 1986, p. 394.)

May First Exposition Internationale organized by Georges Petit: A committee of foreign painters (Raimondo de Madrazo, Giuseppe de Nittis, and Alfred Stevens) invites artists to participate.
(Distel 1990, p. 38.)

P[aul] R[oulx]'s *Plan—Catalogue complet du Musée du Louvre, salle par salle, avec un répertoire complet donnant la place de chaque tableau* published in Paris, citing works by, among others, Chardin, Monnoyer, Fragonard, Boucher, Hals, Velazquez, Watteau, Murillo, Rubens, and Pater.

Théophile Gautier's *Guide de l'amateur au musée du Louvre, suivi de la vie et les oeuvres de quelques peintres* published in Paris.

1883

April 25 Exhibition of portraits (1783–1883) at the École des Beaux-Arts, Paris.

April 30 Death of Manet.

June 12 The exhibition *Cent Chefs-d'oeuvre des collections parisiennes* opens at the gallery of Georges Petit. It displays old master paintings (among them Boucher, Rembrandt, and Rubens) together with paintings by Camille Corot, Delacroix, and Jean-François Millet.
(Distel 1990, p. 39.)

July 5 In a letter to his son Lucien, Pissarro writes: "Are you drawing? Do not waste your time, try to make some progress, remember the drawings that you have copied after the Holbeins, he is the true master." (Dessines-tu? Ne perds pas ton temps, tâche de faire des progrès, rappelle-toi les dessins que tu as copiés d'après les Holbein, c'est le vrai maître.)
(Pissarro 1980, pp. 227–28, letter 166.)

Winter Morisot displays her copy (cat. 67, p. 142) of a detail of Boucher's *Venus Asking Vulcan for Arms* (in the Louvre) in her apartment in Paris.
(Clairet, Montalant, and Rouart 1997, p. 57.)

Eugène Müntz's *Les Historiens et les critiques de Raphaël, 1483–1883. Essai bibliographique pour servir d'appendice à l'ouvrage de Passavant; avec un choix de documents inédits ou peu connus* published in Paris.

1884

January 6–28 An exhibition of Manet's works is held at the École Nationale des Beaux-Arts, before the auction at the Hôtel Drouot on February 4 and 5.

May 15 First Salon des Indépendants opens: the exhibition is organized by the Groupe des Artistes Indépendants, founded in Paris with the purpose of holding exhibitions without juries or awards.
(Ann Arbor 1980, p. XI.)

December The Groupe des Artistes Indépendants is replaced by a new organization, the Société des Artistes Indépendants.

Blanc's *Collection d'objets d'art de M. Thiers léguée au musée du Louvre* published in Paris. A chapter entitled "Copies d'après les grands maîtres" lists the copies in Thiers's collection. Blanc writes (p. 79): "What represents the originality of the *cabinet* Thiers is that he owns pictures in reduced format of all that is most beautiful in the world as far as sculpture and painting, and that nothing of what it contains is at the Louvre. As far as painting, these pictures are versions of an absolute accuracy; I say versions, because the means utilized are not quite the same." (Ce qui constitue l'originalité du cabinet Thiers, c'est qu'il possède des images réduites de tout ce qu'il y a de plus beau dans le monde en fait de sculpture et de peinture, et que rien de ce qu'il renferme n'est au Louvre. Pour ce qui est de la peinture, ces images sont des traductions d'une fidélités absolue, je dis des traductions, parce que les moyens employés ne sont pas tout à fait les mêmes.) The copies were made by members of the Academie de France in Rome or by painters chosen for their abilities; the medium is mainly pencil (crayon) and watercolor (aquarelle). The artists most copied are Michelangelo, Raphael, and the artists of the Florentine School, but there are copies as well after Titian, Rubens, and Velázquez.

1885

April 20 Second exhibition of portraits at the École des Beaux-Arts, Paris.

May 18–30 Sale of the comte de la Béraudière's collection of old master paintings, drawings, and engravings at 12, rue de Poitiers. In the introduction of the catalogue, the baron J. Pichon writes (p. 10): "God does not like that I underestimate the great and true talents of our artists and artisans of today, but is it the fault of us, lovers and friends of antiquity, if we are less touched by the beauty of a new object than by the beauty of an antique one?" (A Dieu ne plaise que je méconnaisse les talents très grands et très réels de nos artistes et de nos artisans d'aujourd'hui, mais est-ce notre faute a nous, amateurs et amis de l'antiquité, si nous sommes moins touchés par la beauté d'un objet nouveau que par celle d'un objet ancien?) Among the artists represented: Boucher (3 paintings), Fragonard (2 paintings), and Vallayer-Coster (4 paintings).

Autumn Morisot travels to Belgium and Holland, visiting the museums in Antwerp, Amsterdam, Rotterdam, and Haarlem. She admires Rubens in particular.
(Clairet, Montalant, and Rouart 1997, pp. 58–59.)

Marie de Besneray's *Les Grandes Époques de la peinture: Le Poussin, Ruysdaël, Claude Lorrain* published in Paris.

Duret's *Critique d'avant-garde* published in Paris.

1886

April 27–May 6 Monet visits Holland.

May 15–June 15 Eighth Impressionist exhibition opens at 1, rue Lafitte. Seventeen participants: Marie Bracquemond, Cassatt, Degas, Forain, Gauguin, Guillaumin, Morisot, Pissarro, Lucien Pissarro, Odilon Redon, Rouart, Émile Schuffenecker, Georges Seurat, Paul Signac, Tillot, Vignon, Zandomeneghi.
(San Francisco 1986, pp. 443–47.)

Félix Fénéon's *Les Impressionnistes de 1886* published in Paris.

Zola's *L'Oeuvre* (*The Masterpiece*) published in Paris.

Georges Lafenestre's *La Vie et l'oeuvre de Titien* published in Paris.

1887

March 3 First volume of the Goncourts' *Journal* published in Paris.

October 21 Second volume of the Goncourts' *Journal* published in Paris.

1888

April 24 Third volume of the Goncourts' *Journal* published in Paris.

Lefort's *Velasquez* published in Paris.

1889

March 31–April 30 *Exposition Watteau* at the Palais Rameau, Lille.

May 20–October 31 The Exposition Universelle opens in Paris; the Tour Eiffel is built for the occasion.

July 1 Sale of M. E. Secrétan's collection of paintings, watercolors, and drawings by modern and old masters at Charles Sedelmeyer's galleries, Paris.

September 8 Degas, together with the Italian painter Giovanni Boldini, arrives in Madrid and visits the Prado that same day.
(Paris 1988, p. 392.)

Blanc's two-volume *Histoire de la renaissance artistique en Italie* published in Paris.

Roger Portalis's two-volume *Honoré Fragonard, sa vie et son oeuvre* published in Paris.

1890

May 21–24 Sale of Eugène Piot's collection at the Hôtel Drouot.

May 29–31 Sale of Gustave Rothan's collection of old master paintings at the gallery of Georges Petit, 8, rue de Sèze.

June 4 Sale of Ernest May's collection of old and modern paintings, watercolors, pastels, and drawings at the gallery of Georges Petit.
(Distel 1990, pp. 227, 229.)

October 6 Fourth volume of the Goncourts' *Journal* published in Paris.

Félix Naquet's *Les Artistes célèbres: Fragonard* published in Paris.

1891

February Fifth volume of the Goncourts' *Journal* published in Paris.

June 8 Sale of Henri Hecht's collection at the gallery of Georges Petit. Among the old masters were works by Hendrik Avercamp (*Les Patineurs*), Fragonard (attributed to, *Les Baisers*), Hals (*Conversation galante;* attributed to Hals: *Le Musicien*, *La Femme à la collerette*), and Velázquez (*Portrait de don Balthazar Carlos, fils de Philippe IV*, ill.). "The same portrait [of Don Carlos], with some variations, particularly in the landscape, appears at the Museum of Madrid." (Le même portrait avec des variantes, notamment dans le paysage, figure au Musée de Madrid).
(Distel 1990, p. 72.)

June 23 In a letter to his son Lucien, Pissarro refers to the sale of seventy drawings from the collection of Miss James: "I saw the annoucement of the sale of Watteau's drawings in the *Art dans les deux mondes* [June 13], which I will send you." (J'ai vu annoncer la vente de dessins de Watteau dans l'Art dans les deux mondes que je t'enverrai.)
(Pissarro 1988, pp. 98–99, letter 669.)

November 22 In a letter to Octave Mirbeau, Pissarro refers to the Louvre's instituting an entrance fee: "Did you read in our newspapers that the government . . . is going to make us pay for the right to contemplate the Botticellis at the Louvre." (Avez-vous lu dans nos journaux que le gouvernement . . . va nous faire payer le droit de contempler les Botticelli au Louvre.)
(Pissarro 1988, p. 148, letter 713.)

1892

February 23 Sixth volume of the Goncourts' *Journal* published in Paris.

May 16–17 Sale of the comte Daupias de Lisbonne's collection at the gallery of Georges Petit. Among the artists represented are Boucher (3 artworks), Fragonard (6), Greuze (3), Oudry (1), Pater (1).

May–June Renoir travels to Spain. Vollard reports the artist's comments about Madrid: "If it hadn't been for the Prado, I should have turned round and come right home the same day. But I couldn't miss Velasquez. . . . It's commonplace enough to say that El Greco is a very great painter. . . . His faults only serve to strengthen my natural preference for Velasquez. What I love so much is that aristocratic quality that you find over and over again in Velasquez. . . . All of the art of painting is in the little pink sash of the Infanta Margherita in the Louvre! . . . I know that the critics find fault with Velasquez for his too great facility. . . . Only the painter, who knows his business thoroughly, can create the impression that a picture was done at one stroke. . . . Wasn't it Charles Blanc who said that Velasquez was too matter-of-fact? Why do people always look for ideas in painting? When I look at a masterpiece, I am satisfied simply to enjoy it. . . . Goya's *Royal Family* is worth the trip to Madrid alone." And about Titian, Rubens, and Poussin at the Prado: "Titian has everything. . . . Rubens is just a shell beside him, nothing but surface. . . . You see how I love Titian; but in spite of everything I always come back to Velasquez. . . . Another thing which struck me particularly at the museum in Madrid was a Poussin which has remained as fresh as a Boucher, whereas in the Louvre and the other galleries, the Poussins are so dirty."
(Vollard 1934, pp. 126–31.)

July Georges Lecomte's *L'Art impressionniste d'après la collection de Paul Durand-Ruel* published in Paris.

Autumn Morisot visits the Musée des Beaux-Arts in Tours and copies Boucher's *Apollo Revealing His Divinity to Isis* (detail) and Mantegna's *Resurrection*.
(Clairet, Montalant, and Rouart 1997, pp. 70, 272.)

Lefort's *Murillo et ses élèves, suivi du catalogue raisonné de ses principaux ouvrages* published in Paris.

1893

March 2 Cassatt is in Siena and, in a letter to Samuel P. Avery, explains her intentions to go "to Padua & to the Villa Giacomelli to see the frescoes by Paul Veronese." She hopes, though, to be back in Paris by the end of March, since "by that time I will have had enough of the 'Grand Old Masters.'"
(Mathews 1984, p. 247.)

1894

February 21 Death of Caillebotte.

The Goncourts' *L'Italie d'hier,* a reminiscence of their trip to Italy in 1855–56, published in Paris.

June 23 Seventh volume of the Goncourts' *Journal* published in Paris.

June 25–October Pissarro is in Belgium with his son Félix. During his stay, he visits, among other cities, Brussels, Antwerp, and Bruges. In letters he reports having visited the museum in Brussels and seen there a Van Eyck, some Jordaens, and Rubens; in Ghent, another Van Eyck.
(Pissarro 1988, pp. 465–66, letter 1020; Pissarro and Durand-Ruel Snollaerts 2005, pp. 250, 251.)

1895

February–March Monet is in Norway. He explores the area around Oslo to find places to paint.

March 2 Death of Morisot.

May 8 Eighth volume of the Goncourts' *Journal* published in Paris.

November Exhibition of works by Cézanne at the gallery of Ambroise Vollard.

1896

February In a letter to Eugenie Heller, Cassatt talks about her visit to St. Quentin to see the pastels of Maurice Quentin de La Tour: "My sister-in-law, Miss Hallowell, & I are going this week to St Quentin for the day. In the Musée of St Quentin are eighty pastels of Latour which I very much wish to see. . . . There are Latour's in the Louvre, but the St Quentin ones are celebrated. He was an artist, most simple most sincere, no 'brio', no facility of execution, but his portraits are living & full of character."
(Mathews 1984, p. 263.)

March 5–23 Posthumous exhibition of Berthe Morisot's oeuvre, *Berthe Morisot (Madame Eugène Manet): Exposition de son oeuvre,* at the Galerie Durand-Ruel, Paris.

March 6 In his article in the newspaper *Le Figaro,* "L'Oeuvre de Mme Berthe Morisot," the critic Alexandre Arsène writes (p. 5): "The Louvre is the object of frequent visits; Berthe Morisot spends long hours there copying the *Little Cavaliers* by Vélazquez, the *Calvary* by Veronese [see 1858] and some other paintings again by the Venetian master, who happens to perfectly satisfy the colorist instinct of the beginner." (Le Louvre est l'objet de fréquentes visites; Berthe Morisot emploie de longues heures à y copier les 'Petits Cavaliers' de Vélasquez, le 'Calvaire' de Véronèse et d'autres tableaux encore du maître vénitien, lequel se trouve satisfaire à merveille l'instinct coloriste de la débutante.)
(Lille 2002, p. 102.)

March 26 Sale of Emmanuel Chabrier's collection at the Hôtel Drouot. He had more paintings by Manet, Monet, Renoir, and Sisley than by any other artists.

May 26 Ninth and last volume of the Goncourts' *Journal* published in Paris.

June 8 Sale of paintings and drawings by old and modern masters at the gallery of Georges Petit (8, rue de Sèze), including Goya (*Course de taureaux*) and Ruisdael (*Les Ruines* and *Bords de l'Yssel*).

July 15 Renoir leaves for Germany. He visits Dresden and its museums, recalling: "As to architecture, Dresden is rather weak, aside from the Catholic church and the Museum, two buildings of a charming kind of rococo."
(Vollard 1934, p. 107.)

1897

February A selection of artworks (about forty) from the Caillebotte bequest is shown to the public in the Luxembourg Museum. Caillebotte, who had died on February 21, 1894, included in his will a bequest to the Luxembourg Museum, and then to the Louvre, of a collection of about sixty Impressionist works. Part of the collection was refused by the French State administrators, and only a selection was displayed in the new gallery opened for it in the Luxembourg Museum.

1898

January 13 Zola publishes his letter "J'accuse" about the scandal implicating Captain Dreyfus, who was accused of espionage.

March 23 Pissarro writes to his son Lucien from Paris, expressing his views on the individuality of the artist as well as the influence of the old masters: "[Louis] Anquetin exhibits at Hessele rue Laffitte, only drawings. Another one who rummages in the masters' sketches! It is Michelangelo that he robs impudently, but slavishly and clumsily; . . . it is a matter of personality, individuality, nobody will think of denying the very characteristic individuality of a Rembrandt and even in Manet who derives from Goya, but who brings a different vision, a very special and modern approach that Goya could not conceive; Corot originates in and reflects Le Lorrain, it is evident, but what a transformation that is entirely his genius: his figures, how modern! All in all, it is only here that we have the tradition of the masters, without plagiarizing them." (Anquetin fait une exposition chez Hessèle rue Laffitte, des dessins seulement. Encore un qui fouille dans les cartons des maîtres! C'est Michel-Ange qu'il chipe effrontément, mais servilement et maladroitement; . . . il s'agit de personnalité, d'individualité, il ne viendra à personne l'idée de nier l'individualité très caractéristique d'un Rembrandt, et même dans Manet qui procède de Goya, mais qui apporte une vision autre, un esprit très spécial et moderne que Goya ne pouvait concevoir; Corot procède et reflète Le Lorraine, c'est évident, mais aussi quelle transformation qui est tout son génie: ses figures, est-ce assez moderne! En somme, il n'y a qu'ici ou l'on ait la tradition des maîtres, sans les piller.)
(Pissarro 1989, pp. 462–63, letter 1527.)

July 5 Pissarro writes to his son Lucien from Lyon, where he visited the museum: "In the museum, some superb Primitives [Early Netherlandish], some Tintoretto, some Veronese, one Greco, some Claude Lorrain, etc." (Dans le musée, des Primitifs superbes, des Tintoret, des Véronèse, un Greco, des Claude Le Lorraine, etc.)
(Pissarro 1989, p. 498, letter 1566.)

September 1 Maurice Tourneux's article "Petits Maîtres oubliés: Jean-Baptiste et Jean-François Colson" is published in the *Gazette des Beaux-Arts.* Jean-François Colson's *Le Repos* (Musée de Dijon) is reproduced.

October 13 In a letter to his son Lucien, Pissarro talks about his intention to see the Rembrandt exhibition in Amsterdam: "When I arrive in Paris within a few days, here is what I intend to do: take advantage of the exhibition of the Rembrandts in Amsterdam to go there and see whether there might be something to do thereabouts." (En arrivant à Paris dans quelques jours, voici ce que je compte faire: profiter de l'exposition des Rembrandt à Amsterdam pour y aller et voir s'il n'y aurait pas quelque chose à faire par là.)
(Pissarro 1989, p. 512, letter 1590.)

October 22 Renoir leaves for Holland, where he visits The Hague and Amsterdam. "I love Rembrandt, but I find him a little 'stuffy'. For my part I have a predilection for painting that lends joyousness to a wall."
(Vollard 1934, p. 136.)

November 1 To his son Lucien, Pissarro briefly comments on the Rembrandt exhibition he saw in Amsterdam: "The exhibition of Rembrandt includes about forty first-rate artworks; the city museum is truly very interesting." (L'exposition de Rembrandt renferme une quarantaine d'œuvres de premier ordre; le musée de la ville est vraiment fort intéressant.)
(Pissarro 1989, p. 516, letter 1596.)

November 22 In another letter to his son Lucien, Pissarro talks more extensively on the influence of the art of the past: "I did not have the time to write to you what I have felt in seeing the masterpieces of Rembrandt: it is admirable and the thought I had after having seen not only the Rembrandts, but the Frans Hals, the Van der Meers [Vermeers] and many other great artists, it is that we, the moderns, are absolutely right in seeking, or rather feeling differently, because we are different and that besides it is an art so typical of a time that it is absurd to try to follow this path. Also, as I have often told you, I mistrust those artful painters who are able to imitate the old masters; I certainly do

not have the same esteem for these artful ones as I have for those who, even if they are not creating masterpieces, look at them with their own eyes! How can I describe to you the portraits of Rembrandt, the Hals and this canal by Van der Mer, a masterpiece that comes closer to the Impressionists; I came back from Holland more than ever an admirer of the Monets, the Degas, the Renoirs, the Sisleys." (Je n'ai pas eu le temps de t'écrire ce que j'ai éprouvé en voyant les chefs-d'œuvre de Rembrandt: c'est admirable, et la réflexion qui m'est venue après avoir vu non seulement les Rembrandt, mais les Frans Hals, les Van der Meer [Vermeer], et tant d'autres grands artistes, c'est que nous, modernes, nous avons rudement raison de chercher, ou plutôt de sentir autrement, puisque nous sommes autres et que du reste c'est un art tellement particulier d'une époque que c'est absurde d'essayer de marcher dans cette voie. Aussi, comme je te l'ai dit souvent, je me méfie des peintres adroits qui savent pasticher les vieux maîtres, je n'ai certainement pas la même estime pour ces adroits comme j'en ai pour ceux qui, même en ne faisant pas de chefs-d'œuvre, regardent avec leur yeux a eux! Comment te décrire les portraits de Rembrandt, les Hals et ce Canal de Van der Mer, chef-d'œuvre qui se rapproche des impressionnistes; je suis revenu de Hollande plus que jamais admirateur des Monet, Degas, Renoir, Sisley.)
(Pissarro 1989, p. 520, letter 1601.)

Aureliano de Beruete's *Velazquez* published in Paris.

Jules Maurice Audéoud donates to the Louvre the sketch *Voeu à l'amour* by Fragonard and two drawings by Boucher and Fragonard. He also makes a bequest of a group of drawings by Rembrandt, Tiepolo, Watteau, Saint-Aubin, and Lawrence.
(*Donateurs* 1989, p. 139.)

1899

January 29 Death of Sisley.

May 4–5, 8–9 Sale of the comte Armand Doria's collection at the gallery of Georges Petit. Of the Impressionists he had owned works by Cézanne, Manet, Monet, Morisot, Pissarro, Renoir, and Sisley.
(Distel 1990, p. 171.)

May 15–18 Sale of M. G. Mühlbacher's collection of eighteenth-century French paintings, drawings, watercolors, and pastels at the gallery of Georges Petit. Among the artists represented: Boucher (1 painting, 6 drawings), Fragonard (8 paintings, 11 drawings), Greuze (1 painting, 1 drawing), Huet (2 pendant paintings, 7 drawings of which 4 are 2 sets of pendants), Pater (4 drawings of which 2 are pendants), Vallayer-Coster (1 painting, 1 drawing).

June 8–10 Sale of Charles Stein's collection at the gallery of Georges Petit. The collection included paintings by Boucher (1), Chardin (2), and Rubens (1).

July 1, 3–4 Sale of Victor Chocquet's collection at the gallery of Georges Petit. Among the Impressionists represented were Cézanne, Manet, Monet, Renoir, and Sisley.

September–October Monet is in London, where he starts painting his series of the Charing Cross Bridge and Waterloo Bridge.
(Stevens 2001, p. 143.)

1900

February–April Monet returns to London, where he continues his series of Charing Cross Bridge and Waterloo Bridge. In addition, he starts painting the Houses of Parliament.
(Stevens 2001, p. 143.)

April 15–November 12 Exposition Universelle in Paris.

1901

January–March Monet visits London for the third time since September 1899.
(Stevens 2001, p. 143.)

January–April Cassatt visits Spain and Italy with Mr. and Mrs. Henry O. Havemeyer and suggests that they acquire paintings by El Greco and Goya.
(Chicago 1998, p. 345; Clement, Houzé, and Erbolato-Ramsey 2000, p. 27.)

1902

February 3 In a letter to Charles Camoin, Cézanne writes: "Since you are now in Paris and the masters of the Louvre attract you, if it appeals to you, make some studies after the great decorative masters Veronese and Rubens, but as you would do from nature—a thing I myself was only able to do inadequately.—But you do well above all to study from nature."
(Cézanne 1976, p. 282.)

1903

Announcement of the donation to the Louvre of Isaac de Camondo's collection (it will be effective in 1912) in which the Impressionists are strongly represented. The collection also includes artworks from the medieval and Renaissance periods.
(*Donateurs* 1989, p. 29.)

May 8 In a letter to his son Lucien, Camille Pissarro talks about the influence of the old masters on the Impressionists: "This Mr. Dewhurst hasn't understood a thing about the Impressionist movement. . . . All he sees is a method of execution, and he mixes up the names. . . . He leaves out the influence of Claude le Lorrain, Corot, the entire eighteenth century, especially Chardin." (Ce M. Dewhurst n'a rien compris du mouvement impressionniste. . . . Il ne voit qu'en procédé d'exécution et il mélange les noms, . . . il supprime l'influence de Claude le Lorraine, Corot, tout le XVIII siècle, Chardin surtout.)
(Pissarro 1991, pp. 336–37, letter 2016; Pissarro and Durand-Ruel Snollaerts 2005, p. 113.)

September 13 In a letter to Charles Camoin, Cézanne invokes the teaching of Thomas Couture: "Couture used to say to his pupils: 'Keep good company, that is: go to the Louvre. But after having seen the great masters who repose there, we must hasten out and by contact with nature revive within ourselves the instincts, the artistic sensations which live in us.'"
(Cézanne 1976, pp. 297–98.)

November 13 Death of Pissarro.

1904

May 12 In a letter to Émile Bernard, Cézanne writes: "The Louvre is a good book to consult but it must be only an intermediary. The real and immense study to be undertaken is the manifold picture of nature."
(Cézanne 1976, pp. 302–3.)

October Monet travels to Madrid, where he visits the museums in the city and admires artworks by Velázquez. After Madrid he travels to Toledo and there sees paintings by El Greco.
(Chicago 1995, p. 237.)

December 9 In a letter to Camoin, Cézanne compares Michelangelo and Raphael: "what you must strive to achieve is a good method of construction. Drawing is merely the outline of what you see. Michelangelo is a constructor, and Raphael an artist who, great as he may be, is always tied to the model.—When he tries to become a thinker he sinks below his great rival."
(Cézanne 1976, p. 309.)

December 23 In a letter to Bernard, Cézanne comments on the Venetian masters: "Yes, I approve of your admiration for the strongest of the Venetians; we praise Tintoretto. . . . and on the day you find them [your own means of expression], be convinced you will rediscover without effort, in front of nature, the means employed by the four or five

great ones of Venice." In the same letter he refers more generally to the old masters: "During this period (I am necessarily repeating myself a little) we turn towards the admirable works that have been handed down to us through the ages, where we find comfort, support, such as a plank provides for the bather."
(Cézanne 1976, pp. 309–10.)

Gaston Schéfer's *Chardin: biographie critique* published in Paris.

1905

January 23 In a letter to Roger Marx, Cézanne writes: "My age and health will never allow me to realize my dream of art that I have been pursuing all my life. . . . To my mind one does not put oneself in place of the past, one only adds a new link. With a painter's temperament and an artistic ideal, that is to say a conception of nature, sufficient powers of expression would have been necessary to be intelligible to the general public and to occupy a fitting position in the history of art."
(Cézanne 1976, pp. 313–14.)

From Aix-en-Provence Cézanne writes once again to Bernard about the Louvre and nature: "The Louvre is the book in which we learn to read. We must not, however, be satisfied with retaining the beautiful formulas of our illustrious predecessors. Let us go forth to study beautiful nature, let us try to free our minds from them, let us strive to express ourselves according to our personal temperament. Time and reflection, moreover, modify little by little our vision, and at last comprehension comes to us."
(Cézanne 1976, p. 315.)

1906

September 13 To his son, Cézanne writes about "Emilio Bernardinos" (presumably Émile Bernard): "in his drawings he produces nothing but old-fashioned rubbish which smacks of his artistic dreams, based not on the emotional experience of nature, but on what he has been able to see in the museums, and more still on a philosophic attitude of mind which comes from his excessive knowledge of the masters he admires."
(Cézanne 1976, p. 328.)

September 26 To his son, Cézanne writes again about learning from nature compared to learning from the art of the past: "[Émile Bernard] . . . is an intellectual constipated by recollections of museums, but who does not look enough at nature, and that is the great thing, to make himself free from the school and indeed from all schools.—So that Pissarro was not mistaken, though he went a little too far, when he said that all the necropoles of art should be burned down."
(Cézanne 1976, p. 332.)

October 23 Death of Cézanne.

Duret's *Histoire des peintres impressionnistes* published in Paris.

In 1906 and 1907 Étienne Moreau-Nélaton donates to the Louvre about 100 paintings and about 60 drawings of the nineteenth century. Among the artists represented: Corot, Delacroix, Manet, Monet, Morisot, Pissarro, and Sisley.
(*Donateurs* 1989, p. 277.)

1907

February 25 A new presentation of Rembrandt's paintings is inaugurated at the Louvre.
(Archives du Louvre, P1, February 25, 1907.)

Exhibition of works by Chardin and Fragonard organized by the Galerie Georges Petit.

The *Catalogue of the Rodolphe Kann Collection: Pictures* published in Paris. Volume 1 lists the pictures of the seventeenth-century Flemish and Dutch Schools; volume 2, the fifteenth- and sixteenth-century Netherlandish and German Schools.

1908

October–December Monet is in Venice. On his way back to Giverny he stops in Genoa and Bordighera.

Jean Guiffrey's *Catalogue raisonné de l'oeuvre peint et dessiné de J.-B. Siméon Chardin: suivi de la liste des gravures executes d'après ses ouvrages* published in Paris.

Armand Dayot and Léandre Vaillat's *L'Oeuvre de J.-B.-S. Chardin et de J.-H. Fragonard* published in Paris.

Jean Martin and Ch. Masson's *Catalogue raisonné de l'oeuvre peint et dessiné de Jean-Baptiste Greuze: suivi de la liste des gravures executes d'après des ouvrages* published in Paris.

Paul Lafond's *Murillo* published in Paris.

1909

Edmond Pilon's *Chardin* published in Paris.

1910

April 18–30 *D'après les maîtres,* exhibition at the Galerie Bernheim-Jeune, Paris, presented artists' copies after Titian, Rubens, and Veronese by such different artists as Delacroix, Manet, and Odilon Redon.
(Groom 1993, p. 243 n. 60.)

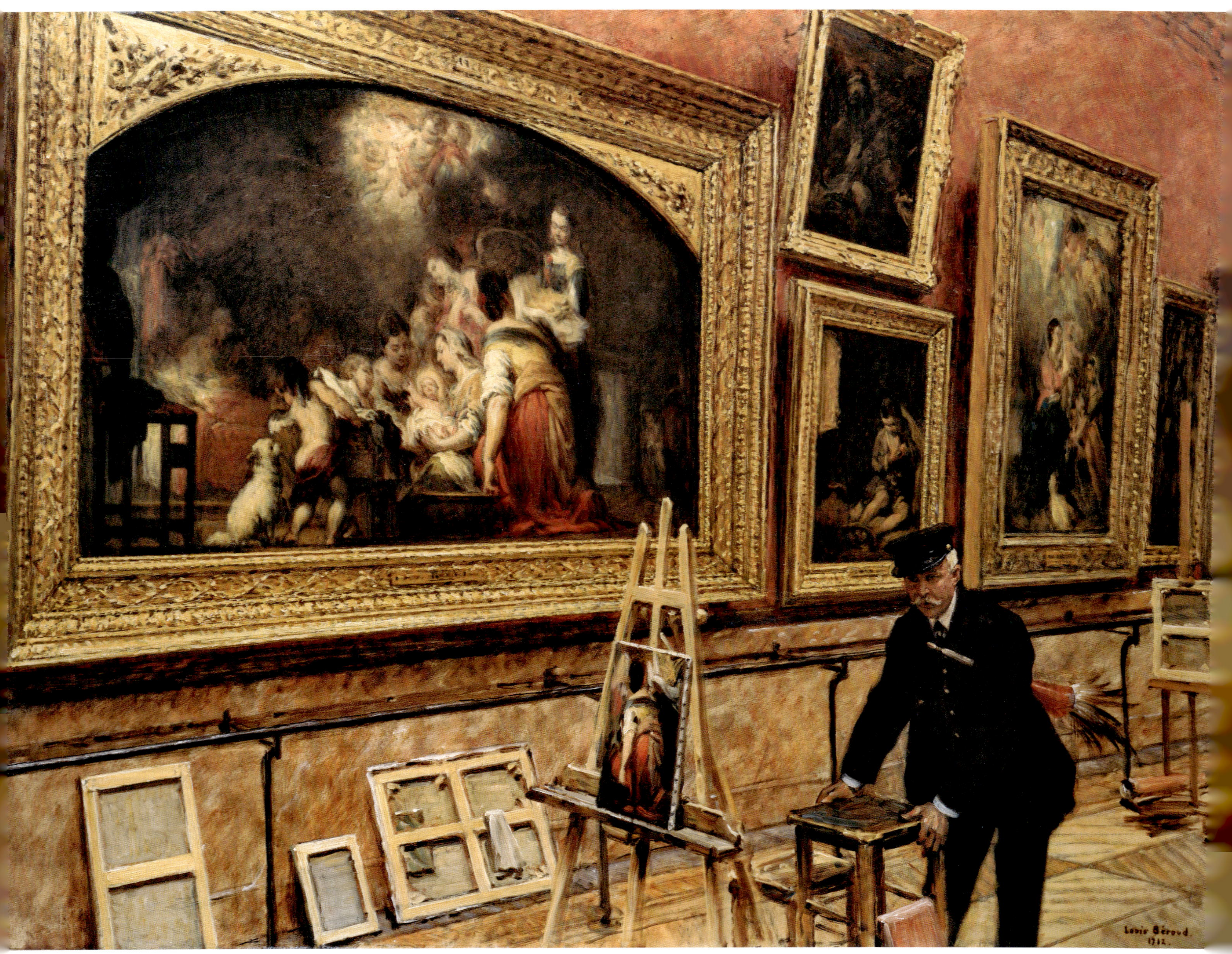
Louis Béroud.
1912.

Checklist of the Exhibition

1. Ludolf Backhuysen (1630–1708)
The "Koning Willem III" and Other Ships in the Sea-lanes off Texel, c. 1690
Oil on canvas, 22 × 28 in. (55.9 × 71.1 cm)
Richard Green Gallery

2. Frédéric Bazille (1841–1870)
The Beach at Sainte-Adresse, 1865
Oil on canvas, 23 × 55⅛ in. (58.4 × 140 cm)
High Museum of Art, Atlanta, Georgia; Gift of the Forward Arts Foundation in honor of Frances Floyd Cocke, 1980.62

3. Frédéric Bazille (1841–1870)
The Heron, 1867
Oil on canvas, 38⅜ × 30¾ in. (97.5 × 78 cm)
Musée Fabre, Montpellier Agglomération

4. Frédéric Bazille (1841–1870)
Flowers, 1868
Oil on canvas, 51⅛ × 38⅛ in. (130 × 97 cm)
Musée de Grenoble, France, Gift of the Teulon Family in 1940, Inv. MG 2911

5. Louis Beroud (1852–1930)
An Evening in the Louvre, 1912
Oil on canvas, 38 × 51½ in. (96.5 × 130.8 cm)
Collection of Rhoda and David T. Chase

6. Abraham Hendricksz van Beyeren (1620/21–1690)
Banquet Still Life, c. 1653–55
Oil on canvas, 42⅛ × 45½ in. (107 × 115.5 cm)
Seattle Art Museum, Gift of the Samuel H. Kress Foundation, 61.146
(Denver and Seattle only)

Cat. 5
Louis Beroud
An Evening in the Louvre, 1912

7. Cornelis Bisschop (1634–1674)
The Seamstress, 17th century
Oil on canvas, 20⅞ × 17¾ in. (53 × 45 cm)
Nasjonalmuseet for Kunst, Arkitektur og Design, Oslo, Norway, NG.M. 01391

8. François Boucher (1703–1770)
Seated Nude, 1749
Black, red, and white chalk on paper, 11¾ × 8¾ in. (29.8 × 22.2 cm)
The Berger Collection at the Denver Art Museum, TL-17498

9. François Boucher (1703–1770)
Vulcan Presenting Arms to Venus for Aeneas, 1756
Oil on canvas, 24 × 25 in. (61 × 63.5 cm)
Sterling and Francine Clark Art Institute, Williamstown, Massachusetts, 1983.29

10. Mary Cassatt (1844–1926)
Mrs. Duffee Seated on a Striped Sofa, Reading, 1876
Oil on panel, 13½ × 10½ in. (34.2 × 26.6 cm)
Museum of Fine Arts, Boston. Bequest of John T. Spaulding, 48.523

11. Mary Cassatt (1844–1926)
The Family, 1893
Oil on canvas, 32¼ × 26⅛ in. (81.9 × 66.3 cm)
Chrysler Museum of Art, Norfolk, Virginia, Gift of Walter P. Chrysler, Jr., 71.498

12. Paul Cézanne (1839–1906)
Boy Searching for Lice, after Murillo, c. 1882–85
Drawing on paper, 7⅝ × 4¾ in. (19.5 × 12 cm)
Nationalmuseum, Stockholm, NMH 112/2003

13. Paul Cézanne (1839–1906)
Mont Sainte-Victoire, 1886–87
Oil on canvas, 23½ × 28½ in. (59.6 × 72.3 cm)
The Phillips Collection, Washington, D.C., Acquired 1925
(Atlanta and Denver only)

14. Paul Cézanne (1839–1906)
Plaster Cast of a Putto, c. 1890
Pencil on paper, 19⅛ × 12¾ in. (48.7 × 32.4 cm)
Nationalmuseum, Stockholm, NMH 1/1992

15. Paul Cézanne (1839–1906)
The Plaster Cupid (recto) and *Study of Drapery* (verso), 1890–95
Pencil on laid paper, 19¼ × 12¾ in. (48.9 × 32.4 cm)
Brooklyn Museum, Frank L. Babbott Fund, 39.623a–b

16. Paul Cézanne (1839–1906)
Still Life with Statuette, 1894–95
Oil on canvas, 24¾ × 31⅞ in. (63 × 81 cm)
Nationalmuseum, Stockholm, NM 2545

17. Paul Cézanne (1839–1906)
Still Life with Apples and Oranges, c. 1895–1900
Oil on canvas, 28¾ × 36½ in. (73 × 92 cm)
Musée d'Orsay, Paris, France
(Denver and Seattle only)

18. Paul Cézanne (1839–1906)
The Plaster Cupid, 1900–1904
Graphite and watercolor on paper, 18½ × 8⅝ in. (47 × 22 cm)
The Morgan Library & Museum, New York, Thaw Collection
(Atlanta and Denver only)

19. Paul Cézanne (1839–1906)
Mont Sainte-Victoire, 1902–6
Oil on canvas, 25⅛ × 32⅛ in. (63.8 × 81.6 cm)
The Nelson-Atkins Museum of Art, Kansas City, Missouri, Purchase: Nelson Trust, 38-6
(Seattle only)

20. Jean-Siméon Chardin (1699–1779)
The Scullery Maid, 1738
Oil on canvas, 18½ × 15 in. (46.9 × 38.1 cm)
The Corcoran Gallery of Art, Washington, D.C., William A. Clark Collection, 26.39

21. Jean-Siméon Chardin (1699–1779)
Still Life with Dead Pheasant and Hunting Bag, 1760
Oil on canvas, 28⅜ × 22⅞ in. (72 × 58 cm)
Gemäldegalerie, Staatliche Museen zu Berlin, Berlin, Germany

22. Jean-Siméon Chardin (1699–1779)
Basket of Plums, c. 1765
Oil on canvas, 12¾ × 16½ in. (32.3 × 41.9 cm)
Chrysler Museum of Art, Norfolk, Virginia, Gift of Walter P. Chrysler, Jr., 71.506

23. Henri-Pierre Danloux (1753–1809)
Portrait of a Little Girl, 2nd half 18th century
Oil on canvas, 21¾ × 18⅛ in. (55.3 × 46 cm)
Musée Calvet, Avignon, Donation Marcel Puech 1986, inv. 23604

24. Edgar Degas (1834–1917)
Two Figures Standing on a Flight of Steps, after Raphael, c. 1853–54
Graphite on fine-textured white paper, 9⅛ × 5⅞ in. (23.2 × 14.9 cm)
Ashmolean Museum, University of Oxford, England, WA1954.70.36
(Denver and Seattle only)

25. Edgar Degas (1834–1917)
Recto: *Studies of Legs and Feet and of a Figure,* c. 1854
Red chalk and pencil, 8¼ × 11½ in. (21 × 29.3 cm)
Verso: *Studies of Nude Man, a Horse, and a Knee,* c. 1854
Pencil, 11½ × 8¼ in. (29.3 × 21 cm)
Private collection, San Francisco

26. Edgar Degas (1834–1917)
Study of One of the Thieves in Mantegna's "Crucifixion," c. 1855
Pencil on white paper, 12¼ × 5¼ in. (31 × 13.5 cm)
Private collection, San Francisco

27. Edgar Degas (1834–1917)
Head of the Virgin after Solario's "Virgin of the Green Cushion" (Louvre), c. 1857
Graphite on paper, 7¾ × 6½ in. (19.7 × 16.5 cm)
Private collection, San Francisco

28. Edgar Degas (1834–1917)
Self-Portrait in the Style of Filippino Lippi, c. 1858
Graphite on paper, 6¾ × 5⅛ in. (17.1 × 13 cm)
Private collection, San Francisco

29. Edgar Degas (1834–1917)
Studies after Two Italian Madonnas, c. 1859–60
Graphite and red crayon on paper, 10¼ × 13⅜ in. (26.1 × 34 cm)
Fitzwilliam Museum, Cambridge

30. Edgar Degas (1834–1917)
Portrait of a Young Woman, after a 16th-century Florentine drawing, c. 1858–59
Oil on canvas, 25½ × 17⅞ in. (64.7 × 45.4 cm)
National Gallery of Canada, Ottawa
(Denver only)

31. Edgar Degas (1834–1917)
The Daughter of Jephthah, 1859–60
Oil on canvas, 77 × 117½ in. (195.5 × 298.4 cm)
Smith College Museum of Art, Northampton, Massachusetts, Purchased with the Drayton Hillyer Fund, SC 1933:9-1
(Atlanta only)

32. Edgar Degas (1834–1917)
Copy after "The Finding of Moses" by Veronese, late 1860s
Oil on canvas, 12¼ × 6⅞ in. (31.2 × 17.3 cm)
Fitzwilliam Museum, Cambridge

33. Edgar Degas (1834–1917)
The Calvary, copy after Mantegna, 1861
Oil on canvas, 27⅛ × 36⅜ in. (69 × 92.5 cm)
Musée des Beaux-Arts, Tours

34. Edgar Degas (1834–1917)
Infanta Margarita, Copy after Velázquez, 1861–62
Etching and drypoint, 1st state, 5¼ × 4¼ in. (13.2 × 10.8 cm)
Bibliothèque nationale de France, Département des Estampes, Paris
(Denver only)

35. Edgar Degas (1834–1917)
Visit to a Museum, c. 1879–90
Oil on canvas, 36⅛ × 26¾ in. (91.8 × 68 cm)
Museum of Fine Arts, Boston. Gift of Mr. and Mrs. John McAndrew, 69.49

36. After François Du Quesnoy (1597–1643)
Putto
Plaster, 17¾ × 7 × 7½ in. (45 × 18 × 19 cm)
Nationalmuseum, Stockholm, NMSkAv 566

37. Jean-Honoré Fragonard (1732–1806)
Boy with a Peep Show, c. 1780
Oil on canvas, 15½ × 12½ in. (39.4 × 31.8 cm)
Portland Art Museum, Portland, Oregon. Museum Purchase: From the Bowles Estate, with funds from Ella M. Hirsch, Helen Thurston Ayer, Caroline Ladd Pratt, and Museum Auction Funds

38. Jean-Honoré Fragonard (1732–1806)
A Young Girl Reading, c. 1776
Oil on canvas, 32 × 25½ in. (81.2 × 64.7 cm)
National Gallery of Art, Washington, Gift of Mrs. Mellon Bruce in memory of her father, Andrew W. Mellon, 1961.16.1

39. Francisco de Goya (1746–1828)
Still Life with Golden Bream, 1808–12
Oil on canvas, 17⅝ × 24⅝ in. (44.8 × 62.5 cm)
The Museum of Fine Arts, Houston; Museum Purchase with funds provided by the Alice Pratt Brown Museum Fund and the Brown Foundation Accessions Endowment Fund
(Seattle only)

40. El Greco (1541–1614)
Lady in a Fur Wrap, 1577–80
Oil on canvas, 24⅝ × 19¼ in. (62.5 × 48.9 cm)
Glasgow City Council (Museums), The Stirling Maxwell Collection, Pollok House
(Denver and Seattle only)

41. Jean-Baptiste Greuze (1725–1805)
A Schoolboy Sleeping on His Book, 1755
Oil on canvas, 25⅝ × 21½ in. (65 × 54.5 cm)
Musée Fabre, Montpellier Agglomération

42. Frans Hals (1581/85–1666)
Fisher Boy, 1630–32
Oil on canvas, 29⅛ × 24 in. (74 × 61 cm)
Koninklijk Museum voor Schone Kunsten, Antwerp
(Denver only)

43. Frans Hals (1581/85–1666)
Portrait of a Young Woman, c. 1655–60
Oil on canvas, 22½ × 21 in. (57.2 × 53.3 cm)
Ferens Art Gallery, Hull City Museums and Art Galleries

44. Meindert Hobbema (1638–1709)
The Haarlem Lock, Amsterdam, c. 1663–65
Oil on canvas, 30⅜ × 38½ in. (77 × 98 cm)
The National Gallery, London, Miss Beatrice Mildmay Bequest, 1953, NG6138

45. Jean-Baptiste Huet (1745–1811)
Young Couple in a Landscape
Oil on canvas, 24⅝ × 30¾ in. (62.5 × 78 cm)
Nationalmuseum, Stockholm, NM 6673

46. Claude Lorrain (1604/5–1682)
The Rest on the Flight into Egypt, c. 1640
Oil on canvas, 30 × 36¼ in. (76.2 × 92.1 cm)
Joslyn Art Museum, Omaha, Nebraska (JAM1957.17)

47. Bernardino Luini (c. 1480–1532)
Madonna and Child with the Infant Saint John, c. 1515–20
Oil on canvas, transferred from wood, 44 × 34 in. (111.8 × 86.4 cm)
Jocelyn Kress and Jedediah H. Kress Turner

48. Édouard Manet (1832–1883)
The Little Cavaliers, c. 1859–60
Oil on canvas, 18 × 29¾ in. (45.7 × 75.5 cm)
Chrysler Museum of Art, Norfolk, Virginia, Gift of Walter P. Chrysler, Jr., 71.679

49. Édouard Manet (French, 1832–1883)
Les Petits Cavaliers (The Little Cavaliers), pl. 2 from the portfolio *Huit gravures à l'eau-forte par Manet (Eight Etchings by Manet)* (Paris: Cadart, 1862), after a painting attributed to Diego Rodríguez de Silva y Velázquez, 1860
Etching on chine collé, 9¾ × 15⅜ in. (24.7 × 39.1 cm) (image)
Fine Arts Museums of San Francisco, Bruno and Sadie Adriani Collection, 1957.94

50. Édouard Manet (1832–1883)
Study for the "Surprised Nymph," 1860–61
Oil on board, 14 × 18⅛ in. (35.5 × 46 cm)
Nasjonalmuseet for Kunst, Arkitektur og Design, Oslo, Norway, NG.M. 01182

51. Édouard Manet (1832–1883)
Fishing, 1861–63
Oil on canvas, transferred from the original canvas, 30¼ × 48½ in. (76.8 × 123.2 cm)
The Metropolitan Museum of Art, Purchase, Mr. and Mrs. Richard J. Bernhard Gift, 1957 (57.10)

52. Édouard Manet (1832–1883)
Infanta Margarita, after Diego Rodríguez de Silva y Velasquez, 1862
Etching and drypoint, 6¼ × 5¾ in. (16 × 14.6 cm) (image)
The Baltimore Museum of Art: The George A. Lucas Collection, purchased with funds from the State of Maryland, Laurence and Stella Bendann Fund, and contributions from individuals, foundations, and corporations throughout the Baltimore community, BMA 1996.48.5135

53. Édouard Manet (1832–1883)
Gypsy with a Cigarette, c. 1862
Oil on canvas, 36¼ × 28⅞ in. (92 × 73.5 cm)
Princeton University Art Museum. Bequest of Archibald S. Alexander, Class of 1928, y1979-55
(Seattle only)

54. Édouard Manet (1832–1883)
Victorine Meurent, c. 1862
Oil on canvas, 16⅞ × 17¼ in. (42.9 × 43.8 cm)
Museum of Fine Arts, Boston. Gift of Richard C. Paine in memory of his father, Robert Treat Paine 2nd, 46.846

55. Édouard Manet (1832–1883)
Le Saumon (The Salmon), c. 1864–65
Oil on canvas, 28¼ × 36⅛ in. (71.7 × 91.7 cm)
Shelburne Museum, Shelburne, Vermont
(Atlanta and Denver only)

56. Édouard Manet (1832–1883)
Portrait of Théodore Duret, 1868
Oil on canvas, 16⅞ × 13¾ in. (43 × 35 cm)
Petit Palais, Musée des Beaux-Arts de la Ville de Paris

57. Édouard Manet (1832–1883)
Marine in Holland, 1872
Oil on canvas, 19¾ × 23¾ in. (50.2 × 60.3 cm)
Philadelphia Museum of Art: Purchased with the W. P. Wilstach Fund, 1921

57a. Édouard Manet (1832–1883)
Portrait of Berthe Morisot (1841–95) Reclining, 1873
Oil on canvas, 10¼ × 13⅜ in. (26 × 34 cm)
Musée Marmottan Monet, Paris, France
(Atlanta and Denver only)

58. Édouard Manet (1832–1883)
Portrait of Isabelle Lemonnier, c. 1879
Oil on canvas, 36 × 28¾ in. (91.4 × 73 cm)
Dallas Museum of Art, Gift of Mr. and Mrs. Algur H. Meadows and the Meadows Foundation Incorporated

59. Claude Monet (1840–1926)
Still Life with Flowers and Fruit, 1869
Oil on canvas, 39⅜ × 31¾ in. (100 × 80.6 cm)
J. Paul Getty Museum, Los Angeles
(Denver and Seattle only)

60. Claude Monet (1840–1926)
Windmill and Boats near Zaandam, Holland, 1871
Oil on canvas, 18⅞ × 28⅞ in. (47.9 × 73.5 cm)
Ny Carlsberg Glyptotek, Copenhagen
(Atlanta and Denver only)

61. Claude Monet (1840–1926)
Windmills near Zaandam, 1871
Oil on canvas, 16 × 28 in. (40.6 × 72.4 cm)
The Walters Art Museum, Baltimore, 37.894

62. Claude Monet (1840–1926)
Autumn on the Seine, Argenteuil, 1873
Oil on canvas, 21⅜ × 28⅞ in. (54.2 × 73.3 cm)
High Museum of Art, Atlanta, Georgia; Purchase with funds from the Forward Arts Foundation, The Buisson Foundation, Eleanor McDonald Storza Estate, Frances Cheney Boggs Estate, Katherine John Murphy Foundation, and High Museum of Art Enhancement Fund, 2000.205

63. Claude Monet (1840–1926)
Summer, 1874
Oil on canvas, 22⅜ × 31½ in. (57 × 80 cm)
Nationalgalerie, Staatliche Museen zu Berlin, Berlin, Germany
(Denver and Seattle only)

64. Claude Monet (1840–1926)
The Zuiderkerk, Amsterdam (Looking up the Groenburgwal), c. 1874
Oil on canvas, 21⅜ × 25¾ in. (54.4 × 65.4 cm)
Philadelphia Museum of Art: Purchased with the W. P. Wilstach Fund, 1921

65. Jean-Baptiste Monnoyer (c. 1634–1699)
Vase of Flowers on a Marble Table
Oil on canvas, 45⅝ × 35⅜ in. (116 × 90 cm)
Musée de Grenoble, France, Inv. MG 188

66. Berthe Morisot (1841–1895)
The Calvary, 1860
Oil on canvas, 27½ × 27½ in. (69.8 × 69.8 cm)
Private collection

67. Berthe Morisot (1841–1895)
Venus Asking Vulcan for Arms (after the 1757 original by Boucher in the Louvre), 1884
Oil on canvas, 44⅞ × 54⅜ in. (114 × 138 cm)
Private collection

68. Berthe Morisot (1841–1895)
In the Garden at Maurecourt, c. 1884
Oil on canvas, 21¼ × 25⅝ in. (54 × 65 cm)
Toledo Museum of Art, Purchased with funds from the Libbey Endowment, Gift of Edward Drummond Libbey, 1930.9

69. After Bartolomé Esteban Murillo (1617/18–1682)
The Beggar Boy
Oil on canvas, 53½ × 38¼ in. (136 × 97 cm)
Nationalmuseum, Stockholm, NM 753

70. Aert van der Neer (1603–1677)
Skaters on a Frozen Canal by a Village
Oil on panel, 15⅞ × 26¼ in. (40.3 × 71.8 cm)
Dr. Hans Riegel Stiftung, Austria

71. Jean-Baptiste-Joseph Pater (1695–1736)
Country Party, 18th century
Oil on canvas, 25¾ × 32³⁄₁₆ in. (65.4 × 81.8 cm)
Fine Arts Museums of San Francisco, Gift of Brooke Postley, 59.36

72. Camille Pissarro (1830–1903)
The Maidservant, 1867
Oil on canvas, 35½ × 27¾ in. (90.1 × 70.4 cm)
Chrysler Museum of Art, Norfolk, Virginia, Gift of Walter P. Chrysler, Jr., 71.530

73. Camille Pissarro (1830–1903)
The Marly Road, c. 1870
Oil on canvas, 15 × 18⅛ in. (38.1 × 45.9 cm)
High Museum of Art, Atlanta, Georgia; Purchase with High Museum of Art Enhancement Fund, funds from the Livingston Foundation, Hambrick Bequest, Alfred Austell Thornton in memory of Leila Austell Thornton and Albert Edward Thornton, Sr., and Sarah Miller Venable and William Hoyt Venable, the Phoenix Society, and Mr. and Mrs. Jerome Dobson, 2001.1
(Denver and Seattle only)

74. Camille Pissarro (1830–1903)
Bouquet of Flowers, c. 1873
Oil on canvas, 21⅝ × 18¼ in. (54.9 × 46.3 cm)
High Museum of Art, Atlanta, Georgia; Gift of the Forward Arts Foundation in honor of its first president, Mrs. Robert W. Chambers, 74.231

75. Camille Pissarro (1830–1903)
The Little Country Maid, 1882
Oil on canvas, 25 × 20⅞ in. (63.5 × 53 cm)
Tate, London, Bequeathed by Lucien Pissarro, the artist's son, 1944

76. Camille Pissarro (1830–1903)
Morning, Sunlight Effect, Éragny, 1899
Oil on canvas, 26 × 32½ in. (66 × 81.7 cm)
The Israel Museum, Jerusalem, Bequest of Mrs. Neville Blond, O.B.E., London, through the British Friends of the Art Museums of Israel, B87.110

77. Raphael Santi (1483–1520)
Two Men Conversing on a Flight of Steps and *A Head Shouting,* c. 1509
Silverpoint heightened with white bodycolor, on a pale pink preparation, with much oxidation, 11 × 7⅞ in. (27.8 × 20 cm)
Ashmolean Museum, University of Oxford, England, WA1846.191
(Denver and Seattle only)

78. Pierre-Auguste Renoir (1841–1919)
Skaters in the Bois de Boulogne, 1868
Oil on canvas, 28⅜ × 35⅜ in. (72.1 × 89.9 cm)
From the Collection of William I. Koch, Palm Beach, Florida

79. Pierre-Auguste Renoir (1841–1919)
Still Life with Bouquet, 1871
Oil on canvas, 28⅞ × 23¼ in. (73.3 × 58.9 cm)
The Museum of Fine Arts, Houston; The Robert Lee Blaffer Memorial Collection, gift of Sarah Campbell Blaffer

80. Pierre-Auguste Renoir (1841–1919)
Confidences, c. 1873
Oil on canvas, 32 × 23¾ in. (81.2 × 60.3 cm)
Portland Museum of Art, Maine. The Joan Whitney Payson Collection at the Portland Museum of Art. Gift of Joan Whitney Payson, 1991, 1991.62

81. Pierre-Auguste Renoir (1841–1919)
Child with a Hoop, c. 1875
Oil on canvas, 24½ × 19¼ in. (62.3 × 48.9 cm)
The Baltimore Museum of Art: The Helen and Abram Eisenberg Collection, BMA 1976.55.8

82. Pierre-Auguste Renoir (1841–1919)
Still Life with Peaches and Grapes, 1881
Oil on canvas, 21¼ × 25⅝ in. (54 × 65.1 cm)
The Metropolitan Museum of Art, The Mr. and Mrs. Henry Ittleson Jr. Purchase Fund, 1956 (56.218)

83. Pierre-Auguste Renoir (1841–1919)
Studies of the Berard Children, 1881
Oil on canvas, 24⅝ × 32¼ in. (62.5 × 81.9 cm)
Sterling and Francine Clark Art Institute, Williamstown, Massachusetts, 1955.590

84. Pierre-Auguste Renoir (1841–1919)
The Wave, 1882
Oil on canvas, 21 × 25 in. (53.5 × 63.5 cm)
Collection of The Dixon Gallery and Gardens, Memphis, Tennessee; Museum Purchase from Cornelia Ritchie and Ritchie Trust No. 4 Provided through a Gift from the Robinson Family Fund (Denver and Seattle only)

85. Pierre-Auguste Renoir (1841–1919)
A Bather, c. 1885–90
Oil on canvas, 15½ × 11½ in. (39.4 × 29.2 cm)
The National Gallery, London, Presented by Sir Antony and Lady Hornby, 1961, NG6319

86. Pierre-Auguste Renoir (1841–1919)
A Woman Nursing a Child, c. 1893
Oil on canvas, 16¼ × 12¾ in. (41.2 × 32.5 cm)
National Gallery of Scotland (NG2230)

87. Pierre-Auguste Renoir (1841–1919)
Christine Lerolle Embroidering, c. 1895–98
Oil on canvas, 32⅛ × 25⅞ in. (81.5 × 65.7 cm)
Columbus Museum of Art, Ohio: Gift of Howard D. and Babette L. Sirak, the Donors to the Campaign for Enduring Excellence, and the Derby Fund, 1991.001.057

88. Pierre-Auguste Renoir (1841–1919)
The Artist's Son, Jean, Drawing, 1901
Oil on canvas, 17¾ × 21½ in. (45.1 × 54.5 cm)
Virginia Museum of Fine Arts, Richmond, Collection of Mr. and Mrs. Paul Mellon

89. Pierre-Auguste Renoir (1841–1919)
Mother and Child (Madame Thurneyssen and Her Daughter), 1910
Oil on canvas, 39⅜ × 31⅝ in. (100 × 80.3 cm)
By permission of Albright-Knox Art Gallery, General Purchase Funds, 1940

90. Pierre-Auguste Renoir (1841–1919)
Seated Bather, 1914
Oil on canvas, 32¹⁄₁₆ × 26⁹⁄₁₆ in. (81.4 × 67.5 cm)
Mr. and Mrs. Lewis Larned Coburn Endowment; through prior bequest of Annie Swan Coburn to the Mr. and Mrs. Lewis Larned Coburn Memorial Fund; through prior acquisition of the R. A. Waller Fund, 1945.27, The Art Institute of Chicago

91. Pierre-Auguste Renoir (1841–1919)
Nude on a Couch, 1915
Oil on canvas, 21⅜ × 25¾ in. (54.4 × 65.3 cm)
Tate, London, Bequeathed by Mrs. A. F. Kessler, 1983

92. Sir Peter Paul Rubens (1577–1640)
Susannah and the Elders, 1607
Oil on canvas, 37 × 26 in. (94 × 66 cm)
Galleria Borghese, Rome
(Denver only)

93. Follower of Sir Peter Paul Rubens (1577–1640)
Venus and Cupid Warming Themselves (Venus frigida), c. 1610–20
Oil on panel, 14 × 18⅜ in. (35.5 × 46.6 cm)
Dulwich Picture Gallery, London

94. Salomon van Ruysdael (1600/3–1670)
River Landscape, 1644
Oil on panel, 20½ × 33¼ in. (52 × 84.5 cm)
Statens Museum for Kunst, Copenhagen

95. Alfred Sisley (1839–1899)
View of Saint Mammès, 1880
Oil on canvas, 21¼ × 29⅛ in. (54 × 74 cm)
The Walters Art Museum, Baltimore, 37.355

96. Alfred Sisley (1839–1899)
The Pike, 1888
Oil on canvas, 16½ × 31½ in. (42 × 80 cm)
Wadsworth Atheneum Museum of Art, Hartford, Connecticut: Gift in honor of Helene and Mark Eisner, by exchange

97. Titian (c. 1485–1576) and Workshop
Danaë, after 1554
47½ × 66¾ in. (120.6 × 169.5 cm)
Extended loan from the Barker Welfare Foundation, Glen Head, New York, 9.1973, The Art Institute of Chicago

98. Anne Vallayer-Coster (1744–1818)
Vase of Flowers, 1775
Oil on canvas, 18⅛ × 12 in. (46 × 30.4 cm)
Fitzwilliam Museum, Cambridge

99. Diego Rodríguez de Silva y Velázquez (1599–1660) and Workshop
Infanta Margarita Teresa, c. 1664
Oil on canvas, 47⅜ × 37¼ in. (120.5 × 94.5 cm)
Kunsthistorisches Museum, Vienna, Inv. No. GG 3531

100. School of Diego Rodríguez de Silva y Velázquez (1599–1660)
Meeting of Thirteen People
Oil on canvas, 18⅝ × 30⅝ in. (47.2 × 77.9 cm)
Musée du Louvre, Paris, France

101. Jean-Antoine Watteau (1684–1721)
The Robber of the Sparrow's Nest, c. 1712
Oil on paper laid on canvas laid on panel, 8⅝ × 7¼ in. (22.6 × 18.5 cm)
National Gallery of Scotland (NG 370)

Bibliography

Alvarez Lopera and Naverrete Martinez 1990
Alvarez Lopera, J., and E. Naverrete Martinez. "Mena a la sombra de Cano." In *Pedro de Mena y su epoca,* pp. 35–52. Malaga, 1990.

Amsterdam 1986
Monet in Holland. Exh. cat. Amsterdam: Rijksmuseum Vincent van Gogh; Zwolle: Waanders, 1986.

Anderson 1998
Anderson, J. A. "Pedro de Mena, Seventeenth-Century Spanish Sculptor." *Studies in Art and Religious Interpretation,* vol. 22. Lewiston, N.Y.: Edwin Mellen Press, 1998.

Ann Arbor 1980
The Crisis of Impressionism, 1878–1882. Exh. cat. by Joel Isaacson. Ann Arbor: University of Michigan Museum of Art, 1980.

Anon. 1883
"Le Modernisme de Frans Hals." *L'Art Moderne* 38 (September 23, 1883): 301–3.

Armstrong 1991
Armstrong, Carol M. *Odd Man Out: Readings of the Work and Reputation of Edgar Degas*. Chicago: University of Chicago Press, 1991.

Artiste 1893
L'Artiste 6 (August 1893): 99–126.

Astruc 1866
Astruc, Zacharie. "Trésors d'art de Paris." *L'Étendard,* July 23, 1866.

Bailey 1997
Bailey, Colin B. "Portrait of the Artist as a Portrait Painter." In *Renoir's Portraits: Impressions of an Age*. Exh. cat. by Bailey and Linda Nochlin, pp. 1–51. New Haven: Yale University Press, in association with National Gallery of Canada, 1997.

Bailey 1999
Bailey, Colin B. "'Toute seule elle peur remplir et satisfaire l'attention': The Early Appreciation and Marketing of Watteau's Drawings, with an Introduction to the Collecting of Modern French

Drawings during the Reign of Louis XV." In *Watteau and His World: French Drawing from 1700 to 1750*. Exh. cat. by Alan Wintermute, pp. 68–92. New York: Merrell Holberton Publishers, 1999.

Bakker 1986
Bakker, Boudewijn. "Monet als Toerist." In *Monet in Holland*, exh. cat., pp. 15–35. Amsterdam: Rijksmuseum Vincent van Gogh; Zwolle: Waanders, 1986.

Baltimore 2000
Manet: The Still-Life Paintings. Exh. cat. by George Mauner. Paris: Musée d'Orsay; Baltimore: Walters Art Gallery, in association with Harry N. Abrams, 2000.

Barter 1998
Barter, Judith. "Mary Cassatt: Themes, Sources, and the Modern Woman." In *Mary Cassatt: Modern Woman*. Exh. cat. by Barter, pp. 45–107. Chicago: Art Institute of Chicago, 1998.

Baticle and Marinas 1981
Baticle, J., and C. Marinas. *La Galerie espagnole de Louis-Philippe au Louvre, 1838–1848*. Notes et Documents des Musées de France, no. 4. Paris: Éditions de la Réunion des Musées Nationaux, 1981.

Baudelaire 1964
Baudelaire, Charles. "The Painter of Modern Life." In *The Painter of Modern Life and Other Essays*. Translated and edited by Jonathan Mayne, pp. 1–40. London: Phaidon Press, 1964.

Baudelaire 1965
Baudelaire, Charles. *Art in Paris, 1845–1862: Reviews of Salons and Other Exhibitions*. Translated and edited by Jonathan Mayne. London: Phaidon, 1965.

Baudot 1949
Baudot, Jeanne. *Renoir, ses amis, ses modèles*. Paris: Éditions Littéraires de France, 1949.

Baxandall 1985
Baxandall, Michael. *Patterns of Intention: On the Historical Explanation of Pictures*. New Haven: Yale University Press, 1985.

Béguin and Constans 1969
Béguin, Sylvie, and Claire Constans. "Hommage à Louis La Caze (1798–1869)." *La Revue du Louvre et des Musées de France* 19, no. 2 (1969): 115–32.

Bernard 1925
Bernard, Émile. *Souvenirs sur Paul Cézanne et lettres*. Paris, 1925.

Berson 1996
Berson, Ruth, ed. *The New Painting: Impressionism, 1874–1886; Documentation*. 2 vols. San Francisco: Fine Arts Museums of San Francisco, 1996.

Bilbao 2002
Mujeres impresionistas: La otra mirada. Exh. cat. by Xavier Bray et al. Bilbao: Museo de Bellas Artes, 2002.

Blanc 1858
Blanc, Charles. *Le Trésor de la curiosité tiré des catalogues de vente de Tableaux, Dessins, Estampes, Livres, Marbres, Bronzes, Ivoires, Terres Cuites, Vitraux, Médailles, Armes, Porcelaines, Meubles, Emaux, Laques et autres Objets d'Art*. Sale cat. 2 vols. Paris: Vve Jules Renouard, 1858.

Blanc 1861
Blanc, Charles. *Histoire des peintres de toutes les écoles. École hollandaise*. 2 vols. Paris: Librairie Renouard, 1861.

Blanc, "Chardin" 1862
Blanc, Charles. "Chardin." In *Histoire des peintres de toutes les écoles. École française*, vol. 2. Paris: Vve Jules Renouard, 1862.

Blanc, "Le Nain" 1862
Blanc, Charles. "Les Frères Le Nain." In *Histoire des peintres de toutes les écoles. École française*, vol. 1. Paris: Vve Jules Renouard, 1862.

Blanc 1863
Blanc, Charles. Introduction to *Histoire des peintres de toutes les écoles. École hollandaise*, vol. 1. Paris: Vve Jules Renouard, 1862.

Blanc 1865
Blanc, Charles. *Histoire des peintres de toutes les écoles. École française*. Vol. 2. Paris: Vve Jules Renouard, 1865.

Blanc 1866
Blanc, Charles. "Salon de 1866." *Gazette des Beaux-Arts* 1 (June 1866): 497–520.

Blanc 1869
Blanc, Charles. "La Galerie Delessert." *Gazette des Beaux-Arts* 11 (February 1869): 105–27; (March 1869): 201–22.

Blanc et al. 1869
Blanc, Charles, W. Bürger, Paul Mantz, Louis Viardot, and Paul Lefort. *Histoire des peintres de toutes les écoles. École espagnole*. Paris: Vve Jules Renouard, 1869.

Blum 1946
Blum, André. *Vermeer et Thoré*. Geneva: Éditions du Mont-Blanc, 1946.

Bodelsen 1968
Bodelson, Merete. "Early Impressionist Sales, 1874–94, in the Light of Some Unpublished 'Procès-Verbaux.'" *Burlington Magazine* 110 (June 1968): 330–49.

Boggs 1962
Boggs, Jean S. *Portraits by Degas*. Berkeley and Los Angeles: University of California Press, 1962.

Boggs 1994
Boggs, Jean S. "Degas as a Portraitist." In *Degas Portraits*. Exh. cat. edited by Felix Baumann and Marianne Karabelnik, pp. 16–85. London: Merrell Holberton Publishers, 1994.

Boime 1964
Boime, Albert. "Le Musée des copies." *Gazette des Beaux-Arts* 64 (October 1964): 237–47.

Boime 1971
Boime, Albert. *The Academy and French Painting in the Nineteenth Century*. London: Phaidon Press, 1971.

Boime 1976
Boime, Albert. "Entrepreneurial Patronage in Nineteenth-Century France." In *Enterprise and Entrepreneurs in Nineteenth- and Twentieth-Century France*, edited by Edward C. Carter II, Robert Forster, and Joseph N. Moody, pp. 137–207. Baltimore: Johns Hopkins University Press, 1976.

Boone 1995
Boone, M. Elizabeth. "Bullfights and Balconies: Flirtation and Majismo in Mary Cassatt's Spanish Paintings of 1872–73." *American Art* 9 (Spring 1995): 54–71.

Boston 1962
Barbizon Revisited. Exh. cat. by Robert L. Herbert. Boston: Museum of Fine Arts, 1962.

Boston 1984
Edgar Degas: The Painter as Printmaker. Exh. cat. by Sue Welsh Reed and Barbara Stern Shapiro. Boston: Museum of Fine Arts, 1984.

Brame and Reff 1984
Brame, Philippe, and Theodore Reff. *Degas et son oeuvre: A Supplement*. New York: Garland, 1984.

Brejon de Lavergnée, Foucart, and Reynaud 1979
Brejon de Lavergnée, Arnauld, Jacques Foucart, and Nicole Reynaud. *Catalogue sommaire illustré des peintures du musée du Louvre*. Vol. 1, *Écoles flamande et hollandaise*. Paris: Éditions de la Réunion des Musées Nationaux, 1979.

Bréon 1988
Bréon, Emmanuel. *Claude Marie, Édouard et Guillaume Dubufe, portraits d'un siècle d'élégance parisienne*. Paris: Action Artistique de la Ville de Paris, 1988.

Brettell 1990
Brettell, Richard R. *Pissarro and Pontoise: The Painter in a Landscape*. New Haven: Yale University Press, 1990.

Broude 1991
Broude, Norma. *Impressionism: A Feminist Reading*. New York: Rizzoli, 1991.

Brown 1994
Brown, Marilyn R. *Degas and the Business of Art: A Cotton Office in New Orleans*. University Park: Pennsylvania State University Press, 1994.

Brown 2002
Brown, Marilyn R., ed. *Picturing Children: Constructions of Childhood between Rousseau and Freud*. Aldershot: Ashgate, 2002.

Bürger 1857
Bürger, W. *Trésors d'art exposés à Manchester en 1857 et provenant des collections royales, des collections publiques et des collections particulières de Grande Bretagne*. Paris: J. Renouard, 1857. Republished in 1860 and 1865 as *Trésors d'art en Angleterre*. Brussels: Claassen.

Bürger 1858
Bürger, W. *Musées de la Hollande. Amsterdam et La Haye. Études sur l'école hollandaise*. Paris: Vve J. Renouard, 1858. Also published in Brussels: Claassen.

Bürger, *Études* 1860
Bürger, W. *Études sur les peintres hollandais et flamands. Galerie Suermondt à Aix-la-Chapelle, avec le catalogue de la collection par le Dr. Waagen*. Translated by W. B. Brussels: Librairie de F. Claassen, 1860.

Bürger, "Exposition" 1860
Bürger, W. "Exposition de tableaux de l'école française tirés de collections d'amateurs. Deuxième et dernier article." *Gazette des Beaux-Arts* 7 (September 15, 1860): 333–58.

Bürger, *Musées* 1860
Bürger, W. *Musées de la Hollande II. Musée van der Hoop, à Amsterdam et musée de Rotterdam*. Paris: Vve J. Renouard, 1860.

Bürger, "Petit Guide" 1860
Bürger, W. "Petit Guide des artistes en voyage. 1—Hollande." *Annuaire des Artistes et des Amateurs* 1 (1860): 247–64.

Bürger, *Trésors* 1860
Bürger, W. *Trésors d'art en Angleterre*. Brussels: Claassen, 1860.

Bürger 1861
Bürger, W. "Salon de 1861. De l'avenir de l'art." *Revue Germanique* 15 (1861): 248–60.

Bürger 1862
Bürger, W. "Nouvelles Tendances de l'art." *Revue Germanique* 19 (1862): 60–80.

Bürger 1864
Bürger, W. "Galerie de M.M. Pereire." *Gazette des Beaux-Arts* 16 (1864): 193–213, 297–317.

Bürger 1866
Bürger, W. "Van der Meer de Delft." *Gazette des Beaux-Arts* 21 (1866): 197–330, 458–70, 542–75.

Bürger 1867
Bürger, W. "Les Collections particulières." In *Paris Guide part les principaux écrivains et artistes de la France,* vol. 1, pp. 536–51. 2 vols. Paris: Librairie Internationale, 1867.

Bürger 1868
Bürger, W. "Frans Hals." *Gazette des Beaux-Arts* 4 (1868): 219–30, 431–48.

Bürger 1869
Bürger, W. "Nouvelles Études sur la galerie Suermondt à Aix-la-Chapelle." *Gazette des Beaux-Arts,* 2nd per., 1 (January 1, 1869): 5–37.

Burty 1860
Burty, Philippe. *Tableaux de l'école française principalement du XVIIIe siècle tirés de collections d'amateurs et exposés au profit de la caisse de secours des artistes peintres, sculpteurs, architectes et dessinateurs*. 2nd ed. Paris, 1860.

Burty 1867
Burty, Philippe. "Fine Art: The Exhibition of the 'Intransigeants.'" *Academy* 9 (15 April 1876): 363–64.

Cézanne 1937
Cézanne, Paul. *Paul Cézanne Correspondance*. Edited by John Rewald. Paris: Grasset, 1937.

Cézanne 1941
Cézanne, Paul. *Paul Cézanne Letters*. Translated by Marguerite Kay. Edited by John Rewald. London: Bruno Cassirer, 1941.

Cézanne 1976
Cézanne, Paul. *Paul Cézanne Letters*. Translated by Marguerite Kay. Edited by John Rewald. New York: Hacker Art Books, 1976.

Champfleury 1850
Champfleury. *Essai sur la vie et l'oeuvre des Lenain, peintres laonnois*. Laon: Fleury et Chevergny, 1850.

Champfleury 1860
Champfleury. "Nouvelles Recherches sur la vie et l'oeuvre des frères Le Nain," pt. 1. *Gazette des Beaux-Arts* 8 (November 1, 1860): 173–85.

Chaumelin 1867
[Chaumelin, Marius]. "Bürger, (Willem)." In Pierre Larousse, *Grand Dictionnaire universel du XIXè siècle,* vol. 2, pp. 1422–23. Paris: Librairie Classique Larousse et Boyer, 1867.

Chaumelin 1868
Chaumelin, Marius. "Salon de 1868: V." *La Presse,* June 29, 1868.

Chennevières 1879
Chennevières, Philippe de. "Les Dessins des maîtres anciens exposés à l'École des Beaux-Arts." *Gazette des Beaux-Arts* 19 (September 1879): 185–211.

Chennevières 1888–89
Chennevières, Henry de. "Chardin au musée du Louvre." *Gazette des Beaux-Arts,* 2nd per., 38 (July 1888): 54–61; 3rd per., 1 (February 1889): 121–30.

Chicago 1995
Claude Monet, 1840–1926. Exh. cat. by Charles F. Stuckey. Chicago: Art Institute of Chicago, 1995.

Chicago 1998
Mary Cassatt: Modern Woman. Exh. cat. by Judith A. Barter et al. Chicago: Art Institute of Chicago, 1998.

Chu 1974
Chu, Petra ten-Doesschate. *French Realism and the Dutch Masters: The Influence of Dutch Seventeenth-Century Painting on the Development of French Painting between 1830 and 1870*. Utrecht: Haentjens Dekker & Gumbert, 1974.

Chu 1987
Chu, Petra ten-Doesschate. "Nineteenth-Century Visitors to the Frans Hals Museum." In *The Documented Image,* edited by Gabriel P. Weisberg and Laurinda S. Dixon, pp. 111–44. Syracuse, N.Y.: Syracuse University Press, 1987.

Cincinnati 1992
Cavaliers and Cardinals: Nineteenth-Century French Anecdotal Paintings. Exh. cat. by Eric M. Zafran. Cincinnati: Taft Museum, 1992.

Clairet, Montalant, and Rouart 1997
Clairet, Alain, Delphine Montalant, and Yves Rouart. *Berthe Morisot, 1841–1895: Catalogue raisonné de l'oeuvre peint*. Montolivet: Collection le Catalogue, 1997.

Claretie 1867
Claretie, Jules. "Courrier de Paris." *L'Indépendance Belge,* June 15, 1867.

Clark 1984
Clark, T. J. *The Painting of Modern Life: Paris in the Art of Manet and His Contemporaries*. New York: Alfred A. Knopf, 1984.

Clarke 2003
Clarke, Michael. "Monet and Tradition, or How the Past Became the Future." In *Monet: The Seine and the Sea, 1878–1883*. Exh. cat. by Clarke and Richard Thomson, pp. 37–49. Edinburgh: National Galleries of Scotland, 2003.

Clement, Houzé, and Erbolato Ramsey 2000
Clement, Russell T., Annick Houzé, and Christiane Erbolato-Ramsey. *The Women Impressionists: A Sourcebook*. Westport, Conn.: Greenwood Press, 2000.

Cleveland 1979
Chardin and the Still-Life Tradition in France. Exh. cat. by Gabriel P. Weisberg with William S. Talbot. Cleveland: Cleveland Museum of Art, 1979.

Collins 1998
Collins, John. "The Identity of Bastien Lepage's 'Girl with a Sunshade' at the Fitzwilliam Museum, Cambridge." *Burlington Magazine* 140 (May 1998): 323–25.

Collins 2004
Collins, John. *Masterworks of Nineteenth-Century French Realism from the National Gallery of Canada*. Ottawa: National Gallery of Canada, 2004.

Collins 2005
Collins, John. "*Christine Lerolle Embroidering*: Between Genre Painting and Portraiture." In *Renoir's Women*. Exh. cat. by Ann Dumas and Collins, pp. 87–111. Columbus: Columbus Museum of Art, in association with Merrell Publishers, 2005.

Courthion and Cailler 1960
Courthion, Pierre, and Pierre Cailler, eds. *Portrait of Manet by Himself and His Contemporaries*. Translated by Michael Ross. London: Cassell, 1960. First published in two volumes as *Manet raconté par lui-même et par ses amis*. Geneva, 1953.

Cuzin 1993
Cuzin, Jean-Pierre. "Au Louvre, d'après les maîtres." In *Copier/créer: De Turner à Picasso; 300 oeuvres inspirées par les maîtres du Louvre*. Exh. cat., pp. 26–39. Paris: Réunion des Musées Nationaux, 1993.

Degas 1945
Degas, Edgar. *Lettres de Degas*. Edited by Marcel Guérin. Paris: Grasset, 1945.

Degas 1947
Degas, Edgar. *Degas Letters*. Translated by Marguerite Kay. Edited by Marcel Guérin. Oxford: Bruno Cassirer, 1947.

Delteil 1919
Delteil, Loys. *Le Peintre-graveur illustré*. Vol. 9, *Degas*. Paris: Delteil, 1919.

Demény 1874
Demény, Paul. "St. Francois." *Le XIXe Siècle,* August 21, 1874.

Demetz 1963
Demetz, Peter. "Defenses of Dutch Painting and the Theory of Realism." *Comparative Literature* 15, no. 2 (Spring 1963): 97–115.

Denis 1913
Denis, Maurice. *Théories, 1890–1910: Du symbolisme et de Gauguin vers un nouvel ordre classique,* 3rd ed. Paris: Bibliothèque de l'"Occident," 1913.

DeWitt 2003
DeWitt, Lloyd. "Manet and the Dutch Marine Tradition." In *Manet and the Sea*. Exh. cat. by Juliet Wilson-Bareau and David Degener, pp. 1–15. Philadelphia: Philadelphia Museum of Art, 2003.

Distel 1989
Distel, Anne. *Les Collectionneurs des impressionnistes: Amateurs et marchands*. Düdingen, 1989.

Distel 1990
Distel, Anne. *Impressionism: The First Collectors*. New York: Harry N. Abrams, 1990.

Donateurs 1989
Les Donateurs du Louvre. Paris: Éditions des Musées Nationaux, 1989.

Dumas 1988
Dumas, Ann. *Portrait of Mlle. E. F. with Regard to the Ballet Le Source*. Brooklyn: Brooklyn Museum of Art, 1988.

Duranty 1986
Duranty, Edmond. *La Nouvelle Peinture: à propos du groupe d'artistes qui expose dans les Galeries Durand-Ruel*. Translated in *The New Painting: Impressionism, 1874–1886*. Exh. cat. edited by Charles S. Moffett, pp. 37–49. San Francisco: Fine Arts Museums of San Francisco, 1986.

Duret 1902
Duret, Théodore. *Histoire d'Édouard Manet et de son oeuvre*. Paris: H. Floury, 1902.

Duro 1985
Duro, Paul. "Le Musée des Copies de Charles Blanc à l'aube de la IIIe République. Catalogue." *Bulletin de la Société de l'Histoire de l'Art Francais,* année 1985, pp. 283–312.

Duro 1987
Duro, Paul. "'Un Livre ouvert à l'instruction': Study Museums in Paris in the Nineteenth Century." *Oxford Art Journal* 10, no. 1 (1987): 44–58.

Edinburgh 1990
Cézanne and Poussin: The Classical Vision of Landscape. Exh. cat. by Richard Verdi. Edinburgh: National Galleries of Scotland, 1990.

Eisler 1960
Eisler, Colin. "A Chardin in the Grand Manner." *Metropolitan Museum of Art Bulletin,* n.s., 18, no. 6 (February 1960): 202–12.

Félibien 1705
Félibien, André. *Conférences de l'Académie royale de peinture et de sculpture*. London: David Mortier, 1705.

Fevre 1949
Fevre, Jeanne. *Mon Oncle Degas*. Geneva: Pierre Cailler, 1949.

Flescher 1978
Flescher, Sharon. *Zacharie Astruc: Critic, Artist and Japoniste*. New York: Garland, 1978.

Ford 1966
Ford, Richard. *A Handbood for Travellers in Spain and Readers at Home*. 1847. Edited by Ian Robertson. London: Centaur Press, 1966.

Franits 1997
Franits, Wayne, ed. *Looking at Seventeenth-Century Dutch Art: Realism Reconsidered*. Cambridge: Cambridge University Press, 1997.

Fried 1969
Fried, Michael. "Manet's Sources: Aspects of His Art, 1859–1865." *Artforum* 7 (March 1969): 28–82.

Fried 1996
Fried, Michael. *Manet's Modernism, or, The Face of Painting in the 1860s*. Chicago: University of Chicago Press, 1996.

Fromentin 1910
Fromentin, Eugène. *Les Maîtres d'autrefois*. Paris: Plon 1876. New edition, Paris: Plon, 1910.

Fromentin 1963
Fromentin, Eugène. *The Old Masters of Belgium and Holland*. Translated by Mary C. Robbins. Introduction by Meyer Schapiro. New York: Schocken Books, 1963.

Galassi 1991
Galassi, Peter. *Corot in Italy: Open-Air Painting and the Classical-Landscape Tradition*. New Haven: Yale University Press, 1991.

Gasquet 1926
Gasquet, Joachim. *Cézanne*. 2nd ed. Paris: Bernheim-Jeune, 1926.

Gautier 1856
Gautier, Théophile. *Catalogue de la precieuse réunion de tableaux de l'école française provenant du cabinet de M. Barroilhet*. Sale cat. Paris: Hôtel Drouot, March 10, 1856.

Gautier 1860
Gautier, Théophile. "Exposition du boulevard des Italiens." *Le Moniteur Universel,* no. 320 (November 16, 1860).

Gautier 1890
Gautier, Théophile. *Oeuvres de Théophile Gautier. Poésies*. 3 vols. Paris, 1890.

Gautier 1929
Gautier, Théophile. "À Zurbaran." In *España*, edited by René Jasinski, pp. 232–34. Paris: Vuibert, 1929.

Gille 1874
Gille, Philippe. *Le Figaro*, January 19, 1874.

Van Gogh 1958
van Gogh, Vincent. *The Complete Letters of Vincent van Gogh*. 3 vols. London: Thames and Hudson, 1958.

Goncourt 1873
Goncourt, Edmond de, and Jules de Goncourt. *L'Art du dix-huitième siècle*. Paris: Rapilly, 1873.

Goncourt 1882
Goncourt, Edmond de, and Jules de Goncourt. *L'Art du dix-huitième siècle*. 3rd ed. 2 vols. Paris: A. Quantin, 1882.

Goncourt 1948
Goncourt, Edmond de, and Jules de Goncourt. *French Eighteenth-Century Painters*. Translated and edited by Robin Ironside. Oxford: Phaidon, 1948.

Goncourt 1971
Goncourt, Edmond de, and Jules de Goncourt. *Paris and the Arts, 1851–1896: From the Goncourt Journal*. Translated and edited by George J. Becker and Edith Philips. Ithaca, N.Y.: Cornell University Press, 1971.

Goncourt 1981
Goncourt, Edmond de, and Jules de Goncourt. *French Eighteenth-Century Painters*. Ithaca, N.Y.: Cornell University Press, 1981. First published as *Fragonard, étude contenant quatre dessins gravés à l'eau-forte*. Paris: E. Dentu, 1865.

Goncourt 1989
Goncourt, Edmond de, and Jules de Goncourt. *Journal: Mémoires de la vie littéraire*. Paris: Éditions Robert Laffont, 1989.

Grate 1959
Grate, Pontus. *Deux Critiques d'art de l'époque romantique*. Stockholm: Almqvist & Wiksell, 1959.

Groom 1993
Groom, Gloria. *Édouard Vuillard, Painter-Decorator: Patrons and Projects, 1892–1912*. New Haven: Yale University Press, 1993.

Grunchec 1983
Grunchec, Philippe. *Le Grand Prix de peinture: Les concours des Prix de Rome de 1797 à 1863*. Paris: École Nationale Supérieure des Beaux-Arts, 1983.

Hamilton 1986
Hamilton, George Heard. *Manet and His Critics*. New Haven: Yale University Press, 1986.

Hanson 1977
Hanson, Anne Coffiin. *Manet and the Modern Tradition*. New Haven: Yale University Press, 1977.

Haskell 1976
Haskell, Francis. *Rediscoveries in Art: Some Aspects of Taste, Fashion and Collecting in England and France*. Ithaca, N.Y.: Cornell University Press; Oxford: Phaidon Press, 1976.

Haskell 1980
Haskell, Francis. *Rediscoveries in Taste: Some Aspects of Taste, Fashion and Collecting in England and France*. 1976. Oxford: Phaidon Press, 1980.

Haskell 2000
Haskell, Francis. *The Ephemeral Museum: Old Master Paintings and the Rise of the Art Exhibition*. New Haven: Yale University Press, 2000.

Havard 1872–73
Havard, Henry. "Les Chefs d'oeuvre de l'école hollandaise exposés à Amsterdam en 1872." *Gazette des Beaux-Arts,* 2nd per., 6 (1872): 211–24, 295–311, 373–92; 7 (1873): 394–403.

Havard 1879–81
Havard, Henry. *L'Art et les artistes hollandaise*. 4 vols. Paris: Librairie de l'Art, 1879–81.

Havard 1882
Havard, Henry. *Histoire de la peinture hollandaise*. Paris: Maison Quantin, 1882.

Havard 1883
Havard, Henry. "Johannes Vermeer, dit van der Meer de Delft." *Gazette des Beaux-Arts,* 2nd per., 27 (1883): 389–99; 28:213–24.

Havard 1888
Havard, Henry. *Van der Meer de Delft*. Paris: Librairie de l'Art, [1888].

Hecht 1998
Hecht, Peter. "Rembrandt and Raphael Back to Back: The Contribution of Thoré." *Simiolus: Netherlands Quarterly for the History of Art* 26 (1998): 213–24.

Henriet 1876
Henriet, Frédéric. *Le Paysagiste aux champs*. 1866. Paris: A. Lévy, 1876.

Heppner 1938
Heppner, Anton. "Thoré-Bürger en Holland, de ontdekker van Vermeer en zijn liefde voor Neerland's kunst." *Oud-Holland* 55 (1938): 17–34, 67–82, 129–44.

Herbert 1988
Herbert, Robert L. *Impressionism: Art, Leisure and Parisian Society*. New Haven: Yale University Press, 1988.

Herbert 2002
Herbert, Robert L. *From Millet to Léger: Essays in Social Art History*. New Haven: Yale University Press, 2002.

Hertel 1996
Hertel, Christiane. *Vermeer, Reception and Interpretation*. Cambridge: Cambridge University Press, 1996.

Higonnet 1998
Higonnet, Anne. *Picture of Innocence: The History and Crisis of Ideal Childhood*. London: Thames and Hudson, 1998.

Hobsbawm and Ranger 1983
Hobsbawm, Eric, and Terence Ranger, eds. *The Invention of Tradition*. Cambridge: Cambridge University Press, 1983.

Holly 1996
Holly, Michael Ann. *Past Looking: Historical Imagination and the Rhetoric of the Image*. Ithaca, N.Y.: Cornell University Press, 1996.

House 1986
House, John. *Monet: Nature into Art*. New Haven: Yale University Press, 1986.

House 1993
House, John. "Cézanne and Poussin: Myth and History." In *Cézanne and Poussin: A Symposium,* edited by Richard Kendall, pp. 129–49. Sheffield: Sheffield Academic Press, 1993.

House 1997
House, John. *Pierre-Auguste Renoir: La Promenade*. Los Angeles: J. Paul Getty Museum, 1997.

House 1999
House, John. "Impressionism and the Modern Portrait." In *Faces of Impressionism: Portraits from American Collections.* Exh. cat. by Sona Johnston, pp. 11–35. Baltimore: Baltimore Museum of Art, in association with Rizzoli International Publications, 1999.

House, *Impressionism* 2004
House, John. *Impressionism: Paint and Politics*. New Haven: Yale University Press, 2004.

House, "Face to Face" 2004
House, John. "Face to Face with *Le Déjeuner* and *Un Bar aux Folies-Bergère*." In *Manet Face to Face.* Exh. cat. edited by James Cuno and Joachim Kaak, pp. 55–85. London: Courtauld Institute of Art; Munich: Pinakothek-Dumont, 2004.

Huussen 1986
Huussen, A. H., Jr. "Claude Monet in Nederland." In *Monet in Holland,* exh. cat., pp. 36–48. Amsterdam: Rijksmuseum Vincent van Gogh; Zwolle: Waanders, 1986.

Isaacson 1972
Isaacson, Joel. *Monet: Le Déjeuner sur l'herbe*. London: Allen Lane, 1972.

Isaacson 1994
Isaacson, Joel. "Constable, Duranty, Mallarmé, Impressionism, Plein-Air, and Forgetting." *Art Bulletin* 76 (September 1994): 427–50.

de Jongh 2000
de Jongh, Eddy. *Questions of Meaning: Theme and Motif in Dutch Seventeenth-Century Painting*. Translated and edited by Michael Hoyle. Leiden: Primavera Press, 2000.

Jowell 1974
Jowell, Frances Suzman. "Thoré-Bürger and the Revival of Frans Hals." *Art Bulletin* 56 (March 1974): 101–17.

Jowell 1977
Jowell, Frances Suzman. *Thoré-Bürger and the Art of the Past*. Ph.D. diss., Harvard University, 1972. New York: Garland Press, 1977.

Jowell 1989
Jowell, Frances Suzman. "The Rediscovery of Frans Hals." In *Frans Hals*. Exh. cat. by Seymour Slive, pp. 61–85. London: Royal Academy of Arts, in association with Ludion, Brussels, 1989.

Jowell 1995
Jowell, Frances Suzman. "Thoré-Bürger and Vermeer: Critical and Commercial Fortunes." In *Shop Talk: Studies in Honor of Seymour Slive*, edited by Cynthia A. Schnider, William W. Robinson, and Alice I. Davies, pp. 124–27. Cambridge, Mass.: Harvard University Art Museums, 1995.

Jowell, "Géricault" 1996
Jowell, Frances Suzman. "Le voilà en France: Géricault According to Thoré." In *Géricault: Conférence et colloque*, edited by Régis Michel, pp. 779–99. 2 vols. Paris: La Documentation Française, 1996.

Jowell, "Art Market" 1996
Jowell, Frances Suzman. "Thoré-Bürger: A Critical Rôle in the Art Market." *Burlington Magazine* 138 (February 1996): 115–29.

Jowell 1998
Jowell, Frances Suzman. "Vermeer and Thoré-Bürger: Recoveries of Reputation." In *Vermeer Studies*, edited by Ivan Gaskell and Michiel Jonker, pp. 35–57. Studies in the History of Art. Washington, D.C.: National Gallery of Art, 1998.

Jowell 2001
Jowell, Frances Suzman. "From Thoré to Bürger: The Image of Dutch Art before and after the *Musées de la Hollande*." *Bulletin van het Rijksmuseum* 49, no. 1 (2001): 45–60.

Jowell 2003
Jowell, Frances Suzman. "Thoré-Bürger's Art Collection: 'a rather unusual gallery of bric-à-brac.'" *Simiolus: Netherlands Quarterly for the History of Art* 30 (2003): 54–119.

Jubinal 1837
Jubinal, Achille. *Notice sur M. le Baron Taylor et sur les tableaux espagnols achetés par lui d'après les ordres du Roi*. Paris: Chez Édouard Pannier, Éditeur du Musée d'Artillerie Espagnol, 1837.

Kendall 1993
Kendall, Richard, ed. *Cézanne and Poussin: A Symposium*. Sheffield: Sheffield Academic Press, 1993.

Krauss 1967
Krauss, Rosalind. "Manet's Nymph Surprised." *Burlington Magazine* 109 (1967): 622–27.

Lacambre and Lacambre 1973
Lacambre, Geneviève, and Jean Lacambre, eds. Champfleury, *Le Réalisme*. Paris: Collection Savoir, 1973.

Laurent 1863
Laurent, Jean. *Catálogo des la fotografías que se venden en casa de J. Laurent*. Madrid, 1863.

Lebrun 1792–96
Lebrun, J.-P.-B. *Galeries des peintres flamands, hollandais et allemands*. 3 vols. Paris, 1792–96.

Lefort 1879
Lefort, Paul. "Velazquez." *Gazette des Beaux-Arts* 19 (May 1879): 415–29; 20 (September 1879): 229–39; (November 1879): 416–26.

Lemoisne 1946–49
Lemoisne, Paul-André. *Degas et son oeuvre*. 4 vols. Paris: P. Brame et C. M. de Hauke, 1946–49.

Levine 1976
Levine, Steven Z. *Monet and His Critics*. New York: Garland Publishing, 1976.

Levine 1978
Levine, Steven Z. "The Crisis of Resemblance: Portraits and Paintings during the Second Empire." *Arts Magazine* 51 (December 1978): 90–93.

Lhote 1939
Lhote, A. *Traité du paysage*. Paris: Floury, 1939.

Liedtke 2000
Liedtke, Walter. *A View of Delft: Vermeer and His Contemporaries*. Zwolle: Waanders, 2000.

Lille 2002
Berthe Morisot, 1841–1895. Exh. cat. Lille: Musée des Beaux-Arts; Martigny: Fondation Pierre Gianadda, 2002.

Lipschutz 1988
Lipschutz, Ilse Hempel. *La Pintura espanola y los románticos franceses*. Madrid: Taurus, 1988. Revised ed. of *Spanish Painting and the French Romantics*. Cambridge, Mass., 1972.

Lloyd 1981
Lloyd, Christopher. *Camille Pissarro*. New York: Skira, 1981.

Locke 2001
Locke, Nancy. *Manet and the Family Romance*. Princeton: Princeton University Press, 2001.

London 1985
Renoir. Exh. cat. by John House and Anne Distel. London: Arts Council of Great Britain, 1985.

London 1990
Art in the Making: Impressionism. Exh. cat. by David Bomford et al. London: National Gallery, 1990.

London 1992
Alfred Sisley. Exh. cat. edited by MaryAnne Stevens. London: Royal Academy of Arts, 1992.

London 1995
Impressions of France: Monet, Renoir, Pissarro, and Their Rivals. Exh. cat. by John House et al. London: South Bank Centre, 1995.

London 1996
Degas beyond Impressionism. Exh. cat. by Richard Kendall. London: National Gallery, 1996.

London, *Encounters* 2000
Encounters: New Art from Old. Exh. cat. by Richard Morphet. London: National Gallery, 2000.

London, *Impression* 2000
Impression: Painting Quickly in France, 1860–1890. Exh. cat. by Richard R. Brettell. New Haven: Yale University Press, in association with Sterling and Francine Clark Art Institute, 2000.

London 2006
Cézanne in Britain. Exh. cat. by Anne Robbins. London: National Gallery, 2006.

Lostalot 1883
Lostalot, Alfred de. "Exposition internationale de peinture et de sculpture (Galerie Georges Petit)." *Gazette des Beaux Arts*, 2nd ser., 27 (1883): 343–48.

Loyrette 1989
Loyrette, Henri. "Degas entre Gustave Moreau et Duranty. Notes sur les portraits, 1859–1876." *Revue de l'Art*, no. 86 (1989): 16–27.

MacWilliam 1993
MacWilliam, Neil. *Dreams of Happiness: Social Art and the French Left, 1830–1850*. Princeton: Princeton University Press, 1993.

Mainardi 1987
Mainardi, Patricia. *Art and Politics of the Second Empire: The Universal Exhibitions of 1855 and 1867*. New Haven: Yale University Press, 1987.

Mallarmé 1986
Mallarmé, Stéphane. "The Impressionists and Édouard Manet." *Art Monthly Review and Photographic Portfolio: A Magazine Devoted to the Fine and Industrial Arts and Illustrated by Photography* 1, no. 9 (September 1876): pp. 117–22. In *The New Painting: Impressionism, 1874–1886*. Exh. cat. edited by Charles S. Moffett, pp. 27–35. San Francisco: Fine Arts Museums of San Francisco, 1986.

Manchester 1987
The Private Degas. Exh. cat. by Richard Thomson for the Whitworth Art Gallery. London: Herbert Press, 1987.

Manet 1979
Manet, Julie. *Journal (1893–1899): Sa Jeunesse parmi les peintres impressionnistes et les hommes de lettres*. Paris: C. Klincksieck, 1979.

Manet 1988
Manet, Édouard. *Édouard Manet: Voyage en Espagne*. Edited by Juliet Wilson-Bareau. Caen: L'Échoppe, 1988.

Manet 1991
Manet, Édouard. *Manet by Himself: Correspondence and Conversation; Paintings, Pastels, Prints and Drawings*. Edited by Juliet Wilson-Bareau. London: Macdonald and Co., 1991.

Mantz 1868
Mantz, Paul. "Salons de T. Thoré." *Gazette des Beaux-Art* 24 (1868): 400–403.

Mantz 1870
Mantz, Paul. "La Collection La Caze au musée du Louvre." *Gazette des Beaux-Arts,* 2nd per., n.s., 3 (May 1870): 393–406; 4 (July 1870): 2–25.

Mantz 1874
Mantz, Paul. "Exposition en faveur de l'oeuvre des Alsaciens et Lorrains. Peinture. III." *Gazette des Beaux-Arts,* 2nd per., 10 (October 1874): 289–99.

Mantz 1875
Mantz, Paul. "Jan van Goyen." *Gazette des Beaux-Arts,* 2nd per., 12 (August 1875): 138–51; (October 1875): 298–311.

Marc-Bayeux 1985
Marc-Bayeur, Auguste. "Les Copistes du Louvre." 1860. In *Paris qui s'en va et Paris qui vient,* pp. 147–50. Paris: Éditions de Paris, 1985.

Marguery 1926
Marguery, H. "Un Pionnier de l'histoire de l'art: Thoré-Bürger." *Gazette des Beaux-Arts* 67 (1926): 229–45, 295–311, 367–80.

Mathews 1984
Mathews, Nancy Mowll, ed. *Cassatt and Her Circle: Selected Letters*. New York: Abbeville Press, 1984.

Mathews 1994
Mathews, Nancy Mowll. *Mary Cassatt: A Life*. New York: Villard Books, 1994.

Mathews 1996
Mathews, Nancy Mowll, ed. *Cassatt: A Retrospective*. N.p.: Hugh Lauter Levin Associates, 1996.

Mathey 1963
Mathey, Jacques. "Manet as a Pupil of Chardin." *Connoisseur* 154, no. 620 (October 1963): 92–97.

Mauclair 1905
Mauclair, Camille. "De Fragonard à Renoir (Une Leçon de nationalisme pictural)." In *De Watteau à Whistler,* pp. 35–47. Paris: Bibliothèque-Charpentier, 1905.

Mauclair 1921
Mauclair, Camille. *Les États de la peinture française de 1850–1920*. Paris: Payot et Cie, 1921.

McCoubrey 1964
McCoubrey, John W. "The Revival of Chardin in French Still Life Painting, 1815–70." *Art Bulletin* 46 (March 1964): 39–53.

McPherson 2001
McPherson, Heather. *The Modern Portrait in Nineteenth-Century France*. Cambridge: Cambridge University Press, 2001.

McQueen 2003
McQueen, Alison. *The Rise of the Cult of Rembrandt: Reinventing an Old Master in Nineteenth-Century France*. Amsterdam: Amsterdam University Press, 2003.

Meier-Graefe 1911
Meier-Graefe, Julius. "Die Anordnung fordert die alten Meister in die Schranken." In *Auguste Renoir*. Munich: R. Piper, 1911.

Meller 2002
Meller, Peter. "Manet in Italy: Some Newly Identified Sources for His Early Sketchbooks." *Burlington Magazine* 144 (February 2002): 68–110.

Meltzoff, "Vermeer" 1942
Meltzoff, Stanley. "The Rediscovery of Vermeer." *Marsyas* 2 (1942): 145–66.

Meltzoff, "Le Nains" 1942
Meltzoff, Stanley. "The Revival of the Le Nains." *Art Bulletin* 24 (September 1942): 259–86.

Ménard 1873
Ménard, René. "La Collection Laurent-Richard." *Gazette des Beaux-Arts,* 2nd per., 7 (March 1873): 177–96.

Merson 1861
Merson, Olivier. *La Peinture en France: Exposition de 1861*. Paris: Dentu, 1861.

Moore 1890
Moore, George. "Degas: The Painter of Modern Life." *Magazine of Art* 13 (1890): 416–25.

Moreau-Nélaton 1927
Moreau-Nélaton, Étienne. *Bonvin raconté par lui-même*. Paris: Henri Laurens, 1927.

Morisot 1950
Morisot, Berthe. *Correspondance de Berthe Morisot*. Edited by Denis Rouart. Paris: Quatre Chemin Éditart, 1950.

Natanson 1900
Natanson, Thadée. "De Renoir et de la beauté." *La Revue Blanche* 21 (March 1900).

New York 1983
Manet, 1832–1883. Exh. cat. by Françoise Cachin et al. New York: Metropolitan Museum of Art, 1983.

New York, *Degas* 1988
Degas. Exh. cat. by Jean Sutherland Boggs et al. New York: Metropolitan Museum of Art, 1988.

New York, *Fragonard* 1988
Fragonard. Exh. cat. by Pierre Rosenberg. New York: Metropolitan Museum of Art, 1988.

New York 1993
Great French Paintings from the Barnes Foundation: Impressionist, Post-Impressionist, and Early Modern. Exh. cat. New York: Alfred A. Knopf, in association with Lincoln University Press, 1993.

New York 1997
Sotheby's, New York. *Ten Paintings by Paul Cézanne Formerly in the Auguste Pellerin Collection*. November 13, 1997.

New York 1999
Manet's "The Dead Toreador" and "The Bullfight": Fragments of a Lost Salon Painting Reunited. Exh. cat. by Susan Grace Galassi et al. New York: Frick Collection, 1999.

New York 2000
Chardin. Exh. cat. by Pierre Rosenberg. London: Royal Academy of Arts; New York: Metropolitan Museum of Art, 2000.

New York 2003
Manet/Velázquez: The French Taste for Spanish Painting. Exh. cat. by Gary Tinterow and Geneviève Lacambre et al. New York: Metropolitan Museum of Art, 2003.

Nochlin 1992
Nochlin, Linda. "A House Is Not a Home: Degas and the Subversion of the Family." In *Dealing with Degas,* pp. 43–65. New York: Universe, 1992.

Nochlin 1997
Nochlin, Linda. "Impressionist Portraits and the Construction of Modern Identity." In *Renoir's Portraits: Impressions of an Age.* Exh. cat. by Colin B. Bailey and Nochlin, pp. 53–75. Ottawa: National Gallery of Canada, 1997.

Ottawa 1983
Fantin-Latour. Exh. cat. by Dougles Druick and Michel Hoog. Ottawa: National Galleries of Canada, 1983.

Ottawa 1997
Renoir's Portraits: Impressions of an Age. Exh. cat. by Colin B. Bailey and Linda Nochlin. Ottawa: National Gallery of Canada, 1997.

Paris 1866
Exposition retrospective. Tableaux anciens empruntés aux galeries particulières. Paris, Palais des Champs-Élysées, 1866.

Paris 1874
Exposition au profit des alsaciens-lorrains. Paris, Palais Bourbon, 1874.

Paris 1880
Tableaux et dessins de l'école française: oeuvres importantes de Fragonard. Paris, Hôtel Drouot, April 12–16, 1880.

Paris 1883
Catalogue de l'exposition de Portraits du siècle (1783–1883) ouverte au profit de l'oeuvre à l'École des Beaux-Arts. Exh. cat. Paris: Société Philanthropique, 1883.

Paris 1966
Dans la lumière de Vermeer. Exh. cat. Paris: Musée du Louvre–Orangerie des Tuileries, 1966.

Paris 1979
Chardin, 1699–1779. Exh. cat. by Pierre Rosenberg. Paris: Éditions de la Réunion des Musées Nationaux, 1979.

Paris 1983
Manet, 1832–1883. Exh. cat. by Françoise Cachin, Charles S. Moffett, and Juliet Wilson-Bareau. Paris: Éditions de la Réunion des Musées Nationaux, 1983.

Paris 1988
Degas. Exh. cat. by Jean Sutherland Boggs et al. Paris: Éditions de la Réunion des Musées Nationaux, 1988.

Paris 1993
Copier/créer: De Turner à Picasso; 300 oeuvres inspirées par les maîtres du Louvre. Exh. cat. by Jean-Pierre Cuzin and Marie-Anne Dupuy. Paris: Éditions de la Réunion des Musées Nationaux, 1993.

Paris 1994
Impressionnisme: Les Origines, 1859–1869. Exh. cat. Paris: Éditions de la Réunion des Musées Nationaux, 1994.

Philadelphia 2003
Manet and the Sea. Exh. cat. by Juliet Wilson-Bareau and David Degener. Philadelphia: Philadelphia Museum of Art, 2003.

Pickvance 1986
Pickvance, Ronald. "Catalogus." In *Monet in Holland,* exh. cat., pp. 97–175. Amsterdam: Rijksmuseum Vincent van Gogh; Zwolle: Waanders, 1986.

Piles 1708
Piles, Roger de. *Cours de peinture par principes*. Paris: Jacques Estienne, 1708.

Pissarro 1980
Pissarro, Camille. *Correspondance de Camille Pissarro*. Vol. 1, *1865–1885*. Edited by Janine Bailly-Herzberg. Paris: Presses Universitaires de France, 1980.

Pissarro, *Lucien* 1980
Pissarro, Camille. *Camille Pissarro Letters to His Son Lucien*. Edited by John Rewald. London: Routledge and Kegan Paul, 1980.

Pissarro 1988
Pissarro, Camille. *Correspondance de Camille Pissarro*. Vol. 3, *1891–1894*. Edited by Janine Bailly-Herzberg. Paris: Valhermeil, 1988.

Pissarro 1989
Pissarro, Camille. *Correspondance de Camille Pissarro*. Vol. 4, *1895–1898*. Edited by Janine Bailly-Herzberg. Paris: Valhermeil, 1989.

Pissarro 1991
Pissarro, Camille. *Correspondance de Camille Pissarro*. Vol. 5, *1899–1903*. Edited by Janine Bailly-Herzberg. Paris: Valhermeil, 1991.

Pissarro and Durand-Ruel Snollaerts 2005
Pissarro, Joachim, and Claire Durand-Ruel Snollaerts. *Pissarro: Critical Catalogue of Paintings*. Milan: Skira, 2005.

Proust 1913
Proust, Antonin. *Édouard Manet. Souvenirs publiés par A. Barthélemy*. Paris: Renouard et Laurens, 1913.

Proust 1996
Proust, Antonin. *Édouard Manet*. *Souvenirs*. Paris: L'Échoppe, 1996.

Proust 2003
Proust, Marcel. *Time Regained*. 1927. Translated by A. Mayor and T. Kilmartin. New York: Modern Library Paperback, 2003.

Przyblyski 2001
Przyblyski, Jeannene M. "The Makings of Modern Still Life in the 1860's." In *Impressionist Still Life.* Exh. cat. by Eliza E. Rathbone and George T. M. Shackelford, pp. 28–33. Washington, D.C.: Phillips Collection, 2001.

Rebeyrol 1952
Rebeyrol, Philippe. "Art Historians and Art Critics, I: Théophile Thoré." *Burlington Magazine* 94 (1952): 196–200.

Reff, "Reproductions" 1960
Reff, Theodore. "Reproductions and Books in Cézanne's Studio." *Gazette des Beaux-Arts* 56 (November 1960): 303–9.

Reff, "Cézanne and Poussin" 1960
Reff, Theodore. "Cézanne and Poussin." *Journal of the Warburg and Courtauld Institutes* 23 (1960): 150–74.

Reff 1963
Reff, Theodore. "Degas's Copies of Older Art." *Burlington Magazine* 105 (June 1963): 241–51.

Reff, "Copies" 1964
Reff, Theodore. "New Light on Degas's Copies." *Burlington Magazine* 106 (June 1964): 250–59.

Reff, "Louvre" 1964
Reff, Theodore. "Copyists in the Louvre, 1850–1870." *Art Bulletin* 46 (December 1964): 552–59.

Reff, "Pictures" 1968
Reff, Theodore. "The Pictures within Degas's Pictures." *Metropolitan Museum Journal* 1 (1968): 125–66.

Reff, "Unpublished Letters" 1968
Reff, Theodore. "Some Unpublished Letters of Degas." *Art Bulletin* 50 (March 1968): 87–93.

Reff, "Manet's Sources" 1969
Reff, Theodore. "Manet's Sources: A Critical Evaluation." *Artforum* 8 (September 1969): 40–48.

Reff, "More Unpublished Letters" 1969
Reff, Theodore. "More Unpublished Letters of Degas." *Art Bulletin* 51 (September 1969): 281–89.

Reff 1970
Reff, Theodore. "Manet and Blanc's 'Histoire des Peintres.'" *Burlington Magazine* 112 (July 1970): 456–58.

Reff 1971
Reff, Theodore. "Further Thoughts on Degas's Copies." *Burlington Magazine* 113 (September 1971): 534–43.

Reff, *The Artist's Mind* 1976
Reff, Theodore. *Degas: The Artist's Mind*. New York: Metropolitan Museum of Art, 1976.

Reff, *Notebooks* 1976
Reff, Theodore. *The Notebooks of Edgas Degas. A Catalogue of the Thirty-eight Notebooks in the Bibliothèque Nationale and Other Collections*. 2 vols. Oxford: Clarendon Press, 1976.

Reff 1985
Reff, Theodore. *The Notebooks of Edgas Degas. A Catalogue of the Thirty-eight Notebooks in the Bibliothèque Nationale and Other Collections*. 2 vols. New York: Hacker Art Books, 1985.

Renoir 1981
Renoir, Jean. *Pierre-Auguste Renoir mon père*. Paris: Gallimard, 1981.

Renouvier 1863
Renouvier, Jules. *Histoire de l'art pendant la Révolution*. Paris: Jules Renouard, 1863.

Réveil 1828–34
Réveil, Achille. *Musée de peinture et de sculpture, ou Recueil des principaux tableaux, statues et bas-reliefs des collections publiques et particulières de l'Europe; dessiné et gravé à l'eau-forte par Réveil, avec des notices descriptives, critiques et historiques par Duchesne aîné*. 16 vols. Paris: Audot, 1828–34.

Rewald 1946
Rewald, John. *The History of Impressionism*. New York: Museum of Modern Art, 1946.

Rewald 1948
Rewald, John. *Paul Cézanne, a Biography.* New York: Simon and Schuster, 1948.

Rewald 1973
Rewald, John. *The History of Impressionism*. 4th, rev. ed. New York: Museum of Modern Art, 1973.

Richardson 1991
Richardson, John. *A Life of Picasso*. Vol. 1, *1881–1906*. London: Cape, 1991.

Rivero 2003
Rivero, Ignacio Cano. "Seville's Artistic Heritage during the French Occupation." In *Manet/Velázquez: The French Taste for Spanish Painting*. Exh. cat. by Gary Tinterow and Geneviève Lacambre et al., pp. 93–113. New York: Metropolitan Museum of Art, 2003.

Rivière, "Aux femmes" 1877
Rivière, Georges. "Aux femmes." *L'Impressionniste*, no. 3 (April 21, 1877): 2.

Rivière, "Les Intransigeants" 1877
Rivière, Georges. "Les Intransigeants et les impressionnistes. Souvenirs du salon libre de 1877." *L'Artiste*, 1 November 1877, pp. 298–302.

Rivière, "L'Exposition" 1877
Rivière, Georges. "L'Exposition des impressionistes." *L'Impressioniste,* April 14, 1877, pp. 1–4, 6.

Roldán 2003
Roldán, Deborah L. "Chronology." In *Manet/Velázquez: The French Taste for Spanish Painting*. Exh. cat. by Gary Tinterow and Geneviève Lacambre et al., pp. 353–403. New York: Metropolitan Museum of Art, 2003.

Roos 1996
Roos, Jane Mayo. *Early Impressionism and the French State (1866–1874)*. New York: Cambridge University Press, 1996.

Rosen and Zerner 1984
Rosen, Charles, and Henri Zerner. "The Recovery of the Past and the Modern Tradition." In *Romanticism and Realism: The Mythology of Nineteenth-Century Art,* pp. 183–202. New York: Viking Press, 1984.

Rosenberg 1989
Rosenberg, Pierre. *Tout l'oeuvre peint de Fragonard*. Paris: Flammarion, 1989.

Rosenblum 2000
Rosenblum, Robert. "Remembrance of Art Past." In *Encounters: New Art from Old,* exh. cat., pp. 8–23. London: National Gallery, 2000.

Rosenthal 1987
Rosenthal, Léon. *Du romanticisme au réalisme: Essai sur l'évolution de la peinture en France de 1830 à 1848*. 1914. Paris: Macula, 1987.

Rousseau 1762
Rousseau, Jean-Jacques. *Émile ou l'education*. 4 vols. Amsterdam: Jean Néaulme, 1762.

San Francisco 1986
The New Painting: Impressionism, 1874–1886. Exh. cat. edited by Charles S. Moffett. San Francisco: Fine Arts Museums of San Francisco, 1986.

Schapiro 1997
Schapiro, Meyer. "Portraiture and Photography." In *Impressionism: Reflections and Perceptions,* pp. 153–78, 333. New York: George Braziller, 1997.

Schulman 1999
Schulman, Michel. *Théodore Rousseau, 1812–1867. Catalogue raisonné de l'oeuvre peint*. Paris: Éditions de l'Amateur, 1999.

Shackelford 2001
Shackelford, George T. M. "Impressionism and the Still-Life Tradition." In *Impressionist Still Life.* Exh. cat. by Eliza E. Rathbone and Shackelford, pp. 20–27. Washington, D.C.: Phillips Collection, 2001.

Sheriff 1987
Sheriff, Mary. "Invention, Resemblance, and Fragonard's *Portraits de Fantaisie*." *Art Bulletin* 69 (March 1987): 77–87.

Sheriff 1990
Sheriff, Mary. *Fragonard: Art and Eroticism*. Chicago: University of Chicago Press, 1990.

Shiff 1984
Shiff, Richard. *Cézanne and the End of Impressionism*. Chicago: University of Chicago Press, 1984.

Silvestre 1875
Silvestre, Armand, ed. *Le Grand Art chrétien. Opinon de la presse sur la célèbre statue de Saint François d'Assise copiée par M. Zacharie Astruc et reproduite en marbre, bronze et bois par MM. Christofle et Cie*. Paris: Imprimerie de J. Claye, 1875.

Simches 1964
Simches, Seymour O. *Le Romantisme et le goût esthétique du XVIIIème siècle*. Paris: Presses Universitaires de France, 1964.

Slive 1970–74
Slive, Seymour. *Frans Hals*. 3 vols. New York: Phaidon: 1970–74.

South Hadley 1987
Berthe Morisot, Impressionist. Exh. cat. by Charles F. Stuckey and William P. Scott, for Mount Holyoke College Museum of Art. New York: Hudson Hills Press, 1987.

Stevens 2001
Stevens, MaryAnne. "Monet e Londra: Le Esperienze del luogo." In *Monet: I luoghi della pittura.* Exh. cat. by Marco Goldin, pp. 137–60. Conegliano: Linea d'Ombra Libri, 2001.

Stirling-Maxwell 1999
Stirling-Maxwell, William. *Velázquez and His Works*. London, 1855. Madrid: Ayuntamiento de Madrid, 1999.

Sweet 1966
Sweet, Frederick A. *Miss Mary Cassatt: Impressionist from Pennsylvania*. Norman: University of Oklahoma Press, 1966.

Thomson 2000
Thomson, Belinda. *Impressionism: Origins, Practice, Reception*. London: Thames and Hudson, 2000.

Thomson 1988
Thomson, Richard. *Degas: The Nudes*. London: Thames and Hudson, 1988.

Thoré 1835
Thoré, Théophile. "Zurbaran, le Caravage espagnol." *L'Artiste* 9 (1835): 225–26.

Thoré-Bürger 1868
Thoré-Bürger. *Salons de T. Thoré, Salons de 1844, 1845, 1846, 1847, 1848*. Paris: Librairie Internationale, 1868.

Thoré-Bürger 1870
Thoré-Bürger. *Salons de W. Bürger, 1861–1868; avec une préface par T. Thoré*. Introduction by Marius Chaumelin. 2 vols. Paris: Librairie de Vve Jules Renouard, 1870.

Tietze-Conrat 1944
Tietze-Conrat, E. "What Degas Learned from Mantegna." *Gazette des Beaux-Arts* 24 (1944): 413–20.

Tourneux 1907
Tourneux, Maurice. "Philippe Burty." *Gazette des Beaux-Arts*, 3rd per., 37 (May 1907): 388–402.

Tucker 1986
Tucker, Paul. "The First Impressionist Exhibition in Context." In *The New Painting: Impressionism, 1874–1886*. Exh. cat. edited by Charles S. Moffett, pp. 93–117. San Francisco: Fine Arts Museums of San Francisco, 1986.

van der Tuin 1948
van der Tuin, H. *Les Vieux Peintres des Pays-Bas et la critique artistique en France de la première moitié du XIXè siècle*. Paris: Librairie Philosophique J. Vrin, 1948.

Valéry 1989
Valéry, Paul. *Degas Manet Morisot*. Translated by David Paul. Bollingen Series 45, 12. Princeton: Princeton University Press, 1989.

Venturi 1939
Venturi, Lionello. *Les Archives de l'impressionnisme: Lettres de Renoir, Monet, Pissarro, Sisley et autres*. 2 vols. Paris: Durand-Ruel, 1939.

Verbeek 1958
Verbeek, J. "Bezoekers van het Rijksmuseum in het Trippenhuis van 1884–1885." *Bulletin van het Rijksmuseum* (special edition) 6 (1958): 59–71.

Villot 1853
Villot, Frédéric. *Notices des tableaux exposés dans les galleries du Musée impérial du Louvre. 2me partie, Écoles allemande, flamande, hollandaise*. Paris: Vinchon & Fils, 1853.

Vischer 1997
Vischer, Bodo. "Goya's Still Lifes in the Yumuri Inventory." *Burlington Magazine* 139, no. 1127 (February 1997): 121–23.

Vollard 1920
Vollard, Ambroise. *Auguste Renoir, 1841–1919*. Paris: Éditions G. Crès, 1920.

Vollard 1924
Vollard, Ambroise. *Degas*. Paris: G. Crès et Cie, 1924.

Vollard 1925
Vollard, Ambroise. *Renoir: An Intimate Portrait*. Translated by Harold L. Van Doren and Randolph T. Weaver. New York: Alfred A. Knopf, 1925.

Vollard 1934
Vollard, Ambroise. *Renoir: An Intimate Portrait*. New York: Alfred A. Knopf, 1934.

Vollard 1938
Vollard, Ambroise. *En écoutant Cézanne, Degas, Renoir*. Paris: B. Grasset, 1938.

Vosmaer 1873
Vosmaer, C. *Etsen naar Frans Hals avec une étude sur le maitre et ses oeuvres par C. Vosmaer*. Edited by W. Unger. Leiden: A. W. Sijthoff, 1873.

Walker 1933
Walker, John. "Degas et les maîtres anciens." *Gazette des Beaux-Arts* 10 (1933): 173–85.

Washington 1982
Manet and Modern Paris: One Hundred Paintings, Drawings, Prints, and Photographs by Manet and His Contemporaries. Exh. cat. by Theodore Reff. Washington, D.C.: National Gallery of Art, 1982.

Washington 1984
Degas, the Dancers. Exh. cat. by George T. M. Shackelford. Washington, D.C.: National Gallery of Art, 1984.

Washington 1990
Martindale, Meredith. *Lilla Cabot Perry: An American Impressionist*. Exh. cat. Washington, D.C.: National Museum of Women in the Arts, 1990.

Washington 2003
Édouard Vuillard. Exh. cat. by Guy Cogeval et al. Washington, D.C.: National Gallery of Art, 2003.

Weisberg 1993
Weisberg, Gabriel. *The Independent Critic: Philippe Burty and the Visual Arts of Mid-Nineteenth-Century France*. New York: P. Lang, 1993.

Westrheene 1857
Westrheene, Tobias van. *Jan Steen. Étude sur l'art en Hollande*. The Hague: M. Nijhoff, 1857.

Wheelock 2000
Wheelock, Arthur K., Jr. "Dou's Reputation." In *Gerrit Dou, 1613–1675: Master Painter in the Age of Rembrandt*. Exh. cat. by Ronni Baer et al., pp. 12–24. Washington, D.C.: National Gallery of Art, 2000.

Wildenstein 1960
Wildenstein, Georges. *The Paintings of Fragonard*. Garden City, N.Y.: Phaidon, 1960.

Wildenstein 1974
Wildenstein, Daniel. *Claude Monet: Biographie et catalogue raisonné*. Vol. 1, *1840–1881, Peintures*. Lausanne: La Bibliothèque des Arts, 1974.

Wildenstein 1985
Wildenstein, Daniel. *Claude Monet: Biographie et catalogue raisonné*. Vol. 4, *1899–1926, Peintures*. Lausanne: La Bibliothèque des Arts, 1985.

Wilson-Bareau, "Goya" 2003
Wilson-Bareau, Juliet. "Goya and France." In *Manet/Velázquez: The French Taste for Spanish Painting*. Exh. cat. by Gary Tinterow and Geneviève Lacambre et al., pp. 139–61. New York: Metropolitan Museum of Art, 2003.

Wilson-Bareau, "Manet" 2003
Wilson-Bareau, Juliet. "Manet and Spain." In *Manet/Velázquez: The French Taste for Spanish Painting*. Exh. cat. by Gary Tinterow and Geneviève Lacambre et al., pp. 203–57. New York: Metropolitan Museum of Art, 2003.

Wissman 1986
Wissman, Fronia E. "Realists among the Impressionists." In *The New Painting: Impressionism, 1874–1886*. Exh. cat. edited by Charles S. Moffett, pp. 337–52. San Francisco: Fine Arts Museums of San Francisco.

Zola 1970
Zola, Emile. *Mon Salon. Manet. Écrits sur l'art*. Paris: Garnier-Flammarion, 1970.

Zola 1974
Zola, Émile. *Le Bon Combat: de Courbet aux impressionnistes; Anthologie d'écrits sur l'art*. Edited by Jean-Paul Bouillon. Paris: Hermann, 1974.

Zola 1991
Zola, Émile. *Écrits sur l'art*. Paris: Gallimard, 1991.

Index

Index to artists and works discussed in the text. Page references to illustrations appear in *italic* type.

After the Bath (Woman Drying Herself) (Degas), *76*
Alfred Sisley (Renoir), 93, *104*
Alte Museum (Berlin), 17
Arrangement in Gray and Black No. 1 or *The Artist's Mother* (Whistler), 208, *209*
Artist's Family, The (Renoir), 129, *130*, 132
artists' organizations, 149, 228, 249
Artist's Son, Jean, Drawing, The (Renoir), 52
art revivals, 18–19, 249. *See also specific artists, collections, publications, paintings, or eras*
Art Students and Copyists in the Louvre Gallery (Homer), *18*
Assembly in a Park (Watteau), 171, *173*
Astruc, Zacharie, 86, 89, 91, 111, 127, 129
  work by: *Saint Francis Standing* (after the original by Pedro de Mena), 127, *127*, 129
At the Louvre—Copying Murillo (Beroud), *34*
Autopsy, The (Cézanne), 123, *126*, 127
Autumn on the Seine, Argenteuil (Monet), *156*, *177*
Auvray, Louis, 249
Avenue at Middelharnis, The (Hobbema), 93, *99*
Avenue of Chestnut Trees near La Celle-Saint-Cloud, The (Sisley), 160, *164*

Backhuysen, Ludolf, work by: *The "Koning Willem III". . . , 94*
Ball at the Moulin de la Galette (Renoir), 50, *54*, 135
Banquet Still Life (van Beyeren), 40, 188, *189*
Barbizon School, 54, 56, 160, 166
Basket of Plums (Chardin), *45*
Bather, A (Renoir), *74*
Bath of Diana (Boucher), 30, *70*, 71, 139
Baudelaire, Charles, 15, 40, 169, 218, 228, 246
Baugniet, Charles, work by: *Troubled Conscience*, *206*
Bazille, Frédéric, 19, 40
  works by: *The Beach at Sainte-Adresse*, *174*; *Flowers*, 40, *42*; *The Heron*, *191*, 197
Beach at Sainte-Adresse, The (Bazille), *174*
Beggar Boy, The (Murillo), *2*, 30, *35*
Bellay, Charles, 248
Bellelli Family, The (Degas), 210, 222, *223*
Bellelli Sisters, The (Giovanna and Giuliana Bellelli) (Degas), 222, *225*
Beroud, Louis
  works by: *At the Louvre—Copying Murillo*, *34*; *An Evening at the Louvre*, *256*
Bertin, Jean-Victor, 175
Beyeren, Abraham Hendricksz van, 40, 188
  work by: *Banquet Still Life*, *189*
Bisschop, Cornelis, work by: *The Seamstress*, 53
Boldini, Giovanni, 252
Bon Bock, Le (Manet), 86, *88*
Bonnat, Léon, 229, 233, 239
Bonvin, François, 197, 199
Boucher, François, 21, 28, 30, 50, 71, 139
  works by: *Bath of Diana*, 30, *70*, 71, 139; *Seated Nude*, *14*, *71*; *Vulcan Presenting to Venus the Arms for Aeneas*, 140, *143*
Boudin, Eugéne, 92
Bouquet of Flowers (Pissarro), *146*
Boy Searching for Lice, after Murillo (Cézanne), *1*, *35*

Boy with a Peep Show (Fragonard), *148*
Breughel, Pieter, 175
Brioche, The (Chardin), 194–95, *197*
brushwork, 38, 129, 140, 150
Bullring in Madrid (Manet), 123
Bush, The (Ruisdael), *159*

Caillebotte, Gustave, 201, 252, 253
work by: *Fruit Displayed on a Stand*, *200*, 201
Calvary, copy after Mantegna, The (Degas), *24*, 245
Calvary, The (Le Calvaire) (Morisot), *26*, 244
Calvary, The (Mantegna), 21
Cano, Alonso, 242
Carolus-Duran, 229, 233, 239
Carracci, Annibale, 30, 171
work by: *Landscape*, 37
Cassatt, Mary
as copyist in the Prado, Madrid, 129, 248
on Correggio, 248
on de la Tour, 253
Dutch influence on, 249
eighteenth-century French art influence on, 50
Italian influence on, 58, 248
on making copies on commission, 248
on Murillo, 248
old masters influence on, 248
Paris exposition refusals of work by, 247
on Rembrandt, 249
Roman studies of, 248
on Rubens, 249
Rubens influence on, 249
Spanish influence on, 248
on travel and art education, 250
travels of, 108n42, 248, 249, 252, 254
on Velázquez and Spanish School, 248–49
Veronese influence on, 252
works by: *The Family*, 58, *67*; *Lydia at a Tapestry Frame*, *128*, 129; *Mrs. Duffee Seated on a Striped Sofa, Reading*, 50, *229*, *230*; *Reine Lefebvre Holding a Nude Baby*, *238*
Cent Chefs-d'oeuvre des collections parisiennes exhibition, 251
Cézanne, Paul
on academic art education, 18–19
Baroque period and, 16
on Bernard, 255
on breaking away from tradition, 37
as copyist in the Louvre, 19, 244, 246, 247
as Cubism forerunner, 132
death of, 255
Dutch influence on, 40
El Greco influence on, 132
female nude motif and, 71, 76
on his art, 255
on Impressionism, 58
on influence of great masters, 132
on landscape painting, 58
landscapes of, 58
on the Louvre, 19, 255
on Michelangelo and Raphael, 254
on painting, 54
on Paris painting exhibitions, 245
Picasso on, 132
Poussin influence on, 174, 175, 244
on Puget, 58
on relationship with the past, 76
on Rubens, 254
Rubens influence on, 174, 244
solitude and, 132
Spanish influence on, 123, 127
on Stendhal, 250
still lifes of, 187, 188, 192
on studying old masters vs. studying nature, 254, 255
Tintoretto influence on, 174
training, 18–19
on Venetian masters, 254–55
on Veronese, 254
Vollard gallery exhibit of, 253
works by: *The Autopsy*, 123, *126*, 127; *Boy Searching for Lice, after Murillo*, *1*, *35*; *Mont Sainte-Victoire, 1886–87*, *178*; *Mont Sainte-Victoire, 1902–6*, *178*; *Plaster Cast of a Putto*, *64*; *The Plaster Cupid*, 58, *65*; *The Plaster Cupid* (recto) and *Study of Drapery* (verso), 58, *64*; *Still Life with Apples and Oranges*, 40, *192*; *Still Life with Statuette*, 58, *63*, 201
Champaigne, Philippe de, 242
Chardin, Jean-Siméon, 40, 50, 187, 194
works by: *Basket of Plums*, *45*; *The Brioche*, 194–95, *197*; *The Jar of Olives*, 194, 195, *195*; *The Scullery Maid*, *49*; *The Silver Goblet*, 194; *Still Life with Dead Pheasant and Hunting Bag*, 187, *190*, 197
Chardin, Pierre, 150, 153
works by: *Child with a Spinning Top*, 150, *151*
Chardin and His Models (Rousseau), *182*, 197, *198*
Child with a Hoop (Renoir), *234*
Child with a Spinning Top (Chardin), 150, *151*
Christine Lerolle Embroidering (Renoir), 50, *53*
Claesz, Pieter, 40
classical French landscape tradition, 54, 58. *See also* Barbizon School
Claude. *See* Lorrain, Claude
"Collection de M. Camille Marcille, La" (Duplessis), 249
Collection d'objets d'art de M. Thiers (Blanc), 251
composition, 38, 40
Concert champêtre, Le (Titian), 19, *20*, 171
Constable, John, 248
Copy after "The Finding of Moses" by Veronese (Degas), *27*
copying (of older or museum art), 16, *18*, 19, 21, 218, 255. *See also* Musée des Copies; *specific artists*
Copistes du Louvre, Les (Marc-Bayeux), 244–45
Corot, Jean-Baptiste Camille, 16, 117, 133n11, 160
work by: *Memory of Mortefontaine (Oise)*, 169, *170*
Country Party (Pater), *173*
Courbet, Gustave, 82, 160
Cours de peinture par principes (de Piles), 184

Danaë (Titian and Workshop), *73*
D'après les maîtres (exhibition of artists' copies), 255
Daubigny, Charles-François, 54, 57, 169
Daughter of Jephthah, The (Degas), *25*
Dead Soldier, A (Italian), *122*
Dead Toreador, The (L'Homme Mort) (Manet), 122, *123*
Degas, Edgar
childhood influence of Louvre on, 19
on copying the masters, 19, 21
as copyist in National Museum of Naples, 243
as copyist in Roman museums and churches, 243, 244
as copyist in the Bibliothèque Impériale, 243
as copyist in the Louvre, 19, 21, 243, 245, 246, 247
as copyist in the Uffizi Gallery, Florence, 244
Dutch influence on, 210, 222
early portraits of, 219, 222
female nude motif, 71, 76
Goncourt on, 40
on his paintings, 40
on Italian and Dutch masters, 244
Italian influence on, 19, 21, 40, 222, 243
on Italian masters, 244
Italian Renaissance and, 16
Japanese influence on, 40
on links with Dutch art, 207
Lorrain influence on, 244
on Manet and Hals, 86
on Mantegna, 21, 40
on the old masters, 21
Raimondi influence on, 243
Raphael influence on, 243
relationship with earlier art, 16
Spanish influence on, 29, 129, 222, 245
spontaneity vs. tradition in paintings of, 40
training of, 19, 21
on Velázquez, 40
Velázquez influence on, 245
on Veronese, 21
visit to Prado in Madrid, 252
works by: *After the Bath (Woman Drying Herself)*, *76*; *The Bellelli Family*, 210, 222, *223*; *The Bellelli Sisters (Giovanna and Giuliana Bellelli)*, 222, *225*; *The Calvary, copy after Mantegna*, 24, *24*, 245; *Copy after "The Finding of Moses" by Veronese*, *27*; *The Daughter of Jephthah*, *25*; *Double Portrait, after Giovanni Cariani*, *224*; *Head of the Virgin after Solario's "Virgin of the Green Cushion,"* *22*; *Infanta Margarita, Copy after Velázquez*, 29, *117*, 118; *Little Dancer*, 129, 133n34; *Mary Cassatt at the Louvre: The Etruscan Gallery*, 19; *Mary Cassatt at the Louvre: The Paintings Gallery*, 19; *Minerva Chasing Vice from the Garden of Virtue*, 21; *Portrait of a Young Woman*, after a 16th-century Florentine drawing, *23*; *The Rehearsal*, 40; *Self-Portrait*

Degas, Edgar, works by (*continued*) *in the Style of Filippino Lippi*, *222*; *Studies after Two Italian Madonnas*, *22*; *Studies of a Nude Man, a Horse, and a Knee*, *22*; *Studies of Legs and Feet and of a Figure*, *22*; *Study of One of the Thieves in Mantegna's "Crucifixion,"* *25*; *Two Figures Standing on a Flight of Steps, after Raphael*, 40, *41*; *Visit to a Museum*, *4*, *152*, 153
Delacroix, Eugène, 16
De l'origine de la peinture (Félibien), 184
Diffident Still Life, The (La Vie Parisienne), *184*
Disembarkation of Cleopatra at Tarsus, The (Lorrain), *162*
Doña María Tomasa de Palafox, Marquesa de Villafranca (Goya), *227*, 228
Don Mariano Camprubi (Manet), 118
Double Portrait, after Giovanni Cariani (Degas, Edgar), *224*
Dughet, Gaspar, 243
Dupré, Jules, 166
Du Quesnoy, François, 58
  work by: *Putto*, *62*
Durand-Ruel, Paul, 132, 160, 252
Duret, Théodore, 86, 123, 247, 249, 250, 255

ébauche, 154
École des Beaux-Arts, 16–17, 19, 249
École Hollandaise (Blanc), 199
eighteenth-century French art, 21, 28
  influence on Impressionists, 135, 137–40, 145–46, 150, 153–54
  revival in 1860s, 137–39
  See also specific artists
Elémens de Perspective . . . (Valenciennes), 166
El Greco, 29, 132
  work by: *Lady in a Fur Wrap*, *110*
Entombment (Ribera), 127
envoi, 17
Ephrussi, Charles, 229
espagnolisme, 28–29, 111–13, 117, 132. *See also* seventeenth-century Spanish art
esquisse, 150, 153
étude, 150, 153
Eva Gonzalès (Manet), 187, *226*, 228
Evening at the Louvre, An (Beroud), *256*

Expositions Universelles, 160, 243, 247, 250, 252, 254

Family, The (Cassatt), 58, *67*
fantasy portraits, 147, 150
Feast, The (The Orgy) (Cézanne), 21
Félibien, André, 183, 184
Fénéon, Félix, 252
fête champêtre motif, 54
Fifer, The (Manet), 123
Fisher Boy (Hals), *84*
Flandrin, Hippolyte, 21
Fourment, Hélène, 30, 171, 243
Fragonard, Jean-Honoré
  Chardin influence on, 150
  collectors and exhibitions of, 137–38
  Goncourts on, 229
  influence on Cassatt, 50
  influence on Impressionists, 229
  influence on Renoir, 211
  revival of, 21, 28, 242
  sketch aesthetic and, 145, 147, 150, 229
  technique of, 150
  unique qualities of work by, 145, 147, 150
  works by: *Boy with a Peep Show*, *148*; *Girl Playing with Her Dog (La Gimblette)*, 140, *144*, 145; *The Music Lesson*, 138, *139*; *Music: Portrait of M. de la Breteche, Brother of L'Abbé de Saint-Non*, 145, *149*, 150, 154; *The Spanish Singer*, 154; *The Storm (The Stuck Cart)*, 138–39, *140*, 145; *Study*, *136*, 137; *A Young Girl Reading*, 50, 145, 147, *231*
François, Jacques, 187
Frans Halsmuseum, 85
French Rococo painting, 28, 138–39, 145, 154. *See also* eighteenth-century French art; *specific artists*
Fruit Displayed on a Stand (Caillebotte), *200*, 201

Gainsborough, Thomas, 248
Galerie Espagnole, 115, 117
Galerie Martinet, 244, 248
Gauguin, Paul, 233
genre painting, 205, 206–7, 212, 215
Gérôme, Jean-Léon, 169, 205
Getting Out of Bed (Morisot), 140
Ghirlandaio, Domenico, 19
Giorgione, 19

Girard, Paul-Albert, work by: *The Triumph of Silenus*, 169, *170*
Girardon, François, 66
Girl Playing with Her Dog (La Gimblette) (Fragonard), 140, *144*, 145
Gleyre, Charles, 19, 245
Gogh, Vincent van, 150
Goupil, Adolphe, 212
Goya, 247
Goya, Francisco de, 29, 129, 154
  works by: *Doña María Tomasa de Palafox, Marquesa de Villafranca*, *227*, 228; *Still Life with Golden Bream*, 40, *47*
Goyen, Jan van, 82
Greuze, Jean-Baptiste, 50, 113, 245–46
  work by: *A Schoolboy Sleeping on His Book*, *52*
Gypsy, The (Hals), 85, *86*
Gypsy with a Cigarette (Manet), *86*, *87*

Haarlem Lock, Amsterdam, The (Hobbema), *61*
Hals, Frans
  characteristics of paintings of, 83–84
  influence on Impressionist painting, 84–85, 108n51
  influence on Manet, 83, 86, 89, 154
  as inspiration to Impressionists, 86–89
  as Modernist, 108n59
  Paris exhibitions of paintings by, 85–86, 89
  Thoré on, 21, 82
  works by: *La Bohémienne*, 85, *86*; *Fisher Boy*, *84*; *The Gypsy*, 85, *86*; *Jeune paysanne souriante*, 85, *86*; *Merry Drinker*, 86, *87*; *Portrait of a Seated Man*, 93, *105*; *Portrait of a Woman*, 85, *85*; *Portrait of a Young Woman*, 30, *220*; *Singing Boy with Flute*, 84, *85*
Harlequin and Columbine (Watteau), *213*
Head of the Virgin after Solario's "Virgin of the Green Cushion" (Degas), *22*
Heem, Jan Davidsz de, 40
  work by: *A Table of Desserts*, 188, *193*
Hélène Fourment and Her Eldest Son, Frans (Rubens), *69*
Henriet, Frédéric, 169

Heron, The (Bazille), *191*, 197
Herrera, Francisco de, the Younger, 242
history painting, 205–6
Hobbema, Meindert, 160
  works by: *The Avenue at Middelharnis*, 93, *99*; *The Haarlem Lock, Amsterdam*, *61*; *The Oak Forest*, *167*
Hollandaise au clavecin (Dutch Woman at the Harpsichord) (Metsu), 93, *103*, 245
Honoré Fragonard, sa vie et son oeuvre (Portalis), 252
Hooch, Pieter de, 50, 210, 247
House in the Country, The (Laen), *90*, 91
Huet, Jean-Baptiste, 54
  work by: *Young Couple in a Landscape*, *56*
Huysmans, Joris-Karl, 129

Impressionism
  architectural influences on, 37
  characteristics of, 15–16, 38
  composition techniques of, 38, 40
  emergence as new school of painting, 30, 37
  modernity and, 30, 37
  mother and child imagery, 58, 66
  portraiture of, 217–18
  as rejection of artistic traditions, 15–16
  relationships with earlier art, 16, 77n3, 175, 181
  social changes impacting elements of, 37
  surface textures of, 38
  themes of, 92
  women painters of, 187
Impressionistes de 1886, Les (Fénéon), 252
Impressionist group exhibitions
  First: April 15–May 16, 1874, 15, 18, 249
  Second: March 30–April, 1876, 249
  Third: April 4, 1877, 249–50
  Fourth: April 10–May 11, 1879, 250
  Fifth: April 1–30, 1880, 250
  Sixth: April 2–May 1, 1881, 250
  Seventh: March 1–April 2, 1882, 251
  Eighth: May 15–June 15, 1886, 251
Impressionists
  aim of, 123
  anti-academic strategies of, 38–39

associations of, 228, 249
Breughel influence on, 175
brushwork of, 129, 140, 150
contradiction revealed by, 58
Dutch influence on, 93, 100
early training of, 19
eighteenth-century French art influence on, 137
group exhibitions, 15, 18, 249, 250, 251
modernism vs. links to past in, 160
old masters' impact on portraiture of, 239
organizations of, 228, 249
as painters of modern life, 30, 37
plein air painting and, 38, 122
Rembrandt influence on, 175
Rubens influence on, 175, 181
Spanish influence on, 112, 113
techniques and materials of, 37–38, 129, 150, 153
Incident at a Bullfight (Episode d'une course de taureaux) (Manet), 122
Infanta Margarita, after Diego Rodríguez de Silva y Velázquez (Manet), 29, *117*, 118, 245
Infanta Margarita, Copy after Velázquez (Degas), 29, *117*, 118, 245
Infanta Margarita Teresa (Velázquez and Workshop), 29, *32*, 244
Infante Don Baltasar Carlos in Hunting Costume (Velázquez), *237*
Ingres, Jean-Auguste-Dominique, 16, 21
"innocent eye" concept, 54, 56
In the Garden at Maurecourt (Morisot), *57*
Italian Renaissance art, 19, 21, 243. *See also specific artists*

Japanese ukiyo-e prints, 40
Jar of Olives, The (Chardin), 194, 195, *195*
Jean as a Huntsman (Renoir), *237*
Jester Pablo de Valladolid, The (Velázquez), 123, *124*
Jongkind, Johan Barthold, 82
Journal (Goncourts), 252, 253
Judgment of Paris, The (Raimondi), 19, *20*, 171, 243
Julie Pissarro and the Maid at Pontoise (photograph), 50

"Koning Willem III" and Other Ships in the Sea-lanes off Texel, The (Backhuysen), *94*

La Caze, Louis, 137, 138
Lace Maker, The (Netscher), 208, *209*
Lace Maker, The (Vermeer), 83
Laen, Dirk Jan van der, 91
work by: *The House in the Country*, *90*, 91
Lafenestre, Georges, 252
Lamothe, Louis, 21
Lancret, Nicholas, 54
Landscape (Caracci), *37*
Landscape with Buildings (Poussin), 175
Landscape with Burial of Phocion (Poussin), 175, *179*
Landscape with Psyche outside the Palace of Cupid ("The Enchanted Castle") (Lorrain), *163*
Large Bathers, The (Renoir), 66, *70*
Lawrence, Thomas, 248
Lebrun, Jean-Baptiste-Pierre, 107n35
Lecomte, Georges, 252
Leenhoff, Suzanne, 30, 171
Lefort, Paul, 129, 242, 250
Le Nain brothers, 206, 207, 208
l'esprit musée, 17–18
l'Haridon, Octave Penguilly, 169
work by: *Roman City in the Alps, Shortly after the Conquest of Gaul*, *168*
Lhote, André, 175, 181
Libro dell'arte, Il (Cennini), 244
Lisbonne collection, 252
Little Cavaliers, The (Manet), 29, *30*, 77n26, 246
Little Country Maid, The (Pissarro), *48*
Little Dancer (Degas), 129, 133n34
lively sketches, 145, 147, 150
Loge, La (Renoir), 118, *120*, 211
Lola de Valence (Manet), 118
Loo, Carle Van, 171
Lorrain, Claude, 16, 160
works by: *The Disembarkation of Cleopatra at Tarsus*, *162*; *Landscape with Psyche outside the Palace of Cupid ("The Enchanted Castle")*, *163*; *The Rest on the Flight into Egypt*, *158*
Louvre
Cézanne on, 19, 255
copyists of nineteenth century and, 17–18, 246
Galerie Espagnole, 115, 117
La Caze collection acquisition, 247
Monet on, 15–16
Pissarro on, 15, 252
Rembrandt exhibition, 255
seventeenth-century Dutch art collection of, 82, 83
See also specific artists as copyists; specific collections
Luini, Bernardino, work by: *Madonna and Child with the Infant Saint John*, *66*
Luncheon in the Studio (Manet), 91, *92*
Luncheon on the Grass (Manet), 19, *20*, 30, 171, 218, 219
Luncheon on the Grass (Monet), 171, *172*
L'Union, 249
Luxembourg Museum, 253
Lydia at a Tapestry Frame (Cassatt), *128*, 129

Madame Claude Monet Reading (Renoir), *210*
Madame Georges Charpentier and Her Children (Renoir), *233*, 233–34
Madame Manet at the Piano (Manet), 93, *102*
Mademoiselle V . . . in the Costume of an Espada (Manet), *153*, 154
Madonna and Child with the Infant Saint John (Luini), *66*
Maidservant, The (Pissarro), *51*
Manchester Art Treasures Exhibition, 243–44
M. and Mme Auguste Manet, Parents of the Artist (Manet), 218, *219*, 223
Manet, Édouard
Boucher influence on, 30, 242
on breaking away from tradition, 37
on Carpaccio, 249
Chardin influence on, 40
as copyist in the Bibliothèque Impériale, 244
as copyist in the Louvre, 242, 244
death of, 251
as differentiated from Impressionists, 16
Dutch influence on, 30, 40, 93, 108n57, 218
on Dutch painting and Rembrandt, 79
on El Greco, 246
Flemish influence on, 30
Fragonard influence on, 154
on Goya, 246, 249
Hals influence on, 83, 86, 89, 154
on his painting, 154
Holland travels of, 242, 248
Italian influence on, 19, 243, 244
on Murillo, 245
palette of, 154
on the Prado in Madrid, 246
relationship with older art, 16
Rubens influence on, 244
Spanish influence on, 19, 29, 111–12, 117–18, 122–23, 218
on Tintoretto, 249
Tintoretto influence on, 243
on Titian, 249
Titian influence on, 243
training of, 19
on Velázquez, 123, 246, 249
Velázquez influence on, 118, 123, 154, 244, 245
Venice visit of, 249
Vermeer influence on, 83
works by: *Le Bon Bock*, 86, *88*; *Bullring in Madrid*, 123; *The Dead Toreador (L'Homme Mort)*, 122, *123*; *Don Mariano Camprubi*, 118; *Eva Gonzalès*, 187, *226*, 228; *The Fifer*, 123; *Fishing*, 30, *36*, 171; *Gypsy with a Cigarette*, 86, *87*; *Incident at a Bullfight (Episode d'une course de taureaux)*, 122; *Infanta Margarita,* after Diego Rodríguez de Silva y Velázquez, 29, *117*, 118; *The Little Cavaliers*, 29, *30*, 77n26, 118, 246; *Lola de Valence*, 118; *Luncheon in the Studio*, 91, *92*; *Luncheon on the Grass*, 19, *20*, 171, 218, 219; *Madame Manet at the Piano*, 93, *102*; *Mademoiselle V . . . in the Costume of an Espada*, *153*, 154; *M. and Mme Auguste Manet, Parents of the Artist*, 218, *219*, *223*; *Monk in Prayer*, *121*, 122; *Moonlight over Boulogne Harbor*, 92; *Music in the Tuileries Gardens*, 118, *120*; *The Old Musician*, *204*, 208, *208*; *Olympia*, 19, 71; *Peonies with Secateurs*, 93; *Portrait of Berthe Morisot Reclining*, *132*; *Portrait of Isabelle Lemonnier*, 229, *232*; *Portrait of Théodore Duret*, 123, 218–19, *221*; *The Saluting Torero*, 123; *Le*

Manet, Édouard, works by (*continued*) *Saumon (The Salmon)*, 40, *46*; *Spanish Ballet*, 118, 122; *The Spanish Singer*, *112*; *Study for the "Surprised Nymph,"* 30, *38*; *The Surprised Nymph*, 93, *101*; *The Tragic Actor (Rouvière as Hamlet)*, 123, *125*; *Victorine Meurent*, 30, 218, *220*
Manet and the Sea (exhibition), 92
Mantegna, Andrea, 21, 40
Marc-Bayeux, Auguste, 244–45
Marly Road, The (Pissaro), *59*
Marriage at Cana, The (Veronese), 21
Mary Cassatt at the Louvre: The Etruscan Gallery (Degas), 19
Mary Cassatt at the Louvre: The Paintings Gallery (Degas), 19
Meeting of Thirteen People (Velázquez), *28*, 29, 242, 244
Meier-Graefe, Julius, 66
Meissonier, Jean-Louis-Ernest, 206
Memory of Mortefontaine (Oise) (Corot), 169, *170*
Meninas, Las (Velázquez), 123, 129, *131*, 132
Merry Drinker (Hals), 86, *87*
Metsu, Gabriel, work by: *Hollandaise au clavecin (Dutch Woman at the Harpsichord)*, 93, *103*, 245
Michel-Ange et Raphaél (Rio), 247
Michelangelo, 19
Millet, Jean-François, 54, 57
Minerva Chasing Vice from the Garden of Virtue (Degas), 21
Moillon, Louise, 185, 187
work by: *Still Life with Cherries, Strawberries, and Gooseberries*, *185*
Monet, Claude
Barbizon School influence on, 160
Chardin influence on, 40
critical reviews of landscapes by, 175
Dutch influence on, 92, 93, 171, 174, 248
French Rococo influence on, 54
on his paintings, 153
Holland visit of, 251
Italian travels of, 255
London galleries, Pissarro and, 248
London paintings of, 254
on the Louvre, 15–16
Norwegian travels of, 253
on plein air painting, 169
Spain travels of, 254
technique of, 150, 153
training of, 19
on Velázquez, 252
wartime move to Holland, 248
wartime move to London, 248
works by: *Autumn on the Seine, Argenteuil*, *156*, *177*; *Luncheon on the Grass*, 171, *172*; *Morning on the Seine, Giverny*, 160, *161*; *The Road to Chailly (Forest of Fontainebleau)*, 160, *165*; *Still Life: A Quarter of Beef*, 199, *199*; *Still Life with Flowers and Fruit*, 40, *44*; *Summer*, *57*; *View of Rouen*, 93, *98*; *Windmill and Boats near Zaandam, Holland*, 93, *96*; *Windmills near Zaandam*, *78*, 93, *97*; *The Zuiderkerk, Amsterdam (Looking up the Groenburgwal)*, *60*, 93
Monk in Prayer (Manet), *121*, 122
Monnoyer, Jean-Baptiste, 40, 185, 187, 243
work by: *Vase of Flowers on a Marble Table*, 40, *43*
Mont Sainte-Victoire, 1886–87 (Cézanne), *178*
Mont Sainte-Victoire, 1902–6 (Cézanne), *178*
Moonlight over Boulogne Harbor (Manet), 92
Morisot, Berthe
Boucher influence on, 252
as copyist in the Louvre, 244, 246, 253
death of, 253
Fragonard influence on, 140, 145, 229
French Rococo painting influence on, 16, 50, 54, 139–40, 145
Goya influence on, 248
on Hals, 85
Holland and Belgium travels of, 251
Italian visit of, 251
Louvre influence on, 19, 21
Mantegna influence on, 252
posthumous exhibition of, 253
Renoir on Fragonard and, 139
Rubens influence on, 251
Spanish influence on, 248
technique of, 140, 145
Titian influence on, 244
Velázquez influence on, 129, 248, 252
Veronese influence on, 244, 252
works by: *The Calvary (Le Calvaire)*, *26*, 244; *Getting Out of Bed*, 140; *In the Garden at Maurecourt*, *57*; *Venus Asking Vulcan for Arms*, 10, 140, *142*; *Young Woman by a Window (Summer)*, *54*
Morning, Sunlight Effect, Éragny (Pissarro), *179*
Morning on the Seine, Giverny (Monet), 160, *161*
Mother and Child (Madame Thurneyssen and Her Daughter) (Renoir), *68*, *216*, 239
mother and child imagery, 58, 66
Mrs. Duffee Seated on a Striped Sofa, Reading (Cassatt), 50, 229, *230*
Murillo, Bartolomé Esteban, 29, 30, 113, 242, 243
works by: *The Beggar Boy*, *2*, 30, 34; *"Soult" Immaculate Conception*, *113*, 113–14
Musée des Copies, 17–18, 77n7, 127, 248, 249
Musée des Études, 249
Musée du Trocadéro, 19. *See also* Expositions Universelles
Musée Espagnole exhibition, 28
Museo del Prado, 17
Music in the Tuileries Gardens (Manet), 118, *120*
Music: Portrait of M. de la Breteche, Brother of L'Abbé de Saint-Non (Fragonard), 145, *149*, 150, 154

National Gallery (London), 17
Naturalist School, 28, 37, 107n9, 112
Needlewoman (Velázquez), 211, *211*
Neer, Aert van der, work by: *Skaters on a Frozen Canal by a Village*, *180*
Neoclassical school of landscape painting, 166, 169
Netscher, Caspar, 208
work by: *The Lace Maker*, 208, *209*
New Painting, The (Duranty), 228
nineteenth century, 16–19
non-fini, 150, 153
Nouvelle Peinture, La (Duranty), 215
Nude on a Couch (Renoir), 71, *72*

Oak Forest, The (Hobbema), *167*
Old Fife Player, The (after Le Nain), *208*
Old Musician, The (Manet), *204*, 208, *208*
Olympia (Manet), 19, 71
open-air painting, 122, 166, 169
"Painter of Modern Life, The" (Baudelaire), 218, 228
Paris Commune, 248
Park of the Château de Steen (Rubens), 30, *37*
Pater, Jean-Baptiste-Joseph, 54, 171, 245
work by: *Country Party*, *173*
paysage composé, 169
paysage historique, 169
Paysagiste aux champs, Les (Henriet), 169
"Peintre de la vie moderne, Le" (Baudelaire), 246
Peintres français en 1867, Les (Duret), 247
Peintres impressionistes, Les (Duret), 250
Peña, Narcisse Diaz de la, 166
Peonies with Secateurs (Manet), 93
Perry, Lilla Cabot, 30, 37
perspective, 40
Pierre Puget (Lagrange), 247
Piles, Roger de, 183, 184
Pinacoteca di Brera, 17
Pissarro, Camille
on artists and preceding masters, 157
Barbizon School influence on, 160
Belgian travels of, 252
Chardin influence on, 40, 50
as copyist in the Louvre, 245
on Corot and Lorrain, 160
Dutch influence on, 160, 166
on Holbein, 251
on individuality vs. old masters' influence, 253–54
on James collection Watteau sale, 252
London galleries, Monet and, 248
on the Louvre, 15, 252
on Lyon museum, 253
Neoclassical landscape theory and, 166
on other Impressionists, 160
Poussin influence on, 160, 166
on Rembrandt exhibition and seventeenth-century Dutch art, 100, 253
training of, 19
on Vermeer, 160
wartime move to London, 248
works by: *Bouquet of Flowers*, *146*; *The Little Country Maid*, *48*; *The Maidservant*, *51*; *The Marly Road*, *59*; *Morning, Sunlight Effect, Éragny*, *179*; *Towpath*, 166

Plaster Cast of a Putto (Cézanne), 64
Plaster Cupid, The (Cézanne), 58, 65
Plaster Cupid, The, (recto) and *Study of Drapery* (verso) (Cézanne), 58, *64*
plein air painting, 122, 166, 169
pochade, 150, 153, 229
Portrait (de la Tour), 244
Portrait of a Seated Man (Hals), 93, *105*
Portrait of a Woman (Hals), 85, *85*
Portrait of a Young Woman, after a 16th-century Florentine drawing (Degas), *23*
Portrait of a Young Woman (Hals), 30, *220*
Portrait of Berthe Morisot Reclining (Manet), *132*
Portrait of Frédéric Bazille Painting "The Heron with Wings Unfurled" (Renoir), 187, *190*
Portrait of Isabelle Lemonnier (Manet), 229, *232*
Portrait of Jeanne Samary (La Rêverie) (Renoir), 135, *136*, 137, 150, 153, 229
Portrait of the Infanta Margarita, Daughter of Philip IV, King of Spain (Velázquez), 29, *116*, 117–18, 243, 245
Portrait of Théodore Duret (Manet), 123, 218–19, *221*
Poussin, Gaspar, 243
Poussin, Nicolas, 54, 58, 160, 243, 244, 247
  works by: *Landscape with Buildings*, 175; *Landscape with Burial of Phocion*, 175, *179*
Prix de Rome, 17, 169
Puget, Pierre, 58, 246
Putto (after François Du Quesnoy), *62*

Raimondi, Carlo, 248
Raimondi, Marcantonio, 19, 171, 243
  work by: *The Judgment of Paris*, 20, 171, 243
Raphael, 16, 17, 40, 66
  work by: *Two Men Conversing on a Flight of Steps and A Head Shouting*, *41*
Reader, The (Renoir), 211, *211*
Realist Movement, 82
Rehearsal, The (Degas), 40
Reine Lefebvre Holding a Nude Baby (Cassatt), *238*
Rembrandt. *See* Rijn, Rembrandt Harmensz van
Remembrance of Things Past (Proust), 239
Renoir, Pierre-Auguste
  on Carpaccio, 250
  characteristics of work by, 135, 137
  Chardin influence on, 40
  childhood influence of Louvre, 19
  as copyist in the Louvre, 244, 245, 246
  Dutch influence on, 50
  eighteenth-century French art influence on, 137, 139
  on El Greco, 252
  female nude motif and, 66, 71
  fête champêtre tradition and, 211–12
  French Rococo art influence on, 50
  on Germany, 253
  on Goya, 252
  Holland travels of, 253
  on Impressionism, 58
  Italian influence on, 66, 250–51
  Italian travels of, 251
  on Morisot and Fragonard, 139
  mother and child motif, 66
  old masters' influence on, 160
  on Poussin, 252
  on Raphael, 251
  Raphael influence on, 66
  on Rembrandt, 253
  on Rubens, 66, 252
  Rubens influence on, 218
  Spanish influence on, 29, 118, 129, 132
  Spanish trip of, 252
  on subject matter of paintings, 58
  technique of, 137
  on Titian, 71, 251, 252
  training of, 19
  on Velázquez, 29, 129
  Velázquez influence on, 29, 129, 132
  Veronese influence on, 21
  Watteau influence on studies by, 234–35
  works by: *Alfred Sisley*, 93, *104*; *The Artist's Family*, 129, *130*, *132*; *The Artist's Son, Jean, Drawing*, *52*; *Ball at the Moulin de la Galette*, 50, *54*; *A Bather*, *74*; *Child with a Hoop*, *234*; *Christine Lerolle Embroidering*, 50, *53*, 92; *Jean as a Huntsman*, *237*; *The Large Bathers*, 66, *70*; *La Loge*, 118, *120*; *Madame Claude Monet Reading*, *210*; *Madame Georges Charpentier and Her Children*, *233*, 233–34; *Mother and Child (Madame Thurneyssen and Her Daughter)*, *68*, *216*, 239; *Nude on a Couch*, 71, *72*; *Portrait of Frédéric Bazille Painting "The Heron with Wings Unfurled,"* 187, *190*; *Portrait of Jeanne Samary (La Rêverie)*, 135, *136*, 137, 150, 153, 229; *The Reader*, 211, *211*; *Romaine Lacaux*, 29, *32*; *Seated Bather*, 71, *75*; *Skaters in the Bois de Boulogne*, *214*; *Still Life with Bouquet*, 29, *31*; *Still Life with Peaches and Grapes*, 40, *45*; *Studies of the Berard Children*, 234, *236*; *The Swing*, *212*; *The Wave*, *134*, *141*; *A Woman Nursing a Child*, *69*; *Woman Reading*, 92
The Rest on the Flight into Egypt (Lorrain), *158*
revisionist art history, 16
revivals, 28–29
Revue Universelle des Arts, La, 243
Reynolds, Joshua, 84, 248
Ribera, Jusepe de, 113–14, 127, 141, 246
  works by: *Entombment*, 127; *Saint Sebastian Cured by the Holy Women*, *114*, 114–15
Ribot, Théodule, 114, 197
Rijksmuseum, 17
Rijn, Rembrandt Harmensz van, 82, 175
  works by: *Susanna*, 93, *100*; *Syndics (The Sampling Officials)*, 79, *80*
River Landscape (Ruysdael), *176*
Road to Chailly, The (Forest of Fontainebleau) (Monet), 160, *165*
Robber of the Sparrow's Nest, The (Watteau), *213*
Rococo. *See* eighteenth-century French art
Romaine Lacaux (Renoir), 29, *32*
Roman City in the Alps, Shortly after the Conquest of Gaul (l'Haridon), *168*, 169
Rousseau, Jean-Jacques, 187
Rousseau, Philippe, 197
  work by: *Chardin and His Models*, *182*, 197, *198*
Rousseau, Théodore, 54, 57, 160, 166
Royal Academy of Painting and Sculpture, 184–85
Rubens, Peter Paul, 19, 30, 171, 243, 244, 246
  works by: *Hélène Fourment and Her Eldest Son, Frans*, *69*; *Park of the Château de Steen*, 30, *37*; *The Rainbow*, 30, *37*, 246; *Susannah and the Elders*, 30, *39*
Rubens et l'école d'Anvers (Michiel), 250
Ruisdael, Jacob Isaacksz van, 160, 242, 243
  works by: *The Bush*, *159*; *Windmill at Wijk*, 93, *96*
Ruysdael, Salomon van, 171
  work by: *River Landscape*, *176*

Saint Francis in Meditation (Zurbarán), 115, *115*, 117, 122
Saint Francis Standing (Astruc, after the original by Pedro de Mena), 127, *127*, 129
Saint Sebastian Cured by the Holy Women (Ribera), *114*, 114–15
Salon, the, 19, 251
Salon des Refusés, 19, 171, 249
Saluting Torero, The (Manet), 123
Samary, Jeanne, 135, 229, 233
Sarto, Andrea del, 244
Saumon, Le (The Salmon) (Manet), 40, *46*
Sauvageot collection, 243
Schoolboy Sleeping on His Book, A (Greuze), 52
Scullery Maid, The (Chardin), *49*
Seamstress, The (Bisschop), 53
Seated Bather (Renoir), 71, *75*
Seated Nude (Boucher), *14*, *71*
Self-Portrait in the Style of Filippino Lippi (Degas), *222*
Seurat, Georges, 181
seventeenth-century Dutch art
  characteristics of, 81–83
  influence on Impressionists, 83, 86, 89, 91–93, 100
  motifs of, 92
  palette of, 145
  Realist movement influence of, 82
seventeenth-century Spanish art
  appeal to Impressionists, 112–13, 129
  French revival in 19th century, 111–13
  influence on Impressionists, 111–12, 117–18, 122–23, 127, 129, 132
  naturalism of, 112
  overview, 28–30
  as pillaged, purchased, then lost by France, 113, 115
  popularity with French people, 129
  techniques of, 112

Silver Goblet, The (Chardin), 194
Singing Boy with Flute (Hals), 84, *85*
Sisley, Alfred, 19, 40, 160, 254
works by: *The Avenue of Chestnut Trees near La Celle-Saint-Cloud*, 160, *164*; *The Pike*, 40, *47*; *View of Saint Mammès*, *176*
Skaters in the Bois de Boulogne (Renoir), *214*
Skaters on a Frozen Canal by a Village (van der Neer), *180*
Société anonyme coopérative d'artistes peintres, sculpteurs, etc., 228, 249
Société des Artistes Français, 251
Société Nationale des Beaux-Arts, 245
Soult, Jean de Dieu, 113, 242
"Soult" Immaculate Conception (Murillo), *113*, 113–14
Spanish Ballet (Manet), 118, 122
Spanish Golden Age, 112
Spanish Singer, The (Fragonard), 154
Spanish Singer, The (Manet), *112*
Spinners (Velázquez), 129
Standish, Frank Hall, 117
Stein collection, 254
Stendhal (Marie-Henri Beyle), 250
Stevens, Alfred, 118
still life
Dutch masters, Realist School and, 199
as genre for women, 187
marginalization of, 188, 194
"masculine" genre of, 187
modernity and, 201
nineteenth-century perceptions of, 183–84, 187
realist group of, 197
Realist School and, 199
seventeenth-century representations of, 183–85, 187
Still Life: A Quarter of Beef (Monet), 199, *199*
Still Life of Flowers and Fruit (Monnoyer), 185, *186*, 187
Still Life with Apples and Oranges (Cézanne), 40, *192*
Still Life with Bouquet (Renoir), 29, *31*
Still Life with Cherries, Strawberries, and Gooseberries (Moillon), *185*
Still Life with Dead Pheasant and Hunting Bag (Chardin), *190*, 197
Still Life with Flowers and Fruit (Monet), 40, *44*
Still Life with Statuette (Cézanne), 58, *63*, 201
Storm, The (The Stuck Cart) (Fragonard), 138–39, *140*, 145
Street Scene (Vrel), *90*, 91
Studies after Two Italian Madonnas (Degas), *22*
Studies of a Nude Man, a Horse, and a Knee (Degas), *22*
Studies of Legs and Feet and of a Figure (Degas), *22*
Studies of Nine Heads (Watteau), 236
Studies of the Berard Children (Renoir), 234, *236*
Study (Fragonard), *136*, 137, 145, 147
Study for the "Surprised Nymph" (Manet), 30, *38*
Study of One of the Thieves in Mantegna's "Crucifixion" (Degas), *25*
Summer (Monet), *57*
Surprised Nymph, The (Manet), 93, *101*
Susanna (Rembrandt), 93, *100*
Susannah and the Elders (Rubens), 30, *39*
The Swing (Renoir), *212*
Syndics (The Sampling Officials) (Rembrandt), 79, *80*

Table of Desserts, A (Heem), 40, 188, *193*
Taylor, Isidore, 115
Thiers, Louis-Adolphe, 17
Timide Nature morte, La (The Diffident Still Life), *184*
Titian (Tiziano Vecellio), 19, 71, 171, 244
works by: *Le Concert champêtre*, 20, 171; *Danaë*, *73*; *Venus and the Organist*, 71, *73*
Toché, Charles, 249
"To the Wives" (Rivière), 228
Tour, Georges de la, 244
Tour, Maurice Quentin de la, 253
Towpath (Pissarro), 166
Tragic Actor, The (Rouvière as Hamlet) (Manet), 123, *125*
Traité du paysage (Lhote), 175, 181
Triumph of Silenus, The (Girard), 169, *170*
Troubled Conscience (Baugniet), *206*
Turner, J.M., 248
Two Figures Standing on a Flight of Steps, after Raphael (Degas), 40, *41*
Two Men Conversing on a Flight of Steps and A Head Shouting (Raphael), *41*

Uffizi, 21
ukiyo-e prints, 40

Valenciennes, Pierre-Henri de, 166
Vallayer-Coster, 146
Vase of Flowers (Vallayer-Coster), 146
Vase of Flowers on a Marble Table (Monnoyer), 40, *43*
Velázquez, Diego Rodríguez de Silva y
Cassatt on, 248–49
Degas on, 40
influence on Cassatt, 129
influence on Degas, 245
influence on Manet, 29, 118, 123, 154, 244, 245
influence on Morisot, 129
influence on Renoir, 129, 132
Manet on, 123, 246, 249
as modernist, 250
Monet on, 252
Renoir on, 129
revival of, 28, 29
works by: *Infanta Margarita Teresa*, 29, *32*, 244; *Infante Don Baltasar Carlos in Hunting Costume*, *237*; *The Jester Pablo de Valladolid*, 123, *124*; *Meeting of Thirteen People*, *28*, 118, 242, 244; *Las Meninas*, 123, 129, *131*, 132; *Needlewoman*, 211, *211*; *Portrait of the Infanta Margarita, Daughter of Philip IV, King of Spain*, *116*, 117–18, 218, 243, 245; *Spinners*, 129
Venus and the Organist (Titian), 71, *73*
Venus Asking Vulcan for Arms (Morisot), *10*, 140, *142*
Vermeer, Johannes, 21
characteristics of paintings by, 83, 91
first Paris exhibition of, 89
influence on Manet, 83, 91
influence on Renoir, 50, 92
Thoré and, 89, 91–92
Thoré on, 109n70, 208n66, 247
works by: *The Lace Maker*, 83; *View of Delft*, 89, *90*, 92, 160; *A Young Woman Standing at a Virginal*, *89*
Veronese, Paolo, 19, 21, 244
Victorine Meurent (Manet), 30, 218, *220*
Vie Parisienne, La 184
View of Delft (Vermeer), 89, *90*, 92, 160
View of Rouen (Monet), 93, *98*
View of Saint Mammès (Sisley), *176*
Vinci, Leonardo da, 21, 244
Visit to a Museum (Degas), *4*, *152*, 153
Vollon, Antoine, 197
Voyage en Asie (Duret), 249
Vrel, Jacobus, 91
work by: *Street Scene*, *90*, 91
Vulcan Presenting to Venus the Arms for Aeneas (Boucher), 140, *143*

Walferdin, François Hippolyte, 137–38, 145, 250
Watteau, Jean-Antoine, 21, 28, 50, 54, 171
works by: *Assembly in a Park*, 171, *173*; *Harlequin and Columbine*, *213*; *The Robber of the Sparrow's Nest*, *213*; *Studies of Nine Heads*, 236
Wave, The (Renoir), *134*, *141*
Whistler, James McNeill, 208, 209
work by: *Arrangement in Gray and Black No. 1* or *The Artist's Mother*, 208, *209*
Windmill and Boats near Zaandam, Holland (Monet), 93, *96*
Windmill at Wijk (Ruisdael), 93, *96*
Windmills near Zaandam (Monet), *78*, 93, *97*
Woman Nursing a Child, A (Renoir), *69*
Woman Reading (Renoir), 92

Young Couple in a Landscape (Huet), *56*
Young Girl Reading, A (Fragonard), 50, 145, 147, *231*
Young Woman by a Window (Summer) (Morisot), *54*
Young Woman Standing at a Virginal, A (Vermeer), *89*

Zuiderkerk, Amsterdam, The (Looking up the Groenburgwal) (Monet), *60*, 93
Zurbarán, Francisco de, 115, 117, 242
work by: *Saint Francis in Meditation*, 115, *115*, 117, 122

Photographic Credits

In most cases photographs were provided by the owners, as cited in the captions and checklist. Further photographic credits are given below.

© de la Archivio fotografía Museo de Bellas Artes de Bilbao: fig. 44
© The Art Institute of Chicago: cats. 90, 97; fig. 40
© The Barnes Foundation 2007: fig. 57
Photo Bibliothèque nationale de France: figs. 8–10, 93
Bildarchiv Preussicher Kulturbesitz / Art Resource, NY, Photo, Jörg P. Anders: cats. 21, 63; figs. 21, 27
© Joachim Blauel—ARTOTHEK: fig. 63
© Blauel / Gnamm—Kunstdia-archiv ARTOTHEK, Weilheim, Germany: figs. 14, 30
Scott Bowron: cat. 47
The Bridgeman Art Library: fig. 72
© British Library Board. All Rights Reserved: fig. 80
© The Cleveland Museum of Art: fig. 6
© The Samuel Courtauld Trust: fig. 47
© Ferens Art Gallery, Hull City Museums and Art Galleries / The Bridgeman Art Library: cat. 43
© The Israel Museum, Jerusalem: cat. 76
Christian Jean / Jean Schormans: cat. 46
Erich Lessing / Art Resource, NY: fig. 74
© 1979 The Metropolitan Museum of Art: cat. 82
© 1982 The Metropolitan Museum of Art, Photo, Malcolm Varon: fig. 87
© 1992 The Metropolitan Museum of Art: fig. 108
© 1993 The Metropolitan Museum of Art: cat. 51
© 2002 The Metropolitan Museum of Art: figs. 42, 66
© Musée Fabre, Montpellier Agglomération, Photo, Frédéric Jaulmes: cats. 3, 41; figs. 13, 82
© Musée Marmottan Monet, Paris, France / The Bridgeman Art Library: cat. 57a
© Musée du Petit Palais: fig. 109
© Musée du Petit Palais / Roger-Viollet: fig. 38
© Museo Nacional del Prado, Reserved Rights: figs. 17, 43, 52, 58, 107, 111
© 2006 Museum Associates / LACMA: figs. 105, 110
© 2007 Museum of Fine Arts, Boston: cats. 10, 35, 54; figs. 49, 91
Nasjonalmuseet for Kunst, Arkitektur og Design, Oslo, Photo, J. Lathion: cat. 50
© The National Gallery, London: cats. 44, 85; figs. 26, 34, 45, 48, 50, 70, 106
© 2007 Board of Trustees, National Gallery of Art, Washington: cat. 38; figs. 5, 33, 51, 52, 90, 96, 99
© National Gallery of Canada: cat. 30; fig. 41
The Nelson-Atkins Museum of Art, Photo, Jamison Miller: cat. 19
Ny Carlsberg Glyptotek, Copenhagen, Photo, Ole Haupt: cat. 60
Portland Museum of Art, Maine, Photo, Bernard C. Meyers: cat. 80
Reproductiefonds: cat. 42
Réunion des Musées Nationaux / Art Resource, NY: fig. 103
Réunion des Musées Nationaux / Art Resource, NY, Photo, Daniel Arnaudet: figs. 60, 61, 62, 64
Réunion des Musées Nationaux / Art Resource, NY, Photo, J. G. Berizzi: figs. 12, 94
Réunion des Musées Nationaux / Art Resource, NY, Photo, Gérard Blot: fig. 23
Réunion des Musées Nationaux / Art Resource, NY, Photo, G. Blot / C. Jean: fig. 46
Réunion des Musées Nationaux / Art Resource, NY, Photo, Christian Jean / Jean Schormans: fig. 67
Réunion des Musées Nationaux / Art Resource, New York, Photo, Hervé Lewandowski: cats. 17, 100; figs. 3, 4, 16, 37, 71, 83, 86, 88, 89, 98, 100, 102
Réunion des Musées Nationaux / Art Resource, NY, Photo, René-Gabriel Ojéda: figs. 20, 73, 76, 78
Réunion des Musées Nationaux / Art Resource, NY, Photo, Préveral: fig. 90
Réunion des Musées Nationaux / Art Resource, NY, Photo, Franck Raux: fig. 69
Réunion des Musées Nationaux / Art Resource, NY, Photo, Jean Schormans: fig. 65
Scala / Art Resource, New York: figs. 79, 84
Seattle Art Museum, Photo, Paul Macapia: cat. 6
© Shelburne Museum, Shelburne, Vermont: cat. 55
SMK Foto: cat. 94
© The State Pushkin Museum of Fine Arts, Moscow: figs. 59, 77
© Sterling and Francine Clark Art Institute, Williamstown, Massachusetts: cats. 9, 83; fig. 97
© 2007 Tate, London / Art Resource, NY: cats. 75, 91
© Virginia Museum of Fine Arts, Photo, Katherine Wetzel: cat. 88
© By kind permission of the Trustees of the Wallace Collection, London: figs. 95, 101

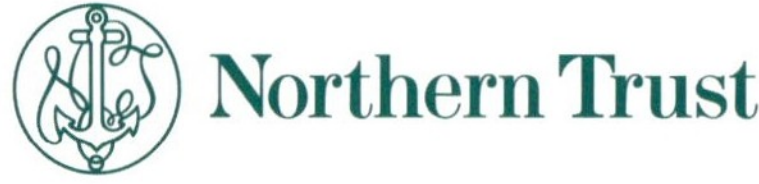

This exhibition was organized by the Denver Art Museum in collaboration with the High Museum of Art, Atlanta, and the Seattle Art Museum.
Northern Trust is the National Tour Sponsor of *Inspiring Impressionism.*
Additional support is provided by the National Endowment for the Humanities, the Samuel H. Kress Foundation, Friends of Painting and Sculpture at the Denver Art Museum, and the Federal Council on the Arts and the Humanities.
Local support in Denver is provided by the Samuel H. Kress Foundation, and the citizens who support the Scientific and Cultural Facilities District.
Promotional support is provided by *The Denver Post.*

High Museum of Art, Atlanta
October 16, 2007–January 13, 2008

Denver Art Museum
February 23–May 25, 2008

Seattle Art Museum
June 19–September 21, 2008

Library of Congress Cataloging-in-Publication Data
Inspiring Impressionism : the Impressionists and the art of the past / edited by Ann Dumas ; with Xavier Bray . . . [et al.].
p. cm.
Includes bibliographical references and index.
ISBN 978-0-300-13132-1 (hardcover : alk. paper)
ISBN 978-0-914738-57-2 (softcover : alk. paper)
1. Impressionism (Art). 2. Art, European. I. Dumas, Ann. II. Bray, Xavier.
ND192.I4I57 2007
759.05'407473—dc22 2007022361

Published by the Denver Art Museum

Distributed by Yale University Press, New Haven and London
www.yalebooks.com

Cover front: Mary Cassatt, *Mrs. Duffee Seated on a Striped Sofa, Reading,* 1876 (detail; cat. 10, p. 230)
Cover back: Jean-Honoré Fragonard, *A Young Girl Reading,* c. 1776 (detail; cat. 38, p. 231)
Endpapers: New Galleries of the Louvre, December 1874; Lithograph; Bibliothèque nationale de France, Paris
Page 1: Paul Cézanne, *Boy Searching for Lice, after Murillo,* c. 1882–85 (cat. 12, p. 35)
Page 2: After Bartolomé Esteban Murillo, *The Beggar Boy* (cat. 69, p. 35)
Page 4: Edgar Degas, *Visit to a Museum,* c. 1879–90 (detail; cat. 35, p. 152)
Page 10: Berthe Morisot, *Venus Asking Vulcan for Arms*, 1884 (detail; cat. 67, p. 142)
Page 14: François Boucher, *Seated Nude,* 1749 (cat. 8, p. 71)
Page 78: Claude Monet, *Windmills near Zaandam,* 1871 (detail; cat. 61, p. 97)
Page 134: Pierre-Auguste Renoir, *The Wave,* 1882 (detail; cat. 84, p. 141)
Page 156: Claude Monet, *Autumn on the Seine, Argenteuil,* 1873 (detail; cat. 62, p. 177)
Page 182: Philippe Rousseau, *Chardin and His Models,* 1867 (detail; fig. 89, p. 198)
Page 204: Édouard Manet, *The Old Musician,* 1862 (detail; fig. 96, p. 208)
Page 216: Pierre-Auguste Renoir, *Mother and Child (Madame Thurneyssen and Her Daughter),* 1910 (cat. 89, p. 68)

Copyedited by Fronia W. Simpson
Proofread by John Pierce
Designed by John Hubbard
Separations by iocolor, Seattle
Produced by Marquand Books, Inc., Seattle
www.marquand.com
Printed and bound by CS Graphics Pte., Ltd., Singapore

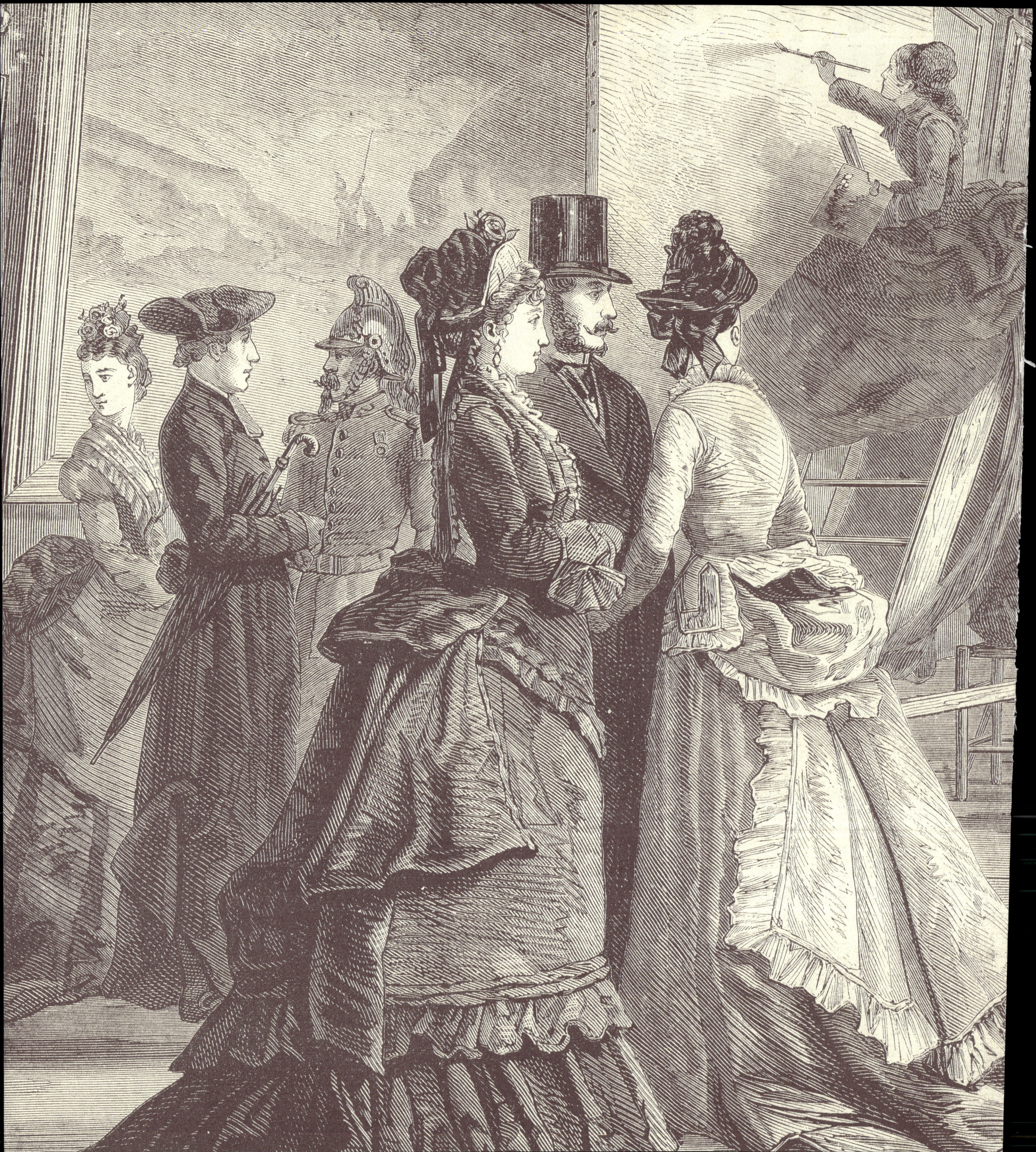